A History of

the Jewish People

THIS BOOK

IS PUBLISHED AT THE DESIRE OF THE LATE

Rosetta M. Ulman

OF WILLIAMSPORT, PENNSYLVANIA

FROM FUNDS CONTRIBUTED FROM HER ESTATE
BY HER EXECUTOR MR. ABRAHAM ERLANGER
MISS ULMAN WISHED THE PUBLICATION OF
THIS VOLUME FOR THE FURTHERANCE
OF TRUTH AND EQUITY

A HISTORY OF
THE JEWISH PEOPLE

BY

MAX L. MARGOLIS AND ALEXANDER MARX

PHILADELPHIA

THE JEWISH PUBLICATION SOCIETY OF AMERICA
5724-1964

PRINTED IN
THE UNITED STATES OF AMERICA

PREFACE

It is a difficult task to tell the story of the life of the Jewish people, from the dim beginnings to the present day, within the limits of a single volume. At every point Jewish history is interwoven with universal history, and this background must be presented. Compression becomes a necessity, considering the wide area embracing practically the whole of the civilized world and the long stretch of time. All those principal centers which have played a part in the unfold, ment of the outer and inner life of the Jewish people must figure in the story. The most advantageous method seemed to be a treatment which would bring into relief the shifting of these centers, from the home country (Book I) to the eastern center (Book II), thence to the West-European centers (Book III), to the emergence of new centers for the fugitives from Spain and Germany (Book IV), and lastly in the Age of Emancipation (Book V) to the new exodus from Eastern Europe and the creation of the center in the ancient homeland.

Places and periods so widely apart must of necessity present different aspects: now it is a record of wars and battles, of victories and defeats, of deportation and restoration, and now of taking root in foreign soil and of being uprooted, of friendly intercourse with the neighbor and of chains of persecutions, of achieving the rights of free citizens and of the reaction expressing itself in German Anti-Semitism and Russian pogroms. All this is told in the present work, but much more. It is the history of the entire people, of the mass; accordingly special stress is laid on its economic and social life. A history of Jewish literature is not the professed purport of this volume. However, letters are a part of the people's many-sided activity and men of letters are personalities, influencing their generation and shaping the future. There is a Jewish life to-day which has its roots in the past; it is an inner life unfolding itself in the long course of the ages under the peculiar circumstances of each period, and the significant moments take on the form of literary creations, of Books: Torah and Holy Writ, Mishnah, Talmud, Midrash, Codes, the Guide of the Perplexed, the Zohar, and so on to our own times.

The authors have endeavored to set forth this story in a manner as dispassionate and detached as possible. They have availed themselves of the great wealth of research done by scholars of all creeds and nationalities in the three-score years that have elapsed since Graetz completed his epoch-making 'History of the Jews.' The reader who is a specialist will readily find that every fact has been tested by recourse to documents and learned publications, but it was not deemed advisable to break the continuity of the narrative by an apparatus of references and footnotes. The present work is intended for the layman and the student. A short Bibliography at the end of the volume has likewise in mind these two classes of readers who may seek to obtain further information. It is not accordingly a register of source-works, and books and articles in the English language wherever obtainable have been given preference. A Chronological Table will enable the reader to survey contemporaneous events synchronously. The Index was prepared by Dr.Louis L. Kaplan.

This volume is the conjoint labor of the two authors. The writing was done by the first of the undersigned, and a good part of it during his year's sojourn in Palestine, and he gratefully records his obligation to his fellow-author for his valuable Lecture Notes on the history of the talmudic and mediæval periods. Moreover, the manuscript was gone over repeatedly by the two authors in joint conference, every fact and date and expression was scrutinized, and 'that which we had hammered was again and again brought back to the anvil.'

M. L. M.
A. M.

TABLE OF CONTENTS

BOOK I

CHAPTER I

THE BEGINNINGS OF THE PEOPLE

(2000–1225 before the Christian era)

CHAPTER II

MOSES. THE EXODUS

(1220)

CHAPTER III

THE CONQUEST OF CANAAN. THE JUDGES

(1180–1100)

CHAPTER IV

THE INROADS OF CANAANITISH RELIGION

CHAPTER V

THE RISE OF THE MONARCHY

(1080–1030)

CHAPTER VI

SAUL AND DAVID

(1030–1013)

CHAPTER XX
MANASSEH. JOSIAH. JEREMIAH
(692–609)

CHAPTER XXI
THE END OF THE KINGDOM OF JUDAH
(608–586)

CHAPTER XXII
THE BABYLONIAN EXILE
(586–538)

CHAPTER XXIII
THE RESTORATION
(538–432)

CHAPTER XXIV
FROM PERSIAN RULE TO GREEK
(424–187)

CHAPTER XXV
HELLENISTS AND PIETISTS. ANTIOCHUS EPIPHANES
(187–165)

CHAPTER XXVI
JUDAH THE MACCABEE AND HIS BROTHERS
(165–142)

CHAPTER XXVII
SIMON. JOHANAN HYRCANUS. ALEXANDER JANNAI
(142–76)

CHAPTER XXVIII
THE LAST HASMONEAN RULERS
(76–37)

CHAPTER XXIX
HEROD THE GREAT
(37–4)

CHAPTER XXX
ROME TIGHTENING ITS HOLD
(4 before–41 after the Christian era)

CHAPTER XXXI
THE WAR WITH ROME
(41–67)

CHAPTER XXXVIII
THE RISE OF MOHAMMEDANISM
(622–858)

CHAPTER XXXIX
THE KARAITE SCHISM
(767–900)

CHAPTER XL
SAADIAH
(882–942)

CHAPTER XLI
THE END OF THE BABYLONIAN SCHOOLS
(943–1038)

CHAPTER XLII
THE KAIRAWAN COMMUNITY
(700–1050)

BOOK III

CHAPTER XLIII
THE JEWS OF ITALY TO THE END OF THE EMPIRE
(139 before–410 after the Christian era)

CHAPTER XLIV
THE JEWS OF ITALY DOWN TO THE TWELFTH CENTURY
(410–1146)

CHAPTER XLV
THE JEWS OF SPAIN UNDER ROMANS, GOTHS AND MOHAMMEDANS
(300–990)

CHAPTER XLVI
SAMUEL THE NAGID AND SOLOMON IBN GABIROL
(993–1069)

CHAPTER XLVII
AL-FASI AND HIS SCHOOL
(1013–1141)

CHAPTER XLVIII
JUDAH HA-LEVI AND ABRAHAM IBN EZRA
(1086–1167)

CHAPTER XLIX
MOSES MAIMONIDES
(1135–1204)

CHAPTER L

THE FRANCO-GERMAN CENTER. GERSHOM OF MAYENCE
(321–1040)

CHAPTER LI

RASHI AND HIS SCHOOL. THE FIRST CRUSADE
(1040–1105)

CHAPTER LII

THE SECOND AND THIRD CRUSADES
(1099–1215)

CHAPTER LIII

THE JEWS OF FRANCE AND GERMANY IN THE THIRTEENTH CENTURY
(1198–1293)

CHAPTER LIV

THE JEWS OF ENGLAND
(1066–1290)

CHAPTER LV
THE JEWS OF PROVENCE
(1100–1394)

CHAPTER LVI
GERMAN JEWS IN THE FOURTEENTH CENTURY
(1298–1407)

CHAPTER LVII
GERMAN JEWS DURING THE FIFTEENTH CENTURY
(1410–1480)

CHAPTER LVIII
JEWS IN CHRISTIAN SPAIN. NAHMANI
(1203–1293)

CHAPTER LIX
THE PROGRESS OF THE CABALA
(1280–1340)

CHAPTER LX
THE DECLINE OF SPANISH JEWRY
(1348–1405)

CHAPTER LXI
THE DISPUTATION AT TORTOSA
(1340–1444)

BOOK 1

IN PALESTINE FROM THE BEGINNINGS TO THE EXTINCTION OF THE PATRIARCHATE

(2,000 BEFORE—425 AFTER THE CHRISTIAN ERA)

CHAPTER I

THE BEGINNINGS OF THE PEOPLE

(2000-1225 BEFORE THE CHRISTIAN ERA)

IN THE stretch of land skirting the western bank of the
Euphrates dwelt of old time the ancestors of the Hebrew
people. Ur of the Chaldees, the home of Terah, the
father of Abraham, lay then much closer to the Persian Gulf
which reached farther north than it does to-day. Toward the
southwest extended the Arabian peninsula, dotted with the
settlements of Arab tribes. These Arabs of pure stock were
reckoned, along with the progenitors of Terah, to the group
of the children of Eber. However, the name Hebrew
(Ibri, Ibrim) clung to Abraham—he was named at the first
Abram—and to his descendants, particularly the Israelites.

The Bible traces Eber to Shem, the son of Noah; from him
were descended likewise the Assyrians and the Arameans.
All these peoples spoke languages closely related, which we
are in the habit of calling Semitic (Shemitic). The speech of
the Canaanites (p. 7) was nearest to that we know as Hebrew;
yet the Bible groups this people, together with the Egyptians, among the descendants of Shem's brother, Ham.

Language and stock are by no means interchangeable
terms. Often the language of one people is acquired by another of a totally different stock. When therefore we speak of
Semites, we have in mind solely their speech and culture, not
the form of the skull or facial expression. If at all there was a
primitive Semitic stock, its earliest habitat is a matter of
conjecture. Nowhere, not even in Arabia, were the people of
Semitic speech indigenous to the soil. It seems probable that
at divers periods in remote antiquity they had migrated from
somewhere in Central Asia. Equally uncertain is the primitive home of the peoples of Indo-European speech, in historical times inhabiting India, the highlands in Iran and north

3

of the Taurus range, and the continent of Europe. It is quite possible that they, too, came from Central Asia and were at one time close neighbors to the Semites, the two sets of peoples trading with one another and exchanging their cultural possessions.

From Ur of the Chaldees an ancient caravan route led to Haran (the Roman Carrhae), a well-cultivated district in northeastern Mesopotamia. There we find the Terahites after their departure from their original home. Their intent was to push on by way of Damascus to the land of Canaan. This destination was reached by Abraham after his father's death. He took with him his brother's son Lot, the father of Moab and Ammon. They left behind the kindred Arameans; they left behind also the gods whom they and their fathers had worshiped. The Bible invests the migration of Abraham with the character of a religious movement. Abraham was 'called' (Isaiah 51.2); by the grace of prophetic inspiration, in obedience to the divine voice, he set foot upon a land which he received as a promise for him and his seed for ever.

This land, which the Jews call the Land of Israel and to which the Romans gave the name of Palestine, was then known as the Land of Canaan. Normally it means the narrow strip of land west of the Jordan, 'from Dan to Beersheba'; it increases in width from twenty miles in the north to sixty in the south and covers an area of six thousand square miles. But from the point of view of actual or contemplated possession, its northern as well as its southern end extended beyond the limits mentioned. Certainly the four thousand square miles east of the Jordan must be comprised within the territory in which the early history of Israel was set.

Physically, likewise, the two halves of Palestine go together. A barrier of mountain chains and table-land, running from north to south, shuts off the Syro-Arabian desert in the east from the Mediterranean, or Great, Sea in the west. A deep chasm merely interposes itself. This great crack sets in with the plain sunk between the Lebanon and the eastern parallel range, the Antilibanus. The southerly extension of the eastern range is the Hermon; in its spurs the river Jordan takes its rise. So far we find ourselves above the level of the Mediterranean. But after the river leaves behind the swampy lakelet Huleh, from the Bridge of the Daughters of Jacob to the pear-shaped Lake of Galilee (Sea of Chinnereth), the river bed falls to a depth of 689 feet; it continues to drop until the Jordan loses itself in the bitter waters of the Dead Sea, the bottom of which is some 2,600 feet below the Mediterranean level. This central Rift formed in ancient geological times a huge inland lake; long before the appearance of man it had dried up, leaving the river and the three lakes. South of the Dead Sea there is a steady rise as we proceed toward the Gulf of Akabah, the eastern arm of the Red Sea.

The abrupt falls of the Jordan, no less than the swift currents and the zigzagging channel, are a hindrance to navigation. In shallow depths the river is fordable. In the spring of the year it overflows its banks. When the water recedes, the river is bordered by a jungle of luxuriant semi-tropical vegetation, the 'pride of the Jordan.' On both sides the ascent is steep. The eastern range is slightly more continuous than the western; it more readily gives itself to table-land formation and maintains a higher average level. From the slopes of Hermon to the valley of the Jarmuch—the river empties its waters into the Jordan just below the Lake of Galilee—Golan, rocky in the north and more arable in the south, stretches itself; a broad prairie to the east is the biblical Bashan, noted for its abundant forests of oak-trees and its rich pasture lands offering nourishment to herds of strong cattle. Another tributary of the Jordan, the Jabbok, intersects the highland of Gilead. Physically, there is a close likeness between Gilead and the corresponding part of western Palestine; the two were also intimately connected historically. The wooded hills of Gilead send forth streams and springs in abundance. The valley of the Jabbok is particularly fruitful; much wheat is grown, and sheep and cattle find rich pasture ground. South of the Jabbok, in the land of Ammon, ridges and forests diminish. Moab is a bleak table-land, broken through by deep river beds; chief of them is that of the Arnon which drains into the Dead Sea.

On the western side, the Lebanon passes over into the plateau of Upper Galilee, walled in by high hills. The hills of Lower Galilee are less elevated; they gradually slope off towards the depression which forms the great break across the main range of the country. This is the Plain of Esdraelon. It is cut off from the Valley of the Jordan by the Gilboa mountains, and from the sea by the range of the Carmel. The cone-shaped peak of Tabor dominates it at the northeastern point. The Kishon is the principal river draining it. This river runs in a northwesterly direction at the foot of the Carmel range; now and again the Galilean hills approach quite closely, leaving but narrow passes through which the river glides along; then the plain widens out towards the Bay of Acre (Acco), which receives the waters of the Kishon through a marshy delta east of Haifa. Between the promontory of the Carmel and the sea there is but a beach of two hundred yards; but gradually the maritime plain increases in extent. It becomes the Sharon, from which passes lead across the Carmel range into the Great Plain, thus connecting sea and Jordan valley and forming the natural route for armies marching south or north, between Egypt and Syria. The Plain of Dothan affords a still wider entrance. It separates the Carmel range from the hill-country of Samaria (Mount Ephraim); the gentle gradients westward and the many broad valleys within, render this central portion of the land far more accessible than the southern hill-country of Judah. From the Philistine coast the Judean Lowland rises imperceptibly with its short and low ranges and the pebbly river beds in its cross valleys; from there the ascent to the Judean mountains and high plateau is steep and abrupt. Between the mountain ridges tortuous and deep defiles interpose. The desolate appearance which the bare stones of the lofty surface present to-day is obviously due to the neglect of ages. Now and again the ruins of terraced masonry show that at one time human hands were at work to conserve the waters of the rainfall and the soil which they moisten. The rough and dreary aspect increases eastward as the terrain falls precipitously towards the Dead Sea. Southward the steppe character becomes pronounced in the dry Southland (Negeb) before it passes into the barren desert.

When Abraham entered the land, he found the Canaanites in possession of a good part thereof; it is they who gave the land its very name. For a long time the traffickers who traded with the Israelites went by the name of Canaanites. Side by side with the Canaanites, who dwelt in the Lowlands, were found the Amorites who occupied the mountainous districts. Both were Semitic, if we remember what the term properly means (p. 3). It is likely that the Amorites were the first settlers. Their early seat was the Lebanon; thence they spread eastward as well as southward. For a time they made themselves masters of Babylon, giving that city its first dynasty of rulers, of whom Hammurapi (about 2100 before the Christian era) was the most illustrious. An energetic administrator, he left an enduring monument in the Code of Laws which he promulgated. The Code testifies to a high degree of civilization, marred by the prevalence of unchaste institutions which are taken for granted and regulated. The penal provisions are strict and oftentimes harsh, as when children are punished for the crime of their fathers. On the whole the Code bears the character of secular legislation, on a par with the tenor of our modern laws; moral injunctions have no place in it.

The Amorite dynasty of Babylon was overthrown by the Hittites. From their plateau across the Taurus they descended into Babylonia as well as Syria; in Abraham's time they had principalities in Palestine. Other smaller nationalities were domiciled in specific parts of the land, so the Hivites about Gibeon, the Jebusites in Jerusalem. Back of all these nations there had been an earlier population which these displaced. The Bible speaks of the Rephaim and Anakim, men of high stature, of whom there were still remnants at the time of the Israelite occupation and even later. Scattered over the country were the structures reared by these 'giants': cyclopean walls of undressed blocks of stone wedged with chips; stone-circles (cromlechs) and crude dome-shaped chambers (dolmens), consisting of a slab supported by upright blocks, for sepulchral purposes. There seems no reason why this older race may not also have been Semitic. At a still earlier period we find evidences of an aboriginal stock of dwarfish stature, who lived in caves and disposed of their dead by cremation.

The pre-Israelite population of Palestine was thus made up of a medley of stocks. The dominant element was clearly Semitic; if there were any other constituents, they had been absorbed. The Philistines occupied the coastland from Jaffa southward. They had come from the southern coast of Asia Minor (or possibly the island of Crete) and dispossessed the Avim. But they had largely surrendered to Canaanite influences. The broken up configuration of the Land, no less than the mixed stocks which formed its population, militated against consolidation of political power. No centralized empire arose. There was a multitude of city-kingdoms; in the face of a common danger a league was hastily formed and it just as soon fell apart. The Philistines alone were permanently federated, though each of their five city-states had its own ruler. So it was easy for powers great and small to overrun the country and impose their suzerainty upon the Palestinian kinglets.

Almost from the dawn of history, the rulers in the Tigris-Euphrates valley had their eye on the 'westland' and boasted of its subjugation. Just as earnestly did the Pharaohs of Egypt strive to bring Syria and Palestine within their sphere of influence. Egyptian armies penetrated into the heart of Palestine during the Middle Empire (from 2160 on). After the twelfth dynasty (1785) the power of Egypt was broken; the tables were turned, and Syrian bedouins (the Hyksos) established themselves in the seat of the Pharaohs (1700–1580). At last the foreign dominion was shaken off. The rulers of the New Empire sought out the remnant of the Hyksos in their Syrian fastnesses. Vigorous military campaigns northward were undertaken by Amenhotep (about 1550) and Thutmose I. (1530). The conquest of Palestine was accomplished by Thutmose III. in a series of expeditions which terminated in 1459. The strong cities were garrisoned with Egyptian soldiery; diplomatic and military officers were

longed for the land of the fathers, which even then harbored a small residue of their people and where the name of Israel had not been forgotten.

CHAPTER II

(1220)

A FRESH revolt broke out in Palestine. The successor of Ramses, Me(r)neptah (1225–1215) quelled it; in a stele, found near Thebes, he boasts of having destroyed Israel. The commotion at home communicated itself to the enslaved Israelites in Goshen. There arose an inspired leader, a personality of incomparable magnitude, to become the liberator of his afflicted brethren from their house of bondage.

Moses the Levite was born at a time when the oppressing Pharaoh ordered all new-born male children of the Hebrews to be cast into the river. The child was exposed in a chest among the bulrushes of the Nile; there the daughter of Pharaoh found him and took him for her son. He grew up in the royal court and was instructed in all the wisdom of the Egyptians. When he came to man's estate, he encountered an Egyptian smiting a Hebrew; the feeling for his own overcame Moses, and he slew the aggressor. But he also witnessed the demoralization among the oppressed, when one Hebrew, striving with another, met the rebuke of Moses with a brazen reference to the killing of the Egyptian. Moses, realizing that the act was known, fled into the land of Midian in the Sinaitic peninsula. There, in an oasis, stood a sanctuary. The fugitive Egyptian—as such he was taken by the Midianite priest—was made welcome; he married one of the priest's daughters and tended his father-in-law's sheep.

On one occasion the shepherd penetrated far into the wilderness, close by the mountain of God (Horeb, Sinai). Suddenly, he beheld a bush burning with fire, and yet the bush was not consumed. It was a vision ushering in his prophetic call. Before he could explain the marvelous sight, he heard a voice calling to him from the bush. The God of the fathers

14

spoke, bidding him undertake the mission of freeing his oppressed people. The patriarchs had known God as the Almighty. To Moses God made Himself known by a new name: I AM THAT I AM, the One whom no definition can exhaust, who is always with His people, a Helper ever ready, a Savior, 'who is afflicted in all their affliction and in His love and in His pity redeemeth them.' Just now the power of God was to manifest itself in freedom for Israel, with Moses as the agent, the first shepherd of God's flock.

The prophetic call which came to Moses made him realize the stupendousness of the task and his own unworthiness. He preferred that someone else might be sent; he knew himself not a man of words, slow of speech, and of a slow tongue. But his was the unquenchable fire, his the prophetic illumination; he would find an interpreter in his brother Aaron, the future priest. It was borne in on the prophet in the sequel how untrustworthy his priestly brother might become, how he would yield to the low religious conceptions of the mass. For the time being Moses accepted his brother's help, when with wife and children he returned from Midian. The two together communicated to the people the divine message, and the people believed. Preparations were made for a hasty departure. The exodus took place in the spring of the year 1220.

The immediate goal was the Mountain of God, where Moses received his revelation and whither the people now resorted for a solemn pilgrimage. They marched in an easterly direction; then they turned southward. It was impossible to round the north of the lakes, to which in high tide the western, or Suez, arm of the Red Sea then extended, for the reason that the frontier was strongly guarded. The Israelites found themselves shut in by the wilderness, between Migdol and the sea. A strong east wind, which blew all night, drove the ebbing waters still further back and uncovered the bed of the sea. In the dry sand the passage was effected towards Baal-zephon on the eastern shore. A detachment of Egyptian horsemen, which pursued the fleeing Israelites, was drowned in the sea when the flood returned. The workings of ebb and flow at the opportune moment were nothing short of a

miracle. The people believed in God and in His appointed
messenger. Triumphantly they sang:

'Sing ye to the Lord, for He is highly exalted;
The horse and his rider hath He thrown into the sea.'

The march went on past the bitter spring of Marah and
the palm grove of Elim. At Rephidim the Amalekites, who
disputed the possession of this fertile strip, were overcome in
battle. Now the road lay open to the Mountain of God,
Horeb or Sinai, close by the territory of Midian, within the
district comprising the oasis of Kadesh with its wide plains
well supplied with springs issuing from the clefts of the rocks.
Both Sinai and Kadesh had long formed sacred centers to
the desert tribes; thither they made their pilgrimages, there
they held their fairs, and there the Midianite priesthood
adjudicated their quarrels according to traditional lore. The
memory of Israel ever after harked back to the time when
Moses brought the people to the foot of the mountain, there
to receive the foundation of their national unity and the
constitution of their religious community.

The inspiration of the prophetic leader communicated
itself to the whole people. A holy enthusiasm possessed them.
They saw God in His spiritual essence, under no manner of
form, and they heard His voice thundering forth the Ten
Words:

'I am the Lord thy God: thou shalt have no other
gods before Me.

Thou shalt not make unto thee a graven image, nor
any manner of likeness.

Thou shalt not take the name of the Lord thy God
in vain.

Remember the sabbath day, to keep it holy.

Honor thy father and thy mother.

Thou shalt not murder.

Thou shalt not commit adultery.

Thou shalt not steal.

Thou shalt not bear false witness.

Thou shalt not covet.'

In their state of exaltation, the people accepted with readiness the prerogatives and duties of the divine election constituting them a holy nation, the priest-people among mankind, guardians of the spiritual interests of humanity. A formal covenant was solemnized by which the people bound themselves to do the will of God. The groundwork of divine revelation must needs be expanded; the Ten Words graven on two tables of stone, the Testimony as they were called, required supplementing in the form of a code of laws regulating the ramified affairs and duties of the nation as well as the life of the individual Israelite. Such a manual of guidance was called Torah, Instruction. The first draft of the Mosaic Torah was read to the people and formally ratified by them. It was therefore named the Book of the Covenant.

The Book of the Covenant, as we now read it in the twenty-first, twenty-second, and twenty-third chapters of the Second Book of Moses or Exodus, is preceded by a prologue at the end of the twentieth chapter and concludes with a peroration. The imageless service of God is inculcated. The new community, during the slow progress of the conquest, will have to contend with the native population and its form of religion. No compromise must be made with either. Anything that will endanger the spiritual life of the nation must be uprooted. The Canaanites have their numerous sanctuaries, scattered throughout the land; so may the Israelites —such was the first thought of Moses—build an altar, of earth or of unhewn stones, not exactly in any place, but wheresoever God has caused His name to be mentioned, in a place hallowed through association with a memorable event in the life of the patriarchs. Thus the names of the Canaanite local deities—the baals—will come to be forgotten. To the sanctuary is brought the Hebrew slave who chooses to remain with his master for life, above the normal term of six years; there oaths are taken in litigations; the manslayer by misadventure seeks sanctuary.

The statutes (mishpatim, 'ordinances') deal with slavery and concubinage, homicide and other crimes punishable with death (like kidnapping, gross unfilial conduct), mayhem, theft, damages to property, seduction, witchcraft, unnatural lust, idolatry. Imperceptibly the little Code proceeds to its second part, the hortatory dicta (debarim, 'words'), that enjoin justice and kindness to the stranger, the widow, and the fatherless, generosity to the impoverished debtor, respect for God and constituted authorities, prompt delivery of the first fruits, abstention from unlawful meat, judicial impartiality, restoration of lost property, humanity to animals, letting the land lie fallow in the sabbatic year that the produce may go to the poor, desisting from labor on the sabbath day that dependents as well as beasts of burden may have rest. Three seasons for pilgrimage, when all male Israelites must present themselves at the sanctuary, are ordained: the feast of unleavened bread in the spring of the year in commemoration of the coming out of Egypt, the feast of harvest, and the feast of ingathering.

A premature attempt was made to enter the promised land from the south; it ended disastrously. After many years there was nothing left but to try the more difficult and circuitous route to reach Canaan from the east. In their wanderings the Israelites carried with them a portable sanctuary, which was taken down and set up from station to station; in its most sacred part rested the Ark of the Covenant, which contained the two tables of stone. The king of Edom refused to let the Israelites pass through his territory. So they were constrained to encircle Edom, going in a southerly direction and then moving up northward. The Amorites, pressed by the Hittites, had pushed the Moabites from their seats north of the Arnon. The Israelites passed by the Moabitish territory far to the east; but so soon as they touched the Amorite frontier, Sihon, whose residence was at Heshbon, met them in battle. The Amorites were defeated and compelled to cede territory to the invaders. A similar victory was obtained over the forces of Og king of Bashan, and the Israelites gained a footing in this fertile district.

The conquest of the country east of the Jordan—only Ammon and Moab held their own—may not have been accomplished all at once; it is likely that the Amorite power was not broken before several generations. The attack was made principally by Reuben, Gad, and half of the tribe Manasseh; they were content to settle in the occupied district which afforded rich grazing ground for their cattle: Reuben and Gad in the southern end, and the Manassite clans of Machir and Jair in Gilead and Bashan. No matter what the custom may have been during the wanderings—the portable sanctuary was within easy access—the beginnings of settled life over an extended area were ordered in accordance with the provisions of the Book of the Covenant. Altars were reared in sundry localities, in any place one saw fit, every man doing whatsoever was right in his own eyes. Moses now realized the danger to the new and spiritual religion of his foundation, when local habits and pagan superstitions of the former inhabitants might creep in. He accordingly revised his earlier legislation in a new Book of the Covenant issued on the eve of his death in the plains of Moab opposite Jericho.

This second thought of the lawgiver sharply distinguished between the unrest attending the period of the conquest when the prevailing procedure might continue in force, and the normal conditions upon the completion of the settlement across the Jordan. He foresaw the natural progress toward centralization, political and religious. The consolidation of national unity and the full expression of Israel's unique piety demanded a central place of worship, a sanctuary one and only, whither men might resort thrice annually and under the eyes of a faithful priesthood be stirred by that which is Israel's chiefest concern, the nearness of God. 'For what great nation is there, that hath God so nigh unto them, as the Lord our God is whensoever we call upon Him?'

The second Code, no less than the first—or for that matter the middle books of the Pentateuch—repeatedly inculcates the duty of caring for the dependent classes, the wandering Levite in the gates, the widow, the fatherless, the hapless stranger, or of succoring the impoverished brother. Even the brute creatures are to be treated with kindness; thus the ox, while treading out the corn, is not to be muzzled. Crime must be punished; but even the criminal shall be spared undue indignity; nor may children be involved in the punishment of offending fathers. Commercial honesty and judicial incorruptibility are insisted upon; all unchaste and unseemly conduct is banned; a holy avoidance of all things impure is demanded, as befits a people serving the Holy God. No form of idolatry shall be tolerated. 'The Lord is God in heaven above and upon the earth beneath; there is none else.

The Unity of God was for Moses not a matter of reasoned speculation; it was morally determined, the most stupendous reality that concerns the Israelite in begetting single-hearted devotion. 'HEAR, O ISRAEL, THE LORD OUR GOD, THE LORD IS ONE. Therefore thou shalt love the Lord thy God with all thy heart, and with all thy soul, and with all thy might.' The Mosaic Torah is summed up in this supreme commandment. The divine law, the prophet exhortingly avers, is neither too hard, nor far off; it is not in heaven, neither is it beyond the sea; the word is very nigh, in one's mouth, and in one's heart.

So spoke the prophet, commending the Torah before he passed away. There is much priestly legislation in the Torah, much of outward ceremonial. It was meant to be there, for piety must needs be organized. But all that is transcended by prophetic inwardness and prophetic persuasiveness. 'By a prophet the Lord brought Israel up out of Egypt, and by a prophet was he kept.' He was also for Israel the greatest of prophets. 'There hath not arisen a prophet since in Israel like unto Moses.' It was not granted him to lead the people into Canaan, but he led them up to its very entrance, and from the heights of Moab's hills he surveyed the land of the fathers which was to be given to their children. The God of the spirits of all flesh would appoint successors to carry on and complete the work of Moses, to win the land for Israel and the Lord. Moses was the creative builder; he laid the foundation; he left a divine programme in the Torah, which ever after remained an inheritance of the congregation of

Jacob. For Moses there was none like unto God, and among nations none like unto Israel; he taught his people the belief in the Unity of God and in Israel's uniqueness.

CHAPTER III

THE CONQUEST OF CANAAN. THE JUDGES

(1180-1100)

AFTER the death of Moses, the leadership of the nation fell to Joshua, an Ephraimite, trained in the arts of warfare and in statecraft. Under his command, the people, organized for military attack, crossed the Jordan at a fordable place facing Gilgal. The strongly fortified Jericho ('Moon-city,' dedicated to the worship of the moon), with its double ring of walls, previously destroyed in the sixteenth century and then rebuilt, was carried by a successful assault. The gateway to the broad plateau in the center of the land was thus opened.

Here the tribe of Judah separated from the northern tribes. While Simeon and the friendly nomadic tribe of the Kenites advanced from the southwest or south, the men of Judah marched from the north to conquer the southern hill-country. The Jebusite king of Jerusalem met them in battle: he was wounded and carried by his people to his residence. Caleb and Othniel succeeded in dislodging the Canaanites from Hebron and Debir. The superior tactics of the in-habitants of the coastal plain, who could move against the invaders with their iron chariots, prevented further occupation of the country down the hills. The Jebusite stronghold and the whole northern belt remained likewise in the hands of the Canaanites. The isolation of Judah was thus made effective for some time to come.

The northern tribes succeeded to the national title of Israelites. Grouped about the sons of Joseph and the Ephra-imite leader, they were at first driven off as they climbed the ascent to Ai; but soon the city was taken by a stratagem. Bethel fell into their hands through the treachery of one of the inhabitants, who betrayed to the Israelite scouts the most advantageous point for an assault. Gibeon with its neighboring localities surrendered peacefully. Adoni-zedek, the king of Jerusalem, organized a coalition of his brother kings against the Israelites and their allies, the Gibeonites. A battle was fought in the Valley of Aijalon; in the descent from upper to nether Beth-horon the fleeing confederates were caught in a hail-storm; the Israelites pursued the enemy relentlessly.

It was a decisive victory for Israel; the day of Gibeon was celebrated in a song, which told how the sun stood still and hasted not to go down about a whole day, until the nation had avenged themselves of their enemies. The heart of the country, the Central Range, was now safe for Israel. The forests of the higher ridges were cut down to afford more soil for the settlers. The leading tribe was Ephraim, in whose territory lay Shechem, where the people assembled for common action, and Shiloh, the resting-place of the Ark. Manasseh dwelt further north, towards the Great Plain; but the Plain itself remained in the possession of the Canaanites. The northern country, Galilee, was opened up to the other tribes after a concerted onslaught by the king of Hazor and his confederates was thwarted at the Waters of Merom.

A good part of the country was thus occupied; but the conquest was in its merest beginnings. The Egyptian overlord by no means relinquished his hold upon the land; Ramses III. (1198–1167) vigorously maintained his Syrian dominions. The struggle between the Israelites and the dispossessed Canaanites appeared to the Pharaohs as an internal feud; so long as the conquerors in their domains and the unsubjected Canaanites in their territories paid their tribute, no attempts were made to interfere on the side of the one against the other.

But soon the Egyptian control of Palestine and Syria grew to be shadowy in the extreme. Israel gained a footing in the land, now by bloody warfare, now by peaceful means. Mutual concessions and accommodations were not infrequent; but as often as one or the other part waxed stronger, there developed renewed friction. The coast was nowhere reached by the invaders; within, the Great Plain, with its fortresses, Taanach, Megiddo, and Beth-shan, constituted a formidable barrier. The Israelite territory was thus split up; each tribe was left to carry on its own adventures. Yet the feeling that they all belonged together was not obliterated; but it required great emergencies and the weight of outstanding personalities to stir them to common action.

The Canaanites once more gathered their forces to strike at Israel. The leading spirit of the new coalition was Sisera. On both sides of the Plain of Jezreel the Israelites were harassed; all power of resistance seemed to be broken in them, 'not a shield or spear was seen among forty thousand of Israel.' Then there arose an inspired mother in Israel, Deborah. She summoned the leaders in Israel, at their head Barak son of Abinoam, to battle on behalf of their people and their God. Of Judah's participation there could be no thought; in the far north Dan and Asher were absorbed in mercantile pursuits; across the Jordan, Reuben dallied irresolute among his sheepfolds and Gilead was indolently impassive. The other tribes, Ephraim, Benjamin, and Manasseh from the south, Zebulun, Naphtali, and Issachar from the north, met in the Plain, where the enemy had massed his hosts near Taanach and Megiddo east of the Carmel (1150).

'The kings came, they fought; then fought the kings of Canaan, they took no gain of money.' It was a combat in which no quarter was given or sought. Boldly did the Israelites rush upon the enemy, 'jeoparding their lives unto the death.' So fierce was the onslaught that the Canaanites, with their chariots and horses, were put to rout in a wild panic. The very stars in their courses seemed to fight against them; in the heavy rainfall, swelling the brook Kishon, their flight was retarded. Sisera escaped on foot; he was parched with thirst. He chanced upon a nomadic encampment of Kenites, the friends of Israel. At one of the tents he asked a drink of water; Jael, the heroic woman of the tent, recognized in him the tormentor of Israel. She offered him milk in a lordly bowl; the weary captain gulped it down. As he was overcome with drowsiness, Jael swiftly struck his head with a heavy hammer; at her feet he fell dead.

The Canaanite opposition was broken for ever. No armed resistance was attempted after that; the Canaanites accommodated themselves to their neighbors and witnessed one portion of the land after another pass out of their possession. Gradually Israel became master; the former inhabitants were reduced to subjection. The complete rout of the enemies of the Lord and Israel was sung in a poem, the 'Song of Deborah,' a quaint document of those early days of storm and stress, glowing with the white heat of praise for the heroic men and women, the rulers in Israel, as they rallied 'to the help of the Lord among the mighty.' The cause of the Lord and of Israel was one, even as in the days of the beginnings, when Sinai quaked and trembled at the presence of the God of Israel.

The Israelite hold on the land, however, was disputed from other quarters. The Moabites had grown ambitious to reconquer their seats wrested from them in Mosaic times; ultimately their activity led to the weakening of Reuben, who dwindled away amid precarious conditions. Some time before Barak's glorious victory over the Canaanites, the tribe of Benjamin in particular had suffered subjection at the hands of Moab, who with the aid of Ammon established himself west of the Jordan in Jericho. It was intolerable to leave the gateway to the central country in the hands of an enemy; the enslaved condition irked the free sons of Benjamin. One of them, the left-handed Ehud, as he ostensibly came to present his people's tribute, sought an audience with the king of Moab at his palace and, unobserved, pierced him with his sword. Ehud's tribesmen responded to his call to arms, and the Moabite garrison was annihilated.

The western country continued to attract the eye of the nomad in the east, ever ready to overrun pastures and farmlands. This time it was the Midianites, a nomad branch of the people settled in the vicinity of Sinai. Having ravaged Edom and Moab, they followed a course northward similar to that taken by Israel under Moses. Now they poured across the Jordan into the fertile valleys of the west. Year after year, just before the harvest, they came, 'as locusts, for multitude,' riding upon their camels, and plundered the crops. The Israelitish peasantry offered no resistance. Fearing for their lives, they fled into the mountains, where the abandoned ancient hill-forts and rock caves afforded a hiding-place. On one occasion the raiders penetrated as far as Mount Tabor. They plundered freely and slew any who ventured into their path. Among the slain were several sons of a Manassite chieftain.

Their brother Jerubbaal, also called Gideon, actuated by the sacred duty of blood revenge and roused by his people's affliction, called the fighting men of his own clan, Abiezer, to arms. The small band of three hundred warriors pitched close by the well of Harod at the foot of the Gilboa mountains, whence the enemy camp northward in the valley could be observed. Suddenly, in the dead of night, Gideon's picked men surprised the enemy; the lurid glow of their torches and their deafening shout ('The sword for the Lord and for Gideon!') threw the Midianites into a panic. The Abiezrites, now reinforced by their brother clans of Manasseh as well as by Naphtali and Asher, pursued the fleeing hordes. The Ephraimites, though they arrived late, intercepted the enemy about to ford the Jordan and slew two of the Midianite chieftains, Oreb and Zeeb.

Once more the Midianites overran the country. This time they made their escape across the Jordan, their camels laden with booty. Gideon and his troops followed in hot pursuit. The men of Succoth and Penuel near the Jabbok refused food to Gideon's hungry men. Gideon marched on toward the south and east, as far as the caravan route on the outskirts of the steppe. The enemy was overtaken and the two kings, Zebah and Zalmunna, were captured. These headstrong sons of the desert freely boasted of killing Gideon's brothers; proudly they refused to die by the hand of Gideon's lad and begged the commander himself to give them the death-stroke ('for as the man is, so is his strength'). Condign punishment was meted out after the victory to the townsfolk of Succoth and Penuel for their unbrotherly conduct to their fellow-Israelites. A boy from Succoth was compelled to write down the names of seventy-seven notables of the town, who were then executed.

The victorious chief led his army of freemen homeward. Gratefully, the people offered him a hereditary kingdom; Gideon declined the royal dignity, for none but the Lord might rule over Israel. However, he maintained at his family seat in Ophrah a semi-regal establishment; the house of Joseph had a king in fact, if not in name. With his portion of the spoil he erected a sanctuary at Ophrah, in which he placed an ephod, a symbolic representation of the deity, made of seventeen hundred shekels of gold. This was clearly a falling away from the Mosaic religion. It shows to what an extent Israel was becoming ensnared by the Canaanite mode of life which persisted in the land after the partial subjection of the natives.

As becoming a ruler of wealth and power, Gideon had a numerous harem. Seventy sons survived him. The expectation was natural that one of these should succeed to his rule. But Gideon had indicated no choice, and the brothers fell out among themselves. The strife served the ambition of Abimelech, the son of a Canaanitish woman in Shechem, whom Gideon had married from political motives. This city was only half-Israelitish; by the side of the new-comers dwelt the Canaanites, among whom the old aristocratic family of the sons of Hamor was the most prominent. There was an ancient sanctuary, dedicated to the god of the city, who was named God (El) or Lord (Baal) of the Covenant, thus uniting the citizens in a covenanted league of peace. Abimelech's kinsmen at Shechem were readily persuaded that it was better for them to be ruled by one of their own bone and flesh. With silver from the treasury of the city-temple he hired a body of adventurers to butcher his threescore and ten brothers. Jotham, the youngest, alone escaped. Abimelech was acclaimed king in the sanctuary, close by the sacred terebinth.

The affection of the Shechemites for their king was of short duration. Jotham emerged from his hiding-place and shamed the Israelite part of the population for their ignoble conduct toward his father and his father's house. From a terrace on Mount Gerizim he mocked their choice of a ruler—the offspring of the subjected Canaanite race—with the famous fable of the trees going forth to find a king for themselves. One after another, the olive-tree, the fig-tree, the vine, declined the honor; the mean bramble alone accepted. Thus discord was sown between the two sets of citizens. Soon enough the Canaanite portion itself cooled toward their kinsman king. Abimelech, after all, felt himself to be an Israelite and preferred a strictly Israelitish city for his residence. Shechem was left in the hands of its governor Zebul.

This official was minded to be loyal, although he could not prevent the malcontents from injuring Abimelech by intercepting caravans and plundering the tribute which they bore for the king. Open rebellion was fostered by a mutinous troop, led by the Israelite Gaal, which was admitted into the city. As the townspeople were making merry over the completion of the vintage and between cups were reviling the absent king, Gaal fomented the seditious spirit by pointing out how little cause the Israelite section had to serve the usurper. The governor of the city, unable to stem the rising tide of revolt, played a double rôle. While ostensibly holding with Gaal and the majority of the population, he secretly apprised Abimelech of the intrigue.

Four royal companies marched in the night against the city. Gaal, urged by Zebul, made a sortie in the morning and suffered heavy losses. He sought safety behind the gates of the city; but Zebul, now openly espousing the king's cause, shut them against him. The infuriated citizens made away with the treacherous governor and took the field against Abimelech. They were attacked in front by three of the royal companies, while the fourth cut off their retreat to the city. For a whole day the fight went on. At length the place was carried by assault. All the inhabitants were put to the sword, and the city was completely destroyed. Abimelech then turned against the Tower of Shechem, a town in the neighborhood of the city, where a body of rebels still held out. As Abimelech advanced against them, they took refuge in an underground chamber of the temple of the God of the Covenant. The king's forces set fire to the sanctuary; a thousand men and women perished in the flames.

Thus the Shechemite rebels were annihilated. But the insurrection had not been put down. It spread to other localities. The king invested the city of Thebez, a few hours' journey from Shechem, on the road to Beth-shan. The citizens had shut themselves in the tower and Abimelech made ready to fire it. But fate overwhelmed him. As he stood before the barred gate of the tower, a woman cast from above a millstone upon his head, injuring him fatally. But he retained consciousness, and as it was ignominy worse than death to perish by the hand of a woman, he called hastily on his armor-bearer to dispatch him. Thus ended the rule of the house of Gideon, the first attempt in northern Israel to establish a monarchy.

The monarchical idea was nevertheless gaining ground, although it went against the grain of the liberty loving Israelites and the Mosaic tradition hardly favored its coming. When an emergency arose, the tribe immediately concerned was content to fight its own battles. All through this period the leaders were lifted into their position by the need of the hour. When their task was done, they still exercised temporary sway over their own section and often enough over contiguous territory. They were known by the title of 'judges,' the name given to their chief magistrates by the Carthaginians, the Canaanite (Phoenician) outpost on the North-African coast. The central Ephraimites naturally looked upon themselves as the backbone in the north; they took time in answering a call to arms when they were not immediately concerned, though when they awoke to the danger somewhat late, as in the case of Gideon, they did their part nobly; they considered it an affront when they were disregarded.

Gilead was hard beset by the Ammonites. The Gileadites turned in their distress to Jephthah, who had been driven from his home and was leading the life of a freebooter. At the sanctuary of Mizpah, he received the homage of his peo-

ple. The campaign was short and decisive; the Ammonite
danger was warded off. Tragedy awaited the returning leader
at home. He had vowed rashly to offer up to the Lord for a
burnt-offering the first that would come forth from the door
of his house to meet him. As it happened, it was his only
child, a daughter, that came joyfully to greet him. The fatal
vow was kept, though it broke the father's heart. The heroic
maiden was content to yield her life, seeing that the enemies
of her people had been humbled.

The Ephraimites declared war against Jephthah, because
they had not been called to join in the campaign against
Ammon. Jephthah accepted the challenge. He went out with
his Gileadite forces against the Ephraimites, who had
crossed the Jordan, and put them to flight. The fugitives
tried to regain the fords. But they were easily betrayed by a
peculiarity of their speech. They pronounced the sound *sh* as
s, saying 'Sibboleth' for 'Shibboleth,' meaning a flood, and
so they were ruthlessly butchered.

CHAPTER IV

THE INROADS OF CANAANITISH RELIGION

THE process of settlement, slow as it was, profoundly altered the mode of life of the Israelites. At the outskirts of the steppe, or wherever else grazing might be found for cattle, the ancient love for the free and haphazard life of the nomad asserted itself. The tent offered a simple abode and scant possessions were moved with ease. Among these pastoral people the old tribal organization persisted longest. Blood relationship, real or fictitious, was the strongest tie; whatever authority was called for was exercised by the elders.

But the nation at large was willing enough to take over a more luxurious and less precarious existence based upon an order of things ready-made. They installed themselves in houses which they had not built, and took possession of fields and orchards which they had not planted. The erstwhile shepherds were transformed into tillers of the soil. They produced grain and wine, oil and figs; the herds yielded them milk and meat. There was more than enough to supply their own needs; the surplus was exchanged with the Phoenician traders for the products of Tyre and Sidon or far-off lands. The Israelites at first lived in open villages; later they gained a foothold in the cities, often alongside of the old Canaanite residents or of stray foreigners. They took to the crafts; warfare was carried on with greater efficiency; industry developed; life took on pleasanter, richer, and more refined forms.

The backbone of the nation was the peasantry, permanently established on the land. The old tribal organization was on the wane; it still made itself felt in the avenging of a kinsman's death, or when members of a clan assembled periodically for the joint sacrificial feast. Tribe and clan names persisted, but they had acquired in the main a local, geographical connotation. In the cities particularly, the government was in the hands of a body of elders from among the aristocratic families, with one or more of their number acting as the executive. These city councils performed also judicial functions; by the side of the lay judges, the priests sat in judgment over matters affecting the religious life and conscience and administered the oath. Into the hands of the priests was committed the Torah of Moses; copies were made and deposited in the sanctuaries; the priests, likewise, collected and committed to writing, in measured lines or in prose, the story of the past life of the nation and its leaders.

The Canaanite inheritance made itself felt also in the religious sphere. Of an out and out adoption of Canaanite polytheism there could be no question. But the worship of the Lord assumed more and more the features of the indigenous Baal cult. In consonance with the first thought of Moses (p. 17), the Canaanite sanctuaries, high places as they were called, like Bethel, Beer-sheba, Shechem, Gilgal, Penuel, Ramah, Mizpah, were reconsecrated to the service of the Lord; it was recalled that the patriarchs or early leaders had worshiped there. It was inevitable that the Canaanite mode of worship lingered; the danger, only too vividly anticipated by the lawgiver, was realized. The Canaanite symbols, like poles and stone pillars, were suffered to remain. We have seen how Gideon erected an ephod of gold in his sanctuary at Ophrah (p. 27); other examples will meet us later. With the ephod was often associated another idol to which human form was given—the teraphim; both were employed in divination. The popular religion gave itself over to all sorts of magic and witchcraft; the Canaanite worship of demons and departed souls was wide-spread. The grossest aberration consisted in the adoption of human sacrifices (p. 11), strictly forbidden by the Mosaic Torah.

A typical instance of the inroads of paganism is the story of Micah's idolatrous shrine. This man, who was of the tribe of Ephraim, confessed to his mother the theft of a substantial sum of silver; the pious mother dedicated a part of the restored treasure, two hundred shekels, to the Lord. A silver-smith was called in to overlay with silver an image carved of wood or stone, which was placed in the family shrine. Micah installed one of his sons to act as priest. 'In those days there was no king in Israel; every man did that which was right in his own eyes.' It happened that an itinerant Levite from Beth-lehem in Judah passed by; overjoyed, Micah turned over the ministry at his shrine to the trained priest, allowing him above his sustenance and raiment ten shekels of silver yearly. The tribe of Dan in the south, pressed back by the Amorites and finding their territory about Zorah and Eshtaol too limited, just then determined to trek northwards; at the springs of the Jordan, they captured the city of Laish and renamed it Dan. On the way they appropriated the image of Micah's shrine and forced the Levitical priest—he was a descendant of one of the sons of Moses—to accompany them. Micah's protestations were of no avail; unwillingly he sub-mitted to being robbed of image—'his god'—and priest alike. It was an advancement for the Levite to be associated with a tribal sanctuary rather than to minister in a private shrine; the Levitical priesthood continued in Dan until the Philistine advance.

Corruption in morals went hand in hand with the lapse into idolatry. Another Ephraimite Levite, fetching his wife back from her father's house in Beth-lehem, and unwilling to spend the night with non-Israelites in Jebusite Jerusalem, found with difficulty a lodging in the house of an old man in Benjamite Gibeah. A mob demanded the surrender of the Levite for the satisfaction of their unnatural lust. The woman was turned over to the rioters, who abused her to the point of death. The outraged husband published the infamous deed through all Israel. In the war that ensued almost the entire tribe of Benjamin was annihilated; only a small remnant of the warriors escaped. Even the women had been slaughtered. Moreover, the Israelites had bound themselves by a solemn oath not to give their daughters in marriage to Benjamites. The prospect of the extinction of a whole tribe in Israel could not be tolerated. As the city of Jabesh in Gilead had not answered the call to arms, it was decided to punish the citizens by wholesale extermination; only four hundred virgin girls were kept alive, and these were turned over to the Benjamites. As even this number did not suffice, the Benjamites were advised, at the time of the annual festival at Shiloh, to carry off as many of the girls as came out to take part in the dances. No guilt could attach to their fathers or brothers on account of the oath since the girls were taken by force.

Amid this general backsliding into Canaanite idolatry and immorality, there were not wanting circles of zealous adherents to the Mosaic teaching. Thus at Shiloh the imageless cult was kept in its purity. This sanctuary housed the national palladium, the Ark of the Covenant; the priesthood that guarded it was the one instituted by Moses, Levites in descent from his brother Aaron. The warlike tribe of patriarchal times had been transformed by Moses into a brotherhood dedicated to the service of God; they bore the Ark, they ministered at the altar, and they blessed the congregation in the name of God. Wherefore the Levites received no allotment of land; they were endowed instead with certain revenues and tithes. Unlike the stray Levites, content to serve in shrines, private or public, where impure rites prevailed, the order at Shiloh was organized and presided over by men imbued with the Mosaic traditions. Naturally even at Shiloh, those of grosser fibre were rapaciously bent upon their emolument, much to the chagrin of the spiritually minded who in the discharge of their office cut themselves loose from all worldly ties or interests, 'knowing neither father nor brother nor their own children,' absorbed in the service of God and in teaching His ordinances in accordance with the Mosaic Torah.

CHAPTER V

THE RISE OF THE MONARCHY

(1080-1030)

TWO tendencies, operative during the period of the Conquest, retarded the realization of the Mosaic programme. Tribal and local separatism, broken through at intervals only, impeded the progress to complete nationhood; the growing spell which the native civilization cast over the simple minds of the Israelites tended to deaden the purer notions of piety inherent in the Mosaic religious institution. The people were roused to the double danger as a new peril from without swept over the nation. The Philistines, established in the coastal plain, invaded the hills and valleys of the Lowlands. It was this advance, coming on top of the Amorite pressure, that drove the Danites to seek for themselves a new home in the north (p. 33).

For years and decades intermittent skirmishing went on between the two peoples; there were raids and counter-raids; each tried to injure the other. The Danite Samson was the heroic figure which this warfare produced. He was possessed of great strength, which was believed to reside in his locks worn long after the manner of consecrated men ('Nazirites,' Numbers, chapter vi). However, he had a weakness for Philistine women. These alliances enabled him to play many a prank upon the enemies of his people, until through the treachery of his last love, Delilah, he was shorn of his locks and strength. The Philistines blinded him and took him to the temple of their god. There they gathered to make sport of him, but, in a final effort, he brought down the edifice, content to die with his enemies.

Soon the Philistines took the offensive. Their aim was clearly the Carmel range, from which access might be gained to the Plain of Jezreel as well as to the hill-country of Ephraim. A pitched battle was fought between Aphek (in

Sharon) and Eben-ezer (in the year 1080). At the very first onslaught, the Israelites were worsted; four thousand dead covered the field of battle. The Israelitish army retreated and then re-formed, this time with the Ark of the Covenant in their midst. The presence of the Ark betokened the seriousness of the hour; with the Lord now among His hosts, courage filled the breasts of the Israelitish warriors. A shout went up, the old battle-cry which was heard in the times of Moses:

'Rise up, O Lord, and let Thine enemies be scattered;
And let them that hate Thee flee before Thee.'

The Philistines fought with grim fierceness; the Israelites were completely routed; there fell of them thirty thousand footmen. The Ark itself was captured by the enemy; its bearers, Hophni and Phinehas, the sons of Eli the priest of Shiloh, lost their lives. The aged father's heart was trembling for the Ark, which he had suffered to go forth; he was sitting upon a seat by the wayside, when the tidings of the crushing defeat reached him. He was moved neither by his people's disaster nor by the death of his sons; but at the mention of the loss of the Ark, he fell backward and died of a broken neck. Israel lamented the capture of the national palladium. 'The glory is departed from Israel.'

Nothing could hinder the Philistine advance. The temple at Shiloh was razed to the ground. Israel was reduced to a state of vassalage. At Gibeah in Benjamin a Philistine governor was in residence. The Israelites were completely disarmed and the smiths were carried away from the country. Husbandmen were compelled to take their implements to Philistia to have them sharpened for a high price. Sometimes as much as two-thirds of a shekel was paid for the filing of a pickaxe. Remnants of the old Hebrew tribes made common cause with the Philistines; later on they broke away and allied themselves with Israel.

It came home to the clear-headed that the cause of the disaster lay in the people's disorganized condition. If the nation, the whole of it and not merely one or two of the principal tribes, felt itself as such and willed to remain one, salvation, not only at a grave crisis but for all time to come, was to be found in the institution of the monarchy. The way out was shown by the aged seer Samuel (1100–1020). In his younger days, not so long before the battle of Aphek, he had been admitted to the temple at Shiloh and there initiated by Eli as an attendant in the sanctuary. After Eli's death, he returned to his native city Ramah in the hill-country of Ephraim and enjoyed the esteem of wide circles as a seer.

In those days the seer was in a manner the type of man that later came to be called a prophet. Yet the change of name indicated a subtle difference; the transition was effected in these troublous times and under the fostering care of Samuel. Prophecy gave to religion a mystic touch · it meant the complete absorption of the human personality in God, bringing with it religious exaltation and a purified and spiritualized piety. Young enthusiasts traversed the country in bands, singing and dancing as they went along and carrying away the people by their ecstasy. The spirit that stirred them was love of God and love of country; religion and patriotism were one.

The movement, in its incipiency, had in it much that was bizarre; to curb its exuberance and to lead it back into the channels of the Mosaic tradition was the work of Samuel. He scrupled long about the increasing demand for a monarchy. All the nations round about had kings, Egypt, Edom, Moab, Ammon, the Philistine cities. The advantages were certain; but so also were the dangers of Oriental despotism. The experiences of the previous attempts under Gideon and Abimelech were not encouraging; the institution itself seemed a perilous innovation. It had no place in the beginnings of the national existence and was provided for in the Mosaic Torah only as an eventuality none too desirable. Yet the necessity of the hour called for a consistent leadership such as only a king could give. Samuel took counsel with the notables of Israel assembled at Mizpah. The monarchy was determined upon; a constitution was drawn up. Then Samuel produced the man in the person of Saul son of Kish, of the tribe of Benjamin, a resident of Gibeah.

Saul was of a commanding appearance, taller than any of his compatriots. His temperament was such as to commend itself to the shrewd seer on short acquaintance. He had been caught early in the movement of the young enthusiasts, much to the surprise of his friends ('Is Saul also among the prophets?'). Samuel's interest in Saul must have been widely known. The Ammonites, still smarting under Jephthah's blow, saw in the weakening of Israel by the Philistine oppression an opportune moment to regain their lost territory and invested the city of Jabesh in Gilead. The citizens appealed to the city of Gibeah for help. The messengers were received by the people with apathy. But Saul happened to be coming home from the fields behind his oxen. He was quick to act. Forthwith he took a yoke of oxen, cut them in pieces, and sent them broadcast throughout Israel, calling the people to arms with the proclamation: 'Whosoever cometh not forth after Saul and after Samuel, so shall it be done unto his oxen.' The summons was obeyed. An army was assembled. At Bezek, on the road from Shechem to Beth-shan, Saul assumed command; in the night they crossed the Jordan; on the morrow the siege of Jabesh was raised. In triumph the people led Saul to Gilgal; there he was acclaimed as ruler. For the first time in Israel the shout was heard: 'Long live the king.'

The people were now ready to follow their chosen leader, and Saul could do 'as his hand found,' in accordance with an earlier suggestion by Samuel. Saul's son, Jonathan, slew the Philistine governor at Gibeah. The signal was thus given for the uprising. The Philistines took up a position opposite Gibeah in the north, the gorge of Michmas separating the two camps. Three divisions of the Philistine army were raiding the country in several directions; only a small outpost guarded the pass of Michmas. Saul had but a force of six hundred men about him. Jonathan, without the knowledge of his father and accompanied only by his armor-bearer, scaled the cliff and slew twenty men of the Philistine outpost. The others, believing that a larger force was behind the two daring Israelites, fled and carried consternation both to the outpost and into the camp of the raiders. The wild flight of the enemy was hastened by an earthquake. From the heights of Gibeah Saul beheld their panic and quickly pursued the retreating foe. His small force was augmented by former deserters, and all those that had sought safety in the caves of the hill-country of Ephraim crawled out from their hiding-places to join in the pursuit, which extended as far as Aijalon on the slopes of the western range. Saul ordered that none should stop to taste food until the evening, and Jonathan, who in ignorance of the command had eaten some honey, might have perished by the hand of his stern father, had not the people intervened on behalf of the hero of the day.

The Philistines forbore to engage in a formal battle; their generals were content to save the greater part of the army and to lead them back home. Saul's success stiffened the backbone of the nation. The territory of Benjamin, probably also of Judah, was cleared of the enemy. Likewise, the Ammonites, Moabites, and Arameans were driven off from the country east of the Jordan. In order to deliver Judah from the raids of the Amalekites, Saul undertook an expedition against the savage southern neighbor. The enemy was crushingly defeated; their king Agag was taken captive and executed at Gilgal. It was recalled how on the way from Egypt the Amalekites had treacherously fallen upon the Israelite women and children (p. 16).

' There had been a cooling off in Samuel's relations to the king of his choice. Saul was soldier enough and patriot, but somehow lacked a deeper understanding of the prophet's religious soul. The breach between the two leaders of the nation cast a gloom on the remainder of the monarch's career; a predisposition to excitability, of the kind which manifested itself early when he threw himself into the movement of the patriotic enthusiasts, developed into a nervous disorder. An evil spirit seemed to possess him; he was given to unreasoning fits of terror and suspicious brooding; a profound melancholy crept over him, darkening his mind. At the sound of music well played, the unhappy monarch gained temporary relief.

CHAPTER VI

SAUL AND DAVID

(1030-1013)

FROM the day of the disaster at Aphek (p. 36) the tribe of Ephraim had lost its leading position in the nation. The center of gravity was moving southward; the capital of the new kingdom was in Benjamin. The Benjamite monarch drew Judah from a prolonged aloofness to take part in the affairs of the nation. The ascendancy of the southern tribe and the part which it came to play it owed to David, the greatest among its sons. This youngest son of Jesse, at Beth-lehem, was goodly in appearance, of ready speech, and a skilled player on the harp. Saul's courtiers discovered him; the king grew fond of him and made him his personal attendant and armor-bearer. A warm friendship sprang up between David and the king's son, the chivalrous Jonathan. David also won the affection of the king's daughter.

War with the Philistines went on. There were repeated encounters, now here, now there. The king was frequently in camp with his army. His armor-bearer was naturally with him. On one of these campaigns David slew the Philistian champion Goliath, who was of giant stature. He also distinguished himself otherwise at the head of a division over which the king had set him in command. The returning hero was received with acclaims. The women sang:

'Saul hath slain his thousands,
And David his ten thousands.'

From that time on the king's jealousy knew no bounds.

One day, Saul, in his raving condition, threw his spear at David, as he was playing for the king. Dexterously David dodged the thrust. He repaired to his own home; the king ordered a guard placed about David's house, that he might be seized in the morning. He was saved by the loving care of his wife Michal, Saul's younger daughter; apprised of her father's evil intention, she let David slip away in the night. She told the guardsmen that her husband was sick in bed. The maddened king sent his henchmen to fetch him, bed and all. But when they entered the bedchamber, they found resting on a pillow the man-like figure of an idol (teraphim, p. 32), which Michal had laid on the couch in the place of David.

Were these attempts on his life the passing mood of a madman, or was the king definitely committed to the fixed notion that here was a rival who must be done away with? David wanted certainty, and Jonathan agreed to test his father's intentions. The new moon was drawing near when, according to wont, David should take his place at the king's table together with Jonathan and Abner, the chief in command of the army. Saul inquired after the missing David; Jonathan excused his absence on the plea that he had been granted leave to participate in a family festival in his native town Beth-lehem. The angry king used vituperative language about his own son as well as the absent David. True friend that he was, Jonathan, who barely escaped being struck by his father's spear, sent word to David by a prearranged signal. The breach with the king was past recall; safety lay in flight.

Naturally David turned southward, to his own home, to the mountains of Judah which he knew so well and which offered so many hiding-places. He was short of food and weapons. He obtained both at Nob, a small town north of Jerusalem. Here the priesthood of Shiloh had settled after the destruction of their sanctuary (p. 36); Ahimelech, Eli's great-grandson, was their head. David pretended that he had left in haste on a secret errand from the king and Ahimelech was accommodating enough to turn over to him the sword of Goliath (p. 40) which had been deposited in the sanctuary. David continued his flight further to the south; he entrenched himself in the stronghold of Adullam. Here he was joined by his father's house; moreover, there gathered about him some four hundred men, a body of malcontents and adventurers;

their number increased as time went on to six hundred, and under the training of their leader they became proficient in the art of warfare.

As soon as Saul heard of the aid which the fugitives had received at Nob, he inflicted exemplary punishment on the priests' city. All the priests, as well as their retainers, were slain; only one of the sons of Ahimelech, Abiathar, escaped the bloody massacre and found refuge with David. The neighboring town of Keilah was being attacked by the Philistines. David fell upon the enemy and carried away much spoil. He was fearful, however, that the townspeople might deliver him up to Saul. Moreover, it was unsafe to remain long in a fixed place. David therefore chose to roam about in the mountains of Hebron which offered many caverns. Here the Calebite clan had its seat. The beautiful and discreet Abigail, the widow of a wealthy member of this clan, became David's wife. This marriage was doubly advantageous for him; he succeeded to much property and was linked to the influential Calebites. But it also served to embitter the king still more and he gave his daughter Michal in marriage to another of his courtiers.

There were not wanting sympathizers with the king against David and his band of outlaws. Repeatedly the loyal army engaged in pursuit of the fugitive general; once or twice Saul was in danger of being harmed by David's men. David, however, was both magnanimous and prudent and spared the king's life. Nevertheless, it was borne in upon David that sooner or later he might fall into the hands of his pursuers. His condition was desperate. He decided that he must quit Israelitish territory and seek safety with his people's enemy. For a full year and four months David placed himself under the protection of Achish king of Gath. The Philistine ruler hoped that David would fight on his side against Saul; nevertheless he was far from trusting him. He kept him away from the capital. David was content to dwell in Ziklag, not far from Gaza. From there he made repeated raids on Arab bedouins; shrewdly he pretended to the king that he was harassing the Judeans in the Negeb.

The Philistines were now making ready to strike at Israel. Achish demanded of his vassal military service in the ranks of the Philistine army. He was summoned to the council of war. Fortunately for David, the other Philistine kings were suspicious of his fidelity. He returned to Ziklag, only to find the place in ashes. The Amalekite bedouins had made good the opportunity, while David and his contingent were away in the capital; they carried off the women and the children as well as all the spoil. David lost no time in pursuing them; an Egyptian slave, whom the Amalekites had left half-dead on the road, consented to act as guide. The enemy was overtaken; all were slain, save four hundred who rode away upon their camels; in addition to recovering all of his own, David carried away much spoil to Ziklag.

As in the days of Eli (p. 35), the Philistine armies poured by way of Sharon into the Plain of Jezreel. Their objective was the spot where the trade-routes to Damascus joined. They had advanced as far as Shunem in the eastern end of the Plain, when Saul somewhat tardily pursued them with his forces. He halted on the slopes of Mount Gilboa. Before giving battle, he would inquire of the will of God. No reassuring answer was to be obtained by means of the priestly oracle or by the word of prophets. Samuel had been long dead. At no time was his counsel more needed than at this critical moment. It must be procured at all hazards, even if his rest in the netherworld was to be disturbed and his spirit brought up by the magic arts of a witch.

Saul, it is true, had banished the wizards from the land. But near-by at En-dor a woman necromancer was still to be found. The king, in disguise, sought her out at night. In his straits he grasped at the very superstition he had swept away. Saul saw not the apparition, but he heard the voice grimly announcing his doom: 'To-morrow shalt thou and thy sons be with me.' Broken in spirit, Saul led his army into the battle. The Israelitish forces were routed; among the slain were Jonathan and his two brothers. The king was hard pressed by the Philistine archers. He begged his armor-bearer to make an end of his life. But the lad refused. So Saul fell upon his own sword (1013). The next day the Philistines came to strip the slain. They found the bodies of Saul and his three sons. They took the king's armor to the temple of Astarte; his head they severed as a trophy, and his trunk they suspended upon the wall of Beth-shan. The inhabitants of Jabesh remembered how Saul had responded to their cry for help (p. 38); in the night they removed his body and gave it honorable burial in their own city. Subsequently, David had the bones of Saul and Jonathan removed to their family sepulcher at Zela in Benjamin.

David mourned the tragic death of the king, 'the anointed of the Lord,' when the tidings came to Ziklag, with unfeigned sincerity. Forgotten was the private feud; David was stirred to his depths by the national calamity; his sorrow over the death of his heroic and chivalrous friend Jonathan was intense, and it found expression in his famous elegy:

'Saul and Jonathan, the lovely and the pleasant
In their lives, even in their death they were not divided.
I am distressed for thee, my brother Jonathan;
Very pleasant hast thou been unto me;
Wonderful was thy love to me,
Passing the love of women.
How are the mighty fallen,
And the weapons of war perished!'

CHAPTER VII

DAVID. THE CAPTURE OF JERUSALEM

(1013-1006)

THE outcome of the battle of Gilboa could mean only a state of vassalage for Israel. It would seem that Benjamite territory was again occupied by the Philistines and that a Philistine governor once more resided in Gibeah. Ishbaal, Saul's fourth son, moved his residence to Mahanaim, north of the Jabbok, across the Jordan. His succession to the throne was tolerated by the Philistines so long as their overlordship was acknowledged. On similar terms David was permitted to mark out a course for himself in the restricted southern area. His ambitions were well known; his superior generalship was feared; it was advantageous to have him as a friend. Moreover, he was a match for the weak Ishbaal; the two would hold each other in check.

David was quick enough to realize the situation. His first act was to send of the rich spoil, which the expedition against the Amalekites had yielded, presents to the elders of Judah in the principal localities visited by him during his flight. Forthwith David removed his harem and his well-trained troop to Hebron, then the chief city of Judah, whence he opened negotiations with the notables of the small country. David commended himself to them as one of their own flesh and bone and by reason of his military prestige during Saul's early campaign against the Philistines. At Hebron David was proclaimed king of Judah; this dignity he maintained for seven years and a half (1013–1006).

But David aimed higher. He looked upon himself as the real successor of Saul, not only in Judah but in all Israel. He sent messages of his accession beyond the tribal boundaries, in particular to the citizens of Jabesh in Gilead, whom he commended for their act of respect to his predecessor. The times, he indicated, called for courage, seeing that Saul was dead; the implication being that Ishbaal was altogether unequal to the situation. And so he was. The real ruler was the commander of his forces, his great-uncle Abner, personally brave and, so long as Ishbaal let him alone, devoted to the house of Saul, but far surpassed by David in shrewd political judgment and military prowess.

Civil war was inevitable. The first encounter took place near Gibeon, in Benjamite territory. Abner and his forces were worsted. David's men were led by Joab son of David's sister Zeruiah; with Joab were his two brothers, Abishai and Asahel. Light-footed, Asahel overtook Abner; the Benjamite commander, who was retreating with his army to Mahanaim, struck the pursuer down, not without reluctance, fearing the blood feud that must ensue between himself and the redoubtable Joab.

The war between the house of Saul and the house of David was a protracted one. From day to day David waxed stronger and Ishbaal weaker. It must have come home to certain sections of the Israelites, despite the antipathy of the northerners for the south, that the interests of the nation would be best served if David became ruler of united Israel. The movement gained strength when Ishbaal and his powerful minister fell out. It was not long before Abner made direct overtures to David. He offered to use his influence with his own tribe and the whole north. David stipulated the restoration of his former wife Michal (p. 42); a formal request was sent to the king at Mahanaim, who generously gave his consent. Michal was conducted to Hebron by an embassy of twenty men led by Abner. At a banquet in their honor Abner renewed his offer to win over the north.

David was well content to let things take their course. The treacherous conduct of the minister was none of his concern; he was pleased by the growing sentiment in his favor; he was never in doubt of his fitness to rule over the entire nation. Joab had been wisely left out of the negotiations; David knew his bitter enmity toward Ishbaal's minister, so he took the precaution to send him away on a foray. The general returned ahead of time; aside from the private feud, he feared the ascendancy of the Benjamite and, moreover, suspected hidden motives to betray David into the hands of his enemies. Without the king's knowledge, he overtook Abner, persuaded him to return to Hebron, and there in the gate he struck him down. David had full reason to be exasperated by this foul deed which threatened to bring to naught his well-laid plans; sincerely he mourned the death of the princely Abner, who fell 'with hands unbound and feet unfettered.' Joab and his brother, however, were far too strong for David to make them pay for their dastardly crime.

It is not evident that it had been the design of Abner and his followers to do away with Ishbaal; but whether or not instigated by higher officials, two Benjamite captains assassinated him while he was taking his noon-time siesta. His cause was collapsing daily, and David was a man who could bide his time. When the murderers brought their king's head to Hebron in the expectation of reward, they met instead condign punishment. Naturally David profited by his rival's untimely death. Of Saul's dynasty there now remained but Jonathan's son Meribaal, a mere boy and a cripple. So the tribes of Israel, represented by their notables, came to Hebron and offered the throne to David. Agreement being reached as to the rights and duties of both monarch and people, David was anointed formally and publicly as king over the entire nation.

The people looked to the new ruler to break the yoke of Philistine bondage. Nor were the Philistines slow to understand the meaning of David's elevation. David was far too weak to take the offensive. The Philistine plan was to act swiftly. Before David had time to assemble an army, Judah was invaded, Beth-lehem occupied, and Hebron menaced. David withdrew to the stronghold of Adullam. This was familiar ground, and here he remained for some time until he could consolidate his fighting forces. With these he made a sortie and was successful in striking tellingly at the enemy encamped in the Giants' Valley southwest of Jerusalem. The Philistines came again; once more they pitched in the same spot. This time David attacked them in the rear, from the east, and drove them northward as far as Gibeon and then toward Gezer, the western frontier of Israelitish territory. Many more battles followed, in which David's chosen warriors distinguished themselves. Once David came near losing his life, when a giant, whose spear weighed three hundred shekels, bore down upon him; but Abishai forestalled the Philistine and slew him. Then David was besought by his faithful companions in arms never to expose himself in battle again, 'that the light of Israel might not be quenched.' At length David struck a decisive blow by capturing the city of Gath. The power of the Philistines was broken. Philistia was not subjugated nor were the Philistines annihilated. The coastland remained in their possession. But no longer did they dare to set foot on Israelitish territory. An enduring peace was made between the two peoples, who lived from now on in neighborly amity. The Philistines had taught David the craft of warfare; principally from them he recruited his body-guard, the Cherethites and Pelethites.

With the Philistine peril removed, Israel was on the road to the period of 'rest' foreseen by Moses. David's genius understood that the moment had arrived for creating a national center in order to provide a tangible expression of political and religious unity which might check the natural propensity to separatism. Hebron was suitable for the capital of a small country like Judah; but its situation far to the south as well as its close associations with David's own tribe unfitted it as a rallying point for the whole nation. Amid the early campaign against the Philistines, David set out to look for a new capital. His fancy was caught by the Jebusite stronghold Jerusalem. No happier choice could have been made. If the roads connecting the Mediterranean and the east as well as Syria and Egypt did not exactly pass by the city, they were nevertheless not too far away; the site might therefore be considered central enough for trade and commerce. Yet it stood sufficiently aloof; save on the north, its weakest spot, it seemed inaccessible and well-nigh impregnable. The resistance which Jerusalem offered successively to Assyrians, Babylonians, and Romans demonstrated how correct was David's estimate of the site as a natural fastness. In ancient times the city's springs and conduits were sufficient for her population. Moreover, the city lay close to the territory of Benjamin and might well be included within its southern border, the line running from the mouth of the Jordan, touching En-rogel at the southeastern end of the city, and then circling around due west.

The Canaanite strip, which for a long time kept Judah severed from the north, had dwindled away in the course of the Philistine campaigns and lost all power of resistance before the attacks of Saul and David. Jerusalem alone had held out. The Jebusites seemed safe in their strongly fortified citadel upon the rocky hill of Zion. David would have preferred to secure the fortress by peaceful negotiations. The Jebusites mockingly replied that if the walls were manned by the blind and the lame any assault would still be a vain undertaking. Joab, however, discovered the tunnel leading from Gihon into the fortress; up that conduit he crawled with his most daring warriors, thus trapping the surprised citizens. David was master of the stronghold; he added still further outworks and named the whole The City of David.

Jerusalem was to be more than a mere royal residence, 'the city where David encamped.' She was to be the City of God, and this sacred character, which has been hers ever since, was stamped upon her by David himself. He was far too human to be a saint; but he was deeply imbued with religious feeling. He had an inkling of his people's destiny; his vision went beyond the immediate foundation to the issues that lay in time to come. He would enhance the prestige of the new national center by linking it to the religious traditions of Samuel and, beyond him, to those of Moses. The ancient national palladium, the Ark, lost by the Ephraimites to the Philistines (p. 36), had after many vicissitudes been lodged in a private dwelling at Baalath in Judah. If Zion could be made the resting-place of the Ark, it would come to be looked upon by the northern tribes as a religious center in legitimate succession to Shiloh. An untoward incident to the driver of the cart upon which the Ark rested filled David with apprehensions; so the Ark remained without the citadel in the house of Obed-edom the Gittite, a Philistine in David's service. Only after three months, when it was seen that divine blessings came to the Philistine by reason of his housing the Ark, did David renew his attempt to transfer it to his own city. In solemn procession, amid the tumultuous joy of the populace, the Ark was carried up the hill of Zion. David, robed in linen vestments such as were worn by priests, led in the dancing of the marchers as they followed the sacred chest toward the palace. Michal, the proud daughter of Saul, condemned the undignified demeanor of the king. David retorted that for the sake of the Lord, who had elevated him above her father's house, he would find honor in still humbler abasement.

The Ark was set down under a tent close by the royal residence. David must already have given thought to providing a more solid structure for its housing. But there was just then much warfare ahead, if the new state was to be put upon a sure footing. Even when security was later achieved, the king gave heed to the counsel of the prophet Nathan to leave the project to his successor. The Lord was content to dwell in a tent; rather than that David should build Him a house, He would build a house for David, that is, a permanent dynasty. Still David was privileged to make preparations for the future Temple; he even found an e'evated place to the north as a site for the sacred edifice.

CHAPTER VIII

THE WARS OF DAVID

(1006-980)

ISRAEL'S neighbors to the east and to the north took alarm at David's steady progress in consolidating the kingdom. The Ammonites, humbled in the days of Saul, had recovered during Ishbaal's weak administration; now they felt strong enough to pick a quarrel of their own accord. On the accession of Hanun to the throne after the death of his father Nahash, David, in obedience to time-honored custom, sent an embassy to the new monarch. The ambassadors were rudely affronted and sent home. The action was tantamount to a declaration of war. The Ammonites formed a coalition with several Aramean principalities (Rehob, Zobah, Maacah) extending as far as the spur of Hermon. When Joab arrived with the Israelitish army, he found himself between two fires; the Ammonites faced him in the open country outside their capital, while the Arameans threatened him in the rear. Quickly he formed his plans. He left half of the army under the command of his brother Abishai to engage the Ammonites; with the other half he threw himself upon their allies. The Arameans were put to flight; the Ammonites, unable to withstand the onslaught of the Israelites, sought safety in their capital.

The campaign, however, was by no means terminated. The Ammonite capital Rabbah (the modern Amman), a naturally strong fortress on the upper Jabbok, was still threatening. Moreover, in the following year the Arameans appeared again. They were commanded by Shobach, the general of Hadadezer king of Zobah, who had now summoned his vassals from all the lands as far as the Euphrates. This time David led his army in person; a decisive battle was fought and the enemy suffered a crushing defeat. A large portion of their cavalry fell into David's hand. Shobach lost his life in the battle; Hadadezer was substantially weakened so that there could be no thought of succoring his Ammonite neighbor. In the third year, Joab invested Rabbah and succeeded in reducing the citadel which protected the water-supply of the city. The capture of the city itself was reserved for David. He possessed himself of much treasure, including the crown of Milcom, the god of the Ammonites, which weighed a talent of gold and was ornamented with precious stones. This crown the victor set upon his own head. The captured citizens were put to hard work at stone-cutting and brickmaking for the building operations in Jerusalem. The Moabites, who must have availed themselves of the initial successes of the Ammonites to harass the Israelites, were cruelly punished; two-thirds of the population were put to death. Moab, like Ammon, became tributary to Israel.

Hadadezer was meanwhile bent upon retrieving his fortunes. His vassals in the northeast, who had made peace with David, must be brought to book. David met him in battle and defeated him; the same fate overtook Damascus which had come to Hadadezer's aid. Both Zobah and Damascus were annexed and governed by resident officers from Jerusalem. David's realm now extended in the north as far as the Lebanon and Hermon, and in the northeast beyond Damascus to the western banks of the Euphrates. Toi, king of Hamath, who had been at war with Hadadezer, sent David a message of congratulation and costly presents. David's friendship was likewise sought by Talmai, king of Geshur, in the Golan, east of the Lake of Galilee; the peace was sealed by David taking to wife Talmai's daughter Maacah, who became the mother of Absalom. Friendly relations were also established between David and Hiram, king of Tyre; they continued under Solomon.

There remained the troublesome neighbors in the south. The Amalekites were completely annihilated and never more heard of afterwards. Edom, defeated in a bloody battle in the Valley of Salt (east of Beer-sheba), was made tributary; Israelitish tax-collectors were placed in the land. Thus David won access to the ports of Ezion-geber and Elath on the Gulf of Akabah. The Edomites yielded for the present to superior force; but they were on the alert to break loose and shake off the yoke of servitude.

It was thus a veritable empire that David succeeded in building. Stretching from the Red Sea to the Euphrates, it commanded the most important trade-routes of the East. The times were propitious. Egypt was in a state of decline and Assyria was an insignificant power; so David was providentially permitted to exercise to the fullest his military genius. In all of his undertakings he was ably seconded by Joab, a warrior intrepid and undismayed, and if not exactly fastidious in his choice of means, a prudent counselor, wholly devoted to the weal of his master.

It is obvious that for such heavy warfare on many fields David must have taken care to perfect his fighting machine. The nucleus of the army consisted of his ever faithful bodyguard of six hundred picked men, who had gathered about him during the days of his outlawry; as gaps occurred, new men were enlisted, chiefly foreigners. This troop was commanded by Benaiah son of Jehoiada, who hailed from the Negeb. A small body of thirty 'mighty men,' ready for the most daring exploits, did service under three captains. But neither all these nor the other mercenaries sufficed for the larger campaigns. The brunt of the fighting fell upon all young Israelites capable of bearing arms. The ancient wont was for these to respond as the emergency arose and the call to arms was issued. Conditions, however, had changed; the security of the nation demanded a standing army. For that purpose Joab was ordered to take a census of the entire population. Three quarters of a year were consumed in completing the count. Shortly thereafter a devastating plague broke out. The people, who had only grumblingly submitted to the census, saw in the calamity a punishment from God. When the plague reached Jerusalem, it was stayed over the threshing-floor of the Jebusite Araunah. As an act of expiation, David purchased this ground for fifty shekels of silver. There David erected an altar, destined as the site of the great altar which Solomon built in the Temple court facing the eastern entrance.

David's attitude to the surviving members of the previous dynasty was dictated by magnanimity coupled with prudence. He turned over to Meribaal, Jonathan's crippled son (p. 47), the family estate at Gibeah, to be administered by a steward for the prince's benefit. The prince himself was recalled from across the Jordan to Jerusalem; here he might remain under the eye of the king, who was circumspect enough to forestall any possible Benjamite uprising; at the same time Meribaal was treated with the utmost kindness and ate at the king's table. Had David wished to rid himself of the surviving offspring of Saul, after the manner of Oriental rulers, willing agents would have been found to do his bidding. It was a different matter with the two sons of Saul by his concubine Rizpah, and his five grandsons, the children of his daughter Merab. The Gibeonites demanded their lives in expiation for the slaughter of their citizens by Saul, in violation of the oath of peace which the Israelites had sworn to them (p. 22). There was a famine in the land; the curse of God seemed to rest upon it. There was nothing left for David but to deliver the victims, whom the Gibeonites put to death. Lovingly, Rizpah kept watch by their remains until the time of the first rains. David had the bones assembled and given burial in the family sepulcher. Force of circumstances had driven him to acquiesce in this wholesale murder; but he carried his point in refusing to yield up Meribaal, the son of his beloved friend Jonathan.

CHAPTER IX

THE REVOLTS OF ABSALOM AND OF SHEBA

(980-973)

THE military successes of David were offset by family troubles. The subjugator of nations was not strong enough to curb his amorous desires. While Joab and the army were investing Rabbah (p. 52), David entered into illicit relations with the wife of one of his captains who was away at the front. To cover up the consequences, David ordered Uriah, the husband, to be sent home on leave. But as the captain refused to spend the night away from the palace, preferring to remain there with the guards, the king sent him back to the front with a sealed letter to the commanding general to place Uriah in an exposed position and then leave him unsupported to his fate. The plot was successful.

Uriah's wife Bath-sheba was now taken into the harem as the king's wife. She gave birth to a son. The scandal aroused public opinion; the prophet Nathan gave voice to it by means of a parable concerning a rich man who had robbed a poor neighbor of his sole possession. When David declared that such an offender ought to die, the prophet confronted him with the rebuke: 'Thou art the man.' Instead of frowning upon the unwelcome meddler, the king showed the depth of his religious nature by remorseful confession of his guilt. The child grew sick and despite David's prayers and fasting died. The grief-stricken father acknowledged the divine judgment. Greater evil was to rise up against him out of his own family, in fulfilment of the doom announced by the prophet.

Life at court must have been opulent; in the wake of luxurious ease followed looseness in morals. David's first-born son Amnon conceived a violent passion for his beautiful half-sister Tamar, Absalom's full sister, and after violating her sent her away in disgrace. David was too indulgent a father to discipline his son; moreover, Amnon was the first-born and therefore heir apparent. So Absalom took it upon himself to avenge the insult to his sister. After two years' waiting, he invited the court to attend a sheep-shearing festivity on his northern estate. Amnon and the other princes came. During the feast, Amnon was struck down by Absalom's orders. David mourned for his son bitterly. Absalom escaped to the court of his grandfather Talmai (p. 52) and remained there three years, until Joab shrewdly worked upon the king's mind. Absalom was permitted to return to Jerusalem; after a lapse of two more years he was received at court, again through Joab's intercession.

Absalom, once more in the king's good graces, was not content to await his father's death in order to succeed him, but instead plotted to supplant him during his lifetime. He was good to look upon; he set out deliberately to captivate the people by his winning manners and to steal their affection for the aging king by insinuating that redress at court was difficult to obtain. For four years he made his secret preparations. When the time seemed ripe for open rebellion, he asked his father's leave to hold a religious festival at Hebron. The old capital was the seat of disaffection among the Judean nobles, who saw themselves pushed into the background by the king's wider national interests. But also in the north the régime of David had given rise to animosities. A considerable number of northerners joined in the rebellion, which must have struck David as a bolt from the blue sky.

The king decided to quit the capital and to seek safety across the Jordan. The east was less given to change; it clung to David, as it had previously stood by the house of Saul. With the king departed his household and his faithful body-guard; whether for life or for death, so his old companions in arms announced, their place was with their lord the king. The priests Zadok and Abiathar, with the Ark, desired to accompany him; David prevailed upon them to return, but arranged that their sons, Ahimaaz and Jonathan, should act as secret spies. He likewise dismissed his intimate friend Hushai, that he might counteract the counsels of Ahithophel, the grandfather of Bath-sheba. Ahithophel was reputed for his judgment as infallible as a divine oracle; he joined the rebellion in order to square the family's account with the seducer of his granddaughter. Absalom found adherents likewise among the Benjamites, who, rightly or wrongly, looked upon the king as the destroyer of the house of Saul. That Meribaal was in sympathy with the rebel, was probably a malicious slander invented by his steward to further his personal interests; but another Benjamite grandee, Shimei son of Gera, openly gloated over the king's misfortunes.

If Absalom was to be successful, he must strike swiftly, before David could gather an army. Such was the sound advice of Ahithophel. Hushai, however, counseled delay. He pointed out that David had with him seasoned soldiers; that they were in an angry mood; it was futile to attempt to trap David; failure at the initial stage would spell disaster. It were better to wait until the whole of the Israelitish army had been recruited, from Dan to Beer-sheba, with Absalom in personal command. Blindly, the rebel prince suffered himself to be duped. Quickly the intelligence was conveyed to David, who lost no time in putting the Jordan between himself and the enemy. The city of Mahanaim served him as a base of operations. Gileadite grandees, as Barzillai and Machir, and even the subjugated Ammonite king, Shobi son of Nahash, supplied the rapidly assembling royal forces with provisions.

The army was formed in three divisions, under the command of Joab, Abishai, and Ittai the Gittite. The rebel army crossed the Jordan, with Absalom and Amasa, a son of David's sister Abigail, in command. David himself remained in the improvised capital, while the two armies met in battle in the Forest of Ephraim, a jungle east of the Jordan. The rebel army was routed; the rocky thickets were fatal to the fugitives, the forest devouring more people than the sword. In the haste of flight, Absalom was caught by the hair, which he was in the habit of wearing long, in the prickly boughs of an oak-tree, and as his head was held fast in the branches, the mule he was riding trotted on, leaving him suspended in the air. Thus he was found by a common soldier of the pursuing army, who informed Joab. The general hastened to the spot and, unmindful of the king's order to spare the life of his rebel son, thrust three darts into the heart of the struggling Absalom. The signal was given for calling off the pursuit; Absalom's body was cast into a pit and covered with stones.

The tidings reached David, as he sat at the gate waiting for the outcome of the battle. The father's grief over the death of his erring, but beloved son was uncontrollable. He shut himself up in the chamber over the gate and sobbed bitterly: 'Would I had died in thy stead, O Absalom, my son, my son!' The victorious army entered the city in hushed silence and stealthily, as if it, and not the enemy, had been defeated. Joab strongly urged the king to show himself to the army. The general had reason on his side, but his harsh language was offensive, and this together with the killing of the king's son left a rankling in David's heart.

The northern part of the nation was the first to come to its senses. On the other hand, the Judeans still sulked. It was, of course, necessary to conciliate them; the king went so far as to offer Amasa the command of the national forces. But it was a dangerous game which David played, to pit north and south against each other; the ill consequences showed themselves only too soon, and after a generation the breach which rent the nation in twain was complete. For the time being the Judeans forestalled their northern brethren in leading the king homeward. At Gilgal the belated representatives of the north came to meet him. They considered themselves slighted, seeing that they had ten shares in the king against the two of Judah and Benjamin.

The loyalty of the Benjamites was by no means a certain matter. Sheba son of Bichri led a fresh revolt; though he could make no headway in Judah, he won a following in Israel. Amasa was commissioned by the king to mobilize the army. The thing was not done speedily enough to suit Joab, who won the king's ear and was sent off in command of the trusted mercenary force. At Gibeon the rival kinsmen met; Joab murdered Amasa in cold blood. He then pursued the rebels who had entrenched themselves at Abel near the springs of the Jordan. Joab made ready to storm the city, when the citizens cut off the head of the rebel leader and cast it over the wall. The revolt had failed.

David was now aged and feeble. The question of succession had not been settled, although there had been a private understanding between the king and Bath-sheba that her son Solomon would reign in his stead. By right of seniority, his elder half-brother Adonijah considered himself heir presumptive. He was supported by Joab and by the priest Abiathar. By the Serpent's Stone, west of En-rogel, Adonijah assembled his following in order to prepare his proclamation as king. The news reached Bath-sheba and her party, to which belonged Benaiah the captain of the body-guard, Zadok the priest, and Nathan the prophet. The king was reminded of his promise, and he gave orders to have Solomon proclaimed king. At the spring Gihon Solomon was anointed with the sacred oil by Zadok and acclaimed by the populace. On his death-bed the old king charged his successor to do away with Joab and the Benjamite Shimei (p. 57); on the other hand, he commended to Solomon's favor the family of his friend Barzillai the Gileadite.

David died in 973, after a reign of forty years, thirty-three years after the foundation of the City of David, where he was buried. He left to his successor a rich heritage, and to his people the memory of glorious achievement. He had his faults; in the full record of his life, which is preserved in Holy Writ, there is no attempt to cover them up or condone them. He could be vindictive and then again magnanimous; he hated his enemies, but also loved his friends; he was an overindulgent father; he was prone to sin, but was quick to repent. He rose to his station by dint of an indomitable energy; a great warrior, he also pursued the gentle arts of song and music; he loved religious pomp and ceremony. Deeply pious by nature, he divined his people's sacred vocation. The holy city of Jerusalem was his foundation, the rocky hill for the rearing of the Temple was his choice. His dynasty continued down to Persian times; patriarchs and exilarchs reckoned themselves to his house. To the last days the hope of Israel is bound up with this great figure, David the king, symbol of the Jew's undying faith.

CHAPTER X

SOLOMON. THE TEMPLE

(973-933)

SOLOMON carried out his father's instructions to the letter. He lost no time in ridding himself of Joab, the supporter of Adonijah, as well as of Adonijah himself. In the place of Joab he appointed Benaiah commander of the army. The maintenance of the fighting machine built up by the father was the son's watchful concern. There were rumblings among the subjugated nations. Hadad, of royal Edomite blood, had fled to Egypt at the time of the conquest of his country by David.

The Pharaohs of the Tanite (twenty-first) dynasty could not but be ill at ease over the rise of the Palestinian empire which they had been powerless to prevent; they were ready enough to sponsor the cause of Israel's enemies. So Hadad was made welcome at the Egyptian court and received one of the royal princesses in marriage. After David's death he returned to his own country and succeeded in wresting certain provinces from Solomon. It is a question whether Hadad was able to maintain himself long; certainly Solomon kept the port of Ezion-geber, which gave him access to the Red Sea.

Egypt seems to have thrown soldiery into southern Palestine, thus renewing her claim to the land. It was politic both for the Pharaoh and for Solomon to come to terms. South of the Lebanon Solomon was by far the strongest potentate of his time; it was well, however, to have Egypt for a friend, and she was quite satisfied with certain commercial concessions. In return, the Pharaoh's soldiers engaged themselves to reduce the fortress of Gezer, the last remnant of Canaanite power; the city was the Pharaoh's present to his daughter, whom Solomon took as wife.

In the north Solomon had difficulties with Rezon son of Eliada, a former general in Hadadezer's army, who succeeded in expelling the Israelitish Resident from Damascus and founded there a kingdom for himself. If Solomon was thus unable to prevent certain losses of territory at the extreme ends of his realm, he bent his efforts all the more upon consolidating the land of Israel proper. To that end he fortified Hazor in Naphtali; Megiddo; then Beth-horon in the pass leading to Jerusalem; lastly the newly won Gezer, as well as other cities through which the caravan routes passed. Store-cities were built which were stocked with ample ammunition, chariots, and horses.

Solomon's reign was preëminently one of enduring peace. Judah and Israel dwelt safely, every man under his vine and under his fig-tree, from Dan to Beer-sheba. Justice, impartial and even-handed, was to be had at the king's court. The fiscal administration of the country was severely regulated. The country was divided into twelve districts, each presided over by a royal officer. The residue of the Canaanites was reduced to serfdom. But forced labor was exacted also of the Israelites. In the Lebanon ten thousand men did labor for the king under Adoniram, the master of the levy. Solomon had inherited great wealth, gold and silver and objects of art, accumulated by David during many wars. For his vast building operations both material and labor were needed; the service of foreign, chiefly Phoenician, craftsmen had to be paid for in products of the soil. The king's subjects were taxed to provide the luxuries of the royal table, as well as barley and straw for the royal stud. The burden grew heavier and heavier; but if disaffection manifested itself, it was put down with a strong hand.

The plain Israelitish husbandman must have been dazzled by the magnificence of the king's court. Solomon was fond of women, costly buildings, luxurious surroundings. But he was alive to the conditions of his time and to the advantages of the geographical situation of Palestine. The commerce of the world, from Egypt, from Arabia, from lands beyond, passed through Israel. It was inevitable that profit should be derived from it. The king took toll of the foreign merchants. But it was open to him to increase his wealth by mercantile undertakings of his own. He imported and exported horses. A fleet of the king's, in coöperation with that of Hiram king of Tyre, visited Ophir, on the coast of southern Arabia or of eastern Africa, and brought home gold and other articles of merchandise. The Israelitish monarch thus entered into connection with the large world without; the queen of Sheba paid him a visit and brought and received costly gifts.

Thus the land of Israel was opened up to the world, and a knowledge of the great world penetrated into Israel. The merchants, whether royal or private, had an outlook upon things transcending the narrow horizon of the stay-at-home. There was a touch of the secular, worldly-wise, about Solomon and his period. Beyond the immediate concerns of the nation, attention was turned to universal experiences of mankind, taking shape in sententious sayings which inculcate a practical lesson. The king himself was known for his wisdom and for his interest in the collection of fables and parables (Proverbs), just as his father was famed as a poet who gave impetus to the lyric song, especially of the religious kind (Psalms).

The erection of the Temple, planned by David, was executed in Solomon's reign. With Solomon it was part of a large scheme of buildings with the object of beautifying Jerusalem. The site for the Temple had been determined by David (p. 53). It was the northern extension of Zion, the area corresponding nearly to what is known to-day as the Haram. The present remains of the western enclosure belong to Herodian times; but its foundation is Solomonic. In Solomon's structure that was an Inner Court, so called to distinguish it from the other Court south, in front of the Palace, and the Great Court encompassing the whole complex of buildings.

The Temple edifice itself lay east and west, with the entrance on the eastern side as in Egyptian temples. It was a rectangular building of large squared stones and cedar beams. It consisted of two apartments, separated by a wall in which was a door made of olive wood. The outer and larger apartment, the 'Hekal' or Nave, accommodated the Table of Showbread, upon which twelve cakes, six in a row, fresh every sabbath, were exposed; the Altar of Incense; ten golden Candlesticks, five on each side, at the entrance of the smaller apartment. The candelabra furnished artificial light, since the windows, narrow without, though widening inwards, high above the ground and with wooden lattices, were not calculated to relieve the darkness. The inner room behind, the 'Debir' or Sanctuary, was lower, a perfect cube. It was the most holy part of the sacred edifice, the Holy of Holies, containing the Ark surmounted by two cherubim of olive wood plated with gold. Throughout the paneling was of cedar, richly adorned with carvings, while the floor was of cypress wood.

In front of the building, the House, as it was called, stood a Porch, with two bronze columns at the entrance. On the other three sides, attached to the thick walls, ran a side-structure consisting of three stories of chambers to a height half that of the House itself. These chambers served as depositories for the Temple utensils and votive offerings, thus constituting the Temple Treasury. Within the Court enclosure stood the Bronze Altar upon which public and private sacrifices were offered. In the Court the worshipers assembled; here the prophets addressed the people. The Temple proper could be entered only by the priests, the Holy of Holies only by the chief priest once a year. The older line of priests of the house of Eli had forfeited their position through Abiathar's participation in Adonijah's intrigue. They were banished to their estates at Anathoth. In their stead Solomon appointed the sons of Zadok, the priest who favored his own accession; these sons of Zadok remained in office until the Maccabees stepped into their place. In the temple of Onias in Egypt the Zadokites continued until the closing of their sanctuary by the Romans (p. 204).

South of the Temple area, the lower terraces of the hill were occupied by the King's House or Palace and by state buildings. The Palace compound contained more than one building; Solomon's Egyptian wife dwelt in a mansion built expressly for her. From the Palace Court one entered another compound in which stood the Hall of Justice and the House of the Forest of Lebanon. The latter structure consisted of two stories. The lower story had forty-five cedar columns, which gave it the appearance of a forest; the large hall served as an assembly room for the elders of Israel. The upper story was used as an arsenal.

The whole complex of buildings, from the Forest House to the Temple, presented an imposing spectacle. The building materials were hauled to Jerusalem from various quarters. The wood was cut down by Israelitish labor in the Lebanon; it was then floated by Phoenician sailors down the coast to Jaffa. The stone was chiseled near the quarries; the bronze was cast in the Valley of the Jordan. Phoenician craftsmen, supplied by Hiram king of Tyre, were depended upon for executing the larger part of the work upon well-established models; the Israelitish artificers proved good pupils. Seven years were consumed in the building of the Temple, and thirteen were spent in the erection of the other structures. Upon the completion of the Temple, a Feast of Dedication was celebrated; it began with the solemn transfer of the Ark to the Debir. The Temple was the everlasting symbol of the Divine Presence in Israel. Near to all that called upon Him, He was yet far removed, above all comparison. The cloud which enveloped the Temple on the day of its dedication betokened God's unfathomable mystery.

Solomon was devoted to the service of the God of his fathers. Reasons of state, however, compelled him to enter into alliances with many foreign powers. His harem contained, in addition to the Egyptian princess, women of the Moabites, Ammonites, Edomites, Sidonians, and Hittites. Jerusalem was in his conception to be a city in which all these nations should feel at home. For their benefit he built chapels in which they might worship their gods. State interests clashed with a rigid interpretation of Mosaism. There was also another reason for disaffection. The northerners, in particular, groaned under the heavy taxes, paid in produce or forced labor. An Ephraimite, Jeroboam son of Nebat, who was in charge of the compulsory labor of the house of Joseph, availed himself of the deep-rooted antipathy of the north for the south to conspire against the king. The plot was abetted by the prophet Ahijah, whose home was at Shiloh. Thus sectional rivalry, innate opposition to task-work, and religious motives combined to prepare the movement for secession. Solomon, so soon as it came to his ears, sought to apprehend the ringleader. Jeroboam, however, escaped to Egypt, where Shishak, the founder of the Libyan (twenty-second) dynasty, had seated himself on the throne of the Pharaohs. There Jeroboam remained until the death of Solomon (933).

CHAPTER XI

THE SECESSION OF THE NORTH

(933-875)

SOLOMON was succeeded by his son Rehoboam. In the
south his accession was taken as a matter of course, so
firmly rooted was the dynastic principle in David's
own home. Not so in the north. Rehoboam consented to go
to Shechem, the center of the disaffected tribes, in order to
parley with them. A delegation presented a request for the
alleviation of the burdens resting upon the people. The elder
statesmen advised the king to yield. But his younger counselors, those that were grown up with him, favored repressive
measures and the use of force. The king's defiant reply was
met by open revolt. Adoniram, the hated master of the levy,
was stoned to death. The king himself barely escaped with
his life. Immediately the north seceded and established the
Kingdom of Israel, in contradistinction to the Kingdom of
Judah in the south. Jeroboam, who had in the meantime
returned from exile, was proclaimed king in Shechem.

Thus the major part of the inheritance from father and
grandfather was lost by the grandson. Only the tribe of Benjamin held to Judah, and of the subjugated nations, Edom
alone. Rehoboam (933–917) continued to regard the seceders
as rebels and mobilized an armed force against them. The
fratricidal war lasted during the whole of his reign. As might
be expected, the disorganized condition of the northern
realm led to reverses. Jeroboam was compelled to move his
capital from Shechem to Penuel across the Jordan. In his
straits he called in the help of Shishak, who was not slow to
respond. The Pharaoh appeared before the gates of Jerusalem, and Rehoboam was forced to buy him off by surrendering to him Temple and palace treasures, including the
golden shields of the king's body-guard. After the withdrawal of the Egyptians, Rehoboam took care to prevent a

similar invasion by fortifying the exposed cities in the south. Though Israel was not reconquered, the territory of Judah was kept intact.

Jeroboam (933–912) was determined upon detaching Israel from Judah both politically and religiously. So much had the Temple of Jerusalem accomplished that it stood for religious centralization, which proved attractive to thoughtful men even in Israel. It was therefore necessary to lead the people back to the idea of religious decentralization such as had anciently prevailed. From now on the north put itself squarely upon the position of the earlier Mosaic legislation which conceded more than one sanctuary in a given period (p. 17). Accordingly Jeroboam made it a point to restore the worship in two sanctuaries of notable standing, the one at Dan (p. 33) and the other at Bethel. Both were endowed as royal shrines. But the very prophetic circles, which had made Jeroboam's cause their own, were alienated from him when he set up in these two sanctuaries miniature bull figures overlaid with gold. These golden calves, as they were called, were derived from the Canaanite religion in which they symbolized the god of the storm and of vegetation. Mosaism received a setback. The religion of the north reverted to Canaanite paganism. It was a fatal step not only on the religious side. The Kingdom of Israel, immersed in idolatry, lost the consciousness of national distinctiveness which from the very beginning was linked to the religious, and thus entered upon a downward course which led to its ruin.

War with Israel continued during the short reign of Rehoboam's son Abijah (917–915). In order to harass his neighbor, the king of Judah concluded an alliance with Hadad son of Tabrimmon, king of Damascus. The Philistines likewise threatened Israel. While Jeroboam's son, Nadab (912–911), was laying siege to their fortress Gibbethon, one of his generals, Baasa, conspired against him and was proclaimed king in his stead. Baasa (911–888) sought to win over Hadad, but he was outbid by Asa of Judah (915–875), with the consequence that several districts in the extreme north were ceded to the king of Damascus. The Aramean invasion called a halt to Baasa's energetic military measures against Asa. He retreated from Ramah which he had been fortifying, and moved his capital to Tirzah. King Asa razed the abandoned fortress and used its material, stone and timber, to fortify the Benjamite towns Gibeah and Mizpah. Thus the tables were turned; Jerusalem, far from being blockaded, was surrounded by a ring of defensive works.

The new dynasty in Israel was as short-lived as that which it had destroyed. It speedily lost the support of the prophetic circles. Baasa's son, Elah (888–887), was assassinated in his capital by one of his captains, Zimri, who mounted the throne. The army was again investing Gibbethon. The general, Omri, won the support of the forces for himself. He marched against Zimri, who, unable to hold out, set fire to the palace and perished in the flames. Another pretender to the throne, Tibni son of Ginath, disputed the claims of Omri. The nation was divided; at last the party of Omri gained the upper hand. Tibni lost his life, and Omri became king of Israel.

Asa died of the gout in old age. It was unfortunate that the successors of David and Solomon resorted to the short-sighted policy of inviting Aramean meddling with the affairs of the divided nation. It merely led to the ascendancy of Damascus, which in the long run could not but affect the fortunes of the southern kingdom itself disastrously. For the time being Judah enjoyed safety. Religiously, all was not well there either. Idolatrous practices crept in. King Asa did away with many abuses, such as religious sodomy. The worship of Astarte had won many devotees among the women; the queen-mother herself was addicted to the shameful cult and had made an image of the goddess. Asa ordered the image destroyed and removed his mother from her dignity. He was, however, powerless to put down the worship in the rural sanctuaries which had been restored by the side of the Temple in Jerusalem. For even in Judah religious decentralization had raised its head, and the high places, as the various sanctuaries in the land were called, disputed the claims of the Temple to sole recognition and continued to be tolerated.

CHAPTER XII

THE LORD OR BAAL?—ELIJAH

(887-851)

THE founder of the third Israelitish dynasty was an able and energetic ruler, with a vision almost equal to David's. Omri (887–876) chose for his capital a new site, a hill six miles northwest of Shechem, rising over three hundred feet high from the valley leading to the coast. As later events proved, the choice was a happy one. Samaria, as the newly founded capital was called, was, in the conditions of warfare then prevailing, well-nigh impregnable and its reduction by an investing army a most protracted affair.

Omri met resolutely the difficulties bequeathed by the former dynasties. Once for all the Philistines were done with; we hear of no further molestation from that quarter. The Moabites had, during the civil war following the secession, shaken off the yoke of Israelitish dominion; but now they were thrown back from Medeba upon their southern holdings and once more reduced to a state of vassalage. The annual tribute rendered by the king of Moab to the king of Israel consisted of enormous quantities of wool from the herds in which that country abounded. Omri was on terms of peace with his neighbor to the south. But it was not so easy to rid the land of aggressions from the north. The Arameans of Damascus, whose intervention had been bought by king Asa of Judah, did not rest content with the open road to Acco which the slice of Israelitish territory previously ceded (p. 68) had secured for them. Omri was forced to concede special quarters in Samaria for the Aramean merchants to set up their bazaars. In order to check further inroads, political and commercial, by the rulers of Damascus, Omri fore-saw the imperative need of an alliance with the Phoenicians; the friendship, interrupted since the days of Solomon, was sealed by the heir to the throne, Ahab, marrying Jezebel, the daughter of Ethbaal, king of Tyre.

This 'brotherly covenant' was mutually beneficial to the two contracting parties. Israel was the natural hinterland upon which the Phoenicians, occupying the narrow coast, depended for their foodstuffs and raw material; the Israelites were glad to barter their excess products for articles of Tyrian manufacture and wares imported from abroad. The alliance was also founded upon political considerations. If Damascus was an unwelcome commercial rival, Phoenician diplomacy saw farther east a warlike power looming up, which was set upon gaining access to the Mediterranean and disputing with Egypt whatever was its title to the narrow strip of land between them both. Towards the end of Omri's reign and in the first years after Ahab's accession, an Assyrian army marched into northern Syria; King Ashurnazirpal received the tribute of Tyre, Sidon, Byblus, and other Phoenician towns.

It was merely a question of time when the Assyrian colossus would penetrate further south. For the time being Ahab was more concerned with the nearer Aramean peril. It was political wisdom to hold fast to the policies inaugurated by his father. Both son and father really followed in the footsteps of Solomon. It is significant that Ahab's contemporary in Judah, Jehoshaphat (875–851), resumed his ancestor's Ophir expeditions; unfortunately the fleet was wrecked off the port of Ezion-geber.

Like Solomon, also, Ahab beautified his capital. The palace erected by his father was considerably enlarged; from the profusion with which ivory was used in paneling, in doors, in chairs and couches, it was known as the Ivory House. Again, like Solomon, to please his Tyrian wife Jezebel and her compatriots resident in the capital, Ahab built a temple to the chief deity of Tyre, Baal Melkarth (the Lord, King of the City). This acute danger to the national religion met with strenuous opposition on the part of the prophets. Jezebel, an imperious person, who knew how to govern, gave orders to exterminate the prophets. But Obadiah, the minister of the household, aided one hundred of them in secreting themselves away in caves.

Since the days of Samuel, there had been a steady growth in the refinement of the character of the Israelitish prophet. The bands of roving enthusiasts had been transformed into brotherhoods or guilds, the members of which, under the guidance of a superior whom they called 'father,' exercised themselves in the arts preparatory to their vocation. These prophet-disciples nurtured the conviction that the national religion must be maintained at all hazards, no matter what the exigencies of statecraft might counsel. Religion was to them the be-all and end-all of national existence; they were jealous for the honor of God, who must be worshiped exclusively since He is the truly One.

The good old times, with their simple life untouched by the newfangled civilization inherited from the Canaanites, had their protagonists also in the circles of the Rechabites. This group clung to the ideals of the nomadic past; they dwelt in tents and abstained from wine. A third group consisted of consecrates (Nazirites), who either for life or for a shorter period took upon themselves the vow of shunning all intoxicating drink. In all of these groups of zealots was concentrated an aversion to the intolerable present, and a fixed resolve to mold the future in conformity to the bygone past.

The root of the evil was the foreign alliance with Tyre. The dynasty was engrossed in the struggle for the land, to keep it intact against aggression, if necessary by support from the Phoenician coast. For the opposition it was a struggle with the land, with the indigenous civilization incompletely suppressed and now in ascendancy by reason of the entry of the Tyrian city-god. Who was to be God in Israel, the Lord who revealed Himself in Horeb, or Baal? Such was the question which presented itself to Elijah of Tishbeh in Gilead, the typical uncompromising religious zealot, easily the greatest figure since Moses.

Unheralded, on a sudden, did this prophet make his appearance. There was no mistaking his calling. He was cloaked in

a hairy mantle, held fast by a leather girdle. From the
steppes he made his way to the capital. With a sovereign
fixity of purpose, he delivered the message of divine displeasure: 'There shall not be dew nor rain these years, except
at my command.' Forthwith he withdrew into the solitude
from which he had emerged. By the brook Cherith he sustained himself with such food as the ravens let drop. When
the brook dried up for want of rain, the prophet took himself out of the country. In the Sidonian town of Zarephath,
a poor widow gave him lodging and scant sustenance. But
the presence of the holy man brought blessing to the hovel.
When the woman's son fell sick and lay all but dead on his
couch, Elijah brought him back to life.

Almost three years had gone by. The drought was unbroken, and famine stalked in the land. The king, accompanied by his minister Obadiah, went forth in search of
provender for the royal stud. On the way they chanced upon
Elijah. The king upbraided the prophet as the 'troubler of
Israel.' Defiantly the prophet retorted: 'Not I, but thou and
thy father's house are the troublers of Israel.' The idolatry of
Baal was the cause of all the evil. The future of the religion
of Israel was in jeopardy. It must be proved to the people
that the Lord, and not Baal, was God. On Mount Carmel
the momentous contest was fought out. The prophets of
Baal laid out an offering upon the altar of their god. But all
their prayers, artifices, and wild contortions availed not to
bring down heavenly fire. At the time when it was the wont
to offer the evening sacrifice, fire came down from heaven
and consumed Elijah's offering upon the repaired altar of the
Lord. A shout went up from the people: 'The Lord, He alone
is God.' The four hundred and fifty prophets of Baal were
taken down to the river Kishon and slain. From the top of
Mount Carmel the prophet could observe the gathering of
clouds. The drought came to an end.

Jezebel, exasperated by the slaughter of her prophets,
determined to put Elijah out of the way. The prophet
escaped by way of Beer-sheba into the southern wilderness.
There on Mount Horeb, the seat of the Mosaic revelation,

the zealot-prophet, well-nigh weary of life, was confirmed in his opposition to the sinful dynasty. If the cult of Baal was to be cut off in Israel once for all, it must be done by the sword. The house of Omri must be done away with. In the person of a young disciple, Elisha son of Shaphat, of Abel-meholah in the Jordan valley, Elijah found the man of political insight and moral fortitude to carry out the programme to a finish.

If anything was needed to make the opposition to the royal house still more determined, it was the outrage perpetrated against a citizen of Jezreel, who owned a plot of land upon which the king had set his heart. Ahab made all sorts of offers, but Naboth refused to part with his vineyard, an inheritance from his fathers. So Jezebel had the man summoned before the elders of the city on a trumped up charge of blasphemy and sentenced to death. As Ahab went down to take possession of the property, which now fell to the Crown by escheat, Elijah confronted him with the damning denunciation: 'Hast thou murdered, and wilt thou also play the heir?' The doom of the house of Ahab was irrevocably sealed.

As suddenly as Elijah had appeared at the first, so did he vanish. At the Jordan, near Jericho, the master divested himself of his mantle which now descended upon Elisha. As the first and foremost of Elijah's disciples, he became heir to two-thirds of the spirit that was in his teacher. Elisha, amid the group of younger prophets, saw an apparition of a chariot of fire drawn by horses of fire, and the master was no more—he was translated to heaven. This prophet of the truly fiery word was from now on the symbol of the deathless religion which he brought back to life while on earth; at the time of the close of prophecy the day of his return to earth was taken to signify the last refining judgment which was to usher in the redemption of Israel.

CHAPTER XIII

AHAB AND THE ARAMEANS

(854-843)

FROM the religious point of view, the contest between Ahab and the puritanical prophets served to bring out the latent forces of Mosaism and to prepare its coming victory over paganism. It was unfortunate that the king was dominated by the evil spirit of his wife and failed to comprehend the character of the opposition. Measured by secular standards, Ahab was eminently successful during the greater part of his reign. The country seemed to enjoy peace and prosperity. The Aramean peril was kept off until near the end of Ahab's life. The clash, however, was inevitable so soon as Damascus conceived the moment opportune.

A son or grandson of the first Ben-hadad, Ben-hadad II., mustered a large force and invested Samaria. Ahab was almost ready to sacrifice his capital upon honorable terms. But as the Aramean king would listen to nothing short of unconditional surrender, Ahab made a sortie and surprised Ben-hadad and his train of vassals while engaged in a drinking-bout, presumably in anticipation of victory. The enemy was routed; only a portion of the cavalry made good their escape with their king.

At the return of the year, the Arameans came back. A formidable army pitched at Aphek, in the valley of Kishon; over against them the Israelitish forces occupied the slope of Mount Ephraim. A battle was joined in the open field, which resulted in a complete victory for Israel. The city was stormed, and Ben-hadad was taken captive. Ahab, however, spared his life. Assyria was ominously threatening in the background; northern Syria was in the hands of Shalmaneser III. (860–825). Ahab was satisfied with the terms offered by Ben-hadad; the Galilean cities previously wrested from Israel were returned, and Ahab received the concession to

75

set up bazaars in Damascus for Israelitish merchants, exactly as Omri had acquiesced in a similar arrangement for the Damascene merchants in Samaria.

To oppose the well-understood designs of Shalmaneser, a coalition, called into life by Osorkon II. of Egypt, prepared to block the Assyrian advance. The lead belonged to the immediately exposed kingdom of Damascus, where Hadad-ezer had mounted the throne, and to Hamath; Ahab occupied third rank, with a contingent of two thousand cavalry and ten thousand foot. Among the other contingents were Cilicians, Phoenicians, and Ammonites. A battle was fought at Karkar, in the Orontes valley (854). The victory claimed by the Assyrian monarch in the famous Monolith Inscription could not have been decisive; certainly for some time to come no Assyrian army visited these parts.

The immediate object being accomplished, the coalition fell apart. Damascus appeared to be sufficiently weakened for Ahab to strike at his former ally. The Gileadite fortress Ramoth was the bone of contention. The cause appealed to Jehoshaphat of Judah who offered to coöperate. The two houses were at the time on amicable terms; Jehoshaphat's son Jehoram had married Athaliah, the daughter of Ahab and Jezebel. The Judean king was not satisfied with the optimistic predictions of the prophets at the court of Samaria. He asked for one of the prophets of the Lord. Micah son of Imlah was summoned. Alone he stood out against the whole body of his brother prophets, whom he pictured as misled by the lying spirit so that Ahab might go up to battle and perish.

Despite Micah's ill-boding message, the two kings ventured into the battle, Ahab in disguise as a common soldier. This very device cost him his life. One of the enemy archers aimed at him quite innocently, in complete ignorance of the fact that the soldier upon whom he inflicted a mortal wound was none other than the king of Israel. Until the fall of night the stricken king remained standing in his chariot. The Israelites lost the day and retreated, so soon as it was known that the king was dead (853). The body was taken in the chariot to Samaria, where it was buried. Ahaziah, Ahab's son and successor, died after a reign of two years (853–852); he was succeeded by his brother Jehoram (852–843).

CHAPTER XIV

ELISHA. JEHU

(843)

THE death of Ahab was the signal for Moab to throw off the yoke of Israel. Mesha, its vigorous king, lost no time in invading the districts wrested from his father by Omri (p. 70). Jehoram invited the coöperation of Jehoshaphat, and the two kings marched against Moab from the south, through the Edomite country which was still subject to the kingdom of Judah. The allied forces experienced a scarcity of water, which Elisha found a means of relieving. A heavy rainfall filled the torrent beds with water. As the sun, shining upon the water, gave it a blood-red appearance, the Moabites concluded that the allies had quarreled and annihilated each other. Mesha gave orders to rush forward, but his forces were routed, and the king himself was forced to retreat to his capital. Driven to desperation, Mesha, in the sight of the besiegers, offered his first-born son to his god Chemosh. Courage returned to the defenders of the city; they made a sortie; the allied kings were just able to extricate their forces and to return home. Mesha celebrated the victory by erecting a commemorative monument (the Moabite Stone).

The example of Moab encouraged the Edomites to proclaim their independence under a native dynasty. Jehoshaphat's successor, Jehoram of Judah (851–844), tried to regain this country so necessary for commerce with Arabia, but was unsuccessful. Surrounded by the enemy, he barely managed to break through; his forces, unable to stand their ground, took to flight. In the southwest of the realm, towards the Philistine territory, the city of Libnah likewise revolted. It was a much shrunken kingdom that Jehoram of Judah left to his successor Ahaziah, who reigned but one year (844-843).

The prophetic party in the northern kingdom, led by Elisha, conceived the time ripe for the long-planned destruction of the Omri dynasty. A change in the dynasty of Damascus, in which Elisha appears to have had a hand, brought the opportunity. Hadadezer, or whatever was the name of the reigning king, was smothered to death on his sick-bed; the throne was usurped by Hazael (843). Jehoram of Israel thought it safe to press his claims in Gilead. Ramoth was again stormed, the Judean king Ahaziah making common cause with his uncle. Jehoram was wounded and taken home to Jezreel, where his nephew came to visit him. The command of the recovered fortress was left in the hands of Jehu, one of the generals.

As Jehu and his brother officers were seated at their mess, a prophet-disciple, commissioned by Elisha, broke in upon them. He took Jehu aside and anointed him king in the name of the Lord. The choice was approved by the garrison, and Jehu was proclaimed king. Forthwith he drove with a small company to Jezreel, leaving the remainder of the army behind him. The two kings hastened to meet him in their chariots. In the stolen plot of Naboth they came face to face with the general. To Jehoram's query whether all was well, came the reply; 'Nothing can be well, so long as Jezebel thy mother has her way with her witchcraft.' Jehoram understood now that it was revolution and turned to flee. Jehu shot at the king and wounded him mortally. The body was cast into the plot of Naboth, where Ahab had heard the doom pronounced upon his house by the prophet Elijah. Jehu then overtook Ahaziah by Ibleam and inflicted upon him a deadly wound. The Judean king lingered until he reached Megiddo, where he died; his body was taken to Jerusalem for burial.

Jehu reëntered Jezreel. There Jezebel was holding court. She realized that her hour had struck. Decked out in royal raiment, with eyes painted and head attired, this proud daughter of Tyre looked out at the window, as Jehu entered the palace gate. 'Is it peace, thou Zimri, thy master's murderer?' she called out. At the command of Jehu, she was put to death by the palace attendants.

Samaria was still in the hands of the Omrids. There, in the well-fortified city, was the principal royal palace, with the chariots and the stud and the arsenal. It was to be feared that one of the surviving brothers of Jehoram, seventy in number, might be proclaimed king. Jehu dispatched a letter to the authorities in the capital, the minister of the household, the governor and elders of the city, and the tutors of the royal princes, asking for the heads of the seventy sons of Ahab. The request was complied with, and the heads, packed in baskets, were delivered to Jehu in Jezreel. All that remained of Ahab's house in that city, the second capital of the dynasty, including all sympathizers, perished at the hands of the revolutionaries.

Now Jehu was free to enter Samaria. On the way he slaughtered forty-two Judean princes, who had come to inquire after the welfare of the Israelitish royal family. Jehu made his entry into the capital in the company of Jehonadab, a Rechabite zealot. The worshipers of Baal were surrounded in their temple and butchered. The temple itself with all its appurtenances was demolished. Thus the cult of the Tyrian god was destroyed, root and branch. The appalling bloodshed with which this destruction was accomplished left a scar upon the people's conscience which a hundred years later was still unhealed.

CHAPTER XV

THE ADVANCE AND RETREAT OF ASSYRIA

(843-746)

A THALIAH, the mother of Ahaziah, was a true daughter of Jezebel. Upon the news of her son's death (p. 79), she seized the reins of government, feeling that the policy pursued by the dead monarch under her guidance would be safest in her own hands. Apparently she was concerned for the interests of her mother's native state, Phoenicia, and for the religious dominance of Tyre at least in the kingdom of Judah. To that end she sought to do away with all that was left of the seed royal in the male line, including her own grandchildren. Only one grandchild escaped, an infant son of Ahaziah, Jehoash, whom his aunt, the princess Jehosheba, wife of the chief priest Jehoiada, carried off. For six years the prince was kept in hiding in the Temple, while Athaliah reigned over the land (843-837).

In the seventh year the priest's plans had matured. He took the captains of the body-guard into his confidence. Half of the guard was always stationed in the Temple, while the other half was on duty in the palace. Every sabbath the Temple guard was relieved by the palace troops. One sabbath, as the palace guard went up to take its station in the Temple, the Temple guard was likewise retained, so that the palace remained unguarded. The young prince was introduced to the soldiers and acclaimed. Athaliah hastened to the Temple, but was just as speedily led back to the palace and put to death. The king was seated upon the throne and received the oath of the army and of the people's representatives. The temple of Baal, with its altars and images, was demolished; Mattan, the chief priest of Baal, was slain.

Jehoash had a long reign (837-798). At first the youthful king must have been completely under the tutelage of his priestly uncle. Throughout his life he was devoted to the

81

Temple, where his early childhood was spent. The sacred edifice was in need of repairs. The king gave orders that all gifts of money received by the priests from the worshipers should be used for the restoration of the Temple. But after a lapse of time it was found that the priests had kept the money for their own uses. Accordingly Jehoash commanded that all pious donations should be dropped into a chest beside the altar. From time to time the chest was opened and the money counted in the presence of the king's chancellor and the high priest. Thus a fund was obtained for keeping the Temple in constant repair.

In Israel, Jehu (843–816) naturally lost the support of Phoenicia. The friendly coöperation of the southern kingdom, which remained in force during the Omri dynasty, was not to be counted upon during the reign of Athaliah. Nor were amicable relations resumed under Jehoash. Jehu, so soon as he was seated upon the throne, appears to have fallen out with the puritanical party by whose aid he had risen to power, whereas in Judah this party gained ground. Left largely to his own resources, Jehu, as early as the second year of his reign (842), deemed it prudent to throw himself on the side of Shalmaneser, who was then campaigning against Damascus. The Black Obelisk of the Assyrian monarch portrays Israelitish ambassadors delivering their king's tribute, ingots of gold and silver, golden vessels, and precious articles of various sorts.

The Assyrian campaign against Damascus failed of its object, both then and three years later (839). The natural result was that Hazael turned with redoubled fury against Israel. The whole of the country east of the Jordan, as far as the river Arnon, fell into the hands of the Arameans. The invaders operated with great cruelty. They set the fortified towns on fire and put the fighting youth to the sword; babes were dashed in pieces, unborn children were not spared. Over the Gileadite prisoners instruments of torture, with sharp iron knives, were drawn. The invasion was by no means confined to the territory of Israel. On one of his expeditions, Hazael captured Gath and made ready to march upon Jerusalem. There was nothing left for Jehoash except to buy his departure with a substantial tribute from the Temple and palace treasures.

The distressful conditions furnished an opportunity for the smaller nations round about to make predatory incursions. Ammonites, Moabites, Edomites, Philistines, and Tyrians enslaved the population of many a village. The misery reached its climax during the reign of Jehu's son, Jehoahaz (816–800). The kingdom of Israel suffered heavy defeats and virtually lost its independence. The suzerain at Damascus compelled it to reduce its fighting forces to fifty horse, ten chariots, and ten thousand foot. Hazael's successor, Ben-hadad III., invested Samaria and brought the beleaguered population to the verge of famine, until mothers ate the flesh of their babes. Suddenly a rumor reached the enemy that Hittite and Egyptian kings were marching to the relief of the hard beset city, and the Arameans fled in a panic.

Ben-hadad, and after him Mari, renewed their attacks against the kingdom of Israel, when Jehoahaz was succeeded by his son Jehoash (800–785). In three successive battles the Arameans were worsted. So complete was the blow which the king of Damascus received at Aphek that he was forced to restore Israelitish territory previously taken. King, Adadnirari IV. of Assyria (810–783) was the 'deliverer'; a heavy indemnity was imposed upon Damascus. Israel, along with other Palestinian principalities, submitted to the Assyrian potentate. Still there was respite from Aram.

In the second year of the Israelite king Jehoash, his Judean namesake was assassinated in the palace at Jerusalem. His son Amaziah (798–780) had the murderers of his father executed, but he spared the lives of their families, in accordance with the humanitarian ordinance in the Mosaic Code (Deuteronomy 24,16). Amaziah gained a signal victory over the Edomites in the Valley of Salt, southwest of the Dead Sea; their rock-bound fortress, renamed Joktheel, was incorporated into Judah, thus opening up the roads to the south. Puffed up by success, Amaziah challenged the king of

Israel to a test of power. Jehoash replied with the fable of the thistle that asked for the hand of the daughter of the mighty cedar and was trodden down by a passing beast. Battle was joined at Beth-shemesh, overlooking the Valley of Sorek. Amaziah was beaten and taken captive. Jehoash entered Jerusalem, broke down a portion of its walls, and despoiled the Temple treasures. The terms of peace were exceedingly humiliating for the defeated king, who was compelled to deliver hostages as a guarantee of his good behavior. The disaffected Jerusalemites conspired against their king; Amaziah fled to Lachish, where he was overtaken and put to death.

Amaziah was succeeded by his son Azariah or Uzziah (780–740), while in Israel Jehoash was followed by his son Jeroboam II. (785–745). These two kings, for nearly half a century, were able, by reason of the happy political situation, to restore the territories of Israel and Judah almost to their extent in the times of David and Solomon. Damascus was weakened by further Assyrian campaigns, and the Assyrian retreat during the reigns of Ashurdan III. (772–755) and Ashur-nirari IV. (755–746) gave the two monarchs in Israel-Judah a free hand. It seems that Jeroboam was the more powerful and energetic ruler, and possibly Uzziah, by reason of his father's unfortunate venture, owed allegiance to the northerner. At any rate they worked in harmony. Uzziah recovered the port of Elath from the Edomites; Jeroboam carried the war into Aramean territory. From the entrance of Hamath in the Orontes down to the Gulf of Akabah, the whole continuous stretch, including the country east of the Jordan and the lands of Ammon, Moab, and Edom, was once more in the hands of the Israelites and Judeans. It was a half-century of tranquillity and prosperity such as had not been enjoyed since the days of Solomon. Monarchs and people must have hugged the feeling of confirmed stability and enduring security.

CHAPTER XVI

LIFE UNDER THE MONARCHY

WE HAVE caught many a glimpse of the life of the people as it had formed itself since the rise of the monarchy; we may pause for a moment to complete the picture. The land was intensively cultivated. In the plains and valleys the husbandman, with ceaseless toil and moil, plowed and harrowed the ground and sowed and harvested his wheat and his barley; the heaps of sheaves he conveyed in a cart to a floor freely exposed to the wind, where he threshed and winnowed; the grain he stored up to be ground into flour and to be baked into bread, while the chopped straw served as provender for his cattle. A yoke of oxen—or, if a man was rich, as many yokes as he could afford—sometimes a team of donkeys, drew the plough and trampled with their hoofs the heaped up sheaves. These beasts were likewise put to use as draught animals. Where pasture land was available and water plentiful, small cattle were raised, herds of sheep and goats. In the terraced hills the vine, the olive, and the fig were cultivated. It was blissful happiness for a man to be able securely to 'sit under his vine and under his fig-tree.' Patches, surrounded by irrigating ditches, were covered with fruit orchards and vegetable gardens.

In the villages life was simple. Domestic labor took care of the ordinary wants. The women assisted the men at harvesting time, and often tended the flocks. The farmer's wife, and for that matter also a woman in the small towns, was kept exceedingly busy. Preparing the daily meals, fetching water, carrying bundles of sticks for fuel, she found time also for spinning and weaving and needlework; she made clothing for her household and increased the family's income by working at fine fabrics which found a ready sale. The men constructed their own simple dwellings of sun-baked bricks upon a clay foundation, and fashioned the wooden furniture, such as tables, chairs, and bedsteads; they also cut the thongs for their sandals and prepared skins for holding water or wine.

In the larger towns and cities there was a demand for specialized handicrafts. Trades were hereditary in certain families; the craftsmen were formed in guilds and occupied definite quarters; there was a bakers' street in Jerusalem, and a road led to the fullers' field outside. The potter turned out earthen jugs, bowls, plates, lamps; it may be that his ware lacked the artistic finish of the imported articles, such as only the very rich could acquire, but he was a good learner and imitator. The smiths and workers in metal supplied the farmer's implements, swords and spears and arrow-points for the soldier and the tools of daily life. Silversmiths and goldsmiths cast the images for private and public idolatrous shrines, and produced rings and seals set with precious stones, upon which figures or written characters were engraved. The pretentious mansions of the wealthy, not to speak of temples and royal palaces, built of hewn stone, gave employment to architects who made the design, masons, stone-cutters, plasterers; the woodwork and paneling were executed by carpenters and wood-carvers. The weaving and embroidering of cloths, hangings, and rugs had reached a high stage of development, even though the models were foreign in origin; so also the art of dyeing.

Altogether life in the large cities, particularly in the capitals, was full and rich. The magnates had their winter houses and their summer villas, within which they were served with choicest viands and strongest wines, while reclining on soft damask couches. The young men of the aristocracy were entertained by male and female singers, and themselves performed on musical instruments. The city bazaars, whether of the domestic or foreign merchant, were filled with luxurious articles of wear and adornment. The matrons of Samaria and the damsels of Jerusalem were decked out in sumptuous finery, vying with their sisters at Tyre and Damascus, Nineveh and Memphis. Their hair artistically waved, their eyes enlarged with paint, and their bodies anointed with perfume, they affected in the streets a tripping gait, attracting attention by the jingle of their anklets.

There was wealth in the country, but it was unevenly distributed. As commerce expanded and capital was accumulated, small holdings were gradually extinguished and land was concentrated in the hands of the few. The impoverished farmer was more and more entangled in the toils of the rich creditor. If he was unable to meet his obligations, his pledged belongings were seized, or he was compelled to suffer his children or himself to be enslaved. Slavery was by no means the fundamental institution that it constituted elsewhere; the Israelitish slave was on the whole mildly treated. But there was a growing number of laborers who hired themselves out for a shorter or longer period, and of the less fortunate who lived from hand to mouth. The capitalist in the city would buy up and sell the produce of grain, both at his own price. Naturally the harsh landlord or cruel creditor was in a position to sway the courts of justice; it need not always have been by direct bribery. Still the case of Naboth of Jezreel shows how ready magistrates and courts were to do the bidding of those in power.

The social rift between rich and poor had a counterpart in the struggle for power between sectional particularism and nationalist centralization. We saw how the unification of the nation and the central system of administration conceived by the first three monarchs were thwarted by the innate jealousies of north and south. The monarchy had taken root; but it was hedged about by limitations which derived their force from old habits and the self-sufficiency of the cities, in which the leading families absorbed all political power. The king was primarily a soldier. In the north, dynasties were made and unmade by ambitious generals, and even in the south, though the dynasty persisted, the kings were victims of repeated plots. The king was supreme judge and maintained in his capital, at least in Jerusalem, a court of appeals made up of priestly and lay judges. The colleges of city-elders acted not only as an administrative body for their district, but also as a court of justice, and the cantonal authorities often clashed with the central power. The king was dependent for his revenues upon the good-will of the provincial magnates. He was merely the greatest magnate of them all. His palace was somewhat more pretentious than the mansions of his wealthy subjects; his chief minister went by the name of master of the household. Sovereignty was vested in the people. During an interregnum or whenever there was a dispute about the succession, the 'people of the land' assumed authority and seated the rightful heir upon the throne. Whatever democratic tendency may have inhered in this institution was stifled by the preponderance of the gentry, and essentially the polity remained aristocratic.

In the spiritual sphere of life, likewise, there were manifold divisions. Education was widely diffused; the mass of the people were able to read and write. The sons of rich houses had their tutors; parents of more modest circumstances taught their own children. Parental discipline was rigid, and the schoolmaster did not spare the rod. There was piety in the land; but in the popular religion it took on forms bordering upon heathenism and retained outworn superstitions. Men were eager to know the will of God, and the priests were the natural keepers of the people's conscience. But there were priests and priests, those that favored image worship and those who opposed it, worthy messengers of God and others who misused their holy office and had an eye only to their emoluments. Counsel might be had also at the hands of wise men and wise women, persons of ripe years and commanding the accumulated experience of generations; their wisdom had a touch of the practical and tended in the direction of a mild scepticism. Over against the ritualist priesthood and the secularist teachers of worldly-wise maxims stood the prophets who saw deeper and truer and farther, brushing aside sacerdotal quibblings and cold reasoning alike, penetrating to the core of things, insisting with all their might and courage on inward piety for the individual and the moral conversion of the nation. But not all prophets

agreed among themselves. There were prophets and prophets—the easy-going preachers who fawned upon the people
and confirmed them in their downward course, and those
mighty heroes of the spirit who stood like isolated rocks
when all about them was tumbling. How these movements
and counter-movements, currents and cross-currents, determined the events that followed, will be shown immediately.

CHAPTER XVII

AMOS AND HOSEA

(760-734)

URING the reign of Jeroboam II., two years before an earthquake which shook the land so severely that it remained ever after in the memory of men, a momentous scene was enacted in the royal sanctuary of Bethel. A large concourse of people was assembled for worship, when the tones of a dirge broke in upon them:

> 'The virgin of Israel is fallen,
> She shall no more rise;
> She is cast down upon the ground,
> There is none to raise her up.'

The message spelt national catastrophe, involving the destruction of the dynasty and the state: 'Jeroboam shall die by the sword, and Israel shall be led away captive out of his land.' The messenger was a Judean, Amos of Tekoa, in the wilderness of Judah by the Dead Sea. He was not a professional prophet, nor did he earn his bread as a prophet-disciple; he stood outside the guilds. While pursuing his ordinary business of life as an owner of herds and sycamore plantations, he heard the call bidding him prophesy. He regarded himself as special envoy amid the regulars who spoke in the name of God.

Prophecy was to Amos an all-impelling force. 'The Lord God hath spoken, who can but prophesy?' If misfortune befalls the state, it is purposed of God; design, and not chance, rules the history of nations. When an action has been determined upon by God, the prophets become privy to the divine council. It is then their duty to forewarn, just as the sentinels sound the alarm on the approach of calamity. Israel is on the brink of ruin, though the ruling classes, immersed in their pleasures, take no thought. A nation—

Amos can only have meant the Assyrians, of whom for the moment fear seemed unlikely—inevitably, irresistibly, will tear down the two houses, the greater (Israel) and the lesser (Judah), and the destroyer is being raised up by God Himself. The very appearance of the prophet is a notice of the enemy's coming; the prophet's mission is to call to repentance. It may be that the Lord will be merciful with the remnant of Joseph and that in the eleventh hour the danger will be averted.

Amos is as thoroughly convinced as any of his people that Israel is God's elect nation among the families of mankind. This distinction carries with it great responsibilities; it entails dread consequences. 'You only have I known of all the families of the earth; therefore I will visit upon you all your iniquities.' The other nations are not free from misdeeds; sin is sin, even when committed by Moab against Judah's inveterate enemy, the Edomites. The prophet knows the delinquencies of his own people best, and is specially concerned with them. The people are pious in their way, but it is the wrong way. With a one-sidedness which is characteristic of Amos, he is impatient with the exaggerated value placed upon temple worship, at Bethel or Dan, at Gilgal or Beer-sheba, the ostentatiousness of rich offerings, the very music of the elaborate service. Seeking God means something entirely different; it means social justice. These very people who parade their piety are at the same time the oppressors of the poor: the rich are rapacious, the courts venal, the luxuries of the aristocratic ladies and the sumptuous appointments of their palaces are bought with the produce exacted from impoverished tenants. 'Let justice well up as waters, and righteousness as a perennial stream.'

If Israel will not be just, then he is no more in God's eyes than the black-skinned Ethiopians. The Lord led up Israel out of Egypt; but so did He guide Philistines and Arameans from their original seats. Amos meets the objections of the optimists who look forward to the Day of the Lord, the day when, with the help of God, the nation will overcome its enemies. No, that day will bring them the very opposite of what they expect; it will be the Day of Judgment, of divine retribution upon the sinful kingdom.

Was the destruction of the nation the ultimate end which Amos contemplated, on the plea perchance that justice must prevail, though Israel perish? By no means. Amos was not a mere doctrinaire, clinging to justice in the abstract; what he desired was a just society, and that could be brought into existence among his people only by the grace of God. Out of the ruin of the present state there would arise the restoration of 'the fallen hut of David,' the old Davidic kingdom glorified and idealized. It is true, nevertheless, that for the time being the aspect of evil predominated in the preaching of Amos. Amaziah, the chief priest of Bethel, was shocked by the prophet's utterance; he denounced him to the king as a traitor and had him banished to his Judean home. A younger prophet arose, who, though equally stern in rebuking sin, complemented Amos by dwelling more emphatically upon divine forgiveness which must come to the penitent nation.

If Amos was essentially a moralist, Hosea had a deeper insight into the nature of religion. He began his career while Jeroboam II. was yet on the throne, but he lived on to witness the disintegration of the state which soon set in. A domestic experience presented itself to the prophet as a symbol of the national situation. His wife proved unworthy of his trust; yet he loved her dearly, and a divine voice bade him take her back. Israel is gone astray from God. The worship is to all intents and purposes Baal worship, on the same plane as in the old Canaanite religion. The name of the Lord is almost forgotten in the land; the blessings of the crops and the increase of the herds are ascribed to the local deities, in whose honor sabbaths, new moons, and festivals are celebrated. The people are misled by a spirit of impurity; upon the high hills, under evergreen trees, the Canaanite sanctuaries are maintained and the homage paid to stocks and stones is attended by obscene rites.

But even in the larger temples there is the abhorrent image worship. The calf of Samaria, the work of the craftsman, is adored, and human beings degrade themselves by paying it homage. The temple priests are eager to accept the people's propitiatory sacrifices which yield them revenue. So long as the ritual is observed, the sum of one's duty to God is thought to have been accomplished. Yet the priests ought to know better; for that matter also the prophets, who ordinarily remain on a low level. The Book of God's Torah is there to teach the true 'knowledge of God,' that which is essential in religion. But even ten thousand such books would remain unhonored. The people transgress all the commandments: they swear falsely, they murder, they steal, they commit adultery. There is no faith in the land, no love of man for man. Yet the thing that God desires is piety touched by love, love of God and love of man, not sacrifices; a right understanding of religious duty, rather than burnt-offerings.

Israel's piety is as unsubstantial and evanescent as a morning cloud, as the mist which the hot sun dispels. Priests, magistrates, and royal courts alike pervert justice. Kings are deposed, and kings are set up; the men change, but their policies remain the same: all they do is to make covenants and break them. Just as a bird blunders into the fowler's net, so Ephraim flutters betwixt Egypt and Assyria. Or, with another of the prophet's similes, Ephraim, as he mixes himself up with the great powers, is as a cake not turned which is burnt to a crisp on one side, while it remains raw on the other. Israel is grown prematurely old; his strength is sapped by courting the favors of foreigners.

The futile leaning upon the stranger, the aping of foreign customs, the want of a national policy, the prevalence of idolatrous worship, and the decay of morals must combine to bring about the catastrophe. The divine anger would be unrelenting. Yet God is not vindictive like man. Hosea operates with the figure of marriage: there will be a new betrothal, in which Israel engages herself to practise justice and kindliness and faith. Or the relation of Israel to God is that of sonship; then God cannot stifle His paternal love. Israel must return to God, give up his idols, cease depending upon Assyria or Egypt. And if exile must come, it shall be followed by a restoration under the lead of a new David.

With Amos and Hosea is ushered in the line of the 'writing prophets.' Men of action they continue to be, like their predecessors; but they are eminently men of the word, of the finished address, which they commit to writing. Apparently they believed that they had a message beyond their immediate generation. It was a literary age. Priests and wisemen, singers and story-tellers had long since begun to make use of the scribe's pen. There were books of the Torah, books of songs and parables (Psalms, Proverbs), and books of history. The kings had their annalists; in the guilds of the prophets the marvelous deeds of Samuel, of Elijah, of Elisha were strung together to form 'lives.' All these activities continued beyond the period at which we have now arrived. But a new literary product sprang up, books no longer about the prophets, but by the prophets, arranged by themselves or under their immediate supervision. This new genre of book stands unrivaled in the world's literature. Posterity cherished these prophetic writings, because it recognized in the prophets the masters of the nation's destiny. The prophets imparted to their people a distinct character which enabled it to survive the loss of statehood. As so often in the history of Israel, the healing process preceded the stroke; the new order was preparing while the old order was wearing out. At this stage of history, it was the prophets who undermined the state that the nation might live on.

CHAPTER XVIII

ISAIAH AND THE ASSYRIAN ADVANCE

(744-720)

THE dynasty of Jehu came to an end when Zechariah, who succeeded his father Jeroboam II., was assassinated, after a reign of six months, by Shallum (744). The conspirator held his seat only for a month, when he was overpowered by Menahem, who marched on Samaria from the old capital Tirzah. It is obvious that the civil war was precipitated by the contest of two rival parties, the one leaning on Egypt, while the other favored Assyria.

With Menahem (744–737) the pro-Assyrian party won the ascendancy. The advances of the powerful Assyrian monarch Tiglath-pileser IV. (745–727) seemed to leave no other choice open. With the rehabilitation of Assyrian power in northern Syria, exemplified by the incorporation of Arpad as a province of the mighty empire (740), Rezin of Damascus and Hiram of Tyre submitted of their own accord. Menahem, likewise, hastened to dispatch to the king of Assyria a tribute of a thousand talents of silver; the amount was raised by taxing sixty thousand men of wealth fifty shekels each. Menahem's son, Pekahiah, sat on the throne barely two years (737–736), when he was murdered by one of his generals, Pekah son of Remaliah, who entered the palace with a body of fifty Gileadites.

The anti-Assyrian party was now at the helm. Egypt was powerless to lend more than moral support; on the other hand, the enemies of Assyria looked for substantial aid to Armenia (Ararat), which rose against Tiglath-pileser at a time when he was busy further east with the Medes. A coalition was formed; Pekah of Israel and Rezin of Damascus were joined by the two Phoenician seaports Tyre and Sidon as well as by several Philistine towns and an Arab queen by the name of Shamsi. But in the north the Phoenicians and, in particular, the Hittites, then the southern principalities, Judah, Ammon, Moab, Edom, and a part of Philistia, refused their participation. War was declared against the recalcitrant states. The allied armies of Israel and Damascus marched into the territory of Judah.

The old king Uzziah had been incapacitated by reason of leprosy, and during the latter part of his reign his son Jotham had acted as regent. The son did not long survive his father; he appears to have died at the onset of the Syro-Ephraimitic war (736). His successor Ahaz (735–720) was a youth of twenty when he ascended the throne. The allied kings, who had won over the Edomites by recovering for them the sea-port Elath, made ready to annex Judah and to place upon the throne a creature of their own. Jerusalem was in a state of panic. The king resolved quickly to appeal to the king of Assyria; ambassadors were dispatched bearing silver and gold from the Temple and palace treasures. In the meantime preparations were made to withstand the siege by conserving the water supply of the city. On a personal tour of inspection, at the end of the conduit of the Upper Pool, the king was confronted by Isaiah son of Amoz, perhaps the greatest of the new order of prophets.

Isaiah was called to the prophetic office in the year of king Uzziah's death. The conditions in Judah were analogous to those which obtained in Israel at the close of Jeroboam's reign. There was prosperity in the land, silver and gold and no end of treasures; the military strength was unimpaired, with a multitude of horses and no end of chariots. But, like Amos, Isaiah was alive to the reverse of the picture: the growth of large estates, the oppression of the poor, the frivolous pursuit of pleasure, the spread of superstitions and of idolatrous practices. Like Amos again, Isaiah stressed the gloomy aspect of the 'Day of the Lord.' God, for Isaiah, was the supremely Holy, sanctified through justice; all that is lofty in nature or in the creations of human ingenuity, the mighty cedars, the high hills, the towering fortifications, the tall ships, must be brought low that God alone may be exalted.

The judgment over Judah was inevitable, but it was not to

come through Ephraim or Damascus. When all Jerusalem was in consternation, the prophet had no fear of the flicker of those two expiring torches. Accompanied by his son Shear-jashub—a symbolic name expressing the prophet's conviction that a Remnant would turn to God and be saved— Isaiah met the king's nervous apprehensions with the counsel of quietistic faith. 'Keep calm, and be quiet; if ye will not have faith (ta'aminu), ye shall not be established (te'amenu).' So certain was this eminently religious personality of the futility of the combined attack that he bade the king ask a sign in confirmation of the prediction, in the netherworld below or in heaven above. As the monarch artfully declined to test God, the prophet unfolded the divine plan in its fulness. This very year, he announced, a young woman will have a son and call his name Immanuel ('God is with us'). Before the boy shall be two or three years old, the allied kings will have departed from Judah. Then evil days will come upon Judah, such as she has not seen since the secession of Ephraim. Egypt and Assyria will lay the land waste. But then the Remnant that is left will return to the simple life of old, and a reign of everlasting peace and justice will be inaugurated by the ideal king who will supplant the present unworthy ruler. Isaiah had clearly in mind the Messiah from the stock of Jesse, a scion of the house of David whose advent he expected within his own lifetime.

The policy of Ahaz, short-sighted though it was, had for the time being the desired effect. It was not difficult for the Assyrian king to break up the coalition. Damascus still offered forceful resistance. But Israel was stripped of Gilead and northeastern Galilee, and the population was deported to Assyria. That was the first act in the Assyrian captivity. Samaria was still left intact, for the reason that the opposition made away with Pekah and placed his assassin, Hoshea son of Elah, upon the throne (734/3). Thus the much shrunken kingdom of Israel was pacified, and Tiglath-pileser was in a position to invest Damascus. The siege lasted two full years, but at length the city was conquered. King Rezin was put to death, and the population deported.

Ahaz had accomplished his immediate purpose, but at the price of complete submission to Assyria. Judah, no less than Israel, was now a vassal state. Annual tribute was exacted of both. At Damascus Ahaz paid homage to the Assyrian conqueror. Here he saw an Assyrian altar; the conquest had naturally been sealed by the introduction of the Assyrian cult. The Judean king showed his obsequiousness by copying the model and sending it on to his priest Uriah in Jerusalem, who had a similar altar erected before the Temple in the place of the Solomonic altar. Ahaz furthermore introduced in Jerusalem the Assyrian worship of the constellations and the sun, which was conducted by an especial priesthood; within the precincts of the Temple itself figures of sacred horses were set up in honor of the Assyrian sun-god. The national religion was eclipsed, as a sequel to the king's pro-Assyrian policy so vigorously opposed by Isaiah the prophet.

CHAPTER XIX

THE FALL OF SAMARIA. HEZEKIAH

(729-692)

TIGLATH-PILESER was now free to turn against the proud city of Babylon, whose king Nabonassar died during the siege of Damascus, leaving the country in confusion and the play of opposing parties. The ambition of the Assyrian monarch was crowned with success, when in 729 he entered Babylon and on the first of Nisan, the day of the Babylonian new year, 'seized the hands of the god Marduk,' thus becoming king of Babylon under the name of Pul. He died in 727 and was succeeded by Shalmaneser V. (727–722). The absence of the Assyrian monarch and the change in rulers stirred in the west hopes of independence which were fostered by Egypt. Thus Hanno king of Gaza left his exile in the Pharaonic country shortly after the accession of Shalmaneser, and Hoshea of Israel reached an understanding with Seve, one of the Egyptian dynasts, and stopped the payment of the annual tribute to Assyria.

Egypt, however, left Hoshea in the lurch, and Shalmaneser had no difficulty in capturing and incarcerating the revolted king. His capital was not minded to surrender. For three years it was able to hold out against the Assyrian army. Shalmaneser died before the siege came to a close; the capture of the city was accomplished by his successor Sargon (722). In accordance with the custom of the Assyrians (p. 97), subsequently practised by the Babylonians, the upper elements of the population of the country, consisting of functionaries and men of wealth, the army and the priesthood, were deported. From Samaria alone nearly thirty thousand were carried away. The exiles were transplanted to Mesopotamia and Media. The great mass of the people was left behind, those who from the start had been friendly to Assyria and others who were too feeble to offer resistance.

The land of Israel became a province of the Assyrian empire
and was administered by an Assyrian governor. Nevertheless the country was far from being pacified.

A fresh revolt was organized by the king of Hamath, who
won the adhesion of Hanno of Gaza, supported as he was by
an Egyptian contingent under Seve. Samaria was drawn into
the venture, perhaps unwillingly, while Judah wisely kept
aloof. Sargon hastened to Syria before the allies effected a
juncture (720). The king of Hamath was beaten at Karkar;
the southern rebels were overwhelmed at Raphia, near Gaza,
south of the Egyptian frontier. To prevent future disturbances, Sargon threw into Samaria foreign settlers, chiefly
from various Babylonian cities but also from Arabia. Thus a
mixed race arose, which came to be known as the Samaritans.
Bethel was still the chief sanctuary, and an Israelitish priest
instructed the new-comers in the cult of the land. At the
same time the religion was inevitably contaminated by the
paganism imported from the former homes of the colonists.

The fall of Samaria, even while it was imminent, filled her
Judean neighbor with apprehensions. 'The evil is come unto
Judah, it reacheth unto the gate of my people, even to Jerusalem,' so expressed himself the prophet Micah at Moresheth
(a town in the Judean Lowland), whose antipathy to mili-
tarism, as well as his denunciation of moral and religious
corruption, equaled that of the Jerusalemite Isaiah. It was
fortunate that Ahaz refused to be involved in the intrigues
against Assyria. Hateful as the initial act of vassalage had
been to Isaiah, the prophet saw that to throw up the allegiance to Assyria now would mean the immediate end of the
Judean state. He was quite clear as to the futility of succor
from Egypt. The course of submission to Assyria commended itself to Isaiah particularly when once more the
throne was occupied by a man in the twenties.

Hezekiah (720–692) may, at his birth, have inspired
Isaiah's song of the Wonderful Child upon the throne of
David, the anointed Prince of Peace; but the young ruler
was far from fulfilling these high Messianic expectations.
Nevertheless, he was thoroughly imbued with the idea of

religious centralization and purification to which the better minds of the people, among priests, prophets, and thoughtful laymen, clung. It may be that there were differences of opinion as to method and compass of the reformation which was being set in motion. Radicals of the type of Isaiah and Micah, with their vision of the Ideal State in which war among nations would be no more and peaceful arbitration take its place, were convinced that at best the sacrificial worship was an indifferent adjunct to spiritual religion. For them the quintessence of the Torah was strictly ethical: 'Do justly, love mercy, walk humbly with God;' 'Seek justice, relieve the oppressed, judge the fatherless, plead for the widow.' Much as they deprecated unmerited, and therefore false reliance upon the help of God, the conviction was rooted in them that God dwelt in Zion and spoke from the Holy Temple. Certainly the practical reformers set great store by abolishing the provincial sanctuaries and concentrating worship in the Jerusalem Temple. The king readily fell in with their ideas; the country sanctuaries were closed; the idolatrous emblems were destroyed; in the Temple itself such stumbling-blocks as the figure of the Brazen Serpent were removed.

Hezekiah did not dare to irritate his Assyrian overlord by doing away with the sun-horses erected by his father; nor was his reformation as thoroughgoing as it might have been. Politically, likewise, Hezekiah was wary, though disposed to break with Assyria at the earliest possible moment. His father's refusal to side with Hanno (p. 100) involved the son in a war with Gaza; fortune was on his side. To prepare Jerusalem more effectively against siege, Hezekiah had the issue of the Upper Gihon stopped and its waters conducted through a circuitous tunnel to a Pool westward of the City of David; the famous Siloam inscription commemorating the undertaking was discovered in 1880.

When Azuri, king of Ashdod, in expectation of aid from Egypt, attempted to rally the southern states against Assyria, Judah was minded to give her adhesion. It required the drastic interposition of Isaiah to induce the king to withdraw from the alliance. The prophet walked through the streets of Jerusalem half-clad and barefoot, in order to symbolize the capitivity in store for the chief instigators of the trouble, the Cushite rulers on the throne of the Pharaohs. Ashdod was captured by Sargon's general-in-chief and its population deported (711).

Things looked more favorable when Sennacherib (705–681) followed his father Sargon at Nineveh. On the one side the Ethiopian dynasts in Egypt kept inciting the Palestinian states to revolt, and on the other, Merodach-baladan, who had raised himself as king of Babylon, was dispatching his embassies to stiffen opposition to the Assyrian empire. No one followed the negotiations with keener apprehension and clearer perception than Isaiah. How could one trust in Egypt, which was willing enough that the northern allies should do the fighting for her, while she remained passive in the background? From the height of his religious conviction, Isaiah counseled implicit faith in God. He spoke to Hezekiah, as he had spoken to Ahaz. 'In sitting still and rest shall be your salvation, in quietness and confidence your strength.' Politically expressed, it meant neutrality. Isaiah was as little pro-Assyrian as he was anti-Assyrian; what he wanted was a national policy.

There was, however, an anti-Assyrian party at court. Hezekiah resolved to fall in with their views. Sidon in the north and Ashkelon in the south declared against Assyria; the king of Ekron, who persisted in his loyalty, was overcome and imprisoned by Hezekiah. Sennacherib wisely attacked the evil at its root; in 702 Babylon was stormed. The next year (701) Sennacherib marched against the west. The Phoenician cities, from Sidon to Acco, were subdued; Ashkelon was captured. At Eltekeh a battle was fought between the Assyrian forces and an Egyptian contingent. Sennacherib won a costly victory which enabled him to proceed against Ekron. Ammon, Edom, and Moab hastened to make peace; Judah alone resisted. So Sennacherib reduced one Judean fortress after another. Hezekiah, shut up in his capital, made offers of submission. Sennacherib demanded an indemnity of three hundred talents of silver and thirty talents of gold. Hezekiah strained his utmost to deliver the tribute to the Assyrian camp at Lachish. Sennacherib, however, dispatched his commander-in-chief to ask also for the surrender of the capital. As the negotiations with Hezekiah's ministers led to no result, the commander proceeded to invest Jerusalem.

The city was in a panic. What could be done hastily to strengthen the fortifications, was done. The king rent his garments in mourning and implored Isaiah's intercession with the Lord. The prophet rose to the occasion not merely as a patriot, but from the depth of his religious interpretation of international politics. To him God was the arbiter of nations; what power was given to Assyria was solely for the purpose of carrying out the divine plan. Asshur was merely the instrument, the rod of the divine anger, to destroy sinful Israel and Judah. But arrogant Assyria considers world-conquest an end in itself and boasts of leveling the boundaries of nations and of amassing endless spoil. 'Should the axe boast itself against him that heweth therewith?' God therefore is jealous for His city. Out of Jerusalem shall go forth a remnant. The king of Assyria shall not come unto the city, nor shoot an arrow there.

Whether it was the rumor of an army marching from Egypt or of fresh disturbances in the east, or because of a pestilence which broke out in the army, or for all these reasons, Sennacherib concluded peace with Egypt. The Palestinian campaign was abruptly terminated. Jerusalem was delivered. The hearth of God on Zion stood inviolate. Isaiah's prophecy was magnificently fulfilled.

CHAPTER XX

MANASSEH. JOSIAH. JEREMIAH

(692-609)

THE Assyrian overlordship, of course, remained in force. Assyria was at the zenith of its power. Tirhakah, the Ethiopian king of Egypt, tried his best to instigate new revolts in the northern lands; but they remained fruitless. Sennacherib's son, Esarhaddon (681–669), and grandson, Ashurbanipal (668–626), carried the war into Egyptian territory; Memphis was conquered in 671 and Thebes in 666. Both these kings strengthened their hold on the province of Samaria by fresh colonization from other countries. In Judah there may have been slight fluctuations; but in the main the pro-Assyrian party had the upper hand.

The long reign of Hezekiah's son, Manasseh (692–638), who ascended the throne at the age of twelve years, was a period of reaction, both politically and religiously. The reforms of the previous reign were wiped out; the reformers paid for their obstinacy with their lives. According to a late legend, the aged prophet Isaiah was cruelly done to death. The rural sanctuaries were reopened and the impure rites reintroduced. Old and gruesome practices were resuscitated. In the valley of Hinnom, west and southwest of Jerusalem, children were passed through the fire; the king offered his own son, exactly as Ahaz had done. The ancient forms of augury and divination, repeatedly suppressed, were revived. The Assyrian cult of the heavenly constellations was particularly favored. In the Temple itself an image of the Assyrian Ishtar, 'the queen of heaven,' was erected. Within the sacred precincts young women offered their bodies in honor of the deity; the proceeds flowed into the Temple treasury, and the children were raised for menial service of the Temple. Mosaism was completely eclipsed, and all copies of the Torah of Moses were destroyed or sequestered.

Manasseh was quite reconciled to vassalage under Assyria; he paid his tribute regularly, and Judean contingents fought among the Assyrian expeditionary force in Egypt. The conquest of Egypt, however, proved illusory. Psammetich I. (664–609) renounced his allegiance to Ashurbanipal (645), at a time when the Assyrian monarch was busy in Elam and the revolt of his own brother in Babylon strained all of his fighting resources. The Assyrian power began rapidly to sink. The Medes had set up an independent kingdom under Deioces before 645 and were threatening from the east; in the west the Cimmerians were held at bay with the aid of the Scythians. Assyrian diplomacy exerted itself in playing off these warlike peoples, all of Aryan stock, one against the other. Naturally the enemies of Assyria could count on Babylonia for support. Well might the reformer-disciples of Isaiah in Judah take heart. Asshur was not invincible. God in Zion was supreme.

When Manasseh was succeeded by his son Amon, the opposition raised its head. Amon was assassinated in the second year of his reign (638). But the 'people of the land' suppressed the revolution and placed upon the throne Amon's son, Josiah, who was but eight years old. The Assyrian power was still to be reckoned with, and the reactionary party was in the saddle. But the Scythian hordes had spread over western Asia, menacing Assyria and Egypt alike. Luckily, they passed along the coast, leaving the interior of Palestine unscathed. The voice of prophecy was once more heard in Judah. Nahum and Zephaniah saw the oncoming of Nineveh's downfall. To the serious mind of the strict followers of Mosaism it meant a world judgment, from which Judah would emerge purified. For there was much that required uprooting: idolatry, aping the foreigner, social injustice.

When King Josiah was come to man's estate, in the eighteenth year of his reign (621), he was ready to give ear to the anti-Assyrian reform party. It so happened that the Temple was again in need of repairs. The chancellor Shaphan was ordered, in conjunction with the high priest Hilkiah, to take the necessary steps. While the restoration was in progress, when much rubbish had been removed and ancient layers uncovered, the priest chanced upon a copy of the Torah of Moses. It may have been the copy sequestered by Manasseh (p. 104) or one immured during the repairs under Jehoash (p. 82), if it was not the volume deposited at the time of the building of the Temple by Solomon. The priest handed the book to the chancellor, who read it. When reporting to the king concerning the progress of the Temple repairs, Shaphan produced the recovered book and read it to the king. Josiah was profoundly impressed. The forecast of evil with which the nation was threatened for its long disobedience moved him to send a deputation, consisting of the priest and the royal ministers, to the prophetess Huldah, that she might intercede on behalf of the penitent king.

Josiah then convoked the elders of Judah and Jerusalem. In the presence of the priests, the prophets, and the assembled people, the Book of the Covenant, which was found in the Temple, was read. From a platform erected in the Temple court the king proclaimed the Torah of Moses as the law of the realm. The people gave solemn assent. Then the king ordered the most thoroughgoing demolition of all idolatrous altars and symbols in the Temple area, in the city, and in its environs. The rural sanctuaries in the realm were rendered unfit for sacrificial service; their priests were granted maintenance from the Temple revenue, but were disqualified from officiating. The king's officers overran the Samaritan province—it shows how little interference could be offered by the Assyrian governor and garrisons—the high places were closed; the temple at Bethel was destroyed. In Jerusalem, the feast of Passover was observed in the purified Temple in accordance with the prescriptions of the Torah.

Among the supporters of the rehabilitation of Mosaism was the young prophet Jeremiah, who belonged to a branch of the priesthood at Anathoth and whose ministry began in the thirteenth year of Josiah (626). It was his fate to be disillusioned as the first enthusiasm died away. The popular religion could not be ruled out of existence by an official act; it came to the surface again. The return to the Lord was seen to be half-hearted; only a definitive judgment from God would bring the nation to penitence. Jeremiah was in line with his great predecessors in the prophetic office when he deprecated the exaggerated value placed on the sacrificial cult, and he even questioned its Mosaic sanction. He believed in no compromise; it was useless to sow among thorns; the soil should be broken up afresh. Like Hosea, he realized the ineffectiveness of the written Torah alone. 'The pen of the scribes hath labored in vain.' The right kind of Torah is the one written in the heart. There must be an inward willingness to obey, a mind receptive of spiritual influences. The voice of the stern moralist was needed in the face of false security. Jeremiah led a lonely life, without wife and children; he knew himself as a man of strife with priests and the ordinary run of prophets. But the fire of true conviction burned within him; there was a compelling force to speak the truth, to chide but also to sustain. He loved his people tenderly; beyond the catastrophe which he knew must come he saw hope. He looked forward to a reunion of deported Israel with Judah; the continued existence of God's elect people was to him as certain as the permanence of heaven and earth.

Clouds were gathering on the political horizon. Such is the game of politics that the Scythian peril had thrown together the former enemies, Egypt and Assyria. Moreover, Egypt hoped to come to terms with Assyria and ensure its own hold on the lands this side of the Euphrates. This plan, the coalition of opposing monarchs, Nabopolassar of Babylon (625–605) and Cyaxares of Media (624–585), resisted with all their force. In the month of Ab, 612, Nineveh fell before the combined attack of Babylonians, Medes, and Scythians. The proud city was turned into a mound and ruin, which it remained ever after. A new capital was established westward in Haran, where the commander of the Assyrian forces, Ashuruballit, assumed the throne. The new ruler was compelled to evacuate the city and retire to Syria (610). In 609 Necoh II., who had just succeeded his father Psammetich, hastened to join forces with the Assyrian monarch in order to advance on Haran.

The Egyptian army marched along the coast. Gaza, which offered resistance, was overcome. As Necoh made ready to descend into the Valley of Jezreel over the Carmel passes, Josiah, who had annexed the Israelitish country and was as little minded as the Philistines of Gaza to forego his independence, sought to prevent the passage by force of arms. A battle was fought at Megiddo; the Judeans were worsted, and Josiah was mortally wounded (609). The body of the dead king was taken to Jerusalem for burial. The 'people of the land' placed upon the throne his son Jehoahaz, who could be trusted to continue his father's policy.

CHAPTER XXI

THE END OF THE KINGDOM OF JUDAH

(608-586)

J EHOAHAZ reigned but three months. He was summoned to the Assyro-Egyptian headquarters in Syria (at Riblah in the province of Hamath) and put in bonds; subsequently he was removed to Egypt, where he died. In his place Necoh set his brother Jehoiakim (608-598) and exacted an indemnity of a hundred talents of silver and one talent of gold. Jehoiakim apparently favored a policy the very reverse of his father's and friendly to Egypt. It also meant a step backward on the religious side. The cult of the 'queen of heaven' was eagerly and openly pursued. The women in particular were addicted to it, and they baked cakes upon which the image of the goddess was formed. Had not misfortune come since they left off worshiping her? so reasoned the common man.

In official circles reliance was placed upon the Temple. Jeremiah thought differently. It was vain to point to the Temple as a guarantee of security, when at the same time there was gross moral corruption and idolatry in the land. Had not Shiloh been destroyed aforetime? So would it fare with the holy house of God in Jerusalem. The outspoken prophet was set upon, and the populace clamored for his death. But his friends intervened, pointing to a similar bold prophecy by Micah in the time of Hezekiah. Jeremiah had apparently a respectable following, while another prophet, Uriah, who was of like mind, was put to death by the king's orders.

Necoh and his Assyrian ally laid siege to Haran, but were repulsed by the Babylonians and Medes. In 605 Necoh again attempted to cross the Euphrates; but he was beaten at Carchemish and driven off for good. Babylon had become the seat of power. The Babylonian forces were commanded by the crown-prince Nebuchadrezzar, who within the same year succeeded his father upon the throne of the new empire. Jeremiah hailed him immediately as the Servant of the Lord, from whom he had received dominion. Jehoiakim gave in to the anti-Egyptian party and swore allegiance to the Babylonian king (601); he must have realized by then that no help was to come from Necoh. But after three years he broke away. At the command of Nebuchadrezzar, Judah was invaded by contingents from the neighboring nations in conjunction with Chaldean troops. Jehoiakim lost his life (598) and was succeeded by his son Jehoiachin. After three months, Nebuchadrezzar appeared in person to direct the siege of the city. Jehoiachin immediately surrendered. Accompanied by the queen-mother, his harem, and his court, he was taken to the enemy's headquarters; thence they were deported as captives to Babylonia. With them were carried away likewise the nobility and the substantial part of the citizenry constituting the army, seven thousand in number, as well as one thousand craftsmen, with their families. A portion of the sacred vessels, along with treasures from the Temple and palace, was also carried off to Babylonia. This was the first Babylonian deportation (597).

The last king on the throne of David was Zedekiah (597–587), another son of Josiah. He bound himself by an especial oath to serve the king of Babylon. But Egypt continued to stir up trouble; the two parties—the loyalists who stood by Babylon and the hotheads who looked to Egypt for help— were pitted against each other to the point of violence and bloodshed. The political division involved religious consequences: on the one side men, and especially women, gave themselves up to the worship of the Babylonian goddess of love (Ishtar) and her son Tammuz, as well as of the sun-god; and on the other side the cult of the sacred animals of Egypt was carried on in an underground chamber. Apparently those who favored leaning on Egypt thought it discretion to plot in secret.

In 594 the court of Jerusalem was visited by embassies from Edom, Ammon, Moab, Tyre, and Sidon, in order to induce Zedekiah to join in a coalition against Babylon. Jeremiah exerted his utmost to keep the king on the side of prudence. False hopes were being raised by ultra-patriotic prophets, both at home and among the deported exiles in Babylonia, who predicted the speedy collapse of the Babylonian power and the restoration of the sacred vessels. Jeremiah appeared with a yoke around his neck, as a symbol of the continued domination of Babylon; but a prophet of the opposition, by the name of Hananiah, broke the yoke in the sight of the people. Jeremiah dispatched letters to the exiles, counseling them to prepare for a protracted stay in captivity —to build houses and make homes for themselves and pray for the welfare of the state in which they dwelt—until God in His own time should lead them back. It was the year of accession of Psammetich II. in Egypt (594–588). In 590 we hear of an Egyptian campaign in Palestine. Psammetich's successor, Hophra (588–569), was more active in pushing his claims. The Phoenician cities yielded to the force of his arms; Zedekiah, half-willingly, threw himself on the side of Egypt.

Nebuchadrezzar was now determined to make an end of the aggressions of the rival power. He established his headquarters at Riblah, exactly as Necoh had done previously. A part of his army was dispatched against Tyre; with his main forces he appeared in the winter 588/7 before the gates of Jerusalem. He proceeded at once to lay siege to the city. The walls were strong and the defenders fought stubbornly. So Nebuchadrezzar built a rampart about the city with a view to starving the population within. An Egyptian army advanced towards the stricken city, and the Babylonians were compelled temporarily to raise the siege. As Jeremiah made his way to his home in Anathoth, he was seized on the charge of deserting to the enemy. He was placed by the war party in a damp subterranean dungeon.

King Zedekiah had the prophet transferred to the guard house. A secret meeting was arranged between the king and the prophet in the Temple precincts. Jeremiah persisted in his advice to save the city by timely surrender. But the war party was too strong for the vacillating king. Jeremiah was once more confined in the guard house; there he received his daily rations as long as bread was to be had in the beleaguered city. The Egyptians had been fought off by Nebuchadrezzar, who now set up his engines against the northern wall. On the ninth day of Tammuz, 586, a breach was effected. Zedekiah fled toward the Jordan, but was overtaken at Jericho. He was conveyed to the enemy's headquarters at Riblah and there witnessed the slaughter of his sons and of members of the Judean nobility. Then his eyes were put out, and the blind king was taken in chains to Babylon.

A month later, on the seventh of Ab, Nebuzaradan, the Babylonian commander-in-chief, came with orders to destroy Jerusalem. The remainder of the sacred vessels was carried away; so also a quantity of bronze from the dismantled columns and basins. The Temple, the royal palace, and many of the mansions of the nobles were set on fire. The walls were razed to the ground. The population was led captive to Babylonia. This was the second Babylonian deportation. The conqueror was resolved not to leave so formidable a fortress standing to thwart the advance on Egypt which he must have contemplated. With the Judean fighting strength destroyed or else in exile under his own eyes in Babylonia, he had no desire to annihilate the Judean nation. On the contrary, it was good policy to consolidate that part of it which from the start had been loyal, as a bulwark against Egyptian machinations. So on the very day on which Jerusalem was destroyed, Nebuzaradan sought out those friendly to Babylonian rule, among them Jeremiah, and set up an autonomous community, with Gedaliah, the grandson of Josiah's chancellor, as governor residing at Mizpah. Thus the restoration had begun, and a Remnant was saved. Jeremiah was rewarded with a pension from the Babylonian king.

But the community was not to last. There had gathered about Gedaliah all of the poorer folk that had not been carried away; Jews—for we must from now on call the people by the English name, which is but a corruption of 'Judeans'—who had fled to the neighboring countries, returned, among them several princes and princesses of blood royal; even remnants of the Israelites in the north attached themselves to the residue of Judah. But the very constitution of the new community was a thorn in the flesh of the Ammonite king Baalis, who had his own designs upon the vanquished country. Accordingly he instigated the murder of Gedaliah by the hands of a member of the defunct royal house, Ishmael son of Nethaniah. The assassins escaped to Ammon. Those who were left behind feared the reprisals of Nebuchadrezzar, seeing that the Babylonian garrison at Mizpah had been butchered. They determined to emigrate to Egypt, much against the advice of Jeremiah, whom they dragged with them into involuntary exile in the land he most thoroughly abhorred.

It was the poorest sort of Jews that took up their abode in the Delta. The Jewish settlement in Egypt was destined to become a center rivaling Babylonia, but Jews had commenced to drift into the land of the Pharaohs at a much earlier period. The constant relations with Egypt since the rise of the Libyan dynasty in the times of Solomon, especially the trade in horses, led to many a Jew settling in that country. Others were carried away as slaves, and still others, among Asiatics in general, found employment as mercenaries in the Pharaonic army. After the expulsion of the Ethiopians, soldier colonies of Jewish descent guarded the southern frontier in Upper Egypt. Thus Jeremiah found Jewish communities both in Upper and in Lower Egypt. These Jews clung to their nationality and practised the religion they had known in the rural districts of Judea from which they came. Jeremiah met with stubborn opposition when he upbraided the Egyptian Jews for their unwillingness to abandon the worship of the 'queen of heaven,' and her cult persisted down to Persian times.

CHAPTER XXII

THE BABYLONIAN EXILE

(586-538)

I T MUST not be supposed for a moment that there were no Jews left in their home country at all. What happened was simply that the repeated deportations to the north and the exodus to the south had thinned the population and left chiefly the poorest classes. Some stretches of the land must have been desolate, and none too friendly neighbors, like the Edomites, moved up into the territory vacated. The loss of statehood and Temple was a staggering blow, which called forth sorrowful lamentations; but time proved a wonderful healer, and life fashioned itself as tolerably as conditions permitted.

The backbone of the nation was, however, in Babylonia. By the rivers and canals of Babylon they sat, they wept. In the first few years they were deluded with the hope of a speedy return. Their king, Jehoiachin, was in custody; but another king was still sitting upon the throne of David, and they watched with beating hearts the developments at home. The news of the catastrophe of 586 produced consternation; now there remained nothing but to heed the counsel of Jeremiah and to make themselves at home in the foreign land. The majority of them were settled in compact colonies or groups. The soil was more fertile than on the rocky hills of Judea; it was well irrigated by a system of canals. One of their settlements was Tel-abib, by the Great Canal (the 'River' Chebar) near Nippur. They enjoyed a complete measure of autonomy; they kept up their old family ties; their internal affairs were ordered by their own bodies of elders. Thus they had their own jurisdiction and felt themselves to be a national group.

What differentiated these new-comers from the Israelites whom the Assyrians had deported more than a century before was just the circumstance that this very respite had intervened. The Israelitish brethren probably were absorbed by the foreign environment—we speak of the 'lost ten tribes'—though some residue must have maintained its identity in the Median highlands and beyond, to be merged later with the Jewish people. The Jews, on the other hand, on their transplantation to Babylonia, had become conscious of the religious uniqueness which set them apart from all other nations. They had witnessed the rehabilitation of the Mosaic Torah; the sabbath and other rites were the 'signs' by which they knew each other and held together; they had been chastened by the stern rebukes of the great prophets, whose lessons they now, as never before, took to heart. It was depressing to think that the present generation was expiating the sins of the fathers ('The fathers have eaten sour grapes, and the children's teeth are set on edge'). Some in despair stumbled and turned to the worship of stocks and stones; but the main body of the people proved penitent and docile. Moreover, they had a prophet among them, such as their brethren in Egypt had not after the death of Jeremiah.

Ezekiel, who had been carried away with the first deportation under Jehoiachin, was a member of the regular Jerusalem priesthood, the sons of Zadok. In his person prophetic imagination, bordering on the fantastical, and priestly soberness of judgment were united in a measure singularly called for by the changed situation. His service to his people consisted, indeed, in the recognition of the imperative need of the moment. He could be a stern preacher after the manner of the ancients; he was much shocked when his audience admired his pleasing voice and then went home to persist in their evil way. There was for him no compromise with sin. But he held out hope to the sinner. Each man, he taught, has in himself the power to be righteous or wicked, irrespective of hereditary predisposition; the individual is master of his own destiny and responsible solely for his own doings. This doctrine opened the possibility to the prophet's generation to turn a new leaf and to look hopefully into the future.

His principal concern, however, was not with the individual Jew, but with the corporate Jewish people. He looked upon Nebuchadrezzar as the instrument in God's hand to chasten His people; he was just as certain that Egypt and other nations would be doomed. The Jewish people were at present as it were in a grave; but the dry bones would be filled with life, and the revivified nation rise from its grave. Ezekiel was the prophet of the undying hope. When the elders came to him and suggested the erection of a Temple on Babylonian soil, he vigorously and relentlessly set himself against such a plan, which apparently meant a renunciation of future restoration at home. Against their own will, if it must come to that, the dispersed were to be gathered back; they must pass again, as in the times of Moses, through the wilderness, the wilderness of nations, that the sinful members might be lopped off. 'For in the holy mountain, that is Zion, there alone shall the Temple be built.' And so, with painstaking detail, he laid out the plan of the new Temple, as well as the lines of the future policy of the nation, based upon the Mosaic Torah, albeit with some modifications. He expected a reunion of Ephraim with Judah, under one shepherd, a glorified David. The supreme condition was national penitence, a new heart and new spirit, which themselves would be the gift of God. The divine honor was at stake, so long as the reproach of desolation rested upon His land and upon His people.

The fortunes of the Babylonian Jews must have greatly improved as time went on. Babylon, 'the city of merchants,' was nigh, and many must have grown opulent 'through mercantile pursuits. They acquired influence in court circles, and when Nebuchadrezzar was followed upon the throne by his son Evil-merodach, his first act was the release of Jehoiachin from prison. The Jewish king was accorded royal honors; the event is the last recorded in the Book of Kings in the Scriptures. Jewish restoration under the old dynasty had been determined upon as a matter of principle. But Evil-merodach reigned only two years; there followed a period of revolt, and the last king, Nabonidus (555–538), was occupied in repelling the attacks of the Medes under Astyages.

The old friendship between Babylonians and Medes had long been broken. When the Medes were vanquished by the Persians, under Cyrus, the change brought no relief to the Babylonians. Cyrus continued the policy of the Medes and, after conquering Lydia and the Ionian cities of Asia Minor, made himself master of Babylon. The Babylonian army, under the command of the crown-prince Belsharuzur (Belshazzar), offered feeble resistance; the city was taken and Cyrus seated himself upon the throne of Babylon (539). A cry of jubilation resounded among the Jews. 'Fallen, fallen is Babylon; how hath the oppressing exactress ceased!' The joy was still greater when, in the spring of 538, Cyrus, from his summer residence at Ecbatana, made declaration in a royal rescript granting permission to the Jews to return to Jerusalem and rebuild the Temple of the God of heaven. The same royal edict ordered that the sacred vessels of the Temple should be returned to the Jews. It is obvious that Cyrus had been approached by Jewish notables, who reminded the king of the steps toward restoration taken by Evil-merodach, his predecessor upon the throne of Babylon. It was the policy of the Achaemenian rulers from Cyrus down, devoted though they were to their own religion, the Zoroastrian, to tolerate the cults of the subjugated nationalities throughout the empire.

Even as the royal declaration was preparing, the meaning of the epoch-making event was grasped by none more exuberantly and profoundly than by the great unknown prophet, whose utterances form the sequel to the Book of the Visions of Isaiah son of Amoz. He appears to have lived in Palestine, whence he observed the goings on in the great world as they affected his central theme, the rhapsody 'Zion Restored.' He did not hesitate to acclaim the victorious Persian king as the Lord's Anointed, the shepherd appointed by God. Though the prophet's own people might be deaf and blind, the heavens, as it were, opened to himself, and a flood of light issued therefrom. The divine purpose, framed in the beginning of time, was revealing itself to the seer's mind, and above the din of battling hosts and the crash of falling fastnesses he heard the voice of God: This is My work. The deliverance of Israel was being wrought in a manner so unwonted, so strange, yet who hath fathomed the spirit of God? If God is One, who else but He was doing it? If Israel is the elect of God, for whose sake else were old empires tottering, was a new polity arising? 'The time is most opportune, the hour propitious: hasten, flee, depart,' so he called to the Jews of Babylonia.

The Unity of God implied for this great poet and teacher the unity of world history. How he scorns the lifeless images of the gods of Babylon, how he mocks the wisdom and star-gazing of the Chaldean soothsayers! how rapturously he sings of the Incomparable God, whom no similitude can portray! Amid the changes of nature, God's word abides immovably; in the flux of the events of history, as nations come and go, a divine purpose stands transcendent. The religion of the Jew is the religion for all mankind, the true world religion. The Jew is its chosen missioner, the elect Servant of God, who vicariously must take upon himself the sins of the world, willingly submit to contumely and martyrdom, be cut off as it were from the land of the living, but just as surely rise from the grave, triumphant with the success of God's work which he was called to accomplish. And because of this Servantship, Israel is indestructible. God's loving covenant with Israel will outlast the tremors by which mountains are moved. In order that Israel may be the teacher of mankind, a light unto the nations, the disseminator of God's Torah, the nation must be redeemed. God, in whose hands is the destiny of nations, offers to the world-conqueror Egypt and Ethiopia as a price. God is paving the way for His people's return across mountains and desert. The prophet bids Jerusalem take heart; he is the bearer of good tidings to Zion, the comforter of his people, the voice that calls out the advent of God. By the hands of Cyrus Jerusalem shall be built, and the foundations of the Temple shall be laid for Israel, God's elect Servant.

CHAPTER XXIII

THE RESTORATION

(538-432)

ALTOGETHER the caravan which left Babylonia consisted of 42,360 persons, not counting 7,337 slaves of both sexes. The home comers were led by Shesh-bazzar, the youthful son of King Jehoiachin, who received the appointment as governor (nasi) of the new community and to whom the sacred vessels had been delivered by the royal treasurer. The territory assigned to them was very small indeed, comprising Jerusalem and the land about it, as far north as Mizpah and Jericho, and as far as Keilah, Beth-zur, and Tekoa in the south. Edom had moved up beyond Hebron; the remnants of the southern Judean clans, like Caleb and Jerahmeel, which had been pushed out, joined themselves to the new settlers. The land was distributed as far as possible according to the former holdings; only that the descendants of the poorer folk, who had never owned land, now received their allotments. There was ample labor in constructing homesteads, in setting things generally to rights, in communal organization. Jerusalem had a scant population of some three thousand souls; there the heads of the fathers' houses or 'elders' had their seat. The religious needs were cared for by the immediate erection of an altar, and preparations were made for the building of the Temple.

It was not possible to do more, what with all the vicissitudes of a new settlement, failing crops and drought, and scarcity of food. Then there was the burden of taxes paid to the king and the assessments going to the maintenance of the governor. Cambyses (530–522) had succeeded Cyrus; his conquest of Egypt (525) and the war it entailed disturbed the peace of which the new community was most in need. Men asked when the divine displeasure, now resting upon the land for close on seventy years, would end; the fast-days commemorating the national calamity of 586 were still observed. Then came momentous happenings. Cambyses had rid himself of his brother Smerdis; but now there appeared a Magian claiming to be the real Smerdis (522), who received the homage of the empire. Darius I. (521-485) overcame the pretender, but had to deal with an uprising in the eastern provinces, above all with two successive revolutions in Babylon led by a new Nebuchadrezzar (521/20, 520/19). 'Heaven and earth' seemed to be in commotion, and the throne of the Persian king to be tottering.

The commotion communicated itself to Jerusalem. Sheshbazzar was dead. His nephew Zerubbabel stepped into his place. He was encouraged by the prophet Haggai to start the building of the Temple, and to hold himself in readiness for kingly station. Saner elements in the community, fearful of evil consequences, were satisfied to vest the headship in the high priest, Joshua. The prophet Zechariah counseled a dual headship, at the same time curbing the ambitions of Zerubbabel, who was admonished to trust not in power or might, but in the spirit. The lamp of God was to be fed from two spouts. A crown of gold had actually been sent as a gift by the Jews of Babylonia; it was to be fashioned into two crowns. On the twenty-fourth day of Chislev, 520, the foundation was laid for the Temple. But the dream of the royalists was not to be. The Persian empire was stronger than ever.

In the spring of 519, Tattenai, satrap of the western provinces, was sent to Jerusalem to study the situation. The royalist agitation had subsided, but he had misgivings about the building of the Temple. There were not wanting denunciations which cast suspicion upon the undertaking. The Jews pointed to the edict of Cyrus, and when the satrap reported back to the king, a copy of the document was found in the archives at Ecbatana. Darius was satisfied that the Jews were too feeble to attempt seriously the winning back of their independence, and that it was best to have them as friends. So he confirmed the charter of Cyrus and gave orders that the Temple should be completed, the cost to be de-

frayed out of the royal revenues from the Jewish community; out of the same funds were to be provided the daily
sacrifices for the welfare of the king and the royal house. On
the twenty-third of Adar, 515, the structure was finished.

The settlers were subjected to fresh hardships. There was
a scarcity of food due to poor crops or to devastation by
locusts. The poverty-stricken peasants were constrained to
mortgage their small holdings in order to buy food and to
pay the heavy royal taxes. Unable to meet their obligations
by reason of the high rate of interest, they often saw no way
out except to surrender to their creditors their sons and their
daughters as slaves. The community was also beset on all
sides by hostile neighbors who did not take kindly to the
rise of the new settlement. The Edomites, it is true, had
been hard hit by an invasion of Arabs; but that was small
comfort to the Jews. The Ammonites were distinctly unfriendly. The old enmity of the north for the south was
inherited by the hybrid colonists of Samaria—the Samaritans—whose religious conditions were quite different from
the new order of things in Jerusalem and who made ready
to build a temple of their own upon Mount Gerizim. There
was no love lost on either side. The Samaritans presented
their grievances to king Xerxes (485–465).

The conditions demanded some sort of an adjustment. The
heads of the laity as well as of the priesthood pursued a
policy of conciliation towards the plotting neighbors. It was
advantageous to have them for friends. The better relations
were cemented by marriage alliances. Altogether the practical tasks absorbed the interests of the community and
there was a weakening of the moral fibre. The wealthier
classes were harshly oppressive towards the poorer folk,
whose plight obliged them to give up their land; injustice
and unkindliness were rampant. The priests were derelict in
their duty as moral guides and forfeited the respect of the
people; there was laxity in the observance of the sabbath;
the offerings brought to the Temple were of an inferior
quality. There was still a small body of those averse to
worldliness who were scrupulously given to fasting and self-

abnegation; but in their quiet conventicles they brooded, questioning whether it was at all profitable to serve God. One of their number, the prophet Malachi, saw no solution save in a day of judgment, a purifying act which none but Elijah, come down from heaven, could inaugurate.

The man that did come was Ezra. The Jews of Babylonia, who had sent off the first settlers with their best wishes and with substantial gifts, were dismayed by the reports of the unsatisfactory conditions in the new community. King Artaxerxes was upon the throne (465–425), and the Babylonian Jews obtained his sanction for sending a mission to look into the affairs of Judea and Jerusalem. The leader was Ezra, a priest well versed in the Torah of Moses, a 'ready scribe' (sopher), that is, a student of the Book (sepher). The decree issued by the king conferred upon him authority to appoint upon his arrival magistrates and judges, with plenary powers of jurisdiction in accordance with the Mosaic Torah. Moreover, he carried rich gifts from the king and his council for the Temple in Jerusalem; its priests and attendants were granted immunity from taxation. Ezra was also permitted to secure funds from the Jews of Babylonia and to lead back as many of them as wished to join.

About eighteen hundred men, not counting women and children, from priestly, Davidic, and other families, including a number of Levites and other subordinate Temple servitors, went up with Ezra. They arrived in Jerusalem in the month of Ab, 458. Four months were spent by Ezra in acquainting himself with the situation. He was horrified to learn of the extent to which intermarriage had gone. On the twentieth day of Chislev he convoked in Jerusalem an assembly of representatives of the entire community: by an overwhelming majority the resolution was carried to have the unlawful marriages dissolved. A commission was appointed, which busied itself during the whole of the winter with drawing up a list of the transgressors. On the first of Nisan, 457, the measure was carried into execution. Naturally, the Samaritans and other nationalities were angered by the affront to their womenfolk. Ezra realized that in order to defend Jerusalem from a sudden attack the city should be fortified and therefore he made preparations to rebuild the walls. That undertaking was in excess of the royal authority granted to him. And so his enemies seized the opportunity to denounce him to the king.

A petition, signed by Rehum, the governor of Samaria, was dispatched to Susa, and the king gave orders for the immediate cessation of the work and for the razing of the part already constructed. News of the calamity was brought near the end of 446 to Nehemiah, who as the king's cup-bearer stood in high favor with the court. He succeeded in obtaining permission to go to Jerusalem and rebuild the walls of the city. Moreover, he was appointed governor of Judea. Three days after his arrival (in the summer of 445), in the dead of night, he rode out to survey the walls. In the morning he called upon the heads of the people to start the work of rebuilding. From all parts of the land, nobles and commoners, warm-hearted supporters and lukewarm magnates, all set themselves to the task, laboring by day and watching in the night. The zeal of Nehemiah communicated itself to the workers. Being a wealthy man, he provided out of his own purse for the expenses of his position, waiving the governor's salary. He ordered the canceling of debts and restored to the indigent the land held by their creditors. The Samaritans, led by Sanballat of Beth-horon and Tobiah the Ammonite—both related by marriage with Jewish noble families—as well as Geshem the Arab, at first made mock of the feeble fortifications; then they came forward with open threats or plotted in the dark. They planned, with the aid of the neighboring nations and of their sympathizers within the walls, to attack the builders or to lure Nehemiah out of the city and lay hold on his person. Hired Jewish agents, prophets so called, spread the malicious rumor that Nehemiah was thinking of having himself proclaimed king in Jerusalem. All these plots were foiled by the wisdom and courage of Nehemiah. Within fifty-two days the walls were finished.

Now the time was come for Ezra to join forces with the resolute governor, the Jewish lay head of the community.

On the first of Tishri, 445, Ezra read sections of the Torah to the assembled people, the Levites making the rounds and elucidating the text. On the twenty-fourth day a fast was observed, and the people solemnly bound themselves to order their life in accordance with the Torah. A document of ratification was drawn up and subscribed by Nehemiah the governor, then by representatives of priests, Levites, and laity. Those prescriptions of the Torah which were particularly timely were given specific mention. Thus it was stipulated that no marriages should be contracted with the surrounding nations; that the land should lie fallow and all debts be remitted every seventh year; that the prescribed dues for the upkeep of the Temple worship and the maintenance of priests and Levites should be regularly paid. As the written word of the Torah was often too general and undefined, it was expressly made plain that the sabbath and holy days must be so honored as to exclude any manner of business transaction even with non-Jewish traders.

It was unfortunate that in 433 Nehemiah was recalled to the court of Artaxerxes. During his absence the opposition raised its head. Nehemiah therefore obtained from the king leave to return to Jerusalem. He found that Tobiah had been domiciled by the priest Eliashib in one of the Temple chambers; he immediately ordered his removal. He also learned that the Levites had not been paid their tithes and had therefore withdrawn from the Temple service; he reinstated them in their positions and emoluments. As trading on the sabbath with the Tyrian fish-mongers had been resumed, Nehemiah ordered the gates of the city kept closed from the eve of the sabbath to its outgoing. The strict rules against intermarriage had again been broken, and Nehemiah saw the danger not only to religion, but also to the purity and the very life of the Hebrew speech among children of mothers from Philistine Ashdod or from Ammon and Moab. The evil was prevalent in the higher priestly families. Manasseh, a grandson of Eliashib the high priest, was married to a daughter of Sanballat, the governor of Samaria. Nehemiah had him expelled from Jerusalem. The refractory priest organized the service in the rival temple on Mount Gerizim, in complete emancipation from the novel interpretations which were put on the letter of the Torah in Jerusalem. The split between the two communities was thus made permanent.

CHAPTER XXIV

FROM PERSIAN RULE TO GREEK

(424-187)

NEHEMIAH was succeeded in the governorship of Judea by a Persian official Bagohi. The internal administration was in the hands of the high priest and a council of elders, among whom descendants of the Davidic family held a conspicuous place. During the reign of Darius II. (424–404) the high priest was Eliashib's grandson Johanan, the brother of the expelled Manasseh, while the latter's brothers-in-law ruled Samaria after the death of their father Sanballat. Another brother, Jeshua, conspired with the governor for the high priestly office; the two brothers quarreled in the Temple, and Johnanan slew his brother. Bagohi imposed upon the Jews a fine of fifty shekels for every lamb offered in the daily sacrifice; he even entered the Temple, and when the Jews raised objection he bluntly answered that he considered himself purer than the fratricide priest.

In the year 410, a calamity befell the Jewish military colony of Jeb (Elephantine), on an island of the Nile south of the first cataract. This and the other settlement right opposite on the western bank of the river, at Syene (Assuan), had been established before the Persian conquest of Egypt; long before the coming of Cambyses, there had been built a temple in which the Jews of the island made sacrifices to the Lord. As the result of a conspiracy on the part of the priests of the Egyptian god Khnub, in conjunction with a subordinate Persian official, this Jewish temple was laid in ruins. Petitions were sent to the governor of Judea, to Johanan the high priest, and to the rulers at Samaria. The Jerusalemite priesthood were unwilling to accord to the Egyptian Jews the full rights appertaining to their own Temple; they might build a modest altar-house and offer meal-offerings and frankincense, but no animal sacrifices. The worship of these Jews was not free from an admixture of heathenish conceptions such as their fathers had carried away from their rural Judean homes. But the times apparently were not propitious for a rebuilding of the sanctuary. Soon Egypt was in revolt, and Amyrtaeus regained independence for his country (404).

A greater calamity threatened the Jews of the eastern provinces during the reign of Artaxerxes II. (404–361), if we may identify him with the Ahasuerus of the Book of Esther. The story is typical in its main outlines of the long chain of persecutions to which the Jews in the Dispersion have been subjected. Mordecai, a rich Jew, rises to power and influence with the court; his niece, the beautiful Esther, is taken into the harem and becomes the king's favorite. Haman, the new minister at court, because of a grudge against Mordecai the Jew, vents his spleen on the Jewish people as a whole. He presents them to the king as a dangerous people, 'scattered and dispersed throughout the empire, distinct in their laws from all other people, and refusing to obey the king's laws.' Haman obtains the king's signature to an act ordering a massacre of the Jews; a lot (pur) is cast, and the day of the execution is set for the thirteenth of Adar. The Jews of Susa fast and pray; Mordecai conveys the information to Queen Esther, whose Jewish antecedents have remained unknown at court. She invites the king and his minister to a feast, and then pleads with her royal spouse for the life of her people. As the laws of the Persians and Medes cannot be altered, a new act is promulgated by the king, giving the Jews the right to organize themselves for self-defense ('standing for their lives'). Thus the calamity is averted. In commemoration of the event the festival of Purim is instituted.

How far Judea was drawn into the revolt of the Phoenician cities which started in 365 and led to the destruction of Sidon in 350 by Artaxerxes III. (361–337), it is impossible to tell. The punitive campaign against Egypt came nearer home, but it does not seem that the Jews were in any wise affected. They had all reason to keep faith with the Persian rulers, maintaining their loyalty to the very last, when

Alexander the Great had crossed the Hellespont (334), conquered Asia Minor, worsted Darius III. in the battle of Issus (333), and was proceeding to occupy the Phoenician coast. Tyre, and afterwards Gaza, which offered stubborn resistance, were overcome (332); in Egypt Alexander was received as a liberator from the hated Persian dominion. The Egyptian Jews rendered assistance to the Macedonian king in the foundation of Alexandria and were rewarded by a grant of extensive privileges which—so at least it was construed by the Jews—placed them on an equal footing with the Greeks. In the spring of 331, Alexander was ready to strike at the heart of the Persian empire. He passed through Palestine and Syria, which he had left in the care of Andromachus. The Jews accepted the change of masters, while the Samaritans, who murdered Andromachus, were punished severely, and the city of Samaria was compelled to admit Macedonian settlers.

After the death of Alexander the Great (323), the disruption of the empire and the wars among his generals led to a renewal of the age-long dispute for the possession of Palestine between the north and the south. The general commanding Egypt, Ptolemy, invaded the country in 320; Jerusalem was surprised on a sabbath and taken without resistance. Palestine was lost to the rival general Antigonus in 315; but the battle of Gaza (312) gave it back to Ptolemy. Another of Alexander's generals, Seleucus, who coöperated with Ptolemy, made himself master of Babylon. That year was reckoned as the beginning of the Seleucid empire, and the new era, setting in with the autumn, was long in use among the Jews; it is still employed by them in certain parts of the East. The battle of Ipsus (301), which cost Antigonus his life, was the occasion for Ptolemy (I. Soter, 305–285) to seize Palestine. The victory, however, had been won chiefly by Seleucus (I., 305–280), who now ruled Syria from his residence at Antioch.

The son and successor of Seleucus, Antiochus I. (280–261), accordingly, attempted to wrest the country from Ptolemy II. (Philadelphus, 285–247) in 275. Antiochus II. (261–247) concluded an arrangement by which he agreed to receive in marriage Berenice, the daughter of Ptolemy(249), and with her the rights to Palestine. After the death of her father, Antiochus divorced Berenice; but the former queen, Laodice, whom he took back, procured his death by poison, and then had her rival together with her infant child murdered. In revenge, her brother Ptolemy III. (Euergetes, 247–222) invaded the Seleucid realm and carried home an immense quantity of spoil. War with Egypt was resumed on a large scale by Antiochus III. (the Great, 222–187); in the campaigns of 219 and 218 he carried his arms almost to the confines of Egypt. However, after the defeat in the battle of Raphia (217) at the hands of Ptolemy IV. (Philopator, 222–205), he was forced to evacuate Palestine. The accession of Ptolemy V. (Epiphanes) at the age of four years was an opportune moment for Antiochus to resume warfare; by 200 he was in possession of Palestine. It was recovered shortly afterwards by Scopas, a mercenary in the service of Ptolemy, who subdued the Jewish nation and left a garrison in the citadel of the Holy City. But in 198 Scopas was crushingly defeated by Antiochus in the battle of Panium, near the sources of the Jordan. Palestine was definitely transferred to Seleucid rule.

On his first invasion of Palestine, Ptolemy I. had carried away to Egypt many Jewish captives, and the number grew into the thousands in the subsequent expeditions. As many as could bear arms were settled for garrison duty in the fortresses; the remainder served as menials of the king's soldiers. These slaves regained their freedom by an order of Ptolemy II., who was well disposed towards his Jewish subjects. The Jewish population of Alexandria had grown apace; they resided in a compact quarter of their own, in the northeastern part of the city, close by the royal palace. The younger generation spoke Greek, casting behind them the Hebrew speech, or the Aramaic which then had begun to displace Hebrew at home, at least in the rural districts. To make the Word of God accessible to the Greek-speaking community was the purpose of the undertaking known as the Septuagint version of the Scriptures (Translation of the Seventy). Naturally, the Torah was the first and foremost part demanding to be set forth. It is probable enough, as the story goes, that the king, who was a patron of learning, from the very start evinced an interest in procuring a transcript of the translation for his famous library and that he entered into negotiations with the high priest Eleazar to send on a copy of the Torah to Alexandria as well as the requisite number of translators (seventy-two elders—for short, seventy). Or, if the initiative proceeded from the Jews of Alexandria themselves, royal sanction was obtained for the translation and a copy presented to the library. Certainly, another motive played into the work—to convince the world that the Jews possessed a literature rivaling the wisdom of the Greeks. The step was the first in the propagandist activity of the Dispersion to set forth the true nature of the Jewish conception of God and of Jewish morality.

At home, in Judea, the change of masters, from Persian to Greek, from Syrian to Egyptian and back again, produced no appreciable difference in the status of the community. It lacked political independence, sovereignty, statehood, such as (so it was hoped) would come back in God's own time, when the dispersed would be gathered and the visions of the prophets realized in all their truth. Otherwise the community possessed all the attributes that mark nationhood: a contiguous territory, a national speech, a constitution divinely ordained, an autonomous government. The head of the nation was the high priest; as such he was recognized by the foreign ruler, who held him responsible for the preservation of order and for the delivery of the taxes. The high priest was assisted by the Council or Senate, an aristocratic body of priestly and lay elders. The Temple was the visible embodiment of the national sanctities. There was pomp and ceremony, and the people loved it: the music and song of the Levitical singers, the ministrations of hundreds of priests, the gorgeous vestments of the high priest as he stood and blessed the prostrate people amid profound silence. The three festivals, Passover, Weeks (the season of the Giving of the Law), Tabernacles, brought throngs of pilgrims, and

each had its stated sacrifices and ceremonial; the Jerusalemites were happy to witness the awe-inspiring service on New
Year's Day and especially on the Day of Atonement, the
keystone in the structure of Judaism as developed in the
Torah.

The Torah, however, was concerned not merely with the
Temple service, but with the entire life of the Jew. By the
act of Ezra, the first 'scribe' or teacher, the Torah had been
taken out of the keeping of the priests and placed into the
hands of the people. A body of devoted teachers made it
their earnest business to train the Jewish people in the ways
of the Torah, the children and the youth in schools both
elementary and higher, the adults in their meeting houses
(batte keneseth, synagogues). Not only did the Torah require explanation, but the provisions had to be applied to
constantly changing conditions. It was brought home to the
spiritual leaders that in order to safeguard the scrupulous
fulfilment of injunctions expressly commanded in the Torah
they should be hedged about by preventive inhibitions not
originally contemplated. 'Make a fence about the Torah'
was the watchword of the new orientation. Assemblies, like
the one convoked by Ezra, would meet from time to time to
interpret existing laws or to enact new ordinances.   The
institution continued into the third century and was known
as the Great Assembly (or Synagogue). One of its last representatives was the high priest Simon I., surnamed the Just,
a man of singular piety, devoted alike to the Torah, to the
Temple worship, and to deeds of kindness. In the light of
the corruption in high places which subsequently set in, he
stood out as the shining exemplar of a period which had
closed. But also in his own day it was a matter deserving
comment that this high aristocratic dignitary allied himself
with the democratic tendencies operative among the ranks
of humble scholars and teachers.

Prophecy was extinct, for the simple reason that it had
done its work, to prepare for the triumph of Mosaism, the
reign of the Torah. The prophetic writings stood collected, a
worthy second to the Torah, itself instinct with the proph-

etic spirit. The words of the prophets were expounded alongside of the Torah. The subject-matter lent itself to sermonic amplification; the teacher turned preacher, deepening outward formalism by the call to inward piety. The written word, whether of Torah or Prophets, was not a dead letter, but, by reason of the interpretation to which it was constantly submitted, it was made to keep pace with the newer religious experiences, and these were read into the ancient texts. The trend of the times was in the direction of stressing the religious needs and questionings of the individual. The old conception of national solidarity had not lost ground, and men found consolation in the immortality of the race. 'The days of Israel are without number.' The disciples of Wisdom, that third branch of spiritual guidance which had been in the nation from of old, probed the problem of undeserved suffering and of the fate of the individual. In the height of mystic exaltation they put forth tentatively, gropingly, the vision of divine vindication after death. Some of the wise, like Ben Sira, a younger contemporary of Simon the Just, evinced an unconcern with the things hidden, and still others were given to sceptical doubt as to the moral order of the universe and resigned themselves to everyday wisdom: 'Fear God, and keep His commandments; for this is all that man needs to know.'

From this enlightened searching, which still left room for conformity, there was but a step to the worldly-mindedness rife among the wealthier classes. The merchants, whose business journeys took them abroad, and particularly the tax-farmers who were brought in contact with foreign courts and their ministers, held cosmopolitan notions which resolved national differences, and religion sat lightly upon them. They looked superciliously upon Jewish exclusiveness by which they were hampered in taking their place in the larger world for which wealth and station fitted them. This hankering after foreign culture was nothing new; it had engaged all the fiery zeal of the prophetic opposition. Now, as before, the contemners of the national mind were confronted with a counter-movement which rose from below.

But there was this weighty difference: Mosaism had taken root among the common folk, it had stamped itself deep on the national character, thanks to the assiduous labors of generations of teachers. Groups were forming themselves in all stillness, countering insincerity with single-mindedness, pride with humility, worldliness with piety. Their opponents might regard them as Pietists (hasidim); they gloried in their saintliness. They were anchored to Temple and Torah, their inward devotion aquiver with doubt and depression, but ecstatic with childlike trust and new-born exaltation. In heaven they had none but God, and beside Him they desired none upon earth; to be near to God was the highest good. The rift kept ever widening between the men of the world and the lovers of God. The clash was precipitated by the Seleucid conquest of Palestine and the impetus it gave to the sympathizers with Greek culture in high Jewish quarters.

CHAPTER XXV

HELLENISTS AND PIETISTS. ANTIOCHUS
EPIPHANES

(187-165)

THE religious division had, as its concomitant, political factionalism. The two sets of interests acted one upon the other and often blended, though the religious problem overshadowed all else. Scopas, on subduing the Jewish nation (p. 129), found in Jerusalem a strong party with leanings towards the Seleucids. Such was the influential and well-connected house of the Tobiads. The founder Tobiah had married a sister of the high priest Onias II. (son of Simon the Just), and their son Joseph amassed a great fortune as farmer of the taxes during the Ptolemaic dominion. Of Joseph's large family Hyrcanus alone, his father's favorite, threw his wealth and influence on the side of Egypt. Ptolemy V. set up the claim that, when he married Cleopatra, the daughter of Antiochus the Great, Palestine had been promised her as a dowry. Seleucus IV. was now reigning in Antioch (187–176). Hyrcanus made overtures to Ptolemy and promised to advance his cause in Jerusalem. He was worsted in a clash of arms with his brothers and was expelled from the city by order of the high priest Simon II. Hyrcanus returned to his estates across the Jordan, where he built a castle—the ruins are still extant (Arak-el-Emir)—and waged war with the Arabs.

The Seleucid party had the upper hand in Jerusalem. One of their number, Simon, had been appointed administrator of the Temple treasury, which contained large private deposits. The finances of the court at Antioch were at a low ebb; Simon let it be known in friendly quarters how they might help themselves to much money that lay idle in the Temple, especially to the sums left there by Hyrcanus. The scheme was opposed by the high priest Onias III., who sought support among the party friendly to Egypt. Seleucus sent down his treasurer Heliodorus to Jerusalem; but Onias succeeded in thwarting his plans. At the instigation of Simon, the governor of Southern Syria made ready to step in. The matter came before the king, and Onias departed for Antioch to present his case.

Seleucus was murdered by Heliodorus in 176. His brother Antiochus IV. (175–164), who succeeded him, had been kept as a hostage in Rome since 189, one year after his father's defeat by Rome in the battle of Magnesia and the resulting loss of Asia Minor north of the Taurus. Shortly before the death of Seleucus, the Romans had let him go in exchange for the eldest son of Seleucus, Demetrius, a boy of twelve years. At Athens, Antiochus received the news of his brother's death and hastened home, in order to secure the throne for himself. The Seleucid rulers in general were admirers of Greek culture; but this Antiochus, who surnamed himself Epiphanes (the God Made Manifest), was an enthusiast, proud of his Athenian citizenship, and bent upon spreading Hellenic civilization in his domains through settling Greeks in the principal cities. He built temples to Apollo and Jupiter, the Olympian as well as the Capitoline, and erected statues of enormous size; he loved to celebrate with magnificence Greek religious festivities. He strove for popularity among his subjects, but was perfectly unscrupulous as to the means he employed to obtain the funds his lavishness required. Energetic and ambitious, he was given to whims; serious and sober men judged him half-crazed (Epimanes).

Immediately upon the accession of Antiochus, Hyrcanus perceived that he could not hold out in his fastness and took his own life; his property was confiscated by the king. Onias was still in Antioch. His brother Jeshua (or, in Grecised form, Jason), leader of the extreme Hellenizers in Jerusalem, promised Antiochus, who was in need of money, a higher tribute and was nominated to the high priestly office. He worked upon the king's susceptibilities to Greek manners and offered to introduce in Jerusalem the paraphernalia of

Greek civilization. The price paid to the Jews was the privilege to be registered as Antiochian citizens. Under the very
Citadel of David, a place of exercise (gymnasium) was set
up, where the youth from the best families, completely
stripped, wearing only the broad-brimmed hat with figures
of Mercury, wrestled and disported themselves as Greek
athletes. Such was the extreme of Greek fashions that the
young priests forsook the Temple service and ran down at
the first signal to witness the games. Jason went in his liberalism still further. On the occasion of the games in honor of
the Tyrian sun-god, which the king graced by his presence,
the Jewish high priest was represented by a delegation with
gifts for offerings. However, the envoys shrank from so gross
an offense and turned over the money for the building of
ships in the royal navy.

While Rome was throttling Macedonia and laying the
foundation for world dominion, Antiochus learned of warlike preparations in Egypt. Ptolemy VI. (Philometor, 181–
146) renewed his claims upon Palestine. Jerusalem seemed to
be loyal, and when Antiochus visited it, he was accorded a
magnificent reception. But soon an Egyptian party raised
its head in the city. Jason was no longer trusted by the
king. He was replaced by Menelaus, brother of the Temple
treasurer Simon (p. 134), who offered a still higher tribute.
Jason took refuge in the Ammonite country.

The new high priest belonged to another branch of the
priesthood, the class of Miniamin. He was committed to his
predecessor's policies, both in repressing political opposition
and in furthering Hellenizing measures. It was not so easy to
raise the money he had promised. The king's representative
in Jerusalem pressed for payment, but the moneyed men
resisted increased taxation. Menelaus was summoned to
Antioch. Here he was charged by Onias with sacrilege.
Menelaus had helped himself to Temple treasure and bribed
Andronicus, who acted as regent during the absence of the
king, to lure Onias from his refuge in a sanctuary at Daphne,
near Antioch, and to slay him. In the meantime Lysimachus,
the brother of Menelaus, suffered death in Jerusalem because

of his continued depredations of the Temple. Charges were preferred against Menelaus, but his gold won the court over to his side, and he returned to Jerusalem to tyrannize over his enemies. On his return from his first Egyptian expedition (169), the king entered Jerusalem with a large suite; Menelaus conducted him into the Holy of Holies and permitted the thorough spoliation of the Temple.

The next year Antiochus invaded Egypt for the second time. The success of his arms was complete, but he was robbed of the fruits of victory by the intervention of Rome. An ultimatum was presented by the envoy C. Popilius Laenas, who drew a circle in the sand about the king and bade him decide on the spot. Rumors were circulated that Antiochus was dead. Jason hastened to Jerusalem with a force of a thousand men and drove Menelaus into the Citadel. Antiochus was very much alive; deeply hurt by the humiliating outcome of his campaign he was determined to vent his spleen on the Jews. Jason fled betimes and ultimately reached Egypt. The king ordered Apollonius to advance upon Jerusalem. He entered the city on a sabbath. The unresisting inhabitants were butchered; the soldiers pillaged at will and carried off women and children to be sold as slaves. The walls of the city were razed; the citadel south of the Temple hill was fortified, and there the apostate Jews, who were friendly to the king's cause, were quartered together with non-Jewish residents.

A royal edict was proclaimed suspending the practice of the Jewish religion on pain of death. The rescript was couched in general terms commanding the fusion of all nationalities in the realm into one people and the acceptance of the Greek religion by all; but that was only a blind. The force of the proclamation was directed against the Jews and the Samaritans. Accordingly the Temple in Jerusalem was converted into a sanctuary of Jupiter the Olympian, while that on Mount Gerizim was dedicated to Jupiter Xenius (the Defender of Visitors). On the fifteenth day of Chislev, 168, a statue of the god was set up on the altar, the image of the 'lord of heaven,' which the pious Jews spoke of as 'the

abominable thing causing horror'; on the twenty-fifth day of
the month heathen sacrifices were offered on what had been
the altar of God. The Temple was filled with riots and
revelings; within the sacred precincts men dallied with
harlots; swine's blood was poured upon the altar

Heathen altars were also erected in the country towns.
Every month the king's birthday was celebrated, and the
Jews were constrained to eat of the sacrifices; on the feast of
Bacchus they were made to go in procession wearing wreaths
of ivy. It was unlawful for anyone to keep the sabbath and
festivals ordained in the Torah, or to profess himself at all
to be a Jew. The king's appointed overseers saw to the strict
carrying out of the new order of things. Torah scrolls were
rent in pieces and burned; their owners were put to death.
Women, who had their children circumcised, were led publicly round about the city and then cast headlong from the
walls. Eleazar, an aged teacher, who refused to eat swine's
flesh, was tortured to death. A group of pious people who
had fled to a cave near Jerusalem in order to keep the sabbath secretly were surprised and committed to the flames;
they chose to die rather than to desecrate the sabbath by
offering resistance.

The leaders of the Hellenist movement in Jerusalem had,
of course, not expected that things would come to this pass.
Their idea had been to liberalize Judaism and to meet Greek
culture half way. The new course of things overwhelmed
them; temporizing was impossible; they were too worldly-
minded for martyrdom; conscience was stifled. There were
naturally those who had no scruples at all and embraced
heathenism to its utter limit. At the other end, the extreme
Pietists were resigned to passive resistance. Their duty, as
they saw it, was to live as their fathers had lived and to let
God take care of the issue. It was a quietistic attitude, not
different from that of Isaiah centuries before. The visionary
who wrote the Book of Daniel—the last to enter the collection of Holy Scriptures—reasoned that the present was the
final onslaught on God's people and the Holy City. Four
world empires, one more ruthless than the other, had held

sway since Nebuchadrezzar's conquest of Judea: the Babylonian, the Median, the Persian, the Greek. This was now the end: the Messianic kingdom of the saints of the Most High was coming with the clouds of heaven at the appointed time. The seventy years, at the end of which the prophet Jeremiah had set the restoration of Israel, meant seven weeks of years. Now was the seventh and last week, ushering in the judgment, in which the righteous would rise to everlasting life and the wicked to shame and everlasting contempt. Why resort to arms, when Michael, the patron angel of Israel on high, was warring to overthrow the heathen power and to accomplish the deliverance of the Jewish people?

So mused the visionary. A deliverer did come in the person of Judah the Maccabee (the Hammerer), who believed in active resistance. He was one of the five sons of a country priest of the class of Jehoiarib, Mattathiah the Hasmonean, residing in Modein (a small town northwest of Jerusalem, on the road to Jaffa). The aged father had slain both the king's commissary and the first Jew who approached the heathen altar in the town. With his sons and other faithful Jews, the priest had fled into the mountains and convinced the Pietists that it was lawful, when attacked, to defend themselves on the sabbath day. But Mattathiah soon died, and the leadership fell to Judah, who collected a body of resolute warriors from among the scattered Jews. The uprising was started. The Syrian government, taking this disturbance lightly, sent detachments of regular troops first from Samaria under Apollonius, and then from Syria under Seron, to: quell the rebellion. Judah, notwithstanding his small and as yet unorganized forces, proved more than a match for them. He surprised the enemy in night attacks and with a small picked force routed the Syrian host in the pass of Beth-horon. The spoil which fell into the hands of the Jews supplied them with weapons. When Judah moved up to Mizpah (north of Jerusalem), he commanded a considerable force, which he organized in companies a thousand, a hundred, fifty, and ten strong. By fasting and prayers they prepared themselves for the unequal combat.

The Jewish rising was in a measure part of a general revolt of the East against the West. The Parthian province (southeast of the Caspian Sea) had under its own kings been expanding at the cost of the Seleucid empire; now Mithradates I. (about 170–138) was on the way to founding an empire of his own. Antiochus departed for the east to set things to rights, leaving the government of Syria proper in the hands of Lysias with instructions to crush the Jewish rebellion in a war of extermination. An army of forty thousand foot and seven thousand horse, commanded by Ptolemy, Nicanor, and Gorgias, marched down the coast and was advancing towards Jerusalem. With a body of three thousand stout-hearted warriors Judah, dexterously dodging a night attack by Gorgias in the mountains, flung himself upon Nicanor's army encamped at Emmaus. The discomfited Syrian forces fled into the plain. There was no time to plunder the deserted camp; Gorgias was descending with his detachment of five thousand men. So the camp was set on fire. At the sight of the flames, the forces of Gorgias likewise took to flight, leaving rich spoil behind.

A fresh Syrian army, under the command of Timotheus and Bacchides, was ordered to march on Jerusalem by way of Idumea from the south. At Beth-zur, some four miles above Hebron, Judah met them and won another victory. He was now free to move up towards Jerusalem. It proved impossible to dislodge the Syrian garrison from the Citadel. But the Temple hill was forthwith occupied. It was a sorry sight that met the eye: the sanctuary desolate, the altar profaned, the gates burned up, shrubs growing in the courts as in a forest, the priests' chambers pulled down. With the aid of faithful priests the sacred place was cleansed. The heathen altars and places of worship were demolished. The great Altar, which had been desecrated, was pulled down, and its stones removed to a chamber without the Temple courts, until there should come a prophet to tell what was to be done with them. A new altar was built of whole stones, and new holy vessels were made. On the twenty-fifth day of Chislev, 165, exactly three years after its desecration, the

Temple was solemnly rededicated; the morning sacrifice was offered on the new altar, and the lamps upon the golden candlestick were lighted. For eight days the Feast of Dedication (Hanukkah) was kept with sacrifices and prayers of thanksgiving, with music and song, with processions in which palm branches were borne, and with kindling of lights. It was ordained that this feast should be kept annually at this season in commemoration of the rekindling of the lamps in the House of God. Judaism was saved by the heroic zeal of the priest's son of Modein.

CHAPTER XXVI

JUDAH THE MACCABEE AND HIS BROTHERS

(165-142)

LYSIAS was now convinced that the coercive measures against the religion of the Jews had proved a failure. The Hellenists in Jerusalem likewise desired the termination of the state of war. A hint from Rome sufficed to bring the two sides together. Without awaiting the pleasure of the monarch who was still in the east, Lysias obtained from the young prince Antiochus V. (Eupator), whose guardian the regent was, a rescript guaranteeing to the Jews freedom of worship and bidding them return to their peaceful occupations. With Menelaus as go-between, it was hoped to detach the loyal subjects from the rebels and then to outlaw the irreconcilables.

These half-measures were not calculated to satisfy Judah on the one side or the enemies of the Jews on the other. The persecution initiated by the Seleucid monarch had revived the ancient animosities against the Jews among their neighbors to the south and to the east. The Greek cities, which had been growing in number since the times of Alexander the Great, had become fresh centers of virulent hatred of the Jews. Judah left the Temple mount strongly fortified so as to frustrate any attack from the Citadel. He likewise surrounded Beth-zur with walls; this fortress served him as a base of operations against the Idumeans, who made raids upon the Jewish insurgents, at the same time offering a refuge to fugitive Hellenists. The Idumeans were driven into their strongholds, which were captured by Judah and set on fire. The chastisement of the Idumeans brought comfort to their inveterate enemies, the Arab Nabateans, who made common cause with Judah.

News reached Jerusalem from all sides of the sore plight of the scattered Jewish settlements outside the small, but

142

compact territory of Judea. Thus the Ammonites, in league with Greeks and Arabs, were preparing to exterminate the Jews who had entrenched themselves in the Gileadite fortress Ramoth; further up north, near the sources of the Jordan, a thousand Jews had been massacred and their women and children carried away into slavery. With a force of eight thousand men, Judah and his brother Jonathan marched beyond the Jordan; they surprised the enemy in the rear and dispersed them. The rescued Jews were taken to Jerusalem by way of Beth-shan (Scythopolis), the only half-Greek city friendly to the Jews.

Meanwhile Simon, Judah's elder brother, was achieving success in Galilee. At the head of three thousand men, he forced the heathen to retreat to the coast, as far as Acco (Ptolemais); the delivered Jews were again taken to Jerusalem. On the other hand, an attack on Jabneh, led by Joseph son of Zechariah and Azariah, whom Judah had left in command of Judea during these expeditions, was repulsed by Gorgias; the loss to the Jews in the number of slain was considerable. A second expedition by Judah against the Idumeans resulted in the capture of Hebron. Equally successful was his campaign against the Philistine coast; Ashdod was destroyed and its sanctuaries with their statues were demolished. Two hundred Jews, among them women and children, had been lured by the citizens of Jaffa (Joppe) on ships to the high sea and then cast overboard; Judah surprised the two ports of Jaffa and Jabneh by night and set their ships on fire.

All these reprisals were made possible by the preoccupations of the regent arising out of his strained relations with Antiochus Epiphanes and then by reason of the death of the monarch in 164. When in 163 Judah made ready to assail the Citadel with its Syrian garrison, Lysias determined to resume the war against the Jews. Menelaus paid with his life for the unfavorable turn events had taken; he was replaced by Alcimus (Jakim) from among the loyalist priestly families. A vast army marched into Judea from the south; Beth-zur was invested. Judah interrupted the siege of the

Citadel and met the enemy at Beth-zechariah, half-way between the Syrian camp and Jerusalem. Despite acts of bravery such as cost Eleazar, the fourth of the Hasmonean brothers, his life, the Jews were unable to break through the enemy lines with their high-towered elephants and squadrons of horsemen covering the foot soldiers. Judah was compelled to retreat to the Temple mount where he in turn was besieged. Beth-zur was starved into surrender; it was the seventh year, when the land lay fallow and food was scarce. Fortunately Philip, whom the dying monarch had set up as regent in the place of Lysias, had advanced from the east and occupied Antioch. Lysias, in order to meet his opponent at home, concluded peace; a new governor was appointed over Palestine, while the internal administration of the Jewish community was left in the hands of Alcimus. Though Judah was comprised among the beneficiaries of the royal amnesty, he was forced to leave the city.

Philip was overcome, but Lysias and his royal ward were compelled to make way before Demetrius I., the son of Seleucus IV., who seized the throne in 162. Alcimus, whom the partisans of Judah kept from access to the Temple, implored the aid of the new king. Bacchides, the governor of Northern Syria, was sent to Jerusalem. He convened a body of teachers, among them several of the Pietists, who announced that they were satisfied with Alcimus, since he was descended from the legitimate high priestly families. The Pietists reasoned that the object, for which they had joined the uprising, had been achieved; it seemed to them that Judah was now engaged in a dynastic struggle with the lawful head of the nation. They were soon undeceived; to Alcimus they appeared as at one with the irreconcilables, and he had sixty of them seized and executed. Bacchides left a detachment of troops for his protection. But after his act of cruelty the new high priest was distrusted by the faithful; the old antagonism broke out afresh; Judah and his brothers resumed their offensive and the hard-beset priest once more turned to the king for help.

Demetrius sent Nicanor with the charge to capture Judah

and his brothers, dead or alive. Judah was wary; a skirmish near one of the coastal villages resulted in defeat for Nicanor, who commanded but a small force—the main army was needed by the king elsewhere—with which a levy from the loyalist Jews coöperated. Nicanor was enraged and threatened to destroy the Temple unless the rebels were delivered to him. On the thirteenth of Adar, 161, battle was joined between Nicanor, who stood at Beth-horon, and Judah, who encamped at Hadashah, not far from Modein. Nicanor fell in the battle, and his host dispersed toward the coast. Judah entered Jerusalem in triumph, bearing the vanquished commander's head and right arm; they were suspended from the wall in the sight of the Citadel. The day of the victory over Nicanor was ordained as an annual festival.

Judah had proved himself a victorious general. He was at the height of his career, and in reality the head of the nation. To safeguard the national mode of life, mere toleration and the grant of internal autonomy did not suffice. What the nation needed was political independence. As a step towards wresting from the tottering Seleucid empire complete freedom, the statesman Judah entered into negotiations with the Roman Senate, whose word was beginning to be law in Antioch. An embassy was sent to Rome, headed by the priest Eupolemus son of Johanan and Jason son of Eleazar, and it met with a friendly reception. A treaty of amity was concluded with the Senate; the Jews were recognized as a nation; as friends and confederates of the Roman republic they were to be let alone by Demetrius.

Antioch, however, knew Rome better. Roman emissaries were doing their best to give countenance to any disturber of the peace in the east who was just as speedily left in the lurch when he failed. Before the Jewish embassy returned from Rome, Demetrius had quelled the rebellion of the satrap of Media, Timarchus, and then hurriedly dispatched Bacchides into Judea with a formidable force, thus forestalling Roman intervention. Judah met him with a band of eight hundred men, which was completely routed (at a place north of Upper Beth-horon); the leader himself fell in the battle (160). His faithful followers rescued his body and gave it burial in the family sepulcher at Modein.

With the death of the hero, everything seemed to be lost for the nationalists. Alcimus held sway by the grace of the Syrian king and found support even among the moderates, who were satisfied that religious freedom had been restored. Resistance was put down with a high hand, and the rebels were delivered to Bacchides for execution. Nevertheless the nationalists rallied about Jonathan, the youngest of the Hasmonean brothers. There was no safety in Judea, where Bacchides had left heavy garrisons in various localities, compelling at the same time the leading citizens to surrender their sons as hostages. Jonathan withdrew across the Jordan. His brother Johanan departed with the baggage to the friendly Nabateans; but on his way he was intercepted by Arabs and slain. Jonathan surprised the Arabs and made them pay for the death of his brother; but on his return he was met by a Syrian detachment near the Jordan. The small band saved themselves by swimming across the river; with their leader they maintained themselves under precarious conditions in the jungles of the western shore.

Alcimus proved his submissiveness to the Syrian masters by having the wall which separated the inner from the outer court of the Temple torn down. When soon thereafter he died of a stroke (159), it was interpreted as a punishment from God. The high priestly office was left vacant. Bacchides returned home, since the country seemed pacified. Two years later he was recalled by the Hellenists, who had hopes of trapping Jonathan. The attempt failed; Jonathan and his brother Simon had entrenched themselves in a fastness of the wilderness; moreover, they inflicted a heavy defeat upon their assailants. Bacchides, thoroughly disgusted with the Jews who summoned him, accepted Jonathan's overtures for peace. The nationalist leader was not permitted to maintain an army, but he took up his residence at Michmas and gradually won over the moderate elements.

The Seleucid dominion seemed to be well established. But soon Demetrius was embroiled in feuds within and without;

a pretender, Alexander Balas, gave himself out as a son of Antiochus Epiphanes and found support among the king's powerful enemies. In 152 he landed at Ptolemais and was acknowledged by the garrison. Demetrius was in sore straits. Both parties made a bid for Jonathan's friendship. Demetrius withdrew the Syrian garrisons from all fortresses save the Citadel in Jerusalem and Beth-zur, and gave Jonathan leave to return to Jerusalem and fortify it. When Alexander conferred upon Jonathan the dignity of high priest, Demetrius bestowed further privileges upon the Jewish people and the Temple; the Citadel was to be placed under the high priest's control, three Samaritan districts and disloyal Ptolemais were ceded to the Jews. Jonathan, distrustful of Demetrius, made common cause with Alexander; on the Feast of Tabernacles, 152, Jonathan put on the high priest's robe. Two years later Demetrius fell in battle, and Alexander mounted the throne. In Ptolemais the nuptials of the new king with the daughter of Ptolemy Philometor were celebrated. Jonathan was an invited guest. Both kings honored him; the Jewish high priest sat at Alexander's side clothed in royal purple and had the title of general and administrator of Judea conferred upon him.

Alexander alienated the affections of his subjects by his self-indulgence and the ruthless acts of his minister against the friends of the late king. In 147 the son of Demetrius landed in Cilicia and assumed the title of king as Demetrius II. In Palestine, Jonathan alone held to Alexander and improved the opportunity by capturing Jaffa and several cities on the Philistine coast; in Ashdod he had the temple of Dagon set on fire. The grateful Alexander added as a gift the city of Ekron. Ptolemy Philometor was likewise gracious to Jonathan. This monarch was quite friendly to the Jews in Egypt, whose number was now enlarged by fresh migrations from the homeland. Onias, the son of Onias III. (p. 135), obtained permission from the king to build a temple, after the pattern of the Temple in Jerusalem, in Leontopolis (near Heliopolis), where his descendants kept up the service until the sanctuary was closed by the Romans (p. 204). His son or another Onias, together with Dositheus, rose to the high position of general in the king's army; the Jewish philosopher Aristobulus dedicated a free reproduction of the Torah to the king.

The Egyptian monarch cherished the hope of regaining Southern Syria for himself. Soon he broke with his son-in-law, who was overwhelmingly beaten in Cilicia (146). Jonathan was compelled to desist from his designs on the Citadel. However, he won over Demetrius II. by rich gifts and was confirmed in the honors and in the territorial expansion previously conceded by the king's father. An uprising in Antioch was put down by the aid of Jonathan, who in return received leave to invest the Citadel and to recapture Beth-zur.

The disaffected Syrian subjects went over to the side of Tryphon, an officer of the former king, who produced Alexander's young son and had him proclaimed king under the name of Antiochus VI. (145). Tryphon conferred high honors upon Jonathan and his brother Simon. Jonathan made good the opportunity by occupying Beth-zur, Jaffa, Ashkelon, and Gaza; he also fortified the Temple mount and blocked up the Citadel. An embassy to Rome brought back a renewal of the treaty formerly concluded with his brother Judah.

Despite Jonathan's valiant campaigns against Demetrius, Tryphon grew suspicious of his increasing power. Jonathan was lured to meet the minister at Ptolemais, where he was treacherously seized and his body-guard slain. An attempt to surprise two thousand picked men of Jonathan's forces in the Plain of Esdraelon miscarried; nor were Tryphon's troops successful in invading Judea, where Simon assumed control. At Tryphon's demand, Simon sent a hundred talents and Jonathan's two sons as hostages to secure their father's release. But the Syrian broke his word. After a second attempt to succor the hard-pressed garrison in the Citadel had come to naught by reason of a heavy snowfall, he marched across the Jordan and there slew Jonathan. The body was recovered by Simon and buried at Modein by the side of his father and three brothers. A magnificent sepulchral structure with seven pyramids, colonnades, and trophies of armor and ships carved upon the pillars, commemorated the valorous deeds of the heroic family. The monument was of such lofty dimensions that it was visible from the sea.

The boy-king Antiochus was murdered by Tryphon, who then seated himself upon the throne. Simon entered into negotiations with Demetrius, who accepted from the Jewish leader a golden crown and palm branch and granted the Jews a general amnesty and immunities from all taxes due the Syrian monarch and from all future tribute. Thus practical independence was won and the yoke of the heathen removed from Israel (142). From that year on the Jews began to date their documents after the years of Simon, their high priest, captain, and leader.

CHAPTER XXVII

SIMON. JOHANAN HYRCANUS.

ALEXANDER JANNAI

(142-76)

SIMON (142–135) set great store by his acquisition of the seaport Jaffa. In order to safeguard the road thereto, he captured Gezer, at the lower end of the valley of Aijalon. The heathen inhabitants were driven out and all traces of idolatry removed; the place was strongly fortified and a garrison of faithful Jews thrown into it, under the command of Simon's son, Johanan. The Citadel, the bulwark of heathenism in Jerusalem, passed at last into the hands of the nationalists. On the twenty-third of Ijar, 142, Simon entered in festal procession, and ever after this day was kept as a holiday. Subsequently the hill upon which the Citadel stood was cut down, so that the Temple mount rose high above it.

An embassy was sent to Rome to renew the treaty of amity between the Senate and Judea. In Jerusalem a great convocation of priests and laity, high functionaries and elders met; a decree was passed, engraved on a bronze tablet, and publicly set up, which named Simon prince, commander, and high priest for ever (Elul 18, 141). These dignities were to be hereditary in his family, until such time as a true prophet should arise. The ambassadors to Rome, who took with them as a gift a golden shield of a thousand pounds, brought back a senatorial decree, signed in the year 139, which recognized the independence of the Jewish state and commended the Jewish people to the friendship of all kingdoms and principalities in the East within the Roman sphere of power.

The new state was, however, soon involved in the political complications at Antioch. Demetrius II. was defeated by the Parthian Mithradates I. and captured (139). His brother, Antiochus VII (Sidetes, 138–129), took up the fight against

150

Tryphon. At first he was eager to gain Simon's friendship and assistance, in return for which he confirmed him in his position, adding the right of coinage. But so soon as Antiochus had gathered a substantial force of his own, he completely veered round. He declined Simon's proffer of two thousand soldiers, subsidies of money, and siegeworks, and demanded a return of the occupied cities and an indemnity of five hundred talents in arrears. When Tryphon was overcome, Antiochus ordered his general Cendebaeus to invade Judea. Simon dispatched his sons Judah and Johanan to meet the enemy; a battle was fought near Jabneh which resulted in a rout of the Syrian forces. Judah was wounded, but Johanan completed the pursuit (137).

During Simon's reign the people were happy in the freedom to live their own life. Material prosperity increased, strict justice was to be had in the courts, apostasy was suppressed, the laws of the Jewish religion were faithfully obeyed. But Simon's life was cut short through the treachery of his ambitious son-in-law, Ptolemy, the governor of Jericho. When Simon with his wife and their two sons Mattathiah and Judah visited him in the fortress Dok (near Jericho), he gave them a banquet and then had the three men murdered (135). Thus the last of the Maccabean brothers also met with a violent death.

Simon's surviving son, Johanan Hyrcanus (135–104), thwarted his brother-in-law's designs upon his own life and hastened to Jerusalem before Ptolemy could move against the city. Hyrcanus laid siege to the fortress in which Ptolemy was entrenched, but as his mother was still held by the governor, he had to proceed slowly; moreover, the sabbatic year terminated the operations entirely. At length, Ptolemy slew his mother-in-law and fled the country.

Antiochus VII. had by now established order in his realm and took the conduct of the war against the Jews into his own hands. Jerusalem was thoroughly invested; food began to be scarce within; those that could not bear arms were sent ready to capitulate. Counsel was divided in the camp of the enemy; but in the end Antiochus realized that the Greek party was extinct and that behind the high priest stood now the entire people. He granted a seven days' armistice and besides sent in cattle and incense for offerings. Peace was concluded on condition that the Jews were to recognize the Syrian overlordship, pay an annual tribute over and above an indemnity of five hundred talents, and surrender Jaffa, Gezer, and the other occupied cities. Antiochus was minded to place a garrison in Jerusalem, but upon the representations of the high priest he accepted instead hostages, among them the brother of Hyrcanus.

A turn for the better came with the death of Antiochus in his campaign against the Parthians (129). Demetrius II., who had been released from his Parthian captivity, was involved in war with Ptolemy VII. (Physcon) and with the pretender Alexander Zabinas; when Demetrius was murdered (125), his descendants fought with those of Antiochus Sidetes for the possession of the throne (Antiochus VIII. Grypus 125–113 and again 111–96—Antiochus IX. Cyzicenus 113–95). Practically Syria was powerless to act and therefore Judea was once more an independent state. Hyrcanus, taking advantage of his opportunities, not only reoccupied the cities of the coast, but, reinforcing his army of Jews with mercenary troops, he prosecuted the policy of territorial expansion begun by his predecessors. The Idumeans, the old enemy on the south, were subdued and forced to accept Judaism. East of the Jordan, Medeba and the neighboring localities were conquered. The hated Samaritans were overcome, their temple on Mount Gerizim was razed to the ground; despite the repeated intervention of Cyzicenus, Samaria was taken by the sons of Hyrcanus, Antigonus and Aristobulus, and completely destroyed. A legend narrates that intelligence of the decisive victory of his sons was conveyed to the high priest, as he was officiating in the Temple, by a heavenly voice. Further northward, Scythopolis (Bethshan) fell into the hands of the Jews through the treachery of the Syrian general.

The dynastic principle was now established and Johanan Hyrcanus had his own name stamped on coins. He designated himself both as high priest and head of the Jewish commonwealth. This dual dignity did not commend itself to those Jews who, like the Pietists, willing enough to fight for the free exercise of their religion, recoiled, now that the struggle was over, from the more and more pronouncedly secular character of the dynasty. We have seen (p. 144) how the Pietists were ready to accept Alcimus simply because his descent entitled him to the high priestly office. The principle of legitimacy or prior claim was paramount. On the other hand, the old aristocratic, even priestly, families, habituated to political power, had made peace with the new dynasty and saw no objection to the sovereign uniting in himself the sacerdotal and secular functions. For the time being, the stricter elements in the Council of State were in the minority, and so they withdrew from participation in the government constituting themselves the Opposition. Hence they became known as Pharisees or Separatists, while those who allied themselves with the government, being recruited chiefly from the priests belonging to the family of Zadok (p. 64), were called Sadducees. The rift, begun in the days of Hyrcanus, widened under his immediate successors.

When Hyrcanus died, the boundaries of Judea had been expanded to the compass of the Solomonic kingdom. According to the terms of his will, his wife was charged with the government, and the eldest of his five sons, Judah Aristobulus, with the high priesthood. Aristobulus (104–103), however, was ambitious; he threw his mother and his brothers, all but one, into prison and assumed the government. To his brother Antigonus he turned over part of the administrative duties. This preferred position proved the undoing of the prince. Jealous courtiers accused him of designs to seat himself upon the throne; Aristobulus summoned his brother to come to the palace unarmed, and at the same time gave order to his body-guard to fall upon Antigonus if he bore arms. The enemies of Antigonus bribed the messengers to tell him that the sovereign wished to see him in his new armor. Thus Antigonus lost his life.

Aristobulus assumed the title of king, but forbore to place it on the coins struck by him. Though he affected friendship for Greek manners—he called himself Philhellen, a Lover of the Greeks—he followed in the footsteps of his father by conquering and Judaizing the northern districts of Palestine —not only Galilee, but also a part of the Lebanon country occupied by the Itureans. He died of a painful disease after a reign lasting but a year.

His widow, Salome Alexandra, immediately gave orders to release from prison the king's three brothers. Since no issue was left, Jewish law prescribed that she should take to husband the eldest brother, Alexander Jannai (Jonathan), who succeeded both to the throne and to the high priesthood. He reigned twenty-seven years (103–76), during which time he was constantly engaged in warfare. His first act was to invest Acco (Ptolemais); the inhabitants called in the aid of Ptolemy Lathurus, who had been driven from the throne of Egypt by his mother Cleopatra III. and was ruling over Cyprus. Alexander was forced to raise the siege and to conclude peace with Ptolemy; but secretly he entered into negotiations with Cleopatra, and possessed himself of the coast cities Straton's Tower (renamed Caesarea by Herod) and Dor. Ptolemy, resentful of Alexander's breach of faith, marched into Galilee, took the town of Shihin (Asochis, near Sepphoris) on a sabbath, and signally defeated Alexander's forces at Amathus (Zaphon) near the Jordan. Ptolemy was robbed of the fruits of his victory by the advance of Cleopatra's army, commanded by Hananiah and Hilkiah, sons of Onias IV. (p. 147). The Egyptian queen was minded to reunite the Jewish territory with her own dominion; but she was persuaded by her Jewish generals to desist. Alexander was once more master in his land.

Across the Jordan, in the northern part, Alexander conquered Gadara and the fortress Amathus. He also possessed himself of the Philistine coast as far as the Egyptian border; Raphia. Anthedon, and, most important of all, Gaza were annexed (96); Ashkelon alone remained a free city under an autonomous government. These warlike successes, carried out largely by means of mercenary troops, served only to widen the breach between the king and the Pharisee opposition. On the king's return from one of these campaigns, he gave a feast, to which both Sadducees and Pharisees were invited. One of the Sadducees advised the king to appear in his high priestly robes, with the diadem bearing the divine name on his forehead. Forthwith a man from among the Pharisees protested, bidding the king to be content with the royal crown and leave the crown of priesthood to the legitimate seed of Aaron. The specific charge made by the Pharisees was that the king's mother had once been a captive, thus, according to Jewish law, disqualifying her son for the priesthood. Though the rumor could not be substantiated, the Pharisees persisted in their antagonism to Alexander. They had the people on their side, being nearer the common man who was taught by their teachers and imbued with dislike for the aristocratic circles. On the Feast of Tabernacles, during the ceremony of water libation, it was observed that Alexander poured the water on the ground instead of against the altar as was the teaching of the Pharisees; the people pelted the king, in the rôle of high priest, with their citrons and reviled him as the son of a captive mother. The enraged king commanded his mercenaries to throw themselves upon the worshipers, and six thousand people lost their lives. The king went over completely to the Sadducee party; several of the most noted Pharisee teachers, like Joshua son of Perahiah, exiled themselves to Alexandria.

Alexander pursued his conquests beyond the Jordan. Certain Arab tribes were brought under subjection; Amathus, which had revolted, was destroyed. These undertakings led to a conflict with the Arab chieftain Ubaid, and Alexander fell into an ambush from which he barely escaped with his life. Discredited, he returned to Jerusalem, to find the city in open rebellion. For six full years civil war raged in the land. Fifty thousand Jews are said to have perished at the hands of the king's Pisidian and Cilician mercenaries. But the royal forces were likewise exhausted, and the king sued for peace. The Pharisees answered by a curt demand for his death. At the same time they made overtures to Demetrius III. Eucaerus, son of Antiochus Grypus. Clearly the opposition was prepared for extreme measures, involving perchance the surrender of national independence, in preference to the hated king.

Demetrius came with an army (88). The Jewish popular party joined him at Shechem; Alexander was overwhelmingly beaten, losing all of his mercenaries and saving his own life only by flight into the mountains. Now the Jews became ashamed of the betrayal of their king, who was after all a Hasmonean. Six thousand went over to Alexander, and Demetrius retreated to his own dominions. The irreconcilables continued to push the war to the bitter end; but they were defeated in several battles and many of them slain. Their ringleaders were seized by Alexander and brought captive to Jerusalem; there, while feasting with the women of his harem, he had them, eight hundred in number, crucified, and, while they were still alive, the throats of their wives and children were cut before their eyes. Some eight thousand of the Opposition fled the country and remained away until the king's death.

Antiochus XII., the youngest of the sons of Grypus, undertook an expedition against the Arabs and marched through Judea. Alexander sought to check his passage by raising a wall with wooden towers from Jaffa to Chepharsaba; but the Syrian king burned the whole of it down. Antiochus met his death in battle; the Arab king Aretas III. extended his dominion as far as Damascus and from now on became the most powerful and dangerous neighbor of the Jews. Alexander was unsuccessful in an attack upon this Arab king; he was forced to retreat to Hadid, east of Lod, and to conclude peace by offering concessions. Alexander was more fortunate in the regions beyond the Jordan; he conquered a number of cities—Pella, Dium, Gerasa in Gilead, Golan, Seleucia, and the strong fortress Gamala in

Bashan (83–80). The whole stretch of the eastern country from Lake Huleh to the Dead Sea was Jewish territory.

This time, when the king returned to Jerusalem, he was joyfully received. Shortly thereafter he fell into a disease, brought on by hard drinking, which afflicted him during the last three years of his life (79–76). While laying siege to the fortress of Ragab, in the district of Gerasa, his strength was exhausted and he succumbed to the fever (76). The dying king had grown repentant of his antagonism to the Pharisaic party; he counseled his wife to make peace with them, bidding her fear neither the Pharisees nor their opponents, but only the hypocrites who, pretending to be Pharisees, did the deeds of Zimri (Numbers 25, 6–14) and demanded the reward of Phinehas.

CHAPTER XXVIII

THE LAST HASMONEAN RULERS

(76-37)

NOT all Pharisees were alike, as the worldly-minded Jannai shrewdly perceived. Some cloaked themselves in the mantle of Pharisaism and overawed the people by an ostentatious display of piety, by their sanctimonious mien, by boasting of having left nothing undone that duty required, by making fear the highest motive for the service of God. But that was a perversion of an ideal for which the system was in no wise responsible, though no organized piety can ever wholly escape it. The true Pharisee made love of God and love of the neighbor the chief commandments, the sum and substance of the Torah from which all else flowed. He recognized no other sovereignty but the Kingdom of God, no other rule but that prescribed by the divine commandments.

The collection of Holy Scriptures was now sealed, with nothing to add and nothing to subtract. It had grown with the ages, representing the clash of movements and countermovements. Priests, prophets, and wise men had woven its multifarious web. The dominant position was accorded to the Torah, the five books of Moses. A second division (Prophets, Nebiim) was made up of the historical books, Joshua, Judges, Samuel, and Kings, continuing the history of the nation down to the Babylonian exile; then of the collected addresses of the prophets Isaiah, Jeremiah, and Ezekiel in three books and of Hosea, Joel, Amos, Obadiah, Jonah, Micah, Nahum, Habakkuk, Zephaniah, Haggai, Zechariah, and Malachi in one. In a third class (Writings, Ketubim) were comprised supplementary historical works which carried the narrative down to early Greek times (Ruth, Chronicles, Ezra-Nehemiah, Esther), but principally poetic works, whether lyric, like the Psalter, the Song of Songs, and

Lamentations, or didactic, like Proverbs, Job, and (the partly poetic) Koheleth. As we had occasion to remark (p. 138), Daniel was the last book to enter the collection enshrining the Word of God as it had come through the channel of a triple inspiration—priestly instruction, prophetic admonition, and the teaching of singers and wise men.

To the Sadducee the Written Word was the all in all. He was the conservative, who adhered closely to the letter. Innovations, whether in practice or doctrine, were rejected by him. His religious outlook was bounded by conceptions which were the normal, but not the latest, in the Scriptures. Though the names, by which the two parties went, were new, the division had long been in preparation and antedated the closing of Holy Writ. For the Pharisee, the Written Word was supplemented by the Oral, the tradition of the fathers, the Words of the Scribes, that is, the measures introduced in the course of ages and especially by the teachers from Ezra on. Scripture was the truth, but authority was vested in the chain of its appointed interpreters. What came to be held as true, was read into the Scriptural word. The means by which this interpretation was effected might often be forced and apparently removed from the original intent. The point is that the Bible remained a living book, instinct with the beliefs and hopes of each new generation. Thus the Pharisees made a dogma of the belief in the Resurrection of the Body and of a judgment of the soul after death, ideas nascent in the Psalter and more fully developed in Daniel. In Daniel we meet likewise with a developed belief in angels, specialized entities with individual names. The Pharisees believed in the Providential ordering of the affairs of man; but instead of letting this doctrine be hardened into an absolute determinism, they held irrefragably to freedom of the will and human accountability. In the present world there is a mixture of good and evil; in the future order of the world all will be good, iniquity will vanish like smoke, and God alone will reign. The Kingdom of God will be fully realized in the Messianic era; but even now the pious enter upon it, register themselves as its citizens, by submitting to its rule.

It therefore behooves the Jew so to order his life as to become worthy of the heavenly Kingdom, though the end itself is with God, who will bring it on in His own time. All that the Jew can do is to pray that it may come soon. 'Magnified and hallowed be His Name in the world which He created 'according to His will, and may He cause His Kingdom to come speedily and in the near future'—thus runs the 'Kaddish' prayer, rooted in ideas and phraseology which mount up to earliest Pharisaism.

These hopes were cherished by the nation in its darkest moments and by the individual struggling with life's vicissitudes. God transcends the world. He is incomparably Holy. But He is not distant—He is quite near to those who call upon Him, near with all manner of nearness. God is a stern Judge, but also a loving Father, whose very chastisements are chastisements of love. The Pharisaic religion brought comfort to the lowly; the Pharisee teachers were beloved of the common people. In the meeting houses, or synagogues, they taught and preached, set forth the ordinances of the Torah touching the right conduct of man towards God and his fellow-man, and fired the imagination with the blessedness of the world to come. The synagogues vied with the Temple in ministering to the spiritual needs of the people, and in the synagogues the service was unsacrificial, unsacramental, a service of the heart, of prayer and benediction. Of a truth, under the guidance of the Pharisees, the synagogues came to be schools of every kind of virtue, and from Palestine they soon spread to all confines of the Dispersion. The new worship was decentralized, in quite a different manner from that of the days before Josiah when every city had its sanctuary and altar.

Salome Alexandra (76–67) left the command of the army in the hands of her younger son Aristobulus, while her elder son Hyrcanus acted as high priest. She surrounded herself with advisers from among the Pharisees. Their chief leader was Simon son of Shetah, presumably the queen's brother. The high Council of State, combining legislative and supreme judicial functions. was reorganized so as to admit a large number of Pharisees. So powerful was now their influence that they demanded summary punishment of those who had instigated the murder of members of their party in the reign of Alexander. But they had to give way to the interposition of their opponents, with whom Aristobulus was in sympathy. Altogether the reign of the queen was one of peace within and without. An expedition against Damascus was undertaken by Aristobulus, but led to no result. The Syrian empire was now in the hands of the Armenian king Tigranes. He prepared to invade Palestine, but was bought off by rich presents; moreover, the Romans, under Lucullus, were menacing his own country. When the queen, at the age of seventy-three years, became ill, Aristobulus forestalled his brother by starting a rebellion. The queen died before she could take steps to quell it (67).

Of the two brothers, Aristobulus was by far the more energetic. When Hyrcanus, by reason of his birthright, mounted the throne, Aristobulus marched against him with an army. A battle was fought at Jericho; many of the soldiers of Hyrcanus went over to his brother, who thereupon gained a victory. Hyrcanus fled to Jerusalem, but was forced to surrender. Peace was concluded, and the sluggish elder brother resigned both the royal and the high priestly dignity in favor of the younger. All promised to go well, had not the Idumean Antipater, whose father had been appointed governor of his own country by Alexander, worked upon the susceptibilities of Hyrcanus. In order to further his own ambitions by the side of the weaker brother, the crafty Idumean won support for him among the most prominent Jews, at the same time persuading the prince that his life was in danger so long as Aristobulus was in power. Accordingly, Hyrcanus, in the company of Antipater, fled to the Nabatean Aretas, who marched against Aristobulus and defeated him in battle. A great part of the troops of Aristobulus went over to Hyrcanus; only the fewest remained with Aristobulus, who retreated within the Temple fortifications. Hyrcanus and the Arab king laid siege to the Temple. There was a pious man, Onias by name, who had made himself famous by his successful intercessions for rain during a period of drought. He was besought by the besiegers to pray for the frustration of the adversary's plans. The saintly Onias stepped forward and prayed thus: 'O God, King of the universe, since those that are within and without are both Thy people, accept Thou the prayers of neither faction!" The disappointed soldiers stoned him to death. Passover was now approaching, and the besieged were short of cattle for offerings. The besiegers demanded a heavy price, and when the sum was passed to them through a chink in the wall they pocketed the money, but withheld the cattle.

In the meantime Pompey, sent by Rome to Asia, had crushed Mithradates VI. of Pontus and his son-in-law Tigranes (66). His attention was drawn to the complications in Antioch and Jerusalem and he charged Scaurus with the regulation of these affairs. Pompey's emissary made a quick decision in favor of the capable Aristobulus and ordered the Arabs to raise the siege (65). Aristobulus pursued the retreating Arab king and inflicted upon him a telling defeat. He set out to ingratiate himself with Pompey and sent him a costly present, a vine wrought of gold and worth five hundred talents. When the Roman general arrived in Damascus (63), deputations waited upon him from the two brothers, and a third from the nation itself, begging the abolition of royalty and a restoration of the old priestly constitution. Pompey reserved his decision, but suffered Aristobulus to accompany him on the expedition against the Nabateans. Suddenly Aristobulus separated from him and fled to the fortress of Alexandrium (63); he was compelled to surrender the stronghold, but managed to escape to Jerusalem. When Pompey appeared before the city, Aristobulus lost heart; he repaired to the Roman camp and offered to deliver the city.

When Gabinius was sent to take over the city, the gates were shut in his face. Pompey, enraged, ordered an advance towards the walls, while Aristobulus was made prisoner. His following within the city were determined to defend themselves to the bitter end. Hyrcanus had the majority behind him and gave up the city to the Romans. The war party had entrenched themselves behind the Temple forts. The siege lasted three months. At last a breach was made in the walls. The Roman soldiers entered, and a terrible massacre ensued. The priests who would not interrupt the sacrificial service were struck down at the altar. Fully twelve thousand Jews lost their lives. The day was the sabbath or, according to other accounts, the Day of Atonement.

The victorious Roman general entered the Holy of Holies. The Temple treasures were left intact, and the service was ordered to be continued. The originators of the war were executed; the capital and the country were made tributary to the Romans. All of the coast cities from Raphia to Dor, the Greek cities beyond the Jordan, as well as Scythopolis and Samaria, were taken away from the Jews and annexed to the Roman province of Syria. Hyrcanus II. was reinstated as high priest without the title of king. Pompey carried away Aristobulus, with his two daughters, his sons Alexander and Antigonus, and a great number of Jewish captives, to Rome; the proud scion of the Hasmoneans was there led before the triumphal chariot of the general (61).

Hyrcanus II. (63–40) was confronted, after a few years of undisturbed peace, by his nephew Alexander, who had escaped on the way to Rome and gathered a considerable force. Gabinius, the proconsul of Syria, overcame Alexander in battle and forced him to surrender three of the strongest fortresses which had fallen into his hands. This led to a new regulation of Palestinian affairs by which Hyrcanus was shorn of his political powers. The land was divided into five districts, each immediately subject to the governor of Syria and answerable for the taxes; Hyrcanus retained the custody of the Temple (57). Aristobulus and his son Antigonus, who had escaped from Rome, were still less successful in regaining power than Alexander had been (56). While Gabinius was away in Egypt, a fresh revolt broke out, which was led by Alexander and failed just as signally (55). Gabinius was succeeded by Crassus, who had entered into a coalition, the so-called First Triumvirate, with Pompey and Caesar. This rapacious proconsul plundered the Temple and carried away two thousand talents in coin and costly vessels worth eight thousand talents (54). It is not to be wondered at that after his departure the discontented elements broke loose; thirty thousand of them were sold into slavery and their leader Pitholaus was executed by Longinus, the new governor of Syria (53–51).

Palestine, with the entire East, was affected by the break between Pompey and Caesar in 49 and the ensuing civil war. Caesar equipped Aristobulus with two legions, but the Jewish prince was poisoned by the partisans of Pompey before he set sail for Syria. His son Alexander was beheaded at Antioch by the express order of Pompey. After the battle of Pharsalus and the death of Pompey (48), Hyrcanus and his minister Antipater openly espoused the cause of Caesar. When hard pressed in Egypt, Caesar was aided by a Jewish auxiliary force of three thousand men, which, together with the contingents of neighboring rulers and the army of Mithradates of Pergamum, assisted in the taking of Pelusium. Moreover, the Jewish high priest used his influence with the Egyptian Jews to bring them over to the side of Caesar in his war with Ptolemy XIV. Caesar showed his gratitude by restoring the political position of Hyrcanus, who was named hereditary head of the Jewish nation (ethnarch) and received back the territory taken away by Pompey, especially the important port of Jaffa (47–44). Antipater was granted as a reward Roman citizenship and immunity from taxation. By the favor of Caesar, the Jews outside Palestine received valuable privileges; the Jews of Alexandria were confirmed in their rights.

Hyrcanus was but the nominal ruler; the government was really in the hands of the astute Antipater, who appointed his sons as prefects, Phezahel in Jerusalem and Herod in Galilee. Herod was then a young man of twenty-five years and gave proof of the energy which subsequently placed him upon the throne. In Galilee, a patriotic movement was forming, having for its aim the complete restoration of Jewish independence. Just then a small band was disturbing the peace of the district by the use of forcible means against

those who were opposed to their extreme position. Herod
seized the leader Hezekiah and a number of his followers and
had them executed. This summary action met with the dis-
approval of the Council of State in Jerusalem or, as it was
now called by a Greek name, the Sanhedrin. Herod was summoned to stand trial. He appeared clothed in purple and
with a body-guard. The Pharisee Shemaiah, a noted teacher,
moved for condemnation. However, Hyrcanus had received
a peremptory order from Sextus Caesar, the governor of
Syria, for Herod's acquittal. He therefore adjourned the
sitting and advised Herod to remove himself secretly from
the city. Herod had meanwhile been named by the Roman
governor prefect of the whole of Southern Syria; he came
back to Jerusalem with an army, but was persuaded by his
father to abandon his plans for revenge.

After the assassination of Caesar (on the Ides of March,
44), Mark Antony formed with Lepidus and young Octavian
the coalition known as the Second Triumvirate (43). Cassius,
one of the conspirators against Caesar, had made himself
master of Syria; Palestine was compelled to deliver for the
maintenance of the rebel army a sum of nearly seven thousand talents, which was raised through the efforts of Antipater and his son Herod. Soon thereafter Antipater died by
poison as the victim of a personal feud (43); Herod quickly
avenged his father's death. When Antigonus, with the aid
of the king of Chalcis, attempted to regain the throne, he
was defeated by Herod, who, however, was unable to prevent Mari of Tyre from annexing certain parts of Galilean
territory.

In the battle of Philippi the combined forces of Octavian
and Antony destroyed the last hopes of the republican party
(42). Antony was now master of the whole of Asia. Repeatedly
Jewish deputations appeared before him with complaints
about Herod and his elder brother; but Herod's personal
charm, coupled with Antony's friendship for the father,
whose hospitality he had previously enjoyed, and a good
word from Hyrcanus, turned the scales in favor of the two
brothers. These were appointed tetrarchs (co-rulers) of the

Jewish territory, thus succeeding to the political functions held by Hyrcanus, albeit nominally. Antony granted freedom to the Jews enslaved by Cassius for failure to contribute their share towards the maintenance of his army and ordered the Tyrian ruler to restore the annexed localities.

While Antony was detained in Egypt by the charms of Cleopatra (VII.), the Parthians invaded Syria and Palestine. Antigonus realized the opportunity for regaining the throne. He allied himself with the Parthians, found supporters among his own people and entered Jerusalem, engaging in daily action with Phezahel and Herod. A Parthian detachment appeared before the city, and Hyrcanus together with Phezahel was inveigled into meeting the Parthian commander at his headquarters. Both were forthwith put in chains. Hyrcanus was mutilated to unfit him for the high priestly function, and was carried away into captivity. Phezahel committed suicide. Herod, however, fled from Jerusalem in good time; the women of his family and the children he sent on to the fortress of Masada (on the western shore of the Dead Sea) in charge of his brother Joseph, while he himself set out for Petra in Arabia.

Mattathiah Antigonus (40–37), by the grace of the Parthians king and high priest, marched against the Idumeans, who as Antipater's kinsmen were unfriendly, and took the important town Mareshah. Even after the expulsion of the Parthians from Syria by Antony's legate Ventidius (39), Antigonus remained unmolested, though a high tribute was exacted of him. Thus the Romans were bought off when they had come within sight of Jerusalem; but Masada remained in the hands of Joseph, who successfully repelled all attacks. In the meantime Herod had embarked from Alexandria for Rome. His lavish gifts and personal adroitness went a long way in winning the favor of those in power, notably of Antony and Octavian, who both recognized in him a devoted friend of Roman rule, ready to bear down all the opposition at home and to assist in warding off the Parthian peril. Accordingly he was named by the Senate in solemn session King of the Jews. He landed at Acco (39).

Though the legate received instructions to aid the new titular king, he met with lukewarm assistance, but was allowed, without hindrance, to gather an army consisting chiefly of Idumean fellow-tribesmen and mercenaries. Galilee, the center of anti-Roman agitation, presented difficulties; but he was able to descend by way of Samaria to Jaffa, which he took, then to march into Judea and raise the siege of Masada. With Idumea in charge of his brother Joseph, he attempted to lay siege to Jerusalem; but the scant help furnished by the Romans made the undertaking hopeless. In the city, Antigonus was in no wise minded to abdicate, certainly not in favor of Herod, who was but a half-Jew.

Herod, however, captured Sepphoris, the most important city in Galilee, won a signal victory over the forces of Antigonus at Arbela, and hunted down the patriots in their hiding-places (38). Roman assistance was still half-hearted, and nothing was accomplished on a second invasion of Judea. So Herod appealed in person to Antony, who had returned to Asia and was encamped at Samosata on the Euphrates. Peremptory orders were given to Sosius, the new governor of Syria, to lend energetic aid to Herod. Joseph had meanwhile fallen in battle with Antigonus and Galilee had revolted. But now Herod had at his disposal two Roman legions; Galilee was reconquered; at Jericho the forces of Antigonus fought bravely and Herod was wounded; but at Jeshanah in the district of Samaria he annihilated a part of the army of Antigonus under Pappus. Now he was able to lay siege to Jerusalem (37). The inhabitants held out for full five months. Herod absented himself for a short period to celebrate at Samaria his nuptials with Miriam, daughter of Alexander son of Aristobulus II., and of Alexandra daughter of Hyrcanus II. The alliance with the Hasmonean house was counted upon to dispel opposition to his royal status on the part of the Jews, and in Jerusalem the Pharisee leaders, who were averse to the union of regal and sacerdotal power in the person of Antigonus, actually counseled surrender. Jerusalem was taken by storm, the Roman soldiers slaying and pillaging freely, until Herod had to call a halt by buying the

Romans off. Antigonus was taken captive and, by order of Antony at the request of Herod, beheaded at Antioch. Thus ended the rule of the Hasmoneans.

CHAPTER XXIX

Herod, surnamed the Great, pursued during his entire reign (37–4) a clear-cut policy of making himself absolute master at home and earning the good-will of the power to which he owed his elevation. It was a difficult position, to which he brought an indomitable will, unscrupulousness in the choice of means, and all of his native shrewdness. In order to break the power of the Hasmonean dynasty and the related nobility, his first act was the execution of forty-five members of the aristocracy and the confiscation of their property. Since he could not hold the high priesthood in his own person, he bestowed the office upon Hananel, a Babylonian Jew of low priestly rank. However, Alexandra, the king's mother-in-law, secured the intervention of Cleopatra, and through her of Antony, in favor of her son, the young Aristobulus. Herod could not set himself in opposition to the wily Cleopatra, who was by no means well-disposed towards him; then his wife Miriam, whom he loved passionately, pleaded her brother's cause. So Hananel was deposed and Aristobulus elevated in his place. When on the Feast of Tabernacles (35) the Hasmonean high priest was openly acclaimed by the people, Herod repented of his imprudence and shortly thereafter invited the high priest to a feast at Jericho, during which the king's hirelings, who were bathing with Aristobulus, held his head under water until he drowned.

Alexandra, undeceived by Herod's simulated mourning, denounced him to Cleopatra, and he was called to account by Antony. Herod no sooner presented himself (naturally, not empty-handed) than he was restored to favor. But conditions at home were far from satisfactory. The remnants of the Hasmonean family were plotting, though not concertedly;

and Herod's uncle Joseph (who at the same time was the husband of his sister Salome), because he had during the king's absence failed to act with due energy, was executed. Both against his inner foes and against troublesome neighbors, Herod rebuilt the fortresses of Hyrcania and Alexandrium and strengthened the fortifications of Masada. In Jerusalem, north of the Temple mount, the citadel Baris, now named Antonia in honor of Antony, was made stronger; without the city a full Roman legion might be counted upon to quell any disturbance.

Cleopatra strove to recover the old Egyptian supremacy over Palestinian territory. Antony met her wishes to the extent that he compelled Herod to cede to her the rich district about Jericho with its palm and balsam forests and then to lease it at a high rental. The queen paid Herod a visit on her way from the Euphrates, whither she had accompanied Antony, and was received with due honors; but Herod kept wary of her coquetry. When in 32 war was declared by Octavian against Cleopatra and Antony, Herod offered military assistance; but in deference to the Egyptian princess, who was jealous of the Jewish king's chances for glory, Antony ordered him to war on the king of the Arabs who had been remiss with the tribute due to Egypt. The shrewd Cleopatra expected that the two kings would wear each other out. Herod's initial successes were checked by Cleopatra's commander, and Herod suffered defeat at the hands of the Arabs. At the same time a severe earthquake shook Palestine in 31, in which thirty thousand persons perished. Herod's overtures of peace being spurned by the Arabs, he met them in battle and completely routed the Arab army which had invaded Jewish Transjordania. The manner in which Herod on this occasion extricated himself out of a perilous situation served subsequently as his best recommendation in the eyes of Rome.

On learning of Octavian's victory in the battle of Actium (September 2, 31), Herod was guided by the instinct of self-preservation to abandon Antony to his fate. A troop of Antony's gladiators was prevented by Herod from reaching

Egypt. As soon as Octavian set out for the East, Herod hastened to present himself in person. So uncertain was he of the outcome that before his departure he had the aged Hyrcanus, who in 36 had been released from Parthian captivity, executed. He sent his children to Masada under the care of his mother Cyprus and his sister Salome, while his Hasmonean wife and her mother Alexandra were placed in the fortress of Alexandrium in charge of the commandant Soëmus, with instructions to put the two women to death if he failed to return. The meeting between Herod and Octavian took place in Rhodes. The abject humility of the king of the Jews, who left off his crown, paved the way for a favorable reception, the more so since the sagacious Roman discerned in him the right man for the difficult border territory. On Octavian's march to Egypt (in the summer of the year 30), Herod rendered valuable assistance in facilitating the provisioning of the army; the grateful Roman, on the successful termination of the campaign in the autumn of the same year, conceded Jericho and Gaza to Herod, then the coastal cities Jaffa and Straton's Tower, as well as the cities of Susitha (Hippus) and Gedar (Gadara) east of the Sea of Galilee. A portion of Cleopatra's Celtic body-guard was likewise turned over to Herod.

There was no love lost between Herod's mother and sister on the one hand and his favorite Hasmonean wife on the other. Miriam showed openly her bitter condemnation of the execution of her maternal grandfather, and the king's family fed his jealousy by trumped up charges of conjugal infidelity with Soëmus and of plotting to poison her husband. Both the queen and her supposed lover were punished with death (29). Herod's grief over the loss of his wife was uncontrollable and he gave himself over to wild dissipation and drinking bouts, until he fell sick and took to bed in Samaria. Alexandra thought the moment opportune to restore the Hasmonean rule and sought to win over the commandants of the Jerusalem citadels; but the king was speedily informed and the dangerous mother of Miriam was executed (28). Similar punishment was meted out to Salome's second husband, the

Idumean Kosgobar, and his confederates, the sons of Baba, a family distantly related to the Hasmoneans (25).

Herod was now at the height of his power. He cultivated assiduously the friendship of Augustus—as Octavian was now called after being invested with imperial powers—and paid him deferential visits in Rome or during the emperor's presence in Syria; he maintained personal contact with Agrippa, the son-in-law of Augustus and his presumptive heir. It was a great honor for Herod to receive the second man of the empire in his own capital and then to accompany him on his expedition to Asia Minor. Herod's position was that of a friend and ally of the Roman people, and, while naturally restricted in the exercise of sovereign powers in external affairs, he possessed unlimited freedom in his own domain, whether in the management of army and navy, in judicial affairs, in the administration of finances, or in matters of internal government. Thanks to repeated grants from his high patrons, the borders of the Land of Israel were again extended to the limits of the Davidic kingdom; Perea, that is, Transjordania, constituted a separate tetrarchy with Pheroras, the king's brother, as administrator. The direct contact with the sea and the construction of ports opened up maritime trade, which in addition to the inland commerce increased the wealth of the country. The soil was intensively cultivated; colonies were settled in the newly won territory to the northeast; barren land was rendered fruitful through large waterworks and aqueducts. The royal revenue, by direct taxation or by imposts, was considerable; in addition the king commanded resources of his own, from private domains, from interest on loans to neighboring rulers, from working the imperial copper mines in Cyprus.

Herod spent money lavishly. Like Solomon he had a passion for building. The old sites which he restored or enlarged and the new cities constructed by him served both strategic and economic purposes. Thus he rebuilt Samaria and called it in honor of Augustus (Sebastos in Greek) Sebaste; on the site of Straton's Tower he built a new city and named it Caesarea; toward Arabia he erected two new fortresses, both of which received the name of Herodium. He erected magnificent residences for himself in various localities, and in Jerusalem, on the western hill (the Upper City), a vast palace, with huge halls, resplendent with gold, marble, and rare stones. The crowning achievement of Herod's building operations was the reconstructed Temple, which was not really completed till six years before its final destruction. It was said that no more beautiful sight was ever seen by man. The ground-plan and interior arrangement were left as they had been, but the Temple proper, or the House, was increased in height. It was built of huge blocks of white stone, and in the construction of those parts inaccessible to laymen, none but priests were employed. In front ran a large Porch, from which twelve broad steps descended to the Court of the Priests with the Altar and the great Laver. Then followed the Court of Israel for men-worshipers, and, separated by a wall, a gallery for women. Lower down, divided by a wall and fenced-off terrace from the Inner Sanctuary, lay the Court of the Gentiles, and a tablet with a Greek inscription warned non-Jews not to trespass within the enclosure on pain of death. All that is left of this glory is the foundation of the outer Western Wall (Kothel Maarabi), the most sacred spot in the world to the Jew. Here to this day he believes himself nearest to the Divine Presence hovering as of yore over the lone relic of Israel's Sanctuary.

Outside Palestine, from Antioch to the isles of the sea and beyond to Athens, Lacedaemon, and Nicopolis (on the site of Actium), Herod was remembered for his foundations of temples, colonnades, and public edifices. He played the part of patron of Greek culture and friend of Caesar both abroad and at home. In Samaria he erected a temple for the worship of the emperor; in the Holy City itself he built a theater and a hippodrome and introduced athletic games. He surrounded himself with pomp; at his court he entertained Greek savants, of whom the most notable was his court-historian Nicholas of Damascus. At an age past fifty the monarch let himself be introduced to Greek philosophy, rhetoric, and history. He had Greek tutors for his sons. To complete their education, he sent them to Rome and had them lodged with prominent Roman families that they might improve their manners and establish connections at the source of political power.

Herod was in reality king of the Jews rather than a Jewish king. It is true that he made concessions to Jewish susceptibilities; he likewise used his influence to better the condition of the Jews in the Dispersion. But just as often he wounded Jewish feeling, as when he had the Temple surmounted by an eagle. He remitted taxation in times of distress, magnanimously perhaps, but just the same with calculated forethought that upon recovery the people would be able to bear the burden so much the more readily afterwards. He named and deposed high priests in quick succession and, by keeping the sacred robes in his own custody, made it understood that the office was subject to kingly authority. His absolute power was felt in the communal administration which was supervised by a royal commissary. Matters of state and jurisdiction over life and death were committed to an inner council of courtiers. The Sanhedrin was shorn of all prerogatives as a participant in executive functions; it was useful as an instrument whereby the king might carry unpopular measures. Its prestige was still weighty, but its activity was more and more confined to the religious sphere.

Herod was not loved by the Jewish people. There was a class of irreconcilables who twice refused the double oath which he demanded to himself and to Caesar. The majority of the Pharisees found satisfaction in the pursuit of the Torah, and Herod was content to have them thus occupied. The two most noted exponents of Pharisaism during the reign of Herod were Shammai and Hillel. The latter came to Palestine from Babylonia, and of the two his influence on the development of Judaism was by far the more lasting. To both piety meant the strict observance of the Torah, the written Word of God and the unwritten teachings of its authoritative interpreters. This body of law constituted the norm of religious obligation (Halakah). In its application Shammai stood for extreme rigorism. He demanded of his young boy, not yet in his teens, that he should fast on the Day of Atonement. When his grandson was born during the Feast of Tabernacles, he had the roof opened so that the infant might sleep in a booth-like dwelling. Hillel, on the other hand, was more lenient and had an eye to changing conditions. The Torah prescribes the remission of debts in the sabbatic year. As a consequence people refrained from making loans on its approach. Hillel therefore devised a formal document by which the creditor assigned to the courts the collection of the debts and thus avoided the risk of losing his money. Hillel made use of definite rules of interpretation (hermeneutic principles) by means of which new laws were deduced from the Torah. Instead of laying aside every good morsel for the coming sabbath, as Shammai was wont to do, Hillel took thought of each day as it came along, content with the blessings which came from God. Hillel was exceedingly patient and meek. Once a heathen approached him and begged to be instructed in the Jewish religion in the shortest possible time. 'Do not unto others what is hateful to thyself; this is the whole of the Torah, all the rest is commentary,' was the answer. The commentary, of course, must be mastered; an ignorant person cannot be pious. Every man should make himself a disciple of Aaron, be a lover of mankind, and by gentle persuasion bring men nigh to the Torah.

The last decade of Herod's reign was overcast with gloom. Warfare with the Arabs led to an estrangement from Augustus; though a reconciliation followed, their relations lacked the original warmth. Palace intrigues, fostered by Salome, involved the king in domestic differences which ended tragically. Herod had intended the sons of his favorite wife, the Hasmonean Miriam, to be his successors. Alexander was married to the Cappadocian princess Glaphyra, and Aristobulus to Salome's daughter Berenice. The king's policy was apparently to weld together the two families, the Idumean and the Hasmonean. The princes of Hasmonean blood looked down with contempt upon those of other strains, and the old mischief-maker Salome did her worst to disturb the peace by her calumnies. At length the king had Alexander and Aristobulus put to trial; they were condemned and strangled to death (7). Antipater, the son of Herod's first wife Doris, who had a hand in the intrigue, was likewise executed shortly before his father's death (4). While the king lay sick, the people, led by two scholars, tore down the eagle from the Temple gate; but despite his illness, the king had enough strength to see to it that the revolt was put down and the chief ringleaders burned alive. Herod died of cancer of the intestine, unmourned by his own and hated by the entire people.

CHAPTER XXX

ROME TIGHTENING ITS HOLD

(4 BEFORE—41 AFTER THE CHRISTIAN ERA)

Y Herod's last will, Archelaus, the elder son of his
Samaritan wife Malthace, was named king, her
younger son Antipas tetrarch of Galilee and Perea,
and Philip, son of another of the king's wives, Cleopatra of
Jerusalem, tetrarch of the northeastern districts. It was
necessary, of course, to obtain for these appointments imperial confirmation. Before Archelaus, as head of the family,
could depart for Rome, the people demanded satisfaction for
the execution of their beloved teachers (p. 176). When this
was refused, a revolt broke out which was suppressed after
much bloodshed. No sooner was Archelaus gone than there
were fresh riots which required the intervention of the Syrian
legate Varus. He left behind a legion to maintain order in
Jerusalem; but in consequence of the ruthless conduct of the
temporary imperial governor of Palestine, Sabinus, there
was a new uprising which led to heavy fighting, especially
about the Temple, between the people and the Roman
soldiers. The Jews offered stubborn resistance; but they were
overwhelmed and the Temple treasury was plundered,
Sabinus alone helping himself to four hundred talents. A
part of the army of Herod now joined the insurgents, and
Sabinus was shut up in Herod's palace. At the same time,
Judah, the son of that Hezekiah whom Herod had executed
(p. 165), gathered a band of patriots, armed them with
weapons from the royal arsenal at Sepphoris, and operated
throughout Galilee. Varus came down with two legions and
with the help of Arab auxiliaries dispersed the Galilean
rebels. The city of Sepphoris was set on fire and the population sold as slaves. Varus then marched into Judea, caught up
the groups of patriots and had as many as two thousand of
them nailed to the cross.

177

Meanwhile, in Rome, Antipas, who in a previous will of Herod's had been designated as his successor, was disputing the claims of his brother Archelaus, while a delegation from the people argued in favor of an autonomous priestly government directly subject to Rome. Augustus, however, confirmed Herod's last will, except that Archelaus was shorn of royal dignity and received the title of ethnarch (ruler). Salome was granted, in accordance with her brother's testament, the palace at Ashkelon and the cities of Jabneh, Ashdod, and Phasaelis, which upon her death she bequeathed to the empress Livia. Of the three rulers, Philip was the only one who led a peaceful and honorable life and died at home (34 of the Christian era); his lands, at first annexed to the Syrian province, were turned over to Agrippa in 37.

The reign of Archelaus lasted but ten years (4 before the Christian era until 6 after). He pursued the absolutistic policy of his father, whom he resembled in character but not in ability. At will he named, and just as quickly deposed, high priests. He avoided on the whole offending Jewish religious sentiment, save when it interfered with satisfying his passions. Thus he wedded his sister-in-law Glaphyra. Not only had she born children to her first husband, but she had since Alexander's death been married to Juba, king of Mauretania. She died shortly after reaching Palestine; the people saw in her death divine retribution for the unlawful marriage. Archelaus must have had ambitious projects which made his loyalty to Rome suspicious; when both the Jews and the Samaritans joined in complaints about his régime, he was banished to Vienne in Gaul where he died some twelve years later. His territory, that is, Judea, Samaria, and Idumea, was annexed and placed under imperial governors or procurators, who took up their residence in Caesarea.

On occasion, especially during the high festivals when masses of pilgrims streamed into the Holy City from all parts of the Dispersion, these procurators repaired to Jerusalem and had their residence in the Herodian palace. Under normal conditions the procurator was master in his own domain; still he was subordinated to the Syrian legate who might intervene in exceptional cases. The procurator had his own troops; garrisons were stationed in the various districts; in Jerusalem there was just one cohort. Furthermore the procurator was administrator of the finances; the taxes, how-, ever, were farmed out to private contractors (publicans). Otherwise, the internal administration was not interfered with. The old aristocratic constitution was restored. The high Sanhedrin in Jerusalem made the laws and acted as a court of appeal; it consisted of seventy members in addition to the presiding officer, who was generally the high priest. In the division of religious affairs, with its own chief and his deputy, the scholars predominated. In the provincial towns there were smaller Sanhedrins of twenty-three members each. The Temple worship was an object of imperial protection. The high priests were appointed by the procura- tor or by the members of the Herodian dynasty; the office remained in the hands of a few families, among which that of Boëthus, whose daughter was one of the wives of Herod, may be specifically mentioned. The high priest's robe was, as a rule, kept in the custody of the appointive power and delivered four times in the year, on the three festivals and on the Day of Atonement. As far as possible, Jewish sus- ceptibilities were respected; the troops entering Jerusalem left behind their standards and imperial images. Still it all depended upon the personal rectitude and good intentions of the procurator, and these often were lacking.

Immediate cause for friction was furnished by the imperial census of the year 6 or 7 for purposes of fiscal assessment. Apart from an innate aversion to being counted (p. 53), the order brought home to the people their ignominious subjec- tion to Rome and met with universal resistance. However, the high priest Joazar showed how futile open rebellion would be, and the majority submitted to the inevitable. But in Galilee, Judah (p. 177), together with the Pharisee Zadok, called for an uprising in the name of religion. Nothing came of it just then, except that a body of intransigent patriots branched off from the large mass of the Pharisees and organized themselves as the party of Zealots. As in the days of the Syrian persecution, the old cleavage came into life. The rank and file of the Pharisees looked for the termination of foreign dominion in God's own time, but the Zealots were determined to accelerate the end by direct action.

Another, and distinctly exaggerated, form of Pharisaism was Essenism, a new name for the old Pietism. The Essenes lived in villages of their own or dwelt together in large establishments in the cities. After a double novitiate they passed to full membership; children were admitted to be trained early in the ways of the Order. Celibacy was an absolute rule, also community of goods. The members tilled the soil or pursued a craft; commerce was shunned. They performed frequent ablutions and wore white garments. Votive offerings were sent to the Temple, but no animal sacrifices; their own meals, eaten in common, partook of the nature of sacraments. They rejected all manner of oaths. The sabbath they observed strictly. They had a secret lore about angels and other mystic matters. They cultivated prophetic clairvoyancy and practised healing in accordance with their studies of the medicinal properties of roots. They conceived the soul as immortal and believed unconditionally in Providence.

Still another variety of Pharisaism was that of the apocalyptists, the revealers of the end of things. With these visionaries the figure of Messiah tended to become more and more other-worldly: a celestial being, preëxistent and eternal, the judge of sin and even demons, and the bearer of salvation to the pious in a transformed world-order. From these or kindred circles came John (Johanan) the Baptist. He announced himself as the forerunner of the Messiah, of one mightier than himself. He summoned the people to repentance and led them to the Jordan for purification through immersion (baptism)—such as the Essenes and other Pietists practised and such as the Torah prescribed for certain cases of impurity. The tetrarch Antipas (4 before the Christian era to 39 after), whose subject the Baptist was, possessed neither the knowledge nor the interest to distinguish between one kind of Messianism and another. He had not perhaps his father's energetic will-power; but he inherited his passion for building—the most notable operation being the foundation of Tiberias—a sensuous nature, a measure of shrewdness. Like his father, he made devotion to Rome the rule of his life. Indifferent to religious motives, he saw in the Messianic movement a danger to the good relations with Rome and so had the Baptist seized. The stern preacher had also remonstrated against the tetrarch's unlawful marriage to Herodias, whom he took away from his living half-brother Herod. Antipas had contracted a political marriage with a daughter of the Nabatean king, whom he now repudiated in order to please the ambitious woman for whom he conceived an overmastering desire. The Baptist was imprisoned in the fortress of Machaerus and there executed (29 after the Christian era).

Among those who had received baptism at the hands of John was the Galilean Jesus (Jeshua), son of a carpenter at Nazareth. The conviction came to him that he was the 'mightier one,' the actual Messiah; but he kept this knowledge at first to himself. He returned to Galilee and repeated John's call to repentance; for 'the time is fulfilled, the Kingdom of God is at hand.' He went about preaching the good tidings in the synagogues and to concourses of the people, by means of parables and by explication of telling passages in Holy Writ, more and more disengaging himself from the accepted manner of the schools and speaking with authority. By virtue of his Messianic consciousness, he expelled demons, in which popular belief saw the source of nervous disorders, and remitted sins. He gathered a group of disciples from among the common folk, and some were attracted to him even from the ultra-patriotic Zealots. But, to the burning question of one's dealings with Rome, he gave the answer: 'Render unto Caesar the things that are Caesar's, and unto God the things that are God's.' The Kingdom of God of which he preached was not of the political sort.

Jesus had points of contact with teachers before him and in his own day. He put morals above ritual, inward piety above ceremonial. To Hillel's Rule he gave a positive turn:

'Whatsoever ye would that men should do unto you, even so
do ye also unto them, for this is the Torah and the Prophets.' Like the school of Shammai, he forbade divorce save
for one cause; like the Essenes, he tolerated no manner of
oath; with the Pharisees, he held to the belief in the resurrection of the body. Yet, unlike the Pharisees, he associated
with publicans; he made light of the washing of the hands
and of fasting. He was averse to the overscrupulous severity
with which the sabbath and the dietary laws were observed
He said that he came to fulfil the Law, to bring out its essen-
tials; but in distinguishing between the weightier matters
and the lighter he set himself in opposition to the Pharisaic
system. He likewise broke with the slow process of Pharisaic
adjustments and thought it futile to put patches on an old
garment. He taught a righteousness that should exceed the
Pharisaic and overdrew the duty of loving one's enemy and
of non-resistance to evil, just as he overemphasized the
divine love as if the good and the evil deserved it alike.

Whether or not Jesus would declare himself openly as the
Messiah, the impressionable circles with which he came in
contact began to regard him as such. Jesus grew wary of
Antipas and fled into the territory of Philip. At Caesarea
Philippi, near the sources of the Jordan, Jesus was acclaimed
as the Messiah by his disciple Simon Peter, whom, nevertheless, he charged to observe silence. Apart from the dangers
which attended an open avowal, Galilee was not the place
for such a declaration; if anywhere, it must be made at
Jerusalem, where a large body of pilgrims was due on the
approaching festival of Passover. Accordingly, Jesus made
his entry into the Holy City, where he presented himself as
the Messiah. He was immediately seized by the authorities
and put on trial before the Sanhedrin. Witnesses reported
him as saying that he would destroy the Temple made with
(human) hands, and in three days build another, heavenly
one, made without hands. The presiding high priest Joseph
Caiaphas put the question to Jesus: 'Art thou the Messiah?'
'I am,' was the answer, 'and ye shall see the Son of Man
sitting at the right hand of God, and coming with the clouds

of heaven.' The assumption of power beside the Deity by one who had made light of the things hallowed by religious sentiment, was blasphemous in the eyes of the court. Jesus was condemned as a false prophet, and was delivered to the procurator Pontius Pilate, then residing in Jerusalem, as a Messianic pretender and therefore a rebel against Rome. As such Jesus was nailed to the cross. He died on the eve of Passover in the year 30.

The administration of Pilate (26–36) was marked by acts of ruthlessness and utter disregard of Jewish susceptibilities. Thus Galilean patriots were executed without trial; an attempt was made to use the Temple funds for the construction of an aqueduct; the troops marching into Jerusalem brought in imperial images. The people offered resistance and were roughly handled by the soldiery; Pilate continued to vex the Jews by depositing in his official Jerusalem residence shields upon which the emperor's name was inscribed. Antipas and the other Herodians joined in a forceful protest to the emperor Tiberius (14–37), and the shields were ordered removed to the temple of Augustus in Caesarea. Samaritans, assembled on Mount Gerizim to witness the discovery of the sacred vessels (supposedly hidden by Moses) which a pseudo-prophet was about to unearth, were dispersed by Pilate and many of them executed. The Syrian legate Vitellius gave heed to their complaints and ordered Pilate to Rome, Marcellus being charged during the procurator's absence with the administration of Palestine.

Antipas had meanwhile been involved in war with the Arabs who prepared to avenge the humiliation of their king's daughter at the hands of the Jewish tetrarch (p. 181); the moment seemed opportune since Rome was at war with the Parthians and Antipas was taking part in the expedition. Though on this occasion friction developed between Vitellius and the tetrarch, the legate received orders on his return to proceed against the Arabs. His march took him through Judea, but he wisely refrained from taking the army with the imperial standards to the Holy City, which he visited in person during the festival of Passover. For three days the legate tarried in Jerusalem, during which time he acted with circumspection and graciousness. On the fourth day news arrived of the death of Tiberius (March 16, 37); Vitellius recalled his army, and the blow which the Arabs had dealt Antipas remained unavenged.

One of the first acts of the new emperor Caius Caligula (37–41) was to appoint his friend Agrippa, the son of Aristobulus (p. 175), king over the vacant tetrarchy of his uncle Philip (p. 178) enlarged by a district in the Lebanon. A year and half later Agrippa set out from Rome by way of Alexandria; the presence of the newly crowned Jewish king in that city (autumn 38) was the immediate occasion for an anti-Jewish manifestation which resulted in an outbreak. There were by that time a million Jews in Egypt. In Alexandria they occupied two compact quarters, while many of the wealthier classes had their residences in other parts of the city. They had numerous synagogues; the largest was a beautiful and magnificently equipped structure. The Jews of Alexandria had enjoyed extensive rights since the foundation of the city, and the Roman rulers since Caesar had confirmed them in these rights. Moreover, owing to their religious beliefs, they had a privileged position which exempted them from participation in the city cult. They spoke, as we have seen (p. 129), the Greek language and absorbed the higher culture of the Greeks. Beginning with the Greek version of the Torah, which in course of time was followed by the translation of the rest of Scripture, they developed an extensive literary activity in the Greek tongue. Their object was to commend to the attention of the Greek the products of the Jewish mind, just as, conversely, they had entered into the spirit of Greek philosophy and convinced themselves that its truth had been anticipated by their own sacred writers. Judaism was glorified by Jewish poets and historians who assumed fictitious names, as if the authors were heathen Greeks convinced of the excellency of the Jewish religion. The majority of the Jews were observant and, because of the close proximity to the mother-country, in touch with Jewish scholarship; but there were not wanting those who had sloughed off some practices that were to them irksome, while a small number forswore their religion entirely. The Greeks of Alexandria were the inveterate enemies of the Jews, determined to dispute their equality as citizens, resentful of their privileged status, envious of their economic prosperity and their social pretensions. The Jews competed with the Greeks in the crafts and industries; one might find them as common laborers, as lessees of public and private domains, as tax-farmers, as bankers, as merchants. A literary feud had been going on for some time, in which Greek writers misconstrued Jewish religious separateness as wilful exclusiveness and the Jewish horror of idolatry as godlessness. When Agrippa arrived with his retinue and was acclaimed by the Jews of Alexandria, the Greeks mocked him in the gymnasium and produced a pantomime in the theater in which a half-witted Greek was dressed up like Agrippa and received the homage of the actors who shouted Mari, Mari (Aramaic for 'my lord'). The excited populace then determined to wound the Jews in their most sensitive spot. It was known that the capricious and manifestly insane emperor took the imperial cult quite seriously, not as a form of homage but as a worship of himself as a deity. The Greeks of Alexandria, like all the other heathen provincials, readily complied; now they demanded that the Jews likewise should put up statues of the emperor in their synagogues. The Roman prefect Flaccus, who was none too sure of the emperor's favor, willingly fell in with the plot. In due course he sanctioned the installation of the statues in the synagogues, and when the Jews resisted he proclaimed in an edict that they were aliens and turned the mob loose upon them. The Jewish quarters were invaded; the shops and dwellings were looted and then set on fire; Jews were clubbed to death and their corpses mutilated; the synagogues were demolished or desecrated. Flaccus not only suppressed a petition of the Jewish community to Rome, but had thirty-eight members of the Jewish communal council dragged in chains to the theater and there publicly scourged. Jewish women were forced before the spectators to partake of swine's flesh.

Agrippa's intervention led to the removal of Flaccus, but the bitter animosities continued under his successor. In the year 40, two embassies sailed for Rome, a Greek deputation led by the Jew-baiter Apion, and a Jewish embassy of which the spokesman was Philo.

Philo belonged to a wealthy and cultured family. His brother Alexander was chief inspector of customs in the eastern district of the Nile. Philo's life was spent in the pursuit of the highest wisdom and in the writing of theological books. He occupies a noteworthy place in the history of Greek philosophy; he greatly influenced the development of Christian dogma; his theories filtered through in course of time among Jewish circles, and the medieval Cabala was profoundly, though indirectly, influenced by them. Philo persuaded himself in all honesty that the teachings of the divine Plato were contained in the Torah. The method by which the harmony was brought about was that of allegorical interpretation. With Philo, God was the transcendent Being, outside and above the world, so far removed that in order to relate Him to the cosmos all sorts of go-betweens were required. These intermediary potencies were a reflex of the Platonic Ideas; they were conceived as personalities and identified with the angels in Scripture; chief among them was the 'Word' of the Palestinian teachers, the Reason (Logos) of Greek philosophers. Philo's system was thoroughly Greek in that it was dualistic: spirit and matter, God and the world stood as opposites, and the contrast was eternal. The approach to the supra-mundane Deity, unknowable, unnamable, yet supremely real, was effected by means of faith, an act of the will. The essence of Philo's ethics gave preponderance to the spiritual in man; piety meant an ecstatic immersion in the Deity, a divine intoxication, a heavenly passion; the glory of Israel was to be recognized by humanity as the regally philosophic people. The workings of God in history were a sealed book to Philo. The heroes of the past were transformed into psychic forces operating in a philosophic present of everlasting rational sameness. Though the ceremonial observances were largely spiritualized, Philo recognized their practical importance and he reproved the upper classes about him for their laxity. At the bidding of the community he forsook the quiet of the study to present the cause of his brethren to the mad emperor.

While the deputation was awaiting an imperial audience, the stupefying news reached Italy of a worse storm in Palestine. The Jews of Jabneh had torn down an altar erected to the emperor by the heathen residents, and when the matter had been reported to Caligula a peremptory command was issued to set up the emperor's image in the Temple. The governor of Syria, Petronius, was instructed to take effective military measures to carry out the order. He summoned the Jewish notables and reasoned with them, but to no purpose. A mass deputation of the people besieged the governor's headquarters at Ptolemais and implored him to abandon the undertaking. Petronius temporized and at length begged the emperor to rescind the unwise order. Meanwhile Agrippa, who had gone to Italy and there learned from the emperor himself the cause of his fury, had succeeded in having the imperial order countermanded. Caligula still contemplated, on his prospective journey to Alexandria, forcing his will on the recalcitrant Jews of Jerusalem. Fortunately for the Jews, as well as for the hesitating governor, Caligula was murdered (January 24, 41); the news of his death reached Palestine nearly a month before the messengers, delayed by unfavorable weather, arrived with sealed orders to Petronius to take his own life in punishment for his disobedience. Thus the life of the wise governor was saved and the Temple preserved from desecration.

The new emperor Claudius (41–54), no less than his predecessor, was favorably disposed to Agrippa. In addition to the tetrarchies originally granted (p. 184), he had received at the hands of Caligula the territory of his brother-in-law Antipas (39). Herodias, the wife of Antipas, was Agrippa's sister. When her brother was deep in debt, she had secured for him the lucrative position of inspector of markets in Tiberias. Upon Agrippa's receiving the royal title, the ambitious woman impelled her husband to seek similar preferment. Both Vitellius and Agrippa denounced him to the emperor for massing war material, and as the explanation he offered was not considered satisfactory he was condemned to banishment in Gaul. Claudius not only confirmed Agrippa in all these possessions, but added Judea and Samaria. Thus the whole of Palestine, as held by Herod the Great, was reunited in the hands of his grandson, in whose veins flowed Hasmonean blood.

CHAPTER XXXI

THE WAR WITH ROME

(41-67)

AGRIPPA I. (41–44) was in many respects his grandfather's double, but somewhat more genial and prudent, and he had a deeper understanding of the Jewish spirit. Whatever his life had been in the past amid diverse vicissitudes, however even now he wished to be regarded abroad as a friend of Greek culture—at home he conformed strictly to Jewish ordinances. The golden chain, which Caligula presented to him in lieu of the iron chains into which Tiberius had cast him, he made over as a votive gift to the Temple. He offered a thanksgiving sacrifice and defrayed the costs incident to the fulfilment of vows by a great number of Nazirites. No day went by that an offering was not made at his expense. Like any ordinary Jew, the king took his first-fruits to the Temple. When his daughter Drusilla was betrothed to a son of the king of Commagene, he exacted of him a promise to submit to the rite of initiation; and when subsequently that was refused, the marriage was broken off. The Pharisees were highly pleased with the conduct of their king, and the people showed him their affection. In the year 41, during the Feast of Tabernacles, in accordance with custom, he read before the assembled worshipers in the Temple the Book of Deuteronomy. As he came to the passage: 'Thou mayest not put a foreigner as king over thee, who is not thy brother,' he wept; but the people cried out: 'Thou art our brother, thou art our brother.'

In line with his deferential attitude to religious scruples was his nationalistic policy. In order to fortify Jerusalem on the weak north side, Agrippa began the construction of the Third Wall, which, if finished, would have made the city impregnable. But the emperor ordered the work stopped. Shortly thereafter Agrippa invited five princes, all vassals of Rome, to a conference at Tiberias. The Syrian governor

Marsus suspected disloyal intentions; he came as an unbidden guest and dispersed the meeting. It was certainly unfortunate that sudden death overtook Agrippa at Caesarea (44). The emperor Claudius was dissuaded from awarding the succession to Agrippa's young son, who bore his father's name. The whole of Palestine was annexed as Roman territory and placed under the rule of procurators, subject to the oversight of the governor of Syria.

For twenty-two years (44–66) these procurators held sway. The best of them had no understanding of Jewish peculiarities, and the worst, by their rapacity and inexorable severity, drove the people to rebellion. The very first, Fadus, made a demand for the custody of the high priest's robes; fortunately Claudius gave ear to the representations of a Jewish deputation, thanks to the intervention of the younger Agrippa. A commotion, started by a would-be prophet Theudas, was cruelly suppressed. This prophet had led the people to the Jordan, which he promised to dry up by his mere word as a proof of his divine mission. Fadus had the assembly surrounded; many were slain and others taken prisoners; the head of the leader was cut off and exhibited at Jerusalem. The successor of Fadus was Tiberius Alexander (until 48), the renegade nephew of Philo; he had the sons of Judah the Galilean (p. 177), Jacob and Simon, crucified. Subsequently he took part in an expedition against the Parthians, became governor of Egypt, and acted as chief adviser of Titus at the siege of Jerusalem.

The disturbances increased under Cumanus (48–52). During the Feast of Passover, a Roman soldier provoked the worshipers in the Temple by an indecent gesture. Cumanus was besought to punish the offender; instead he attempted to minimize the offense. The infuriated mob heaped reproaches upon the procurator, and he ordered the troops to disperse the crowd; in the narrow passages the fleeing Jews were trampled under foot and thousands perished. A second act was brought on by the Jews themselves. An imperial servant was seized on the public road near the city and robbed of all his possessions. In retaliation the procurator had several villages near the scene of the robbery looted. On this occasion, a Roman soldier tore a scroll of the Torah into shreds, at the same time indulging in scurrilous remarks. A mass deputation demanded satisfaction, and Cumanus yielded by putting the offender to death. A third occurrence cost Cumanus his office. Galilean Jews, on their journey to Jerusalem, were slain by Samaritans through whose country they passed. As the procurator, who had been bribed by the Samaritans, would do nothing to punish the malefactors, an armed body of Jews, led by two Zealots, Eleazar and Alexander, marched into Samaria, slew old men, women, and children, and devastated the villages. Cumanus appeared with several regiments and fell upon the Jews who had taken the law into their own hands. Both Samaritans and Jews complained to Quadratus, the governor of Syria, who had a number of Jews crucified or beheaded, at the same time ordering Jewish and Samaritan notables as well as Cumanus to proceed to Rome and there answer for their conduct. Thanks to the intervention of young Agrippa, the Jews were vindicated: the Samaritan representatives were executed and Cumanus was sent into banishment.

Agrippa was in high favor with the emperor. Two years before (50) Claudius had bestowed upon him the vacant kingdom of his uncle Herod in Chalcis (in the Lebanon); but before he had left Rome, the small territory was exchanged for the larger northeastern districts, principally constituting the dominion once held by Philip (p. 177). At the same time Agrippa II., as we must now call him, was charged with the oversight of the Temple and with the appointment of the high priests. At the instance of the high priest Jonathan, who was among the notables sent to Rome, Claudius named as procurator of Palestine one of his favorites, Felix, brother of the all-powerful Pallas. Felix (52–60), like his brother a freedman, betrayed his slave origin by his cruelty and intemperate wantonness. He was thrice married. His second wife was the Jewish princess Drusilla, daughter of Agrippa I. and sister of Agrippa II. She was a very young girl, married to Aziz king of Emesa; but she left her husband and became the wife of the Roman, in violation of Jewish law. As brother of the rich Pallas, he considered himself free to perpetrate any crime with impunity. As a consequence the party of the Zealots won more and more adherents. They were animated by a deep hatred of Rome and of the wealthy Jews who were friendly to Roman rule, absentee landlords by whom the lowly Galilean peasant was exploited. Accordingly they would attack their political opponents and plunder their possessions. Felix had a great number of these 'robbers' seized and crucified; their chief, Eleazar, fell into his hands by treachery and was sent off to Rome.

These harsh measures only served to aggravate the evil. Into the place of the 'robbers' stepped the patriotic faction of the assassins, who, armed with poniards, mixed among the crowds and stealthily struck down the sympathizers with Rome. Among their victims was the high priest Jonathan, who as a timid man of compromise was hated alike by the patriots and by Felix. The crime was indeed perpetrated with the connivance of the procurator, whom the priest often reprimanded for his misconduct, seeing that he was held to account by the people for having lent his influence to the procurator's appointment.

To the political fanatics were joined religious enthusiasts. Felix made short shrift of both groups, with the result that the small faction grew into a large party, traversing the country in small bands and instituting a reign of terror. They would loot the mansions of the rich, murder the occupants, and set whole villages on fire. As if to add to the demoralization, the high priests were unworthy men, who set members of their own family in lucrative positions at the Temple and whose servants clubbed the people. All the revenue went to the highly stationed priests, and those of the lower ranks were robbed of their share to the point of starvation.

Felix was recalled by the emperor Nero (54–68), who also graciously added to the possessions of Agrippa II. important districts of Galilee and Perea, especially the cities Tiberias and Taricheae, both centers of industry and commerce. The

new procurator Festus (60–62), though a just man, was
powerless to remedy the evils promoted by his predecessor.
A brawl between the Syrian and Jewish inhabitants of
Caesarea, which had begun before the recall of Felix, led to
a decision by the emperor denying to the Jews the rights of
citizenship in the city founded by Herod.

Festus died when scarcely two years in his office. Before
the arrival of his successor, Jerusalem was in a state of complete anarchy. The high priest Hanan improved the opportunity by instituting judicial procedure against his enemies
and having them stoned to death. He was speedily removed
from office by Agrippa. The new procurator Albinus (62–64)
left no manner of wickedness untried. Above all he was
rapacious, plundering public and private treasure, taking
money from whatever source, from the friends of Rome and
from the patriots as well. Things went from bad to worse. In
Jerusalem it was the war of all against all. The 'assassins'
plied their trade, and if one of their men was seized, they
secured his release by laying their hands on one of their
opponents and arranging for an exchange. The high priest
Jeshua son of Dannai refused to surrender the office to his
successor Jeshua son of Gamaliel, and there ensued actual
fighting in the streets.

The last procurator Florus (64–66) was the worst. Compared with him, Albinus was looked upon as just and beneficent. Florus boasted openly of his misdeeds. He plundered
whole cities, and many communities were totally ruined.
When Florus dared to appropriate seventeen talents from
the Temple treasury, the people's patience was at an end.
A riot broke out, and baskets were passed around, that the
charitable might drop in coins for poor Florus who was
so much in need of funds. In revenge for this insult, the
procurator turned loose upon the city a detachment of soldiers. Despite the pleadings of the high priest and notables,
a part of the city was given over to looting. A number of
citizens, some among them of the rank of Roman knights,
were scourged and then nailed to the cross. Even Berenice,
the sister of Agrippa, who happened to be in Jerusalem,

was powerless to check the fury of the procurator and his soldiers. Florus demanded that the people should show their penitence by according a solemn reception to two cohorts due from Caesarea. After much persuasion by the high priest, the citizens agreed to this humiliating proposal. But when the soldiers forbore to return the friendly greetings of the Jews, the people gave vent to their hatred of Florus. The soldiers set upon them and drove them into the city. Here a battle was fought in the streets, and the Jews succeeded in obtaining possession of the Temple hill and cutting the connection with the citadel Antonia (66).

Agrippa was then in Alexandria. He set out in all haste for Jerusalem and from his palace addressed an assembly of the people, bidding them earnestly to abandon their futile and unwise opposition. The people declared themselves ready to resume their obedience to the emperor, but refused to have anything to do with Florus. In the meantime the insurgents took over the fortress of Masada. It was now decreed to suspend the customary sacrifices for the emperor. That was tantamount to a declaration of war. The party of peace, consisting of all those who had not lost their heads, the high priestly families, the representative Pharisees, and members of the Herodian house, invited Agrippa to come to their rescue. With the aid of three thousand cavalry sent by Agrippa, they took possession of the upper city, while the insurgents occupied the Temple mount and the lower city. The two sides fought bitterly, but the war element forced the troops of Agrippa to vacate the upper city, whereupon the insurgents set fire to the palaces of the high priest, of Agrippa, and of Berenice.

A few days later (in the month of Ab) the citadel Antonia fell likewise into their hands. The troops of Agrippa were permitted to leave the city, while the Roman cohort sought refuge in the strong towers of the Herodian palace. The remainder of this structure was burned down. The former high priest Hananiah was taken out of his hiding-place and murdered. The Roman cohort, unable to hold out any longer, agreed to lay down their arms; but no sooner had they walked out than they were set upon by the insurgents and killed to the last man (in the month of Elul). Thus Jerusalem was completely in the hands of the war party.

At last Gallus, the governor of Syria, moved into Judea with the twelfth legion, two thousand picked men from other legions, six cohorts, four wings of cavalry, and numerous auxiliaries (among them the troops of Agrippa). The Roman army encamped at Gibeon, and then after repelling a sortie of the insurgents pitched still closer to Jerusalem on Mount Scopus. The northern suburb Bezetha was occupied without resistance and burned down (month of Tishri). However, Gallus realized that with the forces at his disposal he could not possibly hope to reduce the strongly fortified and bravely defended city. Accordingly he gave orders to retreat. In a gorge near Beth-horon the Roman army was surrounded by the Jews; so fierce was the attack that the enemy's retreat was turned into a wild flight. The best part of the Roman force extricated itself only after leaving behind a good portion of the baggage, which served the Jews in good stead. With great jubilation the victors entered Jerusalem (month of Marheshvan).

The effect of the victory was that the peace party ceased to exist. The incorrigible friends of Rome left the city. Every one else was won over by force or by suasion. It is significant that in the first stage of the war the men in power were of the higher classes. Joseph son of Gorion and the former high priest Hanan took over the defense of the capital; Jeshua son of Sappha and Eleazar son of Hananiah were sent to Idumea; lastly, the command of Galilee was conferred upon Joseph son of Mattathiah (the historian Josephus).

Josephus came of a priestly family. He received a thorough education and at the age of nineteen allied himself to the Pharisaic party. He had been in Rome and there had convinced himself of the power of the empire. He was twenty-seven years old when he accepted the important post of commander of Galilee, where it was expected that the Romans would strike first. He forthwith organized a provincial government, collected an army which he proceeded

to train, and took measures to put into a more or less satisfactory state of defense the most important cities of his
district. The extreme patriots, however, were not satisfied
with the tame manner in which Josephus conducted his
preparations; they had grounds to suspect that the aristo-
crat, who had formerly belonged to the peace party, had not
his heart in the undertaking. The soul of the opposition was
Johanan of Gish-halab, a resolute character, committed to
the war cost what it might. It happened that a number of
youths fell upon a steward of king Agrippa's and robbed
him of all he carried, gold, silver, and costly garments.
Josephus took charge of the spoil and was preparing to send
it back to the king. At Taricheae, where Josephus was at the
moment, the angered people behaved menacingly, and he
escaped their fury only by resorting to a stratagem. Some
time later he saved himself from death, at the hands of
assassins sent by Johanan, by flight to Tiberias. At length
Johanan preferred charges against Josephus at Jerusalem. It
was decided to recall the untrustworthy Galilean commander, and four men with twenty-five hundred soldiers
were dispatched to carry out his deposition. But Josephus
manoeuvered to have the decree revoked and when the
ambassadors refused to return he seized their persons and
sent them home by force.

The emperor Nero was determined to quell the Palestinian
rebellion at all hazards, and he gave the chief command to
Vespasian, who had served with distinction in Germany and
Britain. In the winter of 67 Vespasian tarried in Antioch
and made steady preparations for the campaign, while his
son Titus was dispatched to Alexandria to bring up a legion.
In the spring of the year, Vespasian advanced to Ptolemais.
There he received the submission of Sepphoris, the strongest
point in the heart of Galilee, where the peace party outnumbered the patriots. Soon Titus arrived, and Vespasian
had at his disposal three complete legions, twenty-three
cohorts, six wings of cavalry, beside the auxiliary troops of
king Agrippa and other friendly monarchs, all told some
sixty thousand men.

The Jewish troops under Josephus lost heart. The greater number fled in panic; Josephus, with the remnant of his army, retreated in haste to Tiberias. Thus all the flat regions of Galilee lay open to the Romans; only the fortresses were in the hands of the insurgents. Josephus took over in person the defense of the strongly fortified Jodephath, situated on a precipitous hill hidden from view by the surrounding mountains. For over two months the small Jewish garrison, with courage born of desperation, set at naught the superior skill and experience of the besiegers. Once, during a sortie, Vespasian was wounded. At length a deserter brought the knowledge that the exhausted guards were not able to keep awake of a morning. So early one morning Titus with a small body of soldiers stealthily scaled the wall, struck down the sleeping sentinels, and penetrated into the city. The legions followed, and when the garrison became aware of their presence it was no longer possible to push them back. Men and women were ruthlessly killed or carried away into slavery; the city and the fortifications were razed to the ground (month of Tammuz).

Josephus, with forty companions, had hidden himself in a cistern which led to a cave. His associates prevented their commander from surrendering; they must all die together, each by the hand of his fellow, and the last by his own hands. By some deception Josephus was the last survivor; but instead of laying hands on himself, he gave himself up to the Romans. When led before Vespasian, he predicted the general's future elevation to the imperial dignity. Nevertheless, Josephus was put in chains; but he was treated with consideration. Vespasian celebrated the capture of the important fortress at Agrippa's capital for twenty days, during which time the weary army was sent back to the coast for a rest. Titus led the legions from the coast to Tiberias, which voluntarily opened its gates. By a bold stroke, Taricheae likewise fell into the hands of the Romans (month of Elul).

In Galilee only Gish-halab and Mount Tabor were held by the insurgents; similarly, the strongly fortified Gamala in Golan. After repeated assaults and heavy reverses due to the stubborn resistance of the Jews, the city was taken in the month of Tishri; at the same time Tabor was captured. Gish-halab opened its gates to Titus, after Johanan and his zealot body had escaped in the dead of night towards Jerusalem. Thus, by the end of the year 67, the whole of the north of Palestine had been brought under subjection by the Romans.

CHAPTER XXXII

THE NATIONAL DISASTER

(68-73)

THE patriots, quite rightly, ascribed the ill-success in Galilee to the irresolution and apathy of the command. The party of the Zealots, under the leadership of Johanan of Gish-halab, soon obtained the upper hand in Jerusalem. All those suspected of leanings towards peace with Rome were imprisoned and slain. As the high priests had up to that time been members of the aristocracy, it was decided to choose for that position, by the casting of lots, priests from among the lower ranks, who were to serve each for one year only. The first priest thus elevated was a stone-cutter by the name of Phinehas; his brother priests supplied him with the means of maintaining his station. The men of order met the violence of the Zealots by exhorting the people to curb the rampant terrorism. Such were Joseph son of Gorion, the former high priests Hanan and Jeshua son of Gamaliel, and especially Simon son of Gamaliel, a descendant of Hillel, the foremost leader of the Pharisees. The brawls of the street penetrated into the peaceful halls of the school; the force of calm argument was replaced by the clang of arms, and strict measures were passed accentuating the separation between Jews and non-Jews.

The Zealots were still in the minority and retreated to the inner Temple court. So they summoned the martial Idumeans, who succeeded in entering the city at night during a heavy downpour of rain. They forthwith began murdering and looting. The two former high priests were among the victims. The Zealots finished what the Idumeans had begun. Johanan of Gish-halab was at last master in the city. The Nazarenes, that is, those who accepted Jesus of Nazareth as the Messiah, indifferent to the national cause, sought safety in flight from Jerusalem; the small community settled in Pella beyond the Jordan.

Vespasian decided to let the Jews in the capital wear themselves out by internecine conflicts. Meanwhile he subdued towards the end of the winter of 68 practically the whole of Transjordania; in the spring he captured the Judean Lowlands and Idumea; by the beginning of the summer he was able to occupy Jericho. While preparing plans for the siege of the capital, he received in Caesarea the news of the death of Nero (June 9, 68). It was advisable to await developments at home. The murder of the emperor Galba (January 15, 69) acted as a further cause of delay in warlike activity against the Jews.

Johanan, the dictator in Jerusalem, was not idle. He pushed forward the strengthening of the city's fortifications and assembled provisions of food and water. He also entered into correspondence with the Jews of Babylonia, hoping that they would use their influence to set the Parthian rulers against Rome. The methods of Johanan were still considered too moderate by the group of superpatriots who rallied around Simon Bar Giora (son of a proselyte). This Simon took Hebron by surprise and carried away rich spoil.

Vespasian cut short his inactivity (June, 69) in order to reduce Judea still more completely. Hebron, which resisted, was stormed and sacked. With the exception of Jerusalem and the fortresses of Herodium, Machaerus, and Masada, all Palestine was in the hands of the Romans. Simon, prevented from pursuing his raids into Idumea, had meanwhile been admitted into Jerusalem through the treachery of the aristocrats, who hoped thus to rid themselves of Johanan. The result was that instead of one dictator there were two, who fought against each other but were at one in terrorizing the propertied classes. It was an upheaval from below, a reign of the commune, inaugurated by liberating all slaves.

Before the end of July, 69, Vespasian had been proclaimed emperor by the legions stationed in the Orient. He hastened to Rome by way of Alexandria, where the news reached him that Vitellius, elevated to the imperial station by the army of the Rhine, had been murdered (December 20, 69). Vespasian tarried in Alexandria until the beginning of next year's summer. The conduct of the war against the Jews was left to his son Titus.

In Jerusalem a third dictator, Eleazar son of Simon, was contending for power. He was in possession of the inner Temple court, while Johanan held the remainder of the Temple mount and Simon the upper city as well as a large part of the lower. They fought with each other incessantly, each burning up the supply of provisions accumulated by the other. Thus they robbed the city of the very power of resistance and cut into their own flesh.

A few days before Passover of the year 70, Titus with the main part of his army reached the immediate vicinity of Jerusalem. The general, with six hundred cavalry, had gone on ahead to reconnoiter; when he advanced too close to the city, the Jews made a sortie, and Titus was in extreme peril from which he extricated himself by sheer personal bravery. While the Romans were busy fortifying their camp on the Mount of Olives, the Jews threw themselves upon them with such vehemence that, had it not been for the interposition of Titus, they would have been completely routed. Within the city the bloody feuds went on unabated, and Eleazar was practically eliminated.

Only when the enemy's battering rams began to operate against Agrippa's unfinished Third Wall (p. 189), did Johanan and Simon bury the hatchet. On one of their sorties they fought so desperately that the battering machines came near being destroyed. After persistent labor for fifteen days, a breach was made in the wall. Five days later, the Second Wall yielded to the enemy's battering. Titus, on entering with a picked force, was at first repulsed by the Jews, but soon regained his position, which he now held definitively.

A fortnight or so later, four great embankments, laboriously constructed, menaced the upper city and Antonia. All of these were destroyed by the Jews, those directed against Antonia by undermining. In three days the Romans had the whole city surrounded with a stone wall so as to shut it in from all sides. Provisions had begun to be scarce, and now famine was killing off the people. Johanan turned over for common use the stores of consecrated oil and wine. His soldiers fought now with lessened energy, and when they sallied forth in July they were powerless to destroy the new embankments threatening Antonia. When the wall, weakened by the constant battering, collapsed in one spot, the Romans found an inner wall which had been hastily erected by Johanan. A Syrian soldier and several of his companions who tried to scale the walls were killed by the defenders. But soon the attempt was renewed at night; the outposts were slain, and Titus followed quickly and drove the Jews to the Temple square. The Romans were repulsed, but they held Antonia, and soon the citadel was razed to the ground.

Despite war and famine, the daily morning and evening sacrifice had up to this moment been regularly offered. On the seventeenth of Tammuz, it had to be discontinued, not so much on account of the famine as for want of men to perform the sacred office. Titus proceeeded to a regular assault upon the strongly fortified Temple area. While the erection of embankments was in progress, a number of Roman soldiers essayed to scale the outer wall; they had been misled by a feint on the part of the Jews stationed above the western colonnade. As soon as the Romans had risen to the top, the Jews set fire to the inflammable material below and the Romans perished in the flames.

In Ab (August) the embankments were completed, and the battering began. But the stout walls proved too strong. Titus ordered the gates to be set on fire so as to effect an entrance to the outer Temple area. On the ninth of Ab the gates were consumed by fire. The conflagration spread within. Titus hastened to inspect the Temple. But soon the sacred edifice was the prey of the flames which the Romans kept alive. Furiously, ruthlessly, they killed old men and children, priests and laymen, until the place resembled a shambles.

Johanan and his intrepid patriots had escaped to the upper city. Neither he nor Simon would surrender. So Titus had the quarter occupied by his soldiers burned down: the council house, the hall of archives, the whole of the lower city down to the Pool of Siloam. In the month of Elul the upper city was stormed. The Roman soldiers again applied the torch, looting and killing as they went along. Such as had not died by famine or by the sword were executed or sent into the mines; others were destined to meet their death in gladiatorial combats. The most handsome and vigorous men were picked out for the triumphal procession. Among those who had sought escape in subterranean passage-ways and were apprehended was Johanan; he was thrown into prison for life. Simon, who was likewise seized, was reserved to die at the triumph. The city was razed to the ground; only the three towers of the Herodian palace and a part of the wall were left standing, as a monument of the erstwhile strength of the city and to afford protection for the Roman garrison now installed amid the ruins.

After a turn of gay festivities, Titus embarked from Alexandria for Rome with seven hundred Jewish captives of extraordinary beauty. There, together with his father and brother (Domitian), he led the triumphal procession, followed by the vanquished Jewish leader Simon, who then was executed in the prison next to the Forum. Among the spoil carried in triumph were the two precious golden pieces of the Temple furniture: the table of showbread and the seven-armed candlestick. The arch of triumph, upon which these and other sacred symbols were represented, was erected after the death of Titus and stands to this day.

The Jews were still in possession of the fortresses Herodium, Machaerus, and Masada. The first was reduced by Bassus, the governor of Syria, without much difficulty. Of somewhat longer duration was the siege of Machaerus. Masada was held by the ultra-patriots under Eleazar, a descendant of Judah the Galilean. The task of reducing this formidable stronghold fell to Silva, the new governor of Syria. When at length a breach was effected in the wall, there was found within a bulwark of timber and earth erected by the besieged. The Romans set fire to this obstacle. When they entered, they were confronted by the stillness of death: Eleazar and his noble band had killed off their dear ones and then laid hands on each other (April, 73). There was a sequel of Jewish uprisings in Alexandria and the northern coast of Africa; as a consequence the Temple of Onias in Leontopolis was closed.

Thus was ended the seven years' war against the power and brutality of Rome. Once more the daughter of Zion sat and wept for the sanctuary that lay in ashes, for her sons that had fallen by the sword, and for her daughters carried away into slavery and given over to dishonor. The nation had been vanquished, the Land of Israel was a province of the mighty empire; yet there remained one thing that the fury of legions was powerless to destroy, the invincible Torah of the Jew.

CHAPTER XXXIII

SPIRITUAL RECONSTRUCTION.
SPASMS UNDER TRAJAN AND HADRIAN

(70-135)

THOUGH many were carried away into slavery, there was no thought on the part of the conqueror, had it at all been possible, to uproot the Jewish people from their ancient soil. The land, at least in part, was reserved by the emperor as his personal domain; that meant that the occupants were forced to take it on lease. The fitful political independence under Herod I. and Agrippa I. had been a gift from Rome, bestowed upon persons rather than upon the people; once more the country was administered from Caesarea by Roman governors, this time directly answerable to the emperor. It was painful in the extreme that the poll-tax formerly paid to the Temple was now collected for the benefit of the Capitoline Jupiter. The destruction of the Temple and the abrupt ending of the Sanhedrin left a void which was felt most bitterly; yet with them passed away also the aristocratic dominion of the priestly families and the preponderance of Sadduceeism in national affairs. The Zealots had brought on the war and the extreme Pietists gave themselves up to excessive mourning. All parties, save one, stood now discredited. The Pharisees, the men of the Center, alone had a programme ready-made for a constructive policy of spiritual recuperation, and to that task they resolutely applied themselves.

Their leader was Johanan son of Zaccai, a pupil of Hillel. He had left Jerusalem before the final catastrophe. The story is told that he simulated death and had himself carried out in a coffin. He is said to have asked of the Roman general the gift of Jabneh, where he might assemble the scholars of the nation. The foreign power was at one with Herod in the idea that safety lay in the people's mental concentration upon scholastic pursuits. At Jabneh the appalling news reached Johanan that the Sanctuary lay in ashes. The aged teacher rent his garments, but consoled the weeping disciples with the thought that the Jews possessed a substitute for the sacrificial cult in acts of benevolence, as it is written, 'For I desire mercy and not sacrifice' (Hosea 6, 6). Not that the memory of the past glory was allowed to fade away, or the hope of restoration to be dimmed. But the exigencies of the moment made imperative an interim adjustment. Jabneh was invested with the prerogatives formerly belonging to Jerusalem. A supreme court was organized for the whole range of religious law, which included the civil jurisprudence and, as far as could be managed without conflict with the Roman authorities, the criminal as well. To this court the old name of Sanhedrin was attached. Johanan, being himself a duly ordained judge competent to impose fines, took pains to have the chain of succession continued without break by ordaining his disciples, so that they might exercise penal jurisdiction and transmit their authority, in turn, by the same process of ordination.

Johanan retired as president of the Sanhedrin in favor of Gamaliel II., son of Simon and grandson of Gamaliel I. (p. 199), of the family of Hillel. His father appears to have died during the war. At the time of the reorganization in Jabneh the son was too young to be elevated to so great a station. There were other scholars worthier of the dignity, but Gamaliel possessed the prestige of descent from Hillel. His accession does not seem to have met with obstacles on the part of Rome's representative in Caesarea. Gamaliel recognized the importance of ending the strife of the schools (the followers of Shammai and those of Hillel) and thus establishing an authority unquestioned, 'not for his own honor, nor for the honor of his house, but solely for the honor of God, that divisions should not multiply in Israel.' Thus a beginning was made toward presenting a unified version of the traditional law, but in such a manner that opinions on which the schools were divided were cited in the name of their proponents.

Gamaliel's insistence on authority led him into sharp encounters with his colleagues. His brother-in-law, Eliezer son
of Hyrcanus, was one who, in the opinion of his teacher
Johanan, outweighed all his colleagues in the knowledge of
tradition and was likened to 'a plastered cistern, which
loseth not a drop'; nevertheless Gamaliel overruled him. At
another time Gamaliel had set the calendar in accordance
with his prerogative as head of the Sanhedrin; accordingly,
he compelled Joshua son of Hananiah (likewise a disciple of
Johanan) to appear before him, with staff and wallet, on
what was the Day of Atonement according to that scholar's
calculation. Eliezer stubbornly defied the majority of the
scholars and was put under the ban; but Joshua was persuaded by his friends to obey. This submission pleased
Gamaliel. He kissed the scholar on his head and addressed
him as his master in wisdom and his pupil by virtue of
compliance, congratulating the generation in which the great
defer to their inferiors.

On two further occasions Gamaliel humiliated Joshua.
Consequently the scholars met and deposed Gamaliel, who
was replaced by Eleazar son of Azariah. This session (about
the year 90) was a memorable one. Of the measures then
passed the most important was the one delimiting and defin-
ing Scripture. Certain writings, like the Wisdom of Ben Sira,
which were near-Scriptural, were pronounced as outside
Holy Writ, inspiration, which had ceased in the Persian
period, being conceived as the mark of Scripture. Gamaliel
sought out Joshua, whose trade was that of a needle-maker,
and found him in his house blackened with soot. 'I see that
thou usest charcoal,' said Gamaliel. 'Woe to the generation,'
answered Joshua, 'whose leader thou art, seeing thou know-
est not the privations of scholars, nor how they maintain
themselves.' A reconciliation followed, and Gamaliel was
reinstated. In 95 he headed a delegation to emperor Domitian
(81–96) to remonstrate against an edict forbidding Jewish
proselytizing, said to be in preparation following the conversion of the emperor's cousin, Flavius Clemens.

Gamaliel organized divine worship and gave it a stated

form. The principal daily prayer, consisting of seventeen benedictions, was recast, and an additional section, directed against apostates and heretics of the type of the Nazarenes, was inserted. The groundwork of this prayer antedated the destruction of the Temple and was modeled in part after the liturgy in the sacred edifice. It began with an invocation of the God of the Fathers, the Mighty (whose power is revealed in the giving of rain and dew and in the quickening of the dead) and Holy, and concluded with petitions for the acceptance of the Temple worship and of the nation's thanksgiving and for the blessing of peace. The introduction and conclusion are still recited, in the ritual of the synagogue, every day in the year, including the sabbath and festivals. They constitute the oldest framework. The prayer for peace coincided with the priestly blessing in the Temple ('The Lord bless thee, and keep thee; the Lord make His face to shine upon thee, and be gracious unto thee; the Lord lift up His countenance upon thee, and give thee peace,' Numbers 6, 24–26). Between the first and last invocations, it was the wont in the Temple liturgy to insert prayers for the forgiveness of sins through understanding and repentance, for the healing of the sick, for the blessing of the year, for national redemption and the gathering of the dispersed, for the constituted authorities (judges, elders, teachers), for the Holy City. In Gamaliel's revision reference was had to the altered conditions and the prayers were so rephrased that God was petitioned to restore the Temple worship and the ancient polity, to rebuild Jerusalem, and to renew the Davidic kingdom through the Messiah. The Jews were then vexed by the rise of heretics, specifically the Nazarene sect, and the malediction pronounced upon them was grounded in the conditions of the time. On the other hand, the proselytes of righteousness were deemed worthy of affection by the side of the teachers and the pious.

This Prayer *par excellence* (Tephillah, also called Shemoneh-esreh, 'The Eighteen Benedictions') was preceded by the Confession of Faith (the Shema': 'Hear O Israel: the Lord our God, the Lord is One'), which itself was enclosed in a framework of benedictions, for the blessing of daylight (or for the repose of the night), for the election of Israel, and for the past and future redemption. On sabbaths and holy days sections of the Torah and the Prophets were read, the reading being accompanied by translation into the Aramaic vernacular and expositions which took on the nature of sermons. On Mondays and Thursdays, when the villagers came to the markets in the cities, shorter sections of the Torah were read. The Torah scrolls were kept in a chest (the Ark) and clothed in linen wrappers; other chests held the remaining books of the Scriptures. Scripture was also called Lection (Mikra), and those books alone counted as such which might be read publicly in the synagogue. A special desk was provided for these Scripture readings. Any one of the congregation, who possessed a voice, might pass before the Ark and lead in the service. Care was taken that the reader was a man of dignified bearing and suitably garbed. On fast days, especially saintly men were invited to read the service so as to move the worshipers to contrition. The supervision of the service was in the hands of the 'head' of the synagogue. Directly responsible to him was the sexton (hazzan), whose function it was to take the scroll out of the Ark and to replace it. The finances were looked after by a board of managers.

In the villages no regular public daily services were held for want of the required number of men. In the towns ten men of leisure, mostly of the student class, were paid to attend synagogue. In the towns, likewise, provision was made for stated court sessions. So soon as the population included a hundred and twenty male adults, a court of twenty-three members was constituted. Beside one or more synagogues, each community maintained public baths (with basins for ritual immersion) and cisterns. According to the length of residence, individuals were gradually called upon to contribute to the upkeep of the charitable and other communal institutions. The fullest burden rested upon those who had been residents for over a year or owned a dwelling. These alone had a voice in electing the administrative council, which usually consisted of seven men, called 'managers' (parnasim) or 'best men of the town' (tobe ha-'ir). None but men of pure blood might serve on the council. It was an honor sometimes held for life; frequently the son followed the father in the office. The community expected of its managers complete disinterestedness and a dignified bearing; they were installed by the college of judges or by a scholar of repute. The council collected and spent moneys for current needs; bought and disposed of communal property; supervised trade and commerce; fixed measures and weights and the scale of wages; regulated the various charities and maintained courts and schools; saw to safety, sanitation, and order; issued police regulations and imposed fines for disobedience.

The funds for administrative as well as for charitable purposes were collected as the need presented itself and immediately disbursed. Friday was the regular day for weekly grants of aid to the needy (kuppah); the hungry were fed at soup-kitchens (tamhui) any day of the week. It made no difference whether the beneficiaries were residents or outsiders, Jews or non-Jews. Special collections were made on Purim and the funds were used for dowering indigent brides or for ransoming captives. In the synagogues, offerings were made for charity (zedakah). Collections and disbursements were in the hand of commissions, chiefly from among the members of the council, men in whom absolute trust could be reposed and of whom no accounting was asked. Such was the esteem of the charity collector (gabbai) that a priest might take to wife a daughter of his without scrutinizing the pedigree.

Every synagogue had a Bible school and a high school for the study of the traditional lore. The community looked to the education of poor or fatherless children. Rich parents engaged tutors at their homes. Teachers might set up private schools, since tuition was paid by the parents. Strictly speaking, the Torah must not be taught for reward; such pay as the teacher received was accounted as compensation for the time which he might employ otherwise or for the care he took of the children. If the teacher fell short in his earnings, the deficit was made good from public funds. It was required of a teacher that he should be a married man, as mothers were in the habit of taking their children to school. Girls were taught as well as boys, but education was compulsory only for the boys from their sixth or seventh year on. Teachers were held in high respect. At the top of the educational system stood the Hall of Study (beth ha-midrash), where the higher scholars were prepared.

The peaceful reconstruction was rudely disturbed towards the end of Trajan's reign (98–117). With the annexation of Nabatean Arabia and the lands about the sources of the Jordan previously held by Agrippa II., the trade routes between East and West were all in the hands of Rome, except for Parthian aggression in Armenia. In 114 the emperor set out for the East, reorganized the eastern fighting forces, subdued Armenia and Mesopotamia and turned them into Roman provinces (115). The next year he crossed the Tigris and annexed Adiabene, whose royal house had embraced Judaism during the reign of Claudius and had fought on the side of the Jews during the Great War. Ctesiphon was likewise taken, and the emperor advanced to the Persian Gulf, contemplating the conquest of India after the manner of Alexander the Great. With an eye to the far-eastern commotion and in direct collusion with the Armenians and Parthians, the Jews of Egypt, Cyrene, and Cyprus rose up against Rome and the Greeks. The spirit of zealotism was not quite dead; driven from Palestine, it fanned the flame of insurrection in the Dispersion.

The Jews fought with the supreme straining of all their powers and by the same ruthless methods their opponents had employed against them. Thousands upon thousands of their enemies were put to death. For a time the Jews in Alexandria had the upper hand, but the Greeks soon succeeded in turning them out with much bloodshed. The insurrection was quelled by Trajan's general Turbo; Cyprus was so completely cleared that not a Jew was afterwards permitted to set foot on the island. But in the rear of the emperor the Jews of Mesopotamia had risen. Against them Trajan dispatched Lusius Quietus, who with barbaric cruelty restored order. How far Palestine itself participated in this Second War (for a war it was) against Rome is uncertain. So much we know that Quietus was sent to Palestine as governor and that he was recalled by Hadrian and subsequently executed. The appalling depression of the spirit among Palestinian Jewry may be gauged from the enactment that brides should show their mourning by forbearing to adorn themselves with wreaths. It was also ordained that the study of the Greek language should be forbidden; an exception was made for the house of Gamaliel because of the necessary dealings with the Roman governors. Greek was the language of diplomatic intercourse and mercantile transactions in the East; spoken by the Jews of the Dispersion, it had begun to invade the Jewish circles of Palestine. The old Greek translation of the Scriptures prepared in Alexandria had by this time been taken over by the Greek converts to Nazarenism, Christianity, as it was now called. A new translation, more exact and more in accordance with the latest development of interpretation, was made on Palestinian soil, under the eye of such masters as Eliezer and Joshua, by Aquila of Pontus, a convert from paganism.

While the Jewish uprising failed, as might have been expected, to shake Rome, it contributed to the collapse of Trajan's eastern campaign. The emperor met with defeat at the hands of the Arabs of the desert (117) and died shortly thereafter in Cilicia. His successor Hadrian (117–138) abandoned the conquests beyond the Euphrates and reverted to the policy of Augustus to consolidate the empire within its limits. The Jews, it would appear, had received, possibly from Trajan, a vague promise that they would be permitted to rebuild the Temple. But this was made nugatory by the opposition of the Samaritans and the new emperor's aversion to foreign cults. Whatever hope the Jews may have cherished was completely shattered by the news that Hadrian was projecting the conversion of Jerusalem into a heathen city. The people were sorely embittered. The aged Joshua sought to allay them by telling the well-known fable of the Lion and the Crane: the Jews might consider themselves fortunate that they emerged with their bare lives out of the jaws of Rome. All peaceful reasoning was to no purpose, when a short time afterwards Hadrian revived an old law forbidding mutilations of the body and incidentally circumcision. Though the decree was not aimed at the Jews, for them it was tantamount to an attack on the Jewish religion which must be met by resistance.

Thus the Third War against Rome was launched. The soul of the uprising was the scholar Akiba son of Joseph. In his youth he had been an illiterate shepherd; he won the love of his rich master's daughter and at her bidding had himself educated. He was trained in the schools of Eliezer and Joshua and became noted for deep erudition and a keen intellect. While his colleague Ishmael, of high priestly descent, held to the plain meaning of Scripture, Akiba built mountains of legal norms upon every letter of the Torah, nay upon its jots and tittles. Neither brooked any compromise with the heretics who by the process of allegorical (so-called spiritual) interpretation threw off all allegiance to the Torah. Ishmael excelled as a preacher and so also did Akiba; nevertheless when Akiba ventured upon sermonizing, his colleagues occasionally bade him return to his own domain of religious jurisprudence. Akiba was the first to arrange the accumulated traditional lore according to subject-matter; it was an advanced step in the codification of the great body of Jewish law handed down by word of mouth, to which was given the name of Mishnah (Rehearsal). He was an exclusivist as regards Israel's peculiar relation to God ('My Beloved is mine, and I am His') for whose sake the Jews are willing to undergo martyrdom and whom they love unto death. The Song of Songs was for Akiba the holiest book in the third division of Scripture, the song of union between God and Israel. Akiba was an ardent patriot. He traveled far and wide to strengthen Jewish national solidarity. When, in the person of Simon of Cozeba, a leader presented himself ready to take up the struggle with Rome, Akiba acclaimed him as the Messiah, though the more timid scholars protested. Simon was for Akiba the Star that had stepped forth out of Jacob (Numbers 24, 17); the heroic chief was renamed Son of the Star (Bar Kokeba), and on the coins struck by him a figure of the Temple was surmounted by a star.

The insurrection broke out in 132, when the emperor had returned to Rome from his travels in Egypt and Syria. But the organization of the revolt had been going on secretly for some time. It spread now all over Palestine. It was natural that the Nazarenes (Christians) should reject the new Messiah; otherwise the people stood united to take up arms for religious and national freedom. They gathered in fortified places, strongholds, caves, and subterranean passages. Avoiding an open battle, they sallied forth from their hiding-places and attacked their enemies. Jerusalem, which was guarded by one legion, was captured; it seems that an altar was erected, at which Simon's uncle, the priest Eleazar, ministered. The conditions of the restoration under Zerubbabel and the priest Joshua (p. 120) appeared to repeat themselves: by the side of the civil head of the nation stood the chief priest. The regained sovereignty was marked by restamping the coinage, and the legends proudly counted First, Second Year after the Liberation of Jerusalem.

The governor Tineius Rufus was not equal to the situation. At last Hadrian dispatched one of his best generals, Severus, whom he recalled from Britain. It was not possible to meet the rebels in pitched battle; but their small units were hunted down in their places of refuge and, their lines of communication cut off, annihilated. It was a protracted guerilla warfare, which brought very heavy losses to the Roman side likewise. Hadrian was for a time present in person to direct the military operations; but by the spring of 134 he was persuaded that he could leave the conclusion safely to his general. Jerusalem was retaken, and on the ninth of Ab a beginning could be made with the foundation of the new city according to the previous plans. In accordance with Roman custom, after the ruins were cleared, the earth was freshly plowed up in token of the new foundation.

Meanwhile the main body of the Jews with their leader had entrenched themselves behind the strong mountain fastness of Beth-ther, southwest of Jerusalem. It was the last gasp of Jewish freedom. After a long and stubborn defense, the fortress fell in 135. Those that had not succumbed to famine were butchered by the victorious legions. But the victory was not cheaply purchased. So great were the Roman losses that the emperor, in reporting to the Senate, omitted the customary formula, 'I and my army are well.' Half a million Jews are said to have perished. A great number were sold as slaves in the market near the terebinth of Hebron—so many that a Jewish slave fetched no more than a horse. Such as were not sold there were taken to Gaza or Egypt, and many died from famine or shipwreck.

Judea resembled a desert. Fifty fortresses and a thousand villages were in ruins. Upon the site of the Holy City now rose the new foundation, Aelia Capitolina (the emperor's first name was Aelius), with its theaters and temples dedicated to Bacchus, Serapis, and Venus; on the mount where formerly stood the Sanctuary was reared the temple of Jupiter Capitolinus. The southern gate of the city was surmounted by the figure of a boar, the emblem of the tenth legion. No Jew might set foot in the city. Once a year, on the ninth of Ab, Jews streamed thither, begging and bribing the Roman guards to permit them to linger and weep. This lament kept alive through the ages the memory of the departed glory. Equally undying was the hope of future restoration.

CHAPTER XXXIV

THE MAKERS OF THE MISHNAH

(135-175)

THE enemy realized that Jewish resistance derived its strength from the Jewish religion and the Jewish religious organization. Hadrian purposed to bring down that inner citadel as Antiochus Epiphanes had sought to do; in the long run Rome was no more successful than Antioch. As soon as the insurrection had become noticeable, an edict was issued forbidding not only circumcision but also the observance of the sabbath, the teaching of the Torah, and the maintenance of the religious organization through ordination. Ten scholars, in especial, are said to have suffered martyrdom. Ishmael and another scholar were seized and executed, while Akiba was detained in prison at the governor's seat Caesarea. From his prison cell Akiba persisted in directing through his disciples the people's religious life; unflinchingly he met death at the executioner's hands. Though his body was being lacerated with combs of iron, he died with the profession of the Unity upon his lips.

A similar fate overtook Hanina son of Teradion. He was detected teaching the Torah; when asked why he did so in disobedience of the imperial edict, he answered: 'Even as the Lord my God commanded me' (Deuteronomy 4, 5). He was wrapped in the scroll and burned at the stake. The last among the martyred scholars was the saintly Judah son of Baba. He defied the emperor by ordaining the leading disciples of Akiba. Before he was apprehended and cruelly done to death, he persuaded them to seek safety in flight. They escaped to Babylonia, where Hananiah, Joshua's nephew, had established a school near Nehardea. This scholar contemplated assuming the spiritual leadership of the Jewish people. But the time of Babylonia had not come yet; as soon as the Palestinian schools were reorganized they successfully reasserted their supremacy.

216

The scholastic center at Jabneh had been broken up. So long as Hadrian's edicts remained in force, clashes with the Roman authorities were unavoidable. Antoninus Pius (138–161) was placed before the choice of yielding to Jewish susceptibilities or else of exterminating the Jewish people. He chose the former course. The intolerant laws were revoked, and the Jews were permitted to practise the rite of circumcision, but only on persons of their own race. The fugitive disciples of Akiba returned and set themselves to the task of reconstructing the religious life. At the first opportunity they gathered at Usha in Galilee and reëstablished the Sanhedrin; among the most important measures there enacted were those pertaining to the reorganization of the lower schools and the enforcement of discipline, the maintenance of minor children as a matter of legal obligation, the restriction of charitable gifts to a fifth of one's income as a maximum, and the exemption of scholars from the process of excommunication.

Simon son of Gamaliel, who had escaped during the persecution under Hadrian, succeeded his father as head of the Sanhedrin. Though less scholarly than several of his colleagues and otherwise a modest man, he was a stickler for the distinctive honors due to his station, believing that position to be a great influence towards maintaining the unity of Israel. His deputy Nathan, whose father was the Babylonian exilarch, and the third in rank, the counselor (hakam) Meir, conspired to expose Simon's inferior scholarship in public session. Simon, however, learned of this and prepared himself. Nathan, being a peaceful man, effected a reconciliation with his chief, but Meir persisted in his estrangement. Had it not been for the measure carried at Usha, Meir would have been excommunicated. As it was, the two conspirators were disciplined to the extent that they were not mentioned by name in the scholastic discussions but referred to anonymously ('some say,' 'others say').

Simon was tolerant towards the Samaritans, whom he placed on an equal footing with Jews in every respect, lauding their strictness in such religious duties as had been accepted by them, which exceeded that of the Jews. Similarly he insisted on impartial justice to non-Jews and recognized the validity of documents executed in a non-Jewish court and witnessed by non-Jews. He was averse to burdening the people with new regulations which it was beyond their power to observe; every one should follow the customs of his own district. Whenever possible, he made legal exceptions in favor of women; he held that one was obliged to ransom a captive slave as much as a captive freeman. How truly the conditions of the period are mirrored in his remark that his own contemporaries were as grateful as the ancients for deliverances from persecutions, but that the calamities were now so frequent that one could barely recount them! Just as all waters are gathered together in the ocean, so, he was certain, Jerusalem would some day become the place of assembly for the whole world.

The time was rich in great scholars, particularly from the school of Akiba. Meir was easily the first among them. He had also studied with Ishmael; nor had he disdained the instruction of Elisha son of Abuiah, who had lost himself in esoteric speculations and turned heretic. Meir was satisfied that he knew how to throw away the husk, while he absorbed the kernel, and he honored his apostate teacher beyond the grave. In the same manner, in maturer years, he was on intimate terms of friendship with the heathen philosopher Oenomaus of Gadara. Meir held that a non-Jew who is a student of the Torah is on a par with the high priest, just as he taught the unconditional character of Israel's relation to God ('Ye are the sons of the Lord your God—whether ye act or act not as sons'). Meir was a master of the dialectic art: playfully he would advance reasons for pronouncing a thing clean when it was unclean and the reverse, so much so that his colleagues sometimes could not follow him. His legal opinions therefore were not accepted save in the matter of restrictions which partook of the nature of preventive measures. In point of fact, however, his decisions were free from casuistry and unprofitable hair-splitting. On the whole, he adhered to Akiba's system of clear-cut statements, which he

perfected, just as he revised the body of traditional lore
assembled by his master (p. 213). That was the third step in
the codification of the Mishnah. Meir's lectures were so
arranged that the time was evenly divided between matters
of law, sententious sayings, and fables. His sermons on the
eve of the sabbath in the synagogue of Tiberias were listened to with delight. He earned his livelihood through his
penmanship; a Bible copy written by his hand was highly
prized. His wife, Beruriah, the daughter of the martyred
Hanina (p. 216), was herself a scholar, whose legal opinions
were recorded in the schools. Her husband was vexed by
unworthy neighbors; 'Pray,' said the wife, 'for the destruction of sin rather than for the death of the sinner.' Their two
boys died on a sabbath afternoon while the husband was
lecturing in the synagogue. When he came home, she hid
from him the tragedy until he had recited the blessings over
the parting of the sabbath. Then she asked him whether it
was meet to return a deposit called for by the owner. 'Why,
of course,' answered the unsuspecting husband. 'Come then
to the children's sleeping room; they were given to us for
safe-keeping, now God has recalled them.'

Meir's colleague, with whom he differed on so many points
of law, was Judah son of Ilai. He was deferred to as a chief
authority by the other scholars and was well thought of by
the patriarch. Some three thousand sayings of his are on
record. Through his father, who was a pupil of Eliezer (p.
207), he absorbed much of that scholar's lore; he handed
down also the opinions of others of that early circle; but in
the main he rested on the teaching of Akiba, by means of
which he contributed to the expansion of the material transmitted to the next generation. Study, however, he held to be
but the means to good works, and he would interrupt his
scholastic pursuits to pay his respects to the dead or to
gladden a bridal couple at their marriage feast. He was a
man of the golden mean. 'This Torah is likened unto two
roads, one of fire and one of ice; if you walk in the one, you
will be burned, and if in the other, you will be frozen. What
shall one do? Walk in the middle '

Judah's home was at Usha. At Sepphoris resided his colleague Jose son of Halaphtha. Both he and his fellow-student Simon son of Johai sought to penetrate to the underlying reasons of the teachings they had received from their masters. Simon was of a more independent disposition and often rejected the opinions of his predecessors. Nor was his attitude to Rome as conciliatory as that of the other members of that entire group. A derogatory remark was brought to the attention of the Roman authorities and he was sentenced to death. With his son Eleazar he hid himself in a cave and remained there for thirteen years. Those were the times when the empire had begun to be on the defensive. Under Marcus Aurelius (161–180) and the co-emperor Verus (161–169), the Parthian king Vologaeses III. invaded Cappadocia and Syria. It seems that among certain elements of the Jews in Palestine an attempt was made to turn these complications to their advantage. The Parthians, however, were beaten, and Verus punished the Jews by depriving them of their autonomous judiciary and imposing other restrictions. These exceptional laws were rescinded after the death of Verus (169).

A year later, Judah I. was inducted into the patriarchate, left vacant by the death of his father Simon son of Gamaliel some years previously. Patriarch (nasi) was now the accepted title for the head of the Sanhedrin, recognized as such by the imperial government. The dignity of the patriarch was nothing short of that of an actual monarch. Judah was carefully trained in his father's house by private tutors and for short periods attended the schools of Akiba's great pupils, such as Judah at Usha and Simon son of Johai at Tekoa (northwest of Safed). In contradistinction to his father and grandfather he was the greatest scholar of the period. He surrounded himself by colleagues and disciples. 'Much,' he said, 'I learned from my teachers, more from my associates, and most of all from my pupils.' He had a particularly high opinion of his student Hiya, a Babylonian by birth, whom he designated as his 'counselor from a far country' (Isaiah 46, 11). In Judah, it was said, Torah and high station were united as they had not been since the days of Moses. Judah possessed great wealth of which he gave freely to poor scholars. His high standard of conduct merited for him the appellation of the Saint, just as for his learning he was spoken of as the Master (Rabbi) *par excellence.*

Judah enjoyed the good-will of the Antonine emperors, with one of whom (possibly Marcus Aurelius) he is said to have been on intimate terms. With all his humility, which was highly praised, he filled his position with dignity and distinction. The right of ordination he reserved for himself. His strong personality dominated the Sanhedrin, though he was not always able to carry a point in the face of opposition. Thus he was minded to abolish the irksome observance of the sabbatic year which was attended by much hardship, especially in those days so close to the dire persecutions. Phinehas son of Jair, who was reputed for his great saintliness, swayed the majority of the scholars, and Judah was content with introducing some measures of alleviation. Judah favored the Hebrew speech which in all but certain nooks and corners had receded from the mouth of the people in favor of Aramaic. Hebrew was spoken in the patriarch's home, and the young scholars learned the meaning of many an obscure word of the Scriptures by listening to the living speech of the domestics in Judah's household. The seat of the patriarchate was principally at Beth-shearim (northeast of Tabor), but the last seventeen years of his life Judah spent at Sepphoris, which because of its high altitude afforded him relief from his ailments.

Judah's activity covered a half century. He brought to a finish the codification of the Mishnah, the first steps towards which had been taken at Jabneh (p. 206) and then by Akiba (p. 213) and Meir (p. 219). As a matter of fact, the other scholars, whether among the contemporaries of Akiba or his disciples, had each a Mishnah, that is, the sum of traditional lore taught by him. The point about the final redaction was that it constituted a corporate effort, embodying the conclusions of Judah and his associates, some older and some younger than himself. The material culled from the earlier sources was rounded out and rendered more complete. Also the arrangement of the contents was perfected, though to a large extent the order had been well established. The Code, as it has come down, contains additions introduced in the next generation, but on the whole its compass is nearly as Judah left it. The work is arranged in six Orders; each Order is divided into Tractates, and each Tractate into chapters and paragraphs. The Orders are named Seeds (religious laws pertaining to agriculture, preceded by the Tractate 'Blessings' which treats of the daily prayers and the blessings on partaking of food), Seasons (sabbath, festivals, fasts), Women (laws of marriage and divorce and vows), Damages (civil and criminal legislation; in this Order is incorporated the Tractate 'Fathers,' giving the ethical sayings of the teachers from the times of the Great Synagogue on), Holy Things (laws concerning ritual slaughtering, sacrifices and consecrated things, the Temple and Temple worship), and Purities (laws of ceremonial impurity).

The language of the Mishnah is the Hebrew as it had developed naturally in the centuries since Nehemiah. The diction is concise. The aim of the work was clearly to furnish a text-book for the guidance of judges and religious teachers. Whatever had been settled in the past or in Judah's own school, by majority vote or through the preponderating influence of one in authority, was entered as a decision anonymously. The formulation was mainly taken over from Meir's Mishnah; but as a rule Judah put down in the same form an opinion reached by himself, generally with the concurrence of the patriarchal court. Thus the compilation, to a limited extent, assumed the form of a Code. Dissenting opinions were carefully set down, together with the names of their sponsors. The accepted view was placed last; the opposing opinion was recorded in order to show that it had been considered but failed of acceptance. Altogether a hundred and forty-eight scholars are mentioned by name and these and the other teachers of the period from Hillel to Judah were called Tannaim, Mishnah teachers.

Side by side with the compilations in the form of Mishnah, the sayings of the Tannaim, whether in the domain of law

(Halakah) or of preaching (Haggadah), were assembled in the shape of a commentary on the Pentateuch. Such a commentary was called Midrash (Searching). None was prepared for the book of Genesis, since it contains practically no legal matter. Those on the other books of the Torah circulated in two versions, as they emanated from the school of Akiba or that of Ishmael. The final compilation of these commentaries, so far as they are extant, was effected in the age following the completion of the Mishnah. In the same period also were made independent Mishnah compilations in the form of Supplement (Tosephta), of which those ascribed to Hiya and Hoshaiah enjoyed special authority. All Tannaitic statements excluded from the Mishnah were designated as Extraneous Mishnah (Baraitha).

CHAPTER XXXV

THE LAST PATRIARCHS

(180-425)

URING Judah's patriarchate, the conditions in Palestine were on the whole tolerable, even though rapacious governors might tax the people too heavily, the emperor being too far away to afford redress. Thus, under Commodus (180–192), Niger told a Jewish deputation that he was sorry he could not tax the very air they breathed. Certainly, the Jews had no reason to favor Niger in his contest with Septimius Severus for the imperial position (193/194), as was charged. It is possible that some hotheads among the Jews plotted to rid themselves of both. Whatever the disturbance was, it was quelled rapidly by Severus; but the Parthian campaign, on which he now started, prompted a conciliatory attitude towards the Jews of Palestine, in order not to arouse the opposition of their brethren in Babylonia. Thus the Jews in Palestine might hold honorary civic offices in so far as they did not conflict with their religious obligations. Severus, it is true, forbade Jewish proselytism; but in the same manner he barred Christian propaganda. By the act of the emperor Caracalla (212), the Jews, along with all free inhabitants of the empire, became full Roman citizens; the hardships, consisting in additional burdens of taxation, affected but the wealthier classes and were outweighed by the advantage of being placed on a footing of political and legal equality with the non-Jews.

Compared with the rule of the Sassanid kings of Persia (p. 240), the Roman dominion appeared as the lesser of two evils. Thus the Jews of Cappadocia fought on the side of the emperor Alexander Severus (222–235) against Ardashir I. Nor were the Jews of the empire inclined to support Shapur I. (241–272) in his efforts to push the Romans out of Asia. The campaign in which the emperor Valerian was taken captive (260) affected Palestine, which after the check to the Persian arms inflicted by Odainath, prince of Palmyra, passed under the sway of the latter. This dominion was terminated so soon as the Palmyrenes, at first acting in concert with the Romans, had begun to encroach upon territory of the empire; Odainath's widow, the energetic queen Zenobia, was dethroned by emperor Aurelian (272). Palestine thus was brought back under the rule of Rome. Carus (282) led a successful campaign against the Persians; but the increasing cost of defending the frontiers bore heavily upon the taxpayers, and conditions in Palestine, as elsewhere in the empire, were wretched indeed.

Judah died about 217. He was succeeded by his eldest son Gamaliel III. (217–225). The reign of Gamaliel's son, Judah II., was a much longer one (225–255). The seat of the patriarchate was now removed to Tiberias. The position was still one of glamor; though the second Judah did not possess his grandfather's learning and though there were superior scholars among his contemporaries, he was looked upon as a leader and found ample scope in fruitful communal activity. Thus he endeavored to perfect elementary education by organizing schools in all towns and villages, holding that the world is sustained by the breath of school children and that their instruction must not be interrupted even for so worthy a cause as the building of the Temple. In order to alleviate the distress of the people by reason of the devastation of the country resulting from the Hadrianic war, Judah and his colleagues gave permission to buy oil from non-Jews, thus revoking an earlier measure.

The successors of Judah II. were Gamaliel IV. (255–275) and Judah III. (275–320). Neither commanded the position held by their predecessors; the leadership in the school passed more and more into the hands of prominent contemporary scholars. Judah III. followed his grandfather's example in improving elementary education. It was charged against the patriarch that he appointed as judges unworthy men who bought their positions. One of the younger scholars applied to such an appointee the Scriptural verse (Habak-

kuk 2, 19): 'Woe unto him that saith to the wood, Awake,
to the dumb stone, Arise! Can this teach? behold, it is overlaid with gold and silver, and there is no spirit at all therein.'
When once the patriarch complained about the extortionate
practices of the Roman governor and how difficult it was
always to meet them, a scholar advised him to take nothing
if he wished to give nothing. Gifts poured in from all parts of
the Dispersion and were largely appropriated for the maintenance of the patriarchal station. The scholars who received
but a meager share grumbled, the more so since they were
not exempted from contributing to the support of communal institutions along with other more opulent persons.

Under these conditions the scholastic leadership passed
out of the control of the patriarch. The students frequented
the schools of those teachers who stood out preëminently by
virtue of their knowledge and intellect. The lectures turned
now not so much upon absorbing the traditional matter (that
was now available in the Mishnah which every scholar was
expected to know by heart), as upon its discussion for the
purpose of reaching new deductions and of formulating the
law. Such instruction was called Talmud (Dialectical Exposition); the language in which the argumentation was carried
on was the popular speech, which was the Aramaic as spoken
in Galilee. The greatest master in this art was Johanan,
whose father was a humble smith (hence the son was called
Bar Nappaha, the smith's son). Left orphaned in early childhood, he had a hard struggle, and for a time engaged in business; but he realized that his vocation was to be a scholar,
though it entailed a life of privation. As he humorously said,
he must prove in his own person the truth that 'the poor
shall never cease out of the land.' In his early youth he had
been among the youngest pupils of Judah I., sitting some
seventeen rows behind the Babylonian Rab (p. 236) and
quite unable to follow the discussion. His principal teacher
was Jannai; he also attended the lectures of Hanina and for
thirteen years or more those of Hoshaiah at Caesarea.

Johanan taught at first at Sepphoris, and then at Tiberias.
Of all the contemporary scholars. he was the only one to

whom the patriarch Judah II. deferred, humoring him in his dislike of opposition and bestowing upon him a pension. Yet this scholar who was often overbearing towards his equals, was kindly to the meanest person, even a slave. He was tolerant of the Samaritan dissenters and even of apostates, being willing to accept words of wisdom from non-Jews. He had a high conception of scholarship and demanded of the true scholar absolute devotion to the Torah for her own sake. He made much of public worship. He was loved by the people whom he sustained by his preaching, and he practised what he preached. He had a large circle of students whom he taught how to sift the matter of the Mishnah, how to be exact in its exposition, and how to expand the traditional lore and secure its hold upon the people. Johanan's authority was unquestioned beyond the confines of his own country, just as he admired the scholarship of the Babylonian teachers. He lived to a ripe old age, his death occurring about 279, and left the foundations of the Palestinian Talmud, which in its completed form (if ever it was completed) dates from the time of the extinction of the patriarchate and the closing of the higher scholastic institutions.

Johanan's colleague, Simon son of Lakish, was a man of powerful physique, who in his younger days was thrown in with gladiators. Johanan prevailed upon him to abandon his occupation, gave him his sister in marriage, and made of him a scholar. The erstwhile master swordsman approved himself as keen a debater, skilful in parrying arguments. He would truckle to none, whether the patriarch or any of his colleagues or even his teacher Johanan. Many a time he listened to the praises which a ripe scholar like Jannai sang of his brother-in-law, and then insisted that Johanan was wrong after all. Nor would Simon put up with any and every extraneous Mishnah unless it could be proved trustworthy. He was also free in his opinions on Scriptural matter, as when he pronounced the narrative concerning Job, including the controversy between God and Satan, a poetic fiction. He was a thorough Palestinian and looked down upon the Babylonian Jews, their boasted pedigrees as well as their pretensions to learning. He spoke quite deprecatingly of even so notable a Babylonian teacher as Rab. Still the man who, though the equal neither of Johanan in founding a school nor of Simon in argumentative skill, was a worthy third, hailed from Babylonia. Eleazar son of Pedath received his early education at home; in Palestine he attended the lectures of Hiya, Hoshaiah, and Jannai; when Johanan passed away he took his place, and his countrymen in Babylonia referred to him with pride as the master of the Land of Israel.

The scholars that followed, whether at Tiberias or elsewhere in Palestine, were for the most part either Babylonians by birth or studied for some time in Babylonia. Occupation with the talmudic development of the traditional lore continued, but the branch upon which the Palestinian teachers of the later generations threw themselves with particular zest was the collection of homilies. The patriarchs, with one exception, were men of mediocre caliber who exerted no appreciable influence upon the spiritual life of the people; but as functionaries they enjoyed the recognition of the emperors. During the administration of Judah III., Palestine with Syria was ruled by Diocletian (284–305), who granted to the Jews immunity from taking part in the state cult. The Samaritans, who had to submit to such participation, were henceforth treated by the Jews as heathens. Thus the conciliatory policy, which it had still been possible for Johanan to maintain, was definitely abandoned.

Then, under Constantine the Great (311–337), came that momentous turn which in the long run subjected the Jews of the empire to the dominion of the cross. Among the early followers of Jesus there were Jews who came from the Dispersion and were given to a freer interpretation of Judaism. The seeds sown by them ripened at Antioch; there the name 'Christian' sprang up, and there the first Gentile church was founded. There, too, the new religion was created when the scruples of the conservative Peter were overcome and Paul of Tarsus proclaimed the abrogation of the Mosaic Law. The 'apostle to the Gentiles' envisaged the Church of God as one and dual at the same time, in which Jew and Greek had each his place. He therefore left the prerogatives of Israel untouched; the ancient gifts of grace and the election were irrevocable. The inherent logic of the Pauline position, however, made for a dethronement of the Jewish people. The new Christian people claimed that the election from the start was for themselves. They appropriated the Old Testament as their own and no longer the Jews' possession, and the mother thus despoiled was cast off by the daughter. With these pretensions the Church, intrinsically a transformed Judaism, offered itself to the world. Despite persecutions, as under Nero and then under Diocletian (284–305), it captured a humanity weary of the hollowness of paganism by a residue of the Jewish truth stripped of Jewish ceremonies and national limitations.

What the victory at the Milvian Bridge (312) had done for the ascendancy of Christianity in the West, the defeat of the co-emperor Licinius at Adrianople (323) accomplished in the East. By the edict of toleration issued at Milan (313), all subjects of the empire, hence also the Jews, had been given the freedom to profess whatever religion they chose. Judaism continued to be a licit religion, even after the first steps had been taken at the Council of Nicea (325) to establish Christianity as the state religion. But Judaism was to be practised by those who were born Jews; conversion to Judaism as well as the molestation of Jewish converts to Christianity was strictly forbidden. Oppression by imperial underlings was a frequent cause of friction.

Under Constantius II. (337–361), when the emperor's brother-in-law Gallus was ruler in the East, collisions between Jews and the army led to local outbreaks which were put down by the commander Ursicinus with fearful severity (351). Tiberias, Sepphoris, and Lod were destroyed. Thus the seats of Jewish learning received their death-blow. The patriarch Hillel II. (320–365) was the last outstanding figure in the long line of the illustrious family founded by his namesake Hillel the Elder.

A favorable interlude of all too short duration was afforded by the pagan reaction under Julian the Apostate (361–363).

Though distinctly hostile to Christianity and regarding the pagan philosophies as superior truths, he was tolerant of Judaism. In a letter addressed to the Jewish nation, he announced that he had committed to the flames the tax-rolls in which the Jews were charged with heavy burdens towards the imperial exchequer. As an evidence of further favor, which the Jews had little reason to be grateful for, he mentioned an order to his 'brother, the venerable patriarch Hillel,' to put a stop to collections of money through messengers for the upkeep of the patriarchate. The emperor, who was preparing a campaign against the Persians, hoped to enlist Jewish sympathies still further by the promise to rebuild the Temple upon his return. Unfortunately he died before this promise could be made good.

The principle of toleration for the Jewish religion was maintained by the subsequent Christian emperors, notably by Theodosius I. (the Great, 379–395) and Theodosius II. (408–450). But under the influence of fanatical ecclesiastics, the Jews were subjected to increasingly vexatious regulations with a view to reducing their number by conversions. It was entirely in the spirit of the churchmen that the Jews were designated as perverse and wicked and their sect as vile and bestial. In addition, Christian merchants and traders desired to rid themselves of Jewish competition. It became unlawful for Jews to circumcise their slaves or to own Christian slaves. Jews were not to exercise authority over Christians and must therefore be debarred from public office. Intermarriage between Jews and Christians was made a criminal offense. Palestine was more and more overrun by Christians, and Jewish economic life was rendered precarious. The schools were closed for lack of support. Hillel II. was succeeded by Gamaliel V. (365–385), and he in turn by Judah IV. (385–400); but when Gamaliel VI. (400–425) died without male issue, the emperor Theodosius II. abolished the patriarchal office altogether. Thus the last semblance of visible national organization, maintained in Palestine for upward of three centuries, was no more, and the headship in Jewish affairs passed over from the mother-country to other centers.

BOOK II

THE EASTERN CENTER UNTIL THE EXTINCTION OF THE GAONATE

(175–1038)

CHAPTER XXXVI

RAB AND SAMUEL

(175-254)

NEXT to Palestine, and in a manner surpassing all the Jewish settlements in the west, the Babylonian center produced most far-reaching influences, which strengthened Jewish resistance and shaped Jewish life. This eastern seat of Jewry had its beginnings in the two Babylonian deportations (p. 110, 112). We saw how the transplanted Jews, the best part of the nation, fared during the first fifty years (p. 114–117). When with Sheshbazzar (p. 119) and subsequently with Ezra (p. 122) colonies went forth from Babylonia to repeople the waste places of Judea, the great majority remained behind. They supplied those that returned with funds (p. 122); they took pride in the restored community and ever after contributed to the maintenance of the Temple. They accepted the lead of Palestine as a matter of course. It is therefore not to be wondered at that, down to the times of the patriarch Judah I., Babylonian Jewry remained in the background and had as it were no history of its own.

Yet in Roman times the Jews beyond the Euphrates were counted by millions. The most important communities were those of Nehardea, at the junction of the Euphrates and the Royal Canal; Nisibis and Mahoza on the same canal; Pumbeditha; Sura, also called Mahaseia. But Jews lived also outside the large cities, in villages and hamlets. Farming and cattle-raising were their principal occupations. The ground was owned by the rich and leased at exorbitant rates. The men who tilled the soil underwent great hardships, as they toiled to convey the waters from the canals to the irrigation ditches or strove to keep them from overflowing. Taxes were high, and the tax-gatherers ruthless. Yet, in the popular estimation, 'a yoke of arable land was worth more than a store of merchandise.'

The artisan accounted himself a happier man: 'seven years of famine, but never did it cross the threshold of the craftsman.' Jews labored as bakers and brewers, weavers, dyers, and tailors, ship-builders and wood-cutters; we find among them blacksmiths and tanners, fishermen, sailors, and porters. The farmer took his produce to town once a week; in the market, each trade had its own stall, and a market inspector watched over the measures and weights and settled disputes according to law and custom. There were street-vendors and retail traffickers, eking out a modest living, and then the princes of commerce who exported grain, wine, wool, and flax, and imported silks, iron, and precious stones. The man of business suffered less at the hands of the government and lived better; the rich merchants, who traveled by water or by caravan route to distant marts, led a life of luxury, amid a retinue of slaves and menials.

Slaves were frequently made free. It occasionally happened that a freedman married a Jewess, or that a Jew took to wife a former slave. But such alliances were frowned upon, and a public record of them was kept in order that none might marry into the disgraced family. Purity of blood was made much of by the Babylonian Jews. People married early in life, the young men between eighteen and twenty, and the girls still younger. Marriage followed betrothal after a twelve months' interval or a shorter period, when the bride was led to the home of her husband with music and lighted tapers amid great festivity. Frequently a father bestowed a house upon his son; it was not good form to dwell in the home of one's father-in-law. The women were given to personal adornment and the use of cosmetics; it was a mark of modesty for a woman to paint but one eye. The women folk had their own chambers, and the tasks of the household absorbed their attention. Mothers looked to the education of their children. The wife was held in high esteem. Polygamy, it seems, was rare. Life was not exactly free from care; but on the whole the people were merry, good-natured, and sociable. They appreciated humor and were fond of music; the holidays were occasions of veritable joy.

The communal life was ordered on the whole after the Palestinian pattern (p. 209 ff.). The highest official of Babylonian Jewry was the exilarch (Resh Galutha, 'Head of the Captivity'). This office marked the culminating point of Jewish autonomy. Those who held it traced their ancestry to the house of David in the male line. The Jews looked up with pride to this dignitary and willingly submitted to his authority. The Persian court considered him as the representative of Jewry, answerable for whatever taxes were levied upon them. His investiture was a highly solemn act. It was participated in by leaders lay and spiritual, with laying on of hands and blowing of trumpets; on the sabbath following the elevation an elaborate service was held when the new prince was acclaimed.

Enriched by gifts from his devoted people and in possession of extensive estates, the exilarch maintained an almost regal establishment. At his table rich and varied dishes were served and wine flowed freely. The company included a host of poor scholars who wore a badge as his dependents; the more punctilious would as often as feasible keep away because they suspected ritual irregularities in the preparation of the food. On the festivals the people thronged about the palace. The prince was always richly clad. When he appeared at court, as for example on the occasion of the Persian new year when he carried with him a gift of money, he wore a wide belt inwoven with gold and silver threads. The members of his suite disported themselves in silk garments. The prince's seal bore the heraldic device of a fly. So at least in later times; but at an earlier period the seal was adorned with the design of a lion, the lion of Judah.

Certain of these princes were unquestionably learned men. Thus the patriarch Judah I. bowed in reverence before the exilarch Huna; Ukba II. was a disciple of Samuel (p. 238). For the most part the exilarchs depended upon the counsel of the heads of the colleges, who at a later period composed for them their inaugural addresses, until at last the speech was delivered by the 'Excellency' (Gaon) of Sura. But the prince was duly advised of weighty decisions in spiritual matters.

In his palace sat one of the high courts of appeals. He rarely presided over this court. Still the 'judges of the gate' dispensed justice in his name; his word was law in all matters of internal administration and his authority unquestioned, to impose fines, to chastise and imprison delinquents. It was a harsh rule which at times led to mutterings; but even then it was the abuse of power by subordinate officials rather than the office itself that aroused opposition.

Any learned man in a community was competent to decide civil suits (criminal cases were heard before a college of three judges); still one confirmed by the exilarch or directly appointed by him had the advantage that he could not be sued for damages for an error of judgment. The judges, unsalaried and barred from accepting fees, had the power to inflict corporal punishment or to imprison and to pronounce the ban; if they were properly authorized, also to impose fines. It was furthermore within the province of a judge to remove the communal council, to appoint physicians and collectors of charity, and to proclaim fast days.

The man who laid the foundation upon which the life of the Babylonian Jews rested and gave it direction was Rab, 'Master' *par excellence*, as his admirers called him. His name was Abba. He was of towering stature (hence he was surnamed Arika, 'the Tall'); he once remarked jestingly that he had a commanding range of vision. Though affable and agreeable, he was not given to compromise. Of Babylonian birth and the son of well-to-do parents, he passed under the tutelage of his uncle Hiya who had settled in Palestine. There Rab was privileged to sit at the feet of Judah I. and to amass a stock of knowledge which made him a 'full man in all things.' For some reason or other he failed of obtaining complete ordination; his efforts, even at a later period, to have the scope of his authority widened somehow proved futile. Unlike Hiya, as soon as his apprenticeship was over, he returned to his native land. He was eagerly received by such men as the judge Karna and Samuel; for a while he assisted Shila, then presiding over the academy of Nehardea, as 'interpreter' (Amora), expounding the master's lectures.

When Shila passed away, Rab was to be his successor; but he retired in favor of his younger colleague Samuel, who was a Nehardean by birth. Rab had previously been appointed by the exilarch inspector of markets, and this position afforded him an opportunity for travel and for observing the lax religious conditions among the country folk. A conflict with the exilarch resulted in his imprisonment, but his friend Karna intervened to set him free.

Rab determined to create a sphere of activity for himself. In the far-off Sura, where he knew that dense ignorance prevailed, he founded a new school, which eclipsed the older seat of learning at Nehardea and lasted with slight interruptions for nearly eight centuries. It was well said of Rab that 'he found an open plain and left it fenced in.' He led the people to a strict observance of Judaism and compelled posterity to give assent to the prohibitions by which he sought to overcome ritual laxity. In the early morning and late at night Rab taught a host of pupils, who during the day earned their living as farm hands out of town. In the two months preceding spring and autumn, the Kalla months (March and September), some twelve thousand students day in and day out, from morning till evening, gathered about their master. In the week before the spring and autumn festivals, public discourses on matters of Jewish law were delivered before enormous crowds of laymen.

The subject taught in the school was the whole body of tradition as it lay codified in the Mishnah which Rab had brought with him from Palestine. Up to that time the Jews of Babylonia, as elsewhere in the Dispersion, had been wholly dependent upon the Palestinian patriarch and his Sanhedrin for decisions in regard to religious questions, since in numberless instances scholars were far apart in their opinions. All therefore that could be taught in the schools of distant lands was confined to acknowledged practice rather than theory. Now that in the main a definitive settlement of all past disputes had been reached and stood recorded, the schools anywhere might busy themselves with the Why and the Wherefore, with an exposition of the underlying theory, of ramifications and deductions, in short with the whole range of Talmud as supplementary to the Mishnah. A decision arrived at by Rab would accordingly be as binding as any proceeding from the Palestinian schools. Rab elucidated to his compatriots many an unfamiliar and archaic expression in the Mishnah by recourse to the Scriptures. Similarly he found in the Scriptural word unlooked-for foundation for novel deductions and all sorts of regulations, in part perhaps called for by the local conditions.

Thus, whether as teacher or preacher or active judge, Rab endeavored to regulate judicial procedure, to induce men of learning to serve as judges, to improve the people's morals by lending sanctity to marriage and rendering divorce more difficult. In his own home he exercised infinite patience with his contentious wife; humble and forgiving, he was beloved of all men, and his school with its synagogue was spoken of as a 'little sanctuary' (Ezekiel 11, 16). His death in 247 was universally mourned; all of his pupils followed his body to the grave. For a year the myrtle and the boughs of the palmtree were dispensed with at weddings. As religious questions came up which baffled the ingenuity of the younger generation, it was realized all too keenly that the father of Jewish learning in Babylonia was gone.

Rab's superiority was recognized by none more readily than by his former classmate and lifelong friend, Samuel. 'The man is departed, of whom I stood in awe.' And yet Samuel possessed a fund of qualities which made him a notable complement to his colleague. He was for one thing more versatile. Even before his student years in the school of Rabbi he had begun his studies in medicine; he prescribed for his teacher when troubled with an affection of his sight, and the patriarch was grieved that somehow he was denied the opportunity of naming Samuel master through the process of ordination. A salve for the eyes prepared by Samuel was much in demand; through dissection, practised on the dead bodies of executed slaves, he became a master of anatomy, and the ailments of women engrossed his attention. Above all he was given to the study of astronomy, and he could boast that he was as familiar with the paths of the sky as with the streets of his own Nehardea; only the erratic movements of shooting stars went beyond his ken. Unlike his Gentile friend Ablat, he repudiated all astrological superstitions. His knowledge of astronomy stood him in good stead in working out by calculation a fixed calendar, which he sent to Johanan son of Nappaha in Palestine. Johanan, however, preferred the ancient method of determining the dates of new moons and festivals from year to year.

In the field of jurisprudence, Samuel specialized in civil cases, and his early appointment to the bench enlarged his experience and deepened his understanding of legal principles so that his decisions, as well as his pronouncements later during his career as a teacher, became authoritative in this branch of the law. A far-reaching legal maxim of his makes the law of the state, in all matters not affecting religious practice, binding upon the Jew. After the death of Shila, when Rab declined the invitation to become his successor, Samuel presided over the school of his native city with great dignity and efficiency, excelling as he did in the handling of men and being on terms of friendship with the house of the exilarch. After the death of Rab, when for a number of years the office of head of the new school at Sura remained vacant, Samuel was the acknowledged spiritual leader of Babylonian Jewry. Both these scholars found leisure to establish uniformity in the order of public service; the wording of many an old prayer was modified to express the people's deepest yearnings, and the Book of Prayer was enriched by new compositions from their own pen. Thus the shorter form of the Eighteen Benedictions was composed by Samuel, while Rab wrote the Adoration (Alenu) for the Day of the New Year, a rhythmic poem embodying Israel's hope in the advent of the Kingdom of God.

CHAPTER XXXVII

THE times of Rab and Samuel, at least at the beginning of their careers, were propitious enough to prove helpful to their plans. The ruling dynasty of the Arsacids was favorably inclined to the Jews. Artaban IV. was personally acquainted with Rab and entertained a high regard for the Jewish scholar. When in 226 the Arsacid empire, which had endured for three centuries and a half, made way for the Sassanian or Neo-Persian, Rab exclaimed: 'The bond is broken.' The foreboding seemed all too well founded. The new king, Ardashir I. (226–241), had grown up under the influence of the fire-worshiping Magians, who scrupulously observed the expanded Zoroastrian ritual and were intolerant of all other creeds. The priests forbade the killing of animals for food unless certain parts were offered on their altars, thus practically making it impossible for the Jews to eat meat. As the Parsees were enjoined not to pollute the earth with corpses, the dead in Jewish burial-grounds were exhumed and cast out to the vultures and dogs; synagogues were destroyed and religious practices, like immersion, forbidden. The Jews accepted these visitations as a token of their sinfulness and were disposed to heed the admonitions of their teachers to redouble their zeal for their own faith.

Samuel did his utmost to conciliate the government. His efforts met with success under the reign of Shapur I. (241–272), who was in need of money for his campaigns against the Roman provinces to the west and who, moreover, had a warm regard for Samuel. Out of deference to him, the king spared the lives of Jews in the conquered countries unless they offered resistance. When Samuel died in 254, Shapur had the whole of Syria in his hands; the emperor Valerian, who marched to encounter him, was defeated and made prisoner (260). But this victory was soon frustrated by Odainath, prince of Palmyra (p. 225), who twice forced the Persians back to their capital Ctesiphon (263–265). As the Jews fought the Palmyrenes with particular bitterness, the invaders spent their fury upon Nehardea in which the Jewish population predominated, and razed the flourishing city to the ground. The blow proved fatal to the school built up by Samuel and now presided over by one of his pupils, Nahman son of Jacob. When at length the school found a resting place at Mahoza, a new seat of learning had been founded by Judah son of Ezekiel at Pumbeditha; this school soon rivaled in importance Rab's foundation at Sura, by the side of which it continued for eight centuries.

There were ups and downs in the life of these two principal academies. Outstanding personalities shed lustre upon the particular school with which they were connected and often attracted students from the other institution. In times of interregnum, as when Huna, Rab's successor, died after an activity stretching over forty years (257–297), the orphaned school recognized the head of the sister institution. The Pumbedithans were known for their keen intellect; often their subtlety led them into hair-splitting casuistry; it was said of them that they made an elephant pass through the eye of a needle. Rabbah son of Nahmani (309–330) was famed as a dialectician, a veritable 'mover of mountains'; his appointment as head of the Pumbeditha academy hung in the balance. Palestine, being consulted, threw in its influence on the side of his colleague Joseph, for the reason that he commanded a vast erudition, garnered in as one 'garners wheat'. Nevertheless Joseph stepped aside and his more brilliant contemporary obtained the post; after Rabbah's death he succeeded him for the brief period of three years.

The two scholars differed also temperamentally: Joseph was of a mild disposition, while Rabbah was harsh and entirely preoccupied with his studies. But Rabbah proved himself an ideal administrator and a magnetic teacher; so many thousands of students flocked to his lectures that he was de-

nounced to the government for withdrawing them twice in
the year from active work and thus entailing a loss in taxes
to the treasury. The teacher fled, fearing punishment, and
died on his flight. As legend has it, there was a division of
opinion in the heavenly academy between God and the
angels concerning a matter of impurity, God declaring it to
be pure. It was agreed to refer the question to Rabbah who
had specialized in the subject of pure and impure, though it
had no longer any practical bearing upon life. As he pronounced, Pure, he expired, and a voice from heaven called
out: 'Happy art thou, Rabbah son of Nahmani, for thy body
is pure, and thy soul is gone forth in purity.' Posterity ruled
that, with but few exceptions, the opinion of Rabbah was to
be followed over the dissent of his colleague. Joseph's
strength lay in other directions. He was at home in the Scriptures as very few of the teachers were; he was also familiar
with the Aramaic version which had been imported from
Palestine, and he was a preacher of marked impressiveness.

The mantle of Rabbah fell upon his brother's son Nahmani, better known by his other name Abaye. He was left
orphaned in his infancy and was cared for by his uncle, who
early sought to develop and sharpen his reasoning faculties.
But the young scholar soon passed over to the school of
Joseph, and this teacher's influence proved the stronger.
Abaye, it is true, did not quite share Joseph's disparagement of the dialectic method, and he held that a man might
be a great scholar though one or the other tradition escaped
him. But on the whole he set store by comprehensive knowledge. He lived in poverty and suffered privation, tilling his
small plot of land in the night that he might be free to study
all day long. His scrupulous honesty and charitable disposition made him beloved of the people. He took an eager
delight in the progress of any and all of his students; nevertheless the number had dwindled considerably from what it
had been under his predecessor. Young men were told that
instead of munching bones with Abaye they might rather
partake of rich meat with Raba at the new school which he
maintained in Mahoza.

Both these men had studied together from early childhood. In order to test the intelligence of the two boys, their
teacher once put to them the question: 'Who is it that we
pray to?'—'The Merciful One (God).'—'But where is God?'
—Abaye pointed to the sky, but Raba just raised his finger
toward the ceiling. The blunter intelligence of Abaye was
not able to cope with the keen intellect of his colleague, close
as their friendship was; barring six points of law, the ruling
of Raba was accepted as norm. When Abaye passed away
(338), the Pumbeditha school was closed and the students
sought out Raba at Mahoza, since he preferred to stay in his
own native town though he was recognized as official head
in succession to his colleague. In Raba were united all the
threads of the intellectual activity of the past generations.
He carried on the traditions of the school of Pumbeditha as
well as of that of Sura; he was linked to Pumbeditha through
his associations with Rabbah and Joseph, and in Sura he had
been trained by Hisda, whose daughter, the widow of a
fellow-student, he eventually married.

Under his hands the mass of comment upon the matter of
the Mishnah grew enormously. His acute mind detected
analogies in the most unpromising quarters, and the Scriptural word, whether in the Torah or elsewhere, yielded support for traditional regulations. Seriously as he took his
scholastic work, it was his custom on sabbath afternoons to
address the large public assembled for worship in the synagogue, bringing down to the comprehension of the laity the
things they must needs know in order to observe them. He
would punctuate his remarks with homely sayings and
quaint parables, and would drive home lessons in conduct
and in religious steadfastness drawn from texts in Psalms,
Proverbs, Job, and other Scriptural books. Nothing delighted
him as much as the concluding prayer (the 'Kaddish') in
which the congregation fervently joined, hallowing the name
of God. Of his students he demanded utmost sincerity;
thought should harmonize with outward conduct, just as the
Ark of the covenant was covered with gold within and without. Mere learning, unless the fear of God were coupled

therewith, would not ensure everlasting life. He said of himself that he prayed for wisdom such as Huna's and wealth such as Hisda enjoyed, and they were granted to him; but it was not given to him to be humble. This self-reproach must not be taken literally; he had no false pride about retracting a decision when convinced of its error.

The times were not exactly favorable for study: one day's evil was surpassed by the next day's. The policy of Shapur II. (310–379), like that of his predecessors, was bent upon strengthening the national religion, and conflicts, though not serious ones, arose. Raba was fortunate in possessing the confidence of the royal court, and the king's mother, Ifra Hormizd, who was particularly devoted to the Jewish scholar, saved many an uncomfortable situation. It is significant that the prestige of the heads of the schools was beginning to overshadow the position of the exilarch, both in matters of representation at the court and in the eyes of Jewry within, so much so that official notifications concerning the calendar from Palestine were sent direct to Raba.

Among the successors of Raba (died in 352), first at Mahoza and then in the older seat at Pumbeditha, there were no outstanding personalities, and they were completely left in the background by the illustrious master of Sura, Ashi (375–427). The school building, erected in 293 under Hisda, had fallen into decay; the new structure, as it rose under the personal supervision of the young master, overtopped all other dwellings in the city. The school regained the prestige which it had enjoyed under Rab; it is here that the exilarch presented himself to receive the homage of his people, and the master of Sura outranked the head of Pumbeditha. Like Rabbi, Ashi commanded both learning and affluence. The times were tranquil, and for more than fifty years he presided over the school, taking up in the semi-annual Kalla sessions by turn one tractate after another so that by the time of his death the ground was not only covered wholly but also gone over a second time. The accumulated sum of discussions had become so unwieldy that memory had to be aided by all sorts of mnemonic devices.

It is the merit of Ashi that he created order out of chaos and by a more systematic arrangement of the material caused the complex of questions and answers, of arguments and counter-arguments to hang together. Ashi laid the foundation for that gigantic work, the Babylonian Talmud, and his successors merely put the finishing touches thereto by incorporating the opinions of Ashi himself and of teachers after him.

The close of the activity of the Amoraim, as these builders of the Talmud were called, was hastened by a chain of persecutions which had set in during the reign of Jazdegerd II. (438–457), who made it unlawful for the Jews to keep sabbath and festivals or even to recite the Confession of the Unity (Shema'). Peroz (457–484) proceeded still more virulently. Because of a charge that two Magians had been slain by Jews, one half of the Jewish population in Ispahan was put to death. Jewish children were taken away by force and brought up in the Zoroastrian religion. The large convocations of students were interdicted, and several leading men, among them the reigning exilarch, were executed. The fear for the continuity of the oral lore in the face of these untoward circumstances led to a momentous step which was taken by the Suran master Rabina II. (474–499). Hitherto there had been objections to committing the discussions to writing. Many a scholar had in his hands stray notes in a much abbreviated form which, however, were never publicly exhibited; the feeling had been that there was to be but one written Torah. Now at last it seemed that the mass of tradition could not be entrusted to memory alone and the pen of the scribe was given free scope. Thus the scholastic activity of three centuries and of more than a thousand scholars was turned into a book, the Talmud of Babylon.

The Talmud is primarily a legal commentary upon the Mishnah. Naturally, the interpretation of difficult words or expressions forms a part of this commentary; but in the main the concern is with the legal matter (halakah). Every statement is scrutinized, every division of opinion traced to its source and principle. The discussion, as it grew in the

course of generations, is faithfully reproduced, thus presenting a picture of cumulative layers of argumentation. The
reader is taken into the atmosphere of the schools; he is made
to witness the strenuous mental contests as proponent and
opponent engage in thrusts and counter-thrusts. Constantly
one is led from one subject to another, the very variety keeping the mind agile. The curt phraseology, half Hebrew half
Aramaic, yields now and then to the easy flow of the Aramaic
vernacular; the legal tone is dropped, and the strain is
relieved by a succession of sententious sayings and quaint
tales (haggadah). Sometimes the lighter matter covers several pages and even complete chapters. As a result of the
ease with which transitions are effected, the Talmud becomes
a veritable encyclopaedia, in which, over and above jurisprudence, there are found imbedded theology and esoteric
theosophy, moral and natural science, medicine, mathematics, astronomy, history, legend, folklore. There are two
sides to the Talmud—the one rigidly legalistic and intellectual, the product of critical analysis which penetrates to
the bottom of things; and the other ethical, spiritual, appealing to the emotions. Jewish life as it developed came to rest
wholly on the Talmud; by it religious practice was regulated,
Jewish piety in every act and in every thought molded, and
Jewish mentality kept wide-awake even in the darkest
periods of general stagnation.

The immediate successors of the Amoraim called themselves Ponderers (Saboraim). It is by their hands that redac-
tional improvements and a few additions were introduced
into the body of the Talmud. During this transitional period,
which lasted forty years (500–540), the Jews were subjected
to fresh persecutions by the Persians. Kavadh I. (488–531)
was a vigorous ruler and favored the communistic teachings
of Mazdak which served him as a weapon against the nobles.
The exilarch somehow clashed with this sovereign and was
put to death. Nothing untoward happened during the reign
of the orthodox Khosrau I. (531–579), called Anushirvan
(the Blessed). His adjustment of the imperial taxation, which
was later adopted by the Arabs, was equitable, and if for a

time it brought hardships, the Jews were not the only ones that were affected. Conditions changed for the worse under his son Hormizd IV. (579–590); the Jews favored the general Bahram who led a conspiracy against the king. The schools were reopened (589) and were now presided over by the successors of the Saboraim who called themselves Gaons—Geonim, Excellencies; an abbreviated title for 'Head of the College, which is the Excellency of Jacob.'

The rebels were eventually discomfited and the prince Khosrau mounted the throne by the aid of the Byzantine emperor Maurice, whose daughter he had taken to wife. In the course of their invasion the Roman troops massacred a great portion of the Jewish population of Mahoza. Khosrau (II., surnamed Parvez, the Conqueror, 590–628) was supported in all his vicissitudes by his Jewish subjects and they accompanied him on his campaigns of revenge against the assassins of Maurice which led him as far as Jerusalem (614). Great disorders followed after the murder of the king by his own son, Kavadh II. (628). The struggle between the Byzantine empire and Persia enduring for a hundred years had enfeebled both. A new enemy and a new power stood at the door, and when the last Persian ruler, Jazdegerd III., ascended the throne (632), the Arab hosts were marching against his land under the banner of a new faith, Islam.

CHAPTER XXXVIII

THE RISE OF MOHAMMEDANISM

(622-858)

ONCE again Judaism gave rise to a new religious movement which in turn determined the course of Jewish history and made itself felt in the development of Jewish life and Jewish thought. It were idle to deny to the prophet of Arabia the power of an original personality; nor is it necessary to disparage the stimulus which came to him from Christianity and other ancient lore. But it is just as unmistakable that Mohammed's central message, and still more potently his ordering of the state-church, rested upon direct borrowings from Judaism or upon imitations of Jewish originals. Whether it is the Jewish Scriptures or the embellishments spun out by Jewish haggadists, a knowledge of them could come to the illiterate prophet only through the Jewish mentors whom he had near at hand.

Long before the advent of Mohammed Jews had settled in Arabia, a remnant broken off from the main body and carried thither on the wave of dispersion which set in after the legions of Rome had laid waste the Holy City. In the southwest corner, the rich and fruitful Yemen, their industry and enterprising spirit helped to revive the prosperity-of the country. They instigated the native Himyarites to repel the invasions from Christian Abyssinia, thus seconding the policy of the Sassanian rulers to prevent Christianity from obtaining a foothold in southern Arabia. For a time it seemed as if Judaism might make headway. In the fifth century there arose a new kingdom, half-Jewish, half-Sabean, whose most illustrious ruler, Dhu-Nuwas, became converted to Judaism and took the name of Joseph. But a renewed attack by the Abyssinians, supported by the Byzantine emperor, made an end of this kingdom in 525. The Abyssinian occupation, however, did not last long, and in 575 the Persians established their suzerainty over the land.

In the northwest of the peninsula the Jews occupied the oases on the line of the caravan route running from north to south. Taima, Fadak, Khaibar, Wadi-l-Kura (Vale of Villages) were in their hands, and Yathrib (the later Medina, the Prophet's City) was in all probability founded by them. These settlements consisted of aggregates of plantations, villages, and strong castle-like houses which, now closer together, now wider apart, lay amid scattered palm groves, orchards, and cultivated fields. It appears that the culture of the date-palm was introduced into Arabia by the Jews. They also engaged in commerce, and as jewelers and goldsmiths they were in great demand. They formed compact communities, enlarged by accessions from among the natives, who were attracted to Judaism. Quite after the manner of the Arabs, the Jews were divided into a number of tribes, principal among which were the Kainuka', the Nadhir, and the Kuraiza; the latter two were spoken of as the 'priestly' clans, that is, of Aaronitic descent. Another trait in which they resembled the pure Arabs was that the diverse tribes engaged in perpetual feuds with one another, and it is this disunion which marked them as an easy prey for attack.

When the southern Arabs began to move up northward in the third Christian century, the Aus and Khazraj clans wrested Yathrib from the hands of the Jews, who now became their dependents. The Jews, according as they leaned upon either clan, took part in the internecine warfare, with the result that Jew was pitted against Jew. Nevertheless, when a Jew was taken captive and was about to be sold, the Jews of both sides would unite to buy him back. When upbraided by their Arab comrades, they answered: God has commanded us to redeem our own people. Thus, in all but their religion, the Jews lived and conducted themselves like their neighbors. They bore for the most part Arab names, their speech was Arabic, and in it they composed their poems which vied with those of other Arabs in nobility and dignity of expression. Of one of these poets, who dwelt in

his castle at Taima, Samuel son of Adiya, it is reported that
he suffered his son to be slain when refusing to surrender the
fortune which Imru-l-Kais, famed as king and poet, had
left with him in trust. Long in after times Arabs were wont
to say: 'More faithful than Samuel.' The treacherous assassination of the Jewish chiefs, by which the Khazraj broke
the power of the Jews of Yathrib, was mourned in verse
by a Jewish poetess with the biblical name Sarah. The
astonishing thing indeed is that these Jews clung to their
religion. Their neighbors knew them as the 'People of the
Book'; they had their religious teachers who taught them,
in the end, to choose exile and death rather than to forswear
their ancestral faith.

When Mohammed, discouraged by the hostilities of his
clansmen in his native city Mecca, fled to Medina in 622
(hijra, hejira), he found the ground well prepared. A number
of citizens, who had grown receptive of monotheism through
their associations with the Jews, were flattered that Allah
had now spoken by the mouth of one of their own, an Arab
prophet. It is true, the more substantial members of the
community kept aloof and at best maintained a neutral attitude; Mohammed styled them 'waverers.' But what he could
not forgive or even understand was that he made no headway at all in winning the Jews over to his faith. Though
some of the weaker members, lured by material considerations, joined Islam, the vast majority heard him and then
went their way, scorning the confused utterances of the Arab
prophet in all that pertained to Judaism, its Scriptures, and
its Messianic hope. And yet he had looked upon his own
advent as the consummation of their hopes. Moreover, like
them he directed his prayers towards Jerusalem (kibla), and
like them he kept the great fast on the tenth of Tishri (Day
of Atonement).

The Jews simply would not merge with his followers.
Cleverly did they make mock of the prophet's foibles and
inconsistencies, thereby estranging some of his stoutest supporters. It soon dawned upon him that a way must be found
to rid himself of the Jews if his heavenly mission to unite

Arabia under the banner of Islam was to prosper. For a time he proceeded cautiously. His immediate task was to weld together the factions at Medina, his own companions in the flight, the new converts, and the Jews, in one community. In the Charter drawn up in the second year of the Flight, the Jews of Yathrib were confirmed in the practice of their religion and in the secure possession of their property. They were dealt with as a group on a par with the other groups, and all bound themselves to act as a unit in the event of an attack directed against any one of the constituent parts. However, as the hope of converting the Jews to the new religion waned, Mohammed moved, farther and farther away from Judaism, in the line of ancient Arab usages. The direction of prayer was changed towards the Kaaba at Mecca, the old national sanctuary of the Arabs, and in the place of the one great annual fast the believers were enjoined to abstain from food and drink during the whole month of Ramadhan, each day from sunrise to sunset.

The victory over the Meccans in the battle of Badr (624), celebrated in the Koran as the 'Day of Deliverance,' served to heighten the prestige of Mohammed and to consolidate his power over his adherents at Medina. The time was ripe now to strike at the hated Kainuka', who had their quarters in a strongly built suburb. When Mohammed bade them acknowledge him as their prophet, they refused, and defied him to do his worst. 'Thou wilt see that we are men.' For fifteen days they were besieged. At last, despairing of aid from their Khazraj allies, they surrendered. Only the intervention of the Khazrajite Abdallah ibn Ubaiy prevented a massacre. They were sent into exile and, assisted by their coreligionists of Wadi-l-Kura, they emigrated to Palestine. The spoil, consisting chiefly of armor and goldsmiths' tools, was distributed among the army, Mohammed reserving for himself a choice of arms. As one of the Khazrajites remarked : 'Hearts have changed. Islam hath blotted out all treaties.'

Twelve months later the Meccans inflicted a severe defeat on Mohammed's forces in the battle of Uhud, and the prophet himself was wounded. His cause seemed discredited, and so the Jews were made to pay the piper. A charge was trumped up against the Banu Nadhir that they plotted against the prophet's life—so the angel Gabriel had told him —and when they spurned banishment and no help was forthcoming either from the Khazrajites or their brethren in faith, the Kuraiza, they resolved to trust to the strength of their fortress. Gallantly they held out for a fortnight. To hasten their surrender, Mohammed ordered the surrounding date trees to be cut down. The expedient shocked even the believers, and a special revelation was required to justify it. At last the Jews were ready to capitulate, with the stipulation that they might emigrate with their wives and children and take with them their chattels, any thing that could be laden upon their camels, even to their doors and lintels; only their arms they were forced to leave behind them. Thus they set out, with tabrets and music, a few taking refuge with their brethren at Khaibar, the large majority proceeding to the highlands east of the Jordan. The whole of the confiscated lands was apportioned among Mohammed's companions in his flight to Medina, who thus were advanced to a position of independence and affluence.

In 627 the Meccans, roused by Mohammed's growing power, formed a coalition of the bedouin tribes of the neighborhood with the intent to stamp out Islam. At the advice of a Persian convert, Mohammed had a wide and deep trench dug on the open sides of the city. This foreign artifice disconcerted the besiegers, and they opened negotiations with the Jewish clan of the Kuraiza, whose quarters lay in the section of the city least capable of defense. Mohammed's emissaries were received by the Jews in a sullen mood, and in his alarm the prophet resorted to artful deception in order to sow discord between the Jews and their allies. Disheartened by their long drawn out operations, which were rendered still less effectual by the winter storms, the confederates dispersed. As soon as the siege was raised, the Jews were invested in their fortress; they defended themselves bravely, but at last, brought to the verge of starvation, they surrendered, hoping to escape with their lives. As the Aus would not tolerate the destruction of their ancient allies, Mohammed treacherously left the decision to an Ausite chief, and more than six hundred men were butchered in cold blood. The women and children were sold among the bedouins in exchange for horses and arms. One beautiful Jewess, Rihana, whose husband had perished in the massacre, was spared to be added to the prophet's harem. The enormous booty was appropriated by Mohammed for himself and the army.

Quite unprovoked was Mohammed's attack on the rich Jewish settlement of Khaibar in the following year. The Jews fought desperately from within their strong fortresses or sallied forth to meet their foes without. Doughty Jewish warriors, like Marhab and his brother, met their death in single combat with Moslem men of prowess such as Ali and Zubair. But the enemy carried one fort after another. The Jewish chief Kinana was subjected to cruel torture and then put to death; his comely wife Safia Mohammed took for his own. But another Jewess, Zainab, the sister of the slain Marhab, revenged the death of her kin by putting in the prophet's food poison from the effects of which he suffered to the day of his death. Such remaining fortresses as had not been sacked capitulated. The lands of the Jews were left in their hands, subject to a tax of half the produce. Fadak and Wadi-l-Kura submitted to a like fate. practically without resistance.

Mohammed had achieved his purpose and no Jew in Arabia dared to lift his hand against him or openly to dispute his claims. The prophet was now bent upon detaching his religion completely from Judaism. Mecca was proclaimed as the true seat of Allah on earth; the pilgrimage to Mecca and even the kissing of the black stone were sanctioned; by removing the idols Mohammed claimed that he restored the cult as it had been established in that sanctuary by the first preacher of Islam, Abraham the father of Ishmael.

Mohammed died in 632. The dying prophet is reported to have said: 'Two religions cannot exist in Arabia.' Accordingly the caliph Omar (634–644) expelled all Jews and Christians from the peninsula; nevertheless centuries later flourishing Jewish communities were still to be found in Taima and Wadi-l-Kura. Within a short space of time the compact national Arab state expanded into an empire: Damascus was taken in 635; in the battle on the Jarmuch (636) the remainder of Syria as well as Palestine was won. The battle of Kadisiya (637) drove the Persians back to their ancient seat in Iran; Egypt was conquered in 640, and in the battle of Nehawend (641) Iran itself was subdued. The caliph had now to deal with vast numbers of Jewish and Christian subjects. Omar and his immediate successors left the unbelievers in the possession of their lands, but imposed upon the landlords a heavy ground tax in addition to the poll-tax levied upon every unbeliever whether he owned property or not.

It was stipulated that those of other faiths should refrain from reviling the prophet or mocking the Mohammedan worship; Moslems were not to be lured away from their faith; non-Moslems should not be prevented from embracing Islam; a distinctive dress was prescribed for unbelievers. Nor were non-Moslems permitted to bear arms or ride on horses (they might use mules or donkeys), raise their dwellings above those of Moslems, conduct their worship in a loud voice, build new houses of worship or restore those in decay. These vexatious regulations, for disregard of which varying fines were imposed, were often allowed to lapse. As Moslems and Jews or Christians habituated themselves to one another, much of the harshness disappeared. On the whole, the local administration was left in the hands of the native population, and the Mohammedan rulers confirmed both Christian and Jewish dignitaries in their vested positions.

The first exilarch to hold office under Mohammedan rule was Bustani (or Bustanai). As one version would have it, he was elevated to this dignity by none other than the general who conquered Irak (Babylonia). About the birth of Bustani there cluster legends which are reminiscent of the story of the birth of Cyrus. A Persian king, bent upon exterminating the royal seed of the house of David, dreams that he is having all the trees of a park (bustan) cut down. Just as he makes ready to strike at a tender sprig, the axe is snatched from his hand by a venerable old man and hurled at his forehead with such force that blood spurts over his countenance and beard. He prays for mercy and must promise to nurse the twig that it may shoot up into a leafy tree. On awaking he beholds the blood on his face and, convinced that the dream has significance, summons a Jew known for his skill in interpreting dreams.

The daughter of this man had married a scion of the exilarch's house and was with child. The father sees in the dream a reference to the unborn child who may be the last offspring of the princely house. The king orders that the mother be surrounded with all care, and when a boy is born he is named Bustani. As he grows up he distinguishes himself by learning and intellect. Summoned before the king, he proves himself well mannered, for though he is stung by a wasp or fly (hence the design on the exilarch's seal), he forbears to drive it away by so much as the movement of a finger out of deference to his royal master. The king showers gifts upon him and installs him as head of the captivity. According to another version, the incident with the fly takes place in the presence of Omar who orders an older man to vacate the princely office in favor of Bustani, a stripling of sixteen years. It is further reported that the caliph bestowed upon him one of the captive Persian princesses, Izdundad by name, whom he married. Naturally he had other wives; subsequently their children sought to discredit the legitimacy of their brothers whom the Persian princess had born, on the ground that as a captive her status was that of a slave. But the Gaons ruled that Bustani must have made her a free woman and a convert before the marriage.

The decision is recorded by a later Gaon in answer to a query with reference to a similar case, real or hypothetical. Answering queries (in the form of Responsa), coming from far and near throughout the confines of the Dispersion, constituted one of the chief activities of the two academies of Sura and Pumbeditha. The questions were much diversified.

They touched upon the whole range of law and upon the conclusions to be drawn from the extended discussions in the Talmud, or upon the plain meaning of a talmudic phrase, halakic or haggadic. Some centered around a word or point in the Scriptures; still others turned on the order of worship, or a dogmatic point, or even history. Copies of the answers were in all likelihood kept; naturally they were cherished by the recipients who often read them in public and permitted transcripts to be made and carried from one seat of learning to another. Subsequently these were assembled by various hands under divers titles, and upon their basis the early and later codes were constructed.

The Talmud was altogether too unwieldy a work for average minds to make practical use of in order to arrive at concrete conclusions. The earliest compendious code, which followed the unsystematic order of the Talmud, was composed by Jehudai, a blind scholar, who succeeded to the Gaonate of Sura in 760. Of a different order is a contemporaneous work known as 'Discussions' (Sheeltoth) by Aha of Shabha, who left for Palestine when a younger colleague was named master at Pumbeditha. It consisted of a series of weekly discourses following the order of the Torah, in which legal matter was intermixed with homilies. On the basis of these two works there arose the 'Great Halakoth,' which passed through various stages of compilation and enjoyed such popularity that students were loath to consult the Talmud at first hand.

There was much uncertainty in the far-away communities as to the order of the synagogue service. A brief arrangement of the daily blessings had been prepared by Natronai, the Gaon of Sura (853–856), at the request of the community of Lucena in Spain. The first complete Order of Prayers was compiled for the use of the communities in Spain by his successor Amram, Gaon of Sura (856–874). Though the liturgical pieces are reproduced in full, the real purport of the work, answering to the need of the distant communities, was to incorporate all the regulations appertaining to the service. The material was culled from both Talmuds and the homiletical Midrashim, and the custom obtaining in the two schools as well as in Rab's old synagogue at Sura was cited. From the sister academy also the Spanish communities received spiritual guidance and instruction. The Gaon of Pumbeditha, Paltoi (842–858), sent them a copy of the Talmud and talmudic explanations. Thus a unifying influence radiated from the eastern seats of learning, and the farthest communities of the west were brought under the sway of an age-long tradition of which the Talmud was the authoritative expression.

CHAPTER XXXIX

THE KARAITE SCHISM

(767-900)

THE Jewish intellect, fully occupied with legal deductions, disdained to probe the things secret, to lift the
veil from 'what is above and what is below, what
was before and what shall be in the end.' Yet imagination
could not be starved, and speculation, rife among the sects
on the border of Christianity, enticed some of the best men.
The common people came in contact with the crude superstitions of Chaldaic lore which even the learned could not
entirely shake off. The very soil was impregnated with a
succession of religious systems in which, as in Manicheism,
mystic notions were blended, for the elect to take hold on.
Jewish mysticism in the times of the Gaons reveled in the
contemplation of the divine majesty, which took on grossly
anthropomorphic forms. Those of sober mind were hostile to
the fantastic writings of this genre. Nevertheless the boast
of mystic profundity and of intimate intercourse with the
prophet Elijah secured in 814 the headship of the school at
Pumbeditha to the aged Joseph son of Abba. His successor
Abraham son of Sherira (816–828) was reputed to be able to
prognosticate events from the soft murmur of palms on calm
days.

Deep in the people's soul burned the spark of the Messianic hope, ready to be fanned into flame by any one who
appealed to their imagination. There were those who were
given to 'calculating the end' by deftly manipulating the
obscure numbers in Daniel. In the more distant provinces of
Persia, the Shiite sect of Islam had its seat; its tenets centered in the exaltation of the religious head in succession to
the Prophet and in the belief in the 'hidden imam' and his
'return.' Here in the eighth century the Jewish masses were
stirred by a pretender to the Messianic dignity who came

from a place named Shirin. He held out the promise of a
miraculous restoration of Palestine and bade his followers
abandon their possessions. The Jews were the more readily
beguiled as the reigning caliph, Omar II. (717–720), had
introduced severe regulations for non-believers and many
sought refuge in Islam. However, his successor Yazid II.
(720–724) made short shrift of the would-be Messiah, who
lamely pretended that he had only made mock of the Jews,
and delivered him into the hands of those he had duped.

Some time later another Messianic movement was led by
Abu Isa Obadiah of Ispahan. This time Palestine was to be
regained by force of arms, and the bellicose leader, who gave
himself out for the last of the forerunners of the Messiah,
seriously believed in his mission and placed himself at the
head of an armed host of some ten thousand Jews. The time
seemed propitious, for the Mohammedan empire was torn
by internal strife and another dynasty, that of the Abbasids,
made ready to wrest the caliphate from the Omayyad Mer-
wan II. (744–750). The new monarch, Abu-l-Abbas (750–
754), was far too much occupied to deal with the Jewish
rebel. But when Mansur (754–775) ascended the throne,
Abu Isa fled with his band northward, under the pretence
that he would find succor there at the hands of mythical
Jews, believed to be descended from Moses and hidden somewhere. In reality he purposed to join forces with a Persian
chieftain who led a revolt against the caliph. The rebel forces
were subdued by the Mohammedans, and Abu Isa, mounted
on a horse, fell under their strokes on venturing all too con-
fidently beyond the lines (755).

Nothing daunted, his followers persisted in believing that
he would reappear. A disciple, Yudghan of Hamadan, announced himself as a prophet and another forerunner of the
Messiah, and he was acclaimed as 'shepherd' by a number of
believing Jews. One or the other of these pretenders made
light of certain rabbinic precepts or even ruled that the
observance of the sabbath and festivals was not obligatory
in the exile. In the main, however, they were given to ascetic
exercises and abstained from meat and wine or increased the

number of daily prayers. Their followers lingered on, but gradually dwindled away and were absorbed either by the mass of Jewry or by the new sect which, starting from entirely different premises, had its rise likewise in the eighth century and persists until the present day.

Unlike the Messianists, this sect was in no wise Utopian. Its entire momentum lay in its opposition to the Talmud and the line of traditional development which this work connoted. The earlier anti-traditional tendencies had not entirely died out. After the destruction of the Temple, it is true, the Sadducees ceased to wield any influence as an organized party, and Pharisaism was in the seat of undisputed leadership. But the Sadducee tendencies continued to manifest themselves, however inaudibly, through the centuries. The large mass of the Jewish people willingly bent their neck to the yoke of the Torah as interpreted by the bearers of the principle of tradition. Nevertheless, now and again there were mutterings against the ascendancy of rigorism and the reign of tradition which had so little to rest upon in the written Torah itself. 'What good have the teachers done to us? Not so much as to make it lawful to partake of a raven!' When at length a personality arose who sounded the keynote for deliverance from tradition, there was a chance for the movement to make headway.

The story goes that Anan son of David was in the line of succession to the exilarchate. The Gaons, who had reasons to suspect his orthodoxy—he had lived for some time in Persia at the center of Jewish heresies—had his younger brother Hananiah, a man of inferior scholarship, elected in his stead. The election was confirmed by the caliph. Deeply hurt, Anan was urged by his friends to resistance; in secret conclave he was made a counter-exilarch (767). The government got wind of the rebellion and threw Anan into prison. There, the story continues, he had for a fellow-prisoner the famous Mohammedan student of jurisprudence Abu Hanifa, founder of the Hanafite system of law. He advised Anan to bribe the vizir, seek trial in the presence of the caliph, and pray for recognition as the representative of another body of Jews. 'Is it meet that my brother should rule over two religious communities?' The caliph was won over by Anan's stressing the points which would appeal to a Moslem ruler, that his faction revered Mohammed as a prophet and held to a calendar very much like the Mohammedan, inasmuch as the lunar phases were ascertained by observation from month to month rather than by calculation.

Thus the open breach with the main body of Jewry was effected. In all matters of belief or dogma Anan was at one with those he left behind. What differentiated him was his dissent from Tradition. 'Forsake the words of Mishnah and Talmud, and I will make unto you a Talmud of my own.' He failed to realize that the Talmud was not made; it had grown by a natural process. So Anan fell back upon the remnants of Sadducee lore and gathered up from the Talmud those opinions which had been rejected. Moreover, he could not quite escape the influence of the hated work. He took over its rules and methods and in his legal deductions carried the principle of analogy to the most absurd point.

His tendency to asceticism inclined him to a rigorous interpretation of the law. Like the despondent witnesses of the destruction of the Temple, with whom the Tannaite Joshua was obliged to remonstrate, he forbade all meat except that of deer (Deuteronomy 12, 15), all fowl except pigeons. It was of small consequence that he made it lawful to eat meat with butter. None might leave the house on the sabbath, but anything might be carried unless it were laden on the shoulder. No lights might be kindled to illumine the home on the eve of sabbath, and all food on the day of rest was to be served cold. Fast days were multiplied. The forbidden degrees of propinquity as a bar to marriage were extended. The killing of animals for food was carried out with great solemnity. In illness, no physician might be consulted: 'for I am the Lord that healeth thee.' Certain practices were altered just for the sake of establishing difference. Tradition, however, could not be discarded wholly. Anan's own code, of which only scant remains have been recovered, resembles in style very much those of the Gaons. A small group followed the pathfinder, the first man 'who found the whole truth,' in every particular; but in course of time the 'Ananites' disappeared, making way for those that governed their life in accordance with newer teachings.

It was the boast of the new sect that no two of its members agreed. Anan himself undermined authority by his double precept: 'Search the Scriptures diligently, and lean not upon my opinion.' Any one might interpret Scripture according to his own lights, and no one's ruling need be accepted by others. Still Anan was venerated by later generations among those who attached themselves to his movement; he was looked up to as the 'principal teacher' and invested with a legendary halo. It was narrated that an attempt had been made upon his life, whereupon he escaped to the Holy City. Here, somewhat anachronistically, he was received kindly by Omar (640!) who gave him permission to erect a synagogue facing the western wall of the Temple.

The movement started by Anan was solidified by Benjamin of Nehawend (830) with whom the new sect assumed a fixed appellation, 'Children of Scripture' (Bene Mikra). Subsequently they came to be called 'Scripturists,' 'Karaites' (Karaim), while their traditionist opponents were named 'Rabbanites' (Rabbanim). Benjamin abandoned artificial opposition and now and then ranged himself on the side of the Rabbanites against Anan. 'I have compiled for you this Code—he wrote it in Hebrew and called it 'Benjamin's Portion'—that you may judge your Scripturist brethren. I cite in every instance the Scriptural source. As for those laws which the Rabbanites follow, but for which I was not able to find support in the Scriptures, I wrote them down likewise, that you might follow them if you so chose.' He held that none but an Israelite might judge a fellow-Israelite. He regarded it as lawful to leave one's dwelling on the sabbath for a necessary cause, particularly in order to go to synagogue or the house of study, but not beyond a sabbath day's journey. Even when he agreed with the Traditionists, he used his own deductions, and the prophetic writings in Scripture were drawn upon for support. His calendar was made up by intercalating a month every year. He taught that the Creator of the world was not God Himself, but an angel created by Him; by this angel was likewise the Law revealed—it seems that somehow, through translation into some Oriental tongue, the writings of Philo had reached him. He also indulged in forecasting the advent of the Messiah who, he thought, was due to appear in 1350. Though he did much to place the Karaite sect upon a firmer basis, yet, true Karaite that he was, he left his followers free to disregard his own authority.

A third teacher, greatly commended by the Karaites, was Daniel son of Moses al-Kumisi (about 900). In his later years he was violently opposed to Anan and the Ananites. In contrast to Benjamin, he rejected reason as a means of deciding questions of religious law. He spurned the allegorical method and strictly adhered to the simple, natural sense of the Scriptural word. He tended to a stricter interpretation of religious laws and sedulously maintained all the regulations concerning ritual purity. He would in no way tolerate calculation to enter into the make-up of the calendar. The new year was to begin with the tenth of Tishri (Day of Atonement), and not with the first of that month.

With Daniel al-Kumisi the first period in the life of the Karaite sect closed. Thus far it had sought to arrive at a measure of fixity in religious observance, yet all the time fearful to commit itself to the reign of authority. The sect which the Gaon Jehudai knew only by hearsay, had grown to be a menace to traditional Judaism when it met with a formidable foe—the great master who confined the contagion within its narrow bounds.

CHAPTER XL

SAADIAH

(882-942)

IT WAS altogether an unprecedented event when in the year 928 there was placed in the seat of the Gaon of Sura a scholar who was not a native of the country, especially since for about two centuries the office had been in the almost exclusive possession of three families. The dearth of outstanding personalities had brought the institution to a low ebb. When Yom Tob Kahana, a weaver by trade, passed away after a tenure of but two years (926–928), the exilarch David son of Zaccai thought of closing the school altogether. This would have been quite to the satisfaction of the ambitious head of the rival school at Pumbeditha, Cohen-Zedek II. (917–936). However, a nominal head was appointed in the person of Nathan son of Jehudai, whose sudden death was taken as a warning that it would be sinful to terminate the existence of the venerable seat of learning.

The choice narrowed itself down to Zemah son of Shahin, who belonged to an old family, and Saadiah son of Joseph (882–942) who came from the Fayum in Upper Egypt. The exilarch sought the advice of Nissi Naharwani, who had formerly been helpful in healing the breach between the dignitary and the refractory master of Pumbeditha. Nissi, who disinterestedly declined the honor for himself because of blindness, favored Saadiah's rival. 'It is true that Saadiah excels in wisdom, piety, and eloquence; but he is firm and unbending, of a combative disposition, and when once he has made up his mind he will recoil before none.' However, the exilarch had resolved upon Saadiah, and so he was duly inducted into office, after giving his word that he would defer to the authority of the head of the captivity.

The foundation for the new Gaon's vast erudition must have been laid in the land of his birth, where since the Mohammedan occupation (640) there had been a revival of Jewish communal life. The largest and most flourishing settlement was found in the capital Fustat (Old Cairo) and was presided over in 850 by a Babylonian Jew, Abu-Ali Hasan of Bagdad. The Jews spoke the language of the governing Arab classes, and the Jewish youth absorbed eagerly the culture to which Mohammedan rule had given impetus. Naturally there must have been facilities for acquiring strictly Jewish learning. An older contemporary of Saadiah's, with whom the younger scholar corresponded on learned subjects, was his compatriot Isaac son of Solomon Israeli. He was an eminent physician, subsequently in attendance upon the court at Kairawan, and wrote not only on medicine but on philosophy as well. The Karaites had likewise established themselves in Egypt, and there, as in Palestine, they carried on propaganda for their tenets. Saadiah's fighting blood was aroused, and a lively literary feud ensued between the doughty protagonist of Rabbanism and the schismatics. Sympathetic towards his position as those of his own persuasion may have been, the disturbance of communal peace filled them with apprehensions. Saadiah, actuated also by a desire to perfect his knowledge, wandered forth to the Holy Land, which the Tulunid governors of Egypt had annexed to their country (878).

We possess but scant information about the fortunes of Palestinian Jewry after the extinction of the patriarchate (425). In consequence of the discriminatory laws of the emperors and the expansion of Christian influence in the land, there had been a gradual thinning out of the Jewish population; the ruins, laid bare in recent times, tell mutely their tale of the once magnificent Galilean synagogues. The Code of Justinian I. (527–565) meddled with the internal affairs of the Synagogue and regulated which Greek translation of the Scriptures might or might not be read. The midrashic discourses based on the successive oral tradition fell entirely under the ban. Yet we hear of 'archipherekites' (masters of courses, reshe phirke) as feeble successors to the patriarchs, among the first of whom may be reckoned Zutra —his father, who bore the same name, was exilarch in Babylonia—who emigrated to Palestine in 520. In the struggles between Heraclius (610–641) and Khosrau II. the Jews of Palestine, led by Benjamin, a man of great wealth at Tiberias, took sides with the Persian invaders.

But it is only with the Arab conquest (636–638) that repose came to the Jews in the land of their fathers. As the Gaon Jehudai expressed himself, 'when the Ishmaelites came, they left them free to occupy themselves with the Torah.' When Jerusalem surrendered, the patriarch Sophronius stipulated that no Jews should be allowed to reside in the Holy City; but very soon a Jewish community sprang up. Jews were also attracted to Ramleh (near Ludd) where an Arab garrison was quartered. The Galilean schools were reorganized. Tiberias was the center of scholastic activity, 'which, following its earlier wont, addressed itself in particular to careful watchfulness over the received text of the Scriptures in order that no jot or tittle should be altered. Lovingly did the humble teachers in elementary grades count every word and letter, draw up lists of irregular or unusual spellings, and build up those safeguards for the preservation of the Scriptural word which make up the Masorah. A system of notation, by means of points or figures above and below the letters, was devised to mark vowels and stops. Thus was perpetuated the traditional pronunciation and interpretation.

Over against the Western (Palestinian) school stood the Eastern (Babylonian); the two diverged as regards textual readings and the method of marking the vowels and stops. Even in Palestine, Tiberias developed a system apart from that obtaining elsewhere in the land. The men of Tiberias were looked up to as authorities in this their chosen field. They accounted themselves carriers of a tradition ascending to Ezra the scribe; at the end they were recruited almost from one family. The last and most renowned member of this group, whose rulings were accepted by the entire West, was Aaron son of Moses son of Asher, an older contemporary of Saadiah.

It is significant that in matters pertaining to the letter of Scripture the Babylonian Amoraim deferred to the Palestinians. 'They are experts, we are not.' Another point about which the Palestinian scholars were sensitive was the regulation of the calendar. Anciently, of course, when the empirical method prevailed of accepting the evidence of any one who chanced to see the new moon in a clear sky, it had been the prerogative of the patriarchal court to sanctify the new moon. Similarly, when, owing to discrepancy between the solar and the lunar calendar, the vernal season would have occurred at too early a date, it had been the rule of the patriarch to postpone the Passover festival by intercalating a thirteenth month before Nisan. During the period when observation gave way to calculation, the intricacies of computation were still attended by mystery and the teachers of Babylonia betook themselves to Palestine to be instructed. As late as the year 835 the exilarch recognized as an ancient custom for the supreme lay ruler, in company with the heads of the schools, the scholars, and all Israel, to accept the calendar as sent out by the authorities in Palestine. But in the sequel, owing partly to the ascendancy of the Babylonian schools and partly to the uniformly established computation, the practice fell into disuse, and Babylonia made itself independent of the Holy Land.

In the first quarter of the tenth century, Palestine witnessed a revival of the higher schools of learning, and the masters, like their Babylonian colleagues, styled themselves Gaons. One such zealous dignitary, Aaron Ben Meir, conceived a small improvement in the calendar and sought to reëstablish the ancient authority of the mother country. Accordingly, in the autumn of the year 921, the rectified calendar was proclaimed, as had been the wont, from the Mount of Olives. The news reached Saadiah, who was then sojourning at Aleppo, and he immediately remonstrated with the Palestinian master by letter. Ben Meir had previously visited Bagdad and won the adherence of the master of Pumbeditha, Mebasser, by the support which he lent him against his rival Cohen-Zedek, who was the exilarch's choice. When Saadiah arrived on the scene, he found that the internal quarrel had been composed, and he was able to move the authorities to address a joint letter to the author of the new calendar. It was couched in civil terms, asking him to withdraw his proclamation that the coming Passover would fall on Sunday instead of Tuesday. However, Ben Meir would not yield; incriminations and recriminations passed between Babylonia and Palestine; the tone of the missives grew in sharpness. The holidays were actually celebrated on different days and the confusion created thereby was noticed even by non-Jews. Palestine kept insisting on its time-honored prerogative, and Babylonia urged the danger of disunion in the face of the rift between the Rabbanites and the Karaite schismatics.

The brunt of the battle was borne by Saadiah; he loved a combat, and he had it. He met invective by invective, though he forbore to descend to personal abuse such as his opponent heaped upon him and his. It mattered little that his former pupils in Egypt fell away from him and that in his new environment Ben Meir found supporters. Saadiah proved his mettle in this controversy, in which he demonstrated his vast learning and his grasp of an intricate subject. He had the ear of the exilarch and enjoyed his confidence. At the bidding of this dignitary the forceful protagonist of the prestige of the Babylonian schools composed a 'Book of Seasons' refuting the assertions of Ben Meir. It was written in biblical diction, and like the Bible was supplied with vowel and accent signs. Promulgated throughout the communities far and near, it was to be recited annually in the month preceding the new year. Ben Meir was worsted, and the prize of the victory was the elevation of Saadiah to the Sura Gaonate.

For two years all went well, but the blind counselor's forebodings proved true only too soon. The immediate occasion for the rupture between David son of Zaccai and Saadiah was a lawsuit which involved the settlement of a large estate. It seems that the exilarch was not quite disinterested in pronouncing judgment. In order to give validity to the verdict, the two Gaons were invited to countersign the document. Saadiah evasively directed the parties to the contest to secure first the signature of his colleague. The obsequious Cohen-Zedek complied, but Saadiah refused to affix his signature and on being importuned gave his reason. The exilarch became insistent. He repeatedly dispatched his son Judah with the peremptory request that the headstrong Gaon should subscribe his name. But neither entreaties nor threats were of avail. Once Judah admonished him to sign and not act as a fool; another time he raised his hand to strike the inflexible master and was unceremoniously put out. At last the exasperated head of the captivity deposed the Gaon and appointed Joseph son of Jacob Bar Satia to the vacant seat. Moreover, the ban was pronounced upon the recalcitrant master, who retaliated by issuing an order removing the exilarch and appointing his younger brother, Hasan (Josiah), to succeed him.

Whether it was that Hasan soon died or that the caliph, who was appealed to, sustained David, the unfortunate strife between the two opposing factions endured for seven years. The majority of the wealthy and prominent families, especially the Netira family, sided with Saadiah. The exilarch, however, was abetted by his friends, chief among whom was Aaron Ibn Sarjado, scholarly, ambitious, and enormously wealthy. Saadiah lived in retirement at Bagdad and utilized his enforced leisure to write some of his greatest works. At length the people wearied of the strife and, when the exilarch declined to sustain an appeal to Saadiah on the part of a Suran litigant and had him flogged, there was a universal clamor for peace. Bishr son of Aaron, Aaron's father-in-law, was prevailed upon to interfere. On the Fast of Esther of the year 937 the two adversaries were brought together, and they embraced. On the next day, Purim, Saadiah was a guest at the exilarchal mansion. He was reinstated in his office and cordial relations were restored. When David died (940) Saadiah used his influence to have his son Judah appointed exilarch. But Judah held the office for barely seven months when he died, leaving a boy of twelve years. Saadiah took the grandson of his erstwhile bitter enemy into his house and watched over him with fatherly care. Two years later (942) Saadiah passed away.

To posterity Saadiah was known as the first master in all the branches of Jewish learning. With him Jewish scholarship assumed a diversified aspect. He cultivated the Halakah and codified talmudic law, both civil and ritual. For the first time a systematic presentation was attempted with the subject-matter properly classified and the principles outlined in a deductive manner, the sources being left unindicated. He also wrote an Introduction to the Talmud. His order of Prayers embodied the rite of his native country and incorporated along with the ancient liturgical pieces the poetic (paitanic) hymns of Jose son of Jose, a Palestinian of the first half of the seventh century, and some original compositions. Saadiah was likewise acquainted with the productions of Jannai and of his celebrated pupil, Eleazar Kalir.

It was the habit of these poets and their imitators to embellish their productions with acrostics—forming the names of the author, or running over the letters of the alphabet in their order, as is the case even in certain parts of Scripture—and rhymes. Saadiah early in life composed a rhyming dictionary, intended to facilitate versification, which he called 'Assembler.' He tried his hand at versification of his own, as for example when he gathered up the six hundred and thirteen Commandments to be recited on the Festival of the Giving of the Law (Shabuoth), or composed a penitential poem for the Day of Atonement. But withal Saadiah, like the earlier authors of liturgical poems, was no poet. His construction is far too artificial and his diction labored, both characteristic of the age, with its unnatural taste for bizarre word-formations defying the rules of the structure of the Hebrew tongue. Yet Saadiah was the first to write a Hebrew Grammar, thus opening up a fruitful study which revolutionized the course of Jewish education and letters and marked a return to the Scriptures as the fountainhead of

Judaism. This work was done in a manner totally different from the crude groping after the past on the part of the Karaites.

Both by temperament and the vicissitudes of his career Saadiah was drawn to polemics. His 'Book of the Seasons' dates, as we have seen, from the time of his controversy with Ben Meir. His altercation with the exilarch gave rise to 'The Open Book' or 'The Book that Refutes,' in which, aside from the specific narrative of the unfortunate affair, he generalized on the evils of despotic rulership. In contrast to this he pointed out the providential order by which at critical periods a teacher appears in order to guide the people aright. A sceptical traducer of the Scriptures, Hayawaihi (Hiwi) of Balkh, who seems to have had a leaning towards Christian and Zoroastrian speculations and whose teachings found their way into the schools, met with refutation on the part of Saadiah in a book written some time before he was called to the Gaonate.

But the bitterest polemics were reserved for Anan and the writings of Saadiah's own contemporaries belonging to the Karaite persuasion. Early and late in life, by means of specific treatises and throughout his other writings, he waged war with the opponents of tradition. From the arsenal of the Gaon's polemics the succeeding generations borrowed their weapons in this everlasting warfare with Karaite adversaries, just as the Karaites ever after leveled their shafts at the redoubtable master-controversialist whose very name they held in execration. It seems probable that a treatise on Chronology by the Gaon was likewise aimed at offsetting Karaite attacks on the authority of tradition.

The epoch-making literary undertakings for which the Gaon is justly famed were his translation of the Scriptures into Arabic and his theological work in the defense of the cardinal truths of Judaism. The version of the Scriptures was accompanied in certain books or parts of books by a commentary. The translation was intended for the people, the Jews in the vast domain of Arab culture, and to this day it is read by Yemenite Jews. The forced interpretation, so often indulged in by the rabbis, was discarded. Thus ground was broken for a rational exposition. The work yielded stores of information to successive generations of Bible students. They were equally indebted to the Gaon for the happy suggestions in an independent treatise dealing with some ninety words which are found but once or rarely in the Bible, 'having neither brother nor friend,' but capable of being understood by the aid of the later Hebrew or the cognate Arabic.

Both his linguistic studies and his philosophic interests led Saadiah to expound the fantastic 'Book of Creation,' a product of early gaonic times which attaches mystic significance to letters and numbers. However, the crowning work, in which the Gaon brought to play all his many-sided powers, was his apology of Judaism as a system of faith, to which he gave the name of 'Beliefs (religious doctrines) and Opinions (based on rational, philosophic thinking).' The aim was clearly to link together the basic doctrines of Judaism as revealed in Scripture and the truths grounded on human reasoning. In terms of Mohammedan dogmatics, which supplied him with method and orientation, Saadiah was a rationalist thinker upon an orthodox basis, or an orthodox theologian given to rationalism. He presented a perfectly consistent system in which reason has its part and revelation is not impugned, in which the individual works out his destiny and corporate Israel reaches her goal. This work, like the majority of Saadiah's writings, was composed in the Arabic language and written in the Arabic script. Moslem theologians read and appreciated this theological treatise. Naturally it was studied as well by the Jewish readers, especially after it had been translated into Hebrew (under the title of 'Emunoth we-Deoth'); they were impressed by the positive tone and the harmonious welding together of religion and philosophy, of revelation and reason, in a work which was the first of its kind in the age of Arab-Jewish culture.

CHAPTER XLI

THE END OF THE BABYLONIAN SCHOOLS

(943-1038)

THE lustre which the brief administration of Saadiah shed upon the school at Sura could arrest only for a while the decline to which it was hastening. Saadiah's successor Joseph Bar Satia was a feeble match even for his colleague of Pumbeditha, Aaron son of Joseph Ibn Sarjado. This erstwhile opponent of the Fayumite, through his wealth and influence, mounted the seat vacated by Sherira's father, Hananiah son of Judah (943). Aaron, as Sherira reports, did not belong to the class of scholars, but to that of merchants. Though he had been ordained by Mebasser, he was much inferior to Amram, the brother of Sherira's mother, who was set aside through intimidation. Aaron bore himself magisterially and would brook no contradiction from his subordinates. Dissatisfaction was rife, and Nehemiah son of Cohen-Zedek led a revolt against the overbearing master, charging him with untruthfulness, gross peculation in the administration of the school funds, favoritism towards fawning students, and general malfeasance.

The exilarch Solomon (David's grandson) stepped in to recover in part at least the moneys received from Spain and diverted by Aaron to his own uses. Conditions were exceedingly precarious. One province after the other had fallen away from the empire and was in the hands of independent rulers. The capital was a prey to masterful chiefs who made of the caliphs mere puppets. The country was ravaged, and the Jewish seat of learning found itself shorn of its landed property and practically dependent upon pious gifts from abroad. 'Naught is left to us,' complains a scholar at this time, 'but the writings of our fathers.' Nor was the internal strife calculated to improve conditions. Aaron and Nehemiah had each his following; many thought the former the worthier of the two men. Upon the death of Aaron (960), Nehemiah succeeded him. Sherira alone stood out in withholding recognition, though he held on to his office as president of the court which placed him next in rank.

When Nehemiah passed away in 968, Sherira mounted the chief seat which his father and grandfather had occupied before him. For thirty years he labored assiduously to check the collapse now ominously threatening. He had himself lent a willing hand to the planting of the Torah in the lands toward the going down of the sun. But he justly contended that the parent institutions in the East must not be crippled, 'for how could the body be healthy, if the head were hurt?' To such lengths had apparently gone the process of decentralization. Yet from the farthest corners queries in matters of law were addressed to the Gaon, and he followed implicitly the rulings of the Talmud. The homilies (haggadahs) of the rabbis, however, he considered less binding; they were to be accepted only when supported by reason and Scripture.

As if to render account of a period now closing, in reply to a request of the Kairawan community (p. 280), Sherira composed the justly famed Epistle bearing his name in which he delineated the origins of Mishnah and Talmud. With masterly erudition, aided by the school archives, the Gaon established the unbroken succession of the bearers of Tradition from the remote beginnings down to his own day. After a lapse of centuries, in the face of the rift between the upholders of Tradition and their Scripturist antagonists, Jewish historiography was resumed, and Sherira's chronicle served as a source and model for many future undertakings.

Sherira had his enemies who denounced him to the caliph Kadir. The aged Gaon and his son Hai, whom he had placed as next in rank, were cast into prison and their property was confiscated; through the intervention of friends they were released. Sherira, broken in health, retired in favor of his son in 998, and after a few years he passed away at the age of almost one hundred. On the sabbath of Hai's installation a signal honor was paid to father and son in that, by suitable selections from the Scriptures, it was brought home to the people that 'the God of the spirits of all flesh' had set in the seat of the retired master as worthy a successor as Joshua had been to Moses, or Solomon to King David.

The Sura school had meanwhile been reopened and was presided over first by Zemah son of Isaac and then by Samuel son of Hophni, a grandson of Cohen-Zedek. At first there was friction between him and Sherira, but shortly before the latter's death peace had been made, and it was sealed by Hai marrying a daughter of Samuel. It was agreed that all incoming gifts of money, unless a preference was specified by the donors, should be divided equally between the two schools. Samuel followed in the footsteps of Saadiah and rendered the Scriptures anew into Arabic. The version was likewise accompanied by a commentary which, though striving after the simple sense, was rather verbose and frequently wandered away from the immediate subject. Samuel was succeeded by Saadiah's aged son Dosa who held the office for a brief period (1013–1017). Others followed him, but by the middle of the eleventh century the ancient foundation created by Rab had practically ceased to exist after an activity of eight centuries. It is possible that it was transferred to Egypt.

Nor did the Pumbeditha or rather Bagdad school long outlive the sister institution. Hai was the last Gaon of eminence, worthily summing up a creative period in the life of the Jewish people. Like his father, he attained a hoary age, and for forty years (998–1038) he disseminated knowledge among near disciples and inquirers from afar. He mastered many tongues: Hebrew, Aramaic, Arabic, Greek, and Persian, and he turned them all to good account in elucidating obscurities in Scripture or Talmud. He enjoyed the friendship of the head of the Eastern Church, who resided at Bagdad, and sought information from him as to how a difficult verse in the Bible was rendered in the Syriac version. He possessed erudition and a profound and incisive mind. His codification of the civil law of the Talmud was of fundamental importance for all posterity. We possess from his hand nearly a thousand answers to queries, and the range of subjects discussed is a most varied one, including matters of philosophical and theological moment. He laid down the rule, ever followed in after times, that when the Palestinian Talmud clashed with the Babylonian the latter alone was authoritative.

But what marks off Hai as the exponent of a new age is that with him began the series of commentators on a large scale. The literary works in which Tradition exhausted itself, Mishnah and Talmud above all, were felt to belong to a period quite remote. It was necessary to bring their sense home to latter generations by means of paraphrase and succinct, but nevertheless much needed elucidation. Hai was outstripped by more successful masters in the art of interpretation; but he had shown both the way and the need. He knew well how to distinguish between a talmudic ruling of binding force and a casual remark which must not be taken literally. He taught his followers to exercise tolerance towards the Karaites. When he passed away, a poet in far-off Spain mournfully lamented the loss of 'a pure body, a saintly heart, one resplendent like Moses.'

The exilarch Hezekiah, a descendant of David son of Zaccai, took over the Gaonate. But the Babylonian center had by this time been eclipsed. Other centers had arisen or were in the process of formation. The creative work of Babylonian Jewry was done. Its achievements passed on as a heritage to the communities of the West. In the halls of learning of northern Africa and Europe reverberated the discussions of Rab and Samuel, of Rabbah and Joseph, of Abaye and Raba. There men rehearsed codes and commentaries and theological treatises of the Gaons of Sura and Pumbeditha, who had blazed the path and given direction to Jewish life for centuries to come.

CHAPTER XLII

THE KAIRAWAN COMMUNITY

(700-1050)

ALL along the northern coast of Africa, not merely in Egypt, Jewish settlements sprang up in the wake of the Mohammedan conquest. The foremost community gathered in the capital of the eastern province (Ifrikiya), in the city of luxuriant gardens and olive groves founded by Ukba Ibn Nafi in 673 and named by him Kairawan (The Camp). Here the Aghlabid princes ruled from 800 to 908 in nominal dependence on the Abbasid caliphs. When the Fatimites established their empire over the whole of North Africa, they removed the seat of government to Egypt. In 972, they turned over the western provinces (including Maghreb, previously in the hands of the Idrisids) to the native dynasty of the Zirids. About 1050 Muizz the Zirid transferred his quite nominal allegiance to the Abbasids, thus inviting constant raids from the Fatimites. In 1148 the Zirid dynasty was extinguished by Roger I. of Sicily, who established his authority over all the Tunisian coast.

Jewish settlers were drawn to the flourishing capital early in its history. By the middle of the eighth century there was an organized community very much alive to spiritual interests. From the times of Jehudai Gaon (760–764) on, almost every Gaon of eminence, whether of Sura or of Pumbeditha, was consulted by this African community on a variety of subjects, mostly of course of a religious character. The Babylonian masters spoke of the men of Kairawan as a group in whom Torah and wisdom, Jewish and secular learning were singularly blended. The community maintained relations also with Egypt and Palestine, with Spain and Italy. Pious gifts were forwarded to the Babylonian schools as well as to those in the Holy Land.

At the head of the community stood a lay dignitary, who had the title of Nagid (princely leader) and who, in addition to supervising the internal affairs, acted as his people's spokesman at court. Such a one, in the first half of the eleventh century, was Abraham son of Nathan Ibn Ata, a highly respected physician, who hailed from Apulia (in Italy) and to whom the Gaon Hai addressed a versified epistle; during the lifetime of this Gaon another Nagid, Jacob son of Amram, presided over the community. The spiritual affairs and the higher education were in the hands of learned men who achieved fame in their own day and won for themselves an abiding place in the forward movement of Jewish letters. The high standing of the community induced the exilarch Ukba, when he was driven from Bagdad through the machinations of the ambitious Gaon of Pumbeditha, Cohen-Zedek II. (917–936), to seek shelter in Kairawan. He was received with high honors and a seat was prepared for him in the synagogue next to the Ark.

Some forty years earlier another visitor was entertained by the Jews of Kairawan. Eldad son of Mahli the Danite alleged that he was a descendant of the tribe of Dan. He related that this tribe had emigrated from their Palestinian home so as not to take part in the civil war at the time of Jeroboam's secession, and were residing in the land of Havilah beyond the rivers of Ethiopia. Three other tribes, Naphtali, Gad, and Asher, were with them; these had joined them in the times of Sennacherib. Opposite them lived the Children of Moses, sprung from those Levites who had mutilated the fingers of their right hand rather than to sing the songs of Zion by the rivers of Babylon and had then been translated by a cloud to their present abode. His own people, so Eldad continued, were able to communicate with them only from afar, since they were cut off from one another by a waterless torrent which carried masses of sand and rubble with such terrific force that it could crush an iron mountain. This impassable river rested on the sabbath day, when it was enveloped in a thick mist; hence the river was named Sambation.

The four tribes were made up of brave warriors and, alternately for three months in the year, each tribe was under arms in order to ward off enemy attacks, if necessary also on the sabbath. They were ruled by a common king and a common chief judge; when Eldad left his home, the one bore the name Uzziel (or Adiel), while the other was named Abdon. They exercised criminal jurisdiction even when it involved capital punishment. When not busy with warfare, they occupied themselves with the study of the Torah. They had the entire body of Scriptures barring Esther and Lamentations. They knew neither of Mishnah nor of Talmud; but they had a Talmud of their own in which all the laws were cited in the name of Joshua son of Nun as he had received them at the hands of Moses. Eldad exhibited a Ritual dealing mostly with the rules pertaining to the killing of animals for food. It was written in a Hebrew containing many strange expressions with a slight Arabic coloring, though Eldad himself professed that he knew no other tongue but Hebrew, in which alone he conversed.

Eldad was given a hearing in the presence of the spiritual and lay leaders of the Kairawan community, and he regaled his audience with a weird story of his adventures. He told how the boat he traveled on was shipwrecked, how he found himself among cannibals and how by cunning he escaped, how then he chanced upon the other remnants of the ten tribes, until at last he found himself in Egypt. It is probable enough that in his narrative much fancy was intermixed with reality and that possibly he had come across an isolated Jewish settlement in some outlying corner. The Gaon Zemah son of Hayim in Sura (882–887) was appealed to and the answer was cautious but on the whole reassuring. He pointed out that ritual differences might be expected and that some should be charged to a lapse of memory on the part of the sorely tried traveler. But withal he exhorted the African brethren to adhere steadfastly to the traditions of the Babylonian schools. Eldad's ritual continued nevertheless to be cited by scholars of repute in the subsequent ages. His account of the existence of other tribes of Israel sustained in many Jews the hope of a complete restoration.

In the times of Saadiah (p. 265) his fellow-countryman Isaac Israeli was court physician to the Aghlabid prince Ziyadat-Allah III. (903–909). In the same capacity Israeli ministered to the Fatimite prince Ubaidallah al-Mahdi (910–934), when he set himself in the place of the overthrown dynasty, and to his successors. Israeli was present at the death-bed of Manzur (935); shortly thereafter he passed away himself in extreme old age. He had never married and said once by way of pleasantry that his learned works on medicine would keep his memory alive far more effectively than son or daughter. He did not overestimate his merits; his treatises on fevers and dietetics were highly prized and were made accessible in Europe through Latin translations. He was spoken of as a monarch in the realm of medicine. Among his disciples one was a Mohammedan, the other a coreligionist by the name of Abu Sahl Dunash (Adonim) son of Tamim, who hailed from Babylonia. He was likewise employed as a physician by Manzur, to whom he dedicated a work on astronomy in which principles of astrology were refuted. He also wrote a commentary on the Book of Creation and a treatise on Hebrew grammar.

Jacob son of Nissim son of Josiah, to whom Sherira addressed his famous Chronicle-Epistle (p. 274), founded a school for talmudic learning and had many disciples. One of them, Joseph son of Berechiah, acted as assistant master and was highly respected by Hai and his father-in-law Samuel son of Hophni, with both of whom he corresponded. Another school was founded by Hushiel son of Elhanan. This scholar came from Italy and was on his way to Egypt to join a friend, Shemariah son of Elhanan, who had formerly studied at Pumbeditha and was now presiding over a school at Fustat. While waiting for his son to join him, Hushiel yielded to the entreaties of the Kairawan community to remain with them. Hushiel, it seems, did little writing; at any rate no literary remains have come to light. But such was his impress upon his generation that his death was pub-

licly mourned in the Spanish communities. Samuel ha-Nagid
(p. 315), who had maintained a literary correspondence with
the Kairawan scholar, addressed a consolatory letter to his
son Hananel, who worthily filled his father's place.

The son was more fortunately situated than the father in
that he possessed great wealth. He commanded still greater
riches of the spirit. Three streams of learned tradition united
in him: the eastern or Babylonian, principally through the
writings of Hai to whose authority he markedly deferred, the
European in which he was reared by his father, and the
Palestinian with which the Italians had always been in
touch. Hananel survived the Babylonian Gaon—he was
still alive in 1053—and it is as carrier of a tradition dried up
at its source that posterity valued him most, confident that
any remark of his rested on an authentic background. He
wrote in Hebrew; his diction was simple and concise. It was
known that both he and his father used in their school copies
of the Talmud which were free from the corruptions dis-
figuring the text in more distant localities.

Hananel wrote a commentary on the Talmud with verbal
explanations, but mainly with a view to simplifying the
intricate talmudic discussions and arriving at conclusions
for the guidance of practice. This work, which he modeled
after the commentaries of the Babylonian Geonim, met one
of the greatest needs of the time, facilitating as it did the
study and the understanding of the Talmud. Hananel served
in this respect as a model for the epitomizers who followed.
His attitude toward the Haggadah was a rational one, and
he averred that there was nothing in the Talmud to suggest
ascription of bodily form to God. Like Saadiah, he relied
upon a combination of reason, Scripture, and Tradition; his
explanatory notes on the Bible—on some books he wrote an
extended commentary—stressed the simple sense.

Side by side with Hananel labored Jacob's son, Nissim.
He had enjoyed the double advantage of being taught both
by Hushiel and by his own father, and was also profoundly
influenced by the writings of the Gaon Hai. His sound learning was recognized and his school attracted students from

Spain. Samuel ha-Nagid hailed him as a veritable Gaon; the friendship which linked the two men was further cemented when the Nagid's son, Joseph, married a daughter of Nissim. On the occasion of these nuptials the Kairawan master visited Granada and a number of younger scholars came under his influence, among them the poet Ibn Gabirol (p. 318), who accounted himself a pupil 'in whose heart the master dwelt.' Nissim, who wrote in Arabic, united secular erudition with talmudic learning. His principal work was a 'Key to the Talmud' with a view to assembling parallel passages bearing on a given statement and with attention to the methodology of talmudic disputation. Like Hananel, he had an eye for correct readings.

Neither Hananel nor Nissim left sons to take their places. The voice of Torah and wisdom was hushed, and the community itself soon crumbled away in consequence of Mohammedan fanaticism, which ruled that none might enter Kairawan, the holiest city in Africa, who was not a Moslem. But in the eleventh century there were other Jewish communities in northwestern Africa beside that in Kairawan. Thus Jews lived in Cabes, Tahert, Tlemcen, Fez, Sijilmasa, for the most part in organized communities, with courts for internal jurisdiction, schools, and men of learning.

Some, if not all of these communities, had come into existence a good deal earlier. Thus Tahert was the birthplace of the grammarian Judah Ibn Kuraish; an older contemporary of Saadiah, he had dealings with the fantastic Eldad the Danite. In an epistle addressed to the community of Fez, among whom he came to dwell, he stressed the importance of a knowledge of the Aramaic tongue in which the Targum was written. He pointed out the similarity in structure and in vocabulary between that language, the Hebrew, and the Arabic, thus laying the foundation for fruitful researches in the period immediately following and throughout the ensuing centuries down to our own days. Fez was the birthplace of the epitomizer Isaac al-Fasi (p. 322), whose activity, however, was chiefly exercised in Spain. Before we trace the history of Spanish Jewry, to whom those of northern Africa were closely knitted, we may cast a glance at the Italian communities, which likewise were drawn into relations with Africa at the height of its Jewish life and which, in Europe, antedated every other Jewish settlement.

BOOK III

THE WEST-EUROPEAN CENTERS TO THE EXPULSION FROM SPAIN

139 BEFORE TO 1492 AFTER THE CHRISTIAN ERA

CHAPTER XLIII

THE JEWS OF ITALY TO THE END OF THE EMPIRE

(139 BEFORE—410 AFTER THE CHRISTIAN ERA)

The earliest Jewish settlement in Italy was located in Rome. As early as the second century before the Christian era there were temporary Jewish residents in the city. In the year 139, a number of Jews, possibly those who came in the train of the embassy sent by Simon the Maccabee (p. 150), were expelled from Rome. It was reported that they had sought to infect the Romans with their own cult. So little did the defenders of the Roman religion know about Judaism that they confounded Sabaoth (Lord of hosts, Almighty) with a Phrygian (Thracian) deity of a name sounding somewhat similarly (Sabazius).

But the decree of expulsion was soon forgotten. Certainly in the early decades of the first pre-Christian century a considerable number of Jews lived in Rome and other cities of Italy; annually they dispatched their Temple dues to Jerusalem. A still larger increase in the Jewish population was brought about by Pompey's conquest of Jerusalem (63), when numerous captives were carried to Rome to be led in the triumphal procession of the victorious general. There they were sold into slavery, but soon regained their freedom. Their steadfast cleaving to their ancestral mode of life proved inconvenient to their masters, and the older residents of their own faith were only too eager to redeem them. As freedmen (libertini) they became Roman citizens; they soon constituted an important group, inhabiting a quarter across the Tiber (Trastevere). Here, near the landing place of Phoenician and Greek ships, there resided all the petty traders and shopkeepers doing business with the sailors.

The native Romans, torn by party strife, were impressed with the sense of solidarity among the Jewish colony. The importance, real or imaginary, which the Jews appeared to

287

acquire in the popular assemblies, irritated Cicero, the leader of the substantial burgesses. When in 59 he defended Flaccus, who among other things had diverted to his own use moneys collected by the Jews of Asia Minor for the Temple, the adroit pleader pretended that he must not speak above a whisper lest the enmity of the numerous Jews present should be aroused. It was quite natural for these new citizens to range themselves on the side of the popular party, and when the old constitution gave way under the impact of Caesar, the Jews everywhere rallied to his support.

In the new order of things that was preparing, the Jewish element, in consequence of world-wide diffusion, fitted into the imperialistic state in which national distinctions were leveled so as to make room for a world-embracing humanity. The dictator understood the peculiar religious position of the Jewish people; at the bidding of Hyrcanus II. (p. 164), he guaranteed to the Jews of the empire freedom to form religious associations and to forward their contributions to the Temple at Jerusalem. They were exempted from military service, since they could not bear arms or march on the sabbath, nor was it lawful for them to partake of forbidden food. They were not subject to Roman jurisdiction in civil suits between one Jew and another. When Caesar was assassinated on the Ides of March in the year 44, the Jews mourned deeply; in Rome they gathered by night to weep over his funeral pile.

The privileges accorded by him, in what has been called rightly a veritable 'Great Charter,' were confirmed by Augustus, who otherwise was not favorably disposed toward the Jews. At the instigation of Sejanus, the emperor Tiberius expelled the Jews from Rome and Italy in the year 19 of the Christian era. The occasion was a fraudulent transaction on the part of some unscrupulous Jews who had obtained large sums of money from a noble proselyte lady under the pretense that this money would be forwarded as a gift to the Temple at Jerusalem. The size of the Roman community may be gauged from the fact that four thousand Jews, capable of bearing arms, were deported to Sardinia, there to combat the brigands. As many as refused to do service on the sabbath submitted to heavy punishments. In 31, when Sejanus was removed from office, the Jews were allowed to return; by the time of Caligula (37–41) a substantial community had gathered again in the capital. Claudius (41–54) began his reign with a general edict of toleration for the Jews. Towards the end of his reign, however, owing to disturbances created by Jewish opposition to the Christian propagandists, gatherings in the synagogues were forbidden and as a consequence many Jews left Rome. But that was only a temporary measure. The community, though again and again repressed, grew apace in number and power and achieved complete liberty to live its own religious life.

Contemptuous as was the attitude of the intellectuals among the Romans toward the Jewish people, which they dubbed execrable, and toward the Jewish religion, in which they saw an outlandish superstition, the very Jewish rites which they described as bizarre and morose fascinated wide circles of Roman society. Writers scorned Jewish abstention from pork, the strict observance of the sabbath, and the imageless worship of God, embellishing their accounts of this strange people with puerile myths and malicious slander. The emperors strove with might and main to prop up the crumbling pagan religion. Nevertheless the appeal of the Jewish system of morals, anchored in the veneration of the One and Holy God, attracted many converts. Whatever the regulations with which Judaism was hedged about—a substantial part did not apply outside Palestine—at the core was the prophetic sublimation of the Jewish truth. This pointed beyond the confines of Jewish nationality and offered itself as a light to those without.

The propaganda drew its strength mainly from the sheer consistency with which the Jews clung to their faith and the effect exerted by their pure worship. It gathered further potency from the fact that the Jews held it a duty to bring the willing outsider under the wings of the Divine Presence. From earliest times the synagogues had been visited by Romans. Many attached themselves with varying degrees of intensity, ranging from casual observance of one or the other rite to complete fusion with the Jewish community. The greater number renounced polytheism and image worship, frequented the synagogue, abstained from forbidden food, and kept the sabbath. Such were known as 'they who feared God.' But now and again, either outright or by gradual steps, men and women were admitted to full membership in the household of Israel by submitting to the prescribed initiatory rites and by accepting the whole of Jewish religious life. These were called 'proselytes (of righteousness).' Frequently enough a parent remained on the fringe, while the children became full Jews.

Those who knocked at the doors of Judaism were not all of lowly station. Fulvia, in the times of Tiberius, was a senator's wife; the proselyte Flavius Clemens was a nephew of the emperor Domitian; the empress Poppea, wife of Nero, was favorably disposed toward Judaism and a friend of the Jewish people. Often the converts assumed Hebrew names; thus Beturia Paulina, who turned Jewess at the age of seventy, was renamed Sarah, and such was her zeal for the new faith that the title of 'synagogue mother' was conferred on her. The youthful Aemilius Valens, who died at the age of fifteen years a semi-convert, was of the order of knights. In many a Roman home were the sabbath lights kindled; thus, as Seneca grudgingly admitted, 'the vanquished imposed their laws upon the victors.'

Neither the crushing blow which fell upon the Jewish people in the year 70 nor the cruel severity with which the convulsions at home and abroad were put down by Trajan (p. 211) and Hadrian (p. 214) could break the Jewish will to live. Jews, outside Palestine, who enjoyed Greek or Roman citizenship, continued in their previous status. It was recognized that Judaism was a matter of birth and that the Jewish religious organization partook of an ethnic character. From the times of Caracalla (p. 224), all distinctions between the Jews at home and abroad fell away. Moreover, Alexander Severus (222–235) emphatically confirmed the Jews in their privileges so as to safeguard their separate existence.

They were free to live their own life, though they were thrown back upon themselves and a halt was called upon their missionary activity.

A far more galling humiliation which rested upon the people was the special poll-tax which all Jews of the empire were ordered to pay to the temple of Jupiter Capitolinus. This took the place of the annual contribution of half a shekel which it had been their wont to send to their own Temple at Jerusalem. Not only was Jewish sentiment outraged, but the ordinance, rigorously enforced, led to mean persecutions at the hands of informers. These outrages were stopped by Nerva (96–98), but the tax continued to be levied even in the times of the Christian emperors, until it was abolished by Julian the Apostate (p. 229). However, the Jews were permitted to collect and forward contributions for the maintenance of the patriarchate in Palestine.

After the wars with Rome Jewish captives who escaped with their lives were speedily ransomed. The community was thus considerably enlarged, despite the falling off of proselytes, the missionary activity having been arrested by the steady progress of Christianity. The gradual enlargement of the community made it necessary for Jewish residents to spread beyond the original quarter. During the reign of Domitian a second Jewish quarter had sprung up outside the gate of Capena along the Appian Way. This settlement extended as far as the Grove of Egeria. There the greater number of Jews resided during the times of the empire; they were to be found also in the Martian Field and in the Subura clear to the Esquiline.

Outside Rome and its immediate environs, by the beginning of the Christian era at the latest, Jews had settled in Puteoli, the chief port for commerce between Italy and the Orient; Pompeii, had Jewish inhabitants when in 79 of the Christian era it was buried beneath the lava and cinders from Mount Vesuvius. In late imperial times Jews were thickly settled in lower Italy; thus in the fourth century it was impossible in many localities of Apulia and Calabria to fill the municipal offices regularly since the Jews refused to serve. Jews were to be found in the sixth century at Venusia (Venosa, the birthplace of Horace), also in Tarentum, Capua, and Naples, and in all the large cities of Sicily, as Syracuse, Palermo, Agrigentum; so also in the larger cities of upper Italy, as Ravenna, Aquileia, Bologna, Brescia, Milan, Genoa.

The great mass of the people, especially in the pioneer days, lived by petty trade as they hawked their baskets of wares through the streets; Jewish women offered to interpret dreams for the smallest of coins. Mendicants thronged about the synagogues begging alms of those more fortunately placed. There were artisans, butchers and bakers, makers of garments, weavers. Others were painters, sculptors, actors (Alityrus, Faustina). Jews owned land and tilled the soil. Some grew opulent by engaging in the shipping trade, by importing grain, by banking, by trafficking in slaves. A number of Jews took to soldiering. But when the Christian Church became dominant, the vexatious laws and the animosity of the clergy made for insecurity of Jewish fortunes; Christians were bidden to refrain from patronizing Jewish merchants. Jewish energy was sapped or borne down by local persecutions, and the harassed Jew was forced again and again to seek newer and safer domiciles. These very migrations threw the Jews back upon international commerce, and the densest Jewish settlements were along the frontiers whence they could always pass on to calmer quarters away from the raging fury of excited mobs.

From the start the Jewish mode of life in the capital contrasted very sharply with the ever growing luxuriousness and moral decadence of the native Romans. The Jews were industrious, moderate in eating and drinking, charitable, peaceable. The family life was pure, excesses were rare and touched only the fringe; husbands and wives, parents and children, brothers and sisters loved each other ardently. Girls were married off quite young—at the age of fifteen or so. Widows frequently remarried; a woman was prized when she had passed her life in single marriage and was lamented by the husband of her youth.

The language spoken by the Jews was Greek and at a later period Latin, though the Hebrew and Aramaic which they had brought with them were not suffered to slip away entirely. The names found on tumular inscriptions are for the most part Greek or Latin, very few are Hebrew or distinctly Jewish; sometimes Jewish children were given two names, one Jewish and the other Roman. Often father and son, mother and daughter went by the same name; a daughter would be given a name corresponding to that of the father and a son one answering to that of the mother; generally, however, grandsons were named after their grandfathers.

The religious training of the children was an object of assiduous care. When in the year 95 the patriarch Gamaliel (p. 207) and three other scholars visited Rome, they encountered on the way from the port a group of children playing with sandpiles, one of which they called 'the priests' heave' and the other 'the Levites' tithe,' exactly as their fathers had done in Judea with the piles of produce. The ceremonial laws were strictly observed, the sabbath rest and the dietary injunctions rigorously kept; the prescribed fasts were respected; the festivals were occasions of joy, and in the poorest home savory dishes were served. On the night of the Passover it was the custom of the Jews in Rome to partake of a roast lamb prepared according to the prescriptions observed in Temple times; though the scholars in Palestine demurred, the custom, introduced by Theudas, a teacher noted for learning and piety, remained in force.

There were numerous synagogues in the city; the newcomers naturally clung to their immediate circles; nevertheless it frequently occurred that a person held membership in several synagogues. These synagogues were named after emperors or other distinguished Romans to whom the communities were indebted for gracious acts of benevolence. One such synagogue, named after the emperor Alexander Severus, had a Torah scroll which was prized as having come from Jerusalem down to late medieval times. Other synagogues received their appellations from the locality in which they were situated; still others marked off their membership as Hebrew speaking, or native, or recruited from a certain craft (as for example the synagogue of the lime burners). The fiscal administration of each synagogue was in the hands of executive officers (archons, gabbaim) each of whom had charge of a distinct branch (the treasury, the care of the poor, and so on) and served as a rule from year to year. Sometimes they held office for life and the position tended more and more to become hereditary. The archons were chosen from the body of elders, the trusted leaders in each congregation, presided over by a chief (parnas). The person who supervised the service and often preached on sabbaths was known as the 'head of the synagogue' (archisynagogus, rosh ha-keneseth); an attendant (hazzan) performed the subordinate tasks.

The communities maintained scribes (sopherim) who wrote out the scrolls and such legal documents as deeds of sale, marriage contracts, bills of divorcement, and the like. These men were held in high honor and often belonged to the best families; frequently the son followed his father in this profession. There were schools for higher learning, and the disciples listened eagerly to addresses by visiting scholars; there were also distinguished native teachers spoken of as rabbis. The founder of Jewish learning in Rome was apparently Matthiah son of Heresh who emigrated from Palestine at the onset of the Hadrianic persecution. As he landed on Italian soil, he rent his garments and shed tears at the remembrance of the Holy Land which he reluctantly forsook. His residence in Rome led to the establishment of a communal court of justice to deal with internal disputes, and he labored zealously to advance the religious conditions in his new home by teaching and by preaching.

Beside the synagogues, other communal institutions were maintained. Public baths were kept up for ritual purification in accordance with prescribed regulations. Each community had its own place for burial. These cemeteries, some of them recently discovered, were constructed under ground (catacombs). A deep shaft would be sunk and then galleries opened with recesses for the entombment of the dead. As a gallery was filled, another and a third were opened still further below. The tombs were closed with slabs of stone, marked with inscriptions and ornamental representations. The former were composed in Greek or Latin, with an occasional Hebrew phrase (as 'Peace be upon Israel'); the latter consisted of reproductions of Jewish symbols, such as the seven-branched candlestick, palm branches, the Ark, and the like, but also of all sorts of animal figures. The chambers which served for family graves were decorated with paintings of mythological figures in which even the human form was not absent. Thus the Jews of Rome had absorbed the culture of their environment, so much so that in indicating the time of death of their departed they made use of the Roman calendar. Ever after it remained a mark of the upper class of Italian Jewry that they were orthodox Jews and cultured men at the same time.

As early as the times of Augustus a rhetorician in Rome, Caecilius, was reputed to be of Jewish descent; together with his friend Dionysius of Halicarnassus he belonged to the earliest stylists who affected purism in diction after the manner of the classical period ('Atticists'). A far more prominent man of letters among the Roman Jews was Josephus. We have followed his career at home in Palestine as far as the termination of the war with Rome (66–70) in which he ignominiously betrayed his people. It remains to tell that he accompanied Titus to Rome and there basked in the sunshine of imperial favor. He accepted a pension and was domiciled in an imperial palace; in gratitude to the three Flavian emperors he surnamed himself Flavius. During thirty or more years of ample leisure he gave himself to literary work, by which he rendered a signal service to his people. In his 'Wars of the Jews,' it is true, he strove to flatter the conqueror and cold-bloodedly narrated the triumphal procession which he witnessed. But at least he thought that he was serving the Jewish people by shifting the blame for the catastrophe to irresponsible fanatics. In this view he knew himself at one with Agrippa and other Jewish dignitaries who espoused the victorious cause.

More effectively did Josephus defend the Jewish name against the slanders of the Alexandrian schoolmaster Apion and his coterie of Jew-baiters. He was truest to Jewish sentiment, which neither the veneer of Greek learning nor his Roman prepossessions could stifle, in the 'Antiquities of the Jews,' in which work he invested the long history of his people, from the first to the last, with a halo of veneration. Such weaknesses as this historical work contains must be judged by the standards of the time. There is no need to quarrel with his rhetorical embellishments of the biblical history nor with his practice of excerpting his predecessors. He had a wide range of information, and but for him a good part of the Jewish history nearer his own day would remain unknown. Certainly the historical work of his rival, Justus of Tiberias, who appears to have presented the Jewish side in the contest with Rome, would have stood us in better stead had it only been preserved; apparently it was not to the liking of the Roman world nor of the Christian monks who found in the detached Josephus a more kindred spirit. Altogether, Josephus was rooted in the broad cosmopolitan ideas of the Dispersion.

CHAPTER XLIV

THE JEWS OF ITALY DOWN TO THE
TWELFTH CENTURY

(410-1140)

THE treasures of the Temple which had been carried
to Rome fell into the hands of Alaric, when with
his Visigoths he sacked the city in the year 410.
What remained of the Temple vessels was taken to Carthage
by the Vandals when they in turn sacked Rome in 455.
Twenty years later Odoacer put an end to the western
empire. Under the tutelage of the emperor of the east he
made himself king of Italy. His reign was of short duration;
the Italian kingdom was wrested from his hands in 489 by
Theodoric, king of the Ostrogoths. Nominally the kingdom
acknowledged the supremacy of the emperor at Constantinople. The Ostrogoths, however, being Arian, were tolerant. In an edict, issued in 500, Theodoric confirmed the
Jews in their ancient privileges and granted them internal
jurisdiction in civil suits. Repeatedly the king protected the
Jews and their synagogues against encroachments by the
Catholic clergy and from mob violence.

The Gothic kingdom fell before the onslaught of Justin·
ian's generals, Belisarius and Narses. The Jews of Naples
defended the city bravely, side by side with their Gothic
neighbors. At length all-Italy was conquered (555); an imperial lieutenant (exarch) was established at Ravenna and
the chief provincial cities were ruled by Greek dukes subordinate to him. The Code of Justinian was promulgated
throughout Italy, supplanting that of Theodoric. This code,
with all its severities toward the Jews, remained in force in
all parts of the land and on the island of Sicily until the
Saracen invasion and greatly affected the legal status of the
Jews all through the Middle Ages. The rule of the Lombards
(566–774), at first Arian, later converted to orthodoxy, was
at no time complete; large parts of the country remained

unsubdued. With the emperor too far away to offer assistance, there ensued a general political break-up in which many cities attained a degree of independence. The conditions were favorable for the bishops of Rome to rear the stupendous structure of spiritual supremacy in western Europe and of temporal power in Rome and gradually also in certain other parts of Italy.

Gregory I., surnamed the Great (590–604), 'the real father of the medieval papacy,' typified in his treatment of the Jews that attitude which on the whole marked the policy of his successors in the seat of St. Peter. He had no liking for Judaism, which meant to him 'Jewish depravity;' the Jewish method of understanding Scripture in its literalness was a 'perverse' one; the Jewish arguments against Christianity were 'nonsense.' The Jews should be won over to Christianity by reason and gentle persuasion; willing converts were to be offered inducements and protected against molestation by their former coreligionists. Forcible measures must not be used, for he who is thus led to baptism will at the first opportunity revert to his earlier 'superstitious' beliefs. The Jews should therefore be suffered to practise their own religion and live in accordance with the rights granted to them by the Roman Law. But under no circumstances should they be permitted to acquire and keep Christian slaves or Christian employees; such slaves as were held by them on their estates might remain as tenants bound to the soil. A certain Jew, by the name of Basilius, who had his sons baptized, that they might claim his Christian slaves as their own, was strictly enjoined that these must under no circumstances live in his house. They might minister to him, however, to the extent that his sons were bound by their filial duty to attend on him. Not that Gregory frowned upon the institution of slavery as such, for he himself had Anglo-Saxon slaves purchased in the market for ecclesiastical service. He merely thought it unseemly that Jews should bear rule over Christians.

The see of Rome acquired new authority through the compact with the Frankish kings whom the popes called

in against the Lombards, just as the latter had previously
been played off against the Greeks. The compact was sealed
by the coronation of Charlemagne at Rome in 800. The
south of Italy, however, continued under Byzantine rule. In
827 Sicily was occupied by the Saracens, and they held the
island together with certain dominions across the straits
for more than two centuries. In 982 Mohammedan Sicily
was threatened by emperor Otto II. It is reported that when
the emperor, who had lost his horse, was in danger of capture
by the Saracens, a faithful Jew bade him mount his own
horse and flee for his life; the emperor escaped. The Saracen
rule was terminated in 1061 when Roger I. took Messina;
soon the whole of the island was his. His successor, Roger II.
(1101–1154), joined thereto the dominions on the mainland
acquired by his brother, Robert Guiscard. In 1130 Roger
was crowned king of Sicily and Italy by the authority of the
anti-pope Anacletus, of the Pierleoni family. This family
was of Jewish extraction, and this circumstance led to the
widely spread legend of a Jew on the papal throne.

From the fifth century on a more intense Jewish spirit
developed in the Italian communities. On the tombstone
inscriptions Greek and Latin gradually gave way to Hebrew
outright, or the Greek was expressed in Hebrew letters; the
years were counted as time went on from the destruction
of the Temple or the creation of the world. The communities
were led by learned men (rabbis); at Venosa a collegiate
institution (yeshibah) was presided over by Nathan son of
Ephraim (died in 846). Fresh impulses were coming from
Palestine and the Babylonian schools. Especially did these
influences manifest themselves in southern Italy: 'from Bari
went forth the law, and the word of the Lord from Otranto.'
It is here that Aaron of Bagdad is supposed to have taught
the occult mysteries of the Cabala and to have wrought
miracles. Among his disciples in other parts of Italy is said
to have been Calonymus of Lucca, whose descendants carried the master's teachings to Mayence, thus planting in
the Rhenish provinces the seed of learning which bore rich
fruit in after times.

Not less of a wonder-worker was another of Aaron's pupils, Shephatiah son of Amittai at Oria. He had shown early his gifts as an exorcist when he restored to sanity a daughter of the emperor Basil I. (867–886). The empress presented him with some of her own jewels. The grateful emperor, moreover, was ready to bestow on him cities and provinces. The healer, however, only begged that the cruel edict forbidding Jewish worship through the provinces of the empire might be revoked. Though the emperor could not be induced to take this step, Shephatiah secured at least for his own native city the freedom to practise Judaism. On this occasion he composed a penitential poem. 'Israel,' thus cried the poet, 'that was saved by the Lord with an everlasting salvation, may they be saved this day also at Thy word, O Thou that dwellest on high!' His son Amittai likewise wrote poems, on occasions of joy and of sorrow, as well as for the public service. A daughter, Cassia, was married to her cousin Hasadiah, who, together with nine other pious and scholarly members of the community, lost his life at the hands of the Saracens when in 923 they captured Oria.

Among his kindred was Sabbatai son of Abraham Donnolo (913–982), widely traveled and a student of astronomy and physics. His practice of medicine brought him into friendly relations with Saint Nilus and the prefect Eupraxius. He was the first European Jewish author known to us by name; he wrote a commentary on the 'Book of Creation' and a medical treatise. Around the same time an unknown Italian Jew wrote, in fluent Hebrew, under the name of Josippon, or Little Josephus, a digest of the history by Josephus brought up to date. It was read with great avidity by the generations that came after; for nearly one thousand years, almost all the information the Jews had concerning the events from Nehemiah to the destruction of the Second Temple was derived from that book. A great grandson of Hasadiah, Samuel son of Hananel (died in 1008), was collector of revenues and director of the mint at Capua; he erected synagogues and lavished benefactions upon his coreligionists.

To still higher eminence rose his cousin Paltiel; the Fatimite Muizz (953–975), the conqueror of Sicily, made him his vizir. In this capacity he aided his royal master in the seizure of Egypt, and when the caliph died he commended his faithful adviser, whom the Mohammedans knew by the name of Jauhar, to his son and successor Aziz (975–996). Paltiel, however, did not long survive his master; his body was taken by his son Samuel for burial to Jerusalem. Both father and son made pious donations with princely liberality and their names were held in veneration by their coreligionists at home and abroad. The record of this remarkable family was still fresh in 1054 when a grandson of Paltiel's cousin, Ahimaaz, penned the account of its achievements during two centuries.

Several compilations of homilies by the hands of unknown authors were produced in Italy during that period. Situated as the Italian Jewish communities were between Palestine, the Jewish settlements in Africa, and those to the north of the Alps, there was the opportunity for much give and take in spiritual possessions. Schools for the study of the Talmud arose everywhere, notably in Rome, and such were the high attainments of the masters that the far northern communities turned to them for information. In the eleventh century the school at Rome was presided over by Jehiel son of Abraham, who was ably assisted by his three sons, 'the three excellencies of the house of Jehiel.' Of these, Nathan rose to greatest fame. Taught by his father, he also sat at the feet of Mazliah Ibn al-Bazak in Sicily who had attended the courses of the Gaon Hai at Bagdad. At Narbonne in Provence Nathan was instructed by Moses the Preacher (p. 356) who commanded the wide range of ancient homiletical (haggadic) material.

Upon the death of his father (about 1070), Nathan conjointly with his brothers took over the headship of the Roman college. Here he completed in 1101 a great work which even to this day is prized highly by Semitic scholars. Until the nineteenth century it was virtually the only work of its kind. What al-Fasi in Spain (p. 322) did for epitomizing the legal matter of the Talmud, what Rashi in northern France (p. 357) accomplished for its elucidation, Nathan, the contemporary of both, achieved on the side of lexicography by his dictionary, to which he gave the name 'Aruk,' 'Set in order.' In this work he stored the entire linguistic material of Mishnah and Midrash, of the Talmuds and the Targums, in fact all of the Hebrew and Aramaic that had been written by Jews since the close of the Scriptures. What renders Nathan's effort worthy of the scholar's attention even now is the circumstance that behind the definitions there stands a tradition brought together from many sources, not the least among them being the responsa of the Geonim, the commentaries of Hananel of Kairawan (p. 281), and the works of the school of Gershom of Mayence (p. 354).

In the same year in which Nathan finished his Dictionary, a synagogue erected by himself and his younger brother was completed. Their nephew Solomon took Nathan's place as head of the college which still went by the grandfather's name. Solomon's colleague in the rabbinate was Menahem son of Judah, who together with his son Moses befriended Abraham Ibn Ezra when in 1140 he visited Rome. Thus Rome came into contact with Spanish Jewry.

CHAPTER XLV

THE JEWS OF SPAIN UNDER ROMANS, GOTHS, AND MOHAMMEDANS

(300-990)

THE peculiar romantic charm which attaches to Spain, the land and the people, geographically and historically, is also characteristic of Jewish history in the Iberian peninsula. What the Mohammedans called Andalus, the Jews called Sepharad, a biblical name (Obadiah 20) originally designating Sardis in Asia Minor. This name was quite early transferred to the far western domicile, the land 'where, ere we were plucked out in anger and in wrath, thrones were set for the Jews, where they rose to be princes and counselors of the land.' Proud Jewish families, rooted in the land, imagined themselves of royal Davidic blood. They told fantastic stories that Adoniram, Solomon's master of the levy (p. 62), had died while collecting revenue in Spain, and that his tomb had been found in that country. Others, like the Albalias, rested content with a less remote ancestry. They traced their pedigree to a noble Jew, whose occupation in Palestine had been to weave the veils for the sanctuary. At the bidding of the Roman governor, he was said to have been sent by Titus to Spain, where he settled at Merida (Augusta Emerita). It is certain that Jews were in Spain, at the latest about 300, before the irruption of the Vandals and their associates (409) and their displacement by the Visigoths (412).

Jews lived in the cities and on the open land. They cultivated the soil either by their own hands or by employing slaves, possessed vineyards and olive plantations, carried on trade and commerce. Jewish merchants shipped their wares to the adjacent African coast. As freemen they enjoyed the rights of citizenship like other Roman provincials, and no irksome legal discrimination set up a barrier between them and the rest of the population. Such of the natives as had become Christians lived in amity with their Jewish neighbors, and many a peasant, unable to distinguish between the mother religion and its daughter, saw no reason why his field might not be blessed just as well by a pious Jew as by a cleric of his own. Intermarriages between Jews and their neighbors occurred likewise. The oldest record of Spanish Christianity (the canons of the Council of Elvira, 313) witnesses to a determined effort on the part of the bishops to break down this peaceful intercourse. At this early period there came to light the double picture characteristic of Spanish Christianity of all times, gross worldliness among the laity and fanatical severity among the higher clergy.

The Visigoths, being Germans and Christians of the Arian creed, looked upon the Catholics as Romans; they suffered them, as well as the Romanized pagans, to live in accordance with the Roman system of jurisprudence. Similarly the Jews were left in their previous status, regulated by Roman enactments made before the invasion. Alaric II. (485–507) enforced the restrictions against the Jews imposed by the Code of Theodosius the Great (379–395), 'the first Christian Inquisitor,' but on the whole in a spirit free from acrimony and with toleration toward the Jewish religion. There was mutual trust between the Gothic masters and their Jewish subjects; the Jews at the foot of the Pyrenees guarded effectively the frontier against the repeated invasions of the Frankish neighbor in the north.

The kings were not only harassed from without; within, the nobles were untractable, ever on the alert to keep the throne elective. The Catholic metropolitans were not slow to improve their opportunity, as the Crown leaned more and more for support on the rulers of the Church who in all but name came to be the sovereigns of the realm. The astute and masterful Leander, bishop of Seville, plotted against Leovigild (568–586) and lent his powerful support to the prince Hermenegild on his renouncing Arianism. At the Third Council of Toledo (589), presided over by Leander, King Reccared I. (586–601) formally announced his conversion to the Catholic faith and established Catholicism as the religion of the state.

Whatever the step meant for the subsequent fortunes of the Spanish people, the effect of the change on the Jews was immediate. The Council set itself against intermarriages between Jews and Christians; the offspring of such unions were to be forcibly brought to baptism. No Christian slaves might be held by Jews; Jews should be excluded from any public office; in burying their dead, they must refrain from intoning psalms publicly. In vain did the slave-owning Jews strive to avert the blow which spelt ruin for them as farmers. The monarch was obdurate; he spurned a large offer of money and was commended by pope Gregory I. for his steadfastness. Still the people, and especially the nobles who were all-powerful within their domains, were rather well-disposed toward the Jews, and under Reccared's immediate successors the severe measures largely fell into abeyance. They were reënacted and ruthlessly executed by Sisebut (612–620), who, moreover, saw to it that in numerous cases Jews were baptized by force. Thousands fled the realm to France and Africa, but 'many were they who stumbled' and accepted Christianity, unwilling to abandon the possessions which they and their fathers had held for generations. Isidore of Seville, the learned brother and successor of Leander, although quite inimical to Jews and Judaism, strongly disapproved of the forcible conversions, since the unbelievers should be brought to the Christian truth by reason.

Persecution abated under the mild and just Swinthila (621–631), the 'Catholic Leovigild.' The exiled Jews returned to their homes and those who had submitted to baptism returned to the fold. But when Swinthila was overthrown by Sisinand (631–636), this bishops' man gave sanction to the draconic enactments of the Fourth Council of Toledo (633). In principle, compulsory baptisms were discountenanced; but those Jews who had received baptism, no matter under what conditions, were to stay Christians. Backsliding entailed 'correction' and converts were enjoined to avoid the society of their former coreligionists under pain of forfeiting their personal freedom. Moreover, the children of suspects were to be separated by force from their parents and brought up in convents or in orthodox Christian homes. Connivance on the part of the lower clergy, who were propitiated by gifts, led to the drastic decree at the Sixth Council (638), convoked by Chintila (636–640), that none but Catholics might reside in the realm. Receswinth (649–672), the promulgator of a new code which did away with all previous digests, and Euric (680–687) placed the converted Jews under the special control of the bishops and the ecclesiastical courts. The Twelfth Council of Toledo (681) was presided over by the commanding metropolitan Julian, whose Jewish parents had been converted to Christianity. The son, nurtured in the bosom of Catholicism, believed that it was the good right of truly Christian kings to keep down unbelievers, and he made mock of the Jews who, without a kingdom of their own or altar or priesthood, vainly calculated the date of the advent of the Messiah, whereas Christ reigned supreme. Jews were still to be found in Spain, of both sorts, in communion with the Church and outside. Frequently despoiled, they nevertheless were opulent; they sought their salvation in abetting pretenders who held out the promise of more lenient treatment, and just as often found themselves on the losing side. It was rumored that they were conspiring with their brethren beyond the sea, and even with the Saracens, already in Africa.

King Egica (687–701) still more viciously turned against the Jews, whom a hundred years of ruthless persecution had converted from law-abiding citizens into a discontented and discordant element in the state. All the Jews of Spain were declared slaves in perpetuity, their goods confiscated, and they themselves uprooted from their homes and scattered through the provinces. The exercise of the rites of the Jewish religion was strictly forbidden. Moreover, the children from seven years and upwards were taken away from their parents and brought up in Christian homes so as to be united in wedlock with Christian men and women. Little relief came to the hapless people during the reign of Witiza (701–710), much as he strove to check the absolute power of the bishops. But the hour of deliverance struck in 711, when the Visigothic dominion, enfeebled by inner dissensions, the decay of martial prowess, and the ascendancy of the priests, crumbled away before a small host of Berber and Arab invaders.

It is by no means certain that the Jews lent active assistance in the early period of the invasion. Beginning with a foray the previous year, it developed into an expedition when Tarik set foot on the rock now bearing his name (Gibraltar). After the victory at Xerez de la Frontera (July, 711), within the short period of four years, practically the whole country fell into the hands of the Mohammedans. The Jews naturally rejoiced; nor were they the only ones who were benefited by the change of masters. If Jews were suffered to live according to their own laws and to practise freely their religion, so were the Christians. Property rights were on the whole respected, and the poll-tax, which, in accordance with the laws of Omar, the unbelievers were obliged to pay to the treasury, fell upon Jews and Christians alike. Certainly the altered conditions brought to the Jews prosperity, and many rose to power. Yet, we hear nowhere that, in their newly won freedom, they in any wise oppressed their former persecutors.

The brilliant activity which emanated from the court of the Ummaiyad rulers, from the first Abdarrahman (755–788) down, made of the kingdom by far the most enlightened country in Europe. The capital Cordova became a magnificent seat of culture, with its basins and parks, its glittering palaces and mosques. Nor was the splendor entirely of the material kind. The court attracted and patronized poets and philosophers, men of letters and scientists. The Jews responded with alacrity; they threw themselves with zest into general culture and drew from it the inspiration to revive their own. The flickering light of Jewish learning in the far-off east was rekindled in the west. When at the last the Babylonian center crumbled away, the leading position passed on to Spanish Jewry, to be maintained for half a millennium. The crowning epoch, however, lasted only three centuries, from the tenth to the twelfth. It was ushered in by a commanding person, typifying in himself the happy combination of high worldly station and the love of learning, of true humanism and fervent Judaism, which marked the leaders of Jewish thought in Mohammedan Spain.

Hasdai son of Isaac Ibn Shaprut of Jaen served under Abdarrahman III. (912–961) and his successor Hakam II. (961–976) in the double capacity of physician and inspector-general of customs. To all practical purposes he was the diplomatic adviser of these two caliphs. His mastery of the Latin tongue and his knowledge of affairs stood him in good stead on more than one occasion. The caliphate was bordered on the north by a number of Christian kingdoms; frequent incursions into the Arab domain led to sanguinary battles. Ramiro II., king of Leon (930–950), had routed Abdarrahman's hosts; but upon the king's death, civil war broke out over the succession to the Leonese crown. Hasdai, along with a Mohammedan emissary, made an advantageous compact with Ordoño III., who was beset by his brother Sancho (955); two years later Ordoño died and Sancho succeeded him, but he was unseated by a fresh plot. The unfortunate king, who had not one powerful friend in his late kingdom, was received by his loving grandmother, Tota, the queen-regent of Navarre. He suffered from excessive corpulence, which made of him a laughing-stock. Tota swallowed her pride and appealed to the caliph, who dispatched Hasdai to the court of Navarre. Hasdai cured the king's malady and won his confidence so that he obtained for Abdarrahman favorable terms in return for armed help against the rebels. With still greater adroitness the Jewish statesman prevailed upon the haughty lady and her luckless grandson to present themselves in person at the caliph's palace in Cordova. It was a spectacle gratifying to the national pride of the Moslems, sweeter still to the Jews, since a man of their own faith had brought it about.

Not long before, an ambassador, sent from the court of the German emperor Otto I. (936–973), had declared that he had never met with a subtler diplomat than was this Jew Hasdai. On another occasion, the Byzantine emperor Romanus II. (959–963) courted the favor of the western caliph by rich gifts, among which was a copy of a medical work in Greek by Dioscorides. Hasdai, on behalf of his master, requested from the eastern monarch the dispatch of a monk learned in Greek and Latin. As the Greek read off the work in Latin translation, the Jew, aided by Mohammedan scholars, prepared an Arabic rendition, to the delight of the court. Not the least satisfied was Hasdai himself, who was greatly interested in pharmacology. He is said to have been the first to discover a certain drug useful in preparing the compound known as theriac. His connections with the Byzantine court led him to enter into correspondence on his own account with another ruler, a Jewish monarch. The Hebrew missives exchanged were of immediate concern to Jewry.

The taunt was frequently hurled at the Jews, by Christians and Mohammedans alike, that 'the scepter was departed from Judah' and that the chosen people had been rejected by God for ever. This assertion was galling to the homeless wanderers. It is for this reason that the Jews listened with avidity to any tale concerning an independent Jewish state anywhere, and that Eldad's fantastic story (p. 278) appealed to the Jewish imagination. Rumors of a Jewish king in the extreme East had floated to Spain in Visigothic times, and Isidore of Seville peevishly gave them the lie. But now definite news reached Hasdai that a Jewish king was actually reigning in the land of the Chazars (p. 526). Hasdai dispatched a trusted messenger, Isaac son of Nathan, to Constantinople, whence he was to set out for the Chazar capital. The Byzantine officials, however, suspicious as to Hasdai's designs, were not eager to assist the emissary on his journey, and at length he returned to Spain having failed of his purpose. It was fortunate that in the train of the embassy sent by emperor Otto there were two Jews, Saul and Joseph. On learning of Hasdai's disappointment over the failure of the mission to the Chazar king, they advised that the letter

should be sent over Germany by the hands of Jews traveling
to Hungary, whence it would be forwarded through Russia
and Bulgaria to its destination. As a matter of fact, a German Jew, by the name of Isaac son of Eliezer, conveyed the
carefully prepared epistle and placed it in the hands of the
Chazar king. It told of the turn in the fortunes of Spanish
Jewry wrought by the coming of the Mohammedans, of the
greatness of the western caliph, of Hasdai's station at court
and his great longing to learn every detail of the rise and
present condition of the Jewish kingdom.

The two rulers whom Hasdai served were distinguished by
their culture and zeal for learning. Hakam himself was no
mean scholar, employing agents all through the East to
copy or buy up ancient and modern manuscripts. Authors
from afar sent him copies of their works with dedicatory
poems; scholars, drawn by his liberality, flocked to his court.
At the university of Cordova all branches of learning were
cultivated, and some of the most eminent writers on Arabic
grammar taught there. In like manner Hasdai held court
among his own people. He surrounded himself with men
proficient in Hebrew learning, who vied with one another to
win and to hold his favor. His father had likewise befriended
writers of elegant Hebrew.

One of these was Menahem son of Saruk of Tortosa (c.
910–970). When the elder Shaprut, an opulent and charitable man, had a synagogue erected, it was Menahem's pen
that composed the laudatory inscription which was engraved
upon a memorial tablet. His services were sought by Hasdai,
both on the occasion of his mother's death and later when
his father passed away, to write suitable elegies for recital
during the days of mourning. At Cordova, whither Hasdai
bade him come, Menahem was maintained in comfort and
attached to the household of the statesman. Menahem had
charge of Hasdai's Hebrew correspondence (thus the letter
addressed to the Chazar king was largely of his composition), and acted as a teacher of the holy tongue.

In these years of freedom from care, Menahem occupied
himself with producing a dictionary of biblical Hebrew and

Aramaic. It was practically the first complete work of its kind; it commended itself at once by its concise definitions and the grouping of meanings under classes, duly illustrated by suitable quotations from the Scriptures. Since it was written in the Hebrew language, it became immediately popular beyond the Pyrenees, in France and in Italy. Menahem clearly aimed at an understanding of the Scriptural vocabulary from the Scriptures themselves without avowed recourse to extraneous aid, such as a comparison of the cognate Arabic tongue might have provided. Notable as the advance was upon his predecessors, Menahem was misled by a faulty theory, in utter misconception of the true structure of the language.

Menahem met with a doughty critic in the person of Dunash (Adonim) son of Labrat (c. 920–990), who at Bagdad had been taught by Saadiah and later on removed from Fez to Cordova at the bidding of Hasdai. Criticism was his *métier;* he exercised it against his Babylonian master no less harshly than against the Spanish lexicographer, nor was the right always on his side. Over and above the specific points of word meaning and interpretation, on some of which modern students are equally divided, there was a basic difference which again was the subject of no less acrimonious contention in the nineteenth century. Dunash stressed the importance of looking to the Aramaic and Arabic tongues for the elucidation of obscure Hebrew words and of consulting that ancient depository of Scriptural understanding, the Aramaic Targum. In this respect Dunash was most true to his Babylonian traditions, and he looked down somewhat superciliously on the native wisdom of Spain.

It was an unedifying literary feud between the two grammarians, carried on in verse and in prose. Their contemporaries enjoyed it as an entertaining intellectual tournament. It answered entirely to the manners of the time and place that the opponents did not shrink from personal abuse calculated to do material harm. The prize was the good-will of the patron; for a time Menahem was eclipsed, he was even set upon by the magnate's too zealous retainers and evicted from his dwelling on a sabbath day. Both rivals wrote verses; there was a novelty about those of Dunash that they were composed in regular meter, in exact accordance with the rules of Arab versification. In the memory of posterity this innovation remained connected with the lifetime of the patron-inspirer ('in the days of Hasdai they began to chirp').

At first it was looked at askance, but it took root. The older verse of the piyut genre, abstruse in matter and unseemly in form, was discarded, and in its stead a new poetry was developed, at once graceful and pleasing to the ear, pure in diction and diversified in content, dealing with themes secular as well as sacred. As the Scriptural language was made to live once more on the lips of the singers, as they artfully (sometimes, it is true, in a labored fashion) applied the ancient expressions to the immediate purposes of the occasion, they deepened at the same time an understanding of the Scriptures. One and all devoted themselves to Bible study and painstakingly strove to penetrate to the original intent of the sacred word, freed from the age-long fancies of preachers and homilists (haggadists). The process of perfecting the new song and the new Bible interpretation was a lengthy one and many and varied minds exercised themselves therein; but the beginnings date from the times of Hasdai, who thus became the inaugurator of a new era.

CHAPTER XLVI

SAMUEL THE NAGID AND SOLOMON IBN GABIROL

(993-1069)

UNDER the patronage of Hasdai talmudic studies likewise took on new life. The Talmud had of course
been known in Spain for a long time. A more penetrating and thoroughgoing method of instruction came with
the advent of Moses son of Enoch. He was a Babylonian;
the vessel on which he set sail with his wife and young son
was seized by Abdarrahman's admiral, Ibn Rumahis. The
mother, fearing dishonor, cast herself into the sea; the boy
and his father were taken captive and brought to Cordova,
where they were ransomed by the Jewish community. The
teacher from the distant East came at an opportune moment.
The western caliphs were eager to see their Jewish subjects
detached from eastern tutelage and no longer sending moneys
to the land of their enemies, the caliphs of the East. It was
gratifying that a man of the caliber of Moses, the peer of his
Babylonian colleagues, should undertake the religious guidance of the West. Accordingly, through the instrumentality
of the far-seeing Hasdai, Moses was installed as spiritual
head. His fame spread, and from all Spain and North Africa
students flocked to the first higher Jewish college in Spain.
For use in this school, the bountiful magnate had correct
copies of the Talmud procured from the disintegrating academy of Sura.

The community could well afford to maintain master and
students in a dignified manner, considering that it counted
numerous wealthy families that vied with the Mohammedans in magnificence. Rich Jews might be seen appareled in
silks, with precious turbans on their heads, riding in gorgeous
carriages or mounted on horseback in true knightly fashion.
The chief source of their wealth was the trade in slaves; they
supplied the harems with inmates and with eunuchs to guard

them, and the army with recruits. Thus large numbers of Slavs—taken in warfare by Germanic nations and then sold to the Saracens; the name came to be applied to other Europeans, and even Africans, similarly acquired—were imported, and whole regiments as well as the caliph's bodyguard were formed of them. As these mercenaries rose to power, they precipitated many an uprising; they and the Berbers between them brought about the disintegration of Moslem power in Spain and the fall of the Cordova caliphate.

At the death of Moses (c. 965), the community was divided as regards the succession. An influential part favored the native Joseph son of Isaac Ibn Abithor, who had been taught by Moses and was gifted as a liturgical poet. But others gave the preference to Moses' son, Enoch. Hasdai declared for the latter, and he remained in undisputed tenure so long as the statesman was alive. The question was reopened after the death of Hasdai, Abithor being supported by his own kinsmen and by the two brothers Ibn Jau, wealthy silk manufacturers and purveyors of military banners. However, the caliph Hakam sustained Enoch; his rival was placed under the ban and practically banished from Spain.

With the accession of Hisham II. (976–1013) and the reign of his all-powerful minister Ibn Abi Amir (called Almanzur), the elder of the two Ibn Jau brothers, Jacob, received the appointment as prince and chief judge over all the Jewish communities on both sides of the straits, from Sijilmasa in Africa to the Duero in Spain. Enoch was deposed, and steps were taken to recall his rival from exile. Abithor, however, declined the honor, and upbraided the community for ill-treating so worthy a man as Enoch. The exile continued his wanderings as far as the Orient; the Gaon Hai refused to see the excommunicated rabbi, and at length his life came to an end in Damascus. Enoch lived to witness the decline of Cordova and died on the concluding day of Tabernacles in the year 1014, when the pulpit in the synagogue which he had ascended collapsed.

With the sack of Cordova by the Berbers in 1012 and the ensuing dissolution of the caliphate, Moslem Spain broke up into a number of petty kingdoms. The Hammudites, though they claimed rights over all Arab Spain, actually possessed only the city of Malaga and its territory; at Granada, their powerful vassals, Zawi and his nephew and successor Habbus (1019–1038), reigned, and in 1055 Badis (1038–1073) annexed Malaga to his realm. In this ascendancy of the principality of Granada a distinguished Jew had his part and rose to the exalted position of vizir. Samuel ha-Levi son of Joseph (Ibn Naghdela) was born in 993 at Cordova, whither his father had removed from Merida. He underwent a thorough training in Talmud at the school of Enoch; he perfected himself in the study of Hebrew grammar by assiduous perusal of the treatises of Judah Hayyuj, the 'first grammarian,' as later generations called him. By dint of his knowledge of Arabic grammar, Hayyuj had laid the foundation for an understanding of the structure of the Hebrew language (about the year 1000).

Samuel was well versed in the mathematical sciences and philosophy. He spoke and wrote seven languages; his mastery of the Arab speech and literature was complete and he excelled in penmanship—something prized in those days—and composition. To these latter accomplishments he owed his rise to distinction. Both at Cordova and afterwards at Malaga, whither he betook himself after the capture of his native city, he kept a small shop in which he sold spices. Close by was the castle of the vizir of King Habbus. The inmates of the palace, being illiterate themselves, availed themselves again and again of the services of the Jewish shopkeeper to write their letters to their master. The vizir, enchanted by the beautiful handwriting as well as by the style, sought out the writer and prevailed upon him to become his secretary. Thus Samuel was taken to Granada; there he won the esteem of the minister by his political insight and his sound advice upon matters of state. On his death-bed, the minister commended Samuel to the king, who, as a Berber, had no scruples about appointing the Jew outright as his vizir. This position Samuel filled with dignity and singular discretion. Completely at his ease in

the halls of the splendid Alhambra, tactful and urbane in
his demeanor, an entertaining conversationalist, he was
quite devoid of arrogant self-assertion, and the candor
with which he spoke of his former lowly estate silenced his
very detractors.

Granada had a large and influential body of Jews. By way
of exaggeration, the city was spoken of as 'The Jews' City.'
When Habbus died (in 1038), Jews and Berbers alike were
divided, a portion wishing to confer the throne on a younger
son, while others, among them Samuel, favored the elder
Badis. When the younger brother renounced his candida-
ture, his Jewish supporters—like Joseph Ibn Megas, Isaac
son of Leon, Nehemiah Escafa—fled to Seville, whose prince
was none too friendly to the king of Granada. Samuel's
espousal of the cause of Badis was rewarded in that he was
retained by the grateful monarch as his minister. It was no
small task to serve this bloodthirsty tyrant, who after his
drinking bouts was unamenable to reason or suasion. So
wisely did the Jewish minister govern that the land, in its
enjoyment of security and of an administration free from
irregularities, soon ranked foremost among the Spanish
principalities. Samuel's life was full of activity; again and
again he personally directed military operations from his
quarters close to the battlefields, and on several occasions he
narrowly escaped death. He lived to see the downfall and
violent death of a number of his enemies, like the arrogant
Arab vizir in the Slav state of Almeria, who detested Jews
and Berbers alike, and the Berber minister at the court of
Malaga. Both were balked by the policies of the all-powerful
and sagacious Jewish adviser of Badis and both vainly
plotted to overthrow him by calumnies.

For some thirty years this statesman shed lustre upon the
Jewish community of Granada, which at an early date bestowed upon him the title of Nagid, or Prince in Israel. His
bounty extended to poor Jewish scholars, not only in Spain,
but also in Africa, in Sicily, at Jerusalem, at Bagdad. He
had copies made of the Mishnah and the Talmud and presented them to needy students; he also imported copies from

the defunct academy at Sura and was the possessor of a large collection of books. His fondness for the land of the fathers was demonstrated by supplying the synagogues in the Holy City year by year with olive-oil from his own plantations. He maintained friendly relations with celebrities at home and abroad; so with the Gaon Hai, with the exilarch Hezekiah, with Daniel, head of a school at Jerusalem, with Hushiel, the father of Hananel, and with Jacob son of Nissim, both at Kairawan. A daughter of the latter became the wife of his son and successor, Joseph.

Samuel presided over a college of his own; his mastery of talmudic learning is shown in two works of which only fragments have come down to us: one an Introduction to the Talmud dealing with its methodology, and another, named 'Mighty Halakoth,' a compendium anticipating that of Isaac al-Fasi. In grammar and the interpretation of the Scriptures he was excelled by his contemporary Jonah Ibn Janah (985–1040) at Saragossa, the author of a complete grammar and dictionary of the biblical Hebrew, who deepened the studies of Hayyuj. With him the Nagid carried on a literary controversy. Samuel also wrote a work, called 'The Book of Riches,' which was a full dictionary of the biblical Hebrew in which all that bore on the meaning of words was presented in a manner to leave nothing unsaid. Succeeding grammarians and commentators cited the Nagid with deference, and in some of his observations he anticipated discoveries nearer our own time. Still in this field he lacked the genius, if not the erudition, of Ibn Janah, 'the greatest of medieval Hebraists.' As a poet, the Nagid ranks below his friend and contemporary, Ibn Gabirol. Though the Hebrew language was handled by the Nagid with great skill, his poems were weighted with allusions, baffling even to scholars, and lacked depth of feeling. Samuel died in old age (some time after 1056) and was mourned by all Jewry. The most eminent scholars and poets eulogized him in verse, and the historians said of him that he wore four crowns: the crown of the Torah, the crown of high station, the crown of Levitical descent, and, above all, the crown of good deeds.

Solomon son of Judah Ibn Gabirol (1021–1069) was born at Malaga, whither his father had removed from Cordova during the unfortunate upheaval of 1012. There had been versifiers before Gabirol; there were poets in his own day; but in the estimate of critics he surpassed them all as the Knight of Style, his nation's King of Songs, and the poet Heine in the nineteenth century named this eleventh century singer the Nightingale of Piety. At Saragossa Jekuthiel Ibn Hasan befriended the forlorn youth, supplying him with material means, but also compelling a mind innately introspective to look out upon a world in which there was beauty and joys to delight a sensitive poetic nature. The young poet's gratitude was expressed in eulogizing his benefactor both in life and in death. The loss of his friend enhanced Ibn Gabirol's bitter contempt for the Jewish community of Saragossa who neglected the holy tongue, half of them speaking the language of Edom (Spanish) and half the obscure tongue of Kedar (Arabic). After wandering about the peninsula, he found a refuge with the congenial Nagid of Granada.

Ibn Gabirol sang of wine when a miser forbore to serve it to his guests and offered water instead. Woman had no attraction for him, and he seems to have remained unmarried. His love was for things divine, for the truth which he spent his life to search out. The language of the Scriptures became fluid at his touch; acrostic, meter, and rhyme presented themselves as if without labor. Integral passages from the Book were woven into his verse to round off a stanza, adding piquancy by the very unwonted yet suitable use to which they were put. It was a feat when at the age of nineteen he gave poetic form, in four hundred verses, to a subject so unpoetic as the rules of Hebrew grammar; one of his earliest efforts was a versification of the six hundred and thirteen Commandments, which is still recited in synagogues of the Sephardic ritual. Many more of Gabirol's poems passed into the liturgy, composed as they were for that very purpose. In these the poet expressed, on the one hand, the deep longing of Israel, crushed by the bear (Edom) and pursued by the wild ass (Ishmael), for redemption, and, on the other, the anguish of the human soul defiled by the sinfulness of the body and yearning for reunion with its Maker. The best known of his hymns is the one to which the poet gave the name of 'Royal Crown.' One is enchanted alike by the beauty of its diction and the depth of its thought. What there is in it of a scientific view of the universe, moves along lines made obsolete by the Copernican system. The place assigned to Reason in the sphere nearest to God and resplendent with pure intelligences, likewise the home of the human soul to which it returns after death, is ultimately of Platonic origin. But the sublimity of the monotheistic idea, which is impaired as soon as God is spoken of in terms applicable to man only, is Jewish to the core. God is One, but not in a numerical sense; His is the most perfect Oneness, baffling definition, above human imagination. God is the only true Existence; with the grandeur of God is contrasted the littleness of man—a truly prophetic, Isaianic, conception. Just as surely prophetic is the insistence on the divine grace of Forgiveness and the ascent of man through a contrite return to God. The conviction uttered by the prophet Malachi that the One God is worshiped by all mankind though under different appellations, is reiterated by Gabirol in the most unmistakable manner. 'Thou art God, and all things created are Thy servants and worshipers; nor is Thy glory diminished by reason of those that worship aught beside Thee, for the intention of them all is to attain unto Thee.'

The very poetic form in which this philosopher cast his metaphysical speculations brought them necessarily near the Jewish, biblical, conceptions of God and the world, which are essentially poetic. But when we abstract from the form and penetrate to the essence of the thought there is revealed an originality which perhaps cannot be expressed in terms strictly Jewish. This the poet-philosopher appears to have felt, for he wrote a thoroughly philosophical work, in Arabic, which he called 'The Fountain of Life' and in which, without so much as quoting a verse of the Scriptures or a saying of the rabbis, he outlined his full system. Here he teaches universality of matter, emanating from God as the primal substance, and universality of form proceeding from the will of God as a creative aspect. Gabirol was influenced by Neo-Platonic speculations; but he was also indebted to the 'Book of Creation.' Substantially he expressed the basic thought of his philosophy in a Hebrew couplet in which he traced the origin of universal matter to the All-containing God: Matter is a semblance of existence, longing to become true existence through form, as a lover longs for the beloved. Ibn Gabirol's philosophical treatise was translated into Latin in 1150; it was much studied by the scholastics with whom the author's name underwent all sorts of corruptions (Avencebrol, Avicebron, etc.), and for a long time, down to the nineteenth century, students believed the 'Fountain of Life' to be the work of some Christian philosopher.

Ibn Gabirol wrote two other works in Arabic: one on Ethics ('The Improvement of the Moral Qualities') and the other, a collection of sententious sayings, known as 'The Choice of Pearls.' Truly, this gifted man, who sang songs to make the soul rejoice and deliver the heart from sorrow, had reason to speak of wisdom as his mother and his sister, who chose him of all men as theirs.

A contemporary of the grammarian Ibn Janah and the poet-philosopher Ibn Gabirol was Bahye son of Joseph Ibn Bakuda, of whose circumstances little is known except that he had the office of assistant rabbi (dayyan, judge) somewhere in Spain, possibly at Saragossa. He is also spoken of as the Saint (hasid). He was the author of a work in Arabic which at an early period was translated into Hebrew and to this day is eagerly read by pious laymen. It is essentially a moralistic book. Its tendency, as the title 'Duties of the Heart' indicates, is to elevate spirituality and inward piety above formalism in religion, love of God and complete trust in Him above 'the actions performed by the parts of the body' and consisting in mere outward observance. There is a distinct preference for asceticism and withdrawal from the world, reminiscent of similar contemporary movements in the Mohammedan world which led to Sufism and the mysticism of the somewhat later Ghazali.

CHAPTER XLVII

AL-FASI AND HIS SCHOOL

(1013-1141)

AT GRANADA, Joseph succeeded his father Samuel both as the king's minister and as head of the Jewish community. He had received a princely training and was well grounded in Jewish lore. But unlike his father, he loved ostentation. He lived in a marble palace, and when he rode beside Badis he rivaled the monarch in magnificent apparel. His arrogant demeanor and his predilection for advancing his own relatives or other coreligionists to public positions aroused the envy of Berbers and Arabs. Goaded on by a jealous poet, they spread abroad false rumors about him and imputed to him many crimes. It was a mere pretext to rid themselves of the hated Jew, who dominated his royal master completely. On a sabbath the palace in which Joseph dwelt was attacked. The minister hid himself in a charcoal cellar where he blackened himself as a disguise; but he was discovered, put to death, and fastened to a cross. The Granadans then proceeded to massacre the other Jews and pillage their dwellings. Nearly four thousand Jews fell victims to the fanatical hatred of the populace (December 30, 1066).

Nevertheless Jewish prestige suffered no decline in the rest of Spain. Joseph Ibn Megas, one of those who had been banished when Badis mounted the throne, occupied a high position in the service of al-Mu'tadid (1042–1069) at Seville. At Saragossa, Muktadir (1047–1081) had for his vizir Hasdai, son of the poet Joseph Ibn Hasdai. Isaac son of Baruch Ibn al-Balia, of a distinguished family, the protégé of Samuel the Nagid and his son Joseph, managed to escape the massacre of Granada. At Cordova he won the favor of the Abbadid prince Abu-l-Kasim Mohammed, who, upon his accession to the throne of Seville under the surname al-

Mu'tamid (1069), summoned his favorite as his court astrologer and adviser. In this capacity he served his royal master for twenty years. Ibn al-Balia was a student of astronomy and wrote a work on the calendar. His talmudical learning commended him to the Jews of the kingdom of Seville, who made him their chief rabbi and protector (nasi).

Talmudic learning was now in the ascendant, and the Spanish teachers were looked up to with deference abroad. An authority of the first order was Isaac son of Jacob al-Fasi (1013–1103). He was born in the vicinity of Fez. His fame had been established, before he migrated to Spain, by his compendium of the Talmud which eliminated all irrelevant discussion and formulated clear-cut decisions in all matters of law applicable also outside the Holy Land. At Lucena he became the spiritual head of the community, succeeding Isaac son of Judah Ibn Ghayyath (died 1089), distinguished alike by his talmudic erudition and liturgical productions. There had been some angry discussions between al-Fasi and Ibn Ghayyath. Another disputant was Ibn al-Balia, who, however, on his death-bed, sought reconciliation with his opponent, and al-Fasi proved a true friend and a second father to his former adversary's son. Both Ibn Ghayyath and al-Fasi left a host of disciples, and the influences that emanated from both these teachers were instrumental in producing the zenith of Spanish Jewish culture. When al-Fasi died, two outstanding poets vied with one another in celebrating him in verse: Moses Ibn Ezra, a pupil of Ibn Ghayyath, and Judah ha-Levi, taught in al-Fasi's own school. The elegy composed by the latter was chosen for an epitaph on the master's tomb. The pupil's admiration was expressed somewhat extravagantly in such words as these:

'It was for thee that the mountains
    shook on the day of Sinai;
For the angels of God met thee
And wrote the Torah on the tables of
    thy heart:
They set the finest of its crowns upon
    thy head.'

The feuds between Badis and Mu'tamid, and in general between the several Mohammedan princes, roused the Christian states in the north, long disunited themselves, to an organized reconquest so soon as a vigorous monarch was able to set up a concentrated empire. Such a ruler was found in Ferdinand I. (1027–1065) and still more so in his son Alphonso VI. (1065–1109). With the three kingdoms—Castile, Leon, and Galicia—in his hands, Alphonso pressed upon Toledo and forced the Andalusian princelings to obtain a respite by paying tribute. Mu'tamid himself was compelled to submit to a recognition of Christian suzerainty. On one occasion the embassy, sent to Seville to receive the annual tribute, was headed by a Jew, Amram son of Isaac Ibn Shalbib. So firm was the Jew in demanding pure gold instead of the debased money which was offered that the incensed Mu'tamid ordered him to be crucified. Jews frequently acted as intermediaries between Christians and Moslems.

Another Jew in the services of Alphonso was one named Cidellus. Jews met with fair treatment in the domains of this Christian king. The old Visigothic discriminations had fallen into disuse and, according to the common law which had developed and was confirmed by Alphonso, Jews and Mohammedans were placed on a footing of equality with Christians before the law, despite the admonitions of pope Gregory VII. (1073–1085) to the king to prevent Jews from bearing rule over Christians. Toledo surrendered in 1085 and was made the capital of Christian Spain. The Jews were left in the possession of all the liberties which they had enjoyed during Moslem rule. The last Mohammedan king, the unfortunate Kadir, was permitted to retire to Valencia; he had for his intimate companion a Jew, who remained faithful to him after his death while his nearest tribesmen betrayed him.

The fall of Toledo greatly shocked the Mohammedan princes of Andalusia. They, therefore, invited the aid of Yusuf Ibn Tashufin, king of the Almoravides, a Berber tribe of North Africa who had been recently converted to Islam and had founded a mighty empire extending from the Senegal to Algiers. It was rather a dangerous step to call in these barbarous and fanatical warriors; but, as Mu'tamid put it, he would rather be a 'camel-driver in Africa than a swineherd in Castile.' The Christians were worsted for the time being. In both camps, the Christian and the Mohammedan, Jews fought side by side with their countrymen.

The Almoravides made themselves at home in Andalusia. They suppressed all the petty monarchs and made of Moslem Spain a province of the African empire. The fakihs (orthodox teachers of religion) had full sway and Christians (Mozarabs) and Jews suffered greatly. A Cordovan fakih came forward with the discovery of a tradition that the Jews had promised Mohammed that at the end of the fifth century after the hijra, if the expected Messiah had not by that time made his appearance, they would become Moslems. Yusuf proceeded to Lucena, a town almost exclusively Jewish, and demanded that the Jews should redeem the pledge of their ancestors and embrace Islam. There was great consternation in the community, and at last the king was bought off by an enormous sum, which was really what he aimed at. As illegal taxes were done away with, the Jews were made to supply the deficiencies in the Moslem treasury. Yet on the whole the Jews were left in peace.

Under the second Almoravide ruler, Ali (1106–1143), Jews were entrusted with gathering the poll-tax from Jews and Christians, and a few distinguished men rose to eminent positions at court. Thus Solomon al-Muallem of Seville served as Ali's court-physician. Another was Abraham son of Meir Ibn Kamnial of Saragossa, whom the poets celebrated as 'his people's protector, dwelling in Spain, but reaching out with his generosity to Babylonia and the land of Egypt.' The poets likewise sang the praises of Abu Ishak Ibn Muhajar and of Solomon Ibn Farusal. The latter seems to have been in the employ of a Christian prince; he was sent on a mission to the court of Murcia. Shortly before the battle of Ucles, where the Moslems once more defeated the Christians, this princely man was assassinated (1108). The poet Judah ha-Levi was just making ready to receive him, on his return from his important mission, with a laudatory poem when the sad news arrived and the song was turned into a lament. A high position at one of the Moslem courts was also held by Abraham son of Hiya (1065–1136) who seems to have been chief of police. He wrote several works (all in Hebrew) on mathematics and astronomy, but also on ethics; he believed in astrology and figured out that the Messiah would appear in 1358.

The period was rich in eminent men of letters. Jewish learning had been well established in Spain and the scholar was self-sufficient and independent of the patronage of the wealthy and influential. Moreover, the contentious rivalries of the previous age had given place to unity of endeavor and a spirit of mutual amity. The Spanish scholar was at all times many-sided; he was a balanced, harmonious personality. The rabbi and talmudical student tried his hand at poetry or philosophy, and the poets and philosophers blended with their interest in human culture a deep concern for strictly Jewish learning. Prominent disciples of al-Fasi were David Ibn Muhajar, associate rabbi at Granada, who found leisure to write on grammar; Eleazar son of Nahman Ibn Azhar, rabbi at Seville, wealthy, highly reputed, and poetically gifted, the friend of Moses Ibn Ezra and Judah ha-Levi; Baruch son of Isaac Ibn al-Balia of Cordova (1077–1124), who raised many disciples, the one who acquired most lasting fame being the historian Abraham Ibn Daud (p. 332).

Surpassing all these in talmudical learning was Joseph son of Meir Ibn Megas ha-Levi (1077–1141), who at the age of twenty-six succeeded al-Fasi in the rabbinate of Lucena. It was the express wish of al-Fasi that this distinguished disciple should fill his place after his death, although the master left behind him an erudite son of his own. It is true, certain members of the community demurred at the succession, but Joseph won, and the victory was commemorated by Judah ha-Levi; the poet devoted to his praise other poems besides. Of the large number of Joseph's disciples the best known is Maimun, the father of Maimonides. The impression which the master made upon the father was put by the son in these words: 'The talmudical learning of this man amazes every one who understands his words and the depth of his speculative spirit; so that it may almost be said of him that his equal has never existed.'

To the genre of essayistic literature, known as 'culture' (adab), belongs the treatise in Arabic, entitled 'Causeries and Notes,' a sort of Hebrew 'Ars Poetica,' quite unique in Jewish literature. The author, Moses son of Jacob Ibn Ezra (died about 1139), was the most distinguished of four gifted brothers, of aristocratic birth, wealthy, cultured. Their father had held office under the Nagid at Granada. Moses was taught by his eldest brother Isaac and also sat at the feet of Ibn Ghayyath at Lucena. He fell in love with his niece, and though the affection was reciprocated, the father gave her in marriage to another uncle. Disconsolate, Moses left his home at Granada and wandered to Portugal and Castile. Here he sang of the pain of his own unrealized love. But he had also his more cheerful moods. The beauty of nature evoked many a lovely stanza. The numerous friendships which he made were celebrated in eulogistic poems. He recognized early the poetic greatness of his contemporary Judah ha-Levi, and no spirit of envy marred the relations of these two poets. Moses wrote more than three hundred Hebrew poems on all sorts of secular occasions and approximately two hundred liturgical pieces which have spread through all the Jewries under Arab dominion. Together with Ibn Gabirol and Judah ha-Levi, the singer 'pure and faultlessly true,' Moses Ibn Ezra was reckoned among the three 'fathers of song, whose sun rose in the west.'

CHAPTER XLVIII

JUDAH HA-LEVI AND ABRAHAM IBN EZRA

(1086-1167)

JUDAH son of Samuel ha-Levi was born at Toledo about 1086 and educated at Lucena in the school of al-Fasi, where he had for his schoolmates Joseph Ibn Megas and Baruch Ibn al-Balia. By profession a physician, he found his vocation in poetry. He won early the admiration of Moses Ibn Ezra who was charmed by the beauty of Judah's verse, whose 'warp and woof was of silken speech.' At Cordova, where the physician-poet spent the greater part of his life, he was surrounded by a circle of friends; thence also he entered into relations with the celebrities of the age. He sang of the sweet juice which his lips drained until his friends thought him a wine-bibber; of love enkindled at the sight of a maiden graceful as a doe; of friendship; of the spring covering the earth with golden beds and causing the flowers to change color like a blushing maiden rapt at the touch of her lover's lips; of the elemental fury of a sea-storm making the craft to toss like a drunken man. The beauties of nature and the joyous occasions in his own life or in the life of his friends stirred his harp; with his verse he gladdened the hearts of the newly wed; the elevation of a friend to a seat of honor transported him with joy, just as the death of a Jewish worthy evoked tones of tender sadness.

Judah exulted in the Torah and the duties it inculcated; the liturgy of the synagogue he enriched with hundreds of hymns. His songs of prayer and penitence vie with the Psalms in depth of emotion and loftiness of diction. He is alike the spokesman of the human soul before its Maker and of the Jewish community before the God of Israel. How he groans with his people, driven to and fro, a prey to the fury of the persecutor. How he dwells incessantly on the longing of the Jew for the end to the protracted exile. Proudly he glories in the Jew's resistance to the enticing voice of Christianity, in his steadfastness in the face of the insults of Ishmael. The singer holds his head high because his people will not bend down before the idols made by men.

This pride was born of the poet's view concerning the worth of Judaism and its peculiar character, which runs like a thread through all his verses and which in particular he elaborated in his theological work, the 'Kozari.' This classical defense of Judaism was written in the Arabic tongue. It was cast in the form of a dialogue between the king of the Chazars, ready to relinquish paganism, and the Jewish teacher, whom he summons because of his dissatisfaction with unemotional philosophy and upon the discovery that both Christians and Mohammedans rest their appeal ultimately upon the Jewish Scriptures. This disdain of philosophy Judah ha-Levi shared with his age, which, as exemplified in Ghazali, had grown sceptical of rationalism and recoiled to mystic absorption in the Deity.

Judah ha-Levi, however, was far from being a mystic. Having broken with Greek wisdom, 'which has no fruit, but only flowers,' which leads men astray on devious paths away from the main road, he, quite realistically, envisaged Judaism as a revealed religion, its evidence resting in the historical fact of the concourse at the foot of Sinai. There Israel, howbeit only for a moment, saw God and heard His voice, by virtue of the prophetic exaltation which was the natural endowment of the seed of Abraham, feebly realized previously in Adam and Noah and Shem. This prophetic gift was an abiding motive force in the formative period of the nation through biblical times. In each prophet it was the spark from the fire which burned in the nation's soul, the innate power of the race brought to reality.

The election of Israel is with the poet-philosopher the cardinal dogma of Judaism. It was a second creation, as miraculous as the first when God created heaven and earth. By a process of selection He fashioned Israel as the instrument for working out His world plan to be consummated in Messianic times. What of the present-day ignoble con-

dition of the Jewish people? Israel is the suffering Servant
of the Lord, who willingly takes upon himself chastisement
that through him the world may be healed. Israel is the very
heart of human kind—like the heart in the body, feeling pain
most keenly, and most robust in health. Israel, to-day, is like
a sick man, of whose recovery the physicians are in despair;
but as by a miracle, he comes to life again.

Like the prophet of the exile, like Ezekiel, Judah ha-Levi
looks for national resurrection; like Isaiah the son of Amoz,
like Jeremiah, and once more like Ezekiel, he believes in the
eternity of Israel and the national restoration to the Holy
Land. As in the mind of Moses, the election of Israel is
bound up with the election of the land, singled out by God,
where alone His glory dwelt aforetimes, and where He will
reveal Himself anew to a prophet or to the whole people.
The Chazar king taunts the Jewish teacher with the lip
devotion of the Jewish people to the future restoration on
Zion. They pray for it daily, yet are loath to relinquish their
possessions in exile. The teacher in shame resolves to expa-
triate himself and settle in the ancestral home.

Judah ha-Levi practised what he preached. Immediately
upon his completion of the 'Kozari,' he made ready to fulfil
the vow he had uttered through the mouth of the Jewish
teacher. The song, hushed for a time, was once more on his
lip, and the burden, reiterated with infinite variation, was
the longing for Zion. In those stirring days, when the Latin
Kingdom had wrested the Holy Land from the Fatimite
Moslems and when at home Christian Castile was bearing
down upon the Mohammedan kingdom, Judah ha-Levi
dreamt the vision of the downfall of Ishmael, whom he
identified with the fourth beast in the prophecy of Daniel.
His dream went on to anticipate the restoration of the
Temple with its ancient cult of sacrifice and praise. His heart
was in the east, though his body was in the uttermost west.
How was he to pay his vows, when Zion was held in the iron
grasp of Christian Edom and himself in the fetters of Arab-
speaking Andalusia? The wealth of all Spain he would
readily part with, only to behold with his eyes the dust of

the sanctuary laid waste. Would that he had the wings of a dove, that he might fly, leave behind north and south and inhale the air of Zion! At last (about 1141) he set out for his journey. His passage through Spain was like a triumphal procession. Cordova and Granada vied with each other to speed him on his travels with presents and laudatory poems. With ample means of his own, and in the company of faithful friends, he embarked for Egypt. It was a stormy voyage, but though the sea raged, his soul within him exulted at the prospect of drawing near unto the sanctuary of God. Finally he set foot in Alexandria, resolved to tarry but a short time. But at the importunate invitation of the chief rabbi and physician Aaron Benzion Ibn Alamani, a wealthy man and a composer of liturgical hymns, he stayed on for three months, enjoying unlimited hospitality and recovering his health. He tore himself away at last and reached the port of Damietta, where he found his friend Abu Said son of Halfon ha-Levi, whom he had known of and esteemed at a distance.

Again the journey was interrupted, for an invitation awaited him from the Jewish Nagid at Fustat, Samuel son of Hananiah Abu Manzur, to visit him. With much reluctance the poet yielded. He was charmed with the Nagid and his household, and he made a friend of the principal of the Fustat college, Nathan son of Samuel. Equipped with letters of introduction—he would accept nothing else, and what hospitality he received he paid back with glowing verses— he once more found himself in Damietta. Though entreated to abide in Egypt, the erstwhile home of Israel and the scene of the first redemption, he begged to be permitted to go to his Master, that he might lodge where his fathers once lodged, fearful lest peradventure an untoward incident should befall him. The untoward incident did befall him; so at least according to the legend which narrates that, as he was pouring out his soul in stirring verses before the Temple mount, he was trodden under foot and stabbed to death by an Arab horseman. The same legend locates his burial place in the Holy Land.

But whether or not he found his rest in the sacred soil—
it seems rather that, saddened by the sight of Christian
occupation, he wandered forth to Tyre and Damascus—his
swansong was the crowning elegy known as the 'Zionide'
which through the confines of Israel to this day is recited on
the ninth of Ab, the day commemorative of the destruction
of the Temple. The poet sends to Zion the greetings of the
captive nation and of himself, held captive by longing, pouring forth his tears like the dew of Hermon. He yearns that
his tears may descend upon the hills of the Holy Land, the
land whose very stones and dust he would fondly cherish,
where it were sweetness to walk barefoot over the wastes
that were once the sanctuary of God and whose very air is
the breath of life. Saddened at the sight of the hardships of
the Jew in the land of his fathers, he rises to the hope that
all the kingdoms of the idols will pass away, but that Zion,
the elect seat of the divine Glory, will outlast them all.
Happy, the singer concludes, is he that will wait until the
time comes when the light will once more arise on Zion and
her dawn break, when the elect people will exult in the joy
of Zion restored to her youthful state. Judah ha-Levi gave
immortal expression to the deepest hope of his people, just
as, far ahead of his time and unique in the entire history of
the Jews since Bible times, he penetrated into the inner core
of Judaism and prepared an understanding of it which called
for steadfastness and faithfulness even unto death. As if
prophetically foreseeing the calamity that ultimately befell
the Spanish center, he pointed the way to concentration
upon the ancient soil.

The Almoravides, enfeebled by enjoyment and completely
demoralized, were overthrown by an insurrection in Africa,
led by Ibn Tumart. This former pupil of the mystic Ghazali
gave himself out for the Mahdi, the God-appointed religious
leader, and founded the sect of the Almohades holding to a
strict conception of the Unity of God (tawhid). In a brief
period the Almohades made themselves masters of the Moslem possessions, to the south and to the north of the Straits
of Gibraltar. Morocco fell into their hands in 1146. The Jews

were given the choice of emigration or of conversion to Islam. Those who chose to remain embraced Mohammedanism in appearance, but secretly practised their own religion. Men like Judah ha-Cohen Ibn Shoshan of Fez, who would not yield, died as martyrs.

The same fate befell the Jews in Spain when in 1148 Cordova, and a year later the whole of Andalusia, was conquered by the fanatical Almohades. The Jewish seats of learning at Seville and Lucena were closed. Many Jews made a pretense of accepting Islam; others, like Meir, the son and successor of Ibn Megas, fled to Christian Toledo, where the emperor Alphonso VII. (1126–1157) granted them a refuge. Henceforth the Christian capital grew to be an important center of Jewish activity and learning. Alphonso availed himself of the services of Judah Ibn Ezra, a nephew of the poet Moses. The Jewish favorite was appointed governor of Calatrava, the frontier fortress between Toledo and Cordova, and later on imperial majordomo. He was given supreme jurisdiction over the Jews of Castile with the title of Nasi (Prince); thanks to his efforts, his coreligionists who fled from the fanatical Almohades were able to secure a foothold in the territory of his Christian master. A school for the study of the Talmud, under the headship of Meir Ibn Megas, was opened in Toledo.

Two eminent scholars in Toledo, quite disparate in experiences and theoretical views, shed lustre on that age. Abraham Ibn Daud (c. 1110–1180), the younger of the two, is best known as a historian. His concise chronicle, 'The Order of Tradition,' was principally directed against the Karaites; it furnishes valuable information on the Spanish period. He also wrote a philosophical work, 'The Sublime Faith.' The fame of Abraham Ibn Ezra (1092–1167) rests mainly on his grammatical and exegetical labors. He was also a poet of no mean distinction, and his hymns found a place in the liturgy of the synagogue. As a philosopher, he inclined to Neo-Platonic speculations. He was a many-sided man, roving over divers fields of knowledge, even as in his restlessness he encompassed many lands.

Ibn Ezra was not encumbered with worldly possessions; he was very poor. Wit that he was, he said of himself that were he to deal in shrouds none would die, and were he to sell candles the sun would never set. Wherever he set foot, he astounded the people by his learning and his acumen. He produced a profound impression which in some localities was kept in remembrance long after his death. Everywhere he made friends and received encouragement from wealthy patrons. To please these, or for the benefit of such pupils as he cared to take, he engaged in literary activity. At Rome, in 1140, he wrote a Hebrew grammar and commentaries on the Five Scrolls and the Book of Job. At Lucca, in 1145, he wrote a defense of the Gaon Saadiah against the criticisms of Dunash Ibn Labrat, a commentary on Isaiah and on a part of the Pentateuch. In the same year, at Mantua, he produced another grammatical work; at Béziers, in 1155, he wrote on the Divine Name. The next years found him at Dreux in France busy with commentaries on Daniel, the Twelve Prophets, Exodus, and the remainder of the Pentateuch. In London, in 1158, he wrote a theological work, 'The Foundation of Fear,' and his 'Epistle on the Sabbath.' Once more in northern France he came in contact with the two brothers, Jacob (Tam) and Samuel (p. 364), grandsons of Rashi. In 1160, at Narbonne, he translated an astronomical work from the Arabic.

All the works of Ibn Ezra were written in Hebrew; it may be said that he created Hebrew prose style for scientific purposes. To the Jews north of the Pyrenees he brought the sum of the lore of his native country. He was a thorough rationalist and believed that a knowledge of grammar was indispensable for an understanding of Holy Writ. He excerpted his predecessors freely, especially Ibn Janah, on whom he was unduly severe for his pointing out corrupt readings in the received form of the Scriptural text. He had freer notions himself as to the exilic origin of the Second Isaiah (an opinion, as he tells us, advanced by Moses Ibn Chiquitilla) and the post-Mosaic date of passages in the Pentateuch. These views he presented guardedly, almost enigmatically.

His exposition of the Scriptures, stimulating throughout, scintillating with keen wit, was prized by the scholars ever after. It remains to this day a source which students of the Bible resort to for useful information and many a telling hint. As if overcome with longing for his native home, the wanderer breathed his last at Calahorra, on the boundary between Navarre and Old Castile. On his death-bed he is said to have applied to himself the Scriptural verse (Genesis 12, 4): 'And Abraham was seventy and five years old when he departed out of the world's wrath (*haron* for *haran*, Haran).'

With the center of Jewish life shifted northward, Jewish communities were spread over the five Christian kingdoms: Castile, Leon, Aragon, Portugal, and Navarre. The outstanding community, counting more than twelve thousand members, was in Toledo. It boasted of several magnificent synagogues. Many of its Jews were men of wealth and culture. They were also distinguished by bravery and were accustomed to the use of weapons; the Jewish youth cultivated the art of fencing and gave themselves a knightly appearance. Alphonso VIII. (1158–1214) employed gifted Jews in the service of the state. Two men stood in particularly high favor at the court of this king (it is narrated that he had a love affair with a beautiful Jewish maiden, Rachel, also called Formosa): Joseph son of Solomon Ibn Shoshan and Abraham Ibn al-Fakhar, the latter of whom was entrusted with a diplomatic mission to the court of the Almohade prince at Morocco. Both were looked up to by their coreligionists; they were lavish in erecting houses of worship and, being scholarly men themselves, in patronizing poor scholars.

Despite the activity of Meir Ibn Megas and his namesake cousin, the Toledans did not take to the study of the Talmud. Philosophic speculation and playing at poetry was more to the liking of these intellectuals. Judah son of Solomon al-Harizi (died about 1230) was a much traveled man and given to observation of men and manners. He gathered up his experiences in a romance, modeled after the famous work of Hariri (which, moreover, Harizi translated into Hebrew). In rhymed prose, interspersed with measured verses, the most trivial and the most weighty matters are discussed with astounding stylistic skill. One of the poems is composed in three languages, Hebrew, Aramaic, and Arabic. The whole of the 'Tahkemoni'—'Wise Instructor'—was meant to entertain rather than to instruct. Nevertheless the author evinces much critical judgment in appraising the Hebrew poets of Spain.

The Jews of Castile shared the vicissitudes of Alphonso's campaigns against the Almohades. When after the ill-fated battle of Alarcos (1195) the king shut himself up in his capital, the Jews vied with the Christian citizens in stubbornly defending the city. The enemy at length retreated before the combined onslaught of Castile and Aragon. The allied armies, marching across the kingdom of Leon, did much damage to this territory. In this campaign the most celebrated Hebrew Bible manuscript of Spain, which went by the name of Hilleli and served as a standard for copyists, fell into the enemy's hands (1197). The Jews of Aragon fared well under King Alphonso II. (1162–1196), himself a patron of poets and scholars. The capital Saragossa had long been the seat of a flourishing Jewish community. At this time it was eclipsed by Barcelona, which, because of its favorable situation near the sea, tended to attract men of enterprise in mercantile pursuits. At the head of the Barcelona community, rich in princely men of high station, stood Shesheth Benveniste (died in 1195). A prince of princes, a physician and statesman, he was employed in diplomatic services by his king, and like Ibn Naghdelah was the friend and patron of Jewish scholars.

The community of Tudela, a small town on the Ebro, the possession of which was contested by Aragon and Navarre on two occasions, secured for themselves by their manly stand parity of treatment with Christians and Moslems. For their protection the Jews had a citadel of their own. This community produced a scholarly traveler, Benjamin son of Jonah of Tudela. From 1160 to 1173 he traversed southern Europe, Asia, and Africa, and his Itinerary is replete with interesting statistics and facts bearing not only on Jewish, but also on universal history. The small community of Gerona on the river Ter in Catalonia was the birthplace of several talmudic scholars. Yet none of these communities could attain to such eminence of position as had characterized the southern seats of Jewry, like Cordova, Granada, Seville, and Lucena, before the Almohade conquest.

CHAPTER XLIX

MOSES MAIMONIDES

(1135-1204)

THE condition of the Jews in Moslem Spain was now a lamentable one. For the most part they accepted Islam for appearance sake, and although in secret they remained attached to Judaism, a fruitful Jewish activity was out of the question. The best and staunchest had fled. Among them was the adjunct rabbi, Maimun, descended from a family which for eight generations counted devoted talmudic scholars. He was a pupil of Joseph Ibn Megas. Uprooted from his home, Maimun took his family to Fez. There he was confronted with a growing weariness of the secret practice of Judaism on the part of a number of his coreligionists, who were making ready to go over completely to Mohammedanism. Maimun sought to sustain them. In a consolatory epistle (1160) he urged the faint-hearted to hold fast to the belief in the election of Israel, the supreme worth of the teachings of Moses, and the sure fulfilment of the divine promises.

Yet Maimun himself determined to seek freedom in the East. In 1165 the family landed in Acco, where the emigrants from Spain met with a kind reception at the hands of the Jewish community and its rabbi, Japheth son of Elijah. The whole of Palestine, which was in Christian hands, counted scarcely more than a thousand Jewish families. In some localities there lived from one or three to twenty families; Tiberias had fifty, and Jerusalem some three hundred. The Jews of the Holy City dwelt in a corner below the Tower of David; the dyeing industry was concentrated in their hands. But after a while all but one of these Jews were driven out of Jerusalem. When in 1187 Saladin, the founder of the Ayyubid dynasty in Egypt, reconquered Palestine from the Latins, the Jews returned to the Holy City.

Maimun remained but three days in Jerusalem; one day the family spent at Hebron in devotion at the graves of the patriarchs; the conditions were altogether unfavorable for a permanent settlement in the Holy Land, and so they proceeded to Egypt. Maimun died soon after his arrival in that country; there his eldest son achieved that fame which marked him out as the unquestioned spiritual leader of Jewry during his lifetime and as the greatest authority for all future ages.

Moses son of Maimun, or, as he is usually called, Maimonides (Maimuni), belonged to Spain by birth and early education. Cordova, where he was born March 30, 1135, in our own day has shown itself proud of this distinction by naming one of its streets after the Jewish philosopher. Carefully nurtured by his father in talmudical learning, and early brought in contact with universal knowledge, he shared the vicissitudes of his family. While yet in Spain, at the age of three and twenty years, he began work on the 'Luminary,' a truly illuminating commentary on the Mishnah in Arabic. Uninterruptedly he kept at it during the family's migrations, laboring under great difficulties, with no adequate material at hand; but such was his mastery of the Talmud that he could rely on his memory.

The work was completed in Egypt in 1168. It was the first of his masterly productions, distinguished by clear and methodical systematization. It was not a running commentary in the manner of the French schools. The talmudic discussions, in so far as they bear on an understanding of the Mishnah, are condensed. Often enough the author goes his own way independently of the Talmud. The reader is prepared for what is to come by summary prefatory remarks which bring out salient points; larger introductions of a systematic character precede the single tractates or Orders. At the head of the whole work there is a lengthy introduction, in which it is taught that only those statements of law are authoritative upon which there is no divergent opinion. With particular predilection those points in the Mishnah are gone into which partake of a scientific character, and the

expounder draws on his fund of knowledge, whether it
be mathematics, astronomy, physics, anatomy, ethics, or
philosophy.

The commentary on the ethical tract of the Mishnah, 'The
Sayings of the Fathers,' has a preface of eight chapters, in
which Aristotelian ethics, as understood by the Arab philosophers, is bodily transplanted on Jewish soil. Maimonides
was thoroughly convinced that the two systems, the Jewish
and the Greek, were equally true. His was a logical mind and
his whole point of view was intellectualist. Thus he freely
operated with philosophical speculations and gave them a foothold amid the essentially legal norms of the traditional Code.

The opening of the tenth chapter in Sanhedrin, in which
the Mishnah excludes from participation in the bliss of the
world to come certain classes of unbelievers, affords Maimonides an opportunity to formulate thirteen articles of the
Jewish Creed. A denial of any one of these on the part of
a Jew carries of itself excommunication from the Jewish
fold. Summaries of these articles have since been incorporated into the liturgy in the form of verse and prose. They
affirm the Existence of God, His indivisible Unity, His
Incorporeality and Immutability, His Eternity and Pre-
mundane Existence, His sole claim to worship; the inspiration of the prophets, the supreme and incomparable prophetic inspiration of Moses, the divine origin and immutability
of the Torah; Divine Providence in rewarding the righteous
and punishing the wicked; the future advent of the Messiah;
the future resurrection of the dead. What was new in this
summary of Judaism was that the tacit assent to its cardinal
dogmas was now turned into an open avowal upon which
the very status of a Jew depended. It also placed emphasis
not only on Jewish life as it manifested itself in a multitude
of religious acts, but on correct belief as well.

The formulation of the Jewish Creed was directed against
the philosophical atheist and the philosophical materialist,
against the polytheist and the trinitarian, against the anti-
nomians of all times who taught the abrogation of the Torah,
against Mohammed who set himself up as the seal of the

prophets, against a predeterminism which negated freedom of the will and made accountability impossible. Lastly, again, it aimed to offset Christianity which, in its apocalyptic beginnings, made of the advent of the Messiah an otherworldly event bound up with the resurrection and with the inauguration of the future world. The whole of the Creed, no matter which of its parts later thinkers accepted or rejected as a fundamental belief, commended itself as a systematic presentation of Judaism in contrast with the gross mythologies of heathendom and the competing systems of Christianity and Islam.

Moslem fanaticism of the Almohade variety in the west, which drove Maimonides from Spain and the Maghreb, found a repercussion in Yemen, where two partisans of the Shiah compelled the Jews to accept Islam under the threat of severe punishments. Here again the Jews accommodated themselves to a lip-profession of Islam. A Jewish renegade appeared preaching to the communities that Mohammed was referred to in the Torah and that Islam was a new, divinely documented revelation superseding Judaism. Moreover, a Jewish visionary came forward proclaiming himself a precursor of the Messiah and summoning the Jews to make ready for the termination of their sufferings by dividing their possessions with the poor.

One of the Yemenite scholars, Jacob al-Fayumi, turned for advice to Maimonides, who, in his Epistle to the Yemenites, reiterated his belief that the root of all the hatred, to which the Jews have been exposed at all times, is opposition to Judaism, to the Jewish religion, to the Torah. Mohammed is so far from being alluded to in the Torah that the Mohammedans have charged the Jews with falsifying Scripture and excising references to their prophet. The relation of the two daughter-religions to the mother-faith, the true revelation in the Torah, is like that of a portrait, no matter how well executed, to the living person. Maimonides deprecates all attempts at ascertaining by calculation the time of redemption, although Saadiah had done so. Instead of the redemption there had come the Almohade persecution, exactly as the Jews of Persia had suffered through the pseudo-Messianic movements at the beginning of Moslem dominion. Nevertheless Maimonides could not forbear to point to a tradition in his family that the year 1216 would be the Messianic year; so deeply rooted was the Messianic hope of ultimate restoration in the heart of the sanest of Jews. The Epistle accomplished its purpose. The Yemenite Jews held fast to their ancestral faith; gratefully they remembered the name of the great leader, who used his influence at the court of Egypt to have the religious persecution stopped. In the Kaddish prayer they phrased the second petition thus: 'May His kingdom come in your lifetime and in the lifetime of our teacher Moses son of Maimun'—an honor heretofore accorded only to the Babylonian exilarch.

The fame of Maimonides spread and from all communities in the East questions were submitted to him for his authoritative decision. Ephraim, the rabbi of Tyre, desired to know whether in his quality of a scholar, though a man of wealth, he might claim exemption from the communal tax. Ephraim's disciples turned to Maimonides in 1177 for advice on a number of points. One of the questions touched the boundaries of the Holy Land, and Maimonides showed himself a poor student of geography. As to the importance of astronomy for the Jewish scholar, that science was his chosen field, and he ruled that he who knows the subject and neglects to turn it to good use is one of those who 'regard not the work of the Lord, neither have they considered the operation of His hands' (Isaiah 5, 12). Might a Jew instruct men of other faiths in the Scriptures? Christians by all means, because they recognize the Jewish Scriptures as divinely inspired; but not Mohammedans, because they deny the authority of the Torah. This view did not prevent Maimonides in another place from conceding that the Moslems were true monotheists; in his opinion both Jesus and Mohammed fulfilled a mission in paving the way for the Messiah who is to come, inasmuch as through them large parts of humanity have been brought nigh unto the knowledge of God and moral perfection.

When Maimonides settled in Fustat, he and his younger brother David maintained themselves by trading in precious stones. The business was actually in the hands of the brother, while Moses was free to devote himself to study. David lost his life on one of his business journeys to India. Moses turned to the practice of medicine for a livelihood. His skill as a physician brought him to the attention of Saladin's vizir, who paid him an annual stipend for his medical services, and from that time on, some twenty years after his settlement in Egypt, he was greatly in demand among the court circle. However, he ministered to high and low, rich and poor, and he was kept busy until late at night.

It is really marvelous how he found time at all for his literary pursuits, considering that at an early date he had taken upon himself the gratuitous burden of presiding over the college of rabbis at the Egyptian capital. In this capacity he strove to correct many abuses, both in the synagogue worship and in the home life. He watched that no Karaite practices should filter through into the religious life of the Rabbanites, but otherwise he enjoined tolerance toward the Karaite dissenters. He declined a call from the Frankish king in Ashkelon, presumably Richard Coeur-de-lion, to become his body-physician. He was satisfied to remain where he was, enjoying the favor of his friend the all-powerful vizir who had Maimonides named head (Nagid) of all Egyptian Jewry. This dignity he employed to protect his coreligionists far and wide, and it remained hereditary in his family down to the fourteenth century.

In 1180 Maimonides completed the second of his great works, the only one which he wrote in the Hebrew language, the 'Double of the Torah' (Mishneh Torah) or 'Strong Hand' (YaD ha-Hazakah; YD standing in Hebrew for 14, the number of books into which the work is divided). Into this Code of Jewish Law Maimonides gathered together the whole of Jewish jurisprudence, religious, civil, and criminal. Moreover, in contradistinction to all his predecessors and successors he also incorporated all matters pertinent to the religious life in Palestine, even the Palestine of the past. No detail escaped him in the sea of the Talmud or in gaonic literature; still more notable is the architectonic structure of the whole, the grouping under heads, and the lucidity of the style. Scientist that he was, he enriched his Code with an elucidation of the principles of Jewish calendar-making in accordance with astronomical knowledge. His philosophical bent of mind found scope to codify Aristotelian ethics and his own refined metaphysical notions concerning God, the human soul, the human destiny, thus making rational cognition of these matters a Jewish duty on a par with all that goes to make Jewish life. The Code opens with the solemn words of the First Book, called 'Knowledge': 'The principle of principles and the pillar of all wisdom is to know that there is a primal Being, who called into existence all that is,' and closes with the prophetic vision of the time when 'the earth shall be full of the knowledge of the Lord, as the waters cover the sea.'

It was inevitable that the work, the first and only one of its kind to embrace the whole of talmudic law, should meet with criticism. The chief opposition came from Bagdad, where the exilarchate had been renewed and the gaonate restored. At the time Samuel son of Ali was Gaon and after the death of the second exilarch aspired also to the dignity of the headship of the Jews in the East. Samuel was jealous of the increasing prestige of Maimonides and sought to belittle his talmudic erudition. There was, however, also honest criticism on the part of those who feared that the Code would lead to a neglect of the study of the Talmud. The sequel, however, proved the apprehension ill-founded.

Though the author reiterated that he aimed only to facilitate decisions for those who were not professional students of the Talmud, there was a tendency in the work to transform the fluid matter of the Talmud into a rigid fixity. This tendency was perhaps instinctively felt by the faultfinders. Then there were omissions, some through inadvertence, others intentional, as in the case of superstitious notions. Lastly, heresy-hunters were scandalized by the fact that there was lacking the traditional belief in bodily resurrection. Maimonides' sublimated conception of Heaven was really only for the elect who by virtue of right cognition obtain a foretaste of it in their mundane existence through participation in the active intellect of God.

The brunt of the attack was borne by the master's favorite pupil, Joseph Ibn Aknin, of Ceuta in the Maghreb. At Fustat he had been inducted by Maimonides into the sciences and philosophy and was now residing in Aleppo. Exasperated by the intrigues against his beloved teacher, Joseph thought of carrying the combat into the enemy's camp by establishing a rival talmudical school at Bagdad. He desisted at the advice of the sage master, who urged him to cling to his medical profession.

To Ibn Aknin Maimonides dedicated his third great work, the 'Guide of the Perplexed,' which he completed about 1195. In this work Maimonides speaks as a philosopher to the philosophically trained, and on it rests his fame in the history of Christian scholasticism to which he gave an important stimulus. In the 'Guide' Maimonides boldly rationalized Jewish theology. He operated with the Aristotelian philosophy as expounded by the Arab thinker Avicenna (Ibn Sina, died 1037); in all matters pertaining to the sublunar world the authority of the Stagirite was with him unimpeachable. Maimonides stopped short of the Aristotelian teachings with regard to the eternity of matter; not because of any difficulty in reading the proposition into Holy Writ, but solely because he considered it philosophically untenable. The cosmological argument for the Existence of God has chiefly a historical interest.

A lasting contribution to Jewish theology was his uncompromising rejection of the literal interpretation of Scriptural anthropomorphisms. In this he stood in line with a long traditional development, most thoroughly embodied in the authoritative Aramaic version of Onkelos. At the hands of Maimonides it became a doctrine of the inadmissibility of all positive attributes to the Deity. What God is not, may be expressed in words; not what He is, at most what He does. The divine Providence is concerned solely with species except in regard to human beings, over each and every one God exercises special, individual care. Prophecy is intellectualized. There is a rational explanation of all the commandments of the Torah; some, like those touching the sacrificial cult, were concessions to the idolatrous propensities of the people. All the precepts bear ultimately upon moral improvement; subservience to reason is the highest maxim of morals, as reasoned cognition of God's Existence and Unity is the highest duty in religion.

In this theological system, the age-long process of welding Hellenic wisdom and Judaic faith, begun in Alexandria, continued by Saadiah in Bagdad and by Ibn Daud in Toledo, was given a touch of finish which betrays sincere belief in the truth of both. The effect of the work upon Jewry was diverse: the liberals acclaimed it with joy, while the conservative elements anathematized it. The combat was a protracted one, lasting more than a century; the two camps warred stubbornly and bitterly.

The aged sage witnessed the gathering storm with philosophical calm. His fame had reached the zenith, his place in the annals of history was assured. Worn out by professional and communal duties as well as by gigantic literary labors, he passed away on December 13, 1204. He was mourned by Jewry the world over. In Jerusalem solemn obsequies were held amid general fasting; from the Torah was read the forecast of national disaster, and from the Book of Samuel the narrative of the capture of the Ark. 'The glory is departed from Israel; for the ark of God is taken.' The remains were entombed in Tiberias, and on his grave an inscription, penned by an unknown hand, likened him to a celestial being descended into this lower world. In his lifetime, the brief but telling adage had been coined by his admirers: 'From Moses (the prophet) to Moses (son of Maimun) there hath arisen none like unto him.' In Provence, the country nearest the land of his birth, a circle of enthusiasts held his name in veneration. At home he left his honor in the keeping of his worthy son, Abraham, born to him in old age, who succeeded his father as head of the Jewry of Egypt and as physician in ordinary to the sultan.

CHAPTER L

(321-1040)

A CENTURY at least before the Germanic tribes overran the Roman province of Gaul, when the imperial legions stood guard over the river Rhine, Jewish settlements, composed of traders following the soldiers to their fortresses, were to be found in the empire's northernmost outpost on the continent. At Cologne (Colonia Agrippina), the colony planted by the emperor Claudius in the year 50, there existed an organized community, with its customary functionaries, in 321. Its beginnings may have dated from the very foundation of the municipality. Under the Christian emperors, the Jews of Gaul suffered a diminution of their rights as full Roman citizens. A curb was set upon their proselytizing. They were excluded from public positions, from owning Christian slaves or employing Christian laborers, and from intermarriage with Christians.

The heathen Franks, when they established themselves in Gaul, treated their Jewish subjects, who spoke the vulgar Latin and bore Roman names, on a par with the Romans; but the Church saw to it that the legislative restrictions remained in force. The Christian laity had to be exhorted again and again not to break bread at a Jewish table and to refrain from giving their daughters in marriage to Jews. Hilary of Poitiers (died 366), it is reported, had a horror of even answering the greetings of a Jewish passer-by in the street. This aversion was shared neither by the lower clergy nor by the Christian laity who freely associated with the Jews. Close contact with the Christian population led some Jews to be beguiled into embracing the Christian faith. But the majority clung steadfastly to their own religion and practised its observances conscientiously. They occupied themselves with agriculture, trade, and commerce. Jewish healers were consulted even by the clergy, and Jews helped to defend Arles when it was besieged by Franks and Burgundians (508).

Clovis (481–511), the true founder of the Frankish monarchy, on his conversion to the Catholic faith, was powerful enough to hold the clergy in submission. Hence under his immediate successors the Jews were unmolested, save for restrictive measures fostered by Church councils. Much harsher was the legislation in Burgundy, according to which bodily injury committed by a Jew on a Christian entailed heavier punishment than when perpetrated by a Christian. Soon the Merovingians likewise yielded to clerical intolerance. The Third Council of Orleans (538) forbade the Jews to appear in public for four days beginning with Holy Thursday, so as not to affront the Christians living under Catholic monarchs; this measure was approved by Childebert I. (511–558).

The soul of this animosity against the Jews was the bishop Avitus of Clermont. He strove with all might to lure the Jews from their faith. On an Easter Day, as a renegade was being led to baptism, he was insulted by his former coreligionists. Consequently, on Ascension Day, the mob destroyed the synagogue. On the morrow the good bishop placed before the Jews the choice, to accept Christianity or to leave the town. For three days the Jews wavered; then five hundred went to the baptismal font, while the rest emigrated to Marseilles (576). The Council of Mâcon (581) forbade the appointment of Jews as judges (as the Council of Clermont in 535 had done previously) or farmers of taxes, lest the Christians should appear subject to them. It was further ordered that the Jews should show proper respect to the clergy and remain standing in their presence unless ordered to be seated. A Jew guilty of converting a Christian slave was to lose him as well as the right to dispose of his own property by will.

The king Chilperic I. (561–584) was eager to convert Jews and acted as godfather to as many as were won over. He had one Jew, Priscus of Paris, as his business agent, but the persuasion of the learned Gregory, bishop of Tours, with whom the king had brought him together, was powerless to move Priscus to forswear his faith. Cast into prison by the irate king, Priscus asked for delay until after his son's marriage with a Jewess of Marseilles. Phatir, one of those converted Jews at whose baptism the king had been godfather, fell upon Priscus on a sabbath day, when he was unarmed, and slew him together with his friends (582). The murderer was pardoned, but the kinsmen of Priscus slew him in revenge.

After the assassination of Chilperic, Guntram of Burgundy became the protector of the realm. At Orleans, the Jews acclaimed him in the Hebrew tongue. He refused, however, to grant their petition that their synagogue, which had been destroyed by Christians, might be rebuilt at public cost, and upbraided them as 'evil, perfidious, and crafty' (585). The bishops of Arles and Marseilles were reprimanded by pope Gregory for the use of force in converting Jews (591). The same pope, however, admonished the queen Brunhild to enact laws against the holding of Christian slaves by Jews (599). Similar requests were made of the kings Theodoric and Theodebert.

The last Merovingian kings, whose power was weakened by concessions to the rich landowners, the bishops, and the aristocracy, gave free rein to vexatious regulations against the Jews and to downright persecution. Chlotar II. sanctioned the enactment at the Fifth Council of Paris (614) that no Jew should hold civil or military office. The Spanish Jews, escaping to France from the persecutions of Sisebut (p. 305), found no refuge. Dagobert I. (628–638), who succeeded Chlotar, spurred on by the emperor Heraclius, ordered all the Jews of France to accept baptism under pain of banishment from his realm (629). The decree seems to have been ruthlessly carried out, and for a century and a half we do not hear of a Jew in the Frankish dominions.

Only in the southern district by the sea, that of Narbonne, where the Visigoths ruled, did the Jews maintain themselves. They lived in the most friendly relations with the

Christian population and took part in the rebellion against king Wamba of Spain. When in 673 the insurrection was put down, the Jews were driven out. Yet in 689 there were still Jewish residents in the city of Narbonne; three children of Paragorus son of Sapaudus, Justus, Matrona, and Dulciorella, died in that year—it is not quite clear whether as victims of an epidemic or of an unrecorded persecution—and received Jewish burial. The Jews returned with the Arabs in 720; when these were driven back beyond the Pyrenees, Jewish owners of land in villages and suburbs were left in their possessions by the Frankish conquerors, much to the dislike of the Church authorities who were grieved to see Christian laborers employed on Jewish plantations.

When the Carolingian dynasty displaced the shadowy Merovingian kings, the Jews throughout the Frankish kingdom shared in the benefits of a firm régime. Under Charles the Great, or Charlemagne (768–814), and his son Louis the Pious (814–840), Jews, thanks to their connections with their brethren abroad, concentrated in their hands almost entirely the commerce of the land, especially the export and import of goods. A Jew, Isaac, was a member of the embassy sent by Charlemagne to Harun ar-Rashid. He was the sole survivor who returned. Christian traders paid into the coffers of the king one-eleventh of their profits, while Jews paid one-tenth. Certain Jewish merchants, who commended themselves to the emperor, were granted special protection; so Domatus and his nephew Samuel, David and Joseph in Lyons, Abraham at Saragossa. An imperial officer, known as 'master of the Jews,' saw to it in every community that these privileges were maintained and life and property made safe. In Lyons, the market day was changed from Saturday to another day of the week because the Jews would not trade on their sabbath.

Restrictions were placed on the trade in produce and wine and on hoarding coin; nor was it lawful for Jews to accept church untensils in pledge or detain a Christian debtor. Offenses against Christian laws or crimes against Christian persons were severely punished. In a lawsuit between a

Christian and a Jew, the number of witnesses required from the latter exceeded that furnished by the former. A special form of oath was prescribed for Jews. As between Jew and Jew, the disputes were adjudicated by Jewish courts. The canonical regulations were allowed to remain a dead letter. New synagogues were erected, and in them sermons were delivered in the vernacular and listened to with pleasure even by Christian visitors.

The chief offense in the eyes of the Church was the Jewish trade in slaves and the employment by Jews of Christian laborers and domestics. Some of the slaves were clearly heathen, and the Jewish masters often performed on them the rite of circumcision. The bishops thought that the slaves ought to submit to baptism, and in general were uneasy about Christian domestics abstaining from labor on the sabbath and performing service on Sunday. Nor were they satisfied that Christians should partake of Jewish food or buy meat and wine of them, considering that the Jews abstained from food prepared by Christians.

Agobard of Lyons, a man otherwise of clear intellect and saintly character, averse to image-worship, adoration of saints, and superstition, was much chagrined by the imperial indulgence towards the Jews. His feelings found vent in connnection with the following incident. The woman-slave of a prominent Jew in Lyons escaped and, in order to secure her freedom, had herself baptized by Agobard. The Jewish owner demanded the surrender of the escaped slave and, when Agobard would not hear of it, appealed to Everard, the Jews' master. On the side of the Jews was the imperial will as manifested in the grant of privileges, which the bishop sought to make inoperative by enlisting the aid of his friends at court who were inimical to the Jews.

In a series of writings Agobard undertook to demonstrate the churchly point of view in dealing with the Jews and to represent the Jewish claims of descent from the patriarchs as unworthy of consideration. The Jewish religion was for him but a tissue of false pretensions and superstitions, and against the Jewish 'insolence' the authority of the older

Frankish kings was invoked. A synod was convoked at Lyons (829) under the presidency of the zealous prelate. The ecclesiastical agitation took on a political aspect when Agobard and his bishops, aided by the minister Wala, supported the cause of the king's sons by his first marriage against the empress Judith, Louis' second wife, who endeavored to secure the inheritance for her own son, Charles. The elder sons revolted in 831, Louis was deposed at the assembly of Compiègne (833); but soon he regained his throne. Agobard was deposed (835), but after a while the emperor reinstated him.

On still another occasion the emperor gave proof of his just and benevolent attitude toward the Jews. The Jew Gaudiocus and his sons Jacob and Vivacius brought complaint that their letters of protection, ensuring to them the possession of their inherited estates, had been taken from them by malevolent persons. Their petition, supported by the emperor's brother, the abbot and chancellor Hugh, was granted (839). The pious monarch, however, was painfully affected by an incident which fell in the same year. The deacon Bodo, a learned cleric of Alemannic descent and brought up at court, had received permission from the empress to make a pilgrimage to Rome. Instead, however, of proceeding to the capital of Christendom, he betook himself, in the company of his nephew, to Saragossa, where he openly embraced Judaism, taking on the name Eleazar and espousing a Jewish maiden. His nephew likewise became a Jew.

These conversions, brought about by the free intercourse between Jews and Christians, led the bishops to insist on social segregation and the curtailing of Jewish privileges. Amulo, Agobard's successor in the bishopric of Lyons, renewed the literary warfare against the Jews. At the councils of Meaux and Paris (845, 846) the old canonical restrictions were reënacted. Neither Charles the Bald (843–877) nor his Carolingian successors in France would go the whole length of the episcopal recommendations. Jewish merchants imported into the land of the Franks spices from the far East

and exported silks, furs, swords, eunuchs, boy and girl slaves.
However, the virus of episcopal fanaticism spread slowly
but surely among princes and people. A slave circumcised by
a Jew became free, whether he had been a Christian or of
another faith. At Béziers, in the week between Palm Sunday
and Easter Monday, the bishops would summon the faithful
to wreak vengeance on the Jewish inhabitants for the passion of Christ; the Christians were permitted to throw staves
at the Jews. At Toulouse, the count of the city had the
practice annually on Good Friday of smiting the cheek of
the syndic, or chief, of the Jewish community. In the beginning of the twelfth century an annual payment was substituted for this shameful custom. It was fabled that the
Jews had once betrayed, or thought of betraying, the city
to the Arabs, though these had never come near Toulouse.
Because of a rumor that the Jews had made common cause
with the Normans, the entire Jewish population of Sens was
banished (875–876). Charles the Simple (898–929) turned
over to the Church estates and vineyards, salt-mines and
houses, owned by Jews in the Duchy of Narbonne and
previously subject to the payment of tithes to the Church.

The decay of royal power and the rise of feudalism exposed
the Jews to the arbitrary will of the nobles who disposed of
them as if they were serfs. Nor did the rise of the Capetian
dynasty in 987 immediately bring to the Jews resident in
France a position of security. The Jews of Limoges were
offered the choice between baptism and exile. A very small
number succumbed; several in despair took their own lives;
the majority, with wives and children, accepted banishment
(1010). Somewhat more tolerable were the conditions in
southern France, in Provence and Languedoc. There, in the
eleventh century, suddenly emerged a spiritual life. The
first important teacher of the Talmud was Judah son of
Meir ha-Cohen (Leon or Leontin). He was far surpassed by
his pupil, Gershom of Mayence, 'the Frenchman in the land
of Germany.'

In Germany, which since the Treaty of Verdun (843) had
been separated from the Frankish empire, the earliest Jewish

communities were to be found all along the Rhine, on both sides of the river, in Lorraine, or among the Franconians and Swabians. Then we find them along the upper course of the Danube in Bavaria and Austria, and on the upper course of the Elbe in Bohemia. Accordingly Jewish Germany followed on the whole the lines of the Roman conquests, the Jews coming from the south, from Italy, and spreading northwards and southwards. Beside Cologne—which, as we saw (p. 346), harbored Jews in the times of Constantine, and where a synagogue, which remained in Jewish hands for 414 years, was erected in 1012—Augsburg and Metz had been inhabited by Jews by the close of the ninth century. In the tenth there are records of Jews in Worms, Mayence, Prague, Magdeburg, Merseburg, Ratisbon.

The feudal organism of the Germanic state made it impossible for the Jews to own land, and so they were thrown completely upon commerce. Jew and merchant were synonymous terms. Thus Otto the Great (936–973) placed under the jurisdiction of the bishop of Magdeburg the Jews and the other merchants of the town (965). Similarly Otto II. (973–983) gave to the bishopric of Merseburg full jurisdiction over all within the walls of the town, including Jews and merchants. We had occasion to narrate (p. 299) how this emperor was saved in his campaign by a faithful Jew in his entourage. The name of this Jew was Calonymus, and it is likely that the migration of the Calonymus family from Lucca to Mayence, which is usually set in the times of Charlemagne, is really connected with that incident. There was an awakening of spiritual interests among the Jews of Germany. In the second half of the tenth century the Rhenish Jews addressed queries, particularly on the subject of the Messianic advent, to Palestine. There was at that time in the Holy Land a college presided over by a priestly family (Joseph ha-Cohen and his descendants). They were successors to the family of Aaron Ben Meir who traced his descent to Hillel. The real founder of talmudic learning in Germany was Gershom son of Judah at Mayence.

Gershom, 'the Luminary of the Exile,' as he was reverently called, was born at Metz about 960; his learning he acquired in France, in the school of Leontin. It is not known what moved him and his brother Machir to settle in Mayence. There Gershom gathered about himself numerous disciples who flocked to him from France, Germany, and Italy The master expounded to them the Talmud plainly and succinctly in the form of a running commentary, which subsequently the pupils, on becoming teachers themselves, committed to writing. Gershom was the acknowledged authority of the three adjacent countries, and queries reached him from many communities. Gershom's fame rests preëminently on a number of regulations promulgated by him under pain of excommunication from the Jewish fold and accepted immediately by all European Jewry. Thus polygamy was prohibited. It was made obligatory for the husband to obtain his wife's consent to a divorce. The secrecy of private correspondence was guarded by the prohibition to open a letter addressed to a third person even when not sealed.

In the early years of the eleventh century a cleric, by the name of Wecelin, embraced Judaism and engaged in a bitter controversy with one of his former pupils. In 1012, emperor Henry II. (1001–1024) ordered the expulsion of the Jews from Mayence. It is possible that under these circumstances many, to save their lives or their fortunes, accepted baptism; among them Gershom's own son. Grieved as the father was over his son's apostasy, he performed all the rites of mourning for him, when shortly thereafter he died a Christian, just as if he had remained in the fold. The public calamity Gershom lamented in a penitential prayer. 'Thy congregation is driven away from her seat and home, faint and prostrate she lifts up her eyes to Thee.'

In a similar strain elegies were composed by Simon son of Isaac, who, however, succeeded in checking the persecution. Many of those who had accepted baptism returned to the fold. Gershom threatened with excommunication any that reminded them of their temporary lapse. Solomon and his wife Rachel were likewise instrumental in having the edict revoked and endeared themselves to the community by the purchase of a new burial-place. The grateful community registered the names of this couple and of its two teachers in its record book for perpetual remembrance during the sabbath service. Gershom's school, in which students of the Talmud from Germany, France, and Italy were trained, flourished for nearly a century.

CHAPTER LI

RASHI AND HIS SCHOOL. THE FIRST CRUSADE

(1040-1105)

JEWISH life was very much the same under the Capetian kings in France or the Franconian emperors in Germany. Local persecutions occurred, as at Lyons (1049) or on the occasion of an expedition of French warriors to Spain to fight the Saracens (1065)—on the way innocent Jews were murdered; the community of Narbonne was saved by the intervention of count Berengar. It was well enough—such was the admonition of pope Alexander II. (1061–1073)—to slay the Saracens who persecuted Christians; but the Jews, who kept the peace, should be let alone.

On both sides of the Rhine talmudic learning was cultivated, and a modest beginning was made in the study of Scripture. At Limousin and Anjou, Joseph son of Samuel Tob-elem (Bonfils) edited older collections of ritual works. Menahem son of Helbo, leaning on Menahem son of Saruk and Dunash Ibn Labrat (p. 311), sought to recover the plain sense of Scripture. At Narbonne, Moses the Preacher collected old homilies. At Worms, a beautiful synagogue in Byzantine style was erected in 1034 through the munificence of a childless couple, Jacob son of David and Rachel. There Isaac son of Eleazar ha-Levi, the father of three scholarly sons, taught. He, as well as Jacob son of Jakar in Mayence and Isaac son of Judah, at first in Worms and then rabbi at Mayence, had been pupils of Gershom, whose traditions they carried on. At their feet sat an illustrious disciple who was destined to transplant the Rhenish learning to his home city in Champagne. He became the epoch-making founder of the French school, distinct from the Spanish, yet rivaling it in importance and fashioning the inner life of Jewry this side of the Pyrenees.

356

Rashi—Solomon son of Isaac—was born in Troyes in 1040, two years after the death of the Gaon Hai, when the old-established seats of learning in the far East had virtually come to a premature end. Troyes was a very important mercantile center, visited by merchants from distant parts of northern Europe, from whom the wide-awake youth learned many interesting facts about foreign countries. With these merchants he traveled to Lorraine. At Worms they still show the bench from which he taught. But legend apart, Rashi tarried in the Rhenish city only during his student days, when 'in want of food, in ragged clothes, and bearing the yoke of matrimony' he imbibed the wisdom of his teachers. At the age of twenty-five, he settled permanently in his native city. If he was named rabbi of Troyes and its environs, he was, according to the custom of the times, unsalaried, sustaining himself and his family as best he might by cultivating a vineyard.

Young as he was, his reputation was immediately established; older men turned to him for scholarly decisions. After the death of his Rhenish teachers (about 1070), young students came to him from France and Germany. On the shelves of his library were copies of Mishnah and the two Talmuds, of Tosephta, of halakic and haggadic Midrashim, of works of the Gaons. As needs might be there were at hand Donnolo's writings, Menahem's Dictionary, the Critique of Dunash—of Hayyuj and Ibn Janah, both of whom wrote in Arabic, no knowledge had reached northern France—latterly also perhaps Nathan's Aruk freshly arrived from Rome. In an even way, disdaining the by-work of dialectic acumen and diffuseness of speech, anticipating as if by divination a difficulty, Rashi expounded the Talmud to the young learners. These expositions he wrote down in note-books forming a Commentary on the Babylonian Talmud, which he submitted to repeated revision. In this Commentary Rashi incorporated the accumulated expository work of the Babylonian and African teachers and especially, nearer home, the immediate traditions of Gershom's school as he had received them from his Rhenish teachers.

Rashi's Commentary surpassed the efforts of all his predecessors. It was a unique work, the like of which had never been seen before, skilful in making plain the most abstruse discussion, masterly in its brevity, taking up the context in brief sections. Aramaic words and expressions are paraphrased in a clear Hebrew and, frequently, in the vernacular French, these renditions figuring among the earliest records of written French. It may be said that without Rashi's Commentary the Talmud would to-day be a sealed book. Rashi also found leisure to write a Commentary on the Bible, which became as popular as his work on the Talmud, chiefly because it maintained an intermediate attitude between the traditional interpretation in Talmud and Midrash and latter-day rational exposition. This Commentary was likewise recast again and again, and in his old age Rashi owned that were he but younger he should make another revision in accordance with the newer interpretation coming up daily.

The Commentary on the Pentateuch, in particular, became in time the most popular and widely used, and ever after the sum of lay education for a Jew consisted in the ability to read his Hummash (Pentateuch) with Rashi. Though the work on the Bible done in France could not measure up to the productions of the Spanish school, a willing exception was always made as regards Rashi, to whom men referred as the Commentator on the Law (Parshandatha). What is most appealing in the two Commentaries, the one on the Talmud which is thoroughly rational and that on the Scriptures which is not quite free from homily, is the touching modesty of the man, who does not scruple to say, 'This I do not understand,' or, 'Concerning this I have no tradition.' With the same modesty he incorporated many a suggestion which came to him from his hearers, whom he apparently drew into his work, making them feel that they were participants rather than recipients.

At the close of the eleventh century, the Church, represented by pope Gregory VII. (1073–1085) and the more diplomatic, but just as vigorous Urban II. (1088–1099), was locked in a deadly combat, over the question of ultimate sovereignty in the Christian world, with the German emperor Henry IV. (1056–1106). Now the emperor was reduced to humiliation (at Canossa, 1077); now Rome had to reckon with this resolute monarch and the anti-pope set up by him. During this time the Jews seemed to be at ease in Germany. Whether it was because the Rhenish provinces in general held with the emperor, or because of the important place the Jews occupied in commerce, they were the recipients of privileges at the hands of bishops and the emperor alike. In 1084, bishop Rüdiger of Spires permitted the Jews to settle in a village incorporated within the city limits, where, for their protection from the populace, they were assigned special quarters fortified by a wall.

The Jews bound themselves to remit to the chapter annually three and a half pounds of Spires coin and were given permission, both in the new settlement and in the city itself, to exchange gold and silver, to buy or sell all manner of goods, and to employ Christian servants. These privileges were ratified in 1090. At the bishop's recommendation, the emperor granted special privileges to Judah son of Calonymus (of the Calonymus family at Mayence), David son of Meshullam, Moses son of Jekuthiel, and other members of the same family. Apparently these Jews were confirmed in their old privileges dating from the time when their ancestors were transplanted from Italy. A similar grant was made to the Jews of Worms under the ministration of Zalman, the 'Jews' bishop.' Little, however, did all these grants, for which the Jews paid considerable sums, avail. Six years later, in the religious zeal engendered by the First Crusade, the populace, on the road to the rescue of the Holy Sepulcher from the infidel Saracen, found victims nearer home—the Jews who stood outside the religious war and, in the eyes of the mob, were accounted enemies of Christianity.

The Jews were not entirely unprepared. Rumors of the threatening danger were heard so soon as the call to the Crusade was sounded by Urban II. at Clermont (in southeastern France) on the 26th of November, 1095. It came to be known that Godfrey of Bouillon had vowed that the blood of Christ would be avenged by the blood of the Jews. Early in January, 1096, the French communities, threatened with extinction if they did not submit to baptism, called on the Rhenish Jews to ordain a general day of fasting and prayer. The Jews on the Rhine felt entirely secure, enjoying as they did the favor of the emperor and of the local rulers. However, they fervently prayed for the safety of their French brethren. The first divisions that poured into Germany were bought off by substantial bribes, which enabled them to procure provisions for the long road. But the frenzy of the mobs, which everywhere formed the advance guard of those that took the cross, was uncontrollable. It was spread abroad that killing a Jew would secure atonement for one's sins. Certain of the leaders took an oath not to leave the country before they had killed a Jew with their own hands.

After the lamentable havoc wrought in Lorraine—in Metz twenty-two Jews, among them Samuel ha-Cohen, lost their lives—the Jews in the Rhenish cities turned for protection to the bishops, in accordance with an earlier rescript of the emperor, then residing in Italy, to the princes, bishops, and counts of the realm. The bishops John at Spires, Adalbert at Worms, Ruthard at Mayence, in response to the solicitations of such Jewish leaders as Moses son of Jekuthiel and Calonymus son of Meshullam, did what was in their power to safeguard Jewish lives and property. As many as could be accommodated in the episcopal palaces were sequestered there; others found a refuge with the secular princes in their castles. The better class of the burghers also took Jews into their homes; all were content to have Jewish property left with them for safe-keeping. The mob overpowered the Jews themselves, though some of them offered armed resistance, and intimidated their protectors.

On May the third, which was a sabbath day, the crusaders surrounded the synagogue of Spires, but the assembled worshipers succeeded in repelling the attack. Then the mob threw itself upon the Jews individually and slew ten of them; one pious Jewess killed herself in order not to fall into the hands of the mob. Apparently, the quick and effective measures taken by the bishop, who had the guilty seized and punished, frightened the mob away. On Sunday, May 18, a larger force, under the leadership of count Emicho, and with the connivance of the burghers, fell upon the Jews of Worms, all such as, counting on promises of protection by the Christian citizens, had remained in their homes. The fewest saved themselves by accepting baptism; the great majority were put to death; many died by their own hands. Jewish dwellings were pillaged and destroyed. The corpses were stripped of their garments, and so they lay until the Jews in the episcopal palace sent to the baptized clothes wherewith to cover the nakedness of the dead martyrs. The children were seized for baptism.

On the following Sunday, the 25th, the crusaders and the burghers, reinforced by the peasants from the neighboring villages, surrounded the Jews in the episcopal palace. After a heavy combat they penetrated within and slew all; many Jews had slain their children and then themselves. The number of those who perished on these two days was about eight hundred souls. The latter Sunday fell upon the new moon of Sivan; the martyrs died singing the 'Hallel' (Psalms 113–118). Isaac son of Eliakim met his death as he was studying Talmud. A prominent Jewess, by the name of Minna, at whose house the best citizens and even princes were wont to gather, was dragged from her hiding-place in the cellar; she spurned the offer of baptism and was immediately put to death. A youth, Simhah Cohen, whose father and seven brothers had been brutally murdered by the crusaders, pretended that he would accept baptism; he was led into the church. At the moment when he was to receive the sacrament, he produced a hidden knife and stabbed the bishop's nephew. It is needless to say that the lad was cut to pieces by the infuriated bystanders.·

From Worms Emicho's army, if army it may be called, moved to Mayence. On the 27th of May, at noon, the city opened its gates to the crusaders who, reinforced by the populace, stormed the hiding-places of the Jews. Such as had not died by their own hands were massacred and the corpses stripped of their garments. The carnage lasted till the evening. The dead, numbering more than a thousand souls, were interred in nine ditches. The cost of burial was defrayed from the moneys left by the Jews with the burghers. Among those who died by their own hands was Jacob son of Shullam, whose mother was a convert. Isaac son of David, the head of the community, who was baptized by force, set fire to his own dwelling as well as to the synagogue, which the crusaders were determined to turn into a church, and perished in the flames. Uri son of Joseph, who had likewise been baptized by compulsion, had planned to aid Isaac in burning down the synagogue; but he was caught and slain.

Only a small number of Jews, Calonymus with fifty-three companions, who had not been discovered in their hiding-place, the treasury of the cathedral, were conveyed in the dead of night by boat to Rüdesheim, where the archbishop with three hundred men in arms awaited them. However, the villagers and the rabble which soon followed could not be fought off. The Jews then proceeded to lay hands on themselves; Calonymus slew his own son Joseph. A few managed to escape to the woods, but were surrounded and done to death. In Cologne, on the 30th of May, the synagogue was destroyed and the dwellings of the Jews were pillaged. One man and two women were slain; the remainder were sent by the archbishop into his castles.

At Treves, in June, archbishop Egilbert was powerless to hold out against the mob. To save himself and the Jewish residents, he advised that they should accept Christianity, and in this he was seconded by the rabbi, whose name was Micah; this man remained a Christian even after the persecution ceased. The women in particular proved steadfast; they were dragged to the churches by force together with the children. Several men and women destroyed themselves by leaping into the river; so Elijah, the brother of Hezekiah, one of the synagogue authorities, the latter's daughter Esther, and two girls from Cologne. Similarly Jews were massacred or brought to self-destruction at Neuss, at Cologne in the castles to which they had fled, Wevelinghofen, Eller, Xanten, Mehr, Kerpen, Geldern. At Ratisbon there were forced baptisms, the whole community standing in the Danube and a priest making the sign of the cross over them; likewise in Bohemia. Altogether the number of Jews who perished was estimated as approaching ten thousand. The readiness with which the Jews accepted the appalling sufferings led a contemporary writer to say that the Lord had chosen that generation for His own portion, since they steadfastly fulfilled His word and sanctified His holy Name in this world.

The paroxysm which had spent itself by the end of July—Emicho's division was scattered to the winds in Hungary and never reached its destination—left a permanent depression of the spirit in the Jewish survivors. They were, however, permitted to return to their old places of residence; in certain localities they were even prevented from emigrating so as not to precipitate a commercial crisis. Stolen property was in a measure restored; but the emperor confiscated for his own use the belongings of the martyred dead. In 1103, a truce was proclaimed, in which the Jews were included. It does not require to be said that heavy sums were paid to the imperial treasury for these acts of grace, as well as for the immediate permission given to all those who had been baptized by force to return to their religion. It appears, however, that these penitents were not always well received by the pious and faithful, and Rashi admonished the latter to refrain from humiliating the penitents and withdrawing from their society. It must have rejoiced the heart of the aged teacher to know that the new synagogue at Mayence, the seat of talmudic learning, was completed and dedicated in 1104; within a year (July 13, 1105) occurred his death. Rashi had no sons, but three daughters, one of whom was so learned in the Talmud that during her father's illness she read to him the incoming talmudic questions and wrote down the answers at dictation. All of these were given in marriage to learned men and were the mothers of scholars of repute.

Two of Rashi's sons-in-law and disciples were Meir son of Samuel of Rameru (a town not far from Troyes) and Judah son of Nathan, who carried on the traditions of the master and laid the foundation for the 'Supplements' (Tosaphoth) to their teacher's Commentary on the Talmud. Judah completed the commentary on one tractate left unfinished at Rashi's death; that on another was finished by Rashi's grandson, Samuel son of Meir, who also wrote commentaries on the Scriptures, stressing the plain meaning. This field was also cultivated by his brother Solomon. An elder brother, Isaac, died at the noontide of his life; both taught their youngest brother, Jacob (called Tam, 'the Perfect,' by the epithet applied to the patriarch Jacob). Jacob Tam was the recognized talmudic authority of his age. Queries were addressed to him not only by the scholars of France, some even older than himself, but also by those of Lorraine, Germany, Italy, Spain, and England. His keen intellect served him in finding difficulties and solving them, although he deprecated extreme casuistry which was then coming into vogue. Idle conjectures, resting on personal opinion and unsupported by any talmudical utterance, were not to his liking.

The multitude of taxes and special contributions to king and feudal lords forced the Jews into lending money on interest. Tam himself engaged in this business, and he sanctioned the method by which money might be lent on interest to a Jew through the agency of a non-Jew. Other timely ordinances issued from his seat at Rameru; he associated with himself his elder brother Samuel and leading French and German rabbis, on one occasion as many as a hundred and fifty. Sometimes they met at Troyes, the seat of Rashi's activity. It was their aim to secure uniformity of practice and to settle questions caused by the new conditions. Jacob Tam was also at home in Hebrew grammar and even tried his hand at versification. He, the shepherd of his people, paid marked deference to Abraham Ibn Ezra when the Spanish scholar tarried in southern France (p. 333). During the Second Crusade, Jacob came near losing his life (p. 367); he was content that his body was spared and his books were left to him.

CHAPTER LII

THE SECOND AND THIRD CRUSADES

(1099-1215)

AFTER the entry of the First Crusaders into the Holy City and the foundation of the Latin Kingdom (1099) there were but few Jews left in the whole of Palestine. It is indeed reported that all the Jewish inhabitants of Jerusalem, whether Rabbanites, Karaites, or Samaritans, were assembled in one synagogue and given over to the flames. When in 1144 Edessa, one of the Latin states in Syria, had fallen into the hands of the Mohammedans, the Latins feared that Antioch and then Jerusalem might be lost. Accordingly they turned for help to the West. Pope Eugenius III. (1145–1153) issued a call for a new Crusade (1146). Soon, in response to the fiery eloquence of St. Bernard of Clairvaux, multitudes gathered about the king of France (Louis VII.) and the German emperor (Conrad III.).

Once more the Jews were the first victims. Not only did the religious enthusiasm beget fanaticism; but this time, in the very wake of the first enterprise which opened up trade with the East, there had arisen a body of Christian merchants, jealous of their Jewish competitors. From this point of view the year 1146 serves as a turning-point in the economic and social life of Franco-German Jewry. Gradually driven out of the sphere of commerce, the Jews perforce took to money-lending, which made of them an object of hate and of social degradation. Up to that time the Church had engaged in this business; but the vigorous ecclesiastical reforms originating in Cluny made an end of it. |So the Jews stepped into the gap. The scenes of the massacres and pillage in 1146 were on a smaller scale than they had been in 1096; otherwise the performance was the same. The bishops sought to protect the Jews. St. Bernard himself would permit no excesses against them—they were neither to be killed **nor** to be expelled. Christian usurers, he urged, were no better than Jewish; however, the Jews should be made to remit interest due from such as took the cross. Jews were compelled by force to accept baptism; many preferred death by their own hands or those of their near relatives.

The instigator of the persecution was the monk Radulph, a pious but otherwise ignorant person. He appeared on the banks of the Rhine and propounded the idea that the Jews, scattered in the cities and villages, were enemies of Christianity and should be killed. The teaching bore immediate fruit in many localities of France and Germany. Some Jews placed themselves under the protection of the king, others emigrated to the imperial city Nuremberg and other places, but many were slain. A Jew, Simeon the Saint, of Treves, was returning from England; on the road, not far from Cologne, he was attacked by the crusaders and, upon his refusal of baptism, done to death. A Jewess of Spires, Minna, had her ears and thumbs cut off. The Jews of Cologne left their dwellings and their property with the bishop. For a consideration he permitted the anxious Jewish community to seek safety in the strongly fortified Wolkenburg in Lorraine. The next year (1147), at Würzburg, the mob attacked the Jews, accusing them of the murder of a Christian whose body was found in the river. Twenty-two Jews, men, women, and children, were massacred, among them the rabbi, Isaac son of Eliakim. At Aschaffenburg, a Jewess, by the name of Guthulda, was drowned in the river because she refused to be baptized. At Stahleck, near Bacharach, Alexander son of Moses, a prominent scholar, Abraham son of Samuel, and Calonymus son of Mordecai were seized on the road and put to death. The Jews of Magdeburg and Halle were expelled.

The disturbances passed on to France. At Ham a hundred and fifty Jews were killed; a number lost their lives at Sully. At Carenton (in the department of Manche) it came to a veritable battle between a body of crusaders and Jews; the latter resisted heroically, but were ultimately destroyed. In France there fell at this time as a martyr Peter, a promising pupil of Samuel son of Meir and his brother Jacob. The community of Rameru was attacked on the second day of the Festival of Shabuoth. Jacob Tam, the most prominent Jew in town, saw his entire possessions seized, a scroll of the Torah which he owned was torn to shreds, and he himself received five wounds in the head to atone for the wounds inflicted on Jesus. Fortunately, a friendly knight passed by who promised help if in exchange he received a well-favored horse. Thus was the scholar saved from the hands of the mob.

Jacob's old age was saddened by the news of the destruction of the community at Blois. It is here that the dastardly calumny of ritual murder was fastened upon the Jews, though the example had been set in England first (p. 384). The entire community, consisting of about forty members, men and women, among them two former disciples of the teachers at Rameru, also a prominent Jewess, Pulcinella, the favorite of count Theobald, were committed to the flames (May 26, 1171). They died confessing the Unity and intoning the Adoration of God (Alenu). Only the fewest saved themselves by baptism. Count Theobald was minded to destroy all the Jews of the county, but he was appeased by a ransom of one thousand pounds. The intermediary was Baruch son of David, who also succeeded in rescuing the scrolls and the other sacred books formerly belonging to the Jews of Blois. Jacob Tam ordered a general day of fasting and mourning, which was observed by the communities through France, Anjou, and the Rhineland. This was his last public act. He died on the ninth of June in the same year.

The two closing decades of the twelfth century marked a turning-point in the fortunes of the Jews of northern France. Louis VII. had dealt with them in a manner of comparative mildness; he was loath to carry into execution the regulations of the Third Lateran Council (1179) which forbade the employment by Jews of Christian domestics. Matters changed for the worse under Philip Augustus (1180–1223). The new king was nurtured in the belief that the Jews used Christian blood in the preparation of their Passover bread— the new legend which had sprung up no one knows where—

and was in addition covetous of Jewish wealth. Soon after his coronation, on a sabbath day, the young monarch ordered all the Jews to be arrested in their synagogues and extorted from them a payment of fifteen thousand silver marks. He was persuaded by a hermit of Vincennes that it was an act of piety to despoil the wicked Jews. Accordingly he declared all debts of Christians to Jews null and void, save a fifth which he claimed for the royal treasury.

Having reduced the wealthier Jews, who were particularly numerous in Paris, to beggary, he issued an edict in April, 1182, driving the entire Jewish population from the royal domains. A respite of three months was granted during which they were to dispose of their personal property; on the other hand, all immovable property, such as dwellings, fields, vineyards, barns, and wine-presses, was confiscated by the king. The deserted synagogues were converted into churches. Only the fewest saved themselves by baptism; the great majority left the realm. Fortunately, the royal domains were confined to a small district about Paris. The remainder of France was in the hands of powerful barons, who molested neither those Jews long settled in their lands nor the refugees from the king's domain.

The most active center of Jewish life was in Champagne. At Rameru, Jacob Tam was succeeded by his pupil, Isaac son of Samuel of Dampierre, Rashi's great-grandson. It was reported in after times that the school of Isaac the Elder (as he was called) counted sixty scholars, of whom each one was not only at home in the whole of the Talmud but in addition knew by heart and thoroughly mastered one specific tractate of the sixty. Following along the lines of his teacher, Isaac subjected Rashi's Commentary to renewed scrutiny. What was left unexplained, was made clear; or imaginary gaps were invented and contradictions unearthed between Talmud passages far apart. Similarly, analogies, derived from seemingly irrelevant dicta, were turned to account in order to reach decisions as new questions presented themselves. This emphasis on practical conclusions constituted one of the characteristic differences between Rashi and the

Tosaphists. The whole took on the form of queries and answers—the Amoraic method, applied to the Mishnah, was now brought to bear upon the Talmud itself, a sort of super-Talmud in continuation of the Talmud. Isaac's own son, Elhanan, died as a martyr to his faith (1184); young as he was, his fame for erudition had been established among the 'Supplementers.'

In a Champagne townlet (Bray) a Jew was murdered by a Christian. The murderer, who happened to be a subject of the king of France, was delivered to the Jews by the reigning countess (Blanche) and hanged on the Festival of Purim. This incident offered Philip Augustus an opportunity to wipe out the Jewish community. Surrounded by royal troops, the Jews were given the choice between death and baptism. Many suffered themselves to be slain by their relatives. Close to a hundred persons were burned alive by the king's henchmen; only children under thirteen were spared (1191). From this massacre the king stepped into the Third Crusade for the recovery of Jerusalem from Saladin, who had captured the Holy City in 1187. Those that took the cross were freed from paying interest on their debts. Debts to Jewish creditors were canceled, and the barons, after thus impoverishing the Jews, drove them out from their territories.

Philip, however, fell out with Richard, king of England, and returned home. He bethought himself of another plan of dealing with the Jews. Perhaps it was in defiance of the pope (Innocent III., 1198–1216), who had placed him under excommunication because of his repudiation of his wife Ingeborg. Or the reason may have been that, statesman and organizer that he was, he favored commerce and recognized the Jewish aptitude therefor. At any rate, contrary to all expectation, he recalled in 1198 the Jews to his domain. Moreover, he gave sanction to their operations in money-lending and determined the legal rate of interest. A tax was put on Jewish trade; the treasury had a special account labeled 'Jewish revenue.' By treaties with the barons, the king restricted the Jews in their domicile; henceforth they were not free to move from one feudal dominion to another. King and barons spoke of the Jews in their territories as 'their Jews,' thus treating them like chattels and obviously as a source of extortion. The penalty for migration was the confiscation of property. Isaac the Elder ruled that no Jew should buy the confiscated goods of another Jew and, if bought, these should be returned to their owner.

Isaac's pupils continued the work on the Talmud in the manner of their master. Samson son of Abraham of Sens, the author of the 'Supplements of Sens' and of commentaries on parts of the Mishnah, together with some three hundred French and English rabbis, settled about 1211 in Palestine. He died at Acre (Acco) and was buried at the foot of mount Carmel. His brother, Isaac the Younger at Dampierre, Judah son of Isaac (Sir Leon) at Paris (1166–1224), and a host of scholars labored incessantly to revise the older collections and enrich them with fresh erudition. From the French schools the 'supplementing' activity spread to Lorraine and the Rhine, to lands 'of (comparative) darkness, dry and weary, where vision was scarce.' At Metz, Eliezer son of Samuel (died 1198), a pupil of Jacob Tam, wrote the 'Book of the Reverent,' in which he set forth the quintessence of religious law according to Torah, Talmud, and authoritative interpretation. Another Tosaphist, Baruch son of Isaac, was born at Worms, but lived in Ratisbon; he was Samson's colleague in the school of Isaac the Elder, and wrote a practical ritual code ('Book of the Heave-offering').

Other scholars devoted themselves to mysticism. Samuel son of Calonymus and his son Judah, of the Italian Calonymus family, were both known as 'Saints.' Thus the Babylonian lore, transplanted by way of Italy, found a home in Germany, and a link was established with the East, distinctly unique and far-reaching in its consequences. Judah (died 1200), the author of the 'Book of Saints,' was like Baruch, a native of Worms and a resident of Ratisbon. His mysticism, far from taking theoretic flights, lost itself in a multitude of odd beliefs which stood near to the popular religion and in turn influenced it among German Jews for times to come. He valued dialectic acumen, but never indulged in it himself; he distinctly set himself in opposition to arguing for the sake of display. The root of the Torah was for every man to know the religious practice. Prayer is greater than good works. Devotion in prayer is the principal thing; the unlearned and women should pray in a language which they understand, instead of honoring God with lip-worship in Hebrew. The saint must deal honestly with all men, Jews and non-Jews, or else the name of God will be profaned. The smallest matters are weighty enough. Thus the liturgical productions of the Spanish poets, cast in non-Jewish meters, must not be sung in German congregations. No landmarks shall be removed in any part of the liturgy; the distinct modes of chanting the diverse parts of Scripture must be preserved. Young men and young women shall not dance together, but each sex by itself. No Jew should disguise himself in the garments of a Christian cleric, or sew a cross on his cloak, to escape persecution.

The Third Crusade, in which the emperor Frederick I. (Barbarossa) met his death by drowning, left the Jews of Germany unscathed. The tidings of the capture of Jerusalem by Saladin produced a commotion against the Jews; but it was nipped in the bud by the timely order of the emperor to the clergy to refrain from preaching against the Jews. The imperial protection cost the Jews a small sum of money delivered to the imperial treasury (camera). Thus a beginning was made in the status of German Jewry, in later times a fixed legal condition, that the emperor had direct jurisdiction over them. The protection granted to the Jews by the central authority was not due to the circumstance that they were considered aliens and therefore rightless, but rather to their defenselessness in the face of popular attacks, so glaringly revealed during the First Crusade. The grant was dependent upon the good-will of the emperor; it was an act of grace on his part. It had to be applied for each time a new emperor mounted the throne.

The consideration in return for the protection was either a fixed annual tax, over and above the taxes paid by the individual Jew, or a special assessment at a given time. As a source of revenue, the Jews were valuable to the emperors. As times went by, the moneys thus received were considerable enough to tempt the territorial princes to acquire for themselves the Jewish tax piecemeal from the emperor in lieu of payments due them. Thus the theory developed that the emperor or territorial lord could arbitrarily dispose of the life and property of the Jews. A crime, actually or supposedly committed by individual Jews, was seized upon as a pretext for extorting 'protection money' from the Jewish communities as a corporate body. In 1179, a number of Jews, traveling from Cologne upward the Rhine and passing Boppard, were accused of the murder of a Christian woman whose body had been found on the banks of the river. The Jews were seized and, on refusing baptism, cast alive into the river. Emperor Frederick exacted from the Jewish communities along the Rhine five hundred pieces of silver, and the archbishop Philip on his own hand received forty-two hundred. Bonn, where there were particularly wealthy Jews, alone contributed four hundred.

A similar occurrence took place at Neuss in 1187. A demented Jew murdered a Christian girl in the sight of the public. The mob avenged themselves on the Jews by pillage and murder, and the community paid the bishop a hundred and twenty pieces of silver. Nevertheless, at Spires and Boppard, where excesses occurred in 1195, Emperor Henry VI. and his brother Otto had those guilty of the murder of Jews executed and restitution made for destroyed property. The act of justice was, of course, well paid for by the Jews. At Vienna, in 1196, Solomon, a pious and charitable man and the business agent of the duke of Austria, was murdered by crusaders. A year later, at Worms, two crusaders attacked the home of Eleazar son of Judah, a pupil of Judah the Saint. They killed his wife Dolza and their two daughters Bellette and Hannah, and left the father severely wounded. In both instances the culprits were duly punished.

The chronicles of the persecutions during the Second and Third Crusades were written by Ephraim son of Jacob of

Bonn (died about 1200). He was himself a witness of the events nearer his home and at one time escaped death, but not loss of property. He also commemorated the sufferings of his people in penitential elegies. At the turn of the century, ere the heavy hand of Pope Innocent III. was laid upon the Jews, a voice of song made itself heard in German Jewry, the voice of the minnesinger Süsskind of Trimberg. However, about 1215, he grew weary of appearing before the courts of princes and amusing the great lords and ladies, and determined to share the humiliation of his brethren.

CHAPTER LIII

THE JEWS OF FRANCE AND GERMANY IN THE
THIRTEENTH CENTURY

(1198-1293)

INNOCENT III. (1198–1216), learned in the law and resolute man of action, zealous in the promotion of unity of faith and sworn enemy of heresy, brought the papacy to that pinnacle of moral prestige, religious authority, and temporal power which characterizes the first half of the thirteenth century. His relation to the Jews was mainly dictated by the general policy of his predecessors. Although he regarded the unbelief of the Jews as in many respects blameworthy, yet he held that, as living witnesses to the truth of Christianity, they must not be oppressed by believers. Accordingly, in 1199, he renewed the privileges granted by Alexander III. (1159–1181), which insured to the Jews inviolability of their faith, of their life and limb, and of their property. This did not prevent him, in the same year, while urging the Christians to take the cross against the Mohammedans in the East, from demanding that Jewish creditors should release the crusaders from payment of interest.

The demand was enacted in the form of law, under pain of exclusion from dealings with Christians, in the Fourth Lateran Council (1215). Another enactment protected Christian debtors against exorbitant, usurious, rates of interest, and insured to the churches the tithes from Christian property even when it had passed into the hands of Jewish creditors. Jewish converts to Christianity were to be restrained by 'salutary compulsion' from secretly practising their old rites. In renewal of the rulings of the Toledo Council (p. 305), no Jew was to hold public office. Moneys paid to Jewish officers by Christians were to be turned over to the Christian poor according to the pleasure of the diocesan bishop. But the most degrading and humiliating enactment, which for centuries placed the Jew in the position of a pariah in Christian society, was the one creating for the Jews of both sexes a special dress or a distinctive sign of shame (badge) to be worn on their garments. This was meant to make them immediately distinguishable from the Christian population, on the plea that sameness of dress had led to Christians marrying Jewesses. This provision included the Saracens, with whom in fact this discrimination against the Jews had originated at an early date. The secular princes, however, were a little slow in carrying this enactment into effect. The badge, usually of yellow color and worn on the breast, for a long time stamped the Jew as dishonored, branded as an outsider, an easily marked victim of popular fury and universal contempt.

Thus the Jews were everywhere at the mercy of the populace. In 1221, some ninety-six Jews were slain at Erfurt. In 1235, the body of a murdered Christian was found between Lauda on the Tauber and Tauberbischofsheim in Baden. For three days the two Jewish communities were attacked by mobs. Dwellings and property were destroyed. Many representative Jews were tortured, cruelly executed, and committed to the flames after their death. Pope Gregory IX. (1227–1241) was entreated by the Jews to renew for them the privileges previously granted by Honorius III. and Alexander III.

The emperor Frederick II. (1215–1250), the arch-enemy of the papacy, a reputed liberal in religion, made his Sicilian court a center of intellectual activity in which Jewish as well as Christian and Mohammedan scholars took part. At the emperor's bidding Judah son of Solomon ha-Cohen (Ibn Matkah) of Toledo, with whom the emperor had carried on a correspondence, settled in 1247 in Tuscany. Jacob son of Abba Mari Anatoli of southern France was invited to Naples, in the vicinity of the university founded in 1224. There, in personal contact with the imperial patron of the sciences and other Christian scholars, he made accessible in Hebrew translation the commentaries of Averroes on Aristotle and several works on astronomy and logic by Averroes and al-Farabi. In his own philosophical commentary on the Pentateuch, the 'Goad to Students,' he cited several suggestions that had come to him from the emperor.

In 1235, a charge of ritual murder led to the slaughter of some thirty-two Jews at Fulda. The emperor, thereupon, in consideration of a sum of money tendered by the Jews, confirmed the privileges granted to them by his predecessors. Moreover, he convoked at Hagenau a diet of princes, nobles, and abbots to investigate the charge that the Jews were using Christian blood for ritual purposes. The emperor personally, on the basis of his own reading, was convinced of the falsity of the charge. But as the diet came to no decision, he invited all the kings of the Occident to send converts who had knowledge of the Jewish law. After prolonged meetings, this commission declared that it was written neither in the Old nor in the New Testament that the Jews made use of human blood and that both the Law of Moses and the Talmud strictly forbid the eating of blood. If the Jews were restrained by law from partaking of animal blood, it was not to be supposed that they would risk life and property for the sake of human blood, not to speak of the horribleness and unnaturalness of the crime. Accordingly the emperor confirmed the verdict of the princes and pronounced the Jews free from the charge. He furthermore forbade any one, whether in preaching or otherwise, to lay this accusation at their door.

Otherwise Frederick yielded to the antipathies of his German subjects, which were largely dictated by economic envy. The Babenberg dukes of Austria, who made of Vienna a center of commerce, culture, and learning, committed the financial administration of the duchy to the hands of Jews. Leopold I. (1177–1194) had the Jew Solomon as his master at the mint, the same Solomon who in 1196 was murdered by the crusaders (p. 372). Leopold II. (1198–1230) had another Jew for his banker, who arranged for him the financial terms with the Magyar king upon the conclusion of peace in 1225. Two brothers, Lublin and Nekele, were counts of the treasury to the dukes of Austria. When the last Babenberg duke, Frederick II. ('the Quarrelsome'), was driven out, the emperor acquiesced in the demand of the citizens of Vienna, now an imperial city, that the Jews should hold no office, 'since by imperial authority they had of old been condemned in expiation of their crime to perpetual slavery' (1237). A similar condition was incorporated into the charter granted to Wiener Neustadt.

Nevertheless the emperor vouchsafed to the Jews of Vienna imperial protection on lines similar to the charter previously issued to the Jews of Germany (1238). Their lives were safeguarded against murderous attacks and their children against enforced baptism. Their trade in wines and medicaments was regulated, and they were allowed internal autonomy under jurisdiction of their rabbis. Scarcely had the emperor left Austria, when duke Frederick returned. The citizens of Wiener Neustadt exacted from him a promise similar to the one which the emperor had conceded to them. It is questionable whether this concession extended beyond the locality mentioned.

However, in 1244, the duke issued a charter for the regulation of Jewish affairs, which on the whole was benevolent in character and served as a model for similar charters which the Jews subsequently obtained in Bohemia, Moravia, Hungary, Silesia, and Poland. The interest permitted to Jewish money-lenders is not to exceed eight farthings a week for each pound; several statutes deal with pledges, mortgages, and the like. The Jews are free to move and to carry their wares from place to place within the ducal territory, their merchandise being subject to the same tolls as Christian merchants are required to pay. No toll is to be levied upon the removal of a corpse from city to city or from province to province. Destruction of a Jewish burial-place is punishable with death and confiscation of property. A fine is imposed upon insults to Jewish synagogues. Jewish children are protected from kidnapping and Jewish maidens from violation. Internal strifes between Jew and Jew may be settled in their own courts; naturally the duke reserves for himself all criminal jurisdiction. As to lawsuits between Jews and Christians, Jewish witnesses must be heard alongside of Christian testimony.

Quite the reverse of friendly was the attitude of the French king, Louis IX. (1226–1270), to his Jews. His warfare on usury and the propensity of the nobles to borrow money was justified enough. However, in line with an older ordinance of his father's, he remitted the interest due on Christian debts to Jews. He even went further and liberated his subjects from a third part of their indebtedness to Jewish creditors. The pious zeal of St. Louis manifested itself in the favor he extended to converts; often he was present in person during such baptisms. The neophytes acted with bitter rancor toward their former coreligionists and the faith upon which they had turned their back.

Particularly vicious was the apostate Nicholas Donin of La Rochelle. He laid before pope Gregory IX. a formal accusation against the Talmud, charging that it contained blasphemies against God, against Jesus, and against Christianity, and that it alone was the cause why the Jews stubbornly refused to submit to baptism. The pope gave orders for the seizure of all copies of the Talmud and for an investigation of its contents. In France, the order was immediately obeyed. On March 3, 1240, while the Jews were in the synagogue, all their books were seized. On June 12 of the same year, a public debate was opened between Donin and four representatives of the Jews led by Jehiel son of Joseph of Paris. A just comprehension of the arguments advanced by the Jewish rabbis could not be expected. A tribunal, composed of dignitaries of the Church, passed judgment upon the Talmud, and on the eve of a sabbath in June, 1242 or 1244, twenty-four cartloads of Hebrew books were committed to the flames in Paris. Though in 1247, at the solicitation of the Jews, the pope was favorable to reopening the case, the Talmud was condemned a second time (1248) by the pope's legate.

The holocaust at Paris evoked bitter strains of lamentation in France and in Germany; the elegy of Meir of Rothenburg, who was present at the event, over the conflagration of the Torah is chanted to this day on the Ninth of Ab. In northern France it meant the inevitable decline of the studies begun by Rashi. The aged Jehiel expounded the Talmud to some three hundred scholars by word of mouth. He assembled the later 'Supplements,' pathetically remarking that he was compelled to fall back upon his memory. The persecutions and various exactions of money drained the resources of the communities. Jehiel was compelled to seek financial support for the French schools from the Holy Land and the neighboring countries. At length the aged teacher translated himself to Acco (1260); he died at Haifa, at the foot of mount Carmel (1268). There remained stragglers at home. Moses of Coucy arranged the religious laws of the Talmud in the order of the Pentateuchal Commandments ('The Great Book of Commandments,' Sepher Mizwoth Gadol, SeMaG). Isaac son of Joseph of Corbeil, Jehiel's son-in-law and pupil, followed suit with 'the Lesser Book of Commandments' (Sepher Mizwoth Katan, SeMaK). Others gathered up the gleanings of 'Supplements.'

The Jews in Germany were likewise overwhelmed by persecutions and lamentable vicissitudes. The Mongol invasion, which reached Germany in 1241, aroused in the minds of many, among Christians and Jews, notions concerning the end of the world and the advent of the Messiah (or second coming of Christ), especially since for the Jews the year coincided with the opening of the sixth millennium according to the era of creation. False rumors were spread about Jewish complicity with the ruthless invaders. It was fabled that the Tatars were none other than the lost ten tribes shut up by Alexander the Great in the Caspian mountains. The popular mind was inflamed; the least provocation was fraught with dire consequences. In the imperial city Frankfort-on-the-Main a Jewish lad, ready to accept baptism, was thwarted by his parents and friends. Christians and Jews came to blows; on May 24, 1241, both sides fought with vehemence. A few Christians fell; on the Jewish side the victims were about a hundred and eighty persons. Those whom the sword had not slain died in the conflagration brought about by the fire which they set to their own dwellings. The fire spread and destroyed almost half of the city; the surviving Jews feared the vengeance of the citizens; twenty-four embraced Christianity. The emperor's son, Conrad IV., graciously granted an amnesty to the citizens of the devoted imperial city, on the plea that whatever damage had been done to the Jews was the result of casual negligence and accident.

At Kitzingen (in Bavaria) several Jews and Jewesses were tortured and then executed (1243). The same year witnessed excesses in Ortenburg (lower Bavaria), in Belitz, in Meiningen; the next year the Jews of Pforzheim were the object of popular fury. Peculiar complications developed in consequence of baptism through necessity. A Jewish girl, betrothed to a Würzburg Jew, had changed her faith during the Frankfort massacre. After a while she returned to the fold, but found that her affianced husband had meantime married. The German rabbis held that the husband was in duty bound to divorce his wife and marry the girl whose claim on him had not been made invalid by her enforced baptism. Isaac son of Moses of Vienna (1180–1250) ruled that baptism disqualifies a woman for marrying a Jew. He was born in Saxony and, after a training in France and Germany, settled in Vienna. He wrote a ritual code ('The Light Sown,' Or Zarua'), and became the intermediate link between the Franco-German centers of talmudic learning and the Slavic countries.

The repeated massacres, largely growing out of the popular legend that the Jews were using Christian blood in the preparation of their Passover bread (p. 367), persuaded the Jewish notables that a pronouncement from the papal see might extirpate the fiction which like a disease was lodged in the people's mind. Innocent IV. (1243–1254) was neither friendly nor unfriendly to the Jews. The old canonical restrictions, he insisted, should be enforced with all rigor; otherwise he reaffirmed the edicts of toleration of Gregory IX. and his predecessors. The pitiful petition of the German

Jews, who reminded the pontiff of the lamentable occurrences at Fulda and elsewhere, led him to declare in a bull, addressed to the archbishops and bishops of Germany (July 5, 1247), that the Jewish law forbade the very thing of which the Jews were wantonly accused, faring in consequence much worse than did their fathers in Egypt under Pharaoh. 'Since we are unwilling that the Jews, whose conversion our Lord in his compassion awaits, should be unjustly tormented, we command the bishops that they deal with them graciously and, as regards all the unfounded undertakings against them by the above mentioned prelates, nobles, and mighty rulers, to restore them to their legal condition, and not to tolerate .in future that in this or in other matters they be unjustly harassed; all attempts to the contrary must be suppressed by ecclesiastical discipline.'

During the Great Interregnum from the death of Conrad IV. (1254) to the election of Rudolph of Habsburg (1273), the Jews along the Rhine, in return for a considerable annual tax, were included in the general peace maintained by the Rhenish Confederation. The Confederation fixed the rate of interest on loans not to exceed one-third of the capital. The duke of Brabant, on the other hand, drew the line between money-lenders and legitimate merchants; the former he ordered to be expelled, whether they were Jews or Christians (1261), unless they turned to commerce. Church councils, like that of Vienna under cardinal Guido (1267), reënacted all the rigorous measures with the intent of cutting off social intercourse between Jews and Christians. Jews were subjected to extortion (at Magdeburg, 1261), to expulsion, to violent attacks on life and limb—as at Arnstadt (1264), at Coblenz (1265) and Sinzig (1266), at Weissenburg (1270).

Rudolph of Habsburg (1273–1291), who needed all the money he could lay his hands on, availed himself of a substantial sum lent by the wealthy Anshel Oppenheimer, and in general accepted gifts, in return for any favor, from the Jews in the empire. He confirmed the community of Ratisbon in their old charter which guaranteed them internal judicial autonomy, but yielded to the bishop in insisting that the Jews should keep indoors during Holy Week. Similarly he reaffirmed the charter held by the Jews of Austria since 1244, but appeased the Christian citizens by disqualifying a Jew for public office. He gave imperial sanction to the bull of Innocent IV. against the libel of ritual murder, as well as to that of Gregory X. (1271–1276) which, in addition, forbade baptism by force. The emperor did what was in his power to bring the guilty to book. Serious excesses occurred along the Rhine, in Franconia, and in Bavaria (1283–1287), thus adding new lists of martyrs from among the sorely tried Jews of Germany.

Many of the wealthier families along the Rhine and Main determined to emigrate to Palestine. The company of exiles was led by Meir son of Baruch of Rothenburg (1220–93), one of the last 'Supplementers,' a pupil of Samuel of Falaise and of Isaac of Vienna. Meir was highly revered through northern France and the German communities for his saintliness and learning. He was by far the greatest authority that had arisen in Germany in a long time. He had a large school and many of his students lived in his house. He had more influence on the religious life of his day than any other German scholar, not so much by his own writings as through his great disciples who carried his teachings to Spain and Austria. While tarrying at Lombardy to await the arrival of the rest of the company, the rabbi was recognized by a converted Jew who was passing through with the bishop of Basel. The bishop had him seized and delivered to Germany where, upon the emperor's order, he was confined in the fortress of Ensisheim, near Colmar, in Upper Alsace (1286).

The voluntary expatriation of so many Jews, subjects of the imperial treasury, was not to the liking of the emperor. Such property as the fugitives had left at home was claimed by Rudolph, though the citizens thought that the inheritance should pass on to themselves. At all events an example was to be made of the rabbi; no restriction was placed upon his freedom, and his disciples were permitted intercourse with him; but he was kept in confinement. The Jews offered

to the emperor the sum of twenty thousand marks in silver
for the release of their leader. The rabbi declined to be set
free thus, lest a precedent should be established whereby any
ruler might extort money from the Jews by seizing their
rabbi. So Meir remained in the fortress until his death in
1293. Even then the body was not surrendered until many
years later, when a heavy ransom was paid by a rich and
generous Jew of Frankfort, Alexander Süsskind Wimpfen.
The remains were interred at Worms, and upon his death,
Wimpfen was laid to rest by the side of the great teacher.

We may pause here for a while to narrate the calamity
which befell Jewry in a land whose political history was
largely interwoven with that of France, and where the cultural conditions marking Jewish life were much the same as
in the Franco-German center.

CHAPTER LIV

THE JEWS OF ENGLAND

(1066-1290)

THE Jews of England, the 'Land of the Isle,' came from northern France and the Rhine valley. Before the Norman conquest casual traders ventured across the Channel; some Jews may have come to Britain in still earlier times, in the train of the Roman legions. However, we know of no permanent settlement before the eleventh century. William the Conqueror (1066–1087) brought over a body of Jews from Rouen. They formed the middle commercial class between the upper and lower classes in England. The presence of the Jews in the land was encouraged. Henry I. (1100–1135) granted a charter to Joseph, rabbi and chief Jew of London, and his followers, under which they were permitted to move freely in the country, together with their chattels, without paying tolls or customs. They could buy whatever was offered them, receive pledges for loans of money, and dispose of them after holding them a year and a day. They were to be tried by their peers, and to be sworn on a scroll of the Law.

The disorders and civil strife under Stephen (1135–1154) could not pass by without disturbing the Jewish community; they were mulcted both by the king and by his rival, the empress Matilda (Maud). An Oxford Jew, who refused to pay his contribution to the king's expenses, had his house burned down. In 1144, on the occasion of the disappearance of a boy, William of Norwich, the Jews were accused of having murdered him. At the same time, a Jewish convert, Theobald of Cambridge, made the general charge that the Jews killed a Christian every year before Passover as a sacrifice, deciding by lot in which city the murder was to take place. So flimsy was the evidence that the Jews were not even required to answer the charge, the sheriff of

Norwich taking them under his protection. Nevertheless, the story subsequently gained credence and the child became a martyred saint. As a consequence, the Jews of Norwich were attacked, some being killed, while the majority fled. When, two years later, the crusaders raged against the Jews on the continent, English Jewry went unscathed thanks to the intervention of King Stephen.

The Jews enjoyed favorable conditions under Henry II. (1154–1189), the first of the Angevin kings, both in his French dominions and in England. As there was no agency for money-lending and the taking of interest was prohibited to Christians by the Church, the Jews, who were barred from the artisan guilds and from holding land, perforce became capitalists or money-lenders, thereby filling a gap in the economic life of England. The king would frequently interfere in their business, at times canceling the debts of Christians due to the Jews in return for a lesser payment to himself. When a Jewish capitalist died, the king became his real heir, and many Christians would allow their debts to stand long beyond the appointed time in the hope that the creditor would die whereupon they could settle with the Crown on favorable terms. Moreover, by laying claim to Christian debts, the king often acquired power over the barons who became indebted to him instead of to the Jews. As a rule, however, the natural heir was permitted to retain a part of the fortune so as to continue the remunerative business which was closed to the king.

Several Jews rose to great opulence. They lived in houses of stone which in magnificence equaled the royal palaces. Aaron of Lincoln built up a vast banking institution stretching over nine counties; he advanced money on land, on corn, on dwellings. Many an abbey and monastery was built through his financial coöperation; the king himself was indebted to him for loans. When he died, Henry seized his property. The actual gold and silver went down in a wreck on being shipped to France, but enough remained in the form of debts owed by several hundred persons for the maintenance of a separate division of the exchequer, 'Aaron's

Exchequer.' The Jews were, moreover, heavily taxed especially when preparations were being made by Henry II. for the Third Crusade. On this single occasion, the immense tallage of sixty thousand pounds, one-fourth of their movable property, was levied on the Jews of England.

In all that pertained to the communal and spiritual life, English Jewry was dominated by France. From France, Abraham Ibn Ezra paid them a visit in 1158. In London taught Jacob of Orleans, a noted pupil of Tam; another distinguished disciple of the teacher of Rameru was Benjamin of Canterbury. Jewish communities were to be found at London, Oxford, Cambridge, Norwich, Bury St. Edmunds, York, Canterbury, Winchester, Newport, Stafford, Windsor, and Reading. The largest body of Jews resided in the capital. Until 1177 the only burial-place the Jews owned was located there.

The Jews were roused from their tranquillity by the storm which broke loose at the coronation of King Richard I. (Coeur-de-lion, 1189–1199). When a Jewish deputation appeared at Westminster Abbey with rich gifts on behalf of all the communities in the realm, they were refused admission. The humiliated representatives of Jewry were hooted by the palace guards; the mob without proceeded to throw stones at them. A false rumor spread that the king had ordered the destruction of the Jews. Unable to penetrate into their strongly fortified stone houses, the populace set fire to the straw roofs of the dwellings. Many who essayed to escape were ruthlessly butchered; others, among them Jacob of Orleans, slew themselves when the alternative was baptism. A few Jews, however, saved themselves by this alternative; one of these, the rich Benedict of York, was later permitted to return to Judaism. The riot lasted twenty-four hours; the chief justice and some noblemen, whom the king sent to quell the disorder, were forced to withdraw. The king, on learning what had happened, had three of the participants hanged. He let it be understood that the Jews must not be molested and had proclamation made to that effect throughout England and his French dominions. Scarcely,

however, had Richard crossed the Channel to join Philip
Augustus in the Crusade, when riots broke out afresh; so at
Lynn, ostensibly because the Jews attacked a baptized coreligionist who had taken refuge in a church; also at Norwich,
at Stamford, at Bury St. Edmunds (1190). The Jews of
Lincoln saved themselves betimes by seeking refuge in the
royal castle.

Most tragic was the massacre at York on the eve of the
Great Sabbath and the dawn of the next day, March 16–17,
1190. Crusaders preparing to follow their king against the
Saracens, burgesses envious of Jewish wealth, barons indebted to the Jews, the fanatical clergy, all conspired to
exterminate the Jews. Several dwellings were set on fire;
the wife and children of Benedict, who had died of wounds
received at the coronation, were burned in their house and
their enormous riches were plundered. The alarmed Jews,
with their leader Joseph, sought shelter in the royal castle.
One day the warden happened to be gone; the Jews were
apprehensive lest he might hand them over to the besieging
mob, and so they denied him admission. The warden called
in the aid of the sheriff of the county; Richard Malebys, a
noble deeply in debt to the Jews, commanded the siege. The
rage of the mob was kept alive by the exhortations of a
monk, who celebrated mass every morning in his white robes
in front of the tower. A stone falling from the battlements
killed the monk; his death infuriated the mob to a still
higher degree.

The hapless Jews were short of rations; surrender spelled
baptism or death by torture. In obedience to the exhortations of their religious leader, Yom Tob of Joigny, they chose
to lay hands on themselves. The lay leader Joseph cut the
throats of his wife Anna and their two children, then he fell
at the hands of the steadfast rabbi; the majority followed
suit after burning or destroying their goods. When at day-
break the citadel was captured, those who were still alive
were put to death. Altogether some five hundred Jews
perished. The mob then returned to the cathedral where the
records of debts due the Jews were in safe-keeping. They

compelled the guardians to turn these over to them to be burned then and there in the sanctuary. This done, the fury of the mob was spent, and the city was restored to its usual order and quiet. Similarly the mobs raged elsewhere; a community of proselytes, numbering twenty families, was wiped out. The chancellor Longchamp was ordered to punish the offenders; but the mob of crusaders had dispersed and the guilty barons escaped to Scotland. The sheriff of York alone was removed from office.

It was not to the interest of the Crown that barons and burgesses should rid themselves of payments of moneys owing to the Jews by such forcible measures. On his return to England, Richard, toward whose ransom the Jews of England were made to contribute three times as much as the whole city of London, introduced a system of registering in duplicate all debts held by Jews. Thus the taxes due to the king were safeguarded, the profit accruing to the Crown as a silent partner in all usurious transactions. Under Richard's successors the Jews continued to be subjected to all kinds of taxes, in the form of 'tallages' on goods, chattels, and debts, of gifts, offerings, ransoms, compositions, licenses, and fines. Payment was exacted through imprisonment, confiscation of property, the seizing of women and children, and even gouging out the eyes and other cruel methods. John Lackland extorted from the Jews sixty-six thousand marks (1210). Abraham of Bristol, who refused to pay his quota of ten thousand marks, had, by the order of the king, seven of his teeth extracted, one a day, till he paid the levied amount. Small wonder that a goodly number of English rabbis joined in the exodus of their French colleagues to the Holy Land (1211).

A still larger exodus was set in operation in 1218, two years after the accession of King Henry III., when, in conformity with the decision of the Fourth Lateran Council, the king enforced the wearing of the badge. In 1222, a provincial synod at Oxford under the archbishop of Canterbury, Stephen Langton, enacted anti-Jewish legislation forbidding Jews to hold Christian slaves, build new synagogues, or mix with Christians. The wearing of the badge, an oblong white patch of two fingerbreadths by four, was to be rigidly enforced, so as to make the isolation certain and complete. However, the king, jealous of his authority, quickly dissolved the injunctions of the ecclesiastical body. Soon, however, the oppressive measures against the Jews were revived and the burdensome taxation levied on them again became the norm. The Jews sued for permission to leave the land. But they were far too valuable a source of income to tolerate their expatriation; orders were given to the wardens of the ports to prevent any Jew from passing out of the country. In 1230, the king levied in taxes one-third of the property of the Jews. The annual taxation grew by leaps and bounds. Between the years 1255 and 1273, upward of four hundred thousand pounds escheated to the Crown from the legacies of deceased Jews. The communities were made collectively responsible for the taxes that were to go to the king. In 1241, a 'Jewish Parliament' was convoked at Worcester, supposedly to consider ways and means of improving the lot of the Jews; it proved to be a new method of regulating the distribution of a tremendous tallage.

The influence of the Church became increasingly marked in the repressive measures against the Jews. The order of January 31, 1253, provided that Jewish worship in the synagogues should be carried on in a low voice, inaudible to Christians; Jews might not employ Christian nurses or domestics; Jews might not eat or buy meat during Lent; no Jew might prevent another Jew from embracing Christianity. A special refuge for baptized Jews had been established in 1233, the House of Converts. Henry III. felt himself complete master of the Jews of the realm. In February, 1255, the king sold them to his brother Richard of Cornwall for five thousand marks, ceding all his rights for one year. Before the year was over, the Jews of Lincoln were made to expiate the murder of a Christian boy (Hugh of Lincoln), upon the forced confession of a Jew near whose dwelling the body had been found. Ninety-one were sent to London to the Tower, eighteen were executed for claiming a trial before a mixed jury, as was their right, and the remainder lingered in prison until the king released them at the request of his brother, the earl of Cornwall. An earlier appeal on behalf of the Jews by the friars—who thus proved the utter falsity of the charge—had failed. During the civil war (1262–1266) London Jewry was sacked. Similar excesses occurred elsewhere.

Restrictive legislation reached its complete measure under Edward I. (1272–1307). His Statute of Judaism of 1275 breathed the same spirit as the edict of Louis IX. of 1254. By the categorical prohibition of usury, the chief, almost the sole, source of income was lost to the Jews. After being successively mulcted to the point of impoverishment, they ceased to be quite as indispensable as they had been, particularly since the great Italian banking firms were just as accommodating and had supplied Edward with funds during his Welsh wars. It made little difference that the Lombards soon made themselves as unpopular as their predecessors had been; the monopoly of the Jewish money-lenders had been broken. The king granted them permission to engage in any other legitimate commerce and handicrafts, and even to take farms for a period not exceeding ten years. But farming could not be taken up at a moment's notice, nor could handicrafts be acquired at once. Moreover, the guilds had practically a monopoly of all skilled labor, and they refused to accept any Jews in their midst. Even to buy and sell in the markets one had to be a member of the Guild Merchant.

The other restrictions tended to preclude all intercourse between Jews and Christians. A supplementary edict of 1279 set capital punishment upon Jewish blasphemy against the Christian religion. In 1280, the Jews were ordered to listen to the conversion sermons of the Dominicans. The Synod of Exeter, in 1281, gave force to the usual churchly enactments against the Jews. Jews were forbidden to employ Christian domestics, nor were they allowed to hold public office. Christians might not eat at Jewish tables or engage the services of Jewish physicians, no new synagogues were to be built, doors and windows were to be shut on Good Friday, the wearing of the badge and the payment of church tithes were made obligatory. Because of the increasing vexations leading to the final catastrophe, the spiritual life of English Jewry moved along modest lines. There were individual scholars given to the study of grammar or to liturgical poetry; several are quoted as authorities in Jewish law. At the head of the whole Jewry stood the 'presbyter of all the Jews of England,' who was chosen by the king and who was in the main the official tax collector.

There was no alternative for the king save the final act of expulsion—the first general expulsion to befall the Jews— which was issued July 18, 1290. The Jews were ordered to leave the realm before All Saints' Day of that year. They were given permission to carry away with them their movables. Their dwellings, with few exceptions, escheated to the king, whose profit in the shape of rental did not exceed one hundred and thirty pounds, while the total debt owed to the Jews—the king could collect only the principal— amounted to nine thousand pounds. Some of the Jews were robbed by the captains who undertook to transport them across the channel; others were drowned on their way to France. Altogether sixteen thousand Jews left England, about one-tenth going to Flanders, the others finding refuge in France.

CHAPTER LV

THE JEWS OF PROVENCE

(1100-1394)

So LONG as Languedoc and Provence in southeastern France were under the rule of the counts of Toulouse and the counts of Provence, the Jews shared in the peaceful condition, the prosperity, and culture of this wealthiest portion of France. The population was of old Roman blood; Christianity sat lightly upon them; the Saracens were near by, now as enemies that must be fought, now as friends. Life was gay; manners, fostered by troubadour poetry, were freer, with scant room for bigotry. What made Jewish existence secure was, in the first instance, the circumstance that the ruling counts were only nominally dependent upon the distant king of France or the equally distant emperor of Germany. Secondly, as in Narbonne, the jurisdiction was divided between the viscount and the bishop, both competing for the revenue brought in by the Jewish subjects. The Jews of that city had their own head, referred to as 'king of the Jews,' and their own 'consuls' or police officers, subject, of course, to the city consuls. Jews owned land and immovable property; they had extensive vineyards. They imported spices and retailed them in market stalls; they were generally engaged in commission business. Only at a late date were they drawn into money-lending, but their transactions were not usurious. At Marseilles, the Jews had equality of status with the Christian citizens, and were admitted to all the professions and trades. At Montpellier, several of the ablest teachers at the school of medicine were Jews.

The mental horizon of the southern French Jews was a much wider one than the confined outlook of their northern brethren. Provence, which for the Jews meant the whole South, was the bridge between Spanish Jewry and the center further north. The Provençal Jews became the carriers of Arab-Jewish culture. Among them we find the first translators who, in the Hebrew tongue, made accessible to wider ' circles the works written in Arabic. In talmudic studies they likewise occupied an intermediating position, striving to unite Spanish system with Franco-German acumen. At Narbonne, which was closest to Spain, Abraham son of Isaac, chief of the rabbinical college (died 1178), codified talmudic jurisprudence ('The book of the Cluster,' Sepher ha-Eshkol). Talmudic learning was cultivated by his pupils, Abraham son of David of Posquières (died 1198) and Zerahiah ha-Levi of Gerona, later at Lunel. The authority of the former was recognized in all Provence. He submitted the Code of Maimonides, to some of whose views he objected, to a searching criticism in which he displayed all his vast learning, his keen mind, and clear intellect. Zerahiah was more original than either his teacher or his fellow-student; he possessed an unusual independence of judgment. Though his writings all centered about the Talmud or al-Fasi's Compendium, he was at home in other branches of learning as well.

Nowhere was Maimonides more honored than in the communities of southern France, and here the battle between the traditionalists and the friends of a rationalized Judaism was fiercest. The Jews of Provence hung upon the word of Maimonides as upon an oracle. When the 'Guide' appeared, the intellectuals of Lunel, headed by Jonathan son of David ha-Cohen, begged the author to send them the book and if possible to translate the work into Hebrew, that they might study it more thoroughly. As a matter of fact, the city had the ready talent at hand. It had the good fortune of possessing in the person of Meshullam son of Jacob (died 1170) a leader, at once wealthy, erudite in talmudic learning, and a friend of culture. Thanks to his encouragement, a circle of prominent intellectuals gathered in this city. To Lunel came Judah son of Saul Ibn Tibbon (died about 1190), a fugitive from the Almohade fanaticism in Granada, by profession a physician, and the possessor of a valuable collection of books. He became the 'father of translators' and rendered successively from Arabic into Hebrew the works of Bahye, Ibn Gabirol, Judah ha-Levi, Ibn Janah, and Saadiah (1161–1186).

His son Samuel (died about 1230) was charged with the translation of the 'Guide.' Later, he translated not only works of Maimonides but also some of the writings of Aristotle and Averroes. While at work on the version of the 'Guide,' he entered into correspondence with the sage at Fustat. He longed to meet the greatest Jewish scholar of the age face to face. Maimonides dissuaded him from undertaking the perilous voyage, especially since, busy as he was, he was hardly able to spare him much time. Instead he gave him sound advice as to how to overcome the difficulties of translation and elucidated a number of difficult passages (1199). On November 30, 1204, fourteen days before the author's demise, Samuel completed the translation of the 'Guide.' This translation enriched the Hebrew language with many new terms coined by the translator, and the style of the Tibbonids became the model of scientific Hebrew during the Middle Ages. Another, less successful, version was made by the poet Judah al-Harizi, whose style excelled that of Samuel but who did not master the subject-matter as thoroughly. Both these men rendered into Hebrew portions of the Commentary on the Mishnah.

The publication of the Hebrew 'Guide' added fuel to the flame in the controversy between liberalism and orthodoxy, Maimunists and anti-Maimunists. The opposition to the 'Code,' which had started in the East (p. 343) and was taken up in the West by Meir son of Todros Abulafia ha-Levi, was nothing as compared with the storm which now broke loose. Some of the friends of philosophic studies had followed the method of allegorical interpretation to great length, thereby shocking many of the orthodox talmudists. Orthodoxy, moreover, scented danger in the rationalism of Maimonides. The talmudist Solomon son of Abraham of Montpellier, in conjunction with his pupils Jonah son of Abraham of Gerona and David son of Saul, tried to set the people against the rationalistic method, while carefully avoiding personal attacks upon Maimonides. As Abulafia had done before him, so Solomon son of Abraham now turned to the northern French scholars. These men were entirely unfamiliar with philosophic speculation, and when they saw the 'Guide,' they unanimously condemned it and pronounced a ban against the study of the 'Guide' and the philosophic portions of the 'Code.' The communities of Provence rose in protest; Lunel, Béziers, and Narbonne met the ban by a counter-ban. The community of Montpellier was itself divided, and liberals and traditionalists came to blows in the streets. The quarrel spread across the Pyrenees. At Gerona, Moses son of Nahman (Nahmani, p. 424) was inclined to a conciliatory, mediating attitude. But Toledo, led by Judah al-Fakhar, physician to king Ferdinand III., stood obdurate. To win, if possible, some of the Spanish Jewish communities to the side of the Maimunian party, the aged David Kimhi set out from Narbonne across the Pyrenees.

The family of the Kimhis originated in Spain. At the time of the Almohade persecution, David's father, Joseph son of Isaac, emigrated to Narbonne. He, like his sons after him, maintained himself by tutoring; a contemporary of Abraham Ibn Ezra and Jacob Tam, he wrote on Hebrew grammar and made translations from the Arabic (died about 1170). His elder son Moses (died about 1190) wrote commentaries on the Scriptures and elementary grammatical treatises. Both he and his young brother David furnished the text-books with which Christian Hebraists, at the revival of learning in the early sixteenth century, trained themselves in the knowledge of Hebrew. David summed up the labors of Spanish Jewish scholars of the last three centuries. He wrote a masterly Hebrew grammar and dictionary. His commentary on the greater part of Scripture became so popular that in this respect it was second only to that of Rashi; through indirect channels it profoundly influenced the Anglican version of 1611 (King James Bible, Authorized Version).

By his training, David was committed to the liberal spirit; naturally he espoused the cause of the Maimunists. At

Avila he was taken ill. In vain did he protest, in his correspondence with al-Fakhar, his own orthodoxy, claiming that he was following merely in the footsteps of the ancient teachers, Sherira and Hai and al-Fasi, in that he held fast to reason at the same time that he was true to tradition. At Burgos, the tidings reached him of the scandal perpetrated by the opponents of Maimonides. Gregory IX., bent upon destroying the last vestige of the Albigensian heresy, had in 1233 conferred upon the Dominican order inquisitorial powers to ferret out and repress heresy. To the Dominicans, accordingly, Solomon of Montpellier and his abetters denounced the writings of Maimonides—the 'Guide' had by that time been translated from the Hebrew (of Harizi) into Latin—and a bonfire was made of them in the public squares of Paris. Kimhi did not long survive this fanatical exhibition (he died in 1235). The act led many of the French rabbis to withdraw their signatures, and there ensued a decided revulsion of feeling. The quarrel, however, was one which could not be settled—the differences were too deep-seated. The commotion subsided for the time being, but it was bound to break out afresh sooner or later.

The bloody crusade against the Albigensians had for its result the destruction of the brilliant Provençal civilization and the annexation to the kingdom of France of all the country from Carcassonne to the Rhone (1229). The Council of Béziers (1246) ratified the usual canonical discriminations against the Jews, including the prohibition for Christians to employ Jewish physicians. Nevertheless, Alphonse of Poitiers, heir of the count of Toulouse, who harassed and despoiled the Jews of his domains, was glad, when afflicted with a disease of the eye, to procure the service of a Jewish physician of Aragon. What was left of Languedoc passed into the possession of Philip III. the Bold, after the death of Alphonse (1271). Philip IV. the Fair, who added Champagne to his possessions (1284), mulcted the Jews again and again. At Troyes, on the charge of ritual murder, thirteen of the richest Jews of the community were condemned to perish in the flames (1288); two poems in old French recount the sufferings of the unfortunate victims. At Paris, on the charge of piercing the host, a Jew and his wife were burned to death (1290). In the same year the king expelled the Jews who were driven from Gascony and England. But the fullest measure of misery for the Jews of France was yet to come.

Outside the dominions of the king of France, at Perpignan, which since 1172 had passed from the counts of Roussillon to the kings of Aragon, the Jews lived in fairly tolerable circumstances. Yet even there they were subjected to certain restrictions and were domiciled in one of the worst quarters of the city. Their inner life reflected the conditions of the neighboring communities. There were the liberals, who dabbled in philosophic studies, and the orthodox, who were shocked at the extreme methods by which Scriptural persons and facts were turned into mere parables. Samuel ha-Sullami, wealthy, charitable, pious, a learned man and a poet, befriended a poor scholar, Levi son of Abraham of Villefranche (1250–1320), an extreme allegorist.

The old quarrel broke out again. A vigorous opponent of philosophy arose in the person of Abba Mari son of Moses of Lunel, later at Montpellier, while in Palestine, at Acco, the agitation against Maimonides was started by Solomon Petit, a cabalist of French origin. Liberalism found its sponsors in Jacob son of Machir Ibn Tibbon (a translator of mathematical and astronomical works, whose astronomical tables and treatises were very popular in Latin translations), and the poet Jedaiah son of Abraham of Béziers. An intermediate position, not unfriendly to the students of philosophy, was maintained by the Perpignan rabbi, Menahem son of Solomon ha-Meiri, author of a voluminous and methodical commentary on the whole of the Talmud. The orthodox appealed to the foremost rabbinical authority of the time, Solomon Ibn Adret at Barcelona (p. 430). On the sabbath before the Fast of Ab (July 31), 1305, this scholar issued a ban, signed by himself and by more than thirty scholars of his city, which proscribed the study of the sciences, save medicine, to any one who was not thirty years old. The liberals answered with a counter-ban. Curiously enough, the governor of Montpellier objected to the ban against the study of philosophy, as it would check the progress of conversion.

The quarrel had by no means been allayed, when French Jewry was overwhelmed by an edict of expulsion, promulgated June 21 and executed July 22, on the tenth of Ab, 1306. The king's treasury was empty; the property of the Jews, real and personal, as well as the debts which Christians owed them, was confiscated. Even the chicken in the pot was not safe from the king, so ran a folk-song. The synagogue at Paris was presented by the king to his coachman. The Jews, about a hundred thousand, were turned out of the country where they had resided nearly one thousand years, with only the clothes on their backs and a small pittance in coin. The impression which this calamity made upon a young student, hailing from Spain, but at the time undergoing training in Montpellier, is pictured in the narrative of Estori Pharhi. He tells us how he was taken out of school, stripped of his garments, driven at the height of his studies from his fatherland, how he cast about in his youth from people to people and from kingdom to kingdom among men of foreign tongue, and at last found rest in the Holy Land, devoting himself to a study of its sites. The majority of the banished settled in adjoining Lorraine, Burgundy, Savoy, Dauphiné, Roussillon, and the part of Provence which was not under French dominion. A few rich Jews were recalled to help in collecting the debts and in locating the treasures hidden by the exiles; but their stay lasted only a few years, till 1311.

Jewish history in France practically came to a conclusion then. It is true, the Jews were recalled by Louis X. in 1315. The people, groaning under the usurers who succeeded them, clamored for their return. The king had himself well paid for the grant of protection stipulated to last for a period of twelve years. The Jews were glad to return to their fatherland, 'their mother.' Unsold property, synagogues, and burial-places were restored to them and they were promised one year's notice if the permission to stay was to be withdrawn.

Philip V. the Tall (1316–1322) continued the policy of his predecessor. But a crusading band of shepherds (Pastoureaux) and peasants overran in 1320 southern France and later northern Spain. They soon turned against the Jews, and the horrors of the earlier crusades were repeated. At Verdun, five hundred Jews took refuge in a stone tower; after a desperate defense, being faced with surrender, they preferred suicide. At Toulouse, the governor vainly tried to protect them and to proceed against the 'holy men'; but the populace took sides with the shepherds, and the Jewish community was annihilated; some were baptized. When the shepherds later turned against the clergy, they were vigorously put down. More than a hundred and twenty Jewish communities of France and Spain had in the meantime been ruthlessly destroyed.

It was a time when the popular mind was an easy prey to all imaginary terrors. In the following year, 1321, it was believed that the lepers had formed a conspiracy to poison the wells. The outcasts, on being tortured, alleged that the Jews, fearing to commit the crime themselves, had instigated the undertaking. Accordingly the Jews were condemned to pay a heavy fine. At Chinon, one hundred and sixty Jews were buried in an enclosed pit. In Paris, only the 'guilty' were put to death; the others were exiled. The richest were retained so as to assure the payment of the enormous fines. The king finally admitted the innocence of the Jews; but five thousand had lost their lives; nor was the money, extorted from the Jews, restored to them. Charles IV., who succeeded Philip in 1322, expelled the Jews a second time from the French realm (June 24, 1322), quite unexpectedly, in spite of the promise of a year's warning.

After the disaster of Poitiers, when John the Good was made prisoner by the English army (1356), the Jews were once more brought back (1359) for a period of twenty years. The conditions, however, were most precarious. Another banishment was narrowly averted in 1368, though Charles V. (1364–1380) on the whole kept to his compact and in many ways conceded privileges, all for fixed payments.

But the popular revolts against heavy taxation, which began under that king and continued during the reign of Charles VI. (1380–1422), coupled with the rise of the national spirit, led to riots against the Jews. The king for a time made a show of protecting them, convenient as they were for filling the treasury, until an incident occurred which brought matters to a head. A Jew of Ville-Parisis, Denis Machault, returned to Judaism after accepting baptism. Immediately the Jews of Paris were ordered to be flogged and then banished. On September 17, 1394, which coincided with the Day of Atonement, the mad king signed the order for all the Jews of the realm to leave the country by November 3. No Jew was thenceforth to live in the domains of France. In Lyons, they remained another twenty-five years, till 1420; in some parts of Provence, for another century. From the papal possessions, including Avignon, the Jews were never expelled.

Under such conditions little of fruitful inner activity was possible between the first recall and the final banishment. We hear of official chief rabbis, such as Mattathiah son of Joseph Treves, who lived in Paris; he had great authority and enjoyed royal favor. Charles V. exempted him from wearing the circular badge. In Provence alone, which was outside the French realm, interest in philosophic studies and in the sciences did not flag. In this nook, Maimonides and Averroes held the minds captive. In commentaries on the 'Guide' as well as on various biblical books, two men carried the ideas of the master farther: the shallow but prolific Joseph son of Abba Mari Caspi (of Argentière, died at Tarascon 1340) and the more erudite Moses son of Joshua Narboni. The latter hailed from Perpignan, but spent the greater part of his life in Spain, where he died some time after 1362.

By far the boldest philosopher of the age was Levi son of Gershon, intermittently at Orange, Perpignan, and Avignon (1288–1344). He excelled as a mathematician and astronomer. He invented an instrument of observation; the part of his astronomical work dealing with that instrument was

translated into Latin by order of pope Clement VI. in 1342.
He also wrote commentaries on Averroes as well as on the
Scriptures. His philosophical system, based largely upon
Aristotelian foundations, he laid down in his principal work,
'The Wars of the Lord'—his opponents called it 'Wars
against the Lord'—written in a Hebrew of utmost precision.
In this work he ventured to go beyond Maimonides, admitting a formless matter before creation. The Divine Providence, as applying to individuals, he maintained, manifested
itself in a graded manner—the more illustrious a person,
the more given to realizing in himself the Active Intellect,
the more he participated in the divine care. It was the most
complete surrender to rationalism, paving the way for the
still more resolute rationalism of Spinoza. Yet for the time
being, and for that matter even in later times, Judaism
necessarily recoiled from the extreme positions thus advanced and sought an expression of its deepest concerns in a
'knowledge' that was Jewish or at least more akin to the
Jewish spirit.

CHAPTER LVI

GERMAN JEWS IN THE FOURTEENTH CENTURY

(1298-1407)

HE 'Jewish Knowledge,' which ripened in Spain (p. 432), had its roots both in France and in Germany. It was mainly a turning away from the exaggerated rationalism of the philosophers. At the same time it was favored by the depression of the Jewish mind in consequence of the growing deterioration of the status of Jewry, economic and social. The eclipse of French Jewry was precipitate; the misfortunes of the German Jews were drawn out for a longer period down into the fifteenth century.

During the civil strife between Albert I. of Habsburg and his rival Adolph of Nassau, shortly before the latter was defeated in battle and slain (1298), the Jews of Röttingen, in Franconia, were charged with the crime of pounding a sacred wafer in a mortar until the blood flowed forth profusely. Such a preposterous story was enough to cause a general uprising. A nobleman, by the name of Rindfleisch, placed himself at the head of a mob, and the whole Jewish community suffered death at the stake (April 20). Rindfleisch and his followers went from town to town and from province to province, spreading terror and slaughter throughout Franconia, Bavaria, and Austria. Nothing remained for the Jews except to die heroically for their faith; only the craven saved their lives by baptism. The large community of Würzburg was exterminated (July 23). At Nuremberg, the Jews sought refuge in the castle, but were overpowered and butchered (August 1). Among the six hundred and twenty-eight martyrs was Mordecai son of Hillel with his wife and their five children. He was a pupil of Meir of Rothenburg and the author of a ritual work in which the decisions of the Franco-German schools were summed up.

402

In the whole of Bavaria only two communities escaped, Ratisbon and Augsburg, thanks to the protection of the magistrates. The slaughter passed on to Austria. All told a hundred and forty Jewish communities were wiped out and one hundred thousand persons slain. Albert I. (1298–1308) imposed heavy fines on the imperial cities in which massacres had occurred. As Roman emperor, in succession to Vespasian, Titus, and Charlemagne, he claimed sole ownership of all Jews. It is said that he even demanded of Philip IV. the surrender of all French Jewry. However, both Albert and his son, the duke Rudolph, dealt much more leniently with the perpetrators of excesses in their own Austrian dominions. It was during these evil times that Asher son of Jehiel, a fellow-student of the martyred Mordecai, together with his family, forsook Germany.

It was next to impossible for the inner life of German Jewry to maintain itself in old vigor under such conditions. The sword of Damocles hung continually over them. During the fearful persecutions in Alsace, Swabia, and Franconia (1336–1338), led by two noblemen, 'Armleder' (so called from the piece of leather which they wore around their arms), the emperor Louis the Bavarian (1314–1347) committed the Jews to the care of the count of Nuremberg. He also warned the other princes that no excesses would be tolerated. Such warnings, however, did not check the bloody riots. In Ratisbon and Vienna the council and citizens protected the Jews. But at Deckendorf (1337), a trumped up charge of desecrating the host led to an attack by the city council in league with the knights of the vicinity. They fell upon the unsuspecting Jews and killed or burned them; they then seized their property, thereby not only ridding themselves of their indebtedness to the Jews but even acquiring riches.

Louis renewed the claim of succession to the Roman emperors. In 1342, he instituted a new levy, the 'golden penny of offering.' This was, aside from any other taxes the Jews were paying, a poll-tax of one gulden a year from every Jew and Jewess, above the age of twelve, possessing property worth at least twenty gulden.

Duke Albert II. of Austria (1330–1358) saw through the real cause of the excesses against the Jews, which was nothing but lust for pillage. In answer to his appeal, Pope Benedict XII. (1334–1342) ordered that charges of Jewish desecration of the host and similar offenses must be substantiated by a court of inquiry and that, failing to support their accusation by evidence, the authors of the dastardly libel should be proceeded against with all canonical rigor. On the other hand, duke Henry of Bavaria granted to the citizens of Deckendorf amnesty for the crimes committed against the Jews. He also exempted them from the payments of debts due to Jewish creditors, and gave them permission to retain all pillaged goods. Yet all these persecutions were trifling as compared with the most general and devastating outbreaks against the Jews in western and central Europe which occurred in 1348 and in the following years, particularly in 1349.

The Black Death, that terrible epidemic, essentially the same as bubonic plague, was imported into the West from India and carried off more than one-third of the population. In the credulous and superstitious minds of the terror-stricken masses the notion arose that the Jews were causing the disease by poisoning the wells and rivers which supplied the drinking-water. As in 1320 and 1322 (p. 399), weird stories were circulated concerning a universal plot on the part of Jewry to destroy the Christians. It was fabled that the conspiracy originated in Toledo, the capital of Castile, and that in southern France certain Jews were commissioned to compound the poison and have it conveyed to all parts of Christendom. The ingredients of the poison were supposed to be spiders, lizards, frogs, human flesh, the hearts of Christians mixed with the dough of sacred hosts. By means of inhuman torture confessions were wrung from some Jews, who confirmed any and every suggestion put to them.

In vain did Pope Clement VI. (1342–1352) set himself against the popular obsession; in vain was the solicitude of the German emperor, Charles IV. (1347–1378), for his serfs of the exchequer. In Strassburg, the mayor and the city council, encouraged by letters from other city councils such as that of Cologne, interposed between the Jew-baiters and their victims. They feared that once the mob had its way with the Jews, it might turn against the patrician masters. As a result of this intercession, the council was charged by the mob with being bribed by the Jews and speedily removed from office. The new council brought the whole Jewish community, eighteen hundred souls, to the cemetery on a sabbath and there burned them all alive. It then ordered all documents bearing on indebtedness to the Jews destroyed, pledges to be returned, and the sums of money left by those massacred to be distributed among the artisans. They also entered into a league with the neighboring princes and lords, who owed money to Strassburg Jews, for mutual protection should they be called to account.

The alleged testimonies of the tortured were spread from city to city. The obsession gained momentum as the dread disease raged through Europe. It made the people restless and fanned the hatred against the Jews, who, because of their abstemious habits of life and their natural segregation, were somewhat less exposed to the ravages of the plague. The populace lusted for the blood of the Jews, and more so for their treasures. A contemporary Christian chronicler honestly confesses that the poison which killed the Jews was their wealth. What took place was in truth a social revolution. The Jews, by their loans to the lower nobility, enabled these to resist successfully the efforts of the cities to gain supremacy. In the cities proper, the Jews sided with the patrician class in its struggle against the guilds. Thus the guilds became the bitter enemies of the Jews and, where they succeeded in getting control of the government as in Strassburg, they destroyed the Jewish community. Yet, the result was not quite as desired, since nobility and patricians, once rid of their debts, became only the stronger. This much was accomplished that every one enriched himself at the expense of the hapless victims.

Unlike earlier persecutions, those of 1348–1349 were generally carried out systematically by the order of the city councils. The deadly massacres started in northern Spain (Barcelona, Cervera, Tarrega, June and July, 1348), passed on to Switzerland (Chillon, Bern, Zurich, in September), thence to Bavaria (Augsburg, Würzburg, Munich, and eighty smaller towns, in November), then up the Rhine (Freiburg in Breisgau, Spires, Strassburg, Worms, Frankfort, Mayence, Cologne, January to August 1349), on to Breslau (in May) and later to Magdeburg and Berlin; the turn of Erfurt and Nuremberg came last. In Austria, thanks to the energetic measures of duke Albert II., after the bloody attack on the Jews of Krems (September 1349), the madness was thoroughly checked. As the epitaph on the tomb of this distinguished prince puts it, the Jews had cause to shed tears over their departed protector.

The emperor Charles IV., however he may have shielded the Jews in his own domains, was both lukewarm and powerless to withstand the upheaval from below. He was ready with amnesties to the good citizens for past wrongs, and in several instances he granted immunity to the attacking forces on the eve of their excesses, or made disposition of the property of the victims ahead of time. In general, the goods left behind by those who met their death in the massacres were confiscated by the emperor or by the reigning prince of the locality. All debts owed to them were canceled or collected by the sovereign; synagogues and burial-places adverted to the communes; Jewish dwellings were sold or bestowed upon the emperor's favorites. The gain was enormous, but still more so was the loss of the rich revenue hitherto paid annually by the Jews. Many a town was in ashes by reason of the conflagration in which the Jews heroically destroyed themselves.

Coincidently with the upheaval produced by the dread disease, the passions of the mobs were further incited against the Jews by the Flagellants. These bands of fanatics went from town to town, in advance of the dread plague, urging the people to piety and penance, and scourging themselves so as to appease the divine wrath and thus stay the plague. Frequently they incited the people to kill the Jews. The death-toll of Jews, cruelly butchered or resorting to self-immolation, was enormous; the loss of property staggering. Sixty large and one hundred and fifty small communities were destroyed. The inheritors of dead Jews' fortunes pleased themselves in enacting statutes that no living Jews should be further admitted as residents in their communes.

Soon, however, princes and magistrates thought better of it and rescinded the drastic measures—not because the Jews were loved, but because taxes were high and credit conditions disorganized. The bishop of Augsburg craved the emperor's permission to receive the Jews and give them a home in his own see. In the constitution of the German empire, known as the Golden Bull, which was promulgated in 1356, the electors, lay and spiritual, obtained for themselves the privilege of keeping Jews and, of course, of taxing them. Characteristically enough they are mentioned in the constitution between the right to exploit mines and to collect taxes. They were a mine out of which precious metal could be won by mere pressure without any work. The emperor, however, still claimed the Jews in the smaller principalities and in the imperial cities as his own subjects, serfs of the treasury, as of old. Scarcely had the princes left the diet of Nuremberg, whence the Golden Bull was issued, when Gerlach, archbishop of Mayence, commissioned a Jew to negotiate with his coreligionists the terms of resettlement in the archiepiscopal domain. Soon the remnant of surviving Jews was established in most of the old seats of Jewry. For nearly three decades they enjoyed tranquillity. They were given a breathing-spell to recover and to gather new fortunes, but their position was greatly impaired. The movement started by the Crusades had reached its culmination in the persecutions of 1348–1349. From that time on, the Jews were enclosed in special quarters, the gates admitting to their abode being locked each night that none might leave or enter. Every city and dukedom enacted laws requiring special 'Jewish oaths' in lawsuits, thus further humiliating the Jews.

On the intellectual side, it was an 'orphaned generation.' Spiritual decay was a natural consequence of the social and economic conditions. Talmudic knowledge among the laity was beginning to be scarce. The rabbis themselves were not always sufficiently trained and often gained their position by the aid of the secular powers. Meir son of Baruch ha-Levi, chief rabbi of Vienna (1393–1408), introduced the system of ordination which conferred upon the holder the title 'Our Teacher' (Morenu) and the right to exercise rabbinical functions. With the schools moribund or quite extinct in France and Germany, the Torah found for itself a nook in Austria. In the capital, by the side of Meir, was active Abraham Klausner. Near by, at Neustadt, Shalom son of Isaac conducted a famous talmudical school. Of his disciples the most distinguished were Jacob Levi Mölln (died 1427), at Mayence, and Israel Isserlein (died 1460), who succeeded his teacher at Neustadt.

All these scholars busied themselves with collecting the ritual customs (minhagim) current in Germany and investing them with authority. It was during this time that the differences in customs between western and eastern Germany developed. Others wrote glosses on older ritual codes; so Samuel son of Aaron Schlettstadt on the code of Mordecai (p. 402). Samuel officiated as rabbi at Strassburg; here he had an informer, by due process of Jewish law, put to death, while an accomplice saved himself by baptism. The Jews of the community placed the responsibility upon the rabbi, who had to seek safety in a castle near Colmar together with his pupils. Later, he went to the Orient with recommendations from the prominent German rabbis and returned armed with a ban issued by Babylonia and Jerusalem against the community which had wronged him. The Jews of Strassburg tried to make amends, but the community was soon subjected to a fresh spoliation of twenty thousand gulden (1386) and a general expulsion (1388) with complete confiscation of their property.

During the disorders under the reign of Wenceslaus (1378–1400), the guilds in some cities overthrew the patrician rulers and shed much Jewish blood at Nördlingen, Windsheim, and Weissenburg (1384). The Swabian federation of cities tried to restore the old régime and to punish the leaders of the outbreaks severely. Nevertheless, at Augsburg, two hundred Jews were seized and made to pay twenty-two thousand gulden; a similar impost had been levied on them in 1381. The Jews of Nuremberg purchased the protection of the council by three voluntary gifts (1384–1385). In Ratisbon the council energetically suppressed the movement and compelled the Jews, who made ready to leave the city, to remain. Nördlingen refused to yield to the Federation and secretly secured amnesty from the emperor. To prevent its complete dissolution, the Federation accepted the proposal of Wenceslaus and, at a diet of the Swabian cities at Ulm in 1385, one-fourth of all debts due to Jews was canceled outright, while the other three-fourths were ordered paid to the cities. The Jews were left in the power of the cities and were to be prevented from emigrating. The emperor was indemnified to the amount of forty thousand gulden. This agreement was made the law of the country and was guaranteed by the emperor. Suddenly the Jews were imprisoned and their deeds and valuable securities were seized by the cities which now made their own arrangements with the individual Jewish capitalists and as often as not retained for themselves the uncanceled residue. The Jews thereby lost practically everything except their ready money, while the cities acquired a powerful weapon against the nobility and withal a large income.

In the meantime the Swabian Federation was defeated in its war against a counter-federation of knights and princes. Wenceslaus went with the victors. Intent on despoiling the Jews, he dissolved the Federation in 1389 and in the following year enacted a new and complete remission of debts due to Jews, this time without regard for the interests of the cities. The heavily indebted nobility was greatly benefited, while the incomes of the cities were considerably reduced. However, separate agreements had to be made with all the powers owning Jews, and these, to prevent the entire disintegration of their Jewries, sometimes insisted on concessions favoring the Jews. Thus Nuremberg did not extend the remission to its own citizens. Much more sweeping was the decree of 1390, which robbed the Jews in the southwestern territories of the empire not only of outstanding debts in the localities in which they resided, but also of any money due them outside these localities. The gain which in this way accrued to burghers and others who were indebted to the Jews was enormous, while the emperor received for himself a goodly portion of the obligations thus canceled. Yet the division of Germany saved the Jews from the complete economic destruction which might have resulted from a simultaneous and thorough carrying out of the policy of Wenceslaus. Moreover, the growing world commerce made Jewish banking indispensable so long as the Church prohibition against usury prevented Christian competition. Thus, between 1385 and 1390 some Jewish bankers, operating with the capital they had retained and whatever money was returned to them, managed to recover parts of their fortune.

Nevertheless, the position of the Jews was becoming more precarious. Remission of debts became a regular occurrence, though the king, as a sign of especial grace, might now and then promise individual communities not to resort to this form of spoliation for a certain number of years. Nor were the Jews immune from mob attacks on their life and property. In 1389, the imperial capital Prague witnessed a bloody massacre on Easter Sunday, which coincided with the last day of Passover. It happened that, during a procession with the host which passed through the Jewish quarter, Jewish children, in play, were throwing sand at each other and the host was accidentally besprinkled with some of it. Immediately the mob surrounded the Jews in their homes, shouting, Death or baptism! Many slew themselves; three thousand were put to death by the populace. The synagogue was burned down; the scrolls were torn to shreds and trampled under foot. Even the dead were exhumed from their burialplace and their tombstones shattered. The property of the slain was confiscated by Wenceslaus as king of Bohemia. In the rest of that kingdom the Jews were imprisoned, but, on the payment of heavy fines, the king ordered their release and afforded them protection.

Fresh troubles beset the Jews as a result of the denunciations of a converted Jew by the name of Peter (his Jewish name had been Pesah). He chose for the target of his accusations the prayer of Adoration (Alenu), which forms an ancient part of the liturgy of the New Year and is also repeated at the conclusion of the three daily prayers. This prayer was declared by the convert to contain aspersions on the founder of the Christian Church. It is true, the expression occurs there: 'For they (that is, the idolaters) bow down and pray to naught and vanity, unto a god that cannot save.' But the language is taken from Isaiah 45, 20, and the prayer was composed by Rab in the first half of the third century (p. 239) in Babylonia, where Christianity was practically non-existent. The Jews were imprisoned (August 3, 1394). Among them was Yom Tob Lipmann of Mühlhausen, a student not only of the Talmud, but also of Latin. He was well versed in Karaite literature and in the New Testament, and author of a controversial work directed against the philosophers who undermine faith, and especially against Christian interpretation of Scriptural passages ('Book of Refutation,' Sepher Nizzahon). Lipmann succeeded in countering the convert's imputations and was set free; seventy-seven of his coreligionists, however, were killed and, three weeks later, three more were burned at the stake (1400).

Rupert, who was now on the imperial throne, neutralized in part the severe measures of his predecessor by granting charters to certain communities, to that of Mayence (1401), for example, giving assurance to Jewish creditors that their claims would be honored by their debtors. Nevertheless, archbishop John II. of Mayence ordered (1405) all debts to Jews to be shorn of one-fifth and the remainder to be payable in four terms. As the emperor met only with a partial recognition in the empire, he took pains to insure the universal levy of the 'golden penny' by appointing two Jews collectors of this tax (1403). There was no other means of coercing the Jews save by excommunication; accordingly Rupert named Israel of Krems, residing at Nuremberg, 'chief master of all rabbis and the Jews and Jewesses of the German empire.' The institution of a chief rabbi by the grace of the emperor met with opposition on the part of the other rabbis, which Rupert, though he imposed a heavy fine upon the recalcitrant Jews (1407), was powerless to overcome.

CHAPTER LVII

GERMAN JEWS DURING THE FIFTEENTH CENTURY

(1410-1480)

SIGISMUND (1410–1437) was particularly inventive in extorting money from the Jews. He thought that his Jewish subjects should meet his own expenses in connection with the Council of Constance. In some places the Jews were asked to give up a third, and in other places as much as half, of their fortunes. At a time when the regular revenue of the empire amounted to thirteen thousand gulden annually, nine Jewish families in Frankfort were required to contribute five thousand gulden. The Jews of Cologne vainly offered twelve thousand, in order to escape the necessity of disclosing the exact sum of their possessions (1414). Martin V., the new pope elected at Constance, issued in 1418 a friendly bull in which the Jews were confirmed in all the old privileges. The emperor, who acted as intermediary, claimed the broker's fee, especially because, as the Jews must themselves know, papal favors were not to be had for nothing. The Hussite wars (1419–1436) brought in their train new troubles to the Jews. Along with the heretics they were set upon by the Catholic party at the instigation of the Dominican preachers.

Fanaticism, coupled with greed of Jewish possessions, led to a similar catastrophe in Austria. Albert V., impoverished as he was, readily lent ear to the popular obsession that the Jews were making common cause with the Hussites. The people's excitement was further fed by a story that a rich Jew, Israel of Enns, had purchased from a sexton's wife a consecrated wafer in order to profane it. At the duke's order, all the Jews of the ducal territory were placed in prison (May 23, 1420). The poor were immediately banished, while the rich remained in custody. Many died by their own hands; of those who had saved themselves by accepting baptism, a few, on reverting to their old faith, were burned at the stake. An appeal to the pope brought forth a renewed bull (December 23) forbidding the baptism of Jewish children under the age of twelve. But the fate of Austrian Jewry could not be averted. As many as had survived the Inquisition and its tortures were burned near Vienna (March 12, 1421); for a long time no Jew was to be found in Austria. The property of the Jews was confiscated by the duke; their houses were bestowed upon Christians. The synagogue at Vienna was destroyed and its stones were turned over to the university for the construction of a new building. Draconic as these measures were, they failed of their effect to keep the Jews out of Austria entirely. The duke himself made exceptions in individual cases; in 1438 he granted to Isserlein a safe-conduct to dwell and go about wherever he chose.

Excesses against the Jews were enacted by the anti-Hussite crusaders in Thuringia, Bavaria, and along the Rhine. Jacob Mölln ordered a public fast of three consecutive days. The pope was once more entreated to check the fanaticism of the Dominican monks (1422). Nevertheless, the Jews of Cologne were banished (1426); expulsion befell also many other communities. The Council of Basel (1431–1443), which was convoked to reform ecclesiastical abuses, found time to reiterate the anti-Jewish measures of former councils. In addition it was ruled that Jews should not be admitted to scholastic degrees in the universities and that baptized Jews should by all means be kept in the Catholic faith and prevented from marrying among themselves. Sigismund's successor, Albert II. of Austria, for a consideration of nine hundred gulden, granted the city of Augsburg the permission to drive out its Jews (1439).

When, in 1450, pope Nicholas V. held a jubilee in Rome, the Jews were fearful that the pilgrims on their way to the eternal city might commit excesses, and Israel Isserlein, the outstanding authority in Germany, ordered a fast day. Nicholas V. and his predecessor Eugenius IV. (1431–1447) had both suffered the fanatical Franciscan monk, John Capistrano, to gain ascendancy over them. Evil days struck

German Jewry when this Capuchin was made legate to the German and Slavonic lands for the purpose of carrying into execution the measures of the Council of Basel against the heretical Hussites and the disbelieving Jews. This eloquent and fiery preacher was called by his admirers 'the scourge of the Jews.' The Bavarian dukes, Louis and Albert, were confirmed by the monk in their unfriendliness against the Jews, whom they therefore banished completely from their duchies. The city of Ratisbon alone refused to let its Jews go, but the duke insisted upon their wearing the Jews' badge, and the city authorities otherwise imposed upon them vexatious discriminations (1452).

Godfrey of Würzburg, the reigning duke of Franconia, who had been friendly to the Jews and had granted them the fullest privileges, was persuaded by Capistrano to expel them (1453). The monk claimed to have performed many miracles. When he came to Neustadt, Israel Isserlein offered to follow him to the burning stake and let God decide between them, provided the emperor would take the necessary precautions to prevent trickery. Capistrano naturally declined the offer. The worst fate befell the Jews of Silesia, where four months after his arrival in Breslau, the inflamed mob readily lent credence to a tale that a wealthy Jew, Meyer by name, had desecrated the host. Immediately the representatives of the Jewish community were placed in prison. Capistrano instituted a court of inquiry in the presence of legates from the court of Vienna. By means of the usual method of torture confessions were extracted, and more than forty Jews suffered death by burning (July 4, 1453) and over three hundred were expelled. Ladislas confirmed the act of perpetual banishment passed by the city council.

It is remarkable that in those evil times, when the Jews of Germany were harassed by malicious persecutions, Jewish studies continued to thrive. Erfurt, Nuremberg, Ratisbon, Prague, and other cities maintained colleges for Jewish studies. One of the outstanding figures of this period was the rabbi of Neustadt near Vienna, Israel Isserlein, whose mother had been one of the Vienna martyrs of 1421. His responsa reflect throughout the uncertain position of the Jews in his day. We hear of strife within German Jewry; to this, the prominent leaders, like Isserlein and others, opposed their full authority.

The impotent reign of Frederick III. (1440–1486; died 1493) during which the central authority was ignored by warring princes and cities, was not conducive to Jewish tranquillity. A Jew, leaving the walls of the city in which he resided, took his life into his hands. The warfare at Mayence between the two rival archbishops, Dietrich II. of Isenburg and Adolph II. of Nassau, ended disastrously for the Jews, who, having espoused the cause of the former, were driven out by the victorious rival (1461). Duke Louis IX. of Bavaria had expelled the Jews from his kingdom and then asked the council of Ratisbon to do similarly with its Jews. The council, prompted by somewhat friendly feelings for the Jews and by an unwillingness to lose this valuable source of income, refused to grant the ducal request. Louis then joined forces with the bishop of Ratisbon, who shared his hatred of the Jews.

Two men, one a converted Jew, placed themselves at their service. Peter Schwarz preached conversionist sermons to which the Jews were forced to listen during the Passover festival. Hans Vayol, the erstwhile Jew, fastened upon the rabbi, Israel Bruna, the libel of ritual murder. The rabbi had come from Brünn at the time of the expulsion of the Jews from that city. At Ratisbon, where he settled, he was opposed by an older incumbent of the rabbinate, Anshel by name. The community was divided until at last Israel, by his great learning, won universal recognition. The aged scholar was imprisoned, charged with the murder of a Christian lad for religious purposes (1474). Both the emperor and Vladislav, king of Poland and Bohemia, who claimed Israel as his 'serf,' gave peremptory orders for the rabbi's release. It was effected after Vayol, having been imprisoned and carefully examined, publicly retracted his accusation. Vayol was then burned alive.

Into the midst of these commotions came the news of the affair at Trent. The Jews of the Tirolean city were living in harmonious and amicable relations with their Christian neighbors, when the fanatical Franciscan monk, Bernardinus of Feltre, came to town. In his Lenten sermons (1475) he endeavored to incite the people against the Jews; when the citizens demurred, he predicted that on the approaching Easter Sunday they would come round to his opinion. A week before Easter, a Christian boy of three years old, Simon by name, was drowned in the river Adige. As soon as he was missed the preacher charged the Jews with having crucified him. Two days later, the body was found on the bank of the river, close to the dwelling of a Jew. The Jew, in order to forestall the accusation so readily fastened upon his people, forthwith apprised the bishop Hinderbach of the gruesome find. The body was taken to the church, and the bishop pointed to the Jews as the murderers of the child. A Jewish apostate testified to the use of Christian blood by the Jews. For many days the accused withstood the most terrible tortures. At last, their power of resistance was broken. The Jew, upon whom chiefly the accusation was fastened, admitted his guilt on the rack, but again and again denied it when taken down. Finally his evidence was so distorted as to facilitate matters for the bishop's court. The result was that all the Jews of Trent, barring four who accepted baptism, were burned at the stake.

Hinderbach and the Dominican monks spread stories of miraculous manifestations at the grave of the 'martyred' boy. It made no difference that an investigation by the papal legate proved the whole affair a tissue of falsehoods and that pope Sixtus IV. in his bull of October 10, 1475 forbade the veneration of the child. A second proceeding also cleared the Jews. Nevertheless, a commission of cardinals, headed by an intimate friend of Bernardinus, found a verdict exculpating the bishop. In a decree of June 20, 1478, the pope gave it confirmation. All through Germany the libel was believed. At Frankfort, by the side of the bridge leading across the Main, a memorial column was erected, with pictures of Christian children being tortured by unsightly Jews and an inscription breathing hatred against the Jewish people.

It happened that bishop Henry of Ratisbon passed through Trent on his way to and from Rome. He was immediately convinced that eight years before a similar deed had been perpetrated by the Jews of Ratisbon. The entire community was imprisoned; later, all but seventeen were freed, and these remained in prison for four years. Henry prevailed upon the city council to put these seventeen Jews to trial, after receiving assurance from the duke that he would stand by him (1476). The usual methods of torture were applied.

The Jews knew that if they were to obtain the intercession of the emperor much money was needed. The rabbis of Bavaria convened at Nuremberg and, under the presidency of Jacob Margalioth, authorized a collection from all the communities under their spiritual guidance for the purpose of effecting a release of the imprisoned Jews at Ratisbon. The emperor found the city councilors obdurate; he threatened the city with the loss of its charter, and summoned the magistrates to appear before the imperial court. In vain did the city authorities appeal to the pope. Though a papal legate was sent to sustain the charges against the Jews, the emperor insisted that the Jews kept in jail should be set free. The Jews, however, were to pay a fine of ten thousand gulden; just for what reason, no one knew. At last the prisoners were set free, on the condition that the Jews would not depart nor take their fortunes out of the city (1480). The dukes of Bavaria bided their time when they might banish all of the Jews from their territory.

CHAPTER LVIII

JEWS IN CHRISTIAN SPAIN. NAHMANI

(1203-1293)

THE scene of Spanish Jewish history during the three centuries preceding the expulsion was mainly Christian Spain, and as the reconquest of Moorish territory progressed the final act was hastened. The thirteenth century opened with the ascendancy of Rome in the affairs of the peninsula. Peter II. of Aragon—the kingdom comprised also the Catalonian coast with the prosperous seaport Barcelona, united to Aragon since 1137—surrendered his kingdom to pope Innocent III. in 1203, and received it back as a fief of the Holy See. On his return from Rome, the Jews met him with scrolls of the Law in their hands, trembling for their fate. The States' Council, however, pronounced the royal surrender null and void. In a pastoral letter, the pope reprimanded Alphonso VIII. of Castile (1158–1214) for favors shown to the Jews (1205). A coalition of Christian forces against the Moslems was led by the Castilian king and ended in the victory in the valley of Tortosa (1212). The crusaders, who at the bidding of the pope had come from across the mountains, made good the opportunity by harassing the Jewish community of Toledo. Arnault, archbishop of Narbonne, did his worst to incite the bloodthirsty mob; but the king put a stop to their fanatic onslaught.

When the Lateran Council was about to be convened, the Jews of Aragon, headed by Isaac Benveniste, physician to king James I. (1213–1276), made common cause with their brethren in Provence to send a delegation to Rome for the purpose of preventing anti-Jewish measures. Their effort was in vain; the dishonoring badge was fastened upon the Jew (p. 375). Nevertheless Benveniste succeeded in having the enforcement of this measure postponed. In Leon, Alphonso IX. (1188–1230) forbore to compel the Jews to wear the badge. Honorius III. (1216–1227) found it necessary to remind the bishop of Valencia (in Aragon) and two other ecclesiastical chiefs of their duty to have the measure carried into effect, incidentally also to keep Jews from public offices (1217). 'It is impossible for disbelievers in the Catholic truth,' argued the pope, 'to serve faithfully the sons of Catholicism.' Therefore he admonished King James not to employ Jews as diplomatic agents between himself and the Mohammedan states.

In Aragon, in the southern part more than in the northern, wealthy Jews owned plantations, which they leased to Saracens; in the north they employed Christian labor. Smaller parcels of land were tilled by the Jewish owners themselves. Jews of wealth also raised cattle, tended by Christian shepherds. Some held in lease from the king salt-pits and mines. The great number engaged in all kinds of manual labor, from the meanest to the most artistic. At Saragossa, in 1336, the Jewish shoe-makers formed an association with activities both religious and social; at Catalayud the weavers had their own synagogue. The dyeing of wool, cotton, and silk was quite a general occupation. Jews worked as smiths, potters, bookbinders, and watch-makers. So considerable was the number of Jewish silversmiths and gold-smiths that, in 1415, pope Benedict XIII. found it necessary to forbid having crosses, chalices, and other church utensils made by Jews. Those that did not work at a trade, trafficked with garments, cloths, and other ware. These objects were sold, in the bazaars, in shops leased by the king to the Jewish traders. The cloth halls of the Jews made up a considerable portion of the community wealth; frequently they were seized by the king when the community was slow in paying a tallage. The Jews acted as brokers and auctioneers; as such they were municipal officials, sworn in by the bailiff.

Beyond their immediate domicile, the Jews carried on an extensive commerce in grain, wine, oil, saffron, flax, wool, and cattle. Often they sought permission to journey across the frontier. At an early period, the Jews of the coast cities put to sea, and during the entire thirteenth and fourteenth centuries they took an active part in Mediterranean commerce. The Jews of the island Mallorca did business with the mainland, but also with Africa and the Orient. Naturally, as elsewhere through the Middle Ages, the capital accumulated in profitable business was invested in loans among the Christian population.

As in Germany and Sicily and exactly in the identical sense, the Jews were regarded as the king's serfs. The individual Jew was not literally unfree; only for certain crimes could his property be confiscated or his person enslaved. Still the king's jurisdiction over him excluded subjection to any other authority. Certainly as a body the Jews were subject to the pleasure of the king, whose protection was obtained through specific charters, always revocable. Taxes and tallages were paid by the Jewish communities corporately; the individual assessments were collected by the communal organizations from the members according to a graded scale. The territorial lords, the municipalities, and the Church levied additional taxes upon the Jews. Suits between Jews and Christians were settled by mixed tribunals consisting of Jewish and Christian judges.

The Jewish community (al-jama) formed an independent corporation, with jurisdiction over its own members in all internal affairs. They had their administrative councils and officers. The synagogue was the natural place for communal meetings; certain communities boasted of a special council house. The council was usually a small body, consisting of six to thirty members. Sometimes the communities met to form a larger organization covering a district, especially for the purpose of an equitable distribution of the royal taxes. The rabbi in each community was elected by the members and confirmed by the king; he was salaried. Though he had no official voice in the administration of the community, his advice was sought by council and judges and his moral influence was paramount.

Gerona, 'a mother-city in Israel,' was the home of Jewish scholarship. It was the birthplace of Jonah son of Abraham (the Elder), a pupil of Solomon of Montpellier (p. 394). He took part in the controversy about Maimonides on the side of his opponents and subsequently lived to regret his opposition to the great teacher. Penitently he vowed that he would depart for the Holy Land and there, on the grave of the peerless scholar, pray for forgiveness. He was, however, detained by the community of Toledo, with whom he remained until his death (1263), surrounded by disciples and engaged in writing books. A still greater son of Gerona was Jonah's kinsman, Moses son of Nahman (Nahmani, Nahmanides), who spent the greater part of his life in his native city as the rabbi of the community.

Nahmani was the outstanding personality in Jewry during the middle of the thirteenth century. Through his teachers, he became heir to the traditions and methods of the Franco-German school of 'Supplementers' (Tosaphists), and he transplanted these to the soil of Spain. From that time on, the study of the Talmud was made in Spain, as had been the case in France and Germany, the principal business of the Jewish students, to which everything else was subordinated. The dialectics of the northerners took root in the southern peninsula, though here they were modified by the secular training of the Spanish Jews. Nahmani had a profound reverence for the 'ancients'; with the teachers in the Mishnah he believed that to learn from the elders was to drink old and seasoned wine. Spaniard that he was, he was greatly impressed with the talmudic epitome of al-Fasi, which he defended against criticism and to which he added his own supplements. At twenty he began his series of commentaries upon the greater part of the Talmud, which partake of the nature of glosses.

True to his Spanish training, again, Nahmani was at home in the secular sciences; as a matter of fact, he practised medicine as a means of livelihood, spurning the emoluments of his rabbinical office. But, unlike Maimonides, he refused to regard philosophy as the touchstone of religious truth. The teachings of Bible and Talmud were for him the ultimate authority, no matter what reason might say. Nature, order of the world—they meant nothing to his religious mind; everything that happens was to him a miraculous working of the Deity. Some miracles were visible, others invisible, but just the same real. Three things he held to be fundamental: the belief in creation out of nothing—the first link in the chain of miracles—God's Providence, and His Omniscience.

The stoic imperturbability of the philosophers, who are affected neither by good nor by evil, was not to his liking. There was joy and sorrow in the life of man, a time for laughter and a time for weeping. Nahmani was impatient with Maimonides, who, with Aristotle, disparaged the body as a hindrance to spiritual perfection. Body and soul were both of God; whatever God created must be accounted pure and good. Judaism, which to the rationalists was an open book, devoid of hidden meanings, was in the opinion of Nahmani full of mysteries, above the comprehension of human reason. Nahmani was still far away from the full-fledged system of the Cabala developed by those who came after him. The time was not come yet for mystic lore to be reduced to writing.

Cabala, as the name indicates, was still an oral tradition, received by word of mouth and secretively guarded by the initiates. It was of ancient antecedents, mounting up to the 'wise men' of Bible times. Some teachers of the Mishnah had been entranced by mystic speculations. The Talmud contains mystic notions serving to bridge over the gulf between God and the world, and conversely to facilitate the passage of the soul to God. It knows of intermediaries and of things pre-mundane; it peoples heaven and earth with good and evil spirits. In gaonic times, the 'Book of Creation' operated with the ten Sephiroth (numberings) as fundamental to all existence. A view was preparing that creation was but a series of graded emanations proceeding from God and taking form in the tangible world. All along there had gone on a belief in the power of favored persons to work miracles through combinations of letters, through amulets and incantations.

This double lore, theosophic and thaumaturgic, had been imported from Babylonia to Italy, and from thence to Germany. Eleazar of Worms (died 1238), pupil of Judah the Saint (p. 370), operated with alphabetical and numerical combinations, but gave himself also to contemplation and to the exaltation of prayer. The Cabala was then given a philosophic turn, in opposition to Aristotelianism, in the schools of Provence. For if Aristotle dominated Jewish rationalism, Platonic thoughts, as worked out by Philo and deepened by Ibn Gabirol, influenced Jewish mysticism. In the work called 'The Bright' (Bahir), the doctrine of emanation was clearly taught. Under the hand of Azriel (1160– 1238), who was largely influenced by Ibn Gabirol, the speculations were still further perfected. God became the One without End, who can be comprehended only by the negation of all attributes, in whom all existence has its being and who radiates it by His free will and makes the potential actual. Azriel, it appears, initiated his younger townsman Nahmani; but the pupil was not quite ready to follow the master the entire length.

It was to be expected of Nahmani, so diametrically at variance with Maimonides intellectually and emotionally, that he would lean to the side of the opponents of philosophical studies in the controversy which was stirred up by the Provençal zealots. Nevertheless, he disliked the quarrel and pleaded for a hearing of both sides before a court. In this sense he addressed a letter to the communities of Aragon, Navarre, and Castile. It had no effect on Saragossa, the chief community in Aragon. Its distinguished head, Bahye son of Moses, physician to King James, cited the encouragement which the ancients had given to the study of secular sciences. As the quarrel increased in virulence and the Provençal rabbis became more and more divided, Nahmani again tried his conciliatory efforts. While acquiescing in the strictures against the 'Guide,' he was horrified at the disparagement of the Maimonidian Code merely on account of its introductory book. He also pleaded with the liberals to concede to the orthodox purity of motive. But the difference was too fundamental to be thus settled by compromise; the bitter feud proceeded to its disastrous end. Jewish liberalism was for the time being strangled by the aid of the Inquisition, which had triumphed over the Albigensian heretics (p. 396) and was now setting out to crush the progress of Christian liberalism, the heretical movements foreshadowing Protestantism.

In 1233, a year before the writings of Maimonides were burned in the streets of Paris, the Inquisition was introduced into Aragon. It was committed to the hands of the friars of the Order established by Dominic. Raymund of Peñaforte, the father-confessor of King James, was appointed by Gregory IX. chief agent of the Inquisition for Aragon and Castile. This Dominican general erected seminaries for the teaching of Hebrew, in order to refute the disbelieving Jews with their own weapons. Among his disciples was a baptized Jew, Pablo Christiani. Failing to make proselytes among the Jews of Provence, he persuaded King James to order Nahmani, who at an advanced age was enjoying universal reputation, to take part in a public disputation at Barcelona (1263). The aged scholar stipulated complete freedom of speech. For four days in July, the theological tournament continued in the presence of the king, the court, and many dignitaries of the Church. At the very start, when the Dominican general admonished the Jewish disputant not to cast aspersions upon the dominant Church, Nahmani retorted: I likewise know the rules of propriety. He commanded the Spanish speech and comported himself with Spanish knightliness. Pablo contended that the Messiah had appeared and called to witness certain haggadic statements. Nahmani, in reply, set forth that, of the three species of literature in the hands of the Jews, only two, the Scriptures and the Talmud—the latter being an exposition of the duties commanded in the Torah—were authoritative, while the third, the Midrash with its haggadahs, represents but homilies, which a Jew may accept if he chooses or reject as merely private opinions. These were heretical words to the apostate, who, possessed but of meager knowledge, had grown up in reverence for all the vagaries of midrashic utterances.

As the disputation progressed, the Jews were apprehensive of danger, no matter how the result came out. They begged Nahmani to discontinue. But the king, after a recess of several days, ordered the contest resumed. Nahmani held his own. He was dismissed by the king with a gift of three hundred maravedis. Pablo, on his side, received permission from the king to renew his disputations with the Jews throughout Aragon and the royal dominions beyond the Pyrenees, the Jews being ordered to defray the expense out of the taxes due to the king and to supply him with books. Unable to make headway in winning over the Jews, he denounced the Talmud to Pope Clement IV. (1265–1268). As a consequence, a censorship was instituted over all books possessed by the Jews, with a view to expurgating all supposed objectionable passages. On the commission of censors there served among others the Dominican Raymund Martini, a scholar widely read in Jewish literature. He wrote polemical works against the Jews; but withal he contended that the Talmud contained many statements in confirmation of the Christian truth and should therefore not be burned entirely.

For Nahmani the disputation had an evil sequel. At the request of the bishop of his native town Gerona, he furnished him an account of the contest. The Dominicans fumed. The author was summoned before the king and was condemned to two years' exile, while his book was ordered to be burned. Nahmani left behind his family and friends and in 1267 arrived in the Holy Land.

The Mongolian invasion of 1260 had left the land waste and its cities in ruins. Jerusalem had suffered most of all. Everywhere was the wrack of demolished dwellings; the city was depopulated. Only two self-supporting Jews were to be found in the Holy City, dyers by trade; in the house of these two brothers ten more men were in the habit of assembling on the sabbath for worship. The other Jews had either been slain by the Tatars or had fled, taking the sacred scrolls with them to Shechem (Nablus). Nahmani had these fetched back. One of the demolished residences, with marble columns and a beautiful cupola, was repaired and made into a synagogue for the benefit of the many pilgrims from Damascus, Aleppo, and elsewhere. On the following New Year the first public worship was held there. In addition, Nahmani opened a school for talmudic studies, which attracted young students from beyond the Euphrates.

His own literary activity, however, during these last three years of his life, was centered not in the Talmud, but in the Scriptures. On the sacred soil of Palestine was completed his commentary on the Pentateuch, which was begun in his native Catalonia. The author had in mind the layman, who, as it happened in those days and in concentrated Jewish settlements for a long time after, possessed both the prerequisite schooling and the interest to desire an exposition of the Word of God. Nahmani's strictures on Ibn Ezra, delivered with 'open rebuke and hidden love,' were often enough quite justified. Nahmani was less subtle and scintillating, but his very plainness carried him more than once beyond the shallow rationalism of his predecessor and much nearer the truth.

Nahmani's activity in the Holy Land was cut short by death (1270); he was laid to rest at Haifa beside the grave of Jehiel of Paris. His brief sojourn served to prop up the Torah among the scant communities in Palestine. At home, in far-away Spain, his teachings had struck root in a circle of disciples. Conditions in the Pyrenean peninsula were not unfavorable to the Jews. Compared with the northern lands, Spain must have seemed a paradise. In Castile, Alphonso X. (1252–1284), already as crown-prince, showed his consideration for the Jewish soldiers who took part in the conquest of Seville (1248) by endowing them with land in a separate settlement known as the 'Village of the Jews.' The Jewish residents of the conquered city, who during the Almohade dominion had been compelled to affect conversion to Islam and in all likelihood had aided the king in the taking of the city, were rewarded by the grant of a large quarter for residence. Three of the mosques were turned over to them for use as synagogues. The grateful Jews presented the victorious prince with a golden key upon which was inscribed in Hebrew and Spanish: 'The King of kings will open, the king of all the earth will enter.'

Upon his accession to the throne, Alphonso surrounded himself with Jewish officials. Meir de Malea and his sons, Isaac (Zag) and Joseph, were in charge of the treasury, while other Jews served as collectors of taxes. A lover of the sciences (he was surnamed 'the Wise'), the king had astronomical and astrological writings translated from Arabic into Spanish by Judah son of Moses Cohen, a physician of Toledo, and by the physicians Abraham and Samuel Levi. Zag (Isaac) Ibn Sid, the reader at the synagogue of Toledo, was the editor of the famous astronomical tables, the Alphonsine Tables, as they were named after the king. All these evidences of friendly relations did not prevent the king from incorporating in the Code (known as the 'Seven Sets') compiled under his direction, all the old and new ecclesiastical canons against the Jews. It was not, however, until a century later that it was promulgated, to remain for centuries the text-book of Spanish jurisprudence with its necessarily baneful influence upon the life of the Jewish people.

Alphonso's younger son Sancho made claim to the succession after the death of his elder brother, though the latter had left issue. Father and son quarreled, and the strife was the cause of bringing the Jews into disfavor with the monarch. Because Zag de Malea, the royal treasurer, had under duress supplied funds to the prince, he was put to death by order of Alphonso and his entire wealth was confiscated (1280). Moreover, on a certain sabbath, all Castilian Jews were arrested and a tribute of twelve thousand gold maravedis was levied upon them.

Sancho IV. (1284–1295) retained as his treasurer one of Zag's sons. The taxes payable by the Jewish communities of Castile were regulated by the king. The apportionment was entrusted to a commission of four Jewish notables, who met at Huete in 1290. They were joined by David Abudarham, the elder of the community of Toledo, for the purpose of accommodating their differences. The yearly tax paid by the Jews of Castile amounted close to three million maravedis. Altogether there were upward of a hundred Jewish communities, the largest being that of Toledo; then came Burgos, Carrion, Valladolid, Cuenca, Avila. The Cortes were none too friendly to the Jews. In 1293, Sancho gave in to their motion forbidding Jews to acquire or own real estate. Still the Castilian Jews were influential enough to have inimical legislation suspended.

Conditions were also rather favorable in Portugal under Alphonso III. (1248–1279) and Diniz (1279–1325). The Jews were not required to pay tithes to the Church or to wear a badge. Diniz employed as his treasurer the chief rabbi Judah, a man of great wealth. But the very favor in which the Jews were held by the king served to incense the clergy, who were not slow to complain to Rome concerning what they called Jewish arrogance and ostentatious luxury.

CHAPTER LIX

THE PROGRESS OF THE CABALA

(1280-1340)

I N THIS period of comparative ease, the inner life of the Jews in the Pyrenean peninsula developed freely, shaping its course in the second half of the thirteenth century along the lines introduced in the first. The foremost authority of the period—people referred to him as 'the rabbi of Spain'—was Solomon son of Abraham Ibn Adret at Barcelona (1235–1310), trained by the Geronese scholars, Jonah, Isaac son of Abraham, and Nahmani. Like his masters, he set store by the dialectics of the Franco-German school, and like them he recognized the authority of the ancients. He codified the body of religious law in a work called 'The Law of the House,' which unlike that of Maimonides was diffuse and argumentative, and the author found it expedient to reissue it in abridged form. His compilation was criticised by Aaron son of Joseph ha-Levi, a descendant of Zerahiah (p. 393), who gathered his strictures in a work named 'The Breaches of the House.' Ibn Adret's opinion was sought on a great number of questions by the communities of Spain, Portugal, Italy, France, Germany, and even Asia Minor. At home his talmudic lectures were attended by a host of disciples, many of whom came from distant places. Though well versed in the secular sciences, he assigned to them a subordinate position in the range of Jewish learning.

In the resuscitated controversy between Maimunists and anti-Maimunists, he favored the side of orthodoxy and lent his authority to the promulgation of a ban to the effect that none below the age of thirty years might take up the study of 'Greek wisdom' (p. 397). The test for Ibn Adret was tradition, that which had been accepted by the Jewish people; even stray haggadic utterances were invested with authority, so long as they stood unrefuted in the Talmud.

430

No amount of philosophizing could impugn whatsoever was laid down in tradition. Like his teacher Nahmani, Ibn Adret defended Judaism against Mohammedan and Christian detractors, in particular against Raymund Martini and his polemical work, 'The Dagger of the Faith.' Again like Nahmani, he believed in the mysteries of the Cabala.

With all his leanings to mysticism, Ibn Adret was resolute enough to check hysterical outgrowths manifesting themselves in an overstimulated imagination on the part of visionaries. Abraham son of Samuel Abulafia (1240–1292), of Saragossa, was a carefully instructed man and with an insatiable desire for knowledge, but cf a fantastic cast of mind. At an early age he took to wandering in search for the mythical river Sambation. On returning to Spain, he immersed himself in the study of 'The Book of Creation' and gave himself to ascetic exercises. At the same time he operated with the combinations and permutations of the letters of the alphabet and of numbers, all with a view to obtaining an intuitive knowledge of the inscrutable essence of God.

He was prompted by an inner voice to go to Rome and seek an audience with the pope (Nicholas III., 1277–1280), in order to convert him to Judaism. The death of the pope intervened before the mad undertaking could be put into effect; by deft recourse to mystifying language the visionary escaped with his skin. In Sicily he played the prophet and gave himself out for the Messiah. The Palermo community turned to Ibn Adret for counsel, and he unmasked the pretender. He called attention to Abulafia's hypertrophied imagination, brought on by auto-suggestion, and to the perversion of the words of Scripture or of the wise teachers by means of numerical manipulations with which a grain of truth, derived from philosophy, was intermixed. Abulafia raged against the rabbi of Barcelona and the students of the Talmud in general to whom talmudic knowledge was the end of all wisdom. But the pretender was discomfited. He left behind him a number of 'prophetic' books, of a character unique in Jewish literature.

He also left disciples. One at Avila predicted the advent of the Messiah for the year 1285. Unlettered though he was, he astounded the people by producing a literary work, indited, as he claimed, by an angel who had revealed himself to him. Ibn Adret had difficulty in explaining the phenomenon, unless it were due to a peculiarly powerful imagination rooted in a natural endowment or else a pure matter of accident. Another pupil, Joseph son of Abraham Chiquitilla (died after 1305), was a prolific writer and strove after deepening the mystic science by philosophic speculation. But among those who emerged from the talmudic school of Ibn Adret there were also men who cultivated the Cabala, though they owed their knowledge to other teachers. Among these were Shem Tob son of Abraham Ibn Gaon (died in Palestine some time after 1330) and the Bible commentator Bahye son of Asher (died 1340), who methodically wove cabalistic notions into his exposition of the Pentateuch. Such was apparently the trend of the time.

Most far-reaching was the influence of Moses son of Shem Tob de Leon (1250–1305). He commanded a wide reading of the Jewish philosophical literature and was at home in the whole range of mystical literature accumulated in past ages. Whatever glimpses of the mysterious lore previous scholars had seen fit to reveal, the feeling obtained that mysticism was by its very nature intended only for the ears of the elect initiates, that it was essentially oral tradition, Cabala (Kabbalah), and should not be divulged before the large reading public. Yet, as in the case of all oral tradition of the past, of Mishnah and Gemara for example, the time appeared to be ripe in the judgment of de Leon to compile the sum of cabalistic teaching. The opinion that he forged the work, that he had nothing to draw upon save his imagination and whatever learning he possessed, may be disposed of as irrelevant. As a matter of fact, the work was issued in parts, which were not assembled until near the age of printing.

The compiler named his work 'Brightness' (Zohar), destined to become the Bible of the mystics and, with slight exceptions, to meet with recognition even outside their circles.

Like so many other writings of antiquity, this Midrash or loose exposition of the Pentateuch in the Aramaic tongue appeared as a pseudepigraph. It was the compiler's honest opinion that the author was the Tanna Simon son of Johai, who, as a talmudic legend has it, spent thirteen years in concealment in a cave. There the mysteries were revealed to him, and these in turn the ecstatic teacher communicated to a group of disciples, the wise that were to 'shine as the brightness of the firmament' (Daniel 12, 3). The tannaitic inductor into the mysteries of heaven is glorified above Moses and accorded divine honors, for to him alone it was granted to open the gates of the secrets of wisdom.

The unsystematic composition makes it certain that the Zohar cannot have been the work of one person or one generation. It abounds in supplementary portions and excerpts from writings under special titles. Much of its contents ascends into gaonic and talmudic times, but the succeeding periods, each with its speculative contribution, impressed themselves upon the work as well—the matter simply grew with the ages. The fundamental conception of the Zohar is that there is nothing trivial in the Torah, but that the whole of it, in its commandments and ordinances as well as in its narratives, has higher, mysterious purposes which constitute its very soul.

With a conception of God which identifies the Supreme Being (almost Non-being) with the emanations proceeding from Him, the Zohar unites a gross anthropomorphism, which dwells on eyes and nose, beard and crown of the head —though this had been attacked by the Karaites in the gaonic period and denounced by Maimonides as un-Jewish. With lurid detail, the book pictures Purgatory and Hell, where the souls of the wicked, of those that die impenitent, are tortured by evil demons afore they are purified to return to their heavenly source. It is imbued with the thought of the everlasting combat of good and evil, truth and falsehood, holiness and profanity, God and Satan, a combat willed by God Himself. The two orders run in parallel lines, making up this side (the good) and the other (the evil), or else the good is the core surrounded on all sides by the husk of evil. On the one side are ranged Israel and all the saints, on the other the primeval Serpent, Cain and Esau, Pharaoh and Haman, Rome and the Romish Church. This will continue until the advent of the Messiah—the date is set prophetically between 1300 and 1306—who will emerge from the Garden of Eden, make his appearance in Galilee which was the first province of Palestine to be laid waste, and undergo the onslaught of many nations until the redemption is effected.

There run through the Zohar lofty thoughts and refined spiritual motives alongside of coarse expressions and indelicate figures of speech. While ostensibly endowing the minutest talmudic prescription with mystic significance, the Zohar sets itself as the mistress above the Mishnah, which it likens to a dry rock devoid of life-giving waters. The Zohar keeps itself close to the people, with their credulity and their hunger for visions from the beyond. It imparts a dramatic touch to the life of man, as the two orders of good and evil contest the possession of his soul. Moreover, it sustains man in making of him an active partner in the world process, since every good deed bends the divine will to beneficent spiritual emanations, and prayer as it were forces the hand of God to create spiritual entities. The metaphysic of Cabalism may have tended to deify the Emanations and to endanger the very conception of the Unity. But the Zohar also produced in its readers an intentness touched by emotion and imparted to their every action and thought the zest of saintly worship, of active participation in the betterment of the world, of willed communion with the heavenly agencies making for righteousness.

Thus the hoary 'Jewish knowledge,' enriched by elements derived from the kindred speculations of Neo-Platonism, triumphed over the unemotional rationalism of the Aristotelians. There were stragglers in the field of pure philosophy, such as Shem Tob son of Joseph Palquera (1225–1290) and Isaac Albalag (died 1292). The latter propounded the theory of the double truth, the speculative and the religious, without endeavoring to effect an adjustment between the two. But these were feeble manifestations of the scientific impulse. The age was dominated by the towering personality of Asher son of Jehiel (1250–1328), the exile from Germany (p. 403), whom the community of Toledo, at the advice of Ibn Adret, had taken for their spiritual leader. He brought to his new home an unquestioning simplicity, a profound piety, and a disdain for the secular sciences, blessing God that he was saved from them, since by syllogisms men were drawn away from faith. Naturally he supported the opposition to philosophical studies on the part of the Provençal fanatics. Still Asher was by no means an uncompromising enemy of the sciences; only he desired them to be subordinated. At his express request, his pupil Isaac son of Joseph Israeli wrote a work on astronomy and on the calendar called 'The Foundation of the World.' This science was worthy enough of attention because it was helpful in the construction of the calendar, hence ancillary to a religious purpose.

Many young men came to Asher's school in Toledo; some from far-away Bohemia and Russia. He at once attained a very eminent position and the government repeatedly called on him to act as judge. In one instance, at the request of the queen, he decided a litigation which had been pending for a long time before Jewish and non-Jewish courts. He wrote commentaries on the first and sixth Orders of the Mishnah and short supplementary notes on certain tractates of the Talmud. His fame rests upon his abstract of the halakic matter of the Talmud, after the example of al-Fasi, but enriched by the opinions of the later authorities, Maimonides and the Franco-German Tosaphists. He attached great weight to the latter school, the traditions of France and Germany being in his judgment superior to those of Spain; nevertheless, he only rarely contradicted the decisions of Maimonides. In general, he held that there was no room for blind respect; every opinion was capable of review in the light of talmudic discussion and of sober sense. Nor did he follow the German teachers in their rigorism; he did not try to introduce their different customs into Spain. When an over-zealous saint thought that one ought to recite the afternoon prayer twice daily, Asher proved his error from Talmud, the decisions of later authorities, and reason. He summed up his opposition in the apt remark: Would that we might be sufficiently devout in reciting the established three daily prayers.

Though originally a man of wealth, he died a poor man. He probably lost a large part of his fortune when he left Germany and subsequently during his travels. He gave much of his money to the needy, especially to poor scholars. Asher was succeeded by his son Judah (1270–1349), in piety, character, and charitable disposition the peer of his father, but because of a weakness of his eyes incapable of doing much literary work. Still his scholarship was generally recognized and his authority was acknowledged all over Castile.

The reigns of Ferdinand IV. (1295–1312) and Alphonso XI. (1312–1350) were the golden period of Castilian Jewry. Quite the reverse were the conditions in Navarre, where, owing to the marriage of Jeanne I. in 1284 with Philip the Fair, king of France, and to the exercise of French suzerainty over the kingdom, the Jews were subjected to economic oppression and payments of heavy taxes. Still worse did they fare in the disturbed conditions under the successors of the royal pair when the Navarrese strove to shake off the northern yoke. Between the two warring camps the Jews found themselves an object of profound hatred, which was fanned into a frenzy by the inflammatory harangues of the Franciscan monk Peter Olligoyen. A horrible massacre was enacted in Estella (March 5, 1328); the Jewish quarter was burned and all its population slain. Similar slaughters occurred in Tudela, Viana, Falces, Funes, Murcilla, and elsewhere; the toll of Jews butchered exceeded six thousand.

The new king, Philip count of Evreux, and his consort, Jeanne II., made a pretense of punishing the instigators of the persecution. Nevertheless the Jews suffered further restrictions of their rights. They were completely separated from the Christians and confined to their narrow streets. The taxes were so exorbitant that it was impossible to raise the sums demanded. On the other hand, in Castile, Jews rose to eminent positions in the kingdom. Ferdinand IV. had for his diplomatic agent the Jew Samuel, who unfortunately displeased the queen-mother Maria and narrowly escaped assassination. Still, when she took the reins of government during the minority of her grandson Alphonso XI., she made the Jew Moses her treasurer. At the request of the Cortes of Burgos and under the influence of the Council of Zamora, she forbade Jews to bear Christian names or to associate with Christians. Yet she refused to accede to the demand of Pope Clement V. (1305–1314) for wholesale cancelation of debts held by Jews; she merely regulated the rate of interest. Maria's successor in the regency, the king's uncle Don John Manuel, had a Jew for his body-physician. Another Jew, Judah son of Isaac Ibn Wakar (of Cordova), stood in high favor with the regent; at his solicitation criminal jurisdiction was restored to the rabbinate.

When the young king took the government into his own hands (1325), Samuel Ibn Wakar became his body-physician and Joseph son of Ephraim Ibn Benveniste de Ecya his treasurer. Each of these two favorites was jealous of the other, and the ascendancy of both was a thorn in the flesh of the Cortes which complained of the usurious methods by which Jewish money-lenders were growing rich. Religious hatred was fanned by the apostate Abner of Burgos (Alphonso of Valladolid), whose epistle justifying his conversion was answered by Isaac son of Joseph Ibn Pulgar in a biting satire. The convert, however, succeeded (1336) in securing a royal decree forbidding the ancient execration of seceders from Judaism which was instituted in Palestine at the time when the Christians formed an inner Jewish sect (p. 208) and in which the word 'Nazarenes' had long been replaced by 'apostates.'

Gonzalo Martinez, who had risen to the position of minister of state largely through the influence of Benveniste, preferred charges against his benefactor as well as against the latter's rival, Samuel, and against a number of their dependents that they had enriched themselves in the king's service. Joseph died in prison, Samuel suffered torture on the rack, while their entire property was confiscated. It cost two other Jews large sums of money to exculpate themselves. Martinez contemplated wholesale confiscation of the property of all Castilian Jews and their expulsion from the country. The powerful commander-in-chief was in need of money to prosecute the campaign against the emir of Granada leagued with the king of Morocco. The archbishop of Toledo, however, thought that the retention of the Jews as a permanent source of income was the wiser policy, and Martinez was obliged to yield. Soon thereafter, the overbearing general, elated by his victories which led to the conquest of the fortress Algeciras (1339), was convicted of high treason and burned at the stake.

The Jews, who had rendered signal services in the war, acclaimed the king on his triumphal return from battle. The king yielded to the Cortes in releasing the Christians of one-fourth of their indebtedness to the Jews. He also forbade the Jews of his kingdom to lend money on interest; but he allowed them to acquire real estate. The times, however, had gone by when Jews of wealth and social station were themselves scholars or had any scholarly interests. A contemporary writer upbraids the communal leaders of his day as vainglorious, boasting of their wealth and their aristocratic descent, making much of their services to their people, punctilious in religious observances, but withal given to luxurious living and cruelly oblivious of the needs of their poor coreligionists.

Such a scholar as Asher's son, Jacob (died 1340), was content to live in poverty, merely regretting that his means did not permit a change of raiment on the sabbath or to honor the day by more than an ordinary meal. During his father's lifetime, he acted together with his brother Judah as dispenser of the paternal charities to the poor. He sought no official position, but was satisfied to pursue his scholarly labors in a private capacity. He was a talmudist pure and simple; secular sciences he ignored, neither approving of them nor disparaging them. His field was the ample domain of religious law. He abbreviated his father's digest, and then set himself to prepare a code of his own in which the whole of religious jurisprudence was methodically arranged in four parts or Rows (Turim).

The first, dealing with the duties of the Jew day by day and in appointed seasons, sabbaths, new moons, and festivals, as he sits in his house or walks by the way or repairs to the synagogue, was named 'The Path of Life' (Orah Hayyim); the second, furnishing instruction in the things forbidden and permitted, 'Teacher of Knowledge' (Yoreh Deah); the third, encompassing the laws pertaining to matrimony and prohibited marriages, 'The Stone of Help' (Eben ha-Ezer); and the fourth, comprising civil jurisprudence and the procedure in courts of justice, 'The Breastplate of Judgment' (Hoshen Mishpat). The Code was meant for the times and conditions in which the majority of the Jews lived. The accumulated material since Maimonides was incorporated. When later authorities were divided, no attempt was made at a decision; but deference was paid to the opinions of the author's great father. The work is distinguished by a clear style and a rational disposition; it is instinct with an excess of humility.

In his ethical testament to his son, Jacob inculcated complete obedience to the written and oral law in all that pertains to religious practice as well as to morals. He further admonished his son to speak ill on account of no person, not to indulge in unnecessary questions in seeking to decide a religious point after the manner of boastful scholars, to be single-hearted with God, and to refrain from all manner of superstition. Thus spoke the true saint, in every respect the talmudic Jew, sincerely devout, given to the minute performance of the commandments and to strict observance of moral obligations. He was simple in his religious beliefs, humble and contented, charitable to his fellow-men. He loved God with all his soul and consecrated his life to learning and teaching.

CHAPTER LX

THE DECLINE OF SPANISH JEWRY

(1348-1405)

THE Black Death of 1348 did not lead to any such disastrous consequences for the Jews in Catalonia and Aragon !as it did in Germany. There was some slaughter and much pillage, but the Jews knew how to defend themselves and thus ward off the attacks of the popu-lace. No excesses occurred in Castile, the Jews merely suffering alike with the Christian population from the dread plague. Many members of the most distinguished Jewish families of Toledo and Seville perished. The disease cut short, likewise, the life of king Alphonso. His successor, Peter (1350–1369), though surnamed 'The Cruel,' was favorably disposed toward the Jews, and it may be said that under him they reached the zenith of their power. They espoused the cause of their sovereign, as he battled against his stepbrother, Henry de Trastamara, Alphonso's illegitimate son by his mistress Leonora de Guzman. However, this very partisanship brought to the Castilian Jews the ill-will of the opposing faction, ultimately bringing about that turn in their fortunes which marked the downhill course of Jewish history in Spain.

The king's tutor and all-powerful minister, John Alphonso de Albuquerque, had for his financial agent Samuel son of Meir ha-Levi, of the distinguished Abulafia family. At the minister's advice Peter appointed Samuel as his chief treasurer. The king's marital entanglements—he was actually married to no less than three wives simultaneously—led to a conflict between the minister and his former protégé Samuel. John, who took sides with Queen Blanche of Bourbon, endeavored to lure the royal bridegroom away from the beautiful Maria de Padilla. The attempt was thwarted by Samuel, and from that time on he practically took the place of the deposed minister. The friends of the Bourbon princess, leagued with the king's stepbrother and his powerful faction, beguiled Peter into the fortress Toro, where he was held prisoner; but thanks to the skill and the ducats of his Jewish treasurer he escaped. Blanche was at the time kept in confinement in the castle at Toledo. Under the pretense of rescuing her, Henry invaded that part of the Jewish quarter called the Alcana and butchered about twelve thousand Jews, sparing neither age nor sex. The attackers, however, were repulsed from the inner quarter by the Jewish inhabitants, who defended themselves with stubborn courage (1355).

Samuel's influence over the king grew apace. By skilful management of the royal finances he was able to place large sums at the disposal of the monarch; he also amassed an immense private fortune. His coreligionists looked up to him as their protector and were beholden to him for many benefactions. At Toledo he erected (1357) at his own cost a beautiful synagogue, subsequently turned into a Christian church and now preserved as a national monument. At length, however, Samuel succumbed to the cabals of his many enemies, among whom, it appears, figured also certain Jews who were jealous of his prosperity. Suddenly, in 1360, the king gave orders to have him seized and confined at Seville, where he soon died on the rack. His enormous fortune, consisting of gold and silver coin and of chests filled with jewelry and costly garments, was confiscated by the state. His palace, in the underground cellars of which his successor in office claimed to have discovered vast hoards of gold and silver, is still shown to-day as 'The Jew's Mansion.'

Samuel's death effected no change in the king's relations to the Jews or in their continued loyalty to his cause. But the assassination of Queen Blanche by command of the king led to reprisals by Henry de Trastamara and his supporters, who called to their aid Bertrand de Guesclin and his French marauders, known as the Free or Grand Companies. At Briviesca, near Burgos, the Jews fought bravely on behalf of their king, but they were unable to withstand the ferocious onslaught of Henry's soldiers. The entire Jewish population, comprising two hundred families, was slain and left unburied. Henry had himself proclaimed king at Calahorra; when he entered Burgos (1366), he levied a tax of fifty thousand doubloons upon the Jewish community. In order to raise this enormous sum, the Jews were compelled to strip the sacred scrolls of their silver ornaments. Many Jews were sold as slaves. The Jews of Segovia and Avila were likewise despoiled, while those of Toledo were fined one million maravedis.

The arrival of the English under Edward the Black Prince, who had been summoned by Peter, forced Henry to retreat to Aragon. But no sooner had the English left than Henry reappeared and was accepted by all of northern Castile. Burgos opened its gates to the conqueror; the Jews alone persisted in their resistance and were fined heavily. Peter was grateful enough to his loyal Jews; on calling the king of Granada to his assistance, he stipulated that the Jews of Castile should suffer no harm. Nevertheless the Jews underwent great distress, at the hands both of friends and of foes. Those of Villadiego, noted for scholarship and beneficence, of Aguilar, and of many other towns were destroyed by the English. At Valladolid, the citizens, who favored Henry's cause, pillaged the Jews and destroyed their eight synagogues.

The king of Granada carried away three hundred Jewish families from Jaen to be sold as slaves. Still worse was the fate of those who fell into the hands of de Guesclin; a few escaped to Navarre, but many who remained were forced to accept Christianity. Most lamentable was the plight of the community at Toledo. During the siege more than ten thousand Jews died by reason of famine or by the sword. Along with the rest of the population the Jews held out for Peter, who was invested by Henry in the castle of Montiel (in La Mancha). The hard-beset king left his retreat in the hope of bribing the French commander, but instead he fell into the hands of his rival, who forthwith slew him (1369).

Henry II. (1369–1379) imposed upon the poverty-stricken Jewish community of the capital a fine of twenty thousand gold doubloons. His orders were that, if any refused to pay, their property, whether movable or immovable, should be sold at public sale, and that the poor who were unable to pay should be sold as slaves. Henry was no friend of the Jewish people. The Cortes, assembled at Toro (1371), clamored for restrictive measures against them. Though the king would not wholly accede to their demands, he gave in on two points which wounded the susceptibilities of the proud Castilian Jews to the quick—that they must wear the badge on their dress and refrain from calling themselves by Christian names. However, the king could not dispense with the services of Jews in the management of his fiscal affairs. Samuel Abrabanel occupied a high station at court and Joseph Pichon was chief tax-collector.

Castilian Jewry was in a state of spiritual degeneration. On the one hand was the impoverished multitude, in the rural districts shockingly ignorant. On the other side were the grandees intriguing against each other, given to a life of luxurious idleness in their palatial mansions, the men swelled with pride and their wives and daughters ostentatious in their finery. The leaders of the communities were not ashamed to throw the burden of taxation upon the poorer folk. A contemporary preacher complains that Judaism all too often sat lightly upon the rich; during sermons in the synagogues they would engage in conversation or else go to sleep; they despised learning. Whereas with the Christians, the preacher continues, it was a point of distinction for the sons of noblemen to take orders, the Jewish rich disdained to make of their sons students of the Torah, and the poor, witnessing the disrepute in which scholarship was held, apprenticed their offspring to the vilest trade rather than to send them to a higher school of learning. The few scholars, such as Moses de Tordesillas at Avila or Shemtob Ibn Shaprut of Toledo, successfully engaged in disputations with apostate controversialists. To sustain the faithful, they wrote out their defenses of the Jewish truth ('The Support of Faith,' 'The Touchstone'), thus making them available sources of information for similar future discussions. For higher talmudical learning one had to go outside Castile—to Aragon and Catalonia.

In the seat of Ibn Adret at Barcelona sat Nissim son of Reuben of Gerona (died after 1380), acknowledged as the undisputed leader of his generation. His school was attended by eager scholars, and from beyond Spain his opinion was sought on all matters of religious law. His fame rests upon his commentaries on al-Fasi's compendium as well as upon his expositions of many tractates of the Talmud, the best known and most original being his commentary on 'Vows,' a tractate neglected since gaonic times. In all of these he strove to lead up to a fixed decision. He was famous also as a preacher. He strenuously opposed determining the Messianic year by futile calculations. For some unknown reason, but apparently in consequence of denunciation, he, together with a number of other scholars and certain lay leaders, was imprisoned (1370) by King Peter IV. (1336–1387) and released only after furnishing bail. The charges, whatever they were, were not substantiated.

Informing was rife among Spanish Jewry. Joseph Pichon was denounced to the king by evil-minded coreligionists who had the royal ear. He was cast into prison and heavily fined, but after a while he was restored to the king's favor. Pichon retaliated with counter-charges against his enemies. While John I. (1379–1390) was celebrating his coronation at Burgos, a Jewish court of law sat in judgment upon Pichon and condemned him to death on the charge of informing and treason. The new king's confirmation of the death-sentence against his father's favorite was obtained by withholding the name of the accused, and he was speedily executed. The king in turn had the rabbi and the other participants in the trial put to death. In consequence, the Cortes, convened at Soria (1380), forbade the rabbinical courts to exercise criminal jurisdiction and condemn any Jew to death, mutilation, or expulsion. The assembled representatives at Valladolid (1385) obtained the royal consent to an act forbidding Jews to live in Christian quarters and to employ Christian domestics. It was furthermore enacted that no Jew or Moor might be appointed treasurer by the king or any member of the royal family. The king, however, declined to curtail the

privileges enjoyed by Jewish money-lenders—such transactions were clearly profitable to the Crown.

A dispute between King John of Castile and his mother-in-
law Leonora, regent of Portugal after the death of her husband, Ferdinand I. (1383), as to the appointment of the chief
rabbi of the realm, cost the Castilian pretender the crown of
Portugal almost within his grasp. The Jews of Portugal,
ever since the foundation of the kingdom in the twelfth century, had little cause to complain. They lived in perfect tranquillity and prosperity, and many of them rose to prominence.
In their internal affairs they had complete autonomy. In
accordance with the regulation of 1274 under Alphonso III.,
the chief rabbi (rabbi mor) was appointed by the Crown and
exercised his juridical functions in the name of the king. On
his tours of inspection he was accompanied by a chief justice,
a chancellor who kept the seal, a secretary who drew up
the protocols, and a messenger who carried out the court
sentences.

In 1384, the office of chief rabbi of Castile became vacant.
Leonora favored the appointment of her favorite Judah,
Ferdinand's chief treasurer. John of Castile, whom she summoned to mount the throne as the husband of her daughter
Beatrice, on the other hand, had in view the wealthy David
Ibn Negro, Ferdinand's collector of customs. The embittered Leonora turned against her son-in-law. The plot was
discovered by Negro and the queen-regent was banished to
a convent. But the efforts of John of Castile to make himself
king of Portugal proved futile, and the crown was assumed
by John of Avis, who ascended the throne as John I. of Portugal (1385).

The friction between the Jews of Spain and the Christian
population grew apace. The friendship of the Jews for King
Peter provoked the Christian supporters of Henry. The murder of Pichon, who hailed from Seville, aroused the anger of
his friends among the Christian townspeople. Inflammatory
speeches against the Jews were delivered by Ferrand Martinez, archdeacon of Seville. He was a man of little learning,
but devout and of indomitable courage. The feeble remon-

strances of the court and the pope availed nothing to silence him; the more resolute intervention by the archbishop of Seville was cut short by his death. Soon thereafter the king succumbed to illness (1390). During the minority of his son, Henry III. (1390–1406), the realm was administered by a council of regents, divided by mutual jealousy and powerless to check lawlessness. Martinez, whom the young king's mother, Leonora, chose as her confessor, resumed his harangues and demanded the destruction of the three and twenty synagogues in the diocese of Seville.

On Ash Wednesday, March 15, 1391, the mob broke into the Jewish quarters of Seville. The governor of the city, John Alphonso de Guzman, and the mayor, his kinsman Alvar Perez de Guzman, had two of the leaders of the mob seized and publicly whipped. This action only served to exasperate the mob. Despite prompt measures by the regency, the Jewish quarter was surrounded by the populace (June 6). Fire was set to the dwellings, and there ensued an orgy of carnage. Four thousand Jews, men, women, and children, were killed outright. Of the great and prosperous community which numbered nearly seven thousand families, the majority sought safety in embracing Christianity—between fire and blood, they chose the waters of baptism. The aged Samuel Abrabanel, once the confidant of Henry II., had not the strength to resist temptation and became a Christian. The synagogues were for the most part destroyed; two of the larger ones in the city were turned into churches.

As the regency took no vigorous action to suppress the disorders, the riots spread from Seville to the neighboring towns. At Ecija and Carmona not a single Jew was left. In Cordova the entire Jewish quarter was burned down. The defenseless Jews were ruthlessly butchered; two thousand corpses lay in heaps in the streets, in the houses, or in the wrecked synagogues. Many saved themselves by submitting to baptism. On June 20, on the fast day of the seventeenth of Tammuz, a frightful butchery took place in Toledo. Among the many martyrs was Judah, a descendant of Asher son of Jehiel; with his own hand he cut the throat of his mother-in-law, his wife, and their children, and then killed himself. A considerable number accepted Christianity. Similar scenes were enacted in seventy Castilian towns.

Though Aragon was detached from Castile, the boundary offered no check to the anti-Jewish excesses. During the outbreak in Valencia (July 9), two hundred and fifty Jews were killed. A great number were baptized, among them the richest and most influential, such as Joseph Abarim and Samuel Abravallo. Not a single Jew remained in the former kingdom of Valencia. Murviedro was the only surviving community, but even there many had accepted baptism. On August 2, the Jews of Palma, on the isle of Majorca, were attacked. Three hundred, including the rabbi, were killed, eight hundred escaped under cover of night to the Barbary States, while the remainder submitted to baptism. As this Jewry was the private property of the queen, she compensated herself by levying a heavy fine on the Christian population. The commercial prosperity of the island was destroyed as a result of this outbreak.

Three days later—on the sabbath, August 5—the infection reached Barcelona. At the first encounter one hundred Jews were killed. Several hundred sought refuge in the citadel. Although the authorities did all in their power to protect them, the fort was stormed by the mob on August 8. More than three hundred Jews lost their lives, among them the only son of Hasdai Crescas, who happened to be in the city waiting to be married. A great number, estimated by some as close to eleven thousand, embraced Christianity; a small number escaped. Similar riots occurred in Catalonia— in Gerona and Lerida. The Geronese Jews for the most part chose death rather than to forswear their faith. In Aragon proper the Jews in the main forestalled the impending doom by the offer of a substantial bribe. Nevertheless excesses were committed in some of the larger communities.

Thus for three months did this bloody epidemic rage throughout Christian Spain. Some fifty thousand Jews were massacred, while the baptized numbered hundreds of thousands. Only in the territory held by the Mohammedans was there safety for the Jews. In Portugal severe persecutions were warded off through the influence of the chief rabbi Moses Navarro. John I. of Aragon had twenty-five of the ringleaders executed. The chief instigator of the anti-Jewish excesses, Martinez, was condemned by Henry III. to light confinement. But after a few years he was set free; his compatriots venerated him as a saint until his death (1404).

The effect of the destruction of so much Jewish property was felt by the country at large. Thousands of Christian laborers, previously employed in the Jewish yarn and leather factories now in ruins, found themselves out of work. Commerce had received a setback; the revenue of the Crown suffered diminution. The very churches and cloisters, hitherto dependent upon rates paid by the Jews, were impoverished.

As for the Jews themselves, more serious than the losses was the ever widening chasm between them and their Christian neighbors, fostered by the fanatical churchmen. Joy had departed out of the life of Spanish Jewry. After the manner of their brethren in Germany, they commemorated their visitation in heartrending lamentations. Their proud spirit was cowed; craven fear settled upon them. The majority smarted under the necessity which forced them to enter into the Christian fold; they hated the new faith and longed to throw off the mask. Such as were fortunate enough to escape to Granada or Portugal or to North Africa, speedily rejoined communion with the Synagogue. But the greater part, who were compelled to remain behind, lived a Jewish life in secret, as far as possible fulfilling the obligations of their ancestral faith, while in public demeaning themselves as Catholics. This dual life was connived at by the civil authorities; but the people at large hated these fictitious Christians or Crypto-Jews, Maranos or 'accursed' as they called them, worse than those who were openly Jews.

There was also a class of Jews who had long grown indifferent to Judaism and for that matter to any religious belief. They were satisfied to accord to the dominant religion of the land a lip-profession, so long as they were able to retain their wealth and social position. It was to their interest to play the devout Christians and to make mock of their former co-religionists, whose steadfastness put them to shame. Many saw no other outlet for their ambitions and decided, once the crucial step had been taken, to throw themselves with full zest into their new life. Not a few of these converts, in their eagerness to display their zeal or because they felt lonely in their new society, sought to drag in fresh elements by extolling Christianity and disparaging Judaism.

The most persistent of these missionaries and the bitterest foe of the religion which he forsook at the ripe age of forty, was Paul de Santa Maria of Burgos, originally Solomon ha-Levi (1352–1435). He was a man of learning, and up to his conversion had been punctiliously devoted to Judaism, filling the position of rabbi. His wealth, however, brought him early into contact with high Christian circles. He was by nature an ambitious man, and in 1391, the year of the fearful massacre, he realized like so many others of his class that as a Christian he might find a wider field for his capabilities. After a course of study at Paris, he received the degree of doctor of theology. Peter de Luna, since 1394, as Benedict XIII., successor to the anti-pope Clement VII. at Avignon, made him archdeacon of Tevino and subsequently canon of the cathedral at Seville. He mounted still higher; he became in turn bishop of Cartagena and archbishop of Burgos, keeper of the royal seal to Henry III., and member of the regency during the minority of John II. (1406–1454). Soon after his baptism he set out to prove, in a letter addressed to Joseph Orabuena, chief rabbi of Navarre and physician to King Charles III., that Judaism had been superseded by Christianity. His calumniations of the Jews met with a setback at the hands of the bishop of Pamplona; the Jews showed their gratitude to the good bishop.

One of Paul's disciples followed his master into the Church under the baptismal name Geronimo de Santa Fé, and like his teacher engaged in anti-Jewish propaganda. Hasdai Crescas wrote in Spanish a concise polemical work (1396), discussing impartially the main differences between the two creeds. Incidentally he propounded the question, Which of the two contending popes is infallible, the one at Rome or his rival at Avignon?

At the request of Crescas, a younger scholar wrote in a similar strain a more comprehensive polemical critique of Christian dogmas under the title 'The Confusion of the Gentiles' (1397). This young man, Isaac son of Moses (Prophiat) Duran, had become by force a sham-convert to Christianity (1391). Together with a friend, David Bonet Bongoron, who shared with him the same plight, he determined to set out to Palestine and there freely to confess Judaism. His friend, however, lingered at Avignon where Paul of Burgos chanced to meet him and immediately prevailed upon him to remain a Christian. The disappointed Prophiat addressed to his light-hearted friend a stinging satire, mockingly upholding him in his determination. 'Be not like unto thy fathers' (Al tehi ka-abotheka), thus each section of the epistle opened. For some time the Christians, who referred to the composition as 'Alteca Boteca,' thought it a genuine defense of Christianity; but soon their minds were disabused and the epistle was burned publicly.

CHAPTER LXI

THE DISPUTATION OF TORTOSA

(1340-1444)

IN A time of cruel persecution and inner demoralization, Hasdai Crescas, together with a fellow-student in the school of Nissim of Gerona, Isaac son of Shesheth Barfat, stood like a veritable rock upholding Judaism and Jewish learning. Barfat (1326–1408) corresponded with upward of seventy rabbis and rabbinical assistants at home. His opinions were sought also abroad, as when he interposed between the chief rabbi of Vienna and the incumbent in the rabbinical office at Paris. The spiritual leaders of Jewry in that period seem to have been hasty with their decrees of excommunication or of pecuniary fines. The lay members frequently set themselves against the authority of the rabbis, and the communities were hotbeds of strife. Barfat himself came into collision with troublesome elements in Saragossa; but he steadfastly stood his ground and was prevailed upon to reconsider his resolution to seek another field of activity. Subsequently, however, he took office in Valencia. The events of 1391 drove him out of Spain; he found a refuge in Algiers where the last years of his life were spent.

Crescas (1340–1410) came from a family of scholars. He was rabbi at Saragossa; he enjoyed the favor of the king and queen of Aragon and of the king of Navarre. His fame as a talmudist imparted authority to his religious counsel. His maturest work, produced in ripe old age and entitled 'The Light of the Lord,' was meant as an introduction to a code of Jewish religious law which, however, was never written. He apparently had Maimonides for his model. Whereas the orthodox perceived in the Maimonidian tenets a danger to faith and the heterodox went beyond Maimonides in swallowing Aristotelian teachings, Crescas laid bare the logical inadequacies of the entire system of Greek wisdom, and fought philosophy with its own weapons.

Crescas counted eight dogmas the denial of which entails renunciation of Judaism. The Jew must believe that the world was created out of nothing by the divine will at a given time; in the immortality of the soul; in retribution; in the resurrection of the dead; in the immutability of the Torah; in its perpetual obligatoriness which cannot be abrogated; in the supremacy of Moses as prophet above those that preceded or followed him; in the inspiration resident in the priest's Urim and Thummim; and in the Messianic redemption. Crescas stressed Divine Providence as extending beyond the species to the individual. Human freedom was with him something conditional instead of absolute. There was a divine purpose in the world, to be accomplished by human perfection—not, as with the intellectualists, along the lines of logical cognition, but through loving obedience to the will of God. The Torah alone, revealed religion, instructs man in the duties which help him to acquire eternal bliss, the highest good which consists in cleaving unto God. Crescas saw no reason for giving up the talmudic belief in spirits, good or evil, and in the efficacy of incantations and amulets; but he hesitated to subscribe to the cabalistic doctrine of the migration of the soul (metempsychosis).

Barfat stood somewhat aloof from the Cabala, citing a remark that the Christians believed in the Trinity but the Cabalists multiplied the number of divine manifestations (emanations) to ten. Of Crescas it is reported that he recognized Moses Botarel, an ascetic Cabalist with a smattering of philosophical reading, who made claim that the prophet Elijah revealed himself to him and appointed him Messiah.

The immersion into mystic speculation served as an anodyne for the unabated misery of the people. In 1405, Henry III. granted the petition of the Cortes and declared all bonds on Christians held by Jews to be void, thus depriving the Jews of a large part of their property. They were compelled to wear badges except when traveling. Only collectors of royal revenues and tax-farmers were exempted from some of these restrictions. Upon the death of Henry III. (1406), the realm was administered in the name of the infant king, John II., by his bigoted mother Catharine and his uncle, who later, as Ferdinand I., sat on the throne of Aragon (1412–1416).

Paul of Burgos, whom Henry had named executor of his will and tutor to his infant successor, was the evil genius who inspired anti-Jewish legislation. In 1408 an old decree was reissued forbidding Jews to hold public office. The ex-rabbi was bent upon wearing out the power of resistance to conversionist tactics in the higher strata of Jewish society.

In 1410, a charge of having desecrated the host was preferred against the Jews of Segovia. Meir Alguadez, physician to the late king, was put to torture, and a confession was wrung from him that he had poisoned his master. The hapless man was quartered; the synagogue was converted into a church, and the event is still commemorated by an annual procession. In the following year, at the instigation of Paul of Burgos, the Dominican friar St. Vincent Ferrer, a friend of the anti-pope Benedict XIII., traversed Castile from one end to the other, urging the Jews to accept baptism. He appeared in synagogues, with the Torah in one arm and a cross in the other, attended by an unruly armed mob, and everywhere the weaker elements surrendered to his impassioned addresses. In Toledo he spent a full month; in the principal synagogue he is said to have won over more than four thousand Jews (1411).

The queen-regent and her princely brother-in-law lent a ready ear to his counsels: what could be done by suave persuasion should be done. A still more efficacious means to force the recalcitrant into the arms of the Church was restrictive legislation. In the name of the child-king a law, consisting of twenty-four clauses and betraying the masterhand of the bishop of Burgos, was promulgated (1412)—a piece of legislation which in every way tended to reduce the Jews to poverty and to humiliate them. They were to keep strictly to their quarters; they were shut out from the professions; nor were they to engage in handicrafts, act as brokers, deal in wine, flour, meat, or bread. They were not permitted to hire Christian help; all social intercourse with Christians was forbidden. They were shorn of the right to settle their internal disputes in their own courts, nor might they, without royal sanction, levy their communal taxes. Jews might not assume the title of 'Don,' nor carry arms, trim their hair or shave their beard. Jews and Jewesses were enjoined to clothe themselves in long mantles of coarse material. No Jew might leave the country, and a heavy fine was placed upon any grandee or knight shielding a fugitive. Transgressors were to be punished by one hundred lashes and heavy fines, one-third of which went to the informer.

These stringent regulations were somewhat mitigated by the queen-regent in a subsequent edict (1414). The Dominican preacher had taken himself off to Aragon. There Ferdinand, who was elevated to the throne through the friar's good offices, gave him every facility to pursue his conversionist activities. The number of converts, both in Castile and in Aragon, is estimated at thirty-five thousand. In this work Ferrer was assisted by the renegade Geronimo, who, as a physician in attendance on the Spanish anti-pope at Avignon, willingly lent himself as a tool in the hands of his patron. The object was nothing short of the destruction of Judaism, and when the schismatic head of the Church was driven back to his Spanish home, he threw his entire energy into his pious work. He hoped that, by successfully converting the whole of Spanish Jewry, his chance for recognition at the impending ecumenical council at Constance would be improved.

With the sanction of Ferdinand, Benedict issued a bull summoning the Jews of Aragon and Catalonia to a public disputation in the city of Tortosa. This most remarkable of all the theological tournaments into which the Jews were forced during the Middle Ages lasted a year and nine months (from February 1413 to November 12, 1414) and was spread over sixty-nine sessions. Benedict presided, surrounded by a brilliant suite of archbishops and bishops and abbots and knights. In the opening session, he made it plain to the twenty-two representatives of the Jews that the truth of the Christian religion was above contention; that the truth of

Judaism was equally admitted up to the time of the rise of Christianity; the Jews were merely to answer whether or not certain passages of the Talmud bore witness to the fact that the Messiah had come before the destruction of the Temple. The apostate Geronimo chose for the text of his sermon the words of Isaiah: 'If ye be willing and obedient, ye shall eat the good of the land; but if ye refuse and rebel, ye shall be devoured with the sword.' The threat was unmistakable,, even as the promise of worldly well-being to renegades like himself was undisguised.

The Jewish spokesman, Vidal Benveniste, answered with a long discourse in the Latin tongue. The Jewish delegates realized only too well that it was a sore business to argue with the wily churchmen. The arguments of the opponents were easily met, but in the official account of the proceedings the Jewish statements were perverted into the very opposite. Geronimo at length changed his tactics. Instead of drawing upon the Talmud for proofs of the Christian position, he, with the aid of other apostates, preferred charges against the Talmud as a pernicious work which should be done away with. In a treatise against the Talmud he assembled all passages unfriendly to non-Jews as well as stray and isolated haggadic dicta which served his purpose. Astruc ha-Levi, in the name of almost all his colleagues, declared, much as Nahmani had done on a previous occasion, that the Jews were not bound by haggadic opinions. The Dominican Ferrer meanwhile pursued his conversionist activities; in the Aragonese communities many Jewish families submitted to baptism. The converts were paraded before the Jewish disputants at Tortosa.

The result of the unequal combat was that the disappointed Benedict issued a bull (May 11, 1415) forbidding the Jews to study the Talmud, to read anti-Christian writings, to have intercourse with Christians, or to disinherit their baptized children. On the lines of the decree promulgated by Catharine and placed on the statute-books of Aragon by Ferdinand, the Jews were denied all rights of internal jurisdiction, nor were they free to proceed against informers and traitors. They might hold no public offices nor follow any handicrafts. The badge of dishonor was made imperative, and thrice a year all Jews over twelve, of both sexes, were forced to listen to a Christian sermon in their own synagogues. The apostate Gonzalo de Santa Maria, a son of Paul of Burgos, was appointed to carry the provisions of the bull into effect.

The question, Did the Messiah come and was he realized in Jesus? so often put to the Jews and latterly at Tortosa, set one of the participants in that disputation to think about the position which the belief in the Messiah occupied in the Jewish religion. Joseph Albo (died 1444) was no original mind; but, unlike his teacher Crescas, he was a clear and fluent writer, with a touch of the preacher in him. His work on 'Dogmas,' completed in 1428, became a popular book. Albo distinguishes fundamental dogmas ('roots') without which Judaism, and for that matter any revealed religion, is unthinkable; derivative beliefs ('secondary roots') which follow from the fundamental dogmas and a denial of which involves a denial of that in which they are rooted; and, lastly, beliefs which, though obligatory upon the Jew, are merely subsidiary ('branches')—Judaism is quite thinkable without them and a Jew who disbelieves in them does not excommunicate himself. Thus one may still be reckoned a Jew though he holds that creation was preceded by primeval matter. Similarly the belief in the Messiah, fundamental with 'others,' that is, Christians, is not central in Judaism. Here it is where Albo and Maimonides clashed. The weakened stress upon the Messianic doctrine was a gesture in the face of Christianity. Albo also admitted on academic grounds the mutability of the Law. But he added that, granted that a future prophet might come forward and declare the Law abrogated—of course, barring the fundamental dogmas—his message would have to be authenticated as in the case of Moses by a similar concourse of all Israel. This was the answer to the apostates, who kept repeating that Judaism terminated with the birth of Christianity, and to the lukewarm Jews, who lent a ready ear to their appeals.

The Jews of Castile fared well enough when John II., after the death of his mother, took into his own hands the reins of government. As a matter of fact, the real ruler of the land was Alvaro de Luna. This favorite was a relative of the indomitable anti-pope and like him a masterful politician, a born intriguer, and fascinating companion, on whom the weak and docile king came wholly to depend. To bring order into the finances of the realm, the powerful chancellor availed himself of the counsel of Abraham Benveniste (1390–1455), a Jew of great wealth who remained faithful to his religion. Diego Gonzales, a Neo-Christian, acted as treasurer. The scholar Joseph Ibn Shem Tob and other Jews were permitted to farm the taxes. Benveniste was appointed chief rabbi of Castile; as such he had the supreme jurisdiction in matters religious and legal. The autonomy, of which Castiian Jewry was deprived by the first John, was thus restored.

The disordered state of the communities called for reorganization. In consequence of the combined oppression by queen, anti-pope, and apostates, Castilian Jewry had become demoralized. Many communities had no regular houses of worship and, where they did, friction between the various factions was so sharp that neither side stopped short of using physical force on its opponents. Schools were closed for lack of sufficient funds to pay teachers. Learning and unity had departed from the life of the Jews. At an assembly of heads, spiritual and lay, which met at Valladolid (1432), steps were taken to put on a solid basis the educational institutions, to allocate the taxes for the support of the communal establishments, to regulate the treatment of traitors and informers, to prescribe modesty in dress so as not to arouse the displeasure of the Christian population by extravagant display of finery.

The Jews knew that they were surrounded by evil-wishers. Old Paul de Santa Maria and his entire family plotted incessantly against their former coreligionists and their protector de Luna, at whose hands these ingrained enemies of Judaism had been willing enough to receive whatever preferments came their way. Alphonso de Santa Maria was sent as a representative of Spain to the Council of Basel; there he brought up the Jewish question for discussion. He also worked on the mind of pope Eugenius IV. with the result that he issued a bull in which all the privileges granted to the Jews by his predecessors were annulled (1442). The bull was published in Toledo without the knowledge and consent of the king. The enemies of the Jews considered themselves free to indulge in oppression and ill-treatment to the point of cutting off all associations between Jew and Christian. De Luna had been eclipsed temporarily, but immediately upon regaining his position, though unable to disavow openly the papal bull, he made it practically ineffective by a liberal interpretation issued as a royal decree (1443).

The civil strife which divided Castile into factions during the long reign of John II. implicated the Maranos. Those who had embraced Christianity unwillingly, longed secretly to escape to a land where they might freely and openly profess Judaism, and therefore kept aloof from Castilian politics. But the Neo-Christians who felt at ease in their new station and were eager for advancement, found their way into the city councils, into judicial positions and the legislative chamber of the nobles, into professorial chairs in the universities and into the highest offices of the Church. In Aragon, the Neo-Christians intermarried with families of the higher and lower nobility to such a point that in two or three generations only one family in the land was accounted free from intermixture with Jewish blood. The Neo-Christians took sides in the partisan divisions of the Christian realms. The true Christians looked askance at their political and social climbing and suspected them of lukewarm adhesion to their new faith. With the professing Jews thoroughly humiliated and driven out of important positions, the animosity formerly directed against them was now diverted to the ambitious and successful neophytes. Particularly was the hatred violent in the southern provinces, Toledo, Andalusia, and Murcia.

The first signs manifested themselves in the Castilian capital, when the Marano tax-collectors were ordered by de

Luna to raise one million maravedis for the defense of the frontier. The city refused to pay this amount. From the tower of the cathedral bells tolled summoning the Christian populace. Christian canons delivered inflammatory addresses calling for acts of violence against the spurious Christians. Immediately the mob set fire to the dwellings of Alonzo da Costa, one of the Neo-Christians. The Maranos armed themselves; led by one of their own, they sought to extinguish the flames. They were surrounded and cruelly slain or trampled under foot, and their dead bodies dangled from trees (1440). The alcalde (chief justice) Peter Sarmiento refused to admit the royal troops which had been sent to punish the malefactors. De Luna himself was rather lukewarm in prosecuting the ringleaders, since he harbored ill-will against the Maranos, suspecting them of intrigues against his own person. Sarmiento had a decree passed by the Cortes forbidding the appointment of Neo-Christians to civil or ecclesiastical offices in Toledo. Remonstrances were of no avail; nor was any heed given the two bulls of pope Nicholas V. (1447–1455) in opposition to the decree. Immediately thirteen Maranos were deposed, among them judges and city councilors, notaries, and one presbyter.

After the death of the queen in 1445, John II. was persuaded by his favorite to espouse in 1450 Isabella of Portugal. From this union sprang Isabella the Catholic, destined to seal the doom of Spanish Jewry. The weak king was prevailed upon by the new queen to rid himself of his powerful chancellor; his fall was abetted by influential Maranos who sat in the court which condemned him to death (1453). The king treated the Toledo decree against the Neo-Christians as a dead letter; the people, however, hated them. Still greater was the ascendancy of the Maranos in Aragon, where they supported the king and the nobles against the common people of Catalonia. But even there the evil day was near at hand.

CHAPTER LXII

THE MARANOS

(1454-1488)

URING the reigns of Henry IV. of Castile (1454–1474) and John II. of Aragon (1458–1479) it seemed as if the Jews might take a hopeful view of their position. Both monarchs had Jews for their physicians: Jacob Ibn Nunez, whom Henry named chief rabbi of Castile, and Abiathar Ibn Crescas, who restored king John's eyesight by two skilful operations. The 'impotent' ruler of Castile was unworthily served by his favorites, among whom were several of Jewish descent. The laws restricting intercourse between Christians and Jews were found by the Christians themselves to be detrimental to their interests. With especial rigor were these laws executed in the cities. As a consequence Jews left the cities and settled in the country, in villages belonging to some count, where the anti-Jewish legislation was honored in the breach.

The neglect of these laws, which had been promulgated under the previous reign, stirred the fanaticism of the Franciscan friar Alphonso de Spina, rector of the university of Salamanca and father-confessor to the Castilian monarch. Henry's troubles, culminating in civil strife and the setting up of his younger brother Alphonso as rival king, made him yield feebly to the demand of the Cortes (1465) for the strict enforcement of the harsh measures against the Jews, dating from the time of his grandmother Catharine. De Spina, who in his 'Stronghold of the Faith' (1460) had heaped upon the Jews all the old calumnies, directed his hatred in particular against the Jews in disguise, those Maranos who, rightly or wrongly, were suspected of keeping up their Judaism in secret. Henry was reinstated on his throne after a promise that he would institute in Castile the Holy Office of the Inquisition. Though a bull was obtained from the pope, the

king hesitated. The report was spread that more than a hundred Maranos had circumcised their children. The accusation proved false, but popular hatred was roused to a high
pitch. At Toledo the quarrels between Old and New Christians were signally virulent. A riot broke out in 1467. One
hundred and thirty of the Maranos lost their lives and some
sixteen hundred dwellings were consigned to the flames.

The death of Alphonso (1468) relieved Henry of a hostile
faction; but a fresh one gathered strength among those who
took sides on behalf of the princess Isabella and her rights
to the succession. At Ocassa (1469) the Cortes again clamored for anti-Jewish restrictions. The next year saw the marriage of Isabella with her cousin Ferdinand of Aragon. This
event, fraught with disastrous results to Spanish Jewry, was
consummated with the aid of the Jew Abraham Senior, who
also effected a reconciliation between Henry and his sister.
The grateful Isabella bestowed upon her Jewish friend an
annual pension of one hundred thousand maravedis for life.
That did not prevent the carnage at Valladolid, instituted
among the Maranos by the friends of the princess and in her
immediate entourage (1470). The king was either too feeble
or unwilling to punish the ringleaders.

Religious fanaticism grew stronger from day to day. Now
it was directed against the Jews, now against the New Christians. A report was spread that, in Holy Week, 1468, the
Jews of Sepulveda, near Segovia, had, by the order of their
rabbi Solomon Picho, tortured and crucified a Christian boy.
The bishop of Segovia, John Arias Davila, a son of Diego the
New Christian, had a number of Jews arrested and sentenced
to death at the stake or at the gallows (1471). A small Jewish
lad was spared after a promise that he would embrace Christianity; but when taken to a convent to be taught his new
religion, he soon escaped. The mob then vented its wrath on
the remaining Jews; the greater number were slain, the
remainder sought safety in flight.

Everywhere open hostility against the Maranos raised its
head. At Cordova, under the auspices of the bishop Peter, a
society was formed, which named itself 'the Christian Broth-

erhood' and from which all New Christians were rigidly excluded. In March, 1473, during a procession in honor of the dedication of the Brotherhood, the cry was raised that a little girl of a Marano family had thrown some foul water from a window, splashing the image of the Virgin. Immediately the mob threw itself upon the residences of the wealthy Maranos and set them on fire. To quell the disturbance, a troop of soldiers was dispatched under the command of Alonso Fernandez de Aguilar, whose wife was a member of a distinguished Marano family. In the ensuing skirmish de Aguilar slew one of the ringleaders, thus adding fuel to the flame. The infuriated mob seized weapons and renewed their attack upon the Maranos. For three days the massacre and pillage went on. From Cordova the attack on the Maranos spread to other cities. At Jaen, the constable, who undertook to protect them, was himself killed in church. At Segovia, a fierce attack was instituted (1474). Corpses lay in heaps in all the streets. Not a single Marano would have been left alive, had not the alcalde Andreas de Cabrera intervened.

Upon the death of king Henry IV., Isabella mounted the throne of Castile (1474), not without opposition on the part of the supporters of Juana, Henry's supposed daughter. Isabella reserved for herself full sovereign authority, although her consort Ferdinand was proclaimed king of Castile along with the queen. Five years later Ferdinand succeeded his father in Aragon, and practically the whole of Christian Spain was united. The 'Catholic sovereigns,' to call them by the title bestowed upon them later by the pope, were both resolute and sagacious, bent upon curbing turbulent nobles in the interest of autocratic centralization. Isabella was devoutly pious, even bigoted. Yet the new rulers jealously guarded the royal prerogatives in the administration of the Spanish Church and brooked interference from Rome only when it suited their purpose. Isabella was quite uncompromising and Ferdinand freely rapacious; the grandees submitted to be shorn of their unlawful revenues, and the empty royal coffers filled with coin.

Concern for national unity, churchly piety, and the greed for further enrichment operated as motives for the royal pair to permit the introduction of the Inquisition in their domains. It was chiefly directed against the New Christians, whom the fanatical Dominicans represented as suspected of relapses and who, upon conviction, might be robbed of their wealth by the process of royal confiscation. Sixtus IV. sent the papal nuncio Niccolo Franco with inquisitorial powers. Alphonso de Hojeda, head of the Dominican monastery at Seville, Torquemada, who had been Isabella's confessor while she was Infanta, and others urged the royal couple to recognize the nuncio. But the Spanish majesties insisted that the Inquisition should be under their authority and not under that of the pope. Thus was the introduction delayed. Finally, the pope yielded and, at the request of Ferdinand and Isabella, issued a bull (November 1, 1478), authorizing the Spanish sovereigns to appoint inquisitors in matters of faith. Isabella, at first reluctant, was now ready to give in. In September, 1480, she appended her signature to the order establishing the Inquisition. Two Dominicans, Miguel de Murillo and Juan de San Martin, assisted by Juan Ruiz de Medina and Diego Merlo, were appointed as the first inquisitors for Seville.

The first operations of the inquisitorial court were begun at Seville. The feeling among the Christian population was divided. The mass of the people acclaimed the Inquisition, but many of the nobility, several of whom were united to the Maranos by marriage, were hostile. A number of Maranos of high station and wealth organized resistance; but the plot was betrayed and speedily suppressed. Some eight thousand Maranos, from Seville, Cordova, and Toledo, had fled to Cadiz. The governor of the province, Rodrigo Ponce de Leon, would gladly have protected them, but he was ordered by the inquisitors to send them back to Seville. So great was the number of Maranos apprehended that the tribunal moved to more spacious quarters in the castle of Triana, near Seville. On February 6, 1481, the first 'act of faith' (auto da fé) was held; six men and six women were burned at the stake. The plague, to which Alphonso de Hojeda fell a victim, stayed for a while the activity of the tribunal. But soon enough the Quemadero, as the stake was called, was illuminated with the burning of Maranos. By the first of November nearly three hundred had perished, while about eighty had been condemned to imprisonment for life. The wealth of all these persons went into the royal coffers. Even those long dead were not spared; charges of having relapsed into Judaism were preferred against them, their bones were exhumed and committed to the flames, while their estates were confiscated. Fugitives were burned in effigy.

Not all Christians looked with an easy conscience upon these horrors. So a respite was granted to all New Christians suspected of reverting to Jewish practices; if, within the specified time, they came forward of their own free will and made confession, their life would be spared and their possessions left to them. In reality it was a trap. When a number of penitents presented themselves, their absolution was made conditional upon revealing to the judges the names of all others known to them to be observing Judaism in secret. In fact, the entire Christian population was enlisted in the intelligence service of the Inquisition, and all such as withheld the names of their suspect friends were threatened with excommunication.

A list was drawn up naming the marks by which 'Judaizers' might be recognized, for example, the use of clean linen on the sabbath, abstaining from lighting fire on that day, or purchasing special wine or meat from Jews. All rites of Judaism, all popular customs of the Jews, all acts of omission as regards Catholic practices were specified in this catalogue. Moreover, the relapses of the New Christians were laid at the door of the professing Jews who were accused of abetting the nominal Christians in their secret return to Judaism. As these abounded in southern Spain, in the dioceses of Seville and Cordova, a decree was issued by the royal couple ordering the removal of all full Jews from Christian Andalusia. Thousands were uprooted from their homes. In their new locations they were strictly segregated in their own quarters, and the wearing of the badge was enforced (1481). Thus intercourse between them and the Christians, whether old or new, was cut off. No Jews except such as were physicians were permitted to visit the Christian quarters.

The Maranos, especially those who had no thought of returning to Judaism and yet were on the lists of suspects, made complaints to Rome. Sixtus IV. lent a willing ear to their representations especially as they were fortified by generous offerings. In a letter to the royal couple (January, 1482), he expressed his dissatisfaction with the two heads of the Spanish Inquisition, whom he was ready to depose but for his deference to their majesties. Before a fortnight was over (February, 1482), the pope appointed six further clerics as inquisitors, among them Thomas de Torquemada. Isabella and Ferdinand procured (May, 1483) a papal bull appointing the archbishop of Seville, Iñigo Manrique, judge of appeals for Spain. Only clerics of pure Christian descent, both on the paternal and on the maternal side, were allowed to act as officials of the Inquisition. In August, the pope responded to the entreaties of the Maranos by ordering that all those who had repented at Rome or had done penance should no longer be persecuted by the Inquisition. Scarcely had copies of this bull been made and spread through Spain, when the concession was withdrawn.

So far the tribunals of the Inquisition had been confined to the southern provinces. Moreover, each acted singly, and a suspect might easily escape to another locality where his home tribunal exercised no jurisdiction. To make the Inquisition universal throughout Spain, all over Castile and beyond it in Aragon, and furthermore to impart to it a centralized direction, was the persistent aim of the court. Both objects were realized October 17, 1483, when Torquemada was appointed Inquisitor General of Aragon, Catalonia, and Valencia; he had previously received this commission for Castile. Of noble lineage, Torquemada had early in life assumed the habit of a Dominican; in course of time he had been made prior of the monastery at Segovia. With high intellectual gifts he combined an austere simplicity of life and moral integrity. His rigidity of purpose brooked no crossing his will and made him insolent. Rejecting honorific preferments, he created for himself a position of supremacy in the Church and in the state. A masterful politician and a fanatical bigot, he clung tenaciously to his determination to rid the country of make-believe Christians, shutting out all considerations to the point of bloodthirstiness. As confessor of the queen, and later on also of the king, he obtained an ascendancy over both. From the pious princess and her astute and rapacious consort he early extracted the promise to lend their power to the destruction of heretics. As councilor of state, he drove the lesson home of the political advantages of religious uniformity.

Torquemada was sixty-three years of age when the engine of the Inquisition was committed to his care. He drafted an inquisitorial constitution (it was issued January 9, 1485), which left no loophole for any suspect to escape the clutches of the tribunals, now established also at Cordova, Jaen, and Ciudad Real. A respite of thirty or forty days was allowed for those accused of Judaizing. All who voluntarily confessed within that time might, on the payment of a small fine and of a gift to the royal treasury, keep their fortunes. The confession was to be made in writing before the inquisitors and witnesses and then followed by a public recantation. Those that confessed after the expiration of the term were punished by confiscation of their property or by imprisonment for life according to the gravity of the offense. Maranos under twenty years of age were left in the possession of their property, but were compelled to wear the penitential garment (the sanbenito) at the auto-da-fé. Those confessing after the publication of the evidence, might be admitted to reconciliation if sentence had not been pronounced, and take their punishment by being imprisoned for life; those that concealed any part of their guilt were burned at the stake. If the evidence for conviction was too slow or uncertain, torture was resorted to—the rack opened the mouths of the unfortunate victims, who were forthwith condemned to death. The prisons, some of which still exist in Spain, were small, dark, and damp, oftentimes underground.

In May, 1485, the tribunal was removed from Villa Real to Toledo. An attack upon the inquisitors was repelled, and the chief conspirators were strangled and hanged. The Maranos were summoned to give themselves up voluntarily within forty days. The rabbis of the community were forced to pronounce the great ban upon all Jews withholding evidence in their possession concerning Judaizing Maranos. It was not easy for the Jews to bring themselves to the betrayal of their former brethren; still the more timid turned informers. Within a year, several autos-da-fé were held. Upward of five thousand Maranos made public confession and were given absolution. They were glad to save their lives, no matter how humiliating the penances and how precarious their existence. To their dying day they were debarred from public office; not so much as the position of doorkeeper in some noble's house was open to them. At the same time the impenitent were burned at the stake. On August 10, 1486, five men, including a city councilor, and fifteen women of the best families perished; twenty-three persons were burned alive in May, 1487, and forty-three in July, 1488. Among the victims were priests and friars; they were first stripped of their canonicals and then given over to the flames. On a single day, the bones of one hundred dead Maranos were exhumed and burned.

There was great opposition to the Inquisition operating or being introduced in Aragon, Catalonia, and Valencia, where the royal powers were more circumscribed. In order to overcome the scruples of the supreme court of justice, presided over by a descendant of a Marano lady, a special act of the Cortes was required and an assembly was convoked at the bidding of Torquemada. Neither the president of the Cortes, who was himself the son of a converted Jew, nor other Maranos who sat in that body offered dissent.

In May, 1485, Peter Arbues, canon at Saragossa, and Gaspar Juglar were appointed inquisitors for Aragon, Peter d'Epila and Martin Iñigo for Valencia. Some of the leading Maranos, joined by Old Christians with whom they were connected by marriage, plotted against the inquisitors.

Arbues was assassinated in his church at Saragossa. The murder redoubled the fury of the tribunal. The ringleaders were dealt with most brutally. Hands were chopped off, then followed beheading, quartering, and burning. Two who had escaped to France were burned in effigy. Nor were the Catalonians successful in warding off the Inquisition. In 1487, the tribunal was instituted at Barcelona; in June, 1488, it began its activities with a solemn auto-da-fé, the first victim being a descendant of Geronimo de Santa Fé, the notorious Jew-hater.

Torquemada had his own way entirely in Old Castile. At Avila charges were made that six Maranos and five Jews had killed a Christian child, by the name of La Guardia, for ritual purposes. The chief witness was Yuce Franco, a youth of limited intellect, from whom a priest, impersonating a rabbi, was said to have received a confession. Upon this flimsy evidence the denounced persons were burned alive. It is now known that there never had been such a child and that the whole story was a fabrication from beginning to end to serve as a pretext for the expulsion of the Jews. To such lengths was the Inquisition ready to go in order to attain its ends. Within eight years seventy persons were burned at Avila. Torquemada spread his net out to involve the bishops John Arias Davila of Segovia and Peter de Aranda of Calahorra, who were of Jewish descent. On appealing to Rome, the first succeeded in extricating himself from the meshes of the special tribunal at Rome, while the second was divested of his dignities and died in prison close by the papal palace.

The vice-chancellor Alphonso de la Caballeria, who was implicated in the murder of Arbues, was suspected as a secret Judaizer. However, he took his case to Rome and established his good standing as a Catholic. But he was powerless to prevent the burning of the exhumed bones of his grandmother. His first wife had to don the sanbenito. Two of his daughters were married to sons of the highest nobility; a son married a granddaughter of King Ferdinand. The fewest of the Spanish nobility could boast of pure Christian descent (limpieza); the majority had undergone fusion with Jewish blood. Such among them as escaped the toils of the Inquisition were sufficiently alienated from their Jewish antecedents to witness with equanimity the catastrophe that overwhelmed the mass of Spanish Jews.

CHAPTER LXIII

THE EXPULSION FROM SPAIN AND PORTUGAL

(1492-1497)

THE last seat of Mohammedan power in Spain, the kingdom of Granada, was in a state of disintegration. Dissensions were rife among the Moslem princes, who intrigued against one another and were ever ready to aid the Christians in the hope of gaining a slice of territory for themselves. In the seven years' war of subjugation, the Catholic sovereigns at first pursued the tactics of delay, meanwhile destroying systematically fields and crops. As Ferdinand was busy with the affairs of the Inquisition and his foreign policy, the brunt of preparations for the final attack fell upon the shoulders of Isabella who took every precaution to secure success. In 1487, a special war tax was levied on every Jewish family in Castile; there were at the time fourteen thousand Jewish families in this province. Malaga fell in August of that year; the entire population of the city was reduced to slavery, among them four hundred and fifty Jews, who were ransomed by their Spanish coreligionists and transported to Africa. At last, by valiant fighting and with the aid of treacherous Moors, the capital, Granada, was forced to surrender (November, 1491). On January 2, 1492, the Catholic sovereigns entered the Moslem capital in triumph, and the cross was set up in the citadel of Alhambra.

The goal of the religious and national policy of the Spanish monarchs was now attained. While the subjugation of the last foothold of Islam in Spain was still in progress, the thought had matured in the minds of the royal pair to rid the country of the entire Jewish population. Pope Innocent VIII. (1484–1492) demurred; but Torquemada made capital of the La Guardia invention and took pains to spread the legend throughout the country. At length, from the palace of Alhambra, on March 30, 1492, the dreadful edict went forth.

By July 30, not a single Jew was to remain in the united realm of Castile and Aragon or in the islands of Sicily and Sardinia constituting Aragonese possession. Any Jew who remained after the expiration of the term was to pay with his life, unless he submitted to baptism. The Jews were permitted to take their movables with them, except gold and silver or coin or any merchandise which it was unlawful to export.

The Jews were stunned by the cruel decree. Abraham Senior and Isaac Abrabanel, who had rendered valuable services in the administration of the royal finances, obtained an audience with the Catholic majesties and offered a substantial sum for the revocation of the edict. Ferdinand was inclined to yield, but the bigoted queen was unbending. The story goes that Torquemada suddenly entered the royal chamber and, throwing a crucifix down before the king and the queen, asked whether, like Judas, they would betray their Lord for money. Thus there was nothing left for the Jews but to prepare for the exodus. The finest mansions, if buyers could at all be found, went for a song; the landed estates were for the most part confiscated to make good the loss in taxes and to pay imaginary debts claimed by the monasteries. Moreover, since it was forbidden to take out coin, the Jews were forced to accept drafts which often went unhonored. Everywhere Dominican preachers urged the Jews to embrace Christianity and thus obtain salvation in this world and the next. The weak, few in number, were beguiled and purchased the right to remain by the sacrifice of their convictions, notably Abraham Senior, chief rabbi and principal farmer of the taxes, and his family. It is said, however, that he acted under compulsion, Queen Isabella threatening further reprisals against his coreligionists unless he yielded. But the great majority were of one mind to hold fast to their faith. 'We will go in the name of the Lord,' they cried resolutely. The rich divided their shrunken wealth with the poor, to furnish them with the means for the journey.

'In the same month in which their Majesties issued the edict that all Jews should be driven out of the kingdom and its territories, in the same month they gave me the order to undertake with sufficient men my expedition of discovery to the Indies.' Thus began the diary of Christopher Columbus. The expedition which led to the discovery of the New World had been made possible by a substantial loan which Luis de Santangel, chancellor of the royal household and controller general of Aragon, advanced out of his own purse to the Catholic majesties. Santangel was of Jewish extraction, as was also Gabriel Sanchez, the chief treasurer of Aragon, who, with other Maranos, was a most zealous patron of Columbus. Among the explorer's companions were several of Jewish stock—Alonso de la Calle, Rodrigo Sanchez, the ship-physician Bernal and the surgeon Marco; also Luis de Torres, who was baptized before sailing and whom the captain employed as an interpreter with the supposedly Asiatic natives because of his knowledge of Oriental languages. Thus a Jew was among the first to set foot on the new land. The money which went from the royal treasury for the second voyage of Columbus was largely derived from the confiscations of Jewish fortunes.

As the day set for the exodus approached, the Jews threw themselves with heartrending cries upon the consecrated graves of their dear departed, of whom they must needs take leave forever. In Toledo, the tombstone inscriptions of the prominent men buried there, were copied at the last moment. In other cities, the Jews turned over all communal property to the municipal authorities on condition that the cemeteries would be preserved. Upward of one hundred and fifty thousand people trudged along the highways toward the seaports to embark for new homes. From Aragon and Catalonia some twelve thousand escaped to neighboring Navarre; but Ferdinand prevailed upon King John to expel them. A body of exiles, among whom was Isaac Abrabanel, found refuge in the kingdom of Naples (p. 501). Those residing in the southern provinces of Spain took ship to the ports of the North-African coast; but not everywhere were they permitted to land. One of the last vessels transporting the exiles passed by the little fleet of Columbus bound in search of another world. Twenty vessels were met off the coast of Fez by pirates, who threatened to enslave all of the human cargo. While negotiations were going on for paying ransom, the captain set sail back toward Spain. Three of the vessels went under in a storm; the others were cast upon the Spanish coast. Five hundred, in despair, threw themselves into the arms of the Catholic Church. The stout-hearted sought passage from a Portuguese port and were permitted to reside in Fez. Here, too, their troubles were not at an end; they were visited by a conflagration and then by a pestilence which carried off more than twenty thousand souls.

Harrowing was the fate of the fugitives on many another vessel. The shipmasters exacted exorbitant sums for the passage, and in many cases cruelly tossed the passengers overboard before they reached their destination. A rumor had got abroad that the fugitives had swallowed jewels and gold pieces, and thousands were ripped up by the greedy knife of brigands who looked for treasure in the mutilated remains. At Genoa they were permitted to land only on receiving baptism; many set foot on Corfu, Candia, and the other Greek isles. Often the shipmasters sold them as slaves, later to be ransomed by their compassionate coreligionists. Those that were fortunate enough to reach the Ottoman dominions were received with open arms. The sultan Bayazid II. gloated over the folly of the Spanish monarchs who impoverished their own country and enriched Turkey.

One hundred thousand emigrants entered Portugal, where neither the state councilors nor the native Jews were willing to receive them. Thirty of the richest families, at the bidding of their rabbi, Isaac Aboab, the last representative of Jewish scholarship in Castile, were permitted to settle in Oporto. Six hundred other families, who were able to pay a tax of one hundred crusados each, as well as a number of craftsmen employed in the making of munitions for the African campaign, were likewise granted the right to remain indefinitely on the payment of a poll-tax of four crusados. The bulk of the emigrants, in consideration of a poll-tax of eight crusados, received permission from King John II. (1481–1495) to tarry eight months in preparation for embarking to other countries. After a long delay, ships were provided; aboard these vessels, the unfortunate Jews endured untold sufferings. Still worse was the fate of those who were left behind for want of space. They were sold as slaves, and their little ones were torn from the bosom of their parents and sent to the newly discovered island of St. Thomas. The majority of these children died during the voyage or were the prey of wild beasts upon their arrival. Only a few populated the island, brothers even marrying their sisters in ignorance of their relationship.

John's successor, his cousin and brother-in-law Emanuel I. (1495–1521), was at first favorably inclined toward the Jews. Abraham Zacuto, the pupil of Aboab, was retained by the new monarch as astronomer. Upon the advice of this scholar, the expedition of Vasco de Gama was started, the vessels being provided with Zacuto's newly perfected astrolabe. Political considerations, however, led to a complete reversal in Emanuel's attitude toward the Jews. The king desired to wed Isabella of Spain, daughter of Ferdinand and Isabella and widow of the Portuguese prince Alphonso. The Catholic majesties gave their consent on the condition that the princess should find the realm purified from the presence of the accursed Jews. On November 30, 1496, the contract of marriage was signed, and on December 4 or 5 of the same year the edict of expulsion was promulgated. The Jews were given time until the end of October 1497 to wind up their affairs.

The Jews entertained the false hope that the king might be amenable to a reconsideration. The monarch himself was loath to let so many wealthy and industrious citizens depart. He just as little could tolerate their remaining professing Jews. Though the noble bishop Ferdinand Coutinho pronounced against enforced baptism, the king was abetted by the apostate Levi son of Shem Tob. On Sunday, the first day of Passover, March 19, 1497, all young Jews up to the age of twenty-five years were seized and led to baptism. Many parents smothered their children in their last embrace or threw them into wells and then killed themselves. Others, unwilling to separate from their children, submitted to baptism along with their offspring.

The time for departure was now fast approaching. The king ordered the Jews to assemble at Lisbon and to embark from that port. Twenty thousand Jews gathered in the capital. But the king, fearful of economic loss to the country and the Crown, would not let them go. They were herded together in one of the royal edifices and detained until the time designated for their departure had elapsed. They were now, so they were told, the king's slaves, and would be dealt with according to his pleasure. He sent to them a converted Jew of the royal entourage and his brother, a churchman, to persuade them to embrace Christianity. When all attempts to shake their attachment to Judaism failed, the king resorted to force and ordered them dragged to the baptismal font. Among those forcibly baptized were several who succeeded in escaping to other lands and there returned to Judaism; so Levi son of Habib, who subsequently ministered as rabbi in Jerusalem, and Isaac son of Joseph Karo, the uncle of Joseph Karo of Safed, the famous codifier. Abraham Zacuto likewise escaped. Only half a dozen kept up open opposition, among them Simon Maimi, the chief rabbi, whom the king had desired to set an example for his flock to follow. Buried up to the neck, the rabbi refused to yield and died after seven days. A few companions, who had held out with him, were then permitted to go to Africa.

The New Christians turned to Pope Alexander VI. for protection and, at his request, the king adopted a milder policy. In the rescript of May 30, 1497, the newly converted Jews were granted a respite of twenty years, during which time they were not to be molested by the Inquisition. The majority continued to live secretly as Jews; such as were able to arrange their affairs embraced the first opportunity to seek refuge in Italy, Africa, and Turkey. A decree of April, 1499, forbade the New Christians to leave Portugal without royal permission. After the riot in April, 1506, when over two thousand secret Jews were slain, the king suffered all who wished to do so, to leave the country with their property; but in 1521, emigration was again forbidden. Under John III. (1521–1557), the Maranos were subjected to fresh molestation; in 1531 the Inquisition was introduced. The Maranos began to flee the country, especially under the reign of Sebastian (1557–1578), who granted them free departure upon payment of two hundred and fifty thousand ducats. Of course, it was not possible for all to depart. To this day, in the vicinity of the capital, there is a settlement of Maranos, in whom a knowledge of their Jewish origin still glimmers.

BOOK IV

THE EMERGENCE OF NEW CENTERS
TO THE EVE OF THE FRENCH REVOLUTION
(1492-1786)

CHAPTER LXIV

THE AGE OF HUMANISM

(1330-1546)

THE end of the fifteenth century found the Jewish center in Spain and Portugal broken up. A century before (1394), France had expelled her Jews; two centuries earlier (1290), England. The end of the eleventh century (1096, First Crusade) had been the turning point in the history of the Jews of Central Europe, entailing a condition constantly deteriorating, so that at the close of the Middle Ages they were left with insecurity of residence and a stunted inner life. European history was at this time entering upon a new period. The transition was marked by the New Learning, which was now spreading from Italy into Germany, and by the discovery of the New World towards the setting of the sun (p. 472).

The Revival of Learning, or Humanism, was destined to rend the Western Church in twain and to destroy the foundation upon which medieval society was reared. The idea of a European commonwealth, rigidly directed by Rome, was receding before the growth of national feeling and the enfranchisement of the individual conscience. In Italy, the home of the Renaissance, the interest in classical antiquity awakened in Christian scholars also the desire for a knowledge of Hebrew and Jewish literature. Jewish scholars, familiar with the New Learning, were at hand as teachers.

In the century following Ibn Ezra's visit (p. 302), talmudical studies had continued to be the absorbing subject in the Jewish schools of Italy. One need mention only the da Tranis —Isaiah the Elder, his son David, his grandson Isaiah (son of Elijah) the Younger; then Zedekiah son of Abraham, of the family Anav, represented in the eleventh century by Nathan of Rome (p. 301). But the impetus given by Ibn Ezra had not been in vain. A further stimulus had been

479

afforded by the writings of Maimonides and the controversy aroused by them. Hillel of Verona (1220–1295) was a warm admirer of the great philosopher, though he freely criticised positions which in his judgment were untenable; his own work, 'The Recompense of the Soul,' struck a middle course between philosophy and tradition.

The age of Dante and Petrarch could not but exert a profound influence in Jewish circles. Immanuel of Rome (1270–1330) introduced in Italy secular Hebrew poetry which had long ago found a home in Spain. He was in no sense a genius comparable to the singer of the 'Divine Comedy,' whom the Jewish poet knew in person. Still he was a good imitator, versatile, and a keen wit. His 'Compositions' (Mahberoth)—twenty-seven in number, in rhymed prose, with interspersed verses—were modeled after Harizi's work (p. 335). They contain also a number of hymns. The supplementary vision of Heaven and Hell was a feeble approach to the Divine Comedy. Immanuel's Heaven, however, was not confined to saints of his own nation and faith—it admitted pious Gentiles as well. The manner in which the holy tongue was used for tales of a frivolous character drew later upon the author the anathema of the orthodox; but one must take into consideration the spirit of the time and the surroundings. Another imitation of the 'Divine Comedy' in Hebrew ('The Lesser Sanctuary') was produced by Moses da Rieti (died some time after 1460). Like his ancestor, the philosophical student Isaac (Maestro Gaio), Moses was a papal physician.

Nothing was more fruitful in the service of letters than the invention of the art of printing, and nowhere more so than in Italy. Hebrew printing was first begun in that country. By 1500, Hebrew presses had been set up in Reggio di Calabria and Naples in the south as well as at Pieve de Sacco, Mantua, Ferrara, Bologna, Rome, Soncino, Casal Maggiore, Brescia, Barco, and elsewhere in the north. The Jewish printers were for the most part learned men. Abraham Conat was a physician at Mantua, whose interest in the new art was shared by his wife Estellina. Like their Italian colleagues of the time, the Jewish printers were in the main immigrants from Germany or else of German immigrant stock. Thus the buying public was able to procure printed editions of the Scriptures, commentaries on the Bible, Mishnah, Talmud (in part), prayer books of the different rites for daily worship and for holidays, codes, grammars, dictionaries, philosophical works, and belles-lettres. Early in the sixteenth century the printing of Hebrew books in Venice passed into the hands of Christians. From the press of Daniel Bomberg (1517–1549) came the first and second editions of the Rabbinic Bible (text with Jewish commentaries), the first complete edition of the Babylonian Talmud, the first edition of the Palestinian Talmud, and other important works.

Despite papal bulls and canonical discrimination, Jews in Italy freely associated with Christians. Jews shared in the high level of culture which made of Italy one large school. It was not to be expected that rabbis of German antecedents, driven into Italy by reason of persecution at home, would be friendly to philosophic studies of which they had barely a notion. Joseph Kolon at Mantua, a talmudical authority of high repute, could not live at peace with Judah Messer Leon, rabbi, physician, Latinist, rhetorician, philosopher. The feud divided the community, and ultimately both were banished from the city (about 1477). Judah Menz (1408–1509) at Padua had no other weapon than the ban against Elijah del Medigo (1460–1497), who was descended from a German family long resident in Candia.

There was a modern air to del Medigo. His 'Examination of Religion' makes a clear distinction between philosophy and religious doctrine. As a matter of fact, the essence of Judaism, he holds, is Deed and not Creed. Religious laws are a necessary part in the system of Judaism, and their exposition in the Talmud is perfectly justified. But not everything in the Talmud rests on tradition; much is founded on a fallible interpretation of Scripture. Still less is it possible to accept such talmudic homilies as are clearly contradictory to reason. There is a deep kernel of truth in many a haggadic utterance, but no authoritative doctrine may be constructed thereon. Judaism has its fundamental principles, which are free from illogical difficulties and are unobjectionable to the philosophical mind. But to strive after a cognition of them by means of philosophical study cannot be made into a religious duty (as Maimonides held). The religious truths of Judaism have nothing to fear from reasoned speculation, but ultimately they rest on revelation.

Del Medigo had the distinction of lecturing on philosophy before the university of Padua. Among his disciples was the humanist Pico della Mirandola, of the illustrious circle about Lorenzo the Magnificent. This keen student aimed at harmonizing ancient philosophy with Christian doctrine and had been taught Cabala by del Medigo as well as by another Jewish teacher, Johanan Alemanno. The humanist was convinced that the Cabala yielded the strongest proof for the divinity of Christ. For the same reason Pope Sixtus IV. (1471–1484) had cabalistic works translated into Latin. The Zohar was rendered into Latin by Baruch of Benevento at the bidding of Cardinal Egidio di Viterbo.

This prince of the Church became the pupil of Elijah Levita, whom he harbored in his palace for thirteen years. Levita (1469–1549) passed through many vicissitudes. In early youth he left his native Bavarian home for Padua. The sack of the city by the League of Cambray in 1509 left him destitute, just as the capture of Rome by the forces of Charles V. in 1527 terminated his years of tranquillity in the cardinal's house. He found employment in the Bomberg printing establishment at Venice as editor and proof-reader. There he spent the remainder of his long life, barring four years during which he was back in Germany teaching and assisting the reformed minister Fagius. Thus Levita was brought in contact with the two divisions of the Church during the process of its splitting up. At Venice Levita had for his friend and pupil another eminent Church dignitary, George de Selve, ambassador of Francis I. and subsequently bishop of Lavaur. This friendship secured for Levita an invitation to occupy the chair of Hebrew at Paris, which the Jewish scholar declined.

Levita became the link between the medieval Jewish grammarians and the Christian Hebraists in the age of the Reformation. He was a versatile man and a painstaking student of
the Hebrew language and the Bible. He gave twenty years of
his life to working out a Concordance on a gigantic scale with
a view to recording the accurate form of every word in the
Hebrew text of the Scriptures. He realized the incomplete
character of the masoretic annotations, just then compiled
for the Bomberg edition by Jacob son of Hayim Ibn
Adonijah (1524–1525). The manuscript, which Levita sent
to de Selve, was never published and still rests in the
National Library at Paris. Levita's Introduction to the
Masorah, printed in 1538, is celebrated for the proposition
that the vowel points of the sacred text date from some time
after the close of the Talmud. The thesis was by no means
new, but no one had offered so convincing a proof.

With Fagius and Sebastian Münster—both taught by
Levita—Christian Hebraic study in Germany entered upon
its second stage. The pioneer had been Conrad Pellicanus
(1478–1556). His older contemporary, Johann Reuchlin
(1455–1522), availed himself of his help in composing his
own Hebrew grammar and dictionary. Reuchlin had two
Jewish teachers: Jacob Loans (physician to the emperor
Frederick III.) and Obadiah Sforno (died at Bologna 1550).
The German Hebraist, no less than the Italian Hebraists of
his time, was drawn to Hebrew and Jewish literature by his
interest in Cabala. But as he progressed, he realized the
deficiencies of the accepted Church version of the Scriptures, the Vulgate, and, with Kimhi and Rashi as guides,
turned to the Scriptures in the original. Thus was forged the
weapon with which the Reformation, bursting upon the
world, assailed the authority of the Roman Church.

Well-informed and high-minded, Reuchlin was averse to
persecution as a means for the conversion of the Jew. He
was convinced that the Jewish misery was a punishment for
the stubborn rejection of Christ; but this error, he held,
should be overcome by persuasion. There were some Jewish
books in his opinion which directly attacked Christianity

and might be condemned to destruction. But the great mass of Jewish literature, after the Bible, he knew, consisted of books indifferent towards Christianity (works on philosophy and the sciences), unimpeachable religious and devotional writings, commentaries indispensable for a knowledge of Scripture, cabalistic treatises useful for supporting Christian dogma. The Talmud, which Reuchlin conceded he had not read, he described as containing many a bizarre and superstitious utterance, but at the same time much excellent matter.

Such was Reuchlin's opinion officially submitted to archbishop Uriel of Mayence (1510) in opposition to Johann Pfefferkorn, a converted Jew of Cologne, who demanded the wholesale suppression of all Hebrew books except copies of the Bible. A mandate to that effect had been secured from the emperor Maximilian (August, 1509); but upon representations of leaders of the Frankfort Jewish community and Christian friends, the emperor ordered the consultation of expert opinion. A virulent literary feud ensued between Reuchlin and Pfefferkorn. Reuchlin was denounced as a traitor to the Church. The onslaught was led by the dean of the Cologne Dominicans, the inquisitor Hochstraten. Deputations and counter-deputations appeared before the temporizing emperor. Reuchlin sought the good offices of the Saxon elector, Frederick the Wise. Luther energetically defended the innocence and learning of Reuchlin. From the sentence of the ecclesiastical court at Mayence Reuchlin appealed to pope Leo X. shortly after his accession (1513). The bishop of Spires, acting for the Medicean pope, acquitted Reuchlin; the decision was confirmed at Rome in 1516. The Dominicans still plotted, and though Reuchlin had the powerful support of Franz von Sickingen and Ulrich von Hutten, the previous judgment was reversed at Rome (1520). But then the case had assumed a more dangerous aspect from its bearing upon the revolt from Rome which proceeded from Wittenberg. Over the body of suspect Jewish literature a battle royal was fought between German humanists and obscurantists. While Luther was preparing for the parting of the ways, the Reuchlinians were battering down Dominican intolerance by the trenchant force of satire ('Letters of Obscure Men,' 1514–1517).

Reuchlin had demanded protection for the Jews on the ground that they were 'members of the Holy Empire and imperial burghers.' Luther, in 1523, at the height of his conflict with Catholicism, considered that Christians 'had treated the Jews as though they were dogs and not men,' in a fashion that 'he who was a good Christian might well have desired to become a Jew.' He was not surprised that the Jews had been unwilling to accept Christianity, considering that it was nothing but 'popery and monkery.' Like Mohammed, Luther had high hopes of converting the Jews; he reasoned that, now that the Gospel had come into its own, the Jews would be drawn to Jesus Christ, who was born a Jew. And like Mohammed, Luther, disappointed in his hopes, inveighed in his closing years against 'the Jews and their lies' and admonished his followers 'to burn their synagogues, force them to work, and treat them with all unmercifulness.' In a sermon, preached at Eisleben shortly before his death (1546), he urged the lords of Christendom not to suffer the Jews, those 'hardened blasphemers,' but to expel them. As, in general, the later views of Luther had a greater force in shaping the Protestant Church than the more liberal opinions of his earlier years, so also with regard to the treatment of the Jews.

CHAPTER LXV

AMSTERDAM AND HAMBURG

(1492-1671)

IN Amsterdam and Hamburg, Naples and Venice, Saloniki and Constantinople, Fez, Tlemcen, Algiers and Tunis, Cairo and Alexandria, Jerusalem and Safed, Damascus and Smyrna—on the coast of the North Sea and on the shores washed by the Mediterranean and Levantine waters, as well as on the new continent of America and its isles, the Portuguese-Galician, Castilian, and Catalan dialects were heard on the lips of the Jewish exiles from the Iberian peninsula. These wanderers were either openly professing Jews, directly affected by the decrees of expulsion of 1492 and 1496, or Maranos who had remained behind and whose existence was made unbearable by the Inquisition. The exodus of the Maranos of Portugal followed immediately upon the introduction of the tribunal in 1531 and assumed greater proportions under King Sebastian (p. 476). Among those who early availed themselves of the edict of Charles V. granting to Maranos the right of residence in the Netherlands (1536), was the rich Francisco Mendes, of the Nasi family. Though he himself remained in Lisbon, he set up a branch of his banking business in Antwerp, the management of which he placed in the hands of his brother Diogo.

The two brothers were married to two sisters of the Benveniste family. When Francisco died, his widow Beatrice de Luna (or, as she called herself later, Gracia Mendez) transferred her entire business and family to Antwerp. She was not happy there, longing for a place where she might openly live as a Jewess. But the death of her brother-in-law, who left the control of the estate to her, did not permit her to carry out her design until 1549, when after winding up affairs she departed with her sister and their children to Venice. This sister, dissatisfied with the manner in which her husband had left herself and her daughter subject to the tutelage of Gracia, denounced her sister to the Signory as a renegade to Catholicism. Gracia was imprisoned and her property confiscated.

It had been her intention to proceed to Turkey. Her nephew, Joseph Nasi, had relations with Moses Hamon, the sultan's physician (p. 513), who enlisted the aid of the Turkish government to set the lady free. Pending negotiations over the restoration of her possessions, Gracia took up her residence in Ferrara. There she returned to Judaism and assisted materially and morally numbers of unfortunate Maranos who followed her example. She was particularly held in veneration by members of the Usque family—Solomon, her agent in business and translator of Petrarch's poems into Spanish; Samuel, author of a prose poem in Portuguese entitled 'Consolation in Israel's Tribulations,' an important source for the history of persecutions; Abraham, who established a printing press and issued, in addition to many Hebrew books, a Spanish translation of the Scriptures (the Ferrara Bible, 1553).

Charles V. introduced the Inquisition into the Netherlands. After the outbreak of the revolt against the Spanish rule of Philip II., the tribunal unfolded its ruthless operations, and there was no possibility for professing Jews to maintain themselves in the Low Countries. The Duke of Alva served notice on the authorities of Arnhem to seize all Jews residing there (1571). Conditions improved after the Union of Utrecht, in which the northern provinces declared their independence (1579), and the destruction by the English of the Spanish Armada which greatly weakened Spain (1588). There followed a fresh influx of Maranos into the new republic. Not all of the provinces were willing to receive them, as for example Zeeland, despite the intercession of Samuel Palache, a Moroccan Jew, who in 1591 was sent by his sovereign as consul to the Netherlands. After an eventful voyage, a small group of Maranos from Portugal, among whom were Lopez Homen, his niece Maria Nuñez, and her brother Manuel, found themselves at Emden in Friesland

and were assisted by the rabbi, Moses Uri ha-Levi, to reach Amsterdam (1593).

The Emden rabbi, who followed them to Amsterdam, received them back into Judaism. On the day of Atonement, 1596, a small congregation of sixteen worshiped in the private dwelling of the consul Palache. So ignorant were the Protestant citizens of the nature of this worship that they fell upon the congregation, thinking it to be Catholic. But Jacob Tirado, who was able to converse in Latin with the city fathers, told them that they were Jews fleeing from the Inquisition, possessed of ample means, and engaged in commercial enterprises which would redound to the welfare of the city. He also obtained permission to erect a small synagogue, which was named in his honor 'House of Jacob' (Beth Jacob, 1598). By 1608 the community had grown, counting among its members the poet Paul de Pina (Rehuel Jesurun) and the cabalist Alonzo (Abraham) de Herrera; the latter had Jewish blood in his veins, but also old Spanish, being descended from Gonzalo de Cordova, conqueror and viceroy of Naples. A second synagogue, 'Habitation of Peace' (Neveh Shalom), was opened, and between 1602 and 1614 two burial-grounds were secured.

To the cemetery at Oudekerk were brought in 1616 the remains of Elijah Montalto. A Portuguese Marano, he had settled in Leghorn and then in Venice. His fame as a physician was brought to the attention of Maria de Medici, second consort of King Henry IV. of France and after his death regent, who invited him to become court physician. Montalto stipulated complete religious freedom and exemption from duties on the sabbath. He died at Tours while accompanying the youthful king Louis XIII., and the queen-regent had his body embalmed and sent for Jewish burial to Amsterdam.

Among those who conducted the remains of the court's favored physician was his pupil, Saul Levi Morteira, who, in the same year, was appointed rabbi of the synagogue Beth Jacob. The other synagogue was ministered to by Isaac Uzziel of Fez. This stern lecturer offended certain members of the congregation by his outspokenness against moral lapses. Under the leadership of David Osorio, they withdrew and formed a third congregation, which was named 'House of Israel' (Beth Israel, 1618). Their rabbis were David Pardo, Samuel Tardiola, and (from 1626 on) Isaac Aboab de Fonseca; at Neveh Shalom, Uzziel was succeeded in 1622 by his pupil Manasseh Ben-Israel.

In 1635, the number of German Jews had sufficiently grown to form a congregation of their own with the aid of their Portuguese brethren. Three years later the three Portuguese congregations were consolidated into one. The oldest synagogue was disposed of, the newest remodeled into a school building (Talmud Torah), while Neveh Shalom served as a common house of worship. When the Polish Jews arrived in 1655 (p. 556), they found as members of the rabbinical college Morteira, Pardo, Manasseh Ben-Israel, and Aboab.

Manasseh Ben-Israel (1604–1657) surpassed his colleagues by his wide, albeit superficial, erudition, his versatility, and his interests which went beyond his immediate community. He was a small boy when his parents, Maranos from Portugal, settled in Amsterdam; he grew up to feel himself Portuguese by descent, but Batavian in spirit. The small income which he received, first as a teacher and then as rabbi or preacher, he sought to augment by setting up a Hebrew press (the first established in Holland, 1626) and later by associating himself with business ventures in Brazil whither he intended to emigrate. It was not, however, given to him to be a man of opulence; he remained the student. As such he entered into relations with an ever-widening circle of scholars and men of letters, Jewish and Christian, at home and abroad; among these was the learned queen Christina of Sweden. A work which occupied him the better part of his mature years was the 'Conciliator' (Conciliador, written in the Spanish tongue) in which contradictions in the Scriptures were reconciled.

The speculations of the Christian millenarians, or Fifth Monarchy men, struck a sympathetic chord in the heart of the Jewish scholar of Amsterdam, just as in turn those dreamers, notably among the Puritans of England, leaned on him for support. On both sides the belief, starting out from the predictions in the Book of Daniel, gained ground that the Kingdom of the Saints, which was to endure a thousand years, was at hand. As a preliminary to that event, the Jewish people, it was held, would be restored to their ancestral home (and, as the Christians added, converted to the religion of Christ). But, in order that the restoration might be complete, it was necessary, in accordance with the Scriptures, that Israel, or the Lost Ten Tribes, should be rejoined to Judah. Where then were the Lost Ten Tribes to be found?

The Amsterdam rabbi had come in contact with Antonio de Montezinos (Aaron Levi), who told a weird tale of American Indians he had come across in his travels in the New World, of their religious practices, and of their tradition that they were of the tribe of Reuben. This tale came to the ears of John Dury, Thomas Thorowgood, and Nathaniel Holmes, English divines interested in missionary labors among the Indians, who were eager for a confirmation of earlier conjectures by Jesuit fathers on the relation of the American aborigines to the Israelitish tribes. A lively correspondence followed between the English puritans and Manasseh, with the double result: a manifestation of friendly concern for the Jewish cause in England, and a conviction in the mind of the Jewish scholar that the day of Jewish deliverance was drawing near.

His reasoning he developed in the tract 'The Hope of Israel' which he wrote in Spanish (1650). With full credence in the story of Montezinos and the evidence culled from Jewish and Christian writers, he arrived at the conclusion that the Israelitish tribes, scattered over many countries, had wandered from Tatary across China to the American continent, thus carrying the dispersion to the farthest parts of the globe. That was in fulfilment of Daniel's prediction that, 'when an end hath been made of breaking in pieces and scattering the holy people,' the redemption shall be accomplished. Moreover, in the Torah there was the promise: 'If any of thee that are dispersed be in the uttermost parts of

heaven, from thence will the Lord thy God gather thee.'
Scripture, the writer argued, tends to prove that the restora·
tion under Cyrus was incomplete and that therefore the
prophecies of a return from the distant parts of the world
must refer to the future deliverance. Signs of its coming are
multiplying: on the one hand the untold sufferings of the
Jewish people, beginning with the expulsion from England
and concluding with the catastrophe in Spain and Portugal,
and on the other hand the divine mercy vouchsafed to illustrious Jews exalted to high station, such as Maimonides,
Abrabanel (the ancestor of Manasseh's wife), Joseph Nasi,
and other worthies nearer his own time.

England had meanwhile become republican (1649). Cromwell, who 'by faith and matchless fortitude to peace and
truth his glorious way was ploughing,' dominated the Council of State. He had an eye to the usefulness of the Jews in
building up British colonial and commercial expansion. A
small number of Maranos had by that time found their way
to London, but their presence in the city had hardly come to
public notice. Cromwell's interest in the Jews was assuming
a practical aspect, and Manasseh's tract came opportunely.
He rewrote it in Latin, with a dedicatory epistle to the English Parliament, in which he besought its favor and good-
will to the scattered Jewish nation.

Had the treaty of coalition proposed to the Netherlands
government not miscarried, the Jewish merchants of Amsterdam would immediately have been able to establish themselves in England. With the Navigation Act passed, aiming
as it did to exclude foreign nations from the colonial trade,
there was a strong desire on the part of Jews carrying on
trade with the West Indies to obtain a foothold in London.
Not all Jews of the Dutch metropolis were in sympathy with
the movement. In the first place there were among them
Royalists who had no love for the regicides across the Channel, and then they shared largely in the Dutch resentment
of the blow to their shipping trade.

Overtures to the Jews had come from the British government, and Manasseh was invited to come to England (1652).

Matters were necessarily suspended during the Dutch war. Upon the conclusion of peace, when the policy of the Navigation Act was practically maintained, Manasseh's brother-in-law, Manuel Martinez (Abraham Abrabanel) Dormido proceeded to England (1654) on his own behalf. He had no difficulty in interesting Cromwell in an effort to secure the restoration of his property seized by the Portuguese at the conquest of Pernambuco. In May, 1655, a second invitation to come to England was conveyed to Manasseh; in October he arrived in London, where he was received as the guest of the Protector of the Commonwealth.

From his lodgings in the Strand, Manasseh submitted to the Protector his 'Humble Addresses' in which he appealed for the readmission of the Jews to England. The Messianic motive was reiterated: 'this Island' was necessary to the completion of the dispersion upon which the deliverance hinged. But in the foreground of the plea were more tangible considerations, the benefits to England's welfare which were to accrue from the presence of the Jews. Cromwell was entirely sympathetic. In his colonial schemes, especially since the acquisition of Jamaica, he had availed himself of the advice of London Maranos, chief among whom was Simon de Caceres, a relative of Spinoza (p. 496), and a mer-chant with large interests in the West Indies. It was even planned to colonize Surinam with the Jewish fugitives from Brazil.

Despite Cromwell's good-will and preponderating influence in the Council of State, Manasseh's appeal met with opposition from narrow-minded divines, who brought up the usual accusations against the Jews, and particularly from the merchants of the City of London who feared Jewish competition in trade. At the national conference held at Whitehall in December, 1655, a formal declaration was elicited from the lawyers present that there was nothing in the English law to prevent the settlement of Jews in England. But the question of desirability still hung in the balance. Prynne's hastily written pamphlet, 'A Short Demurrer,' drew from Manasseh a spirited reply ('Vindiciae Judaeorum,' 1656) in which the Jews were vindicated against hateful charges.

The war with Spain, 'the natural, the providential enemy of England,' brought matters to a climax. The Maranos were nominally Spanish subjects, and pursuant to the proclamation of March, 1656, their possessions were subject to seizure. The case of Antonio Rodrigues Robles, a wealthy Marano and Spanish merchant, was ultimately decided in his favor, on the ground of his being a Jew fleeing from the Inquisition. The Maranos were free to throw off their former allegiance. The Jews, if not openly, were tacitly readmitted; their presence was connived at; it was a sort of backdoor admission. Manasseh, it is true, failed to win for the Jews open readmission into England. He returned to Amsterdam disappointed and broken in spirit. Yet the very failure of his mission brought better results than his success might have made possible. An official act in favor of the Jews would have been accompanied undoubtedly by special legislation, which would have placed them at a disadvantage as compared with other citizens. This the Jews were spared. The Marano families were enabled to live as Jews; an arrangement was made for the holding of divine services, and ground for a burial-place was acquired. The Jews continued to be tolerated during the Restoration. In 1664, Jacob Sasportas, who had accompanied Manasseh on his mission, became minister of the community, but a year later, owing to the outbreak of the plague, he accepted a similar position in Hamburg.

The Jewish community of Hamburg numbered then about one hundred and twenty families. Portuguese Maranos had drifted in during the sixteenth century; by the beginning of the seventeenth their presence had become noticeable, and their right of residence, in consideration of a yearly tax, was granted by the senate. As early as 1611, they possessed a cemetery at Altona; in 1627 they had a small place of worship, styled Talmud Torah, in the house of Elijah Aboab Cardoso. Among other prominent members of the community were the physician Rodrigo de Castro (since 1594).

who by special grant of the senate was permitted to own real estate in the city, and the physician, philosopher, and linguist Benjamin Mussafia. The Portuguese Jews were engaged in the import business and took part in the foundation of the Bank of Hamburg (1619).

By 1652 two other synagogues had been opened, and the three together were consolidated into one large congregation, Beth Israel, with the learned David Cohen de Lara (died 1674) as chief rabbi. Jacob Sasportas was attached to a small synagogue and school (Beth ha-Midrash) founded by Manuel (Isaac) Texeira, minister resident of Queen Christina of Sweden. German Jews were less fortunate in being admitted to the city. Some fifteen of the wealthier families had escaped the order of expulsion of 1648. After 1654 other German Jews drifted in, but for the most part they belonged to the poorer classes, eking out a living as small shopkeepers. Until 1671 the German congregation was subsidized by the Portuguese Jews and remained under their control. A separate organization was effected afterwards, consisting of the three communities, Altona, Hamburg, and Wandsbeck, under the jurisdiction of the chief rabbi of Altona.

CHAPTER LXVI

URIEL DA COSTA AND BARUCH SPINOZA

(1585-1677)

JEWISH life in these northern communities moved in traditional grooves. The Sephardic (Spanish-Portuguese) minister, or haham, could by no means compare in depth of talmudic knowledge with an Ashkenazic (German or Polish) rabbi. There was, however, a higher cultural level in the Portuguese communities, and the men who were their spiritual guides excelled in secular learning. Religious discipline was rigorously maintained. Perhaps it was that the Sephardic Jews, by reason of their early associations with Catholicism, were inured to ecclesiastical control; or the hardships which they had undergone in order to find their way back to the ancestral faith served to enhance the worth of the rewon possession. But it really required neither the one thing nor the other to oppose deviation from practice or belief. The treatment which the community of Amsterdam accorded to two of its dissidents comported in every way with more ancient examples in the Palestinian home.

If the first case ended in tragedy, the second involved the loss to Judaism of a thinker who impressed himself on the philosophic thought of modern times. Uriel da Costa (about 1585–1640) came to Amsterdam from Portugal some time between 1612 and 1615. Of a good family, he had studied canon law and had been appointed treasurer of a church. But like many another of his class, this Marano had experienced a longing for Judaism; in Amsterdam he and his four brothers were admitted into the covenant. The family, it seems, established a branch of its business in Hamburg, and in 1616 we find Uriel there. From Hamburg he sent his 'Proposals against Tradition' to the Sephardic community of Venice, at whose bidding Leon da Modena (p. 510) prepared a refutation. Uriel refused to recant, and as a consequence was publicly excommunicated at Venice (August 14, 1618). The decree was also announced at Hamburg. The heretic, however, had in the meantime returned to Amsterdam. From the very beginning, the ideal Uriel had constructed of Judaism from the reading of the Scriptures, clashed with the realities of Jewish life as they presented themselves in Amsterdam and in Hamburg. He possessed neither the learning nor the insight into history to understand the process of development from the Bible onward. He still operated with the Christian conception of 'Pharisaic' Judaism as the antithesis to biblical prophetism. He could not find in the Scriptures the clear-cut doctrines of the immortality of the soul and of retribution in another world. He was neither a clear thinker nor a strong character. He was denounced to the city government and imprisoned; he recanted (1633) only to lapse back into his errors. From opposition to the oral law he came to disbelief in the Bible. He emancipated himself from accepted religious practices and dreamed of a deistic natural religion with a minimum of obligations. Excommunicated by the rabbinate, he again became penitent and submitted to disciplinary humiliation in the presence of the congregation gathered in the synagogue. This degradation so preyed upon his mind that after writing his 'Exemplar Humanae Vitae,' in which he vindicated himself and bitterly condemned his opponents, he took his own life (1640).

Baruch (Benedict) Spinoza (1632–1677) was born in Amsterdam, of a Marano family which had left Portugal in the first quarter of the century. His father Michael was a merchant in fair circumstances and held repeatedly the office of warden of the synagogue. The young Baruch received his early training under Morteira and Manasseh Ben-Israel, perusing the writings of the rationalists Ibn Ezra and Maimonides, familiarizing himself with the criticisms of the Maimonidian system by Levi son of Gershon and Crescas, and snatching glimpses of the theosophical mysticism of the cabalists. His instruction in Latin Spinoza obtained from the physician Franz van den Ende, a man of erratic and rebellious temperament, who instilled in his pupils a love for the natural sciences and unorthodox opinions. Through the portal of Latin, Spinoza gained access to the writings of Descartes (1596–1650). Thus from two sides came powerful stimuli which operated in developing Spinoza's philosophic thought and resulted in alienating him from the synagogue. Already as a boy of fifteen he plied his rabbinical teachers with questions which indicated the trend of his mind. It came to be bruited about that his unorthodox opinions were translated into a laxity of religious observance. He was summoned by the rabbinical college to give an account of himself, but he declined to recede from his position that he was free to think and conduct himself in accordance with his own lights. He was temporarily excluded from communion with his coreligionists, in the hope that he would repent and thus avoid a public scandal. The lighter disciplinary measure did not weigh heavily on the offender, who had by that time made friends in certain Christian circles. He was offered an annual pension, on condition that he would at least conform outwardly. Spinoza spurned the offer, and when a fanatic made an unsuccessful attempt to stab him in the dark, he left the city and took up his abode in a neighboring village with a friend who belonged to the unorthodox sect of the Collegiants. Thus Spinoza had burned his bridges behind him and had withdrawn from the Jewish communion, before the elders of the synagogue pronounced upon him the rigorous ban. This solemn act took place in the synagogue on Thursday, the sixth of Ab (July 27), 1656, 'with the consent of the Blessed God and this holy congregation, in the presence of the holy scrolls in which are contained six hundred and thirteen commandments,' the faithful being warned against intercourse with the accursed heretic and the reading of his writings.

This excommunication of Spinoza was not merely a matter of maintaining discipline within. It was rather inspired by the motive of throwing off corporate responsibility for views which seemed subversive of all religion, including the Christian. Accordingly, Spinoza was denounced by the elders of the synagogue to the city government. No serious consequences followed immediately, the quarrel apparently being considered an internal one. Spinoza drew up a protest, which was later expanded into the 'Theologico-political Tractate.' The publication of this work anonymously (in 1670) provoked a veritable storm which led to its being condemned by the Church authorities and peremptorily suppressed by the States General. Yet the author showed a studied deference to Jesus and the apostles, and his criticism was leveled against the faith he had forsaken rather than against Christianity into which he would not enter. The plea for liberty of philosophical speculation within the state he supported by a distinction between philosophy, which has to do with knowledge ascertained by logical deduction, and religion, which is concerned with obedience and conduct. Such, he maintained, was the religion of the Old Testament; Mosaism was a polity designed for the Jewish state during its existence in Palestine, inculcating obedience in its citizens and holding out to them the promise of temporal blessings.

Hence the contention that the covenant, by which the Jewish state was created, ceased to be binding (in its entirety, be it noted) with the fall of the state. Hence also the curious notion that the retention of the greater part of the Law by the 'Pharisees' was inspired by opposition to Christianity rather than by the desire to please God. According to Spinoza, the observance of these rites, like circumcision, so contrary to those of other nations and making for separativeness, suffices to account for the universal hatred in which the Jewish people is held as well as for its persistence during so many centuries of dispersion. He adds his conviction that, unless the Jews are weakened by the fundamentals of their religion, it is not at all impossible that, given the opportunity, they will once more erect their state and again become the elect of God. The conviction, be it said, was not the product of theoretical reasoning; it was borne in upon him by the actual events of his day (p. 563) an echo of which reached his quiet study.

In order to leave the philosopher free in the pursuit of truth, Spinoza endeavored to prove that prophecy was not arrived at by the exercise of the reasoning faculties, but by heightened imagination. The notion of what the prophets were should not be based upon theories of our own, but upon the data in the Scriptures themselves. The meaning of Scripture must come from Scripture, no foreign thoughts should be injected into it. Spinoza then proceeds to show how difficult it is to get at the sense of the ambiguous biblical diction, how, moreover, the text is not always in its original form, and, lastly, how books ascribed to certain authors were not written by them at all. Thus, starting with Ibn Ezra's veiled hints, he denies the Mosaic authorship of the Pentateuch. His own thought on the question is to the effect that the historical books of the Bible, beginning with Genesis and ending with the Book of Kings, constitute one book, written, as he believes, by Ezra. It is true that Spinoza laid the foundation for methodical biblical criticism; but the process by which the Hebrew Scriptures came to be is neither as simple as Spinoza thought nor as complicated as his modern successors have made it out to be.

Spinoza followed his host to Rhijnsburg near Leiden; later he removed to a place within reach of the Hague and lastly to the Dutch capital itself. He lived most frugally, sustaining himself by the grinding of lenses; a friend left him a small annuity, which he accepted in part. He had a host of friends and admirers, and was visited by Leibniz. His reputation as a thinker brought him an invitation to become professor of philosophy in the university of Heidelberg. Spinoza declined the honor, preferring the tranquillity of his surroundings, away from the distracting labors of a teacher. He spent his time in concentrated thought and in the preparation of his chief work, 'The Ethics,' which was not printed until after his death.

Spinoza's philosophical system, developed after the manner of mathematical propositions, was a mystical pantheism, which largely rested upon the speculations of his Jewish predecessors. The Unity of God was for him so conclusive that it left no room for the universe outside Him. Whether we say God or Nature, makes no difference; for God is realized in the order of the universe, and the universe is a manifestation of God. God is the one Substance, two of whose attributes are Extension and Thought. He is in the corporeal world and in the mind alike. Nothing outside God can modify Him, but He is capable of infinite self-determining. Man attains freedom only by willing what God wills; complete immersion in God is loving Him intellectually.

Spinoza has been called the 'God-intoxicated' man. Other Jewish thinkers before him had striven to conceive God as in-dwelling (immanent) in the universe, and Spinoza might well have remained within the Jewish communion. Judaism was far from that rigidity with which Spinoza invested it, just as he failed to comprehend the undying power of the community from which he sprang and the rich spiritual life by which it was sustained.

CHAPTER LXVII

THE ITALIAN REFUGE

(1492-1663)

ITALY, by reason of her political disunion which made of her an agglomerate of states, offered herself to the Jewish exiles as a domicile which, if uprooted in one dominion, could be planted in another; at least, they paused there for a while before they passed on to the friendlier empire across the Adriatic. Isaac Abrabanel (1437–1509) turned to the kingdom of Naples when his efforts to avert the Spanish decree of expulsion proved futile. This gifted statesman and scholar came of one of the oldest and most distinguished Jewish families of Spain. He was born in Lisbon, whither his father or grandfather had removed. After the death of Alphonso V. of Portugal, whom he had served as treasurer, he was accused by John II. of abetting the conspiracy of the Duke of Braganza; his fortune and valuable library were confiscated, and he barely escaped with his life to Castile (1483). There he entered the service of the Catholic Sovereigns, availing himself of the intermission to write a commentary on the books of Joshua, Judges, and Samuel. He returned to his work as commentator at Naples when the calamity of his people brought his mind back to the national catastrophe narrated in the Book of Kings.

King Ferdinand I. of Naples (1458–1494) and his successor Alphonso were glad to employ the talented financier. The respite, however, was cut short by the French occupation of the city, and Abrabanel followed the court to Sicily. The death of Alphonso made it necessary for him to flee to Corfu; then he settled at Monopoli in Apulia and lastly in Venice at the house of his son Joseph, who was a physician established at first at Reggio in Calabria. In Venice, the father found once more scope for diplomatic business in negotiating a commercial treaty between the Venetian republic and Portugal. However, he was broken in spirit, with his family scattered and his fortune gone; he found solace in literary work, completing his commentary on the major part of the Bible. He also wrote on philosophy and devoted considerable attention to the Messianic doctrine, the anchor in Israel's tribulations.

His eldest son, Judah Leo Medigo (referred to by Christians as Leo the Hebrew), was physician to Gonzalo de Cordova, the conqueror and viceroy of Naples, who ruled the kingdom in the name of Ferdinand the Catholic. The Great Captain would not countenance the banishment of the Jews of Naples, on the plea that there were not many of them and that those few would transfer their industry and wealth to Venice, thus enriching the rival northern city. However, the immigrant Maranos were not left in peace by Ferdinand, and the Inquisition was set up at Benevento. Soon the viceroy was dismissed (1507); Leo withdrew to Genoa and subsequently rejoined his father at Venice. He was a grief-stricken man, his only son Isaac having been detained in Portugal and forcibly baptized. He followed medicine as a vocation; but his leisure hours were devoted to astronomy, mathematics, and philosophy, and these interests brought him in contact with Pico della Mirandola. Leo caught the spirit of Neo-Platonism then cultivated by Italian humanists; the conception of affection as the basic principle of the universe he made the theme of his Dialogues on Love, written in polished Italian.

The youngest son of Isaac Abrabanel, Samuel (1473–1550), was sent to Saloniki to perfect his talmudical learning. He lived for a time at Ferrara, and then at Naples, where the viceroy Don Pedro de Toledo engaged him as financial agent. He amassed a considerable fortune which he employed generously to relieve distress among his unhappy brethren. Since the community was too small to have a salaried minister, he installed at his own expense David Ibn Yahya, a refugee from Portugal, as rabbi (1518). At Samuel's house this well-instructed scholar delivered learned discourses. Many another student found welcome there. It was said of

Samuel that he was thrice great—in learning, in noble station, and in wealth. His second wife, Benvenida, was noted for piety and courtly manners. The viceroy regarded it as profitable for his daughter Leonora to associate with the cultured Jewess, and the friendship continued after the noble lady had become duchess of Tuscany. Charles V., however, was bent upon expelling the Jews from Naples. Though Samuel and his wife were able to stay the execution of the edict for a short time, at length the distinguished pair retired to Ferrara. The other Jews found a refuge at Ancona or fled to Turkey.

The dukes of the house of Este had welcomed the refugees from Spain in the very year of their expulsion. Hercules I. (1471–1505) admitted to Ferrara twenty-one families that had landed at Genoa, and these were soon joined by Maranos from Portugal. The immigrants took an active part in developing the commerce of the city, but were not spared the ignominy of the distinctive badge. Within the Jewish community, they had their own separate organization, with synagogues, rabbi, school, and burial-ground. In 1531, the German Jews erected their own synagogue, in addition to the Sephardic and native-Italian houses of worship. Ferrara continued to be a bulwark of religious liberty until the extinction of the Estes (1597). The earthquake which visited the city in 1570 made a number of poorer Jews homeless, but they were well taken care of by the wealthier members of the community. The calamity brought the various sections together, and a communal organization was perfected which included the several elements, largely under the leadership of Joseph Abrabanel's son Isaac. The Germans worshiped with the Italians, while the Sephardic Jews clung to their own rite. Joseph Nasi and his aunt Gracia, as we have seen (p. 487), found a refuge in the city; the Usques lived here; so did Azariah dei Rossi (1514–1578), who, however, was of native Italian stock. This scholar was far ahead of his times in applying scientific method to Jewish literary and historical questions, and also in making use of non-Jewish sources in his researches. His work 'The Light of Eyes' (published in Mantua, 1573–1575) is replete with erudition derived from Jewish and Christian books.

In 1597, the duchy was added to the Papal States. Clement VIII. (1592–1605) committed the administration to his nephew, Cardinal Aldobrandini. When he entered the city of Ferrara, the populace shouted: 'Down with the Jews.' About one half of the Jews left for Modena, Venice, and Mantua. Those that remained were subjected to restrictions of all kinds, and in 1624 the ghetto was instituted. As in the other cities in the Papal States, the Jews of Ferrara were compelled to listen regularly to conversionist sermons. Such sermons had been ordered by Nicholas III. in 1278, but it was not till 1584 that Gregory XIII. made weekly attendance of one hundred Jews and fifty Jewesses compulsory. It was part of the Catholic reaction, known as the Counter-Reformation, and the consolidation of the unity of the Roman Church through the Council of Trent (begun in 1545 and closed in 1563).

Back of that period, the situation of the Jews in the Papal States had been on the whole more tolerable than anywhere else in Italy. Alexander VI. (1492–1503), the Borgia pope, was absorbed in the aggrandizement of his family; Julius II. (1503–1513) was occupied with shaking off dependence on France; Leo X. (1513–1521), the humanist in the seat of St. Peter, gave his attention to safeguarding his dynastic interests by playing off France and Germany one against the other. Clement VII. (1523–1534), the second Medicean pope, truly merited the title of a prince gracious to Israel which a Jewish writer of the day bestowed upon him. Not only did this pope confer privileges upon certain Jewish physicians and their families, but he also suffered Marano fugitives from Portugal to settle in Ancona and profess their Judaism openly. Moreover, he gave sanction to a new constitution by which the community of Rome henceforward managed its internal affairs.

With the conquest of two bulwarks of Christendom, Belgrade (1521) and Rhodes (1522), by the sultan Sulaiman II. (1520–1566), it is comprehensible that Clement should have lent an ear to a Jewish adventurer from Arabia who promised to raise among the Jews of the East an army against the Turks. David Reubeni made claim that he was the ambassador of his brother Joseph, supposedly reigning over the descendants of the tribe of Reuben somewhere in Tatary, and that he had been commissioned to obtain munitions from the pope. He was of swarthy complexion, short of stature, but spirited and an expert horseman, at the same time pious and given to frequent fasting. The pope received him in audience (1524) and in due course furnished him with credentials to the kings of Portugal and Abyssinia, since the Portuguese by virtue of their maritime expeditions to the Orient and the Ethiopians by reason of their proximity would best be able to enter into relations with the Jewish kingdom. The Jews of Italy paid marked deference to the ambassador, whom the pope had thus honored. Representatives of the Jewish community of Rome, among them Obadiah Sforno and the physician Judah Ascoli, visited him. Benvenida, the wife of Samuel Abrabanel, and the family of the wealthy Jehiel of Pisa supplied him with means for his voyage to Portugal (1525). King John III. (1521–1557) received him with high honors; the impressed Maranos flocked to him in the belief that he was none other than the Messiah, and some of them even ventured to rise in arms. The Portuguese authorities became alive to the danger, and the 'ambassador' thought it discreet to depart by way of Spain and France to Italy.

The presence of Reubeni in Portugal stirred the imagination of one Marano, Diego Pires. In consequence, he gave up a government post, had himself initiated into the covenant of Abraham, and secretly left his native country. Solomon Molko, as he now called himself, turned to Saloniki and to Safed. His associations with cabalistic circles created in him the belief in his Messianic dignity, and he won many adherents. He was convinced that the place for playing his part must be Italy, the seat of the power inimical to the divine redemption. At Ancona, in 1529, he met with the opposition of the saner elements among the Jews; people,

nevertheless, flocked to hear him preach. A public disputation with a prelate placed him in jeopardy and he accepted
the invitation of the duke of Urbino to take shelter in Pesaro.
He was impelled, however, to go to Rome. Disguised as a
beggar he mixed among the poor and the sick close by the
papal palace; for thus, as an old legend had it, the manifestation of the Messiah was to be enacted.

Molko gained access to the pope and communicated to
him his prophecy of an inundation of the Tiber and an
earthquake in Portugal, accompanied by the appearance of
comets. Though the masses clung to him, he had his enemies
among the influential members of the community; so he betook himself to Venice where he fell in again with Reubeni.
The Signory had the case of the adventurer from Arabia
investigated by Gian Battista Ramusio, the well-known
traveler with pretensions to a knowledge of sundry Oriental
tongues. Molko began to have doubts as to the genuineness
of Reubeni's tale. The predicted overflow of the Tiber actually
came to pass (October 8, 1530). Molko was accorded an
honorable reception by the pope and was domiciled in the
papal palace.

Among his uncompromising opponents was the accomplished physician Jacob Mantino, the favorite of powerful
princes and Church dignitaries, translator of philosophical
and medical books into Latin, the only Jew whom the
Signory of Venice exempted from wearing the distinctive
hat. Mantino chanced upon a writing of Molko in which the
latter had used offensive language against Christianity. He
translated it into Latin and placed the translation in the
hands of the clergy. Molko was condemned by the Inquisition
to death. Clement, however, had conceived a great liking for
the plausible dreamer; so he facilitated his escape by a timely
warning, while a man who resembled the accused in appearance and dress was turned over to the tribunal and burned
alive.

In the meantime Portugal had been shaken by earthquake
(January 26, 1531) and the portended comet had been seen.
But despite papal favor Molko was beset by enemies among

Jews and Christians, and leave was granted him to depart.
He rejoined Reubeni in northern Italy, and the two together
made their way to Ratisbon. With a flying banner, bearing
(in initials) the legend, 'Who is like unto Thee, O Lord,
among the mighty?', they appeared before Charles V. and
endeavored to persuade the emperor to call the Jews to
arms against the Turks. In vain did the sagacious Joseph of
Rosheim (p. 547) remonstrate against their folly. But their
stubborn persistence proved their undoing. The emperor had
them put in chains and conducted in his train to Italy (1532).
Molko was immediately condemned by the Inquisition as a
renegade from Catholicism; he maintained his belief in his
mission to the end and steadfastly died at the stake. His
companion was carried away by Charles to Spain and there
suffered a like fate.

Paul III. (1534–1549) followed in his predecessor's footsteps as far as the Jews of his own states were concerned.
Reluctantly he yielded to the setting up of the Inquisition
in Portugal, but he strove to mitigate its severities to the
unfortunate Maranos. The reaction, however, was fully on
its way, thanks to the ascendancy of Cardinal Caraffa, who
as pope Paul IV. (1555–1559) introduced the strictest canonical restrictions, which crippled the Jews of the papal dominions economically and spiritually and, barring short respites,
remained in force down to the Napoleonic era (p. 611). The
Jews were confined within cramped quarters in the ghettos,
and watches were set to regulate the closing of the gates at
night and their opening at dawn. No real estate could be
owned by a Jew, and all such holdings had to be disposed of
at a sacrifice. Jews were kept from the exercise of the professions; none but the meanest occupations remained open
to them. The yellow hat for men and the yellow veil for
women were obligatory. A community was not permitted to
own more than one synagogue. In theory, no Jew might be
led to the baptismal font against his will; but in practice
enforced conversions were quite frequent. The Jews were
taxed towards the maintenance of houses for the reception
and training of converts. Conversionist preachers, often

renegade Jews, would invade the synagogues during the most solemn service, and the religious feeling was outraged by setting up a cross in the Holy Ark, if it so pleased the zeal of the preacher. The Talmud was repeatedly burned or else mutilated by the censor. Periodic expulsions from this or that locality or from all of the Papal States occurred; in the interest of the papal treasury an exception was made in favor of the communities of Rome and Ancona.

Ancona was an important port and the seat of the Levantine trade, which was largely in the hands of Jews, among them Maranos driven from Naples and others who owed allegiance to Turkey. The privileges granted them by previous popes were rescinded by Paul IV.; the Maranos were particularly subjected to cruel persecution. An order went forth to force them back into Christianity; about sixty-three renounced their faith, while twenty-three men and one woman were burned at the stake for their steadfast perseverance in the religion of their forefathers. Those who could escape fled to Pesaro, where the duke of Urbino offered them protection, hoping thus to draw the important Levantine commerce to his own domains. A serious effort was indeed made to bring this about, but the Jews of Turkey could not all agree to transfer their trade to Pesaro, and so the Maranos were expelled (1558). However, the pope was compelled to comply with the request of Sulaiman II. for the release of all Turkish subjects; but those Maranos who had no such protection languished in dungeons. The ostensible reason for not including the Jews of Ancona in the general decrees of banishment from the papal dominions in 1569 and 1593 was that there, as in Rome, the ecclesiastical authorities had them under their watchful eye. But so great were the vexations that hundreds of Jews left Ancona of their own volition.

Among the victims of those fateful decrees was the historian Gedaliah Ibn Yahya (1515–1587), who was driven out from his native town Imola near Ravenna and, after a temporary residence in Pesaro and Ferrara, wandered about until he settled in Alessandria. In his 'Chain of Tradition,' disparagingly called 'Chain of Lies' because of the large

number of miraculous and impossible stories which the un-
critical author gathered from all kinds of sources, Ibn Yahya
traced the history of his people from Moses to his own day.

Another historian of far greater accuracy was Joseph ha-
Cohen (1496–1578). He was born at Avignon of exiles from
Spain and practised medicine at Genoa. When the Jews
were driven from the city in 1550, he was prevailed upon by
the citizens of Voltaggio to establish himself there. However,
when in 1567 the Jews were ordered to quit the territory of
the Genoese republic, he went to Montferrat; in the last
years of his life he was permitted to return to Genoa. He
was painstaking in his historical researches; in good biblical
style, but with no semblance of arrangement other than the
chronological, he narrated the misfortunes of his people in
his 'Vale of Weeping.' He devoted himself also to general
history, producing a work on the history of the Kings of
France and the Ottoman Rulers, the two opposing forces
representing Europe and Asia, the Cross and the Crescent.
In addition, he translated a Spanish work on America
(India), wherein he told also the history of the conquest of
Mexico.

From 1535 on Milanese territory was governed by Spanish
viceroys. The spirit of intolerance, issuing from Madrid and
supported by Rome, could not be long in manifesting itself.
Friction between the Jews and Christians at Cremona led
to an expulsion of some one thousand souls from that city
as well as from Pavia, Lodi, and other localities (1597).

Conditions in the Venetian republic were precarious.
Venice was the first of Italian cities to introduce the ghetto
(1516) by reviving older statutes which had never been
carried out. In 1527, a partial expulsion took place, but the
exiles were recalled in 1534, when the Jews organized themselves into a corporation consisting of three groups, Levan-
tines, Germans, and Spanish-Portuguese (Occidentals).
Schools were maintained for the teaching of Hebrew and
secular studies. One of the principal societies had to do with
the ransoming of enslaved Jews. The war with Turkey over
the possession of the island of Cyprus, the Venetians sus-

pected, had been brought about at the instigation of influential Jewish advisers of Selim II. After the victory in the battle of Lepanto (1571), the Jews were threatened with a decree of expulsion; but no sooner had it been passed than it was recalled.

Life in the Venetian Jewish community, the second largest in Italy during the seventeenth century, reflected the general decadence in the city worn with much warfare. Questionable pastimes penetrated into the ghetto, but also the taste for letters, at a time when the art of poetry had become a mere exercise. Deborah Ascarelli rendered Hebrew hymns into ornate Italian stanzas; Sarah Copia Sullam (died 1641) wrote verses of her own in elegant Italian. A curious mixture of faith and superstition, of ideal flights and worldly frivolity characterized the gifted, versatile, but unstable Judah (Leon) Modena (1571–1648). He was descended from a family originally located in France. His grandfather Mordecai was a noted physician, whom Charles V. created a knight of the Golden Fleece; his great-uncle Abtalion (died 1611) was a scholarly man and conversed fluently in Latin.

Judah was born in Venice, and in its ghetto he spent the greater part of his life. The family fortunes had dwindled by reason of frequent migrations, and he was compelled to eke out a living by a variety of employments—in all, he enumerated twenty-six—ranging from preaching to teaching children, proof-reading, writing letters for other people, or matchmaking. He had an inveterate passion for card playing. When a ban was pronounced upon it by lay heads of the community, Judah opposed the act with an array of arguments, though in his youthful days he had written against the engrossing pastime under the caption 'Turn away from Evil.' Yet this man, who squandered his earnings and idled away precious time in gaming, composed a penitential prayer for the eve of the new moon (the Lesser Day of Atonement) which has passed into all Jewish rituals. For the benefit of his Christian friends, he wrote in Italian a book on Jewish observances. Against Uriel da Costa (p. 495) he constituted himself defender of talmudic Judaism and the

Torah. Notwithstanding his readiness to prescribe amulets for others, he resolutely set himself against the esoteric lore of the Cabala.

Simhah (Simeone) Luzzatto (1583–1663), Judah Modena's colleague in the rabbinate, was likewise averse to mysticism and assigned to Reason and Authority each its own sphere. In his 'Discourse on the Status of the Jews,' written in the Italian language and printed in 1638, he dwelt on the republic's decline by reason of the unprogressive spirit of its pleasure-loving citizens. He pointed out how its world commerce was slipping away and how it were profitable for the state to protect its native Jews who had connections with the Orient and at the time contributed to the treasury more than two hundred and fifty thousand ducats a year and gave employment to four thousand Christian laborers. At the same time this rabbinical student of political economy held up to the Jews a mirror of their own failings. It is true, he maintained, that the Venetian Jews were superior to their brethren elsewhere. There were, however, traits which were common to all Jews alike: a steadfast devotion to their ancestral faith, purity in their domestic life, charitableness to fellow-Jews. But on the other side there were uncommendable characteristics, as obsequious deference to all except their own, betokening unmanly timidity, and a woeful incapacity in present conditions for self-government, each one being concerned with his own private affairs and caring little for the weal of the corporate body. This criticism of the Jew's innermost self and the hallowed traditions of Jewish life in which the two Venetian rabbis engaged, foreshadowed the internal conflict which was to burst out a century later. For the time being the structure of tradition stood solid and the depressed minds found solace in the very unreasonableness of mysticism.

CHAPTER LXVIII

UNDER THE CRESCENT

(1492-1579)

IN NO country were the exiles from Spain and Portugal received with greater willingness than in the Ottoman empire, then on its course of greatest expansion. Planted on the European side since the capture of Constantinople (1453), the Turks, in rapid succession, made themselves masters of the entire Balkan peninsula, from the Peloponnesus in the south to the lower Danube in the north as far as Buda. Moldavia was snatched from the Poles and Crimea from the Tatar khan; Trebizond, Georgia, Mesopotamia were yielded by the Byzantines and Persians, Syria, Palestine, Egypt by the Mamelukes. Venice lost its islands in the Aegean Sea; the Berber states of North Africa acknowledged the suzerainty of the sultan at Stambul, and the Turkish fleet dominated practically the whole of the Mediterranean and harassed the Portuguese colonies in the Indian Ocean.

In these vast domains the Jew could drop the mask of enforced adhesion to a religion which was not his, and be himself again. The Turks demanded of their subjects the surrender neither of their nationality nor of their religion. The poll-tax, levied on all non-Mohammedans (unbelievers), was not oppressive; the road was open to all to rise to the highest positions in the state. The Jews who arrived from the West soon became the preponderant element in old-established communities. They were more enterprising than the native Jews, who had suffered under the oppression of the bigoted Byzantine rulers. They were wide-awake to the opportunities of commerce on a large scale, trained in the arts and crafts, cultured. These Jews taught the Turks the manufacture of the new firearms, cannon, and gunpowder.

Jewish physicians from the school of Salamanca were much sought after for their skill and discreetness.

In a short time, the community of Constantinople grew to be the largest in Europe, with nearly thirty thousand souls. Each group had its own synagogue and organization; the incoming Jews, whether from near or far, kept to themselves, not merely according to countries or provinces but also according to the cities whence they came. At first, naturally, the natives predominated. Soon after the conquest of Constantinople, Mohammed II. appointed Moses Capsali (1420–1493) chief rabbi. As such he was the recognized head of the whole body of Turkish Jews and had a seat in the divan next to that of the mufti. Capsali was succeeded by Elijah Mizrahi (1455–1526), a thoroughgoing talmudist from the school of Judah Menz at Padua, and a student also of mathematics and astronomy. Of all his works the supercommentary (published in Venice 1527) on Rashi's exposition of the Pentateuch was probably the most important. In early youth he was engaged in a feud with the Karaites resident in Turkey; but as he grew older, he became more conciliatory and resisted with all might the intolerance of the hyperorthodox who pronounced a ban upon the instruction of the dissidents by Rabbanite teachers. The ban, as Mizrahi pointed out, would not be binding upon the incoming Jews from Spain and Portugal.

Of the Spanish exiles who arrived in 1492, Joseph Hamon (1450–1518) soon attained a position of prominence; he became physician to Bayazid II. (1481–1512) and Selim I. (1512–1520). He accompanied Selim on his campaigns; during one of these expeditions in the East, he fell ill and died (1518 at Damascus). His son, Moses Hamon (1490–1565), physician to Sulaiman II. (1520–1566), stood in high favor at court; he had great influence with the sultan and he used this power in the interest of his coreligionists. In 1532, a ritual murder charge was invented against the Jews of Amasia (Asia Minor). At Hamon's request, the sultan ordered an investigation with the result that the calumniators were punished and a firman was issued declaring that in the future all such charges were to be tried in the sultan's own court. It was Moses Hamon, likewise, who interceded on behalf of Gracia and her nephew Joseph Nasi (1550; p. 487). The second largest community was that of Saloniki. It grew rapidly by reason of the influx of Sephardic Jews; in a short time there arose ten congregations, and subsequently the number increased to thirty-six. The Jewish population soon outnumbered the non-Jewish residents, chiefly Greeks; Saloniki was spoken of as a 'mother-city in Israel.' One of the most prominent members of the community was Judah Benveniste, grandson of the Castilian chief rabbi and statesman Abraham (p. 457). He had saved of the family fortune as much as he could and had taken with him his large collection of manuscripts and books, which he generously placed at the disposal of scholars. Thus Jacob Ibn Habib (1460–1516), who hailed from Zamora, was able to produce his collection of the haggadic portions of the Talmud, which appeared under the title 'The Fountain of Jacob' (En Jacob) and came to be a favorite book in lay circles. Cabalistic studies were transplanted to Saloniki by Joseph Taytazak, Samuel Franco, and others. Important Sephardic communities were established also at Adrianople and Nicopolis. At Adrianople, Solomon Ibn Verga, basing himself in part on an earlier work of Judah Ibn Verga, composed the 'Rod of Judah,' an account of the persecutions of the Jews in the various lands and periods down to his own day.

The outstanding figure among the immigrants to Turkey was unquestionably Joseph Nasi (died 1579). We have followed his migrations, in the company of his aunt Gracia, from Portugal to Antwerp and thence to Venice and Ferrara (p. 487). At last the family set foot in Constantinople (1553). Here Gracia established her extensive business and unfolded her rich benevolence; a synagogue which she built still bears her name. Here also her nephew Joseph, to whom she gave her daughter Reyna in marriage, rose to dazzling distinction. Letters of introduction from French statesmen paved the way for his favorable reception at court. Sulaiman II. recognized in him a valuable adviser on political affairs in Christian Europe which he so thoroughly understood and of which he kept himself well informed through his ramified connections. Joseph espoused the cause of prince Selim, whom his father supported with all his power, against the younger brother Bayazid; the grateful prince made of the Jewish diplomat his confidant and had him enrolled in his guard of honor. Sulaiman interested himself in demanding, on behalf of the 'European prince' Joseph, from the French court the restitution of the family's holdings in France which had been wrongfully confiscated. Three years later Selim ordered the confiscation of one-third of every large cargo that came from France to Egypt, in order to reimburse his favorite. The sultan made over to Joseph, as a perpetual gift, a district about Tiberias for the express purpose of turning it into a settlement exclusively for Jewish refugees.

On his accession to the throne, Selim II. (1566–1574) named Joseph duke of Naxos and of a number of other islands in the group of the Cyclades, to be held in fief for a nominal tribute. The duke's official rescripts read: 'We, Joseph Nasi, duke of the Aegean sea, lord of Andros, make known, etc.' No attempt was made by him to settle Jews in these Christian islands, and he secured an order from the sultan forbidding Mohammedans to settle there, in order to prevent friction. The duchy was administered by a Christian governor, a Spanish nobleman by the name of Coronello, in whose veins flowed the blood of the baptized Abraham Senior (p. 471), while the duke himself resided in his beautiful palace at Belvedere, near Constantinople. From here he corresponded with the reformers at Antwerp, holding out the promise of a Turkish war against Philip II.; here Emperor Maximilian II.'s ambassadors, suing for peace with the Porte, waited on the Jewish dignitary to secure his goodwill.

France resented the forceful measures which Joseph took to collect the money due him. There was likewise no love lost between the Venetian republic and the formidable Jew. Both plotted against him with the aid of one of the duke's Jewish agents. and, moreover, they were able to count on the support of the all-powerful grand vizir, Mohammed Sokolli. This shrewd minister, a renegade Bosnian, was personally at odds with Joseph; in addition, he was favorably disposed towards the Venetians. However, Selim overruled the vizir. Upon the news of a disastrous fire in the Venetian arsenal, the Turks speedily descended upon Cyprus, Nicosia was taken by assault, and Famagosta capitulated (1571). It was said at the time that the sultan had promised to make Joseph king of that island.

Mohammed Sokolli, with a view to his own designs, availed himself of the services of an agent, who likewise was a Jew and subsequently supplanted Joseph. Solomon Ashkenazi, of a German Jewish family settled in Udine, had traveled extensively and for a time was physician to King Sigismund Augustus of Poland. As a Venetian subject he placed himself in Constantinople under the protection of the diplomatic representatives of the republic, and these in turn introduced him to the grand vizir. Solomon had a hand in the negotiations for peace between Venice and Turkey; in 1574 he was sent to Venice to offer the support of the whole Turkish army if the republic undertook to go to war with Spain. Thanks to the prestige of the sultan's Jewish agent, the decree of expulsion against the Jews of Venice was revoked (p. 510).

With two so highly stationed men as Solomon and Joseph to protect their interests, the Jews of the Ottoman empire were in a most enviable position. The wealthy Esther Kiera, who stood in high favor with the sultana, was a patroness of Jewish learning; the physician Samuel Shullam, a Spaniard by birth, was beholden to her generosity for the means to publish at Constantinople (1566–1567) the historical work of Abraham Zacuto. After his flight from Portugal (p. 475), King Emanuel's astronomer (p. 474) had found a refuge in Tunis, where he remained until the Spanish invasion. There he wrote an annalistic history, both general and Jewish, 'The Book of Genealogies,' from the beginnings until the year 1500; he died in Turkey about 1520. Historical documents were published by Isaac Akrish. Driven from Spain, this talented man, though lame on both feet, wandered most of his life. From Spain he went to Naples; at Cairo he was befriended by the rabbi David Ibn Abi Zimra, himself a Spanish refugee; Candia held him for a time, until he found rest in the house of the duke of Naxos at Constantinople.

The duke had Tiberias rebuilt with the intention of turning it into a manufacturing center in Palestine. Mulberrytrees were planted for the purpose of raising silkworms, and cloth was imported from Venice. An invitation was addressed to the Jews to settle in the new colony; those of the Papal States, driven to desperation by Paul IV. and more recently by Pius V., were to be transported in Joseph's own ships. Very few, however, reached their destination, the majority being seized by Maltese pirates and sold into slavery. The venture accordingly did not turn out a success, and Joseph was far too busy with his political schemes to give it his full attention. However, his benefactions at home were extended to Jewish students. A college presided over by Joseph Ibn Lab was maintained at the duke's expense, likewise a printing establishment for the publication of Hebrew books which after her husband's death (1579) was carried on by the duchess.

CHAPTER LXIX

PALESTINE

(1488-1628)

THE experiment at Tiberias bears witness to Joseph's comprehension of a general feeling that the Jews, driven hither and thither, must look to the Holy Land as a home from which they might not be dislodged. The statesman, of course, had an eye to political independence under Turkish suzerainty, made feasible, as he thought, by his possession of the small tract about the Lake of Galilee. As a matter of fact, the Jewish population of Palestine had grown considerably since the catastrophe of 1492. In 1488, scarcely seventy families were to be found in the Holy City; within seven years the influx of refugees brought up the number to two hundred, by 1521 to five hundred. The newcomers brought wealth and a higher standard of culture. Their conduct contrasted sharply with the high-handed and oppressive manner in which the affairs of the community had been managed when Obadiah of Bertinoro (in the Italian province of Flori) set foot in Jerusalem (1488). This scholar and gifted preacher, whose toleration extended even to Karaites and Samaritans, introduced salutary measures of reform. Whereas before his advent men of wealth and piety had been constrained to leave the city, now with the improvement of conditions the very kindred of these men returned. Thus Isaac Solal, the last head (nagid) of Egyptian Jewry, transferred his wealth and beneficent activity to Jerusalem (1517), leaving the rabbinate of Cairo in the hands of David Ibn Abi Zimra.

For the great number of incoming Jews, who entered the land from the north, Safed, perched on the loftiest hill of Galilee, proved attractive. Joseph Saragossi, who in the exodus of 1492 wandered to Sicily and thence to Beirut and Sidon, found in Safed but a handful of Jews, whose rabbi kept a small shop to eke out a living. A hundred years later Safed boasted of eighteen talmudical colleges and twenty-one synagogues. What Bertinoro accomplished for Jerusalem, Saragossi did for the Galilean town. He planted the seed, which with the increasing influx of Sephardic Jews soon ripened into a flourishing center. Just as the new-comers excelled the natives in developing trade and various manufactures, so they were instrumental in raising the scholastic level of the community. Eminent men were drawn thither and found scope for their ample learning and rich inner life.

A strong personality was Jacob Berab, who came to Safed about 1534. At the age of eighteen, this exile from Spain, the pupil of Isaac Aboab (p. 473), had landed in Tlemcen and been accepted as rabbi in Fez; after the Spanish invasion he had wandered to Cairo, Jerusalem, and Damascus. He was a man of sixty when he settled in Safed. His wealth, as well as his ripe learning, secured for him a prominent position in the community, which now harbored many distinguished schol-ars, and he conceived a plan to revive the act of Ordination long defunct. During the Hadrianic persecution the practice was forbidden and Judah son of Baba contravened the emperor's edict at the cost of his life (p. 216). Ordination, it should be said, applied to judges, who thus were empowered to impose fines, and only he who was properly ordained himself could ordain others (p. 206). Since the chain had long been broken, Maimonides incorporated in his Code a personal opinion, which, however, he left open to discussion, that if at any time the entire body of Palestinian scholars, with unanimous consent, chose to reinstitute Ordination they were free to do so.

Accordingly, Berab assembled twenty-five rabbis of Safed, who created him their chief with authority to ordain judicial functionaries (1538). Among the first four who were thus ordained were Joseph Karo and Moses da Trani. A declara-tion was drawn up and sent to the chief rabbi at Jerusalem, Levi son of the Saloniki scholar Jacob Ibn Habib, with the request that he might approve of the step and accept ordination for himself. Levi felt that he had been slighted and that, if not for his own dignity, then because of the prestige of the Holy City, he should have been consulted beforehand; moreover, he had legal scruples against the innovation. Berab, as Maimonides before him, had his mind set upon a recreation of the ancient Sanhedrin as a visible expression of religious autonomy in Palestine and as a preparation for the advent of the Messiah. Levi Ibn Habib, supported by his colleague Moses de Castro, was not clear whether the rebuilding of the Temple, in obedience to the order of the Messiah or of an accepted prophet, should not precede the formation of the Sanhedrin. Moreover, he saw no practical need for the convocation of the Sanhedrin, since for the absolution of Maranos returning to Judaism—one of Berab's avowed concerns in taking this step—no penances were required beyond penitent confession. Berab had indulged in offensive allusion to the fact that the Jerusalem rabbi had in childhood undergone forcible baptism. At all events, Ibn Habib's opposition led to a collapse of the whole undertaking, which did not survive the passing away of its originator (1541).

Joseph Karo (1488–1575) was brought to Turkey in early childhood at the time of the exodus from Spain. His father Ephraim, who was his first teacher in Talmud, settled in Nicopolis. Subsequently Joseph removed to Adrianople, where he established a reputation for himself as a thorough talmudist and attracted disciples. At the age of thirty-four, he began his commentary on the 'Four Rows' of Jacob son of Asher (p. 439), which he styled 'The House of Joseph.' For full twenty years (1522–1542) Karo labored to produce this gigantic work of erudition, in which the source for every statement in the Talmud and cognate literature was indicated and the opinions of later authorities quoted; and twelve more years (1542–1554) were spent in revision. Painstaking student that he was, he led an inner life touched by the breath of mysticism. All his days he believed himself attended by a mentor-power, in which he saw the personified Mishnah and which admonished him daily what to do and what not to do, regulating his hours of sleep and imposing upon him ascetic abstemiousness. He came into contact with the cabalistic circles of Saloniki; he had a great veneration for Molko and longed to be worthy of a martyr's death like that which the Messianic dreamer had met. This opportunity did not come Karo's way; but his presentiment that he was called to play a great part took him to the Holy Land.

It may have been the miscarriage of Berab's far-reaching plans that ripened in Karo the determination to solidify the unity of Israel by another means. In 1567 was published the first edition of Karo's Code, 'The Prepared Table' (Shulhan Aruk) as the author called it, which to this day serves as a guide for the religious life of the mass of Jewry. It was meant as an abridgment of the 'Four Rows' with the additions found in his own commentary on that work; it was to be placed into the hands of the tyro rather than of the mature scholar. For the latter there was the author's larger work, where the basis of every decision was given. Thus did Karo escape the criticism which had been directed against the Code of Maimonides. The popularity of the product is attested by the rapidly succeeding editions and its spread to all the confines of the Dispersion. There was room for divergent opinions, but withal the Code eclipsed those of remoter times upon which the last undertaking rested. The Law of Moses opens up majestically with the avowal of God as Creator; the Mishnah takes it for granted that the Jew daily confesses God as One; Maimonides starts in with the fundamental affirmation of the First Cause; the first words in Karo's Code bid the Jew rise betimes and prepare for the service of his Maker. It is this key-note that dominates the whole. If any obsolete and outworn notions were carried into it, they are lost in the sum total which blends the multitudinous fragments of Jewish conduct into a harmonious unit of devotion to God's revealed will and to the hallowed traditions of a long past.

Among Karo's intimate friends at Safed, with whom he took counsel, was the cabalist Solomon Alkabez. Their friendship had been formed while they were yet in Turkey, and it was on a Pentecost night, during the wakeful hours spent in

Scripture reading and the study of the Mishnah, that Karo was urged by his mentor-genius to depart with his friend for the Holy Land. Alkabez infused the mystic longing for the Messianic redemption into the poem he composed for the reception of the sabbath, with its beautiful refrain: 'Come, my Beloved, and let us bid welcome to the Bride.' The poem was speedily accepted by all Jewry. The Safed circle included a number of other kindred spirits, all grouped about their masters as associates and given to a life of inward piety, in which frequent confessions and the exchange of spiritual experiences held a place.

The Safed school of mysticism reached its fullest development in Isaac Luria (1534–1572) and his pupil Hayim Vital (1543–1620). Luria was born in Jerusalem of a German family; hence he was styled the 'Lion' (ARI, abbreviation for Ashkenazi Rabbi Isaac). In early childhood he lost his father and was taken by his mother to her rich brother in Cairo, the tax-farmer Mordecai Francis. He was given a thorough training in Talmud under the care of Ibn Abi Zimra and Bezalel Ashkenazi. But Luria's temperament was not satisfied with the scholastic career. He immersed himself into the study of the cabalistic classic, the Zohar (p. 432), which had just been printed (Mantua and Cremona, 1558). He lived the life of a hermit, withdrawing from human society and visiting his home only on the sabbath day. His ascetic life and devout praying brought on ecstatic visions, and he believed himself to be the prophet Elijah, the forerunner of the Messiah. In Egypt he met with little encouragement; so with his cousin-wife and child he settled in Safed (about 1569). Here he gathered about himself a company of disciples, ranged in two divisions, as novices and initiates; they all, with their families, formed a community apart, occupying dwellings about a common court. From time to time the master would take them to Meron, to the grave of Simon son of Johai (p. 220), the reputed author of the Zohar, and there reënact the imaginary sessions of those far-off days. Luria now believed that he was the Messiah from the tribe of Joseph, who was to usher in the advent of the Messiah of

David's lineage. On the sabbath he was wont to dress himself in white, the color of Grace, and wore a quadruple garment to symbolize the four letters of the Ineffable Name. At the last he surrounded himself with three or four of his disciples; the master's most intimate attendant, before whom he unfolded his innermost thoughts, was Vital.

Hayim Vital was the son of an immigrant from Calabria. He came under the influence of Moses Cordovero and the preacher and Bible commentator Moses al-Sheik; but naturally he was most profoundly stirred by Luria. Altogether their intimate associations covered but a few years, before Luria's career was cut short prematurely by the plague. Vital immediately assumed the leadership of the circle of mystics and believed himself to be heir to the master's rôle as Messianic precursor. In him Luria's teaching found a zealous propagator. It had both a theoretical and a practical side. In effect, Luria was the first to develop the practical, or applied, Cabala, just as he was the first to give tangible form to the doctrine of divine Self-concentration. Emanation, the basic principle in the Cabala, he taught, becomes possible through the Infinite Being contracting Himself into finiteness. Thus the divine effulgence passes over into the part sundered, and then through various gradations into the actual world, 'created, formed, and made.' With each descent there is a dissipation of divine energy, the channels or 'vessels' bursting with their content.

All this theoretical conception of Creation is but a preamble to the practical, that is, ethical, doctrine of World Perfection. All the possible souls were united in the Preexistent Man, that is, the Idea of Man. Through Adam's sin good and evil intermixed; there is not a lower soul that has not something of the higher in it, nor is the best soul free from impurity. In order that the ascent may be made to the original world sundered from God, the most perfect world of the Messianic period, the souls must be purified from all dross. This purification is accomplished, on the one hand, by soul transmigration, the purer souls expiating their imperfections through entering into less refined bodies, even into stocks and stones, and, on the other hand, by soul super-fetation, when in addition to the soul received at birth there is incarnated another which formerly dwelt in some superior person. The ascent should also be facilitated by means of certain practices and ceremonies. This is the applied Cabala, which prescribed especially the thoughts one was to carry in one's mind while praying, so that every word and every letter was 'directed' towards the various scales in Creation. Ecstatic joy was injected into divine worship, the worship that was not confined to the synagogue. The sabbath meals, particularly the third, towards the outgoing of the day of rest, were accompanied by hymns which described in sensuous terms the bliss of the sabbath, itself preëminently a revelation of the Divine Presence, the Infinite made manifest in time.

The teachings and practices of the school of Luria were spread far and wide by the 'Lion's Whelps,' as his disciples and followers were called. The system was fitted into the scheme of talmudic Judaism by the eminently learned and saintly Isaiah Hurwitz (1570–1628), who, after filling rabbinical positions in several German and Polish communities, spent the closing years of his life in Palestine. Conditions in the Holy City were, however, quite lamentable; the learned rabbi and the notables of the community were cast into prison by an oppressive pasha. The Jews of Jerusalem scattered in all directions; Hurwitz escaped to Safed and then to Tiberias, where he completed his work 'The Two Tables of the Covenant,' replete with mystic directions and ethical admonitions. The trend of the age was distinctly towards mysticism. Nor was its hold lessened in the next generation, despite the critical acumen of Leon Modena (p. 510) or the feigned apology by Joseph Solomon del Medigo of Candia (1592–1655), the pupil of Galilei and physician of Prince Radzivil in Poland.

CHAPTER LXX

THE JEWS OF RUSSIA AND POLAND TO THE END OF THE FIFTEENTH CENTURY

(100-1501)

A<small>S FAR</small> back as the first Christian century, Jewish communities were established in Panticapaeum (Kerch) west of the Straits which connect the Black Sea and the Sea of Azov; in Anapa on the eastern side of the Taman peninsula; further north, in Olbia at the mouth of the Dnieper. These Jews, residents of the Bosporan kingdom, spoke the Greek language and must have come at a still earlier period from Asia Minor. They possessed a fully developed communal organization with houses of worship. As in all other early settlements, adherents, from among the pagan population, were attracted to the Jewish faith. About the year 300, pagans and Jews joined in a revolt against the missionary activity of Christian bishops. Even when the northern shore of the Black Sea had passed under the sway of the Christianized Byzantine empire, Christianity was making but slow headway in those regions.

The heavy hand which the Church laid upon the Jews of the eastern empire drove many of them northward. In the eighth century the Jewish population on both sides of the Straits, in Crimea as well as in the Caucasus, had increased considerably. Its principal seat was at Phanagoria (or Tamatarcha), which came to be practically a Jewish town.

A noteworthy achievement was the conversion to Judaism of Bulan, the khakan of the Chazars (about 740). Beginning with the sixth century, the Chazars formed an organized state on the borderland of Europe and Asia, between the Caucasus, the Volga, and the Don. Their main strain was of the white race, but their language and polity were akin to those of the Huns and Turks by whom they were held subject for a time. At the zenith of their power, merchants of many lands and divers peoples met in the marts of their capital Itil, at the mouth of the Volga. A renewed and more lasting turn toward Judaism took place under Obadiah, the first khakan who bore a Hebrew name. From that time until the eclipse of Chazar ascendancy, none but a Jew in religion was permitted to ascend the throne. Those in the immediate entourage of the princes and a substantial part of the people embraced Judaism. The poorest among these converts broke with the custom of their pagan compatriots to sell their children into slavery. Members of other religious bodies were free to live according to their faiths and had their own jurisdiction.

The khakans were held in high regard at the Byzantine court, honored above even the pope and Christian monarchs. One of the emperors married a Chazar princess; her son mounted the throne as Leo IV. (775–780). The khakans protected Jewish interests in adjacent lands. Within their own dominion the Hebrew language was an object of study. It is with the last Chazar ruler, Joseph, that Hasdai Ibn Shaprut corresponded from Spain (p. 310). Shortly after Joseph's reply reached the Jewish statesman, the power of the Chazar nation was broken. The blow was dealt by the Varangian princes of Kiev. Svyatoslav I. (964–973) took the fortress Sarkel (965) and then seized the capital Itil as well as the second largest city, Semender (969). The last vestige of Chazar dominion, which maintained itself for half a century in the Crimea, was blotted out by Mstislav I. in coöperation with the Byzantines (1016).

The friendly relations with Byzantium had been cemented by Mstislav's father, Vladimir the Great, who accepted Christianity in 989 and married a sister of the Greek emperor Basil II. It is said that he spurned alike the overtures of representatives of Judaism and the missionary efforts of Catholic Poland. The preference for Christianity in Greek form was founded on political considerations which led Russia to regard herself as heir to the decaying Roman empire of the East. The spirit of Byzantine intolerance transmitted itself to the dominion of the grand prince of

Kiev. Theodosius, abbot of the Pechera monastery, and Hilarion, the metropolitan of Kiev, preached hatred of the Jews, 'the enemies of God.' Svyatopolk II. (1093–1113) protected the Jewish residents of his capital; some of them served him in the capacity of collectors of the customs. But, during the interregnum which followed his death, riots broke out, and the populace fell to looting Jewish property, until order was restored by the entry of Vladimir II. (Monomachus, 1113–1125). In the twelfth century, the Jews of Russia, who naturally spoke the language of the country, began to be thrown into contact with their brethren of Germany, both through mercantile association and by reason of the influx of western Jews into Slavic countries after the Crusades. Russian Jews now had rabbinical authorities of their own. At Chernigov there was a learned rabbi by the name of Isaac. Moses at Kiev corresponded on matters of law with Samuel son of Ali at Bagdad (p. 343). The Tatars, who conquered Russia in 1240, were tolerant in religious matters, both as idolaters and after they accepted Islam. Commercial intercourse was established between Kiev and the Crimea, and the old Jewish communities of the extreme south were brought into relation with those of the north.

Beginning with the First Crusade (1096) and especially after the Second (1147) and Third (1189–1192), when conditions in Germany became more and more lamentable, the stream of Jewish migration poured into Poland. The provinces nearest the border were the first to be sought out as a refuge: Cracow, Posen, Kalisz, Silesia. These new-comers, whether by weight of number or because of their superior training in Judaism, imposed upon the older residents their culture and their very speech. The German dialect was thus introduced among Polish Jewry. Through isolation from its native home this speech assumed a form of its own, suffering admixture in vocabulary from the Slavic and other tongues, yet retaining despite modifying influences its basic German structure of that time. During the period when Poland was split up into a number of principalities, Jews were protected against mob violence by the princes. Mieczyslav III., duke of Great Poland (Posen and Kalisz) issued an edict forbidding attacks upon the Jews by the students of ecclesiastical colleges (1173). During the reign of his immediate successors, Jews farmed and administered the mints both in Great and in Little Poland, and the coins bore the names of the ruling dukes in Hebrew characters. At the beginning of the thirteenth century Jews owned land in Polish Silesia.

The devastations wrought by the Tatar invasion (since 1241) made it necessary to invite settlers from Germany, and no distinction was made as to Jews and Christians. Between the two fixed classes, the nobility (szlachta) and the peasantry, a middle class element of traders and craftsmen was introduced into Polish society for the first time. The Christian immigrant burghers, organized in guilds, were antagonistic to their Jewish competitors, and the Church strove to make operative the canonical restrictions against the Jews. The rights of the Jews within Poland were defined in a charter issued by Boleslav the Pious (1264); it was largely modeled after the one granted by duke Frederick of Austria in 1244 (p. 377). But the provincial synod, held in Breslau in 1267 under the presidency of the papal legate Guido, introduced for the Polish archdiocese of Gnesen measures calculated to cut off social intercourse between Jews and Christians. With a view to protecting 'the tender plant of Christianity in these regions,' it was recommended that the Jews should be segregated in quarters of their own and always appear with the peculiar headgear prescribed in general council.

The rulers, with an eye to the economic needs of the country, were not swayed by the narrow-minded attitude of Church synods or councils. The butcheries committed by Rindfleisch (1298, p. 402) and the worse massacres at the time of the Black Death (1348, p. 404) brought fresh masses of German Jews. Casimir the Great (1333–1370) ratified the charter of Boleslav. He furthermore placed under the jurisdiction of the Crown all lawsuits between Jews and Christians, since the municipal magistrates were hostile to the Jews. He also granted to the Jews access to the municipal bathing establishments alongside of Christians, as well as the privilege of free transit through the country and of unrestricted domicile in any of the cities or villages. It was made lawful for the Jews to rent or mortgage estates of the nobility, with provisions for enforced settling of debts and foreclosure. The motive of all these enactments was the medieval theory that the Jews were the property of the Crown. It was their business to be moneyed men so that at all times they might be ready to supply the treasury with funds.

Casimir also appointed a Christian official to try Jewish lawsuits in the synagogue or some other place, in accordance with the wishes of the representatives of the Jewish community. Thus was laid the foundation for the régime of internal autonomy as it subsequently developed. Upon the opening of the first Polish university at Cracow (1364), the king appointed a Jewish financier to raise funds for loans to professors and students. The Jewish community of Lemberg originated in the reign of this monarch, who added Red Russia (nearly corresponding to Galicia) to the Polish realm. With the growth of ecclesiastical power under his successors, Louis of Hungary (1370–1382) and the first ruler of the Jagello dynasty, Vladislav II. (1386–1434), persecutions of the Jews began. The archbishop of Posen instituted proceedings against the Jews of Posen on the alleged charge of having procured and desecrated three hosts from the Dominican church. The rabbi and thirteen elders of the Jewish community were roasted alive (1399). Moreover, a fine was imposed upon the Jews of Posen, and this fine was extorted annually by the Dominicans down to the eighteenth century. In 1407, at Easter time, a priest of Cracow made public announcement of a rumor that the Jews had slain a Christian child. The Jewish quarter was immediately attacked, many Jews were killed and their children baptized, property was looted and dwellings were set on fire. The synod of Kalisz (1420) reënacted all the anti-Jewish measures passed at the synod of Breslau.

Vladislav II. was grand duke of Lithuania when he assumed the Polish crown. The two states were now united under one king; yet the grand duchy was administered separately under a prince of its own, Vladislav's cousin Vitovt (or Vitold, 1388–1430). The area of Lithuania had grown steadily since the time of Gedymin, the ancestor of the Jagellos (1316–1341). In the beginning of the fifteenth century it embraced old Russian territory, as far east as Vyazma on the banks of the Moskva river and south to the shores of the Sea of Azov. A number of Jewish communities had come into existence, the most important being found in Grodno, Brest, Vladimir. At Troki and Luczk there were Karaite settlements which had moved up from Crimea. In 1388, the Jews of Brest and other Lithuanian communities obtained from Vitovt a charter of guaranties similar to those bestowed by Boleslav and Casimir the Great.

Casimir IV., Vladislav's second son, both as grand duke of Lithuania and (since 1447) king of Poland, was very much averse to the clerical intrigues against the Jews. In 1453, at the bidding of the communities of Posen, Kalisz, and other cities, the new monarch ratified the charter of Casimir the Great from transcripts of the original document, the latter having been destroyed by a fire in the city of Posen shortly after the coronation. The archbishop of Cracow, Olesnicki, denounced the king for granting protection to the Jews and denied the monarch's right to legislate at will in matters pertaining to the Christian religion. Moreover, he invited to Poland the legate Capistrano, 'the Jews' scourge,' who brought evil days upon the Jews of Germany (p. 415). This fanatical ecclesiastic delivered incendiary speeches against the Jews and demanded the revocation of the 'godless' Jewish privileges.

Casimir was engaged in a truly patriotic enterprise against the Teutonic Knights. The scheme ended in the acquisition of the Baltic seaboard vital to Polish commerce, but it was so little understood by the gentry that obstacles were put in the monarch's path at the most critical junctures. An initial defeat sustained by the army encouraged the nobility to wrest concessions from the king. These were the beginning of the curtailment of the royal powers. The Statute of Nieszava

(1454) marked the ascendancy of the Polish oligarchs; the same Statute abrogated the Jewish charter. The German Jews were much too helpless to come to the aid of their brethren in Poland, the country which had been looked upon as a place of escape for the wandering people. Excesses against the Jews were enacted in Cracow (1455) and Posen (1468); the magistrates, derelict in protecting the Jews from slaughter, were severely fined by the king.

The successors of Casimir IV., his sons John I. in Poland (1492–1501) and Alexander in Lithuania, were both unfriendly to the Jews. John instituted the first ghetto in Poland. A fire had broken out in Cracow in 1494 and destroyed a good part of the city; the Jews were attacked by the populace, upon the baseless accusation that they had caused the misfortune, and were driven from the city. The king ordered the Jews to take up their residence in a separate suburb, which continued as a Jewish ghetto till 1868. Alexander, who needed money for his campaign against Ivan III., the first Muscovite czar (1462–1505), issued in 1495 a decree for the expulsion of all Jews from Lithuania and the confiscation into the grand ducal treasury of liens held by Jews against Christian property. The exiles fled to Poland, where the Jews were too numerous and influential to be subjected to a similar fate. Indeed, when Alexander succeeded his brother on the throne of Poland (1501), he was powerless to discriminate against the Jews of Lithuania, since from this time on the grand duchy was indissolubly united to Poland. Through the intercession of the wealthy Abraham Josefovicz, who embraced Christianity and was ennobled by Alexander, the Lithuanian Jews received permission to return to their former homes. They were made to indemnify the Christians for the liens surrendered to the treasury and obligated themselves to pay a substantial yearly tax to the magistracies of the cities in which they resumed their residence. Alexander incorporated the charters of Boleslav and Casimir the Great as an organic part of the constitution of the realm—not from motives of love for the Jews, he said, but rather in order to protect the Christians.

CHAPTER LXXI

INTERNAL ORGANIZATION. LURIA AND ISSERLES

(1510-1573)

THE number of Jews in Poland and Lithuania kept steadily increasing, from fifty thousand at the beginning of the sixteenth century to half a million in the middle of the seventeenth. During that period this northeastern center attained its highest development, both economically and spiritually. The Jews of Poland were not tied down to money-lending or petty trade; they were actively engaged in various industries as producers and manufacturers. Wealthy Jews farmed the tolls and the excise and were frequently employed as financial agents for the Crown; they leased and administered Crown domains and estates of the gentry. Jewish capitalists worked salt-mines or dealt in timber and Jewish merchants exported the agrarian products of the country beyond the border. The poorer classes were traders, craftsmen, tillers of the soil.

The Church, of course, was always inimical to the presence of the Jews in the country; the burghers saw in them undesirable competitors; the overburdened peasantry had no love for the exploiting nobles or their Jewish agents. The kings and the gentry, in conflict with one another, found the Jews useful as sources of revenue or as creators of their wealth. In order to ensure the collection of the taxes from the Jewish communities, it was expedient to concentrate responsibility in certain lay leaders and to compel the rabbis to support these men by their authority. To facilitate this policy still further, the rabbis were invested with power over members of their flocks, if necessary by means of the ban. Sigismund I. (1506–1548) appointed Michael Josefovicz, the brother of Abraham (p. 531), elder ('senior') of the Jews of Lithuania, and Abraham of Bohemia in the same capacity over the Jews of Poland (1514). But the Jews, it seems, were disinclined to submit to lay authority imposed upon them from above, even when these lay heads had the royal permission to associate with themselves rabbinical advisers. The king readily confirmed the rabbis elected by the various communities. When certain Jews still persisted in taking their cases affecting taxation to the royal bailiffs, they were ordered to put themselves completely under the jurisdiction of their own spiritual judges. In 1541, the king set over the whole province of Little Poland two chief rabbis, Moses Fischel of Cracow and Shalom Shakna of Lublin. The former suffered martyrdom at the stake in the following year, nor did the latter, by reason of the opposition of the Jews, hold his appointment very long.

Shakna (1500–1559) introduced into Poland the new method of Talmud study which goes by the name of 'pilpul.' It is a sort of mental gymnastics, consisting in establishing artificial analogies between divergent themes or in creating distinctions between related parts. The method had its home in the schools of southern Germany; it was perfected by Jacob Pollak of Prague (he was subsequently rabbi in Cracow and died in Palestine about 1532), whose pupil Shakna was. With both these teachers the method served the purpose of developing the acumen of their students. From Shakna's school there went forth scholars whose fame and authority continued beyond their age, even as the community of Lublin became the cradle of the administrative polity of Polish Jewry then preparing.

Much as the king was minded to protect the Jews from violence to their persons, he was powerless to shield them against extortions of officials high and low. The concerted protests of the burghers in Posen, Cracow, and Lemberg against their Jewish business rivals had an effect in restricting the area in which Jews might open their shops. The plea was advanced that, if Jewish places of business were permitted in Christian neighborhoods, the Christians might be enticed away from their religion. The argument carried weight with the devout king. Moreover, the Piotrkov Diet of 1521 passed a law confining the trade of the Jews of Lemberg to wax, furs, cloth, and horned cattle. The burgher class won over to its side the lower gentry, and the Diet which met in 1538 adopted still more stringent measures in the spirit of the Church canons. The Jews were distinctly barred from tax-farming and forbidden to trade in the villages altogether, nor were they free to do business in any locality except by special royal permission and by agreement with the magistracies. As part of the scheme to repress the Jews economically and socially, the statute was renewed compelling the Jews to make themselves recognizable by a specific headgear.

Rumors were afloat that Christians embraced Judaism and found shelter across the Polish border in the homes of Lithuanian Jews. Lutheranism was then making headway in the cities, and it was a matter of policy for the king to stamp out any deviation from Catholicism; hence the redoubled vigilance against Jewish proselytism, which as a matter of fact could not be substantiated. A still graver charge faced the Jews of Lithuania. They were accused of having entered into negotiations with the enemy of Christendom, the sultan of Turkey, planning to emigrate to that country together with the Christians they had converted. Though the accusation proved groundless, the investigation was conducted with gross insults and brutalities, so much so that the king promised to discountenance accusations unsupported by evidence. The Catholic clergy, led by bishop Gamrat, continued to agitate against the Jews by means of slanderous publications. The anti-Jewish measures, passed at the council of Piotrkov in 1542, failed to receive legal sanction; nevertheless, the Church became determined in its attitude and only waited for an opportune moment to carry its programme into effect.

Under these conditions, it was essential for the Jews of Poland to solidify their organization for defensive purposes against inimical aggression from without, as well as for the improvement of the moral and religious life of the communities within. Sigismund Augustus (1548–1572), the last of the Jagellos, had the sagacity to understand that the Jews should be permitted to order their inner affairs in their own way. The edict of August 13, 1551, has been rightly called the 'magna charta' of Jewish self-government in Poland. The Jews of Great Poland and Masovia (the district about Warsaw) were empowered, whensoever a vacancy occurred, to elect their chief rabbi ('senior doctor') and lawful judges with plenary authority to exercise spiritual jurisdiction in accordance with the Jewish law. The chief rabbi thus appointed was answerable only to the king and not amenable to the authority of the royal officials or courts. Jews who resisted the rulings of their spiritual heads were given a month's time to repent on pain of death and loss of property to the royal treasury. By special rescript the community of Posen received permission to appoint for its rabbi a foreign scholar, since according to Jewish law a resident of the city itself might become unfit to pronounce judgment on blood relations.

Between 1559 and 1576 the Talmud was printed at Lublin; the Pentateuch had been printed still earlier (1530) at Cracow. In 1566 Benedict Levita of Cracow was granted the monopoly of importing Hebrew books into Poland from abroad. Royal sanction was obtained in 1567 by the community of Lublin for the erection of a structure to accommodate a synagogue and school for the higher training in the Jewish religion ('gymnasium,' yeshibah). The head master ('rector'), to be chosen by the rabbinate, was vested with all authority and removed from the control of the incumbent rabbi, Shakna's son Israel. It must have been the school organized by Solomon Luria, who had presided for several years over a similar institution at Ostrog (in Volhynia, then part of Lithuania).

Solomon son of Jehiel Luria (1510–1573) received his training at the home of his maternal grandfather Isaac Klauber at Posen. Before going to Ostrog, he had held office as rabbi in Brest Litovsk. He had a profound aversion to the newly introduced method of casuistical hair-splitting, and naturally was out of sympathy with its exponents, such as Shakna and his son and their disciples. Nor was he on cordial terms with any of his contemporaries, save one. He complained that in his generation ordained rabbis were numerous, but the scholars few. These ill-prepared ministers of religion would pounce upon the latest text-book and without examination appropriate novel opinions, so that ordinary men thought they were on a par with their betters. For that reason Luria was little pleased with Karo's commentary on the 'Tur' (p. 520)—the 'Shulhan Aruk' had not yet reached Poland—because in that work the author arbitrated on his own initiative between dissenting authorities, often sanctioning a practice held to be unlawful in Luria's country and, moreover, repeatedly falling short of profundity by reason of the vastness of his enterprise. Similarly he found fault with Maimonides for failing to cite in his Code the sources, so that it frequently appears as if he (Moses son of Maimun) had a direct inspiration from the Almighty.

Luria set greater store by the Tosaphists of the French school; but even beyond them he aimed in his own work, 'The Sea of Solomon,' to revert to the fountainhead of religious law, the Talmud. He found the Talmud itself far from being an open book; difficulties and contradictions were not wanting, and recourse must be had to early and late expounders whom he sedulously consulted. He strove after clarity and brevity of expression; he spent upon his literary effort the better part of his lifetime. It took him two years to dispose of half of one tractate, a full year was devoted to two chapters of another tractate, and half a year to a single chapter in a third. Critical of the opinions of others, no matter if they were recognized authorities of past centuries, Luria was quite diffident about his own worth. It was his wont daily, as if he were an ordinary person, for an hour to listen to the exhortations of a preacher.

Luria disapproved of the prevalent levity as when (be it remarked, at weddings) young men and young women danced together. He was sorely grieved that those who led in prayer in the synagogue were chosen solely on account of a good voice, with no regard to character, and that a student commissioned to officiate as reader would not be accepted, even if a worthy person, simply because he was sent by a rabbi. It is not to be wondered at that the spiritual guides were held in disrepute, considering that, as Luria tells us, many of them were quite unworthy, and those who rose above the average were given to the display of their wits rather than to a pious life of good deeds.

The one contemporary scholar Luria did cultivate as a friend was Moses Isserles (1530–1572), a son-in-law of Shakna. Isserles belonged to a distinguished family; his father, Israel, was lay head of the Cracow community and related to Meir Katzenellenbogen of Padua (died 1565). After completing his early training in Lublin, he settled in his native town, where he maintained at his own expense a college, over which he presided for twenty years. He was a comparatively young man when chosen to act as associate rabbi, and from far-away countries scholars submitted to him questions of religious law. His wide information in all branches of Jewish learning enabled him to furnish the 'Cloth'—so he called his annotations—for Karo's 'Prepared Table.' In these supplementary notes Isserles incorporated the religious customs of Germany and Poland and the decisions of the German authorities where they clashed with the opinions of the Spanish school followed by Karo. Thus only did the new Code obtain a footing among the Jews of Poland and Germany, and the influence of the combined work is manifest in Jewish life to this very day. Isserles was also interested in philosophical studies, which he pursued, as he said by way of excuse to Luria, on sabbaths and festivals, thus diverting himself with 'lighter matters' at a time when other people promenaded in the streets. Luria, who was uncompromisingly opposed to philosophy, rallied his friend on his ungrammatical Hebrew; Isserles humbly confessed that he had never studied grammar. A scroll of the Torah, written by his own hand, is still preserved in Cracow. Isserles was also active in the Council meetings at the annual fairs in Lublin.

This Council had become an established institution by the middle of the sixteenth century. It was known at first as the

Council of Three Lands, that is, of Poland (Great and Little), Lithuania, and Polish Russia. Subsequently (in 1623) Lithuania formed a central organization of her own, for the reason that the grand duchy had a distinct fiscal administration all to itself. The usual appellation for the Polish Council came to be 'Council of Four Lands,' Great Poland, Little Poland, Podolia with Galicia, and Volhynia each figuring as a constituent district. The Council met once a year at Lublin during the spring fair and lasted about a month. Another place of meeting was the Galician town Jaroslav, during the chief fair which took place at the end of the summer. This was so at least at the beginning of the seventeenth century, but soon it became customary to hold two meetings annually, one at Lublin before Passover and the other at Jaroslav before the autumn holidays. In exceptional cases sessions were held in other localities.

The Council consisted of thirty delegates, six of whom were rabbis and the remainder lay leaders. The chief business was to apportion to each district its share in the collective annual tax from the Jews to the government, as well as extraordinary expenditures entailed in propitiating high officials, in the defense of innocent Jews charged with crimes, and in warding off hostile legislation. The Council sent its agents (shtadlanim), representative men who by their wealth and station had access to the court or to the magnates, to watch over Jewish interests during the sessions of the Polish Diet at Warsaw. Especially was it imperative to be in attendance during the 'Coronation Diet,' when a new king ascended the throne and pressure was likely to be exercised by anti-Jewish elements to annul or curtail privileges previously conceded. The Council was constantly on the watch to prevent friction between the government and the Jewish population, or any private altercation between a Jew and a Christian, for fear that it might be perverted into a corporate libel against the whole body of Jews. When the Council, as, in 1580, was powerless to avert the enactment forbidding Jews to engage in farming the royal taxes or customs, it gave effect to the measure by an ordinance of its own, lest the greed of the few might endanger the many. The Council was supremely concerned with the welfare of the Jews as a whole. That alone was paramount, and the individual was forced into submission by the efficacious weapon of the ban which the rabbis were empowered to use by the royal edict of 1551.

To ensure the proper conduct of Jews, and especially of Jewesses, laws were passed against extravagance in dress and adornment, lest it might rouse the envy of the Christian population. It was strictly forbidden for a Jew to surrender his wife or daughter to a Christian in lieu of a debt; nor was a Jewish woman permitted to visit the house of a Christian on business unless accompanied by an adult Jew. The instruction of the young was a particular concern, for 'the fear of the Lord is the beginning of knowledge.' Rules were laid down for the proper supervision of schools and for the curriculum of studies; provision was made for constant rehearsals and periodic examinations. The advanced students were enjoined to assist in instructing beginners, and the rabbis were requested to give preference to pupils from their own immediate districts, when accommodation could not be had for more. So circumscribed was the economic life in the communities that measures were enacted to prevent undue competition. It was imperative to preclude an advance on rents by outbidding and to ensure to the holders of leases their privileges or rights which descended from father to son. Nor was it lawful for outsiders to do business in a community except by consent of the communal officers.

At the Council meetings the mode of the internal administration in the various districts and single communities was prescribed. There were district councils and communal boards (kahals). Disputes between individuals were settled by the local rabbis and their courts; but cases involving communities, whether the other party was a corporate body or an individual, came before the high court of justice which held its sessions at the place and time of the Council assemblies. Thus a system of internal administration was worked out in which nothing was left indefinite. The Jew of Poland and Lithuania was inured to rigid discipline; he was hedged about by prescriptions old and new which made for right living, for equitable dealings as between Jew and Jew and between Jew and Christian, and for a public opinion which meted out punishment to transgressors. The system on the whole was efficient in curbing delinquency in all classes and in presenting a common front when danger lurked and the position of the Jew hung on a slender thread which any untoward event might snap.

CHAPTER LXXII

THE ZENITH OF POLISH JEWRY

(1556-1648)

THE royal authority, weakened by conflicts with the gentry could not always prevent the hostile legislation of the city magistracies. Thus at Posen the limits of the ghetto were strictly defined; only forty-nine houses were allowed to the Jews, so that it became necessary to raise the height of many dwellings by additional stories. The magistracy of Warsaw refused to admit Jewish settlers, and Jewish merchants, visiting the city on business, could not tarry longer than two or three days.

The warfare of the Catholic clergy against Reformers and Anti-Trinitarians, led by the bigoted Nuncio Ludovico Lippomano, incidentally resulted in turning the battle against the Jews. The usual weapon was seized upon. A rumor was set afloat that Jews of Sochaczev had procured a sacred wafer and desecrated it by stabbing it until it bled. Before the king could intervene, three Jews and their supposed accomplice, a Christian woman, were burned at the stake. The Jewish martyrs stoutly professed their innocence, protesting that the Jews do not believe that the host is the divine body nor that God has either body or blood (1556).

Again, in 1564, a Jew was executed at Bielsk in Lithuania on the charge of having killed a Christian girl. The king issued two decrees (1564, 1566) in which, on the basis of papal pronouncements proving the groundlessness of the accusation, it was forbidden for local courts to institute proceedings against the Jews on the charge of ritual murder or desecration of the host. Moreover, in keeping with ancient Jewish privileges, it was ordained that such charges must be substantiated by the testimony of four Christian and three Jewish witnesses and that jurisdiction in all such cases belonged to the king himself.

A similar decree was issued in 1576 by Stephen Báthory, who had been elected king of Poland the year previously. The occasion was a renewed libel in connection with the death of a Christian boy, the son of a squire. Stephen confirmed the ancient Jewish privileges and insisted on an equitable treatment of his Jewish subjects by the Christian population. The magistracy of Posen was enjoined to allow the Jewish residents to conduct their business in any part of the city and to trade even on the days of Christian festivals. When in 1577 the Jewish quarter of Posen was attacked by a mob and looting and bloodshed ensued, the king imposed upon the magistracy a heavy fine, which was revoked only after the city fathers protested that they had been ignorant of the plot. Stephen nevertheless was committed to the Catholic reaction and was instrumental in turning over the educational system to the Jesuits. The newly established academy at Vilna was entirely in their control. From it and similar institutions issued those 'lions of the spirit,' who in the succeeding reign were to reconvert Poland to Catholicism and incidentally to Jew-baiting.

Sigismund III. (1586–1632), of the Vasa dynasty, surrendered himself to the service of Rome and, with the aid of his Jesuit counselors, set himself to purge Poland of heresy. The Jews, it is true, found in the king a protector of their rights. Thus they were permitted to trade in the cities, though with some restrictions. The Jews of Brest were upheld in their opposition to the jurisdiction of the municipal courts (1592). The Brest community possessed an efficient advocate in the person of their head, Saul son of Judah. A contractor of customs in Lithuania, he was influential at court and was honored by the title of 'the king's servitor.'

However, the Jesuitic teaching bore fruit. The very same year witnessed at Vilna an onslaught by the burghers, during which the synagogue was demolished and Jewish dwellings, owned by the gentry, were wrecked. Posen was the hotbed of anti-Jewish agitation; an attack on the Jewish quarter was led by Jesuit teachers and students (1618). Trials on the charge of ritual murder became frequent; namely, at

Lublin, in 1598, and then under the following reign in 1636. The clerical party inflamed the people by the publication of incendiary writings aiming at the expulsion of the Jews. So virulent were the attacks, directed in particular against the rich Jews of Cracow, that Sigismund ordered the confiscation of the libelous 'Mirror of the Polish Crown' by Sebastian Miczinski (1618). In the Diet, which met the same year, this docile pupil of the Jesuits had a number of followers; and though in the end common sense asserted itself, the pernicious seed of hatred was implanted in the minds of the Polish people against the Jews.

The same toleration by the king and the same animosities of the Church met the Jews during the reign of Vladislav IV. (1632–1648). Thus at the Coronation Diet the basic privileges were confirmed, with freedom of trade and judicial autonomy. For the erection of new synagogues or the opening of new cemeteries a royal license was required—a distinct favor, considering that in the previous reign there was an attempt to make such privileges dependent upon the consent of the clergy. But the king's wish to be just to the Jews involved him in difficulties with the municipalities, though the gentry favored the small Jewish traders so as to prevent the rise in the price of staple commodities. At Vilna the king responded to the wishes of the gentry; at the same time, in order to placate the burghers, the Jewish traders were hedged about by severe restrictions which confined their stalls within the boundaries of the Jewish street and barred them entirely from such trades as were pursued by the Christian guilds (1633). No sooner were the Jews of Cracow permitted to engage in export trade than, at the solicitation of the Christian merchants, the order was revoked (1642). The Diet, which met at Warsaw in 1643, fixed the rate of profit at seven per cent. for native Christian traders, five for foreigners, and only three for Jews. The result was that the Jews were compelled to lower the quality of the merchandise, while with their smaller profits they were bound to undermine Christian trade and thus invite the hatred of their competitors.

Beside the case of ritual murder laid at the door of the Jews of Lublin in 1636, a similar trial was engineered at Lenczyca in 1639. Between 1635 and 1637 disaster threatened the community of Cracow because a Pole, having stolen some church vessels, was induced by the municipal judge to testify that he had been persuaded by a Jew to steal a host. It made no difference that the Pole, before execution, exonerated the Jew. A mob invaded the ghetto; forty Jews were seized, of whom seven were thrown into the river, while the others saved themselves by embracing Christianity. All these disturbances, however, were nothing in comparison with the storm which broke loose in the closing year of Vladislav's reign.

The first half of the seventeenth century had been a period in which the inner life of the Jews of Poland and Lithuania reached a height such as was sustained in the other centers at the heyday of their existence. Education was widely diffused. The child was taken in hand early and sent to school—the 'heder' (chamber, usually a room in the private dwelling of the teacher) for pay pupils, and the 'Talmud Torah' (Teaching of the Torah), maintained by the community, for poor children and orphans. It was an all-day session in these schools. The instruction started with the Bible and proceeded to Mishnah and Talmud, care being taken that Bible study continued all along to the upper grades. From these schools those pupils that showed promise advanced to the colleges (yeshiboth), where they were grounded in the Talmud and the vast literature which had grown about it. A minimum of Jewish education was possessed even by the duller children, who dropped out in the lower grades and were apprenticed to learn a trade or put to work in humble service. The colleges were frequented not at all solely by those who aspired to the rabbinical vocation. Rather were these institutions nurseries for the training of the large middle class. The ordinary man in moderate circumstances (baal ha-bayith), not to speak of those who rose to leadership in their communities or in the supreme Council, commanded a fund of Jewish learning. No man went

home from daily services, morning and evening, without taking in a course in Rashi's commentary on the Bible, or in the
Mishnah, or in the laws concerning religious practice.

The school year was divided into two terms, a summer
term from May to the middle of August (fifteenth of Ab)
and a winter term from November to the middle of February
(fifteenth of Shebat). The vacations were spent not in idleness, but in study wherever a student might find himself. In
the higher colleges, during the first quarter of each term, a
page of the Talmud with Rashi's commentary and the supplements of the Tosaphists was read daily by the students,
the younger classmen being coached by the older and these
preparing themselves by their own effort. When the head of
the college arrived, difficulties were presented to him which
he proceeded to straighten out. Then he would lay before
the school discoveries of his own and wind up with a discourse in which the finer distinctions were brought out and
seeming contradictions reconciled. In the second quarter
these discourses were set aside in favor of solid instruction in
the compendium of al-Fasi and, with the highest grade, in
the 'Tur' of Jacob son of Asher. Every Thursday the students were examined by a lay director and every Friday by
the head of the college. This principal was accorded high
honors in his community; he was often the recipient of gifts
from wealthy members. In the synagogue, deference was
paid him in calling him up to the Torah 'third' in order,
unless he was a Cohen or Levite.

The students, who for the most part came from out of
town. were given their meals at the homes of members of the
community, usually each day at a different home, but often
enough regularly in one and the same house throughout the
year. The wealthier and more generous residents had as
many as three students daily at table. There was not a home
throughout Poland in which the Torah was not studied,
either that the master of the house was a scholarly man, or it
might be that the son or son-in-law was a student. Scholarship was highly prized. Rich Jews would choose for their
daughters husbands from among the student class. Matri-

monial matches were made particularly during the Council sessions, when at the fairs great multitudes assembled—merchants, delegates, rabbis of renown, heads of colleges with their advanced students who flocked to the highest institutions of Jewish learning at the seat of the Council.

The period was rich in outstanding scholars who left their mark upon posterity. Mordecai Jaffe (died 1612) was a pupil of both Luria and Isserles and author of the 'Robe,' a digest fuller than Karo's 'Prepared Table' and in opposition to it, supplying 'the salt of reasoning to the rich viands on the table.' Joshua Falk (died 1614), rabbi at Lublin and subsequently head of the Lemberg college, took a particularly prominent position in the meetings of the Council; the ordinances passed in 1607, in part regulating the taking of interest and generally concerned with the furtherance of piety and good morals, were largely framed by him. He wrote a commentary on that part of Karo's work which deals with civil law ('Book of the Enlightenment of the Eyes'). Meir of Lublin (1554–1616) wrote a casuistic commentary on the Talmud and was kept busy replying to inquiries on religious law which came to him from other scholars. Samuel Edels (died 1631) was rabbi in Posen, Lublin, and Ostrog, and was a master of the dialectic method. Joel Serkes (died 1640), who occupied rabbinical positions in a number of communities, is chiefly known by his commentary on the Four Turim ('The New House'). Two commentaries on Karo's Code, which now accompany it in all printed editions, began to appear in 1646: 'The Rows of Gold' on all four parts by David ha-Levi, rabbi in Lemberg and Ostrog, and 'The Lips of the Priest' on two parts by Sabbatai Cohen of Vilna.

CHAPTER LXXIII

THE JEWS OF BOHEMIA

(1579-1654)

To the galaxy of scholars who shed lustre on East-European Jewry in the first half of the seventeenth century an interesting personality must be added, who belonged to Poland by virtue of three rabbinical positions he held successively there during the last twenty-two years of his life. Yom Tob Lipmann Heller was born at Wallerstein in Bavaria in 1579; when he died in 1654, he was rabbi of Cracow. He received his training in the home of his grandfather Moses, chief rabbi of the German communities; in Friedberg, at the hands of Jacob Günzburg; lastly, at Prague. The Jewish community in the Bohemian capital had been in existence since the tenth century. It belonged to the body of German Jews and passed through the vicissitudes which affected these from the first Crusade. During the century which followed the acquisition of the Bohemian crown by the Habsburgs (1526), the Jews of Prague were twice expelled and readmitted (1542 and 1561). On the former occasion they were beholden to the good offices of Joseph (Joselmann) of Rosheim in Alsace.

This official lay head of the German Jews (died 1554) was their indefatigable defender during the reigns of the emperors Maximilian I. (1493–1519) and Charles V. (1519–1556). There was a double front to maintain, the Catholics charging the Jews with being the cause of the Lutheran apostasy, and the Reformers, including Luther himself, being none too friendly. Repeatedly Joseph appeared at the Diets to avert hostile legislation. At any emergency, when the Jews of the empire were threatened, he pleaded their cause—in Alsace during the Peasants' War, in Brandenburg or in Saxony, in Strassburg or Würzburg, and then throughout Germany during the Schmalkaldic War. By his learning he successfully discomfited the apostate Antonius Margarita in a public disputation. His wealth and connections placed him in a position to render notable services to the emperor. He gave freely to stricken Jewish communities beyond the confines of Germany. He interposed between quarreling communities, if necessary at personal risk.

On the second occasion the Jews of Prague were fortunate in having among them Mordecai Zemah, of the family of the Soncino printers. Ferdinand I. (1521–1564) had sworn to drive the Jews out of Bohemia, exactly as he had done to the Jews of Lower Austria and Görz. Mordecai appeared before Pope Pius IV. (1559–1565) and secured papal annulment of the royal oath.

Another influential personage and communal benefactor was Mordecai Meisel (1528–1601). He built the Jewish townhall; the neighboring High Synagogue where the Jewish court sat; the beautiful Meisel Synagogue; a hospital, and other communal structures. His benefactions extended to other Jewish communities. He also contributed a considerable sum of money towards the completion of the Church of the Savior in his own city. On more than one occasion he advanced funds to the emperor and empress and was rewarded with noteworthy privileges. Thus the Meisel Synagogue had a standard with an escutcheon; no officer of the law was permitted to enter the building, and it was exempt from taxation for all time. All these honors did not prevent' the confiscation of his wealth by the Bohemian treasury, at the instigation of Emperor Rudolph II. (1576–1612), when Meisel died childless.

Notwithstanding the expulsions, each time the community quickly recovered and counted a number of very wealthy men. The student Heller made his home with a rich merchant, Aaron Ashkenazi, whose daughter he subsequently took to wife. When scarcely eighteen years old, Heller was appointed associate rabbi of Prague. The principal authority in talmudic learning was Judah Loew son of Bezalel (died 1609), who as head of the college and later as chief rabbi attracted a circle of gifted students. But Talmud was not the sole subject that interested master and pupils; mathematics and astronomy claimed their attention likewise. From Loew's school came David Gans (1541–1613), who in talmudic studies counted as his teacher also Moses Isserles. His predilection for mathematics brought him into contact with Kepler, and Tycho Brahe induced him to translate the Alphonsine Tables from Hebrew into German. His chief work was an annalistic history, both general and Jewish, under the title 'The Sprout of David,' which was published in Prague in 1592. Printing had been introduced into Prague as early as 1513.

Heller became rabbi of Nikolsburg in Moravia in 1624, of Vienna a year later; in 1627, he was called to Prague as head of the rabbinate. The first decade of the Thirty Years' War (1618–1648) was then coming to a close; Ferdinand II. (1619–1637) was emperor, and the military campaigns of his generals Tilly and Wallenstein were costly. A heavy tax was imposed upon the Jews of Bohemia; the community of Prague alone was required to pay an annual tax of forty thousand thalers. A commission, over which the chief rabbi presided, undertook to apportion that sum among the members of the community. Naturally the task was a stupendous one; though the commission acted with strict fairness, the result caused grumbling among certain residents. The disaffected denounced the rabbi to the civil authorities, and the rabbi was censured by the emperor. But his enemies, bent upon his ruin, resorted to calumny, representing to the court at Vienna that Heller had in his published works written against Christianity.

Two of Heller's major works, upon which his scholarly fame rests, had appeared—a commentary on the Mishnah ('The Supplements of Yom Tob') and a double set of notes to the work of Asher of Toledo ('Royal Dainties,' and 'Pleasant Bread'). It was not exactly the title 'Royal Dainties,' as rumor had it, that roused the ire of Ferdinand; the point was that the commentaries contained references to non-Jews. Heller was conveyed to Vienna and incarcerated (1629). In vain did the rabbi protest that the sections referred to idolaters of olden times; that the laws regulating the dealings of Jews with them had been framed in Mishnah and Talmud, two works which were a part of the religious literature studied in Jewish schools. Still, through the intercession of influential friends, Heller was liberated on the payment of a fine of twelve thousand thalers. At the same time he was deposed from his rabbinical office, nor was he permitted to officiate in a like capacity in any of the imperial dominions.

There was nothing left for the impoverished and humiliated scholar but to accept a rabbinical position at Nemirov in Podolia (1632) and then at Vladimir in Volhynia (1635). Here he entered into intimate relations with the best families, one of his grandsons marrying a granddaughter of the greatly honored rabbi of Brest Litovsk, Meir son of Saul Wahl. Heller also took a prominent part in the deliberations of the Council of Four Lands and was instrumental in the renewal of an old decree against the prevailing practice of buying the rabbinical office from the governor. This action served to make for him new enemies, and he was glad to answer the call to Cracow (1643) as rabbi and principal of the college. Five years later the storm broke loose which shattered the fortunes of Poland and brought to the Jews cruel suffering such as they had not experienced since the Crusades.

CHAPTER LXXIV

THE CHMIELNICKI MASSACRES

(1648-1655)

IN the border-land to the east (the Ukraine), behind the falls of the Dnieper, lived the community of the Cossacks, sturdy freebooters recruited from Lithuanian refugees professing the Greek Orthodox faith. Stephen Báthory had organized the Cossacks as a defensive force against the Tatars. The chief of the entire body, or hetman, elected by the Cossacks themselves, received his insignia of office from the Polish kings. With the Catholic reaction at the beginning of the seventeenth century, the Cossacks became restive under the repressive rule of the Polish lords (pans), who were hated doubly, as tyrants and Catholics. Risings occurred in 1635 and 1636 which were put down with cruel severity. The Polish Diet of 1638 abolished the ancient privileges of the Cossacks, including the elective hetmanship, and introduced instead government by a commission of Polish noblemen with absolute power. Vladislav IV. had far-reaching plans of leading the Cossacks, who were devoted to him personally, against the Tatars and, after crushing them, taking the field against the Turks with all the forces of the republic. But he was balked by the Diet of 1647; a year later he died, at the very moment when the tempest conjured up by himself burst with elemental fury.

Fear of the Polish magnates put the notion into the head of the Cossack Bogdan Chmielnicki to unite with the Tatars in a determined onslaught upon Poland. When on April 18, 1648, he was elected hetman by acclamation, the insurrection was set on foot. It was directed against the Polish gentry, who stood forth as economic oppressors, political tyrants, and heretics in religion. Between the two opposing forces the Jew was lodged, professing a religion alien in the eyes of Catholic and Greek Orthodox alike, the middleman who as agent of the pans drew upon himself the hatred of the exploited Ruthenian peasants. The land on the nobleman's estates which the tenants tilled was administered by a Jew; the mill to which the peasant took his grain to be ground into flour, the inn where he obtained his liquor, the pond and the river where he fished—all were leased by Jews. The Jewish go-between collected the multitudinous tolls exacted by the Polish lords, whose greed and bigotry did not stop at the doors of the Greek Orthodox house of worship so that every christening and every mass for the dead was taxed.

In two battles, at Yellow Waters and at Hard Plank (near the river Korsun), on May 19 and 26, Chmielnicki routed the main Polish army. The immediate consequence was that the serfs throughout the Ukraine rose against their masters, the Polish gentry and their Jewish stewards. Estates were devastated, manor-houses reduced to ashes, and human beings barbarously done to death. The victims were flayed and burned alive, mutilated and left to the agony of a linger-ing death. Infants were slit like fish or slaughtered at the breasts of their mothers or cast alive into wells. Women were ripped open and then sewed up again with live cats thrust into their bowels; many, married or unmarried, were violated before the eyes of their menfolk, and those that were comely were carried away. Thousands of Jews perished in the towns east of the Dnieper, like Pereiaslav, Piriatin, Lokhvitza, Lubny. Only those who embraced the Greek Orthodox faith survived. The Jews of the Kiev region fled to the Tatars; these at least spared their lives, satisfied with carrying them off as slaves to Turkey. The Jews of Con-stantinople, with the aid of generous contributions from the Italian communities, paid the ransom to free their enslaved brethren. Funds were also obtained from the communities of Amsterdam and Hamburg.

There was no safety on the open land; accordingly, the Jews of Podolia sought refuge behind the fortified walls of Nemirov, where they outnumbered the Russian residents. The Cossacks could not hope to take the city by storm; they therefore resorted to a ruse. On their march to the city they unfurled Polish banners; the Jews were led to believe that a Polish army had come to their rescue and so they opened the gates (June 10 — Sivan 20). In obedience to the exhortation of their rabbi, the Jews refused to forswear their religion; the Christian townspeople and the Cossacks fell upon them and massacred six thousand. Those that cast themselves into the river were shot as they attempted to swim, until the waters were red with blood. A Cossack apprehended the rabbi, Jehiel Michael son of Eliezer, in the act of crossing the river; willingly he followed the rabbi to his house and was bought off by what of gold and silver had been hidden away. With his aged mother—his wife had been slain—the teacher fled to the burial-grounds, but there he was beaten to death by a Christian townsman, who then dispatched the old woman after she had witnessed the cruel end of her son.

A similar fate befell the Jews gathered together at Tulchin. Here they were betrayed into the hands of their assailants by the Polish gentry of the town. The Jews, who bravely defended the city, could have easily overcome the Poles. At the advice of their rabbi, Aaron son of Meir, who feared the Polish revenge on the rest of the Jewry of Poland, the Jews of Tulchin surrendered all their possessions, which the Polish magnate Czverczinski made over to the Cossacks as ransom for the entire town. The Cossacks then demanded also the life of the Jews, and the Poles readily acquiesced. There was not a single Jew who responded to the invitation to embrace Christianity. With grim determination and the cry of the Unity of God on their lips they suffered martyrdom, fifteen hundred souls, among them three scholars of note. After having done with the Jews, the Cossacks turned against the Poles themselves, with supreme contempt for their base treachery. Only three hundred Jewish souls, crippled with wounds and exhausted by hunger and thirst, were suffered to depart in peace.

Count Visznievecki dealt severely with the townspeople of Nemirov for the part they had played in the massacre of the Jewish residents. He was, however, feebly supported by the commander-in-chief of the Polish forces, and therefore unable to hold his ground before the steady advance of Cossacks and Tatars. Polonnoe in Volhynia was betrayed into their hands by the Greek Orthodox serfs within the city (July 21 — Ab 2); immediately a frightful massacre ensued. The Polish nobility fled betimes on their horses; but the Jews were not allowed to escape, and ten thousand of them were butchered. Three hundred of the Jewish notables, grouped about the venerable cabalist Samson of Ostropol, all clad in shrouds and wrapped in their prayer shawls, awaited the bloodthirsty soldiery in the synagogue and there they were done to death.

The Jews of Zaslav and Ostrog fled hither and thither to escape the oncoming fury; those that remained, about two hundred souls in the one town and six hundred in the other, were ruthlessly slain. Three thousand Jews, among them Asher, formerly rabbi of Polonnoe, perished at Konstantinov, and as many at Bar. At Pildava the Polish army, forty thousand strong, was completely routed by Chmielnicki. All Poland now lay at his feet. The Cossacks and Ruthenian serfs spread in all directions. Up the Dnieper, at Chernigov and Gomel, at Starodub and other towns, the Jewish victims were numbered by the thousands. Westward, in Pinsk and Brest Litovsk, hundreds of poorer Jews who were unable to escape perished. Chmielnicki himself marched on Lemberg; the city saved itself by paying a heavy ransom, the greater part of which was contributed by the Jews. The same happened to Zolkiev and other strongly fortified towns. In order to reach Lublin and thence Warsaw, the Cossack hetman laid siege to the fortress Zamosc. Though unable to take the city, he laid waste many Jewish communities to the south and southeast, and tens of thousands of souls perished.

The newly elected king of Poland, John Casimir (1648–1669), entered into negotiations with the rebel leader, but on account of his extravagant demands war was resumed. In the spring of 1649, fresh atrocities were committed and many more Jewish communities destroyed. A bloody battle was fought at Zborov, with the result that a treaty of peace was concluded (August 21, 1649). Chmielnicki was recognized as a semi-independent prince, and a clause was inserted forbidding Jews to reside in that part of the Ukraine held by the Cossacks.

John Casimir granted permission to the Jews who had been forcibly baptized to return to Judaism. Many women that had been carried off by the Cossacks and likewise baptized were able to rejoin their families. Everywhere there were hundreds of children who had been initiated into the Greek Orthodox religion; the Jewish communities of Poland made an effort to rescue them. As the domestic life had been so terribly disrupted, it became necessary for the Council of Four Lands, at its meeting in Lublin in the winter of 1650, to enact measures for the restoration of the normal condition. The twentieth of Sivan, the day of the massacre at Nemirov, was proclaimed a fast day to be kept year by year. Leading scholars, among them Heller and Sabbatai Cohen, wrote litanies to commemorate the martyrs of 1648 and 1649.

After a respite of eighteen months, fresh hostilities began. Fortune now deserted the Cossack leader, whom the metropolitan of Kiev had hailed as the Maccabee of the Orthodox faith and the archbishop of Corinth had presented with a sword from the Holy Sepulcher. Chmielnicki was defeated at the battle of Beresteczko (July 1, 1651), and a treaty of peace more favorable to Poland was obtained, the right of residence in the Ukraine being restored to the Jews. Three years later, Chmielnicki transferred his allegiance to the czar of Russia, and all of the Cossack region was incorporated into the Muscovite empire (1654). In the same year the Russian army invaded the eastern parts of Poland, and as the cities of White Russia and Lithuania were conquered the Jewish residents were exterminated or expelled. Thus the Jews of Moghilev on the Dnieper were driven out; the commander of czar Alexis (1645–1676) tricked them into believing that they would be transferred into the camp of Prince Radzivil, but as soon as they left the city they were set upon and butchered (1655). The Jews of Vitebsk were robbed of their possessions by the Cossacks, many were slain and as many carried away captive to Pskov, Novgorod, and Kazan.   The Jews of Polock, Minsk, and Kovno experienced a similar fate.

On the approach of the Russians, Vilna was evacuated by Radzivil and his garrison (August, 1655). The majority of the Jewish population sought safety in flight; those that remained behind were killed or banished by the Muscovite conqueror. Among the prominent scholars who were compelled to exile themselves were Moses Rivkes, who settled in Amsterdam and there published annotations ('The Well of Exile') supplying the sources of the combined Code by Karo and Isserles; Sabbatai Cohen, who became a rabbi in Moravia; Samuel Aaron Koidanover, who officiated in a rabbinical capacity in Fürth and then in Frankfort-on-the-Main; and others.

While Lithuania was being ravaged by the Muscovites, the heart of Poland was invaded from the west by Charles X. of Sweden. In quick succession the best part of the land was in the hands of the Swedes. The religious differences between the invaders and the invaded stirred the national and Catholic spirit of the Polish people, especially since the successful defense of the monastery of Czenstochova. The Catholics had ground to be suspicious of their Protestant fellow-nationals; it was an easy step to include with them the Jews. Hence the Polish militia, commanded by Czarniecki, fell upon the Jews as soon as they had reconquered territory occupied by the Swedes. In approved Cossack fashion, the Poles perpetrated frightful massacres among the Jews of Great and Little Poland. Nearly all the Jewish communities of the province of Posen, save the city of Posen, and those in the provinces of Kalisz, Cracow, and Piotrkov were destroyed. Between the Muscovite and Polish horrors the Jews felt, in the language of the prophet Amos, as if they were fleeing from a lion only to meet a bear.

The toll of Jewish lives taken during the decade from 1648 to 1658 was estimated as one hundred thousand at the lowest. Jewish refugees were to be met with all over Europe and Asia. Among them was a young girl, who at the age of six had lost her parents in the Cossack riots and subsequently been baptized by the nuns of a Catholic monastery. As she grew up into womanhood, she was found wandering one night in the Jewish burial-ground, asserting that she had been transferred thither by her dead father in a vision. The Jews, for fear of keeping her, sent her on to Amsterdam to rejoin her exile brother. There she returned to Judaism, assuming the name of Sarah, and then passed on by way of Frankfort to Leghorn, all the time proclaiming herself as the destined spouse of the Messiah. The word reached Cairo at the very moment when the dreamer of Smyrna openly came forward as the Redeemer of Israel, the Anointed of the God of Jacob.

CHAPTER LXXV

SABBATAI ZEVI

(1626–1676)

THE man who made a well-nigh irresistible appeal with his Messianic pretensions was Sabbatai Zevi (Zebi, 1626–1676). He was born in Smyrna, where his father Mordecai, descended from a Spanish family and formerly residing in Morea, acted as broker to an English mercantile firm. Father and son must have heard from those merchants that in Christian millenarian circles the year 1666 was looked upon as the year of grace in which the Jews would be restored to Palestine. In Jewish cabalistic circles, however, the year 1648 was accepted as the date for the Messianic redemption.

Sabbatai's talmudic education was obtained in the rabbinical school of Joseph Escapa. But already the youth was more attracted by the study of the Zohar along the lines of Luria's exposition. He gave himself up to rigid ascetic exercises, mortifying his body and bathing frequently in the sea, by day and by night, in winter as well as in summer. Though married early to a girl not unprepossessing, he shunned her society and willingly agreed to divorce her; this happened a second time with another girl. He attracted to himself a circle of disciples, whom he inducted into the mysteries of the Cabala. At the age of twenty he was the acknowledged master of the small group, impressing everybody with his serious mien. He was tall of stature and engaging in appearance; he possessed also a pleasing voice and sang beautifully Luria's verses or poems of his own composition in the Aramaic tongue, which is the language of the Zohar, and also in Spanish.

The advent of the year of grace, 1648, Sabbatai marked by breaking with the age-long tradition and pronouncing the Ineffable Name. This signified that the power of the

Godhead, impaired as it were by reason of human sin and the low estate of the Jewish people, had been restored and that the perfect moral order of the Messianic era had set in. Sabbatai's daring did not pass unchallenged; Escapa and his rabbinical colleagues excommunicated the offender. The community was divided; certain highly placed members, like Moses Pinheiro, were unshaken in their belief in him. Persecution was accepted as a part of the Messianic career. Sabbatai was furnished with means by his family and left his native city.

In Constantinople he chanced upon Abraham Jakini, a preacher of marked ability and religious enthusiasm, who produced a supposedly ancient writing in which the birth of Sabbatai and his Messianic dignity were predicted. But the capital was not exactly the opportune place for unfolding his activity. Saloniki, a seat of cabalistic study, was a more congenial place. Here Sabbatai celebrated his nuptials with the Torah, the mystic union of the Anointed King with the Heavenly Daughter. This act could not fail to shock the sedate rabbis, who banished him from the city. The excommunicate wandered through Morea, but he found the Jews there unreceptive. In Cairo, however, he was more successful. Raphael Joseph Chelebi, since 1656 Egyptian master of the mint and tax farmer, was given to ascetic exercises under the guidance of Hayim Vital's son Samuel. Fifty scholars and cabalists sat down daily at his table and entertained their host with spiritual conversation. In this circle Sabbatai let drop hints as to his pretensions. He was honestly convinced that he was the Messiah; only he had grown maturer and more circumspect.

It was natural for Sabbatai to go to Jerusalem, where, if anywhere, he might hope for miraculous intervention. His conduct in the Holy City won for him universal respect. He fasted much, prayed devoutly, wept copiously, and chanted psalms through the nights while pacing up and down the floor of his chamber. The community was then in dire circumstances. Pious gifts had ceased to flow from Poland because of the terrible Chmielnicki massacres; moreover, an extortionate pasha was clamoring for funds. Who but the charitable Chelebi could help, and who but Sabbatai, the mint-master's favorite, might be sent? Accordingly, he set out for Egypt.

Sabbatai left Jerusalem as a messenger (shaliah); he returned as the Messiah (mashiah). Cheerfully did Chelebi respond to the needs of the Jerusalem community. At the same time there came the opportunity to its emissary to have his Messianic dreams come true in an unexpected manner. It was then that he first heard of the girl Sarah seeking to meet her mate, the Messiah. It made no difference that rumor was unkind about her free manner of life; even that was part of the Messianic-prophetic programme, for did not the prophet Hosea at the behest of God marry an unchaste woman? Sarah was sent for from Leghorn; at Cairo she bewitched Sabbatai and his circle by her beauty and pertness. None was happier than Chelebi that in his house the Messiah and his bride were wedded. Chelebi placed his fortune at the disposal of Sabbatai and became his first influential upholder. In Gaza, on his return journey, Sabbatai found another ally, the prophet to proclaim the good tidings.

Nathan Benjamin Levi (1644–1680) was the son of Elisha, an immigrant from Germany, whom the community of Jerusalem sent out as a messenger to North Africa and Europe to collect funds for the support of the Jews making their home in the Holy City. The son grew up in Jerusalem, where he attended the talmudical school of Jacob Hagiz (1620–1674), an Italian scholar who taught in a pious foundation of two wealthy Jews of Leghorn. Upon the recommendation of the master, a rich Portuguese Jew, Samuel Lisbona, who had removed from Damascus to Gaza, gave Nathan his daughter (the girl was pretty, but blind in one eye) for a wife. He was but a youth of twenty, and when Sabbatai arrived in Gaza, Nathan immediately announced himself as the prophet Elijah come down to earth to pave the way for the Messiah. He told of a message that had come to him, probably some time in 1665, to the effect that within a year and a few months the Messiah would manifest himself in his glory and establish his kingdom by a peaceful conquest of Turkey. The revelation was sent out broadcast; it was embellished with all sorts of fantastic notions, including a journey of the Messiah to the mythical river Sambation, where the Anointed King would take for his spouse the thirteen year old daughter of Moses and then lead back the ten tribes to the Holy Land.

The common folk in Jerusalem and the adjacent settlements were transported with joy. But Jacob Hagiz was decidedly hostile; his son-in-law, the highly esteemed Moses Galante, wavered. Nathan then was ready with a heavenly message elevating Gaza to the position held by the Holy City. Sabbatai left Jerusalem. Prophets were sent out to herald his advent, among them Sabbatai Raphael of Morea and a cabalist from Germany by the name of Mattathiah Bloch. In Aleppo the pretender was received with triumph. A greater ovation was in store for him in his native city Smyrna, where he arrived in the company of the Jerusalemite Samuel Primo as his secretary in the autumn of 1665. Sabbatai proclaimed himself publicly in the synagogue, amid the blowing of trumpets, as the expected Messiah. The worshipers shouted exultantly: 'Long live our King, our Anointed One!'

The frenzy of the masses was boundless. Staid matrons, young girls, small children fell into a trance and in the language of the Zohar acclaimed Sabbatai as the true Savior. All men prepared themselves for the exodus to the Holy Land; business was at a standstill. On the one hand people submitted themselves to ascetic exercises in order to speed the redemption, and on the other hand indulged in festivities in honor of the Messiah. As often as the pretender appeared in the streets, processions were formed, the mass of marchers thrilled with joy as the sweet voice of the heaven-sent leader rang out: 'The right hand of the Lord is exalted; the right hand of the Lord doeth valiantly.' In Smyrna and elsewhere, particularly in Saloniki, children of the tender age of ten and twelve years were united in wedlock, so that the remainder of unborn souls might enter into bodies and thus the last hindrance to the realization of the redemption be removed.

In the tumultuous jubilation all discipline was broken through. The aged rabbi Aaron Lapapa (died 1674) remonstrated and was speedily deposed by Sabbatai and replaced by Hayim Benveniste (1603–1674). The adhesion of this eminent talmudist was hailed with delight by the believers. All opposition was borne down, if necessary by force. Thus Hayim Peña, a wealthy and influential member of the community, had to flee from the synagogue; as his own daughters joined in the general madness, the father could do no less than acquiesce. Sabbatai was undisputed master of the Smyrna community. The local Turkish authorities were bribed to support him against the rabbis, of whom Lapapa was most inimical.

The scenes of the Jewish quarter at Smyrna were repeated elsewhere. Samuel Primo from Smyrna and Nathan from Gaza flooded the Jewish communities the world over with messages concerning the appearance of the Messiah and his wonderful doings. The Christian agents of Dutch and English firms spread the news to European capitals. The Jews everywhere received the good tidings with joy, and even Christians lent credence to the story. At Venice, Moses Zacuto, a fellow-student of Spinoza, inflamed the minds of the all too credulous Jews; in Leghorn, Sabbatai's early adherent Moses Pinheiro acted with equal zeal.

Among the leading converts in Amsterdam were the rabbis Isaac Aboab and Raphael Moses d'Aguilar; the rich philanthropist and theological writer Abraham Pereyra, for several years president of the community; and Spinoza's other fellow-student Isaac Naar. The presses could not turn out quickly enough prayer-books, in Hebrew and Spanish, with directions for penitential devotions by means of which one might become worthy of participating in the Messianic bliss. In one synagogue the custom was introduced of reciting the priestly blessing every sabbath, whereas normally it was customary for those of priestly descent to pronounce the blessing only on the festivals. Even rationalistic circles were drawn into the movement. The philosophizing Benjamin Mussafia (p. 494), formerly of Hamburg and at one time physician to King Christian IV. of Denmark, was the first to sign the address of homage sent to the Messiah by the Jews of Amsterdam. Nor was the detached Spinoza altogether sceptical about the possibility of Jewish restoration (p. 498).

At Hamburg representative elders of the Portuguese community, like Manuel (Isaac) Texeira (p. 494) and Bendito de Castro, led in the jubilant dances in the synagogue, the young men dressed in their best garments and wearing wide green sashes. Many sold all their possessions so as to be ready when the call came to leave the Dispersion for the Holy Land. Glückel of Hameln (died 1724) tells in her highly interesting autobiography how her father-in-law abandoned his residence with all its contents, removed to Hildesheim, and sent on to Hamburg two large barrels of linens and food in preparation for the journey. The only man who stood out like a veritable rock in the face of the general intoxication was Jacob Sasportas (p. 494). In London, Jews wagered a hundred pounds against ten that within two years Sabbatai would be anointed king of Jerusalem. The small community in papal Avignon made ready to depart for the Kingdom of Judah in the spring of 1666.

This well-nigh universal acclaim of Jewry must have turned the head of Sabbatai. His immediate devotees aggrandized him and, whether with his consent or not, spoke of him in divine terms. These men probably won an ascendancy over the dreamer and pushed him on to extreme action. Samuel Primo issued a manifesto in the name of the Messiah bidding the Jews throughout the world turn the fast day of the tenth of Tebeth into a festival. Naturally the rabbis were dumbfounded. Solomon Algazi, of the Smyrna rabbinical college, barely escaped death at the hands of the believers and fled the city. At last, Sabbatai set sail for Constantinople, in the expectation that the sultan would do homage to him, the highest of the kings of the earth. When the storm-tossed ship put off its passengers on the coast of the Dardanelles, Sabbatai was arrested and taken in chains to Constantinople, where he was kept in prison. The able grand vizir, Ahmad Kiuprili, was then setting out for Candia in order to terminate the long war in which Turkey was engaged with the island. He thought it unwise to provoke the Jews by harsh measures against the man to whom they clung so tenaciously; at the same time it was undesirable to leave him in the capital. So Sabbatai was transferred to the fortress of Abydus, where political prisoners were kept.

The detention was rather of a mild sort; his friends had access to him. Far from losing faith in him, his adherents looked upon the imprisonment as temporary, a necessary step towards the triumph of their cause, and referred to the place of detention mystically as the 'Tower of Strength.' Sabbatai bore himself as the Messiah. On the eve of Passover he had a paschal lamb killed for himself and his companions and he consumed it with the suet in disregard of talmudic law. He gave expression to the abrogation of the laws of Moses and the rabbis by pronouncing a benediction: 'Blessed be God, who looseth (permits) that which is bound (forbidden).' Thanks to the rich presents, which pilgrims from near and far laid at the feet of the pretender, he was able to live in regal splendor. His sovereign superiority to accepted tradition proceeded apace. First the fast day of the seventeenth of Tammuz was done away with, because on that day the Messianic consciousness had come to him for the first time. Then on the seventh day thereafter, which was a Monday, he ordered the Great Sabbath to be kept. Lastly, the ninth of Ab, the fast day in commemoration of the destruction of the Temple, being the anniversary of his birth, was ordained a festival, a day of rejoicing, with a special service of song and thanksgiving. And these orders were obeyed, even as in all the communities, with few exceptions, a blessing was invoked upon 'our Lord and King, the holy and righteous Sabbatai Zevi, the Anointed of the God of Jacob.'

The turning point came about through the visit of two Lemberg Jews, Isaiah, the son of the celebrated David ha-

Levi (p. 546), and his stepbrother. Both were received by the pretender with marked attention. They incidentally narrated to him that in Poland a prophet by the name of Nehemiah Cohen was predicting the nearness of the Messianic kingdom, but not with Sabbatai as the Messianic person. Sabbatai sent by their hand a letter to the Jews of Poland, in which he promised them vindication for the sufferings they had recently endured and peremptorily ordered Nehemiah to his presence. The prophet came, saw the would-be Messiah, and was unconvinced. Some of the bolder believers thought of taking Nehemiah's life, but he escaped to Adrianople and after embracing Islam revealed to the lieutenant-governor what the Sabbatian movement was all about; that Sabbatai was plotting to overthrow the Ottoman rule, and that the constable at Abydus found the coming of so many Jews a profitable business and was therefore keeping his superiors in the dark.

This information was conveyed by the governor to the sultan (Mohammed IV., 1648-1687). Forthwith a council of state was convoked. At the mufti's advice, a renegade Jew, who was physician to the sultan, was dispatched to persuade Sabbatai (he had been removed to Adrianople) to turn Moslem. Whether it was that Sabbatai's courage failed him or because he feared that a terrible catastrophe would befall the Jews of the Ottoman empire, he consented to the change of faith. On September 16, 1666, Sabbatai was brought before the sultan; he immediately cast off his Jewish headgear and accepted the white Turkish turban. Thus the transformation was effected. Sabbatai the 'Jewish Messiah' was no more, for he left the sultan's presence as Mehemet Effendi, His Turkish Majesty's pensioner. It is said that the sultan, even after the conversion, contemplated a wholesale destruction of the would-be Messiah's followers among the Jews and was held back by the sultana-mother on the ground that they had been duped. But on the whole the outcome was quite satisfactory to the Turkish ruler, as without bloodshed the movement might be left to collapse of itself.

The erstwhile Messiah advised his family that he had turned Moslem in obedience to the command of God. His staunch supporters, as soon as they recovered from their first stupor, consoled themselves with the belief that it was not Sabbatai who had become a Turk, but a mere phantom that took on his appearance. The Messiah himself had ascended to heaven or had been translated to the regions of the ten tribes, whence he would come back in glory to accomplish the work of redemption. Nathan, the prophet of Gaza, clung to the notion that it was all an unfathomable mystery, and he traversed Asia Minor, European Turkey, the Greek islands, Italy, everywhere heartening the believers not to lose faith in Sabbatai's Messianic mission. However, the saner people, and especially the rabbis, had come to their senses, and the false prophet was excommunicated and expelled from the various cities he visited, until disheartened but still persevering he returned to Turkey. He is said to have died in Sofia (1680).

Despite the disillusionment, the communities in Asia, Africa, and Europe still harbored groups, now smaller, now larger, desperately refusing to be undeceived. Sabbatai Raphael, the other prophet of the movement, found a welcome in many a city during his wanderings through Germany, Holland, and Poland. In Leghorn, Moses Pinheiro had initiated into the Cabala a Portuguese Marano who had returned to the Jewish fold, the physician Abraham Michael Cardoso (died 1706). This visionary became an enthusiastic propagandist of Sabbatai's Messiahship; the conversion notwithstanding, he won many over to the lost cause, particularly in North Africa, where the ninth of Ab was for a number of years kept as a day of rejoicing.

Sabbatai himself, it seems, lived a dual life. Ostensibly a devoted Moslem, he would chant psalms and expound the Zohar before a small gathering of his Jewish friends, whom he was permitted to admit to his society on the plea that he would gradually bring over his former people to the Mohammedan religion. He was once surprised in the act of psalm singing and banished to Dulcigno, a small Albanian town. There he died; as it was reported subsequently, on the Day of Atonement (1676). Sabbatai was a dreamer, but the dream was that of his people longing for redemption, and the cabalistic framework he found ready-made. He believed in himself and followed after a delusion; but the episode stirred the Jewish soul to its depths and roused the mass to penitence and religious fervor.

CHAPTER LXXVI

THE SABBATIANS. MOSES HAYIM LUZZATTO

(1676-1747)

THE ghost of the Sabbatian movement was long in being laid. The death of the would-be Redeemer was as little of an obstacle to his followers as his apostasy had been in his lifetime. Daniel Israel Bonafoux, an unschooled precentor at Smyrna, proclaimed that Sabbatai was not dead, but had been spirited away and within forty-five years would return to accomplish the redemption. The heads of the community denounced the self-appointed prophet to the local kadi and procured his banishment from the city. In a small neighboring town he rallied about him the believers; here Cardoso, driven from Tripoli, joined the group and by his intellectual attainments won the mastery over it. Cardoso gave himself out as the continuator of the dead Messiah. He taught that the true God of Israel was not the First Cause, a Being devoid of will and powerless to exert influence on the world, but rather the Holy Father, a second Person as it were, the Creator and Giver of the Law, whom alone it is meet to worship. Because the Jewish people had swerved from this truth, it must immerse itself in idolatry. Only from within, so he asserted, can false belief be destroyed, exactly as Sabbatai had turned Mohammedan in order to undermine Islam. Cardoso wandered from one country to another as a heretic, condemned by the rabbis; in Cairo he met his fate, the victim of his nephew's greed (1706). So he died a Jew, while the precentor-prophet Bonafoux sought safety by embracing Islam.

The taint which Sabbatai was to remove by his conversion ascended to the birth of Ishmael by which Abraham's seed was corrupted. So taught an Alsatian Jew, who on returning from the Orient cast his spell on the masses of Bohemia, Moravia, Hungary, and Poland. After the Hungarian town which he made his home, he was called Mordecai of Eisenstadt; but people usually referred to him as Mordecai the Preacher. He had the gift of eloquence as well as a commanding presence; he fasted much, sometimes for as many as eleven days in succession, and earnestly admonished his audiences to repent. He considered himself the veritable Messiah, whose way Sabbatai was sent to prepare; for whereas the Smyrna dreamer was a rich man and therefore imperfect, he, Mordecai, was the poor man who, in the language of Scripture, was to deliver the city, that is, Jerusalem. The Italian Jews invited this new Messiah to visit them. At Modena and Reggio he was received enthusiastically, but on nearer acquaintance a recoil set in. The dreamer developed the notion that he must do with Edom (Rome) what Sabbatai had done with Ishmael. The meaning was unmistakable that he considered a plunge into Christianity in order to expiate in his own person its sinfulness, by which the perfect order was retarded. His opponents prepared to deliver him to the Inquisition, so he thought the better of it and fled the country.

At the seat of Sabbatianism the movement gained a new impetus. The pretender's widow, his last wife whom he married after his conversion, was the daughter of a Saloniki Jew, an enthusiastic believer. She had a brother, by the name of Jacob Querido, a lad of fifteen. She made believe that he was the son of her departed husband, born of a posthumous union with her. Soon devotees in Saloniki rallied about the reincarnate Messiah, but the rabbis saw to it that the Turkish authorities were apprised of their doings. To save themselves, about four hundred of them, with their leader and his father, embraced Islam. Jacob proved his devotion to his new religion by making the pilgrimage to Mecca. On the way back he died in Alexandria. His followers took for their leader his son Berechiah, in whom they believed to see a reincarnation of Sabbatai and his pretended son Jacob. The sect, for such it now was, kept up the Sabbatian cult in secret; while on the surface conducting themselves as Mohammedans and from time to time visiting the mosques to escape suspicion, they married only among themselves and practised certain Jewish rites. To the present day this sect, which the Turks call Dönmeh (Dissidents), still lives on in Saloniki.

Sabbatian missionaries carried the infection into European communities, and in nooks and corners the cult led an existence under cover. Even where the movement had been known only from hearsay, the guardians of tradition became apprehensive at the manifestation of any unwonted religious exaltation. In Poland, Judah the Saint (as he was called) of Dubno, a man of no high intellectuality but guileless, and his cleverer associate Hayim Malak were holding revival meetings in which cabalistic fancies were an adjunct to the preaching of repentance. Saul, the rabbi of Cracow, addressed a letter of inquiry concerning Sabbatianism to Zebi Ashkenazi, then in a minor rabbinical position in Altona. This distinguished scholar (1658–1718), a Moravian by birth, had spent his early youth in Saloniki and Constantinople, where his learning made such an impression upon the Sephardic Jews that they referred to him as 'haham.' This title he retained for himself ever after. For a short time he had been rabbi at Serajevo, after the misfortune of losing his wife and daughter in the bombardment of Buda by the Austrians (1686). He was now married a second time to the daughter of the chief rabbi of the three communities at the mouth of the Elbe. The Haham Zebi, who knew the Sabbatians from personal observation, enlightened the Cracow rabbi and warned him specifically against the questionable doings of Malak.

As a result of rabbinical persecution, Judah and a group of fifteen hundred persons left for the Holy Land in 1700. While the majority congregated in Moravia and Hungary, Judah with a smaller body passed through Germany, by way of Altona and Frankfort-on-the-Main, to Vienna. In the Austrian capital the wealthy banker and court Jew Samuel Oppenheim supplied them with means to continue their journey. The shrunken residue reached Jerusalem. The leader Judah died shortly after. The place in which he and his fellow-pilgrims had established themselves, together with the synagogue, was destroyed by the Arabs in 1720; the enclosure was long known as the Ruin (Hurbah) of Judah the Saint, and the chief synagogue of the Ashkenazim subsequently erected there still bears that name.

The small body found itself stranded, and it scattered in all directions. Two of Judah's nephews went over to Christianity; one of them later on allied himself with a Sabbatian element in Mannheim in southern Germany. Malak, who had come in contact with the aged Primo, placed himself at the head of a Sabbatian society in Jerusalem. At length he was driven out; in Saloniki he associated with the Dönmeh sect and went on a tour of propaganda through Turkey. The rabbinate of Constantinople excommunicated him (1709), and so he made his way back, traversing the communities of Podolia and eastern Galicia and planting the seeds of the Sabbatian heresy.

An arch-impostor was unquestionably Nehemiah Hiya Hayun (died some time after 1726). He was born apparently at Serajevo, though for reasons of his own he pretended to be a Palestinian by birth. His early training he received at Hebron, where he was inoculated with the Sabbatian virus. After a short ministry as rabbi in Uskup near Saloniki, he led an adventurous existence in Turkey and Italy, in Egypt and Palestine. At Smyrna (1708) he captivated certain wealthy people with extracts from a cabalistic work he had ready, in which he developed a doctrine bordering on trinitarianism. The rabbi, Benjamin Levi, scented the heresy and advised the rabbinical college at Jerusalem, whither Hayun was bound. As soon as the cabalist had set foot in the Holy City, he was anathematized by the chief rabbi, Abraham Isaaki, and his work was condemned to be burned without examination. In Venice, however, he succeeded in printing a part of his book with the approbation of the spiritual authorities. A still more cordial reception was accorded to him at Prague (1711 to 1712), where David Oppenheim was chief rabbi.

David Oppenheim (1664–1736) was the nephew of the Vienna court agent Samuel. From his father and father-in-law he had inherited a substantial fortune. He collected a large and marvelous library of Hebrew books and manuscripts; many books were specially printed for him on vellum or blue paper. This library with its rare treasures was acquired by the Bodleian at Oxford in 1829, and there it rests as one of its chief glories to this day. David was a beneficent man, spending a tithe of his fortune in charity. He was somewhat of a cabalist himself, and though he had no time personally to enter into relations with Hayun, his son Joseph was charmed by the pretender. This patronage encouraged Hayun to unfold by deft implication the teachings he had imbibed from the Sabbatian sectaries of Saloniki, that sin must be conquered by an excess of sinfulness and the satisfaction of grossest desires. The people readily believed him when he told them that he was the recipient of communications from heaven by the hand of the prophet Elijah, that he could force the Deity to reveal Himself to him, and that he had the power to bring the dead back to life and create new worlds.

In Berlin Hayun insinuated himself into the good graces of the family of the rich court jeweler Liebmann (p. 590). With their aid and with the approbation of the rabbinical member of the family, Aaron Benjamin Wolf, Hayun published in 1713 his book under the title of 'The Faith of the All.' The text, by some Sabbatian sectary, possibly by Sabbatai himself, was surrounded by a double commentary written by Hayun. While the text taught that the 'Holy Father,' that is, the Messiah, was God incarnate, the commentary inculcated the doctrine of the Trinity, in which God (the Primal Cause), the Holy Father or King, and the Divine Presence (Shekinah) were the three Persons. With this book the author appeared in Amsterdam, purporting to be a messenger from the Holy Land and petitioning the managers of the Portuguese community to allow him to offer his publication for sale.

The Portuguese rabbi, Solomon Ayllon (1664–1728), born in Safed and nurtured in the Cabala, was himself suspected of being a Sabbatian, having come under the influence of the

Saloniki sect together with Hayun in his younger years. Ayllon was not trusted by some members of his own community, since the year before he had expressed a favorable opinion on some work of Cardoso. Hayun's book was therefore submitted to the Haham Zebi, who in 1710 had accepted the call as chief rabbi of the Ashkenazic community at Amsterdam. It was an easy matter to lay one's hand on the palpable heresy in Hayun's books. Moreover, the warning issued by the Jerusalem rabbinate against the plausible cabalist had preceded his arrival in the Dutch metropolis, and Moses Hagiz (1670–1744), a born Jerusalemite, now settled in Amsterdam as preacher and teacher, added the weight of his testimony in disfavor of the questionable publication. Zebi refused to sit on the same commission with Ayllon to pronounce judgment on the author and his work.

Haham Zebi had had serious difficulties with the lay heads of his own community and on those occasions the Portuguese parnasim had strongly supported him. Now through the activity of Ayllon, who claimed that the prestige of the older community was involved, a feud developed between the Portuguese parnasim, among whom Aaron de Pinto took a leading part, and the proud Ashkenazic chief rabbi. While Ayllon and his party were preparing to exonerate Hayun, Zebi in conjunction with Hagiz pronounced the ban over the heretic. The Portuguese answered by publicly acquitting him. Moreover, when the Ashkenazic haham refused to appear before their body, they forbade members of their community to have intercourse with either of their two opponents. Hagiz left for Altona, while Zebi departed to London and then by way of Breslau to Poland (1714). But letters came to Amsterdam from Germany, Italy, Poland, and African communities with anathemas hurled against the heretic. Hayun was therefore prevailed upon to journey to the Orient in order to have his excommunication rescinded. He was well provided with letters of recommendation. In Constantinople he succeeded in enlisting the good offices of the vizir, and the rabbinical college absolved him on con-

dition that he would not engage again in teaching, preaching, or publishing cabalistic matter (1724). However, he
forgot his solemn promise quickly when he returned to
the West; again he was excommunicated (1726). This time
the aged adventurer could not maintain himself in Europe or
in the Orient; he died an exile in North Africa.

Hagiz, from his seat in Altona, took a hand in nipping in
the bud another Messianic movement, though this time it
had not the remotest connection with Sabbatianism. Moses
Hayim Luzzatto (1707–1747) was the son of wealthy parents
in Padua. He received a careful education and mastered
early beside the Hebrew also the Latin tongue. The two
strains united to develop his natural powers as a poet. From
a drama on a biblical theme and a new Psalter on the model
of the Scriptural he advanced to a dramatization of the victory of virtue and love over vice and selfishness. This morality play, 'The Tower of Strength' or 'The Integrity of the
Upright,' was written in honor of the nuptials of his teacher's son. The teacher was Isaiah Bassan, by whom the
impressionable disciple was introduced to the Cabala. Luzzatto was so impregnated with the style and the thought
of the Zohar that he produced a duplicate of his own which
he called 'The Second Zohar.'

Luria's writings turned the poet into a full-fledged mystic.
As he penetrated deeper and deeper into the esoteric lore,
he believed that his illumination was conveyed to him from
above by the voice of a mentor-angel. In the Cabala he
found the complete truth which no other philosophical system could open up. The lower world in which man finds himself has in it spiritual waves, emanating from the higher
worlds and ultimately from the Infinite Source whose modes
these all are. As man is carried on these waves, he is able, by
his acts and thoughts, to stir up motions, which communicate themselves to the loftier spheres for evil or for good. It
is given therefore to man to take an active part in spiritual
perfection; every 'awakening' below produces an 'awakening' above and brings down to earth the sanctity of heaven.
It was a fruitful thought which paved the way for a religious

movement soon to arise in the east of Europe. For Luzzatto the perfection of the world meant the spiritual union of Israel with God, the redemption from the bondage of the long exile. His own new Zohar was the final revelation marking the end, and its author the appointed agent of salvation.

Luzzatto cautiously opened himself up to a small circle of youthful friends. Among them was a young man from Vilna, Jekuthiel Gordon, who was studying medicine at the university of Padua. This elated convert spread the news in letters to his home city and to Vienna. Hagiz came to hear of it and forthwith wrote to the rabbis of Venice to suppress the movement before it reached the masses (1729). Luzzatto heeded the counsel of the Venetian rabbinate and wrote to Hagiz directly. He dissociated himself completely from the Sabbatian heresy—he was neither a prophet nor a prophet's son, nor had he worked miracles; by divine grace he had merely been the recipient of revelations. How could a man who was unmarried and resided far away from the Holy Land come to be thus chosen? was the answer of Hagiz. He therefore turned to three other Italian rabbis and prevailed upon several in Germany to pronounce the ban upon any one who wrote in the language of the Zohar and claimed inspiration by angels. Bassan and other emissaries of the rabbinical college at Venice induced Luzzatto to surrender his cabalistic compositions to the custody of his teacher.

Luzzatto now married and settled down to practical affairs. Soon his father met with business reverses, and the son returned to his cabalistic studies. Rumors came to the ears of the Venetian rabbis and they engaged a spy to report the doings of the suspect. Old and new charges were trumped up; the rabbis were irritated particularly with Luzzatto's sharp criticism of Leon Modena's attacks on the Zohar. So the mystic, now no longer a rich man's son, was excommunicated and his writings were condemned to the flames (1734). Luzzatto left wife and children and sought a refuge beyond the Italian home. At Frankfort he was compelled by the rabbi to refrain from teaching the Zohar, but he reserved for himself the right to take up his favorite pursuits again in the Holy Land when he should have passed the age of forty. Should he break his word, the ban against him was to remain in force. Many rabbis of Germany, Poland, Holland, and Denmark agreed to the terms; naturally Hagiz was one of them, so also the young Jacob Emden (p. 593), like his father, the Haham Zebi, a zealot to the core.

At last Luzzatto found rest among the Portuguese of Amsterdam in the hospitable home of the wealthy Moses de Chaves, whose son he tutored. Soon he was in a position to fetch his family and parents from Italy. He still corresponded with his intimate circle at home and admonished them to devote themselves steadfastly to the quest of mystic truth. The consequence was that the rabbis called in all scraps of Luzzatto's writings still in circulation. The author himself produced in the Amsterdam period two other works, each of which left a mark upon succeeding thought and letters, but with cabalistic matter well submerged. The brief essay on true saintliness ('The Path of the Upright') became a favorite pocket-companion with all men striving after the higher life. It starts with the premise that moral conduct is not something naturally given, but rather requires a stupendous effort to overcome all that thwarts it, in short, that it can be acquired only by training and education. While the ordinary methods of bodily mortification are deprecated, great store is set by solitary communion in retiring from the world. Another thought which was developed with far-reaching effect among the new Pietists (p. 585) stresses the point that with the saintly man even his physical performances are invested with sacredness.

The other work ('Unto the Upright, Glory') was an allegorical poem on the occasion of the nuptials of his pupil Jacob de Chaves. There is little of dramatic action in this composition, but deep thoughts are expressed in beautiful diction. The Hebrew language took on a new lease of life, and to Luzzatto must be accorded the distinction of being the father of modern Hebrew literature. The gifted poet was approaching the fortieth year of his life, and he was seized with longing to return to his mystic preoccupations on the sacred soil of Palestine. But scarcely had he and his family set foot upon the Holy Land when they succumbed to the pestilence (1747). The remains of the poet-mystic were interred in Tiberias.

CHAPTER LXXVII

HASIDISM

(1660-1797)

THE death of Charles X. in 1660 enabled Poland to drive back the Muscovite invader; but rebellion at home forced her to conclude peace upon unfavorable terms. She recovered some of her provinces, but she lost a portion of White Russia and all of Little Russia on the eastern bank of the Dnieper, along with the city of Kiev (1667). Podolia and Volhynia thus remained with Poland. The sufferings undergone by the Jews of these regions, however, had left them without recuperative powers, and the center of Jewish life moved northward.

A number of Jewish communities, it is true, were relieved by John Casimir from taxation so as to rehabilitate themselves. The kings who followed immediately, Michael Wisniowecki (1669–1673) and John Sobieski (1674–1696), the heroic deliverer of Vienna, confirmed to the Jews of the kingdom of Poland and the grand duchy of Lithuania their ancient privileges. The Diets, however, were inimical; the administrators of the cities made royal protection nugatory; the students of Jesuit schools frequently made a pastime of attacking Jews in the streets. Many a Jewish community paid an annual tax to the principals of these schools to prevent excesses. In 1687 hundreds of scholars, joined by the street mob, set upon the Jewish quarter of Posen. The Jews, however, defended themselves bravely, and for three successive days a veritable battle raged between the two camps.

It was small gain that the Saxon kings, Augustus II. (1697–1733) and Augustus III. (1733–1763), upon their accession, ratified Jewish rights. The power of the Crown had completely waned; sovereignty was vested in the Diet, and any single deputy could by his veto abruptly terminate the assemblage long before its fixed term had run out. Poland was heading for dissolution; Russia, courted by king and nobles, was tightening the noose about her neck. The Jewish communal organization was in constant perplexity how to meet its debts. The creditors were either brother Jews who sued the delinquent communities in Polish courts, or Polish nobles. What with the regular tax to the Crown, the imposts by local authorities, and the extraordinary 'gifts' to the clergy and Jesuit convents, there was a growing drain upon the communal exchequers. Moreover, the community was corporately answerable for debts of individuals, real or imaginary. Such was the impoverishment that for the sake of economy laws were passed restricting the outlay on family festivities or the annual number of weddings in a community; salaries of religious functionaries were cut. In 1733, the Piarist monks threatened to seize the Great Synagogue in Vilna for arrears. The community was compelled to pawn the Perpetual Lamp of the synagogue, which was not redeemed until 1746.

The head-tax demanded of the corporate Jewish body kept increasing by leaps and bounds. In 1717 it amounted to two hundred and eighty thousand Polish gulden; some fifty years later it rose to more than a million. The treasury could ill afford to have this source of revenue curtailed. In 1740, the nobility proposed a change in their own favor. It was nothing short of making the Jews hereditary subjects of the lord upon whose land they were domiciled, so that their tax would flow into his own coffers. The monstrous resolution failed of being carried. The rural Jews were nevertheless to all intents and purposes the serfs of their landlords. At their whim, the Jews might any day be turned out of the inns they kept, or their license for selling liquors might be revoked. The rents were frequently raised, and woe to the Jew who could not pay, for his children and women would be taken away from him and often enough reared in the Catholic religion.

There was a veritable recrudescence of ritual murder libels, having their origin in the credulity of the Christian masses and being fostered by the clerics for their own purposes. In Sandomir, a Christian woman threw the dead body of her illegitimate child into the courtyard of a Jewish elder. It was the time near Passover (1698). Despite the agitation of Father Szuchovski, the Jew was acquitted by the lower courts; but the cleric had the case brought up again before the tribunal of Lublin and the unfortunate elder was quartered (1710). Szuchovski, with the aid of a converted Jew, Serafinovicz, wrote a libelous book against the Jews (1716). The renegade was summoned by the Jews to a public disputation, but he failed to attend; nevertheless, the slanderous book was republished twice (1738 and 1760). Upon the finding of the dead body of a Christian child in Posen, the rabbi, Loeb Calahora, together with the communal advocate and two elders, was immediately arrested. Steadfastly the victims asserted their innocence; the rabbi and the lay advocate succumbed to the tortures and died in prison (1736). For four years the trial dragged on, until, through the influence of an outside community, it ended in the acquittal of the suspects. The Jews of Posen found themselves saddled with a debt of sixty thousand gulden, and the Council of Four Lands authorized the community to solicit funds in Great Poland, Germany, and Italy.

A similar case at Zaslav in Volhynia (1747) resulted in the gruesome doing to death of religious functionaries and communal elders. For the next ten years there was an almost annual recurrence of ritual murder trials in one place or another. At last the terrorized Jews of Poland found it intolerable that, as soon as the dead body of a Christian was found anywhere, the crime was at once laid at the door of the Jewish people. They accordingly sent Jacob Zelig as their spokesman to Rome to obtain redress from the apostolic see. The Pope, Benedict XIV. (1740–1758), directed Cardinal Ganganelli to take up the matter most seriously. This just prince of the Church obtained a report from the papal nuncio at Warsaw and then prepared an elaborate memorandum which was submitted to the new pope, Clement XIII. (1758–1769). The document deals exhaustively with the entire question of the blood accusation, both in general and in particular, and comes to the conclusion that the charge is unfounded and that it had been condemned by the popes of the Middle Ages, especially by Innocent IV. in the year 1247. Ganganelli urged that steps should be taken to safeguard the Jews of Poland, exactly as those popes had come to the rescue of the Jews of Germany, 'that the name of Christ might no longer be held in dishonor among the Jews and that the difficulties in converting them might not be increased.' In accordance with an order from Rome, the nuncio Visconti at Warsaw informed Brühl, the minister of Augustus III., that 'the Holy See, having latterly examined all the foundations upon which the opinion rests that the Jews use human blood in the preparation of their unleavened bread and for that reason are guilty of the slaughter of Christian children, has concluded that there is no evidence whatsoever to substantiate this prejudice' (1763).

With the progressive impoverishment of Polish Jewry under the heavy communal burden, brought about by the outlay of money, above the regular corporate tax, for defeating calumny, spiritual life was at a low ebb. In the century following the Cossack massacres, the scholastic institutions but slowly regained some of their former vigor. There was a dearth of outstanding scholarly figures. Abraham Gumbiner in Kalisz (died about 1683) wrote a commentary on the first volume of the Code of Karo and Isserles; Jehiel Heilprin in Minsk (died about 1746) was the author of a useful chronicle ('Order of Generations'). A few men took up the study of Hebrew grammar and even of mathematics. Those that wanted to become physicians sought out foreign universities, in Padua or Halle or Frankfort-on-the-Oder. The mental depression drove learners into the mysticism of Luria's school. There was a feeling that the writing of commentaries and supercommentaries on the Codes left the yearning of the soul for simple and direct communion with God unsatisfied. The reaction arose in forlorn Podolia, where Jewish misery was at its worst, and it took on the form of Pietism (Hasidism).

Hasidism was not a sectarian movement, and the Hasidim had not the least intention of forming a sect. There was no attempt to modify cardinal doctrines or to do away with the smallest detail of accepted observance. Rather was the stress laid upon a new method of serving God, and this method addressed itself to the individual concerned with his own personal salvation. The founder of the movement was Israel Baal Shem Tob (or, by abbreviation, Besht; 1700–1760). The title of Baal Shem was given to a man who worked miraculous cures through the Name of God. But the Besht was more than a healer of bodily ailments; he was a physician of the soul. As such he was referred to as the Man of the Good Name, that is, of good and godly repute, and this title he accepted for himself.

Already the child exhibited the traits which marked out the man. Often he would absent himself from school to seek solitude in the woods. As a lad of twelve he took service in the humble capacity of helper to a schoolmaster, his duties consisting in taking children from their homes to school and back. He loved to conduct them to the synagogue and train them to say their Amens dutifully. Later on he did chores for the synagogue sexton; he would be through with his work in a short time, sleep the rest of the day, and then remain awake the whole night studying and praying. Learning was not his *métier*, and he disdained to parade even his meager attainments. He would not undeceive the brother of his intended wife, who insisted that his sister should marry none but a scholar. However, the bride chose to take him as he was, and the couple set off for the Carpathian mountains. There they eked out a living, the man digging up lime and the woman taking the load on a cart to the city. Thus years were passed in close touch with nature.

But the Besht was not satisfied with complete solitude; he formed a circle of devoted disciples. For eleven years he was their guide in the Podolian town Miedzyboz. He wrote no books. He taught by word of mouth, in pithy sententious sayings, in homilies, and in parables. Nor was his activity confined to his immediate disciples, who stored up in their memory the casual remarks and teachings of the beloved master. He was of the people and mixed among them. It was his belief that it was given to the commonest man to find God; for the Deity was diffused through the entire creation. God has willed it that man should serve Him in all manners. There is no place into which God does not enter, no human occupation but is an act of worship. Every movement, every walk, every talk makes an impression in the spiritual world. One may not arrive at the same degree of union with God as another, but then even a worm serves God to the extent of its powers. Sadness is a hindrance to devotion; all worship must be attended by cheerfulness. It were better not to be distracted by the letter of the prayer-book; one should pray with closed eyes. It is a miracle that man comes to life again after right devotion, since one's soul should go out in the passionate absorption in God. Prayer and study are the very food which sustains the angels; devotion creates spiritual values. All service of God must be done with the burning glow of enthusiasm. Thus did the Besht bring to the meanest life a consciousness of spiritual power and make of religion a joyous immersion in the all-pervading, ever-present Godhead. It was a faith in which evil was but a lesser good, earthly beauty a similitude of the heavenly, and all self submerged when nothing but God mattered.

There was about the Besht none of the lugubrious mortifications practised by Luria, nor of his pretensions to Messianic dignity. But when the Besht did discourse on the person of the Messiah, the listeners were able to visualize the Redeemer as if he stood before them in the flesh. Of Sabbatai Zevi the Besht said that there was in him a 'holy spark' and that his downfall was brought about by his vainglory.

A most unholy spark was now being thrown into the smoldering embers of the Sabbatian aberration. Jacob Leibovicz (died 1791) was a Podolian Jew of very slight education. In Turkey, where he was known as Frank (the name applied in the East to Europeans), he associated with the Dönmeh and conceived the notion that he was the reincarnation of Sabbatai and his successors. With the trinitarian formula he returned to Poland. He announced himself as the Second Person of the Trinity, the 'Santo Senior' or Holy Lord, and gathered a circle of followers from both sexes, who under his guidance indulged in licentious orgies. At the instigation of the shocked Jews the police arrested the celebrants; but Frank, having become a Turkish subject, was banished across the border.

A conference of rabbis from the Four Lands met at Brody in 1756, and the Frankists, as the new sect was called, were solemnly excommunicated. At the same time it was decreed that none should study the Zohar or any other cabalistic writings before the age of thirty (and, even after forty, only those who had mastered talmudic studies). Representatives of the sect took their case to the Catholic bishop Dembovski of Kameniec-Podolsk. They presented a confession of faith which came close to Christianity and proclaimed themselves Zoharists who were at war with the Talmud. The bishop summoned the rabbis to answer the charges against the Talmud in a public disputation (summer of 1757). The rabbis lacked the address such as had distinguished the Spanish protagonists of the Talmud in similar tournaments, and thousands of copies of the Talmud were seized and publicly burned.

Dembovski died suddenly in November, 1757. The Frankists, persecuted by the Jews, recalled their leader. They entered into negotiations with the primate of the Polish Church and the papal nuncio with a view to being received into Christianity. A second disputation, presided over by canon Mikolski, was held at Lemberg (July, 1759). Among the Jewish representatives who participated in the religious debate was also the Besht. Energetically did they stand up against the calumny of their sectarian opponents that the Talmud enjoined upon the Jews the use of Christian blood. After the disputation the Frankists submitted to baptism; Frank's conversion was celebrated with pomp at the capital, the king acting as godfather.

But soon it came to the ears of the clergy that the trinitarian conceptions of the converts were not those of genuine Christianity and that the leader was still regarded by the sect as the Messiah. Frank was arrested and imprisoned in

the citadel of Czenstochova (1760). There he remained for
thirteen years, his followers looking upon his imprisonment
as a necessary part of his Messianic career, of the kind it had
fallen to Sabbatai to go through. They named the place of
detention mystically 'The Gates of Rome' and regarded 'the
religion of Edom,' Christianity, as the portal through which
the Messiah must pass. The 'Holy Lord,' who was bent upon
doing away with all moral restraints, was released by the
Russian commander on the eve of the first partition of
Poland. For nearly twenty years he carried on the cult of
self-deification in Moravia and Germany, as Baron von
Frank in Offenbach. The swindle was continued by his
daughter Eve till 1817.

The fate of Poland had been sealed by the intrigues of
Russia and Prussia. At the dictation of these two powerful
neighbors, the Poles elected for their king in 1764 Stanislav
Poniatovski, the former favorite of Catharine II. (1762–
1796). King and Diet were desirous of maintaining the power
of the Catholic Church, but were compelled to acquiesce in
repealing all laws against the dissidents (1767). The Confederation of Bar (1768), formed by the nobles to restore the
supremacy of Roman Catholicism, only served to unleash
the fury of the Greek Orthodox Ukrainian peasants against
Poles and Jews, and the atrocities of 1648 were repeated in
Podolia. By royal act (1764), the Council of the Four Lands
had ceased to exist. The uprooting of the Jewish communities, thus coming on top of the disruption of the internal
organization, contributed to the hold which Hasidism obtained on the minds of the Jews and its spread beyond its
original home.

The mantle of the founder had fallen upon the 'Preacher
of Mezdyrzecz,' Dob Baer (1710–1772), who by his talmudic
learning won over adherents from among the scholarly elements. The cult of the leader, the Zaddik (the Righteous
One), was developed to its ultimate consequences by one of
the pupils, Elimelech of Lizensk. The Zaddik was conceived
as the intermediary between God and man, a sort of Super-
man, possessed of miraculous gifts which were inherited by

the son from the father. Thus came about the dynasties of Zaddikim, who were visited by pilgrims from the district where they held sway. A more rational spirit dominated the Hasidim in the northern provinces, in Lithuania, where the movement made but slow progress, and in the adjoining eastern territory which since the first partition of Poland (1772) had been annexed by Russia.

The leader of the intellectual Hasidim, or the votaries of Habad (abbreviation for Hokmah, Binah, Deah, 'Wisdom, Understanding, Knowledge'), was another disciple of Baer's school, the learned Shneor Zalman of Liady (1747–1812). It is told of him that when praying he would address God thus: 'Lord of the world, I desire neither thy Garden of Eden (Heaven) nor Thy future world; I desire Thee, Thyself.' As the movement invaded the north, the antagonism of the opponents (protestants, Mithnaggedim) grew stronger. The Hasidim had adopted the Sephardic ritual of Luria, and their method of devotion contrasted with the sober conduct of prayer among the majority. Communities were frequently disrupted and violent quarrels followed. The citadel of opposition was Vilna, a city renowned for its learned men, of whom it now harbored the greatest.

Elijah son of Solomon of Vilna (1720–1797), the glory of eastern Jewry to whom he was simply the Gaon of Vilna, held no official position in the community. His sole occupation was to study by day and far into the night, and to teach a small body of mature students for an hour or two. He lived practically in this house of study, which was fitted up as a place of worship; there he performed his devotions most punctiliously, but with the least loss of time in transition to his appointed task for the long day. At intervals only he would repair to his home and children, both in the care of an understanding wife. Into her hands the community dropped a small allowance; the master himself was ascetically abstemious.

Nor would he suffer his time to be frittered away by communal activity. There were other learned men to attend to judicial functions, but he could not be lured away from his vocation, which was to go over and over again the whole ground of Jewish literature and to jot down illuminating annotations or to dictate longer expositions. By his mastery of the entire body of Jewish lore he was able to produce parallels from remote corners and set aright many a fault in the ordinary prints. He was averse to the display of acumen; the simple sense, by no means always on the surface, engaged his full attention. For days, for weeks he would labor to solve a puzzle; he would partake of no food and bring himself to the verge of illness. Suddenly, through converse with a visiting pupil—for 'two are better than one'—the solution would flash upon his mind and master and student would be happy together. Often an illuminating thought would come to him during his devotions and just as quickly pass out of his mind while he was chiding himself for the unseemly interruption; and his heart would overflow with gratitude to God when the find came back again.

From his teacher Moses Margalioth he learned early to draw within the range of his studies the much neglected Palestinian Talmud. Diligently he read and reread the Scriptures; he wrote commentaries on difficult books and even a concise grammar of the Hebrew language. He knew mathematics and astronomy and turned these sciences to good use in elucidating difficult sections of the Mishnah. He was sovereign in his wide domain, taking frequently an independent view; the ultimate source was paramount, in accordance with which he corrected misusages of long standing. He was a student, with a fame extending beyond his own city; as such he was revered, but at the same time men honored in this intellectual giant the man of saintly conduct, the man who realized in himself the ideal of the Jewish saint.

Such a man could not but look with misgivings upon the Hasidic type of piety which often exhausted itself in externals and seemed to disparage learning. It was against his wont to meddle with public concerns; but it was a time 'when the Torah was made void' and he gave his approval to the forcible procedure of the rabbinical council against the local Hasidim (1772). He issued a manifesto against the Hasidim, signed also by the head of the Vilna rabbinate, in 1781, when Jacob Joseph Cohen published the first manual embodying the Besht's teachings, with its overt attacks on mere learning. The writ was sent to an assembly of rabbis meeting at Zelva and steps were taken to sever all connections with the Hasidim, who were to be expelled from the communities and treated to all intents and purposes as beyond the pale of Judaism.

By the second and third partition of Poland (1793, 1795) the whole of Lithuania with Volhynia and Podolia went to Russia. It was therefore to the Russian government that the Lithuanian Jews, exasperated by the insulting behavior of the Hasidim upon the death of the Gaon (1797), turned with denunciation of the teachers of heresy. Shneor Zalman was twice haled to St. Petersburg (1798, 1800), but each time released since the examination convinced the authorities that his religious teachings were harmless so far as the government was concerned. Each of the two protagonists, the Gaon and the Hasidic leader, left his mark upon the life of Russian Jewry, at a time when in the West the old order was being completely transformed.

CHAPTER LXXVIII

THE JEWS OF PRUSSIA

(1671-1786)

SINCE the Peace of Westphalia (1648) the German empire had become a loose confederation of some three hundred independent principalities and free cities. From certain of these territories the Jews had long been expelled; in others their number was exceedingly small, and in none were they more than tolerated. During the eighteenth century their residence in any part or place was not a matter of right, but of privilege, for which an annual protection-tax was paid. If they traveled from one principality to another or from city to city within the same dominion, they were subjected at every border and at the gate of every town to a body-tax. In the cities they were confined to a circumscribed area, the ghetto or the Jews' quarter, often consisting of one narrow street, in which, as in a few of the larger cities, sometimes as many as five hundred families were crowded together. From the degrading body-tax only certain highly privileged Jews were exempt, but even these, so soon as they set their foot beyond the principality in which the privilege had been acquired, were compelled to pay the obligatory toll even for transient residence.

In each family only one of the sons was permitted to abide in his birthplace; if there were daughters, it was fortunate if they could be married into families possessing the right of residence. A permit, heavily taxed, was required for entrance upon the matrimonial state, and it was granted only to one member in a family. For each child born a special tax was exacted. The principal care of the government was that the Jewish population should be kept to a restricted number which should not be exceeded. It made no difference that families were disrupted and children had to be sent away from the parental roof to such localities as might tolerate their presence or to other countries. But even the reduced families had great hardship in sustaining themselves. The Jew was kept from husbandry; he could not own land; he was excluded from the guilds. Nothing remained for him but petty trade, and what little money he made was lent out on interest, since it could not be invested by the owner in productive industry. Socially the Jews were thrown upon their own; they spoke a corrupt dialect; they were the butt of their Christian neighbors. When a Christian walking in the street met a Jew, no matter how cultured, he would cry out: 'Jew, where are your manners?' (Mach Mores, Jud!), and off went the Jew's hat in humble salutation.

Conditions were much the same in Frankfort or in Hamburg, in Vienna or in Prague, or in the young community of Berlin. The first residents admitted to his capital by the Great Elector, Frederick William (1640–1688), were the Veit and Ries families with their relatives, Austrian Jews from among those that had been exiled from Vienna by the emperor Leopold I. in 1670. It is true that there had been living in Berlin just one Jew, Israel Aaron, purveyor to the elector's army. This specially favored contractor stipulated that the incoming Jews should be well-situated financially and in no wise compete with him in his business. The decree of admission was signed May 21, 1671, fifty families being permitted to settle in the Mark for twenty years. They were granted freedom of commerce and the right to buy or rent houses. Other Jews filtered in, though they had no residence permits. Stringent measures were taken against the new-comers, but the influx continued. By the beginning of the eighteenth century the number of Jewish families in Berlin had risen to seventy. Jost Liebmann, master of the mint to the Great Elector and court jeweler, and his wife, Israel Aaron's widow, were in high favor with Frederick III. (or Frederick the First, as he was called after his coronation as king of Prussia in 1701). Up to 1712, when the foundation was laid for the first public synagogue (it was dedicated in 1714), only private houses of worship had been permitted.

The king acted justly enough when two baptized Jews charged their former coreligionists with blaspheming the founder of Christianity in the concluding prayer of their daily devotions (the Adoration, Alenu). He solicited the opinion of the Halle theologian, Johann Heinrich Michaelis, and since it was favorable to the Jews he cleared them of the charge which, though not new, was unfounded. On the other hand, the king was instrumental in the reprinting of a book which teemed with accusations against the Jews, on the plea that similar works had appeared lately and in no wise hurt the Jews. Moreover, to the royal mind the book was no more than a defense of Christianity intended to prevent apostasy to Judaism. The publication served in the hands of clerical Anti-Semites in the nineteenth century as a convenient source for their vituperations of Jews and Judaism. The author was Johann Andreas Eisenmenger (died 1704), and the work bore the title 'Judaism Uncovered' (Entdecktes Judentum). It was first published in Frankfort-on-the-Main (1700); through the influence of the Jews, especially of the banker Samuel Oppenheim in Vienna, the entire issue was confiscated by imperial order. The author offered to destroy the edition if the Jews paid him thirty thousand thalers. After Eisenmenger's death, the Prussian king supported his heirs in their attempt to print the book; the imperial ban was, of course, inoperative in Prussian Königsberg where the book appeared in 1711.

The rise of Prussia to the level of a Great Power and, in rivalry with Austria, to a dominant position in Germany was the work of Frederick William I. (1713–1740) and still more so of his son, Frederick II., or the Great (1740–1786). During the reign of the father, Prussian Protestantism had a strong pietistic tendency favored by the king; the son, 'the philosopher on the throne,' the friend of Voltaire, was not exactly pious. Both were strict autocrats, and for religious minorities, such as Catholics or Jews, there was no question of equality with members of the Established Church of the kingdom. Jewish affairs were under the control of the home ministry which was also the department of the treasury, and officials of this body were charged with carrying out the draconic legislation of 1750. The Jews of the kingdom were either of the protected class (Schutzjuden) or merely tolerated (geduldete Juden). There were three kinds of protected Jews: those who had a general privilege covering all the members of a family and entitling them to unrestricted residence and trade; ordinary protected Jews with limited rights of residence and occupation, inheritable only by one or at the most two children; extraordinary protected Jews, like physicians, artists, and other professionals, whose limited rights of residence did not pass on to their children. Religious functionaries, the younger children of ordinary and all children of extraordinary protected Jews, domestics and so on, belonged to the merely tolerated class and for one thing could not contract marriages outside their own class, lest by so doing they might raise themselves into the order of the privileged.

By special royal patent, in 1763, there was advanced to the status of a protected Jew one who in the short space of twenty years had made for himself a name in the literary circles at home and abroad. Moses son of Menahem (Mendel) Mendelssohn (1729–1786) was born in Dessau, where his father was a humble writer of Torah scrolls. Like his contemporary, the Gaon of Vilna, Mendelssohn had the good fortune of being trained early by a scholar who also took up the study of the Palestinian Talmud. David Fränkel (1704–1762) was rabbi in Dessau until 1742, when he was called to the rabbinate of his native Berlin. A year later the master was rejoined by his pupil, who gained admission to the city after paying at the gate the obligatory toll. Again, like his Vilna contemporary, Mendelssohn was drawn to the study of mathematics, into which he was initiated by a learned Polish Jew, Israel Zamosz (died 1772). But from this point on Mendelssohn proceeded to a career which was impossible at that time in the Lithuanian bulwark of traditionalism and, had it at all been possible, was farthest from the mentality of the Vilna saint.

Traditionalism was clearly on the wane in the capital of Frederick II. Elsewhere in Germany Judaism was still moving in its beaten tracks. Cultural conditions were much the same as in eastern Europe, whence at least four out of the five leading talmudists in the second half of the century hailed. In Frankfort, Worms and then again in Frankfort, after holding positions in Berlin and Metz, officiated Jacob Joshua Falk (1680–1756), famous for his commentaries on the Talmud. A great celebrity was the rabbi of Prague, Ezekiel Landau (1713–1793), whose responsa still enjoy authority. From a minor position in the Bohemian capital Jonathan Eybeschütz (1690–1764) advanced to the rabbinate of Metz and in 1750 was installed as chief rabbi of the three communities Altona, Hamburg, and Wandsbeck; from 1776 to 1799 the same position was held by Raphael Cohen (died 1803). Jacob Emden (1697–1776), who resided in his birthplace Altona as a private man, was the only scholar of German nativity. We have seen (p. 576) how he displayed against Luzzatto the zealot disposition which he inherited from his father. The coming of Eybeschütz to the communities once ministered to by the Haham Zebi was the cause of opening up another feud in which the son's talents for heresy-hunting found ample scope.

It happened that a number of women had died in childbirth, and the new rabbi was requested to supply amulets to ward off the danger. He had done so previously in other communities. These amulets were written in cipher; it was claimed in circles unfriendly to the rabbi that the reading yielded formulae in which Sabbatai Zevi figured as the Messiah. One of the amulets was shown to Emden, who had himself aspired to the position obtained by Eybeschütz, and he pronounced the writer, whoever he might be, a Sabbatian. For this temerity the elders of the community, who sided with their rabbi, gave orders to close Emden's private synagogue. Emden entered into correspondence with a number of German rabbis, who were all outspoken enemies of Eybeschütz, and secured from them statements derogatory to the rabbi. The elders of the Altona congregation became exceedingly threatening, and Emden was compelled to flee to Amsterdam (1751).

From there he brought charges against his enemies before the Danish courts, for Altona was then under the control of Denmark. The courts ordered all hostile action against Emden to be stopped. The Hamburg senate likewise interposed to make an end of the disturbance, and suspended the suspected rabbi. The feud divided the community, Emden having in the meantime returned. On both sides pamphlets were published, incriminations by Emden and his party and defenses by Eybeschütz and his friends. A former pupil of the rabbi, who had since been converted to Christianity, Carl Anton, professor of Hebrew at Helmstedt, wrote an apology (1752). Eybeschütz himself published letters from his admirers denouncing the charges as slanderous (1755). The rabbi was restored to his position and permitted to end his years in peace. It was not certain that the amulets had been correctly deciphered or who really wrote them. At all events, this was the last echo of the Sabbatian heresy.

In Berlin there was a moving away from orthodoxy. In well-to-do Jewish families there began to manifest itself a hankering after the manners of Christian society, but also a desire for culture. It was from the son of one of these families, Aaron Solomon Gumperz, that young Mendelssohn received lessons in French and English; another friend taught him Latin. The student's years of privation were ended when in 1750 a rich silk-manufacturer, Isaac Bernhard, engaged him as tutor to his children and four years later as his bookkeeper, then subsequently as manager of the business. While conscientiously fulfilling his duties, Mendelssohn continued his studies unceasingly, perfecting himself in letters and philosophy. His first literary effort was produced under the stimulus of Lessing. A warm friendship united the dramatist and critic, who appreciated classicism in poetry and art and humanism in religion, to the Jewish thinker who expressed himself so lucidly in German on esthetics and metaphysics. Thus Mendelssohn was brought together with the circle which included the rationalist Nicolai and the leaders in the movement known as 'Aufklärung' with its revolt against all beliefs and institutions untried by human reason.

When in 1761 Mendelssohn visited Hamburg, he found many admirers both among Jews and Christians; Eybeschütz wrote him a very flattering letter. In Hamburg Mendelssohn met the lady who consented to become his wife. On his return to Berlin he handed in an essay upon a metaphysical theme proposed by the Berlin Academy of Sciences, and the paper was awarded the first prize, above the compositions of two other writers, one of whom was none other than the Königsberg philosopher Immanuel Kant. It was this distinction that won for him the privileged status which rendered his residence in the capital free from police interference. The Jewish community honored him by exempting him from the payment of taxes. After the victory at Leuthen (1757), Mendelssohn prepared the German sermon which the rabbi, his teacher David Fränkel, read in the synagogue; so also after the conclusion of the Seven Years' War by the Peace of Hubertusburg (1763). When Jewish communities in Switzerland and in Saxony were threatened with expulsion, they appealed to the sage of Berlin to use his influence in Christian circles on their behalf.

In Mendelssohn's house, as in the homes of many other Jews of the upper classes, the children spoke the German language instead of the corrupt dialect with its mixture of old German and Hebrew used by the ordinary denizen of the ghetto. The improvement of the speech was the first step in preparing the Jews of German lands for entry into the life about them. By his translation of the Pentateuch into German, printed in Hebrew characters, begun in 1778 and completed in 1783, Mendelssohn pursued a twofold purpose. On the one hand, by habituating Jewish students to the use of German in rendering the Scriptures, it was easy to foresee that they would be led further to the reading of German literature; as a matter of fact, Mendelssohn's translation served as a First German Reader. On the other hand, the new translation and the accompanying Hebrew commentary were conceived in a rational spirit, with stress on the Bible as literature to be esthetically enjoyed. Thus in both respects a far-reaching change in the education of the

Jewish child, so utterly at variance with the methods in vogue, was being promoted. It is not to be wondered at that the guardians of traditionalism, in Prague, Altona, Frankfort, and Fürth, put the translation under the ban. The spiritual authorities of Berlin were more lenient. When, at Mendelssohn's suggestion, the Jewish Free School was opened in the Prussian capital (1781), the curriculum comprised in addition to the Jewish subjects (Bible and Talmud) also the study of German and French.

These internal adjustments to the new age were to pave the way for an improvement in the political and civic conditions of the Jewish people. Lessing had just given to the world in his play 'Nathan the Wise' (1779) the Gospel of Tolerance, and its central figure, as everybody knew, was modeled after his Jewish philosopher-friend. The Jews of Alsace were preparing to lay a petition before the French council of state (p. 608); they asked Mendelssohn to write it for them. At Mendelssohn's request, Christian Wilhelm Dohm, a Prussian councilor of state, published a direct plea for Jewish emancipation (1781). He dealt at length with the miserable conditions of Jewry and argued that if the Jews had faults these were the result of Christian oppression. It was in the interest of every state—and happy the first state that undertook it!—to turn their Jewish subjects into useful and contented citizens.

A beginning in this direction, but only a beginning, was made by Emperor Joseph II. with his Patent of Tolerance (January 2, 1782). There was no thought of placing the Jews of Austria on a civic parity with Christians. The old restrictions of residence still remained in force, and the Jews of Vienna constituted so many tolerated families, but in no wise a community. However, some measure of relief did come to the Jews. For one thing, the offensive body-tax was abolished. In the same way the old rules, which held the Jews to a distinctive dress or forbade their appearance in the streets on the forenoons of Christian festivals, were done away with. Permission was granted to the Jews to engage in commerce on a large scale and to open factories. Jews were free to learn any kind of a trade from Christian masters, but without the right of being called masters themselves. Jews might send their children to the public schools or open similar establishments of their own; Jewish students were to be admitted freely to colleges and universities. The purpose of the whole legislation was avowedly to break down from above Jewish separatism. The Jews were ordered to make use of the German language in their bookkeeping and business correspondence. The state furthermore insisted on its own control of the laws of marriage and divorce to which the rabbis must in the last instance submit.

The complete revolution in the education of the Jewish child contemplated by the emperor was acclaimed by Mendelssohn's circle. Naphthali Herz (Hartwig) Wessely (1725–1805), who collaborated with Mendelssohn in the Hebrew commentary accompanying the German translation of the Pentateuch, was convinced that curriculum and method of instruction for Jewish children must conform to the practical needs of the new generation. It was not possible for all to become proficient in Talmud; the greater number must be taught a trade. Moreover, it was necessary that Jewish school children should have a knowledge of the elementary sciences, history, and geography, and above all learn to speak and write the German language correctly. He himself had through business associations with Christians in his native city Copenhagen and by dint of private industry acquired a store of secular learning. Hebrew poet that he was, he was a stickler for purity of language and for a rational understanding of the Scriptures along the lines of grammatical rules. Wessely enthusiastically welcomed the educational reforms to which Joseph II. gave the force of law and urged their acceptance in a series of epistles to his people. In Triest, where the majority of Jews were of Italian or Portuguese descent, there was immediate readiness to open a school according to the new plan. At the other end of the Austrian dominions, in Galicia, which since 1772 had been joined to them, there was consternation. In his rescript of 1788, the emperor had made it plain that the Jews must divest themselves of such of their laws and customs as ran counter to the imperial legislation. While the Italian rabbis sided with Wessely, others, among them Ezekiel Landau of Prague, were decidedly hostile to all innovations which, they instinctively felt, would break down traditional Jewish life.

The symptoms of such a breakdown were beginning to manifest themselves in Berlin, and it was only through the efforts of representative laymen that Hirschel, the rabbi of the community, was dissuaded from joining in the protest against Wessely. Mendelssohn was concerned with the principle of abstract freedom: 'in these days' one should be free to publish one's honest opinions without let or hindrance. He as well as Wessely conformed in their religious practices; but about them men and women were casting off the 'yoke of the Law.' As in Alexandria in the times of Philo, so in Berlin during Mendelssohn's period, the question was mooted whether the old laws were still binding. Dohm had advocated that the Jewish 'colony' in the Prussian state should have complete autonomy within, with powers to expel recalcitrant, non-conforming members. Mendelssohn energetically opposed the right of excommunication. Ecclesiastical law, he claimed, was contradictory to the nature of religion.

Religion with him was concentrated in eternal truths, which one cannot be commanded to believe since one must necessarily believe them from proof by reason. Judaism, he maintained, is really no religion at all; it has no dogmas. Judaism is a revealed legislation. At a given time God made His voice to be heard and gave Israel specific commandments. These commandments must be obeyed. Of course, some of these, being merely national, ceased to be operative at the destruction of the Temple. Religious infractions were no longer state offenses; no punishment, no penance could come to the sinner except what he voluntarily takes upon himself. The Jews should comply with the customs and the civil constitution of the countries in which they dwell, and at the same time be constant to the religion of their forefathers. 'Indeed, I do not see how those who were born in the house of Jacob can, in any conscientious manner, disencumber themselves of the law. . . . Personal commandments, duties which were imposed on a son of Israel, without any consideration of the Temple service or landed property in Palestine, must be observed until it shall please the Most High to make our conscience easy by loudly and openly proclaiming their abrogation.' If emancipation cannot be obtained except by breaking those laws which are still binding, the Jews will renounce emancipation. But if, as is evident, manifoldness is the design and end favored by Providence, every one in the state who is obedient to civil government ought to be free to pray to God after his own fashion or after that of his forefathers.

Thus wrote Mendelssohn in his 'Jerusalem' (1783). The programme was clear: civic emancipation and fidelity to Judaism. How far the two things could be made to go together, in the opinion of the Jews and of the world, is the question that determined the latest phase of Jewish history which, for Europe, began with the French Revolution and, for America, with the Declaration of Independence.

BOOK V

THE AGE OF EMANCIPATION

(1787-1925)

CHAPTER LXXIX

JEWS IN AMERICA IN COLONIAL AND
REVOLUTIONARY TIMES

(1654-1790)

A T the outbreak of the Revolutionary War in 1775, Jewish communities were to be found in the colonies of Rhode Island, New York, Pennsylvania, South Carolina, and Georgia, with smaller units in some of the other colonies. By extraction the majority were Portuguese Jews, who came from Holland and Dutch Brazil in the seventeenth century, or from England in the eighteenth; as early as the beginning of the latter century they were joined by Jews from Germany and Poland. The Portuguese Jews left their impress upon the communal organization; the Sephardic rite obtained in the congregations, though Ashkenazic Jews had a place in the administration.

The first Jew to settle on Manhattan Island was Jacob Barsimson from the Netherlands (August, 1654). A month later a group of twenty-three, 'poor and healthy,' were landed in what was then New Amsterdam. They had sailed along with their brethren and other Dutch subjects from Pernambuco after its reconquest by the Portuguese; but their vessel was captured by Spanish pirates. A French man-of-war, the St. Charles, rescued the passengers and brought them to New Netherland. Peter Stuyvesant, governor since 1647, austere and inflexible, was not at all pleased with the accession to the colony of 'hateful enemies and blasphemers of the name of Christ.' But the Dutch West India Company, which counted among its shareholders a number of Jews, thought it unfair to exclude the Jews who had sustained considerable loss in the taking of Brazil. So they were allowed to remain, with the proviso that, 'the poor among them should not become a burden to the company or to the community, but be supported by their own nation.'

At every step the small group, slightly enlarged by fresh arrivals from Amsterdam, encountered difficulties at the hands of unfriendly magistrates. But they persevered sturdily. A more cordial reception was accorded the fifteen Jewish families from Holland that are said to have settled in Newport in 1658, augmented later by arrivals from Curaçao. In the Colony of Rhode Island, founded by Roger Williams, religious liberty was complete, and no other test was demanded than obedience to His Majesty's laws. Liberty of conscience was also granted by the English when they succeeded to the Dutch possessions in 1664, and it was incorporated as a principle in the constitution drawn up by William Penn for the colony named after him (Pennsylvania, 1682). Nevertheless, in New York, as New Netherland had been renamed, it was not possible for a Jew to become naturalized up to 1727, when it was no longer obligatory to take the oath 'upon the true faith of a Christian.' By a decree of the Assembly of New York, in 1737, Jews were debarred from voting for members of that body. They were also restricted in retail trading, while those who engaged in wholesale commerce were required to obtain the governor's consent.

Professing Jews do not seem to have gained a foothold at an early date in Puritan Massachusetts. Judah Monis (died 1764), who drifted to Boston in 1715, accepted Christianity in 1722 and was appointed instructor in Hebrew at Harvard College. This post he held for forty years; the first Hebrew Grammar published in America (1735) was his work. Nor were conditions favorable in Maryland; Jacob (John) Lumbrozo, who as early as 1656 practised medicine there, was tried and convicted for denial of the divinity of Jesus and restored to liberty only upon Richard Cromwell's accession to the English protectorate. No difficulties were experienced by some forty well-to-do Jews who were sent from London to Georgia in the very year of the colony's foundation (1733), because James Edward Oglethorpe, director of the colony, befriended them. In 1741 all but three families removed to Charleston in South Carolina and formed the nucleus of a settlement.

From the first, wherever Jews were domiciled, plots were secured for burial purposes. Religious services were conducted at the inception in private dwellings or in small rented quarters; the prayers were read by laymen. But soon congregations were organized and permanent synagogue structures erected. The congregation Shearith (Sheerith) Israel, 'The Remnant of Israel,' in New York, dates its existence from 1655; its first public synagogue was consecrated April 6, 1730. The minister was Moses Lopez de Fonseca, and under his supervision special functionaries watched over the supply of ritually prepared ('kasher') meat for the congregants. The Jews of Savannah, Georgia, immediately upon settling, organized the congregation Mikveh Israel, 'The Hope of Israel'; a similarly named congregation had its beginnings in Philadelphia about 1740; Beth Elohim, 'The House of God,' was formed at Charleston in 1750; the synagogue Jeshuath Israel, 'The Salvation of Israel,' at Newport, was erected in 1763 for a congregation which had existed since 1658.

The commercial activities of the Jews during the colonial period were varied and often on a large scale. These merchants exported wheat and imported tobacco and slaves; others did business in their counting-houses as brokers. Jacob Bueno was commended by the Earl of Bellomont (died 1701) for helping him in matters of colonial finance. Jacob Franks was the king's fiscal agent for the northern colonies; with his son David, who resided in Philadelphia, he supplied the army with provisions during the French and Indian War which ended in the acquisition by the British Crown of Canada and the French possessions east of the Mississippi (1763). Franks took a warm interest in his own congregation at New York, but Trinity Church was also indebted to him for his substantial liberality. Hayman Levy (died 1789) was the owner of a privateer and engaged in the fur trade. Of Aaron Lopez at Newport, Ezra Stiles, subsequently president of Yale College, said that 'for honor and extent of commerce, he was probably surpassed by no merchant of America.' Stiles was also on intimate terms with

Hayim Isaac Carregal, of Hebron, who visited Newport in 1773 and preached to the congregation in Spanish. Isaac Miranda (died 1733), 'apostate Jew or fashionable Christian proselyte,' of Lancaster, Pennsylvania, rose to the position of a judge in the Court of Vice-Admiralty. At Philadelphia, David Franks (1720–1793) enjoyed high standing in commercial and social circles; in 1748 he was a member of the provincial assembly. The two brothers, Bernard (died 1801) and Michael (died 1806) Gratz, traded with the Indians and supplied the government with Indian goods, thus opening the western lands to settlers from the Atlantic seaboard. Benjamin Sheftall and his son Mordecai (died 1797), prominent merchants in Savannah, were members of the Union Society for the education of orphan children founded by five different religious denominations.

In the preliminary actions which led to rupture with England as well as in the war itself, Jews took part along with other Americans, whether as merchants joining in the boycott against English goods or as soldiers in the ranks, commissioned officers, and diplomatic agents. Some Jews, as some of the people in general, were on the side of the loyalists; but the majority were true to the patriot cause. The Declaration of Independence (July 4, 1776), written by Thomas Jefferson, put it down as a truth self-evident that all men are created equal and endowed with certain inalienable rights. The Constitution of the United States of America, which was accepted definitively by the thirteenth of the original states in 1790, ordained that no religious test should be required as a qualification to any office or public trust under the United States. The First Amendment of 1791 prescribed that Congress should make no law respecting an establishment of religion, or prohibiting the free exercise thereof.

During the prosecution of the war, when there was great difficulty in raising money, and many of the public men were without funds, the game was pretty nearly up, to use the language of Washington, unless money and men were at once made available. Robert Morris, the Superintendent of

Finance, was 'the financier of the Revolution.' Among the men on whom Morris relied for the supply of large amounts was Haym Salomon, a Polish Jew in the banking business in Philadelphia.

The British occupation of New York led to an exodus of patriot Jews to Philadelphia. Similarly, there assembled in Philadelphia Jews who had fled from Charleston, Richmond, Savannah, and smaller localities. All these temporary residents worshiped in Mikveh Israel, Gershom Mendes Seixas (1745–1816), of the New York congregation, acting as minister. The crowding made it advisable to build a more commodious place of worship; the new edifice was dedicated September 13, 1782. At the close of the war, Seixas returned to New York, where he resumed his ministry at Shearith Israel. He represented his people with dignity; in 1787 he became a trustee of Columbia College and his name appeared among the incorporators of that institution of learning.

The Philadelphia congregation took the lead (December 13, 1790) in tendering to President Washington, on its own behalf as well as in the name of the sister congregations of New York, Savannah, and Richmond, an address of congratulation. In his reply, George Washington dwelt on the liberality of sentiment of religious denominations in the country 'standing unparalleled in the history of nations.' The congregations at Newport and Charleston also tendered addresses to the first chief magistrate.

CHAPTER LXXX

JEWISH EMANCIPATION IN FRANCE AND
FRENCH DEPENDENCIES

(1787-1811)

JEWISH emancipation in Europe was achieved first in France, but by no means with that ease with which it fell into the lap of the Jews on the other side of the ocean. For one thing, the Jewish population of France was more numerous, counting some fifty thousand souls. The great majority—four-fifths—were living in the eastern and northern provinces, Alsace and Lorraine, under economic and legal restrictions similar to those prevailing in Germany, from which that territory had been wrested (1648-1678). In Strassburg, no Jew had been permitted to live since 1388. In 1767, Cerf (Herz) Berr (1730-1793) was allowed to stay in the city during the winter and, from 1771 on, permanently. In France proper, there were colonies of Portuguese Jews in Bordeaux, Bayonne, Marseilles; these had come as Maranos and then gradually reverted to Judaism, but being wealthy they were not molested. In 1723, they received royal letters patent, legalizing their residence. A small number had found their way to Paris, the well-to-do Portuguese being tolerated by the police, while the poorer Alsatians or Germans were subjected to periodic expulsions.

Before the Revolution had set in, efforts were made by the Jews to secure an amelioration in their condition in view of the edict of 1787 which conferred a small measure of toleration on the Protestants. It was on this occasion that Cerf Berr procured, through the agency of Mendelssohn, Dohm's treatise (p. 596). With Cerf Berr were associated other representatives from Alsace and, on the side of the Sephardim, Abraham Furtado (1756-1816) and David Gradis. But the royal commission, presided over by Malesherbes, was not ready for so radical a reform as Jewish emancipation.

When the States General were convoked in 1789, a few of the Sephardic Jews were among the electors of Bordeaux; Gradis lacked but a small number of votes to be chosen as a deputy. The deputies of Paris in particular were instructed to bring up the question of Jewish rightlessness. On the other hand, in Alsace, among the clergy and nobility, but also among the burghers of Strassburg, there was pronounced hostility to the Jews and a clamor for further restrictions. The growth of the Jewish population was to be curbed; the very existence of the Jewish people was considered a public calamity. The Jews, led by Cerf Berr, held a meeting of their own communal representatives, at which extremely modest demands were prepared. At the very moment when the Bastille had fallen (July 14) and the Jews of Paris and Bordeaux were enlisting in the National Guard, agrarian riots broke out in Alsace. The peasants destroyed the castles and estates of the nobles and pillaged Jewish dwellings. More than a thousand Jews abandoned their homes and fled for safety to Basel.

The Declaration of the Rights of Man and of Citizens in the Constituent Assembly (August 26–November 3), with conscious leaning on the American Declaration of Independence (1776) and Constitution of 1787, established the principle of religious freedom. But the logical consequences in favor of the Jews were not immediately drawn. Complete emancipation was advocated by such able friends of the Jews as Count Mirabeau, who during his travels in Prussia had met the cultured circles of Berlin Jewry; the abbé Gregoire; the Protestant pastor Rabaud-Saint-Etienne; Clermont-Tonnerre; and Robespierre. But against them were arrayed the Alsatian deputy Rewbell, La Fare (the bishop of Nancy), and the abbé Maury. So after many debates decision was postponed (December 22).

The Jews of southern France determined to forward their own interests. A petition signed by two hundred and fifteen heads of families in Bordeaux was favorably reported on by

Bishop Talleyrand, and the Jews of Portuguese extraction and those of Avignon, previously under the Holy See but now preparing to be united to France, were declared full citizens (January 28, 1790). Young Parisian Jews, members of the National Guard, among them a learned Jew from Poland, Zalkind Hourwitz (died 1812), of the Oriental division of the Royal Library and an ardent supporter of the Revolution, appealed to the Paris Commune. The advocate Godard sponsored their earnest pleas; fifty-three out of sixty districts voted in favor of the enfranchisement of all French Jews. Abbé Merlot presented the address of the Commune before the National Assembly (February 25), but the enemies of the Jews brought about another delay. At last, the opposition was overcome. On September 28, 1791, on the motion of Duport, a decree was promulgated granting the Jews of all France complete civic rights on a par with other citizens.

The Jews were exuberant in their gratitude. Enthusiastically they threw themselves into the progress of the Revolution; they volunteered for service and gave freely of their means for the defense of the young republic battling for its existence against the armies of the allied monarchs of Europe (1792–1793). The intoxication turned the heads of the Jews. Jewish teachers led their pupils to the 'Temples of Reason'; Jewish deputations effusively compared the new laws of the Mountain, as the advanced Jacobins were called, with the ancient law given on Mount Sinai; Jewish 'priests' vied with the ecclesiastics who abjured Christianity, acknowledging the God of freedom and the religion of equality. The Republican Calendar, with its system of every tenth day as a feast, made the observance of the sabbath a misdemeanor; difficulty was experienced in procuring unleavened bread for Passover; extremists agitated to have the Abrahamic rite prohibited by law.

Religious compulsion abated with the introduction by Robespierre of the deistic cult of the Supreme Being (1794). But the reign of Terror continued its bloody work. On the least suspicion of falling short of red radicalism, Jews shared the fate of other Frenchmen who languished in dungeons or fell under the guillotine. The moderate forces at last gained ground under the Directory (1795–1799). Meanwhile France, no longer content with safeguarding its own territory, was waging an aggressive war beyond its borders. In quick succession vassal republics were formed: the Batavian (Holland, 1795; Belgium was incorporated downright into the French Republic), the Cisalpine (1797) and Roman (1798) in Italy, the Helvetian (Switzerland, 1798). In Switzerland the number of Jews was small; the new régime brought them some alleviation, but the legislative chambers refused to grant them civic rights.

In Holland, Jewish emancipation was stubbornly contested by unfriendly deputies in the National Assembly, but also by the large conservative majority in the Jewish community which was jealous of its internal autonomy and apprehensive of the dangers to the Jewish mode of life when once the barriers were removed. Nevertheless, thanks to the effective pressure of the French ambassador Noel, the Assembly conferred upon the Jews on September 2, 1796, full citizenship and the right to vote and be voted for in state and communal elections. Two Jews of Amsterdam, Bromet and de Lemon, entered the second National Assembly as deputies (1797), in the subsequent year Isaac da Costa Atias. The liberal members of the Jewish community had now (since 1796) a separate congregation, Adath Jeshurun, with moderate reforms in the ritual strongly resented by the orthodox.

Nowhere was the entry of the French acclaimed with greater jubilation than in the ghetto of Rome. The pope, Pius VI., author of the most inhuman edict (1775) by which the community of seven thousand souls was reduced to abject misery and degradation, was carried off as a prisoner of war. The gates of the ghetto were broken down and the Jews walked out to freedom, as full citizens, divested of the yellow badge of servitude. It was a great satisfaction that the Jew Baraffael entered the republican militia as a major, and another Jew, Ezekiel Morpurgo, sat in the Roman senate. The Jews were made to pay for the part they took in the revolution when the Neapolitan army drove out the French

(1799), so much so that they welcomed the restoration under Pius VII. (1800–1808), who at least did not revert to the harsh régime of his predecessor. In aristocratic Venice the Jews also had a period of freedom, but it was all too short (July-October, 1797); by the peace of Campo Formio, Venice was ceded to Austria and the older order restored.

This compact was signed for France by the commander of the army in Italy, the young Napoleon Bonaparte. His expedition to Egypt and Syria, which was directed against England, brought him for the first time face to face with the Jews. It was a political manoeuver, but nevertheless honestly meant, when after the capture of Gaza and Jaffa (February-March, 1799), he summoned the Jews of Asia and Africa to rally under the French flag and wrest the Holy Land from the Turk for the restored nation to dwell therein. The Jews of Jerusalem ignored the call; resolutely they labored to strengthen the defenses of the city.

At the zenith of his career, Napoleon occupied himself again with the affairs of Jewry and Judaism, still somewhat spectacularly, but now with a well-defined and firm purpose. What of religion there was in him was of the thin, deistic kind. He was willing to accord to religion its place in the scheme of things; but he would have it subordinated to the interests of the state and submissive to Caesar's will. In the Concordat with the Papacy (1801) he had left no room for the domination of Catholicism, the religion of the majority of the French people. Similarly he framed the constitution of French Protestantism so as to prevent the infiltration of foreign influences into France. In the same manner he dealt with the Jews. It were weakness—so he emphatically declared—to expel them when by the imperial word he might convert them into Frenchmen. The Jews must cease to be a nation and become a religious sect. Everything should be done to further their fusion with the French people, if necessary by forcing every third Jew to marry a French woman and every third Jewess to have a French husband.

Napoleon was little edified by the spectacle of small Jewish traders following his armies to buy up the soldiers' loot.

On the occasion of his visit to Strassburg, shortly after the battle of Austerlitz (1805), he gave ear to the complaints of the enemies of the Jews, unreconciled as they were to Jewish equality, about the extortionate practices of Jewish money-lenders in Alsace. From another source it came to the emperor's notice that the Jews were evading conscription. Both charges were exaggerated. However, in a rescript dated May 30, 1806, Napoleon suspended for ¦a year the payment of all debts held by Jews against agriculturists in the eastern departments. At the same time he gave orders for calling together a 'Jewish States-General,' to be followed by a second assembly, the resuscitated ancient Sanhedrin, for the purpose of accepting carefully prepared organic articles which should do away with usury and revive in the Jews 'civic morality, lost during the long centuries of a degrading existence.'

The Assembly of Jewish Notables met in Paris in July, 1806, and immediately after the conclusion of its sessions in February, 1807, the Grand Sanhedrin was convoked. The first body was preponderatingly made up of laymen; it numbered one hundred and eleven deputies from France and the newly formed Kingdom of Italy and was presided over by Furtado. As a matter of fact, the meetings were conducted by imperial commissaries, of whom Molé was not exactly a friend of the Jews. Twelve questions were laid before the Assembly in the open; at the same time there were conveyed, through the president, secretly the clear-cut wishes of the emperor as to how the questions should be answered. The decrees of the Notables were subsequently taken up by the Sanhedrin in order that they might be given doctrinal force. The Grand Sanhedrin was formed after the model of the ancient tribunal at Jerusalem. It consisted of seventy-one members, forty-six rabbis and twenty-five laymen, with David Sinzheim (1745–1812), the rabbi of Strassburg, as president and two Italian rabbis as assessors.

If the imperial councilors had anticipated any difficulties at all, they soon came to a different conclusion. Of course, resistance to the emperor's will was not to be thought of:

the adulation which marked all public utterances certainly pleased the great arbiter of nations and was no more and no less than what came to him universally. The Jews, finding themselves in a situation so unwonted, rose fully to the occasion. The question whether the Jews considered France as their fatherland and recognized the duty of defending it, was answered by a rising vote and the spontaneous cry: 'Aye, even unto death.' The very first question concerning polygamy was easiest to answer, since the European Jews had long been given to monogamy. It was decreed that no rabbi should solemnize a marriage or grant a divorce unless an act by a civil officer in accordance with the law of the land had preceded. It was further decreed that the Jews recognized their fellow-citizens of other faiths as their brethren to whom they owed moral obligations; that the Jews must discard all discreditable occupations; usury was condemned as contrary to Jewish law.

The Preamble made declaration that of the Jewish laws only the religious ones were immutable, while the political regulations, bound up with the life of the nation during the time of its autonomous government in Palestine, had ceased to be operative from the time that the corporate nation became defunct. Accordingly, the rabbis surrendered their internal jurisdiction in civil matters. Moreover, they ruled that the civil and political law of the land was obligatory on the Jew, and, in deference to that law, Jewish soldiers were freed of religious obligations for the time of their service.

One question, that concerning intermarriage, presented a difficulty; yet it was overcome in a manly spirit. The law prohibiting intermarriage, so it was declared, applied only to the ancient peoples inhabiting Palestine who were idolaters. The Christians were not idolaters. Hence intermarriage with Christians was not to be proscribed by the ban. However, no rabbi could solemnize such unions, exactly as no Catholic priest would perform such a ceremony (except under certain conditions). Nor is the final act with which the Notables concluded their sessions to be pronounced one of servility. The vote of thanks to the Holy See for protection afforded to the Jews in past centuries was meant in all sincerity. The Assembly chose to forgive and forget the harsh measures of some popes, like Innocent III., Paul IV., and not so long ago Pius VI. It was a gesture of reconciliation, a hope for future friendliness in mutual forbearance. Israel offered the hand for peace.

The outcome of Jewish submission to the commands of Napoleon was the decree of March 17, 1808, which was benevolent enough so far as it regulated Jewish worship, but deserved the appellation 'infamous' which the Jews applied to it because of the insulting discriminatory measures against them. Provision was made for the creation of consistories, governing bodies consisting of rabbis and laymen, in every department or group of departments where there were two thousand Jews, and of a central consistory in Paris. No salaries were accorded to the rabbis from the state, though the chief function of the consistories was for the purpose of facilitating conscription. That itself was a humiliating condition. Still more so was the legislation, to remain in force for ten years, restricting loans and denying the right of residence in a new department to all but agriculturists. No Jew was to engage in trade without permission from the prefects; no Jewish conscript might offer a substitute for himself, though such a procedure was allowed to Christians. Thus from above and by forcible legislation an improvement in the occupation of Jews was to be effected. By 1811 twenty-two departments had been exempted from the operations of the edict—presumably the method of coercion had accomplished its purpose. Naturally these hardships ruined the economic life of thousands of Jews; but the injury to Jewish feeling was immeasurably greater.

The consistorial organization of Jewish worship was established also in the Italian kingdom which was most closely united to the empire. In the kingdom of Holland, during the reign of Louis Bonaparte (1806–1810), the central consistory of Amsterdam was mainly a governmental department for Jewish affairs, but powerless to unite the divided community with its two elements, the Sephardic and the

Ashkenazic. As in France, the consistory was charged with encouraging Jewish conscription. However, as Jews were not received into the civic militia, a separate Jewish corps was formed, until its units were absorbed into the regular French army when the kingdom was annexed (1810).

During the six years of Napoleon's sway in Germany (1806–1812), the Jews enjoyed temporary equality in several of those states which entered directly into the sphere of French influence. First of all the Jews obtained full emancipation in the kingdom of Westphalia, formed in 1807 with Jerome Bonaparte as ruler. A royal decree, issued January, 1808, placed the Jews, even those who migrated into the kingdom from other lands, on a footing of absolute equality with other subjects.

In accordance with a further decree, of March 31, 1808, a consistory was organized in the capital, Cassel. The government appointed to the presidency of this body Israel Jacobsohn, financial agent to Jerome Bonaparte, who previously had served the duke of Brunswick in a similar capacity. This well-meaning, but somewhat shallow and vain man (1768–1828) was the typical representative of the higher class layman of his age. He was imbued with the ideas of Mendelssohn's circle and hailed with delight the advent of freedom in the wake of the French Revolution and Napoleon's régime. He realized that an inner improvement in culture must go hand in hand with external emancipation. In 1801, he had founded in Seesen a boarding school for boys, which accepted Christian and Jewish scholars alike; his example was followed by his brother-in-law, Isaac Herz Samson, who in 1807 opened a similar school in Wolfenbüttel. With the aid of David Fränkel, head master of the Francis school at Dessau (organized in 1799), Jacobsohn established new schools throughout the Westphalian kingdom. In these schools the general subjects were taught by Christian teachers, while a Jewish instructor gave lessons in Jewish religion and Hebrew language. The consistory also introduced external reforms in the mode of worship, such as choral singing of German hymns, addresses in the vernacular, German prayers by the side of the Hebrew. Boys and girls were confirmed after the Protestant manner, with public examination in the catechism and speeches. The innovations, displeasing to the orthodox, were carried out by consistorial rescripts, and all private worship was abolished, to the end that the official type alone should remain in force. The complaints of the communities were silenced by a royal decree (July 5, 1811). Until the fall of Napoleon (1813), the Jews of the Westphalian kingdom were admitted to public offices and to the professions; many enlisted in the army and a number rose to the positions of captains and quartermasters.

Jacobsohn interested himself also in the condition of his coreligionists of Frankfort, which since 1806 had become the seat of the Confederation of the Rhine under the presidency of the prince primate Karl von Dalberg. New life was stirring in the Frankfort ghetto; in 1804 a group of cultured Jews had founded a modern school (the Philanthropin). Representatives of the community appeared at one of the last sessions of the Grand Sanhedrin and expressed their readiness to accept the decrees of that body as soon as they were able to enjoy equal civic rights. Jacobsohn's address to the prince primate evoked a hostile rejoinder which was printed anonymously, and Goethe, whose birthplace Frankfort was, indulged in a cheap pun on the 'Jacobin son of Israel' to whom his people appeared 'as they should be or become in the future, but not as they now were and would remain for some time.' However, with the constitution of the grand duchy of Frankfort (1810), Dalberg as head of the state removed all the disabilities of the Jews of Frankfort for the payment to the senate of four hundred and forty thousand gulden (December 28, 1811). The sum was computed on the basis of the annual tax for protection which the Jews were in the habit of paying, multiplied by twenty.

Of the other states constituting the Confederation of the Rhine, Baden admitted the Jews to hereditary citizenship upon the condition of their following a useful occupation, thus excluding money-lenders, traders in cattle, and small shopkeepers. The religious affairs were governed by a supreme council of eight persons, consisting of rabbis and communal elders. In Mecklenburg, thanks to the warm recommendation of Tychsen, professor at the university of Rostock, equal rights were conferred upon the Jews short of admission to public offices (1813). Elsewhere the progress of emancipation was retarded or hedged about by unfriendly measures. In Bavaria, where the Jewish population numbered thirty thousand souls, the Jews were made to assume all the obligations of citizenship, but had none of its rights. Agriculturists, artisans, manufacturers, and professional men were accorded special privileges; but the freedom of domicile and marriage was restricted, and it was openly stated that the number of Jewish residents in any locality should rather be diminished than enlarged. Only in the Hanseatic towns, which were directly annexed to France, were the Jews automatically enfranchised (1811); so in Hamburg, but particularly in Lübeck and Bremen, where, after centuries of expulsion, Jews were now permitted to dwell. Thus did French penetration sweep away the cobwebs of the medieval treatment of the Jews on German soil.

CHAPTER LXXXI

EMANCIPATION IN PRUSSIA

(1786-1812)

I N the two largest Germanic states which waged war with revolutionary and imperial France, Prussia and Austria, the entrenched absolutism either moved quite warily in ameliorating the condition of the Jews or was entirely retrograde. The successor of Frederick the Great on the Prussian throne, Frederick William II. (1786–1797), was given to Rosicrucian mysticism and was a champion of orthodoxy. Nevertheless, through his very opposition to his predecessor's policies and because of his general kind-heartedness, he was imbued with the necessity of mitigating the hard lot of the oppressed Jewish people. Without awaiting the opinion of a royal commission appointed immediately after his accession, he granted the request of the Jewish leaders for an abrogation of the body-tax (1787). The report of the commission (1789) conceded certain privileges at the price of tutelage from above and meddling with the internal life of the Jews, but insisted upon the present restrictions remaining in force for a time. It was the commission's opinion that it would take three generations for the Jews to divest themselves of those religious peculiarities which separated them from the Christian population, leaving a small residue of an innocuous or indifferent nature. Then, it was hoped, they might become useful citizens and the restrictions be removed.

The proposed reforms were rejected by the Jewish deputies of the various Prussian communities, in answer to whose petition they had been framed (1790). David Friedländer (1750–1834), son-in-law of the rich banker Daniel Itzig and 'faithful friend and pupil' of Mendelssohn, demanded, on behalf of his fellow-Jews, complete civil and political equality. His representations were brushed aside as so much rhetorical sophistry. The king repeatedly urged his ministers to prepare a law on the basis of the commission's report. At last the draft of the new legislation was presented to him for his signature (April, 1792). It offered civil, but not political equality, and even that at the cost of the destruction of the internal Jewish organization. But the king's signature was never appended, since it was represented to him that any effort to improve the status of the Jew would cause general dissatisfaction among the people. This was particularly undesirable in view of the impending war against the Revolution (the First Coalition, 1793–1797).

The Jews in the eastern provinces, including the city of Warsaw, which fell to Prussia after the second and third partition of Poland (1793, 1795), presented a special problem which was met on the whole in a humane and liberal spirit. The Regulation of April 17, 1797, removed a number of disabilities as regards domicile and choice of occupation. Still the Jews remained subject to all sorts of restrictions. Thus no Jew was permitted to marry under the age of twenty-five years, and then only when he had a fixed income. In the place of the poll-tax, divers contributions were levied on the Jews, for protection or in lieu of personal military service or for permission to marry, and so forth. The communal organization was confined to the strictly religious interests; the rabbinical courts were abrogated. In the Jewish schools the study of the German and Polish languages were made obligatory.

A petition presented to the new king, Frederick William III., who ascended the throne in 1797, led to the meager result of abolishing corporate responsibility for petty offenses committed by Jews. The elaborate regulations, published in 1801, created a censorial commission, consisting of a police-officer, a legally trained member of the magistracy, and a number of Jewish communal leaders, with discretionary powers to punish offenders. The king's ministers admitted a certain harshness in the new legislation. They insisted, however, that this increased police supervision was to be used only to prevent the entry of undesirable foreigners and to facilitate the removing of suspicious elements of the population. As regards the status of the Jews, they considered a change impracticable so long as the Jews stood apart from other subjects of the state. It was not merely a question of dogmatic differences, but principally of divergent rites and customs and an ecclesiastical constitution which made of the Jews 'as it were a state within the state.' It was regretable that, until solid internal reforms made the Jews worthy of citizenship, along with the 'unimproved' mass there must suffer, if at all they did, also the 'innocent members of the nation.' Nevertheless, the regulations were practically abandoned in 1805, owing to the continued opposition of the Jews.

The group of 'innocents,' that is, of intellectuals more or less at dissonance with the Jewish life of the past, had grown apace in the frivolous Prussian capital during the decades preceding the national regeneration. The entrance of the Jews into the general European civilization was all too sudden. The circle of Mendelssohn's admirers edited between 1784 and 1797 a Hebrew periodical, 'The Gatherer' (Ha-Measseph), devoted to the phantom of rationalism and to bold and ruthless warfare with all that was peculiarly Jewish, in a spirit devoid of reverence or of historical comprehension. To the collaborators belonged Isaac Satanov (1732–1804) and Judah Loeb Benzeeb (1764–1811), both versatile Hebrew stylists; the latter wrote a Hebrew grammar and dictionary of much merit which enjoyed great popularity.

More serious students were attracted to Kant's critical philosophy; of these, Solomon Maimon (1753–1800) was by far the most original mind. Translated from the uncouth surroundings of Lithuanian Hasidism into the center of Prussian enlightenment, he broke with all religion, but that did not prevent him from knocking twice at the portals of Christianity. Lazarus Bendavid (1762–1832) regarded Judaism as an unreasonable agglomerate of ritual and superstition and looked to the cultured, who were free from the old credulity and equally from modern infidelism, for restoring the 'pure religion' of Moses divested of all historical 'overgrowth.' Marcus Herz (1747–1803), philosopher and physician, delivered private lectures on philosophy which were attended by generals, ambassadors, ministers, and princes of the blood. His house was frequented by poets and sculptors, theologians and statesmen. Foreigners of eminence deemed it an honor to be invited to the evening entertainments. The attraction, however, was the lady of the house, Henrietta Herz, beautiful, accomplished, scintillating in conversation. By twenty years her husband's junior, she engaged in amatory pastimes with her men friends; long estranged from Judaism, she only awaited her mother's death to embrace Protestantism (1817).

Another circle of intellectuals grouped itself about the unprepossessing, but vivacious Rachel Levin (1771–1833), the daughter of a rich jeweler, who forsook the religion of her fathers on marrying the Prussian diplomat and man of letters, Varnhagen von Ense (1814). There were numerous baptisms in high Jewish society. Mendelssohn's daughter, Dorothea, married to the banker Veit, secured a divorce from her husband in order to marry her lover, Friedrich Schlegel, the leader of the new romantic school and the author of novels in which free love was advocated; subsequently both embraced Catholicism. The sons by her former husband were likewise baptized. Her younger sister, Henrietta Mendelssohn, also became a Catholic. Of the philosopher's sons only the eldest, Joseph, died as a Jew. The second son, Abraham, the father of the composer Felix Mendelssohn-Bartholdy, and all but one of Mendelssohn's grandsons went over to Christianity.

The leap into Christianity was contemplated by the anonymous writer of the Epistle to Pastor Teller (1799). The author was none other than David Friedländer, who, on behalf of 'several heads of families of the Jewish denomination,' petitioned to be received into the fold of the Protestant Church on conditions of their own. So far as the religious ceremonies went, like baptism, they were ready to accept them only as symbols. But they could not conscientiously subscribe to Christian dogmas contrary to reason, as, for example, the belief that Jesus was the Son of God. Of course, they might constitute themselves as a sect, midway between Judaism and Christianity; but they were honest enough to confess that only as members of the Christian Church could they hope to obtain for themselves and their children full citizens' rights. Naturally the good pastor replied that a form of Christianity which left Christ out was meaningless. Nor was this 'Judaizing Christianity' acceptable to Schleiermacher, who in his Discourses on Religion had begun to stress the mystic element in religion, the very thing Friedländer found so unreasonable in Judaism. The world of thought was moving on to a deeper understanding of the religious consciousness, while those of the school of Mendelssohn lagged behind with their 'reasoned verities.'

By the Treaty of Tilsit (1807) Prussia was shorn of much of its territory. The parts west of the Elbe were incorporated into the kingdom of Westphalia, where the Jews had been granted full emancipation. The Polish provinces, turned into the duchy of Warsaw, were administered by the Poles under the king of Saxony. A liberal constitution was introduced and the civil Code Napoleon became the law of the land; but the status of citizens, desired by the progressive Jews and just as stubbornly opposed by the Hasidic element, was denied to the Jewish population. In Prussia itself, the disaster led to a moral regeneration under the liberal régime of Stein and Hardenberg, with Wilhelm von Humboldt in the ministry of education. The reform of municipal government benefited the Jews to the extent that they were admitted to the city councils. David Friedländer, cured of his desire to cut himself off from the Jewish community, was elected a city councilor in Berlin (1808). At last, on March 11, 1812, on the eve of the War of Liberation, the Jews of Prussia received the grant of emancipation. It was still a partial one, government positions being closed to the Jews; but all other disabilities disappeared.

The avowed aim of the government was to destroy the internal communal organization of the Jews, to prevent their flocking to the baptismal font for the sake of escaping civil disabilities, but just the same to welcome voluntary conversions and to prepare the way for their merging with the bulk of the population through the acceptance of the dominant faith. Friedländer and like-minded Jewish leaders came to the conclusion that the gift of emancipation, if it was to be enjoyed by the new generation to the full, must be accompanied by a process of assimilation with a reform of the Jewish synagogue and school. As Prussian citizens the Jews had but one fatherland, Prussia, to pray for, and one native tongue, the German, to pray in. The ancient hope of Palestinian restoration must be cast overboard and the old sacred tongue, the Hebrew, discarded as dead.

In the War of Liberation several hundreds of Jews fought as volunteers, not to count the great number of conscripted youth. Jewish soldiers took part in the various battles; many were killed or wounded in the battle of Leipzig (1813) and at Waterloo (1815). A goodly number distinguished themselves by heroism and were recipients of the iron cross, while some were made officers. The sacrifices of life and fortune availed the Jews but little in the time of restoration subsequent to the fall of Napoleon, when reaction set in.

At any rate, Prussia had gone far in advance of Austria in the treatment of the Jews. The tolerant measures of Joseph II. became a dead letter under his successors. During the long reign of Francis II. (1792–1835; since 1806, after the collapse of the Germanic empire, he went by the name of Francis I., emperor of Austria), the 'tolerated' Jewish families of the capital were required to pay a special toleration tax, though several members of the wealthiest class were ennobled. Other Jews continued to live as dependents, real or feigned, of their privileged coreligionists, or often enough without legal right and subject to expulsion at a moment's notice. A special police department, swept away only by the tide of the 1848 revolution, dealt out permits of residence as it suited the whim of the officer in charge, or for a consideration. No Jew in Vienna was permitted to own a home in his own name. The trade in raw products, salt, grain, furs, was forbidden, nor was a Jew allowed to open an apothecary's shop. It was a special act of grace that the Viennese Jews were given leave in 1811 to construct a synagogue and a school.

In Bohemia and Moravia the number of Jews admitted to residence was definitely prescribed. Fourteen thousand Jewish families lived in the two crown lands; an organized community existed really only in Prague. In Galicia, the former Polish province, the Jewish population was quite dense, numbering a quarter of a million souls. Barring Lemberg and a few other towns, where the Jews were confined in special suburbs, there was no restriction on freedom of domicile. But after 1793 only those Jews were allowed to settle in the villages who were agriculturists or artisans. However, they were forbidden to lease land except on condition that the cultivation of the soil was to be done by them in person and not through hired labor, and so the measure was tantamount to excluding them from the villages. Jews intending to marry were required to pass an examination in the use of the German language as well as in Jewish religious and moral law. As but the fewest could pass, the majority contented themselves with a religious marriage, which was not recognized in law.

The Galician Jews took by no means kindly to the new type of schools forced upon them by the government. Nor was the general inspector possessed of tact or considerateness for the religious scruples of the parents who clung to the old and tried ideas of Jewish education. Herz Homberg (1749–1841) was imbued with the rationalistic spirit of Mendelssohn, in whose house he had been tutor and with whom he had collaborated in the new Hebrew commentary on the Pentateuch (Biur, 'Exposition'). As governmental superintendent of schools, he insisted on a preliminary training of the children in the new schools before they were allowed to apply themselves to the study of the Talmud. Moreover, he was instrumental in saddling the Jews of Galicia with a special tax on the candles used in the homes on sabbaths and festivals. When relieved of his duties as superintendent, he occupied himself with preparing schoolbooks and catechisms which the government forced upon all

Jewish elementary schools. In his capacity as censor of Hebrew books, he was also unduly harsh in not admitting to print new works of a cabalistic or strictly rabbinical type. Altogether Homberg was oppressive to his coreligionists and submissive to the government; he was rewarded by an appointment as inspector of the Jewish schools in Bohemia (1814) which he held to his death.

The Jews of Hungary, seventy-five thousand in number, were tolerated only in certain parts of the country; in many of the free cities they were not permitted to stay longer than was necessary for the transaction of business. The most ordinary civil rights were withheld from them. Both in Galicia and Hungary, the Jews were made to serve in the army. Naturally there were difficulties in the matter of food and because of the desecration of the sabbath which military duties involved. Still the soldier's life reacted favorably upon physical well-being and discipline.

CHAPTER LXXXII

RUSSIAN JEWS UNDER PAUL AND ALEXANDER I.

(1796-1825)

FARTHER to the east, Russia had, by the three partitions of Poland, become heir to the largest and most compact body of Jews. From the outset, the policy of the czarist government was to keep the Jewish mass strictly confined to the newly acquired western provinces and to prevent its spreading into the other parts of the Russian empire. But even within the 'Pale of Settlement' there was a striving to narrow down the sphere of Jewish economic life. The Christian merchants and small burghers were none too friendly to their Jewish competitors, who were placed in a category by themselves, paying a tax twice as large as that required of Christians in the same condition. Only the small number of Karaite Jews, in a few cities of Lithuania and Volhynia, but principally in the Crimea, were exempted from the double tax and in general were placed almost on a footing of equality with the Christian subjects. One could be generous to a negligible minority; it was different with the large majority, so strange to the Russian mind at the first encounter.

Official investigations were set in motion under Paul I. (1796–1801). The marshals of the nobility throughout the southeastern provinces threw the blame for the evil state of the peasantry upon the Jewish tavern-keepers. As a matter of fact, the landed aristocrats were eager to keep to themselves the monopoly of the manufacture and sale of spirits. At the same time they desired the Jewish internal organization to be broken down so as to bring about an amalgamation of the Jews with the rest of the population. Friesel, the governor of Vilna, was himself convinced that the root of the evil lay in the outlandishness of Jewish religious customs. In 1800, Derzhavin, poet and senator, laid before the czar an elaborate memorandum looking to the 'curbing of the avaricious pursuits of the Jews' and their transformation into an element 'useful to the government.' Two projects had been submitted to him by representative Jews. Nathan Shklover, a wealthy merchant at St. Petersburg, advised that the Jews should be drawn to manufacturing enterprises and to agriculture in colonies near the Black Sea ports. A physician by the name of Frank proposed, on Mendelssohnian lines, the opening up of the Russian public schools to Jewish children.

Derzhavin was satisfied that he had hit upon a plan whereby 'the stubborn and cunning tribe might be set to rights.' The Jews should be made to accept family names and register under the four categories of merchants, urban burghers, rural burghers, and agricultural settlers. A special Christian official should be charged with supervising the affairs of the Jews and their gradual transformation. The ordering of the religious life should be in the hands of the separate synagogues, with their rabbis and schoolmen, under a supreme ecclesiastical tribunal in the capital of the empire. The Jewish population should be evenly distributed over the various parts of White Russia and the surplus transferred to other provinces ('governments'). Jews were to be forbidden to keep Christian domestics, nor be allowed to participate in city government. They must abandon their distinct dress and peculiar speech. Jewish children might go to their own religious schools up to the age of twelve; thereafter they must attend the public schools of the state. A government printing-office should publish Jewish religious books 'with philosophic annotations.' It was to be an enlightenment bestowed from above, and the emperor was urged to follow the Gospel commandment, 'Love your enemies, do good to them that hate you.'

Paul died before the report could be acted upon. His successor, Alexander I. (1801–1825), appointed in 1802 a commission for the improvement of Jewish conditions in White Russia and the other provinces acquired from Poland. Jewish deputies were summoned to receive the plan of reforms. Unable to accept certain 'correctional measures,' they were dismissed and ordered to send in their suggestions as to the best means of carrying the reforms into effect. In the commission itself, Speranski was the only statesman who pleaded for a maximum of liberties and a minimum of restrictions, emphasizing the futility of reforms from above. He believed that, if the Jews were left to themselves and all avenues leading to their happiness were thrown open to them, they would accomplish their own improvement. However, the contrary opinion prevailed. Accordingly, the statute laid before the czar and approved in 1804 placed itself squarely upon keeping the Jews out of Russia proper and confining them to thirteen 'governments': five of Lithuania and White Russia, five of the Ukraine or Little Russia, and three of New Russia. In addition, if in the future there should develop Jewish agriculturists, they might settle in two eastern governments, Astrakhan and the Caucasus. On the economic side, Jews should henceforth be forbidden to lease lands or keep taverns in the villages. On the other hand, they might buy unoccupied lands or settle on crown lands in order to engage in tilling the soil.

Thus, while a small number of agriculturists would be created, hundreds of thousands of Jews were meanwhile deprived of means of support. Manufacturers and artisans were exempted from the double tax; merchants and burghers were just tolerated. All Jews belonging to these categories might sojourn temporarily in the interior governments on special passports issued by the governors of their own districts. Rabbis and communal elders were to be elected for three years, subject to ratification by the governors. The rabbis were to look after religious matters and exercise jurisdiction only in matters of religion, but without the right of pronouncing the ban. The communal bodies ('kahals') were charged with responsibility for the regular payment of the state taxes. Free access was granted to the public schools, both elementary and higher; the Jews might also open schools of their own, with one of the three languages, Russian, Polish, or German, as obligatory. It was made incumbent upon the rabbis and lay leaders to acquire proficiency in any one of these languages to the extent of being able to write and speak it.

The projected expulsion from the villages as well as other 'reforms' difficult of realization in the face of centuries old customs filled the Jews with dismay, and the government was flooded with petitions. The czar was fearful of Jewish susceptibility to the Napoleonic spirit. He interpreted the convocation of the Jewish Notables and the Grand San-hedrin (p. 613) as a manoeuver to win ascendancy over the Jews of Prussia, Austria, and Russia. Accordingly, the governors were ordered in 1807 to convoke provincial assemblies of Jewish representatives. But after the Peace of Tilsit, when Alexander and Napoleon had come to an understanding, the expulsion of the Jews from the villages was begun in all ruthlessness. It was to be carried out in three instalments and finished by 1810. But in 1809 a new commission was set to work on the problem, and after three years of labor it came to the realization that the expulsions had not benefited the peasants and were only aggravating the economic ruin of the Jews.

The French legions were now pouring into Russia (1812); it was not advisable to exasperate the Jews. Jewish senti-ment, as voiced by Shneor Zalman, the leader of the White Russian Hasidim (p. 586), was unfavorable to Napoleon, whose gift of civil rights, he thought, might lead to a disin-tegration of the religious life. Civic rightlessness under Alex-ander, so long as it preserved inviolability of Judaism, was preferable. Jewish fidelity to the Russian cause was attested by the governors of the western provinces which constituted the actual theater of the war.

The internal conflict between the Hasidim and their opponents continued, especially since the government saw no reason to interfere. The method of study introduced by the Gaon of Vilna was propagated through the foundation of the school for higher talmudic learning at Volozhin (1803) by the Gaon's foremost pupil, Hayim of Volozhin. In this circle there was even a measure of toleration towards those secular sciences which were helpful to an understanding of the Talmud, such as mathematics and natural history. The revolution of Jewish life, which was preparing in the West under the influence of the school of Mendelssohn, was on the whole powerless to affect these eastern regions. At Warsaw, during the period of Prussian domination, there might be a longing for political emancipation at the price of giving up Jewish separateness; and at St. Petersburg one or the other might leap into the arms of the Greek Orthodox religion. Still the beginnings of the Berlin variety of Enlightenment were discernible in the Russian Pale of Settlement. Mendel Levin of Satanov (1741–1819), who had met Mendelssohn in person, translated into Hebrew a manual of medicine by Tissot, the moral philosophy of Franklin, and Campe's books of travel.

CHAPTER LXXXIII

CULTURAL TRANSFORMATION IN CENTRAL EUROPE

(1814-1823)

FOR the Jews of Central Europe the triumph of the Coalition against Napoleon meant a struggle to rewin their rights, wherever jeopardized or curtailed by reason of the reaction, and at the same time to pursue their efforts at their own cultural transformation. Much as the leaders protested that political rights should not be bought at the cost of religious convictions, the modification of Jewish life, in education and religious worship, went hand in hand with emancipation accomplished or contemplated. The taste for European culture had developed; the entry into the life without, even while preparing, called for adjustments in the life within. There was much precipitate haste; no one calculated what the issue might be; but the first step was taken, and there seemed to be no going back.

The departure of the French before the allied forces brought about everywhere a return to the old treatment of the Jews antedating the occupation. Upon the advice of David Friedländer, the Jews of the Hanseatic cities made common cause; they commissioned a capable and friendly Christian attorney, Carl August Buchholz, of Lübeck, to represent the interests of German Jewry before the statesmen assembled at the Vienna Congress (1814–1815). The Jews of Frankfort sent a deputation of their own, the manufacturer Isaac Joseph Gumprecht and the court-financier Jacob Baruch, father of Ludwig Börne.

Whatever aid came from the highly stationed and socially influential Viennese Jews and their ladies, was for the most part of the indirect kind. The salons of Baroness Fanny, daughter of Daniel Itzig of Berlin and wife of Nathan Adam von Arnstein (1748–1838), and her sister Cecilia, wife of the famous financier Bernhard von Eskeles (1753–1839), were regularly frequented by the Prussian statesmen. The Austrian diplomats were as often the guests of the Baroness' sister-in-law Marianna, wife of Metternich's banker, Leopold Edler von Herz (1743–1825). The representatives of the nations were lavishly entertained; in their hosts and in the other 'new-fashioned' Jews and Jewesses whom they met at these gatherings, they observed a speedy transformation, often resulting in the children being raised in the Christian faith. Judging from these examples, Jewish emancipation, the statesmen thought, should be advantageous to Christian society.

The Prussian Wilhelm von Humboldt was more impressed with the 'old-fashioned' type of Jew. Such a one was Simon von Lämel (1766–1845), formerly of Prague, who, together with Arnstein, Eskeles, Herz, and the Moravian Lazar Auspitz (1772–1853), submitted a petition to Prince Metternich for a moderate improvement in the legal status of the Jews of German Austria. In framing the Constitution for the Germanic Confederation, the Prussian plenipotentiary Hardenberg was in favor of an act which would put the Jews of the several states on a footing of equality with their brethren in Prussia in accordance with the Prussian decree of 1812. The greatest opposition came from Bavaria, Saxony, and the Free Cities. A resolution was finally adopted (June, 1815) recommending to the incoming Federal Assembly to take steps in granting to the Jews the enjoyment of citizens' rights in proportion to their assuming the duties of citizenship. It was provided that until then the Jews should be allowed those privileges at present accorded *by* the confederate states. 'By' was at the last moment substituted for 'in.' This change was insisted on by the opponents who thus hoped to side-track any favorable action, since the emancipation effected by the French 'in' the states had not been granted 'by' the states themselves. It was at the Vienna Congress that for the first time the Jewish question was considered as one of general European politics.

At the very moment when this compromise was reached, Israel Jacobsohn, now that the consistorial organization in

Westphalia had fallen through, removed to Berlin. There he instituted in his home a private service according to the new style, with instrumental music, prayers in German, and a German sermon. A similar private service was called into existence at the home of Jacob Herz Beer, the father of the composer Meyerbeer. Both private chapels were ordered closed by the government, which was averse to sectarian innovations (1816). Of the young men who acted as preachers at those services, Eduard Kley (1789–1867) accepted the post of headmaster of the Jewish Free School at Hamburg. He likewise succeeded in forming a group of liberals who took steps to introduce the new style of service in a permanent edifice of their own. The Hamburg 'Temple,' as it was called, was dedicated in 1818; Kley and Gotthold Salomon (1784–1862) became the Temple preachers.

The service was ordered very much after the pattern of the Berlin experiments. There was choral singing to the accompaniment of the organ; German predominated in the liturgy, though the main prayers were recited in Hebrew. The sabbath portion from the Torah was read in the Portuguese pronunciation and without the customary cantillation. The prayer-book, edited by Meir Israel Bresselau (died 1839) and Seckel Isaac Fränkel (1765–1835), two noted Hebraists, followed on the whole the traditional cast. The omission of late accretions, such as the medieval 'piyutim' of the Ashkenazic rite, was compensated by the introduction of the more poetic pieces of the Sephardic ritual. The excision or rephrasing of those portions of the liturgy which dealt with the hope of the Messianic restoration, was by no means carried out with anything like consistency. Nevertheless it was dictated by a show of complete identification with the surroundings in the struggle for political emancipation. It was a parting of the ways which the orthodox element was bound to view with alarm, considering that the Temple venture was public beyond previous attempts, even though the members remained within the general community.

The rabbinical college of Hamburg denounced the new movement as heretical. The local feud was carried abroad when the friends of reforms at Berlin secured the opinions of two Italian and one Hungarian rabbi, Aaron Chorin, of Arad (1766–1844), favorable to the innovations (1818). The orthodox answered by a counter-publication of condemnatory letters (1819) from the most authoritative rabbis of the day, such as Akiba Eger at Posen (1761–1837), his son-in-law Moses Sofer at Pressburg (1763–1839), Mordecai Benet at Nikolsburg (1763–1829), and many others of lesser renown. They protested particularly against the introduction of the organ which became the dividing line between orthodoxy and reform in Germany. The protagonists of orthodoxy felt instinctively the dangers involved in the break with tradition; but their uncompromising attitude made them blind to such demands of the times as were justifiable.

It was a step in the right direction when the Hamburg community elected in 1821 Isaac Bernays (1792–1849) as chief rabbi (or 'haham,' the title preferred by himself). Possessed of talmudic knowledge and a university education, he was among the first orthodox rabbis to preach in German. He steered his course, not always with the desired clarity, between the extremists on either side. Thus a third variety of Judaism was preparing which, while placing itself squarely upon tradition, reckoned with the exigencies of the new life.

Strain as the Jews might to bring themselves into accord with the world without, their longing for political equality was for the present far from being fulfilled. The heightened nationalism, engendered by the defeat of the French, and still more the reaction which quickly stifled all liberal thought, were not calculated to redeem the promise of 1815 even approximately. In published pamphlets and on the boards of theaters an inimical tone was struck. In the streets of Würzburg, Bamberg, Carlsruhe, Heidelberg, Mannheim, Frankfort, Hamburg, excesses were committed against the Jews with the cry: Hep-hep, death to the Jews! (1819).

In Hesse and to a less extent in Baden and Württemberg, some measure of the acquired rights and the ecclesiastical organization was allowed to remain. Elsewhere the old conditions were resuscitated. Lübeck and Bremen again drove the Jews from the city limits. In Hamburg the burghers would not countenance political rights for the Jews and insisted on restricting them in commerce, handicrafts, and the holding of property. Bavaria put off any legislation in favor of the Jews (1822). Saxony could not prevail upon the trade guilds to admit Jews (1818), but at least conceded to those of Dresden the privilege of maintaining a synagogue (1825). In Saxe-Weimar, Goethe led the agitation for throwing the Jews back into medieval conditions (1823). Similarly did the Jews fare in Hanover and Mecklenburg, and restrictions were heaped upon them in Austria, the hotbed of reaction. The Jews of Frankfort, after a long drawn out contest, acquiesced in being placed in a special category of 'Israelitish citizens,' with no political rights and a number of irksome limitations as regards matrimony, owning of dwellings, and the trade in commodities (1824).

In Prussia the promises for constitutional government made before the war were forgotten. Instead, the old provincial estates were brought to life again, and these representatives of Junkerdom refused to extend the operations of the emancipatory act of 1812 to the reconquered provinces. But even in old Prussian territory an arbitrary interpretation of the law kept the Jews from civil appointments and from such vocations as that of an auctioneer or apothecary. Christian children were forbidden to visit Jewish schools (1819), and Jews were enjoined not to bear Christian names (1828). In Prussia, as elsewhere, the paternal absolutism did not refrain from meddling with the internal affairs of the Jews, and the intervention led to curiously contradictory results. While Saxe-Weimar insisted on forcing the German language upon the synagogue service (1823), Prussia, in the very same year, prescribed that the Jews must conduct their worship after the traditional pattern, with no innovations in language, ceremonies, prayers, or singing. It even forbade the German sermon. On the plea that the main synagogue structure was undergoing repairs, the 'Beer Temple' had led on its existence; now it was definitely shut down. Naturally the orthodox element had instigated the action; the resentment of the liberals led indirectly to a renascence of Jewish scholarship along lines truly epoch-making.

CHAPTER LXXXIV

THE RENASCENCE OF JEWISH SCHOLARSHIP

(1819-1868)

LEOPOLD (Yom Tob Lipmann) Zunz had been a preacher at the Beer Temple. Born in Detmold in 1794, he lived on to a ripe old age of above four-score and ten years and witnessed the stages of the profound transformation in the life of his people during the nineteenth century. At his death in 1886 he was mourned as the Grand Old Man of the new Jewish learning for which in his youth he had laid the foundations. The regular training which he received in the Wolfenbüttel gymnasium and in the universities of Berlin and Halle prepared him admirably for the task which he set himself early in life, to submit the whole of the Jewish literature to a critical study along modern historical lines and to present the results in the living German tongue.

Zunz coined the expression 'Wissenschaft des Judentums,' which meant an understanding of Jewish antiquity in all its parts as far as expressed in literary monuments. Hebrew writing he regarded as having reached its conclusion; a closed period lay behind which demanded an appraisal. The method of study must be disinterested, but by no means detached from the present-day problems which required for their solution a right appreciation of the past.

While yet a university student, in 1819, together with like-minded associates, Zunz founded a society for Jewish culture and study ('Verein für Cultur und Wissenschaft der Juden'). It was hoped that familiarity with Jewish literature and history would stem the tide of apostacy which once more was rife. But the president of the Society, the jurist Eduard Gans, was the first to embrace Christianity for the sake of a university career (1825); his example was followed by an-

other member, the poet Heinrich Heine. Zunz was saved
from the leap by what was more than a 'whim'; he was far
too deeply at home in Jewish literature to be anything but
thoroughly at one with his people. Against the interference
of the Prussian government he proved in a monumental
work ('Die gottesdienstlichen Vorträge der Juden,' 1832)
that the sermon in the spoken language was a continuous
Jewish institution ascending to remote times. The book,
however, was not merely a casual polemic, sharp and convincing as it was for the practical purpose; it was the first
comprehensive historical study of the vast Jewish homiletical
literature and of the early development of the liturgy. With
equal mastery he subsequently threw himself into a delinea-
tion of the liturgical poetry ('piyutim') of the synagogue
(1855–1865).

From the start Zunz favored a reform of the worship
which should admit commendable innovations, like music
and choral singing, and such changes as pertained to content, mode of recitation, and language of the prayers. Above
all he sponsored the idea of rectifying abuses by restoring
the original and vital customs in the place of the decrepit and
lifeless usages. As Zunz grew older and the havoc wrought in
Jewish life stood revealed, he raised his voice in protest
against the suicidal breaking with Talmud, the Messianic
hope, and fundamental institutions like the sabbath and the
Abrahamic covenant (1844). Engrossed in his literary occupations and content with the post of principal of the Jewish
Teachers' College at Berlin, which was opened in 1840,
Zunz looked with disdain upon the professional ministry and
its ecclesiastical pretensions.

Hebrew writing was by no means defunct, as Zunz had
been led to believe. At the two ends of the Austrian agglomerate of states, in the Italian provinces and in Galicia, the
new learning used for its vehicle the Hebrew tongue, thus
taking up the thread where Azariah dei Rossi (p. 503) had
left it. Isaac Samuel Reggio (1784–1855), at Görz, was imbued with the Mendelssohnian spirit and heartily believed
in the compatibility of Torah (Jewish learning) and philo-

sophy (secular knowledge). According to this tenor he edited the works of older scholars with interesting comments and strove to bring out the true sense of the Scriptural word in a new commentary, notably that on the Pentateuch, accompanied by an Italian translation (1821). Reggio's chief merit consisted in his lending a hand to the establishment of an institution for the training of rabbis on modern lines, the 'Istituto Rabbinico' at Padua, which was opened in 1829. It was the first school of the kind, antedating by one year the rabbinical seminary at Metz (transferred to Paris in 1859), which was originally founded as a yeshibah (1704) and then transformed into a Talmud Torah (1820).

The man who made the Padua school renowned was its principal professor, Samuel David Luzzatto (1800–1865). Scion of an ancient family (Moses Hayim Luzzatto was his great-grandfather's brother), he possessed a wide range of Jewish and secular information, and wrote Hebrew with masterly skill. His life's work encompassed original and penetrating contributions to the grammar of Hebrew and Aramaic (1836, 1855–1857, 1865) and to an understanding of the Scriptures (commentaries on Isaiah, the Pentateuch, and other books, 1855 and subsequently). Luzzatto raised biblical studies among the Jews to the dignity of a specialty, requiring the major part of a man's time and pursued as a profession. Other branches of Jewish literature, especially Hebrew poetry, found in him a zealous student who brought to light unpublished works and made clear many an obscurity. He was an uncompromising foe of the innovations among the northern Jews. Again and again he assailed the surrender of the Jewish spirit to the Hellenic, and he was equally severe on medieval worthies, such as Ibn Ezra and Maimonides, for coming to terms with the alien wisdom.

By the side of Zunz, the creator of the history of Jewish literature, and Luzzatto, the restorer of the study of the Hebrew language and Scriptural interpretation, it was the gift of the Galician lay scholar, Nahman Krochmal (1785–1840), to grasp the philosophic meaning of Jewish history with its periods of rise and decline constantly repeating themselves. Under the influence of Hegel's system of philosophy, he saw in Judaism the synthesis of opposing movements making for a consecration to the spiritual in the absolute. The progress of the life-story of the 'everlasting people' presented itself to him as bound up with every movement in the large world. His chief, but unfinished work, posthumously published by Zunz (1851), was characteristically named a 'Guide of the Perplexed of our Generation.' It signified a strengthening of the Jewish consciousness and a reinterpretation of the essence of Judaism in which unreasoned enthusiasm and cold logic are reconciled to form a 'faith refined.'

Another Galician student, who held rabbinical offices in Tarnopol and Prague, Solomon Judah Loeb Rapoport (1790–1867), pointed the way in a number of historical essays to the recovery of creative periods long forgotten or little understood. By dint of a profound knowledge of the talmudic literature and its sequel in the tenth and eleventh centuries, coupled with critical acumen, he reassembled the scattered data from sources known or recently discovered. Thus he vitalized eminent figures in the past by evaluating their significance in the nexus of events and introducing into Jewish history the notion of development. Rapoport's writings were all in Hebrew; Zunz acknowledged them as stimulating; Christian scholars lauded them as mines of information. In richness of content and methodical penetration they were incomparably superior to the shallow rationalism and cold detachment which dominated the historical work of Isaac Marcus Jost (1793–1860), teacher in the Frankfort Philanthropin. It was exactly what Jost signally failed in understanding and Rapoport fully comprehended, that the past must be judged by its own standards, that each age developed that which was necessary to the safeguarding of Jewish life and existence, and that history was a sequence of unfoldments each standing in relation to that which preceded it. Rapoport approached the story of his people from within, even as he repudiated the vagaries of those leaders in his own day who made ready to sacrifice the rich past for the beggarly crumbs of ease in the present surroundings.

CHAPTER LXXXV

AFTER THE JULY REVOLUTION

(1830-1846)

THE bloodless July revolution of 1830, by which the popular Orleanist Louis-Philippe succeeded the arbitrary Bourbon Charles X., affected the Jews of France favorably; still more potent was its effect abroad, in Central Europe and even in insular Britain, eventually leading to Jewish enfranchisement. In France, the law of 1808 (p. 615) had been suffered to fall into desuetude when the time-limit expired in 1818; but the full measure of equality was achieved only in 1831, when Judaism was placed on a par with other religions by the granting of state support to the synagogues and the Jewish ministry. The last vestige of discrimination disappeared in 1846 when the specific form of the Jewish oath ('more Judaico') was abolished, thanks to the efforts of the brilliant advocate Isaac Adolphe Crémieux (1796–1880), since 1831 vice-president of the Central Consistory at Paris and throughout his long life the indefatigable defender of Jewish rights at home and abroad. In 1835 he prevailed upon the French government to discontinue consular relations with the Swiss canton Basel for its refusal to admit an Alsatian Jew to its borders. In 1845, however, when a new expulsion of the Jews from Basel was ordered, the conservative minister of foreign affairs, Guizot, refused to interfere in the internal affairs of a foreign government, exactly as he had been reluctant in 1841 to make representations to Saxony for excluding a Parisian Jew from Dresden.

Internally, the process of Jewish amalgamation with French interests and culture went apace. Jews became prominent in politics, in art, and in letters. Benoît Fould entered the Chamber as a deputy in 1834; in 1842 there followed Max Cerfberr on the conservative benches and Crémieux in the opposition. The composer Halévy (1799–1862), who is best known by his tragic opera 'La Juive,' was born in Paris of Bavarian immigrants; the equally talented and prolific Giacomo Meyerbeer (1791–1864), who befriended Richard Wagner only to be traduced by him in later days, produced his most notable operas in the French capital. From Paris, Heinrich Heine (1797–1856) and Ludwig Börne (1786–1837), both lost to Judaism, yet by no means indifferent to the race from which they sprang, led the movement of 'Young Germany' which prepared the German people for political maturity and unification. The religious life of the French Jews, except in the strictly orthodox communities of Alsace, was of the weakest sort: the cantors in the synagogues sang beautifully and the rabbis were nicely mute. Two brothers of the Cerfberr family were converted to Catholicism—Théodore (in 1826) and Alphonse (in 1842) Ratisbonne, the latter of whom engaged in conversionist activities among the Jews and Mohammedans in Palestine. On the other hand, there were those who rose superior to the general apathy. Adolphe Franck (1809–1893), professor at the Sorbonne and member of the Institute, won recognition for his meritorious sketch of the Cabala (1843). The unassuming Solomon Munk (1803–1867), an emigrant from Silesia, lost his eyesight over his assiduous labors on manuscripts in the field of Oriental and Jewish studies; his greatest achievement was the publication of the Arabic original of the 'Guide' of Maimonides with a French translation in three stout volumes (1856–1866). It was he who recognized in the Avicebron of the Christian scholastics, Solomon Ibn Gabirol, the great Spanish-Jewish poet and philosopher.

In England, the Jewish resettlement in the seventeenth century, as told above (p. 493), was at first rather a matter of connivance. There was no law in England which forbade the return of the Jews, but the Act of Uniformity of 1559, which made any other rites, except those of the Church of England, unlawful, was still in force. However, by virtue of the dispensing power of the Crown, the small Jewish community in London was able to venture into the open with its religious organization. An Order in Council, made by

King James II. on November 13, 1685, formally declared that the Jews should 'quietly enjoy the free exercise of their religion, whilst they behave themselves dutifully and obediently to his government.' By 1701 the Bevis Marks Synagogue was completed. A year later, David Nieto (1654–1728), the most notable among the congregation's spiritual leaders, was installed as haham. He was an Italian by birth and of a philosophical bent of mind; a theological treatise, published in 1704, laid him open to the charge of Spinozism, of which, however, he was cleared by the Haham Zebi. Nieto's chief literary effort was a defense of the oral law against the unbelievers, 'Kozari Part Two,' modeled after Judah ha-Levi's work.

The Sephardic element of London Jews maintained the direction of the growing community to the end of the eighteenth century, though German Jews had begun to arrive as early as 1692 and in 1722 had a place of worship of their own, the Great Synagogue in Duke's Place. Naturally, the newer arrivals could not compare with the Sephardim in wealth or culture. Some of the richest financiers of northern Europe belonged to the Bevis Marks congregation. Such were Sir Solomon de Medina, the first Jew knighted in England, who made himself extremely useful to the Duke of Marlborough on his campaigns (1702–1714), and Samson Abudiente (with his Anglicized name, Samson Gideon, 1699–1762), the friend of Sir Robert Walpole. To such highly stationed families the legal restrictions to which the Jews were subject were irksome. Repeated efforts to provide by an act of Parliament for the naturalization of Jews resident in England, led to no results. A bill passed in 1753 met with popular opposition and was repealed the next year, although an act had been passed as early as 1740 which permitted the naturalization of Jews in the British colonies of America. Jews holding land were accordingly prevented from passing it on to their offspring. Accordingly, Gideon, in his desire to found a landed family, decided to raise his children in the Christian faith, and his example was followed by a number of the leading families.

The Board of Deputies, which was called into existence shortly after the accession of George III. (1760), was powerless to secure an alteration in the political status of the Jews. At the beginning of the nineteenth century a second defection of prominent Sephardic families became wide-spread. It was then that David Ricardo (1772–1823), be it said against his father's will, abandoned Judaism in preparation for his brilliant career as a political economist and member of the House of Commons. In 1813, the scholarly recluse Isaac D'Israeli was fined by the congregation for declining to serve as warden. He preferred to have his name stricken from the list of members and after his father's death (1816) had his son Benjamin baptized. Of course, he was alive to the worldly advantages that lay in the change of religion; but little did he dream to what exalted heights it would carry the precocious boy.

Still the congregation was by no means bereft of important figures. There had been a continuous tradition and an eagerness among the laymen for religious instruction, at a time when the rabbis of the German community could not command a single pupil advanced enough to take up talmudic studies. These rabbis were of the old school. Hirschel Levin tarried in London but eight years (1756–1764); David Tevele Schiff persevered from 1765 to his death in 1792. The ministry of Solomon Hirschel (1802–1840), who, though born in London (as the son of Hirschel Levin), was educated abroad, coincided with the growing ascendancy of the Ashkenazic element, enriched as it was by the advent of the Goldsmids from Holland and of the Rothschilds from Frankfort.

The founder of the House of Rothschild was Mayer Anshel (died 1812), a Frankfort banker, who, chiefly as investor for the landgrave of Hesse-Cassel, built up a lucrative brokerage business. Among his five sons, the one possessing the greatest ability as a financier was the third, Nathan Meyer (1777–1836), since about 1800 located in Manchester and from 1805 on in London. By coöperation with his brothers at Frankfort, Vienna, Paris, and Naples, the head of the London branch undertook vast financial operations embracing practically the whole of Europe. The subsidies paid by England to her continental allies during the war with Napoleon were handled by the Rothschilds; during the years of reconstruction they introduced the method of raising loans for the nations of Europe and South America by passing them on to English investors with a guarantee of a fixed rate of interest. By his marriage to a sister-in-law of Moses Montefiore, Nathan Mayer came into association with the heads of the Sephardic community who maintained financial connections with the Amsterdam bankers. The barriers between Sephardi and Ashkenazi were being let down; Montefiore married the daughter of an Ashkenazi. The combined influence of both sections was a tower of strength for the Jews of England in their battle for civil and political rights.

It was not an easy combat against set prejudice. In 1829 the Catholics achieved the removal of most of their political disabilities. But the declaration, 'upon the true faith of a Christian,' now required of persons elected to an office in lieu of taking the sacrament, while it relieved Christian dissenters, accentuated the exclusion of Jews. The Jewish issue was forced by David Salomons (1797–1873). In 1835 he was elected sheriff of London. Upon refusal to make the prescribed declaration, the difficulty was solved by an act of Parliament dispensing with the declaration for the particular office of sheriff of a city which was a county by itself, such as the city of London was. But when in the same year he was elected alderman for a ward of the municipality of London, the courts pronounced the election void because the alderman-elect had refused to sign the prescribed declaration. His reëlection to the same office in 1844 and his repeated refusal to subscribe the declaration in the form unacceptable to a professing Jew, led to an act of Parliament, passed in 1845, which created a new form of oath for Jews elected to municipal offices. Thus one of the disabilities was swept away.

The office of sheriff in the county of London had meanwhile been held by another Jew (1837), whom the young queen Victoria (1837–1901) knighted on that occasion. Sir

Moses Montefiore (1784–1885) illustrated through his long life the fine combination of unswerving devotion to queen and country and of whole-hearted concern for the welfare of his coreligionists throughout the world. He assumed the British traditions to the full and remained at all time a scrupulously observant Jew.

While in the mother-country the contest for the removal of Jewish disabilities was just commencing, a bill extending the same political rights to Jews as to Christians was introduced in the Legislative Assembly of Canada (1831), and after passing both the Assembly and Council received the royal assent (1832).

CHAPTER LXXXVI

RELIGIOUS DEVELOPMENTS AMONG THE JEWS OF THE UNITED STATES

(1802-1868)

EXCEPT in the state of Maryland the political status of the Jews of the United States was on a par with that of all other citizens. The exception was removed in 1825 when the Jews of Maryland became eligible to offices by subscribing to a special declaration of their belief in future reward and punishment. The measure of relief was due to the influential position of the Jews of Baltimore—among whom the Cohen family was the most prominent—to their patriotic service in the defense of Baltimore during the war of 1812, and to the sympathies of a distinguished group of Christian citizens.

As the Ashkenazi element grew in numbers, whether they came straight from Germany and Poland or by way of England, the difference of ritual and Hebrew pronunciation led to the establishment of separate congregations. Thus arose Rodeph Shalom, 'Pursuer of Peace,' in Philadelphia (1802), and Bene Jeshurun in the city of New York (1825). Still more naturally was the Ashkenazi ritual followed in new communities like Cincinnati, where a body of young English Jews organized the congregation Bene Israel in the same year. The mode of worship was in keeping with the traditions which the new-comers brought with them.

It was among the Portuguese families of the south, in process of fuller identification with the life about them, that the first stirrings were manifested for reforms in the synagogue service. In 1824, twelve members of the Beth Elohim congregation in Charleston, South Carolina, led by the journalist Isaac Harby (1788–1828), seceded to constitute the Reformed Society of Israelites and organized an abridged service of which portions were read in the English language.

Sermons were delivered by the lay members, and the congregation worshiped with uncovered heads. The experiment, however, was of short duration. Only with the coming of Gustav Poznanski to the parent congregation as preacher (1836) were reforms introduced on the lines of the Hamburg Temple, although not without opposition from the conservative element. The new synagogue structure, dedicated in 1841, was equipped with an organ. In his dedicatory sermon the minister exultantly declared: 'This country is our Palestine, this city our Jerusalem, this house of God our Temple.'

A plea for relief from certain 'burdensome' ceremonies and improvements in the synagogue worship of the sort effected by 'a set of Jews' in Germany was made also in New York. The occasion was the dedication of the third synagogue edifice erected by the congregation Shearith Israel in Crosby Street in 1834; the speaker was Mordecai Manuel Noah (1785–1851), distinguished as a journalist, playwright, and politician. He had served his country as consul in Tunis and traveled in the Barbary States and through western Europe. Brought face to face with Jewish misery and rightlessness in most countries of the Old World, the thought had matured in him to transplant the Jews to America. In 1825 he purchased a tract of land on Grand Island in the state of New York and issued a manifesto to the Jews of the world to found a government of their own in this refuge to which he gave the name of Ararat. The corner-stone of the new city was laid with great pomp and ceremony, but the scheme fell through.

Neither at that time nor subsequently when he advocated reforms of the synagogue did Noah for a moment relinquish the Jewish hope of restoration in Palestine. In point of fact, the political events in the neighborhood of Palestine just at that period suggested to him the possibility of a disintegration of the Turkish empire and of the turning over of Palestine to its rightful owners, the Jews, with the consent of the Christian powers. He realized that there would be difficulties in effecting civic cohesion among the diverse elements of Jewry; he therefore planned the venture in America as the first step in organizing the government of the Jews. In a

'Discourse on the Restoration of the Jews,' delivered in 1844, he called on the free people of America to aid the Jews in their efforts to regain Palestine. The Jews must learn that it is their duty to prepare the fulfilment of the divine promises actively by human agency, and the power and influence of their Christian brethren must be invoked in carrying out the great work of restoration. The Messiah is yet to come, and 'if he has not come, we are bound to seek him, not here, but in our own land, which has been given to us as a perpetual inheritance, and which we dare not surrender without at once surrendering our faith.'

Thus the alinements, developed in Germany, repeated themselves in America. The nascent American reformatory movement received a counterbalance when in 1829 the congregation Mikveh Israel in Philadelphia elected as its minister a man thoroughly alive to constructive work. Isaac Leeser (1806–1868) came to America at the age of seventeen. He had received his secular education in a secondary school at Münster in Westphalia and had read several tractates of the Talmud; but in the main he was a self-taught man. He found before him virgin soil. The children were in need of Hebrew spelling-books and of manuals of religious doctrine; men and women required prayer-books correctly printed and adequately rendered into English. The indefatigable leader applied himself to the task of supplying all these needs. His crowning literary effort was the English translation of the Scriptures (1853), which until superseded by the new version of 1917 was the authorized translation for the Jews of America. Beginning with 1830, and then regularly from 1843 on, he preached to his congregation in English. Fearlessly, consistently, implacably he fought the progress of reform with his vigorous pen in his monthly magazine 'The Occident,' which he edited from 1843 to his death. He took a leading part in the creation of charitable and educational institutions, and his influence went beyond his own community. It was by a member of Leeser's congregation, Rebecca Gratz (1781–1869), that the first Sunday School for Jewish children was started in 1838.

CHAPTER LXXXVII

THE DAMASCUS LIBEL

(1840)

IN 1840 an event which profoundly stirred the Jewish world took place in Damascus. On February 5, Father Thomas, superior of the Franciscan convent, suddenly disappeared. Although it was known that a Turkish muleteer had threatened to kill him, his brother monks spread the rumor that he had been slain by the Jews for ritual purposes, merely on the score of his having been seen in the Jewish quarter the day before his disappearance. The French consul, Ratti Menton, with the aid of the governor, Sherif Pasha, had several arrests made in the Jewish quarter. A confession was extorted from a Jewish barber by means of torture in true medieval fashion, and seven notables of the community were arrested and tortured. One of them, Joseph Lañado, a feeble old man, died under the cruel treatment; Moses Abulafia embraced Islam; the others, unable to endure the torture, took upon themselves the blame for a crime which neither they nor their fellow-Jews had committed. Even small children, sixty in number, were confined in prison and left without food. Three of the rabbis and other prominent Jews, jailed at the instigation of the French consul, remained steadfast; Isaac Levi Picciotto, an Austrian subject, escaped, thanks to the interposition of the Austrian consul Merlato.

The French consul did his worst to poison public opinion abroad by libelous publications in the French press. He prepared to make short shrift of the detained Jews. The governor, equally desirous of executing them, sought authorization from his master Mehemet Ali, the rebellious Pasha of Egypt, who had possessed himself of Palestine and Syria in 1832. France was pursuing a policy friendly to the usurper. Crémieux's representations to Louis-Philippe and his minister Thiers met with lukewarm replies, and he was forced to own: 'France is against us.' Upon the urgent requests of Palmerston, the British secretary of state for foreign affairs, and Metternich, the Austrian chancellor, Mehemet Ali was willing to turn over the case to a special court of the consular agents of England, Austria, Russia, and Prussia. The French consul-general at Alexandria, however, did all in his power to prevent a reopening.

In the House of Commons, on June 22, Lord Palmerston announced that he had duly served notice on Mehemet Ali concerning the impression which the barbaric treatment of the Jews of Damascus was bound to arouse in Europe. On July 3, a great meeting was held in the Mansion House in London, at which members of Parliament and representatives of the Christian clergy vigorously protested against the medieval libel. Meetings of protest were held by the Jews in New York City (August 19) and in Philadelphia (August 27) at Mikveh Israel, where, besides Leeser, three Christian clergymen spoke. On behalf of President Van Buren, secretary of state John Forsyth gave out the information that letters had been sent to the consul at Alexandria and the minister to Turkey with instructions to use their good offices in preventing or mitigating those horrors 'the bare recital of which has caused a shudder throughout the civilized world.'

At an assembly of representative Jews in London which was attended by Crémieux, it had been resolved to send a deputation to the East, consisting of Montefiore, Crémieux, and Solomon Munk. The French consul interposed all possible obstacles, but French influence in Egypt was now on the wane. A collective note from nine other European consuls forced Mehemet Ali to order the release of those Jewish martyrs who had not succumbed to death (September 6). In October, Damascus and all of Syria were freed from the dominion of Mehemet Ali; shortly afterwards Syria was restored to Turkey. Montefiore and Crémieux were received in audience by the sultan Abdul-Mejid (1839–1861), who graciously issued a firman pronouncing ritual murder a base libel on the Jewish people and confirming the inviolability of Jewish persons and property in the Ottoman empire. The united action of the Jews far and wide which the dastardly affair provoked served as a proof that, with all their divisions, political, cultural, and religious, the Jews had a common bond which nothing could destroy.

CHAPTER LXXXVIII

THE STRUGGLE FOR EMANCIPATION IN WESTERN EUROPE

(1830-1858)

IN THE states comprising the Germanic Confederation, the immediate effect of the July revolution was but meager. This much, however, was accomplished: the governments were ill at ease and gave in here and there; above all, men spoke out their mind freely and prepared the larger upheaval of 1848 which came in the wake of another revolution in France. One German Jew, preëminently, understood that the righting of the Jewish conditions was a part of the general liberal movement, and that point was with him pivotal in the life-long warfare he waged on behalf of his coreligionists.

Gabriel Riesser (1806–1863) was a grandson of Raphael Cohen, the chief rabbi of Altona and the two sister congregations, who had joined in the ban against Mendelssohn's translation of the Pentateuch (p. 596). The change that had come about within three generations showed itself in the grandson; he was sent early to a secondary school and passed on regularly to the university from which he was graduated as a doctor of laws. Riesser felt himself thoroughly a German. He longed for the career of a university teacher, but he would not stoop to change of religion. He could enumerate twenty or more who had followed the line of least resistance; he would not question their motives, believing as he did in the right of the individual to be answerable to his own conscience. But he scathingly rebuked the governments for thinking so lightly of religious convictions as if they could be changed like a cloak, and of Christianity as if its profession were a mere civic affair and its expansion a matter of state reason indifferent to conscious assent.

Riesser firmly believed that there was no such thing as a

Jewish nation with a corporate existence of its own; the ceremonial laws and even the Messianic hope were in his judgment not of a purely political, but rather of a religious character. Moreover, he considered the medieval form of Judaism as irrevocably passing away. Nevertheless he demanded political emancipation for orthodox and reformers alike. He had no patience with the 'dogma' that the Talmud must be absolutely condemned or that this or that observance should be bartered away for the rights of citizenship. He would not listen to discarding the name of 'Jew'; under that very title he published, from 1832 on, a periodical 'for religion and liberty of conscience.'

Riesser's pen and voice were active whenever there was an opportunity to battle for Jewish rights, and at no time would he rest content with half-measures. So he counseled the Jews of Baden to reject outright the condition proposed by the diet of 1831 that they first should rid themselves of certain 'religious hindrances' to their emancipation. Despite a memorial prepared by Riesser, the same condition was insisted upon by the diet of 1833, the liberal minister Rotteck hoping that the Jews would accept the proviso which they had repudiated.

Riesser followed hopefully the developments in the Bavarian legislature in 1831. The home ministry ordered provincial assemblies of Jewish rabbis, teachers, and laymen, who, however, were divided on the question of religious doctrines and observances. The Würzburg convocation would hold only to the old traditions as found in the Talmud and Shulhan Aruk; so, too, the assemblies of Ansbach and Munich, while that of Bayreuth favored the abolition of the 'second days' of festivals customary outside Palestine (1836). All, however, opposed the transfer of the sabbath to Sunday. In the face of such disunion the government put off any measures of improvement in the civil situation of the Jews. Moreover, the liberal ministry was succeeded by a reactionary one, which informed the Jewish communities that the government would not tolerate any newfangled changes in Jewish doctrine or religious practice (1838).

The action of electoral Hesse in granting the Jews unconditional emancipation (1833) was acclaimed by Riesser with joy. Elsewhere in the smaller states no appreciable change in the status of the Jewish population occurred before 1848. In Prussia, the phantom of a 'Christian' state operated inimically against Jewish hopes of amelioration. By the regulation of 1833 the Jews of Posen were divided into two categories, those who were deserving of naturalization and those who were not. After the accession of Frederick William IV. (1840–1861), a project was in preparation (1842) to segregate the Jews in corporations by themselves and, specifically, to keep them from all government offices and even from military service. Riesser entered the arena by tearing off the mask behind which the illiberal designs of the government were hidden. The state was not obligated to move a finger to further the amalgamation of the Jews with the other inhabitants; but it should not step in to hinder. It was misunderstanding the Jewish cohesion to invest it with the character of a nationality long defunct. If the dictionary had no word by which to denote Jewish separateness, it was because nothing like it exists in the world. The Jews are held together solely by the religious idea; everything else is subordinate to it; whatever there lingers of a corporate order is the result of oppression from without and is being rapidly sloughed off.

However, the king of Prussia was constrained to introduce a semblance of constitutional government. In the spring of 1847 the Combined Provincial Diets were convoked, and a compromise measure was passed regulating Jewish affairs (July 23). The Jews were granted equality with Christian subjects, except where the law as it stood established another ruling. Accordingly, Jews were not eligible as deputies in the diets; nor were they to serve as judges, police or administrative officers. In the universities Jews might teach languages, mathematics, and natural sciences, but by no means be members of the senate or deans. In each town or city the Jews were to be organized as a religious community, with the right to elect their own executives and ministers.

These communities were to remain units without a central organization comprising them all, such as the Jews of France had. The government would not meddle with the internal affairs and would leave the Jews free to settle their religious differences. Schools could be established only for religious instruction; in exceptional cases elementary schools might be created for the teaching of other subjects, but in general Jewish children should frequent the schools alongside of Christian scholars. Each community was to maintain itself financially by its own means, subject, however, to government control.

Full emancipation came when the French revolution of February 1848 swept eastward. In Paris, the Provisional Government, set up in the place of the Orleanist monarchy, included Crémieux as minister of justice. In March, insurrections broke out in Vienna and Berlin. In the collisions with the troops several hundreds of the insurgents, among them a number of Jews, fell, and the victims, Jews and Christians, were buried in common graves, rabbis and Christian clergymen joining in performing the sad rites. Similar uprisings occurred all over Germany as well as in Hungary. Everywhere liberal constitutions were wrested from the monarchs, and all, save that of Bavaria, included clauses removing Jewish disabilities. The German National Assembly, which convened in May at Frankfort, numbered four Jewish deputies, among them Riesser, who subsequently was elected a vice-president. Riesser nobly defended his coreligionists against aspersions on their fitness as citizens. The fundamental rights of German citizenship, passed by the Assembly and incorporated into the Constitution of the empire, abrogated all distinctions on account of religion.

But the joy was short-lived. The larger states were by no means minded to be bound by the 'fundamental rights' which they refused to proclaim as law. In fact, the liberal constitutions severally granted or promised were withdrawn or made nugatory. The deputies of the National Assembly were dispersed; the old Confederation and its Diet of delegates representing the several sovereigns were reëstablished (1850).

It was small comfort to the Jews that the privilege of sitting in the legislatures was not taken away from them, when by arbitrary interpretation their civil rights were constantly infringed. Jewish emancipation in Prussia, Austria, and the smaller states was allowed to remain on paper, but was far from actual. In Hungary, the collapse of Kossuth's republican government through Austro-Russian intervention resulted in the Jews being compelled to pay a special indemnity for their participation in the revolution. By the grace of Emperor Francis Joseph (1848–1916) the amount was reduced to a million florins and subsequently used as a fund for Jewish educational purposes.

In England, Baron Lionel de Rothschild (1806–1879), eldest son of Nathan Mayer, was elected to Parliament in 1847. It was not, however, till 1858 that he was permitted to take his seat, the form of the oath being so amended as to relieve the scruples of professing Jews. The leader of the conservative majority in the House of Commons was then Benjamin Disraeli (1804–1881), who, whatever he thought of Jewish participation in politics, was glad that the question, awkward as it was for him as a born Jew, was at last disposed of.

CHAPTER LXXXIX

REFORM AND COUNTER-REFORM

(1841-1860)

IN 1841, a strife was precipitated over the new edition of the prayer-book of the Hamburg Temple. Bernays condemned it outright, while a number of like-minded rabbis supported their colleagues in Hamburg. The principal point in dispute was the omission of the prayers for national restoration in Palestine. The Temple leaders protested that the restoration did not imply that each and every Jew would necessarily abandon his present abode, exactly as at the time of the return from the Babylonian exile not all the Jews returned. Isaac Noah Mannheimer (1793-1865) discountenanced the omissions, being a firm believer in the national restoration; but he was free to confess that he had outgrown the idea of the reinstitution of the sacrificial ritual. He favored certain innovations, like confirmation for children which he had introduced in Copenhagen. At Vienna, in the new synagogue constructed in 1823, he labored on conservative lines, in coöperation with the celebrated cantor Solomon Sulzer (1804-1890), to render the service attractive and to edify the congregation with his sermons, gifted preacher that he was. He was averse to interference with the Hamburg congregation which was leading back to the house of God many that had been alienated.

Still the pivotal matter was the desire to accentuate Jewish patriotism by mere equivocation as regards rehabilitation in Palestine. It was becoming manifest that a cleavage had been reached, and that an adjustment was preparing which accepted the dispersion as definitive. The Jew was to surrender completely his own national aspirations, become denationalized; the question was, how completely. The most radical proponent of a denationalized Judaism was Samuel Holdheim (1806-1860). With ruthless logic and talmudic dialectic art he battered at the edifice of talmudic Judaism and the residue of rabbinical jurisdiction. His basic premise was, 'The law of the state is supreme,' and he drew the conclusion that the Jewish laws of marriage and divorce must go. In his later years he had no scruples about officiating at mixed marriages. Still with Holdheim Judaism had an eternally binding element that was not national in character; there was a limit to its elasticity. He could not therefore go the whole length with the programme of the Frankfort Reform Society, a group of laymen in consultation with the mathematician M. A. Stern of Göttingen. Their Declaration, issued in 1843, pronounced for unlimited development of the Mosaic religion, threw over the Talmud as devoid of dogmatic or practical authority, and rejected the Messianic restoration of the Jewish people in Palestine. In the original draft a paragraph had been inserted to the effect that the members of the Society did not consider circumcision binding.

There had occurred some fatalities by reason of the rite, and a senate regulation was promulgated that all such parents as desired to have their children circumcised should employ only persons authorized by the city to perform the operation. The optional character of the rite, it was thought, was thus recognized by the city authorities, and a father actually neglected to have his child circumcised. The rabbi of the community, Solomon Abraham Trier, addressed a circular letter to a number of colleagues and scholars, among them Luzzatto and Rapoport, all of whom expressed their horror at the breach, though diverging on the disciplinary measures against transgressors. Holdheim wrote a treatise declaring the rite to be not a national but a religious one, and therefore obligatory. Riesser, while not quite sympathizing with the Frankfort hotheads, insisted that no pressure should be exercised upon the individual consciences of parents. Zunz (p. 639) unmistakably and forcibly castigated the vagaries of the Frankfort group. So positive a stand on the 'bloody and barbaric' rite of initiation was irritating to Geiger; he wondered whether it was true that the master had—as a matter of principle, not merely of conformity— reintroduced in his home a 'kosher' table. Zunz replied with dignity and firmness. 'I leave it to those who take a delight in it to attack defenseless Judaism from motives inimical to religion. The rule for the religious can be only the religious, that which is held in universal acceptance and as a living tradition. It is ourselves that we must reform, not religion.'

Abraham Geiger (1810–1874) was quite as radical as Holdheim. Geiger, however, was a scholar of encyclopedic erudition and methodical training. The chief literary work, which achieved a fame outlasting the author's generation, had for its subject the development of religious ideas in Judaism traceable in the form which Holy Writ assumed in the original text and in the early versions ('Urschrift und Übersetzungen der Bibel,' 1857). Many of the conclusions lent themselves to correction by subsequent research, but the main contention was brilliantly conceived. 'The Bible,' wrote Geiger, 'is and at all times was a Word full of fresh life, not a dead book. This everlasting Word belonged not to a particular age; it could not be dependent for its meaning on the time when it was written down. . . Hence every period, every school, every individuality introduced into the Bible its own way of regarding the contents of the Bible. . . Thus the Bible became the full expression of the higher life of the people. That which seemed deficient in the text of the holy book the national spirit innocently supplied.' This thought, which elevates the fluid historical development above the fixity of the written letter, was borne in upon Geiger by his activity as a reformer, just as in its turn it imparted to his practical work rule and direction.

Judaism thus presented itself to Geiger under the historical aspect. Ideas and institutions came to be and had not been before; hence they were subject to change, they could pass away, replaced by newer modes of expression. Geiger therefore believed in the capacity of Judaism for new development, though perhaps not to the unlimited extent of the Frankfort group. But where he and Holdheim parted company was that the latter in the end allied himself with a private group in Berlin, similar in origin and perhaps also in its intent to the Frankfort society. The Berlin Reform

Association was called into being by a number of radicals in 1845. On promulgating their creed and taking steps for a curtailed ritual, almost wholly in German, they were bitterly opposed by the newly elected rabbi of the community, Michael Sachs (1808–1864), a modern man of high scholarship, but thoroughly conservative. The pulpit in what a few years later became the Berlin Reform Synagogue was at first offered to Geiger, who, however, declined, while Holdheim accepted it (1847). Geiger would hardly have consented to the transfer of the sabbath to Sunday, as was done in the Berlin Reform Synagogue under Holdheim's ministry. Geiger would have considered it a concession to Christianity, whose claims to superiority he intrepidly fought. At all events he would not separate himself from the main community, within which he desired to carry out his reforms. As the law in Prussia stood then, the Reform Synagogue remained a private society and no more.

Thus Geiger worked within the Breslau community, the first large position he held after his youthful charge at Wiesbaden (1833–1838). He craved recognition as a member of the rabbinical college; from the start he was involved in a bitter feud with the orthodox senior rabbi, Solomon Tiktin (died 1843), who refused to admit his junior to functions of a legal-religious character. All the time Geiger was bent upon reforming the service and connived at the omission of certain essential rites on the part of liberal members. He furthermore placed himself in communication with those rabbis who were of his way of thinking and he was the acknowledged leader in the rabbinical conferences (1844 at Brunswick, 1845 at Frankfort, 1846 at Breslau).

The men who gathered at these assemblies were far apart. The most practical among them was Ludwig Philippson (1811–1889), founder in 1837 of the first Jewish weekly in German ('Allgemeine Zeitung des Judentums,' continued till 1922) and author of a German translation of the Scriptures with explanatory notes, a labor of fifteen years (1839–1853). There were practical questions to be considered, as for example the problem of school children carrying their books to school and writing on the sabbath day. The liberals advocated accommodating theory to practice, squaring doctrine with life; in other words, giving in to laxity when once it had become wide-spread. It was on the third day of the Frankfort Conference that the Dresden rabbi, Zechariah Frankel (1801–1875), registered his dissent by withdrawing.

By the side of Geiger, Frankel was the most distinguished scholar in the assembly. He had come half-heartedly; on the very first day he defined his attitude as being positive-historical. He placed himself squarely upon historical continuity, differing from Geiger in that, while allowing for critical researches into the past, he held that what had come to be must be honored as a permanent institution from which it were treason to part. Thus he considered the retention of the Hebrew language in the public worship absolutely essential instead of merely advisable as the Conference voted.

Geiger had for many years advocated the establishment of a rabbinical seminary. He was largely instrumental in securing an endowment from a member of his own community; but when, in 1854, the institution was opened in Breslau, he felt it as a humiliating blow that he had been completely passed over. Frankel became the first director of the new seminary and imparted to it the conservative character which remained with it in after times and marked it as the center between the two extreme positions on the left and on the right.

Indeed, there was an extreme right. Not the old-fashioned orthodoxy, but one that was reared anew, a foe worthy of the modernists' steel. Samson Raphael Hirsch (1808–1888) was Geiger's fellow-student at Bonn. But his was a temperament given to mysticism, intensified by the teachings of Bernays, the haham of his native city. The conclusion ripened in Hirsch early and gave direction to his life-long ministry—at Oldenburg, Emden, Nikolsburg, and Frankfort—that Judaism and humanism, Jewish piety and modern culture were compatible ideals.

In the 'Nineteen Letters of Ben Uzziel,' published in 1836, he outlined his full programme, which in his subsequent writings was merely worked out in detail. The trouble with the young generation was, he contended, that it did not know Judaism, and with the elders that for them piety was a mechanical performance. Judaism stood for the spiritual perfection of every Jew and every Jewess; instead of trimming the Torah to the measure of the age, it was rather life that must be consecrated by the conscious fulfilment of all the commandments, each and every one of which is a necessary part of an organic whole. Yes, Israel has a mission to the world; but in order to accomplish it, God has imposed upon the Jews moral and spiritual separateness. Israel's national existence was conditioned by a life according to the Torah; it was forfeited when that life was not realized. It will come back in order that the fulness of the God-willed conduct may be achieved, but come back in God's own time, and must not be accelerated by human agency. Then the whole human race will be converted to the Jewish view of life and acknowledge God as One. The goal is the universal brotherhood of man. For that goal Israel must wait and work and live, live the full Jewish life. Humanity will be the loser if the Jew, instead of developing his own individuality, will yield to the hollow sentimentality of the age and accept conceptions from without which are not his. For the sake of the very mission the Jew must persevere in his aloofness, not from hostility to the world, but as an act of service to the highest interests of human kind. Jewish steadfastness calls for sacrifice upon the altar of duty; convenience is an unworthy rule of life. Emancipation is to be welcomed; the Jew may now rise to his full stature of manhood, be man and Jew at once, full man and full Jew.

In 1840, a reform congregation of the moderate type was organized in London. It took the name of the 'West London Synagogue of British Jews.' The step was combated by the orthodox authorities, particularly by Nathan Marcus Adler (1803–1890), who was installed chief rabbi of the Ashkenazim in 1845. However, in 1856, the reform synagogue was authorized by an act of Parliament to register marriage ceremonies.

CHAPTER XC

POLITICAL AND CULTURAL CONDITIONS
IN EASTERN EUROPE

(1815-1855)

ETWEEN the Vienna Congress (1815) and the seating of Rothschild in the British House of Commons (1858), the Jews of Confederate Germany and the Austrian dependencies, of France, of England, and across the Atlantic passed through a period of external and internal development which proceeded along more or less similar lines. Their political and cultural status was sufficiently marked to divide off the Jews of the West from their brethren in the East.

What was left of the grand duchy of Warsaw, after the slices recovered by Prussia and Austria, was bound to Russia as a new kingdom of Poland with the czars as its hereditary kings. The constitution of 1815 was a liberal document, except that the Jews were left out in the cold. A commission, while recognizing in theory that the Jews should receive civil and political rights, considered their immediate emancipation as harmful. The Jews must first wean themselves from their present occupations and take to tilling the soil, rid themselves of their communal separateness and change their system of education. The Polish viceroy refused to fall in even with this modest project. Novosiltsov, the czar's representative, who had a seat in the Administrative Council, proposed that the Jews should be granted civil rights coincidently with a transformation of their habits of life. But the Polish members of the Council answered: 'Let them first become Poles' (1817). So the Council proceeded to 'reform' the Jews by expelling them from towns from which, in accordance with their ancient charters, Jews were barred, or at least by confining them in special quarters.

Nor were the Jews admitted to military service, in lieu of which a fixed conscription tax was exacted.

The displeasure of the Poles with Jewish separateness was seconded from within by a group of assimilationists, wealthy bankers and merchants in the capital, who labeled themselves 'Votaries of the Old Testament' or 'Poles of the Mosaic Persuasion.' The government was not slow to frame a law, which was sanctioned by an imperial ukase (1822), abolishing the 'kahal' administration and replacing it by communal boards strictly confined to the ordering of religious and charitable affairs. In Warsaw the assimilationists obtained control of the management of the community. They were close to the powers in the government and coöperated with them in civilizing the Jews and modernizing Judaism. The very first thing they did was to open a school for the training of rabbis (1826). The language of instruction was Polish; most of the teachers of the secular subjects were Christians. The post of principal was held by Anton Eisenbaum, an extreme assimilator; Hebrew and Bible were taught by Abraham Buchner, who had published a pamphlet setting forth 'the worthlessness of the Talmud.'

The repudiation of what was sacred to hundreds of thousands of their brethren availed these Jews but little. When in 1830, at the outbreak of the revolution, they offered themselves as volunteers for service in defense of the fatherland, they were told that Jewish blood could not be allowed to mingle with the noble blood of the Poles. Nevertheless Joseph Berkovicz, whose father Berek had fought as a colonel under Kosciusko in 1794, called upon his coreligionists to fight for Polish independence. The communal leaders set themselves against the formation of a separate Jewish regiment. In the sequel Jews were admitted to military service, but only in the militia, not in the regular army. However, since the commander of the National Guard insisted that the Jewish guardsmen should shave their beards, a special 'bearded' section of the metropolitan guard was formed, comprising eight hundred and fifty Jews. The collapse of the revolution and the iron rule of the Russian viceroy Paskevich after 1832 introduced no appreciable changes in the status of the Jews, which was regulated by the former Polish law. But in 1842 the Jews of Poland were placed on a par with their brethren in Russia, both being forced to discharge military service in person. Three years later the law forbidding the traditional Jewish mode of dress was made operative in Poland likewise.

In Russia proper, the last ten years of the reign of Alexander I. (1815–1825) brought to the Jews a mixture of benevolent paternalism and severe repression. The former was exemplified by the creation of a 'Society of Israelitish Christians,' which held out substantial privileges to whole communes of converted Jews. However, the scheme was finally dropped for the very reason that all told there were reported only thirty-seven families from Odessa, neither possessing certificates of baptism nor able to produce passports. Instead of Jews being converted to Christianity, there came to light a heretical movement of dissidents from the Greek Orthodox Church, who observed the seventh day sabbath ('Subbotniki') and professed doctrines akin to Judaism. The Jews, of course, had nothing to do with the movement, since it occurred in remote provinces where no Jews resided. Nevertheless it was ordered that the Jews should be expelled from any place where the 'Judaizing' sect had made its appearance.

The alleged proselytism of the Jews served as a pretext for strict measures forbidding Jews to employ Christian domestics or to lease manorial estates and thus become masters of serfs. In 1821, White Russia was stricken by a famine; naturally the Jews were affected as well. The government harked back to the policy, previously interrupted, of banishing all Jews from the villages of the governments of Moghilev and Vitebsk. The order was ruthlessly carried out; by the beginning of 1824 more than twenty thousand Jews had been expelled. The college of six Jewish deputies was powerless to avert the calamity. This body was created in 1818 as a sort of advisory board in Jewish matters, accredited to the ministry of ecclesiastical affairs. In 1825, the board was altogether disbanded. The government considered the deputies undesirable go-betweens, who ferreted out its intentions and prematurely divulged them to the communities in the Pale. The imperial policy was plainly to reduce the number of Russian Jews. Even the progressive elements among the Russian people were distinctly inimical. The revolutionist Pestel—he subsequently paid the penalty of death as one of the leaders in the December uprising upon the accession of Nicholas I.—proposed to curb the Jews by means of correctional measures or to assist them in setting up a state of their own in some portion of Asia Minor.

Nicholas I. (1825–1855) pursued a determined policy, which he carried through with inflexible thoroughness, to uphold autocracy, orthodoxy, and Russian nationality. Not only was Russia to shut itself off against western European influences, but within also all national differences were to be wiped out before the dominant race. It was proper enough to extend conscription to the Jews equally with all elements and classes of the population. The ukase of 1827 gave expression to the hope that the training acquired by the Jewish recruits would, upon their return, communicate itself to their families. The unmistakable meaning was made clear beyond doubt by an elaborate statute of ninety-five clauses. The time of service was to be twenty-five years. Jewish recruits, however, might be taken at the tender age of twelve years. All boys below the age of eighteen were to be trained in preparatory establishments, the actual duration of the service being reckoned from the time they reached the nineteenth year. These 'cantonists,' as they were called, were sent away into the farthest provinces, at a distance from their home surroundings and influences. The sturdiest children alone reached their destination, the weaker ones succumbed during the long journey. Every method of torture was used to induce the children to embrace Christianity. They were starved, or they were made to eat salted fish and then denied water; they were kept forcibly awake and were mercilessly flogged. Small wonder that few remained steadfast.

The Jewish communes ('kahals') were answerable for the number of conscripts each was to supply. Exempt were certain classes of merchants, artisans and mechanics, agricultural colonists, rabbis, and the small number of graduates from Russian educational institutions. If the community fell short of its quota, the communal agents made a regular hunt to catch (hence they were called 'catchers') any one available, often enough children under twelve years, in which case their age was misstated. The burden fell chiefly upon the poor, who had no means to pay the high license fees required of merchants, or who were not sufficiently well-connected to escape the hunting agent. In 1834 and the beginning of 1835, a rumor was spread that the government would prohibit early marriages and that those married before the law went into effect would not be conscripted. A panic seized the communities, and boys and girls were joined in marriage in their early teens. The law of 1835 did forbid marriages below the age of eighteen, but of course offered no exemption to those already married. Thus the number of families whose husbands and fathers were conscripted, was unduly increased.

The Statute concerning the Jews, of which the law just cited was the least harsh, had the word 'Forbidden' written almost all over it. The Pale of Settlement was considerably narrowed down. It comprised Lithuania (Kovno, Vilna, Grodno, Minsk), the southwestern provinces (Volhynia, Podolia), White Russia (Vitebsk, Moghilev) minus the villages, Little Russia (Chernigov, Poltava) minus the crown hamlets, New Russia (Kherson, Ekaterinoslav, Taurida, Bessarabia) except Nikolaev and Sevastopol, the government of Kiev exclusive of the city of Kiev. In the Baltic provinces, only the old settlers were permitted to reside. The villages on the entire fifty verst zone along the western frontier were closed to new-comers. As to the interior provinces, only temporary furloughs, limited to six weeks, were to be granted to holders of gubernatorial passports, on condition that the travelers were dressed in the Russian instead of the Jewish garb. Licensed merchants of the first two classes paying the highest tax might visit the two capital cities, the seaports, and the fairs at Nizhni-Novgorod and other cities.

The Jews were forbidden to employ Christian domestics for permanent work. It was permissible to hire Christians for temporary service, provided the laborers were accommodated in quarters of their own. The Russian language was made obligatory in public documents. The 'kahals' were charged with the duty of seeing to it that the instructions of the authorities were carried out with precision and that all taxes were correctly paid. Barring the city of Vilna, where the Jews were wholly excluded from municipal self-government, those Jews who were able to read and write Russian were eligible as members of the town councils and magistracies. Synagogues were not to be erected in the vicinity of churches. Jewish children were admitted to Russian schools of all grades, without compulsion to change their religion. A strict censorship was exercised over all books published in Hebrew.

In 1840, the Council of State, principally won over by the ministers of instruction and of home affairs, Uvarov and Stroganov, came to the conclusion that the 'Jewish evil' must be attacked at its root. The 'evil' consisted in Jewish separateness, and the 'root' was the Jewish educational system. Imperial sanction was obtained for the establishment of a committee to define measures for the radical transformation of the Jews of Russia. As an initial step Uvarov's project was accepted to create in all the cities of the Pale elementary schools in which Jewish children were to be taught the Russian language, secular subjects, Hebrew, and religion according to Holy Writ. Thus the growing generation would be weaned from the Talmud, in which, according to the opinion of the Russian statesmen, resided the chief cause for keeping the Jews estranged from their compatriots by the 'perverse' religious traditions which it inculcated. It was foreseen that the Jews would not take kindly to the reforms from above, however their ultimate purpose might be disguised. It was necessary that the 'obstinate' people should be taught to trust the 'benevolent' intentions of the government. Uvarov soon found the desired man for the task in the person of a young German Jew, who had just come to Russia to take up the post of preacher and director of a modern school in the Jewish community of Riga.

Max Lilienthal (1815–1882) was a graduate of the university of Munich and a sympathizer with religious reforms of the moderate sort. His success at the Riga school brought him an invitation from Uvarov, by whom he had been previously received, to visit the cities of the Pale and there, with the coöperation of the enlightened circles, to influence the masses in favor of the proposed school reform. Those that called themselves 'enlightened' (maskilim), or friends of 'enlightenment' (haskalah), were then exactly at the stage of the Mendelssohnians in Germany at the end of the preceding century. They were for the most part self-taught men, who acquired a measure of European culture and often enough achieved erudition which they then proceeded to disseminate by means of literary efforts in the Hebrew tongue. But whereas in Germany the movement had issued in the destruction of Hebrew writing, its counterpart in Russia produced a renascence both of the Hebrew language and of Hebrew letters which eventually struck deep roots among the people.

The first place among the leaders in this movement belonged to Isaac Baer Levinsohn (1788–1860), at Kremenez. His literary efforts, carried on amid privations and with inadequate library facilities, lacked profundity. Yet, under the conditions of his time and place, the very commonplaces he uttered, whether in the defense of Judaism or in advocacy of secular education, were novelties at which the bigoted looked askance. He rather naively believed in the good intentions of the government and was flattered by tokens of appreciation from highly stationed officials and ministers of state. The recurrence of ritual murder trials he met by a timely publication which proved its usefulness even on subsequent occasions. Among the other bearers of enlightenment may be singled out the prose writer Mordecai Aaron

Günsburg (1795–1846) and the poet Abraham Dob Lebensohn (1789–1878). Groups of men of the newer orientation were to be found in the Lithuanian metropolis Vilna and in the newer community of Odessa which became a very focus of modernity.

Lilienthal met with a friendly reception in these circles, but it was uphill work to convince the old-fashioned that there were no evil designs lurking in the government scheme and that the old schools were not imperiled. Still he experienced no difficulty with the head of the Volozhin yeshibah, Isaac, successor to his father Hayim, the founder of the school (p. 630). The venerable scholar consented to serve on the commission of rabbis and laymen summoned to St. Petersburg in 1843. The other members were the leader of the Hasidim in White Russia, Mendel Shneorsohn, grandson of Shneor Zalman (p. 586); the Berdiczev banker Halperin; lastly, Bezalel Stern, principal of a modern school at Odessa. The two rabbinical members vigorously stipulated that the schools of the old type should be preserved intact alongside of the new institutions planned by the government. An imperial rescript of 1844 ordered the establishment of Jewish elementary schools of two grades and the opening of two rabbinical institutes (these were subsequently located in Vilna and Zhitomir). In a secret communication to the minister of public instruction it was made plain that the old schools were to be closed gradually. The announced purpose was to bring the Jews nearer to the Christian population by destroying the study of the Talmud and the prejudices fostered by it. Before the plan was realized, Lilienthal, in 1845, had left Russia and emigrated to America. He had given his solemn pledge to the notables of the Vilna community that he would not be a party to any sinister motive on the part of the Russian government; he kept his word as soon as its insincerity was borne in upon him.

Inexorably did the government proceed to the complete realization of its programme which encompassed the destruction of Jewish communal organization and the enactment of repressive measures calculated to involve the broad masses in economic ruin. The 'kahals' were stripped of their internal administrative function; Jewish affairs were placed entirely in the hands of the police and the municipal government. But the government was by no means minded to dispense with Jewish fiscal agents to serve as tax-collectors for the imperial treasury among their own people. In addition to the regular taxes, the Jews were required to pay a special tax on 'kosher' meat and on sabbath candles. The disposition of these revenues lay in the hands of the provincial governors or the ministry of public education. These additional funds were to make up for shortages in the ordinary tax and to pay for the maintenance of the new schools. At the same time the law driving the Jews out of the frontier zone was made to cover also cities and towns, and not merely the villages as previously ordained. Furthermore, the Jews of the Pale were divided into two categories, the useful and the useless. This second class, which included the petty tradesmen and the large mass who lived from hand to mouth, was subjected to increased disabilities.

The plight of Russian Jewry stirred the influential Jewish circles abroad. In London it was determined that Montefiore should go to Russia. He came in 1846, was received in audience by the czar and conferred with the minister in charge of Jewish affairs. He was given every facility to travel in the Pale and was bidden to submit a report based on his personal observations. The tour was marked by enthusiasm on the part of the Jewish masses; but their hope that any change in the government's attitude would result from the mission was doomed to disappointment.

A Jewish merchant from Marseilles, Isaac Altaras, arrived in the same year in Russia with a project to transplant a certain number of Jews from Russia to Algeria; but the scheme fell through. The government was preparing in 1852 drastic measures against the huge mass of Jewish proletarians. However, the country was soon plunged into the Crimean War (1853–1856), and the measures were dropped. Fresh horrors resulted from the shortage of Jewish recruits. The order went forth that all Jews without passports—often enough they were made to part with them by the trickery of the appointed captors—might be seized for the army. At the very eve of the war, the government found scope for harassing the Jews by commanding European style of dress, while Jewesses were enjoined from cutting off their hair when entering upon marriage. On the top of all Jewish misery, the Jews of Saratov had to undergo trial on the charge of ritual murder. One of the imprisoned innocent sufferers—two had meanwhile committed suicide and the others were physical wrecks unable to discharge their penal servitude—was pardoned by Alexander II. in 1867, thanks to the intercession of Crémieux.

CHAPTER XCI

PROGRESS OF THE REFORM MOVEMENT IN AMERICA AND IN EUROPE

(1845-1876)

WHEN Lilienthal landed in New York in 1845, it was beyond the reach of his vision that the closing year of his life would witness the first mass migration of Russian Jews to America. Small bodies of Polish Jews, either by way of England or straight from home, had long been arriving, and they were followed soon by venturesome individuals from Russia. But beginning with 1830 and then continually in ever increasing numbers, in the period of reaction preceding and following 1848, there was an inpouring of Jews from Germany, particularly from Bavaria and Baden. The first comers were favored with little of worldly goods; until they learned the strange language, they eked out a living by peddling and rose but slowly to a competence. Only those that came after 1848 counted a number of better situated families, and there were many possessed of culture. The new land offered many opportunities of which these immigrants were quick to avail themselves; theirs was the freedom, denied at home, to establish families and to engage in mercantile pursuits leading to prosperity. The discovery of gold in California lured some of the more enterprising to the far western coast.

These German Jews kept their native speech for a considerable period, both in their homes and in public gatherings. Their number was large; some had come from the same village or town, others hailed from a neighboring locality, and there was a decided homogeneity about them all. They were furthermore divided from the old Portuguese settlers as well as from the more recent Polish arrivals by their ritual (minhag), which was the Ashkenazic in vogue in southern Germany and somewhat distinct from the one obtaining north of the Elbe and farther east. In New York City, where the largest number of German Jews resided, there were by 1842 three German congregations, which in 1845 united by electing Lilienthal as their joint rabbi. In the same year the congregation Emanuel was organized, which from the beginning showed an inclination towards reforms in the worship. Religious differences were developing; in order to create a common meeting-ground along educational and philanthropic lines, a group of German Jews founded in 1843 the Order B'nai B'rith (Bene Berith, 'Sons of the Covenant'), which rapidly spread over the United States and in time also to Europe and the Orient.

The movement for reform throughout the land, whether in new congregations starting out with that definite object in view or in older synagogues which had begun on orthodox lines, was an importation from Germany. It was destined to outstrip the German model, so that what was exceptional there became the normal practice here. There was in America no possible interference from without, nor were the congregations, each an independent corporation, amenable to a central communal authority. Rabbis fresh from Germany, imbued with the spirit for innovations and notably those who had taken part in the early reforming conferences, were free to change the ritual and religious practices, usually step by step, but sometimes quite precipitately. By dint of an organizing ability akin to that which distinguished Ludwig Philippson in Germany, Isaac Mayer Wise (1819–1900) became the leader of American reform. Of a commanding presence, a forceful preacher, genial to his friends, a fighter when any one crossed his path, he above all entered into the spirit and temper of his adopted country, while many of his co-workers remained German to their dying days. His initial ministry was in Albany, in the state of New York (1846–1854); in 1850 he had a clash with his old charge because of a doctrinal point and his friends organized for him a new congregation. The remainder of his long life he spent in Cincinnati as preacher, teacher, editor, author, and organizer. Through him that city became the seat of reform in America.

Wise had made early plans for a new ritual (Minhag America); it was consummated after the Cleveland Conference in 1855. The key-note of that gathering, which was attended by Leeser (p. 650), was union. Concessions were made to the right wing by reaffirming the authority of the Talmud, while the progressives were satisfied that they could get round the Talmud by interpretation. The compromise was denounced by the ultra-orthodox on the one hand and by the extreme reformers on the other. David Einhorn (1809–1879) had just been installed in Baltimore after a reforming career in Germany and for a brief time in Hungary, in the course of which he developed radical tendencies unacceptable to those rooted in the old traditions. He immediately launched a protest on behalf of his own congregation, concurred in by Temple Emanuel of New York, against upholding the authority of the Talmud and the 'hierarchical' designs in the west. This controversy laid the foundation for the split between east and west which lingered on for decades; the two camps of reform now came together, now fell apart again, until in the end the power of organization prevailed, not without concessions to the theorists.

Still more accentuated grew the division between the reformers and the traditionalists, the latter among themselves likewise representing various shades. There were fresh adhesions on either side. But soon the country was engrossed in the gigantic struggle for the saving of the Union during the Civil War (1861–1865). The Jews of the north and of the south fought along with their compatriots in the opposing camps; naturally the northern states had the larger number of Jews, and even the recent immigrants threw themselves with zeal into the combat. The Jews of the south occupied prominent posts in the Confederate army and government; among the most distinguished men in Jefferson Davis' Cabinet was Judah P. Benjamin (1811–1884), who served as attorney general and subsequently as secretary of state.

On the continent of Europe, likewise, a momentous struggle was preparing which, when it terminated in 1870, accomplished the unification of Italy under the king of Sardinia and of Germany under the leadership of Prussia. At the same time it swept out of power Napoleon III. (1852–1870), who had made the cause of the oppressed nationalities his own. In the course of the upheaval the Jews of Central Europe received their complete emancipation: in Austria in 1868, after the collapse of absolutism in consequence of her defeat by Prussia; north of the Main in 1869 by constitutional enactment of the North German Confederation; in southern Germany as soon as Bavaria joined the German Empire in 1871 (in Baden and Württemberg full equality to the Jews had been conceded in 1862 and 1864). The consummation was achieved only after repeated and concentrated efforts of the Jewish communities which, thanks to the energy of Ludwig Philippson, besieged with their petitions the several legislatures at every opportune moment. Nevertheless the success was entirely due to the advocacy by the liberal groups, often in the face of the government's opposition. The Jews of Italy had the greatest cause to rejoice when in 1870 the papal states ceased to exist and Rome became the capital of the united kingdom.

It was not so long ago that an outrage had been committed in Bologna against the most sacred rights of Jewish parenthood by the agents of Pius IX. (1846–1877), the reactionary enemy of modern civilization. In 1858, papal gendarmes carried away by force the six-year-old son of a Jewish family, Edgar Mortara. The child had been christened during illness by his Catholic nurse. The Church insisted that the baptism once administered made the boy a Catholic and that he must be brought up as such against the will of his parents. This truly medieval act shocked the civilized world. It made no difference to the pope that the Jews everywhere, in freed Piedmont, in Germany, in England, in America, raised their voices in protest. Montefiore came to Rome and made a personal appeal to the vicar of Christ—he remained obdurate even to the representations of the Catholic monarchs Napoleon III. and Francis Joseph. The child remained in the hands of his captors, who systematically imbued him with hatred for Judaism, so that when he attained majority he refused to return to the faith of his fathers.

The Mortara affair served to strengthen Jewish solidarity; as an outcome there was called into being in Paris in 1860 the 'Alliance Israélite Universelle,' which made as its chief programme the defense of Jewish rights wheresoever attacked. Crémieux was the president of the new organization with brief interruptions from 1863 to 1880.

The rise of the national spirit in Europe awakened in the minds of some Jews the conception that the Jewish people itself was a nation, in fact of all nations the most oppressed, which must look for repatriation in its ancestral home. This view ran counter to the doctrine of the reformers, just as it set itself against the platform of the newer type of orthodoxy by its advocacy of human and diplomatic agencies. The rabbi of Thorn, Zebi Hirsch Kalischer (1795–1874), a pupil of Akiba Eger (p. 635), published in 1862 a pamphlet in which he endeavored to prove that the Messianic redemption must be preceded by Jewish rehabilitation in Palestine. He called for the foundation of a colonizing society to effect the settling of Jewish tillers of the soil in the ancient homeland. As a direct result of Kalischer's agitation, the 'Alliance' founded in 1870 the agricultural school Mikveh Israel, near Jaffa, under the supervision of Charles Netter (1828–1882).

Kalischer's plea for restoring Palestine to the Jewish people was taken up immediately by Moses Hess (1812–1875). This 'communist rabbi,' as he was ironically called, had passed through a revolutionary career during which, as anarchist and socialist in turn, he was absorbed by the problem of the European proletariate. The Damascus and Mortara affairs brought him back to his own people. In his book 'Rome and Jerusalem,' published in 1862, he boldly attacked the reformers and the orthodox of the Samson Raphael Hirsch type for having sacrificed the Jewish national idea. He expressed the hope that a Jewish Congress would take in hand the colonizing of Palestine and pointed to renationalization as the only means of solving the Jewish question.

Hess owned himself powerfully stimulated by the early volumes of Graetz's 'History of the Jews' which had then appeared. Heinrich (Hirsch) Graetz (1817–1891) enjoyed in his early years the tuition and friendship of Samson Raphael Hirsch, both in the latter's Oldenburg home and later in or near Nikolsburg. But his sober, critical mind recoiled from Hirsch's symbolism. He was drawn rather to the party of Zechariah Frankel, under whom he accepted in 1854 a position on the teaching staff of the Breslau seminary. Graetz devoted himself in his latter years to biblical studies; but his chief fame rests on his work as historian. His 'History,' completed in 1870, was distinguished by vast erudition, a critical handling of the sources, and especially the happy instinct for discovering in the most unpromising material a mine of information. Moreover, the presentation was vivid and the narrative had warmth. He told the story of his people from within, with the large world as a background and no more. He spoke to all Israel and found a unity of purpose across the diverse periods. He had his prejudices and shortcomings; but what Hess admired and others found fault with was the unmistakable romanticism which he spread over the tale and the staying conviction that even in the times succeeding the formation of the Talmud Jewish history retained its national character.

The difference between Hess and his critics among the reformers was that the former operated with the newer ideas championed by Napoleon III., while the latter followed the tendencies in vogue since Napoleon I., the great leveler of nations, who made Jewish emancipation conditional upon the surrender of Jewish nationality. Thus the reformers steadfastly and unflinchingly kept to their course. They were the leading spirits in the Synods of Leipzig (1869) and Augsburg (1871), gatherings of laymen and rabbis, chiefly from Germany and Austria, but also (at Leipzig) from Switzerland, Belgium, England, and America. The aim was to create a world-embracing clearing-house for mooted religious questions in Jewry. The orthodox, however, kept away, and at the conclusion dissociated themselves from the general tone of the assemblies and from the specific resolutions carried there. The presiding officer of both gatherings was the Berlin philosopher Moritz Lazarus (1824–1903), who throughout his life spent his best efforts to prove that fidelity to Judaism in no wise precludes identification with the culture of the environment. He recognized for himself and for other German Jews but one nationality to which they belonged, the German. On both occasions Geiger was the first vice-president. In the same year in which the Leipzig Synod was convened, the American reformers met in Philadelphia and carried similar doctrinal and practical resolutions.

The need of an American institution for the training of rabbis had long been felt. While the eastern and western reformers continued at cross-purposes, the conservative forces forestalled them by creating in 1867 Maimonides College, which had a short existence of six years. Leeser, its head professor, was removed by death in the first academic year. But the college was fortunate to have on its faculty two zealous scholars: Sabato Morais (1823–1897), who in 1851 had succeeded Leeser at Mikveh Israel, and Marcus Jastrow (1829–1903), since 1866 rabbi at Rodeph Shalom. Shortly before his death, Jastrow completed a Dictionary of the Talmud in English, a model of painstaking labor and a credit to American Jewish scholarship. After the closing of Maimonides College, Wise renewed his efforts to establish a rabbinical school. In 1875 the Hebrew Union College at Cincinnati was opened, with Wise as president; the chair of Talmud was worthily occupied from 1879 on by Moses Mielziner (1828–1903), who in 1894 published a valuable Introduction to the Talmud in English.

In Germany, neither the progressives nor the orthodox were entirely satisfied with the Breslau seminary. Yet it served as the model for the rabbinical school at Budapest, which was set up in 1877. Among the first teachers in the Hungarian school were two graduates of the older institution, Wilhelm Bacher (1850-1913) and David Kaufmann (1852-1899), both versatile scholars who enriched Jewish scholarship with lasting contributions. The School for Jewish Learning ('Hochschule für die Wissenschaft des Judentums'), which was opened in Berlin in 1872 chiefly through the instrumentality of Ludwig Philippson, had among its first teachers Geiger, the historian David Cassel (1818–1893), the critical student of the Talmud Israel Lewy (1847–1917), the profound thinker Heymann Steinthal (1823–1899). It was intended that the institution should be strictly scholastic and that the teachers and students should be free to identify themselves with any expression of Judaism. Such a programme was unacceptable to the orthodox; a year later they created in the same city a seminary of their own, thanks to the efforts of Israel Hildesheimer (1820–1899). He was a man of modern culture and deep Jewish learning, who had previously conducted a yeshibah on modern lines in Eisenstadt, Hungary; he associated with himself in the new venture the talmudist David Hoffmann (1843–1921), who subsequently succeeded to the principalship, the historian Adolph (Abraham) Berliner (1833–1915), the Arabist Jacob Barth (1851–1914). The split between the reformers and the orthodox grew ever wider; in 1876 a law was passed by the Prussian government which enabled the orthodox to set up their own congregations as independent corporations.

CHAPTER XCII

THE JEWS OF RUSSIA AND RUMANIA

(1855-1878)

A SEEMING peace settled upon the Jews of the West, with political equality achieved and the religious conscience satisfied by the very separation of orthodox and progressives. The era of political reforms in the first ten years of the reign of Alexander II. (1855–1881), during which the Jews in Russia were, as they thought, on the eve of better days, was accompanied by an inner crisis, similar in some respects to the western and quite dissimilar in other ways. For one thing, juvenile conscription came to an end at the very commencement of the reign. The age-limit for recruits was made the same for Jews and Christians, though some discriminations still remained. If there was at all a definite policy amid much vacillation, it meant fusing Jews and Russians along cultural lines—the attempt to bring about religious sameness had been given up as hopeless. The Jews were to be 'Russified,' and privileges were granted to those who were ready for the process.

The inner provinces of the empire were opened for permanent residence to merchants of the highest class, graduates of universities, and mechanics. Wealth, education, and skill were welcome enough in furtherance of the industrial development of the country and as helpful to certain parts of the military machine. The Jewish capitalists supplied money and material for the construction of railroads, Jewish physicians and surgeons were needed in the army and in civil life. The law of 1864 made it possible for Jews to be admitted to the legal profession and in rare cases even to a judicial career.

But the great mass, without means to pay the high merchants' licenses or to afford costly education, remained penned up within the dense Pale, unable to advance economically. While a few hundred found their way to secondary and higher educational institutions, hundreds of thousands frequented the old-fashioned schools (heder and yeshibah) against which the government battled to no purpose until at length it left them in peace. Nor was the government able to drive out the old-style rabbis; in the end the two rabbinical seminaries were transformed into teachers' institutes to supply teachers for the Jewish crown schools.

Just as at St. Petersburg the official circles were bent upon Russifying the Jews, so at Warsaw the Poles, now preparing another revolution (1860–1863), were obsessed with the idea of Polonizing them. Suddenly it dawned upon the Polish leaders that Jewish friendship ought to be cultivated, and their approaches met with a hearty response not merely from the group of intellectuals eager for assimilation, but from the orthodox as well. The venerable spiritual head of the Warsaw community, Berush Meisels (1800–1870), vied with his younger colleague Marcus Jastrow (p. 681), then preacher in a semi-reformed Warsaw synagogue, in espousing the Polish cause. When in 1861 several Poles and Jews were shot down by Cossacks during a street demonstration, both these rabbis marched behind the coffins alongside with the Catholic clergy. Both were sent to prison by the Russian viceroy, but were subsequently released.

The concession which the czar was persuaded by Marquis Vielopolski to grant to the Poles provided for the removal of sundry Jewish disabilities. Nevertheless the revolution broke out in 1863 and was put down with severity. Many Jewish youths died in the battles or fell into the hands of the Russians as prisoners. Russia was now determined to obliterate every vestige of Polish autonomy. The whole of the western provinces was Russianized with vigor, and a period of reaction set in over the empire.

The Jews were made to feel the change in two ways. Because a number of Jews had grown rich in consequence of the industrial development of the country, the cry was raised that they were 'exploiters,' a menace to the real 'producers.' Then a fresh onslaught was launched against the 'kahals.' As a matter of fact, nothing remained but a shadow of the old organization. However, an apostate, Jacob Brafman, seized upon the minutes of the kahal of Minsk, dating from the time of its legitimate existence. By gross misrepresentation and with wilful malice he made it appear that the Jews were banded together for the exploitation of the Gentile world, that the organization was still secretly kept up, and that the Paris 'Alliance' was but a part of a universal Jewish 'kahal' aiming at world domination. The official circles immediately set about to destroy the communal cohesion of the Jews (1870).

A new municipal statute placed a check upon Jewish participation in town government. Even in places with a preponderating Jewish population, only one third in the city councils could be Jews, and no Jew was eligible to the post of burgomaster. Similarly, the law of 1874, establishing general military service, discriminated against Jews by directing that in the case of Jewish recruits shorter measurements of stature and chest should be adopted, and that those rejected as unfit should be replaced by other Jews, even if they were the only sons of their parents. The ritual murder legend was revived by Hippolyte Lutostanski, a convert from Roman Catholicism to the Greek Orthodox Church; soon a trial occurred in Kutais, a government in the Caucasus (1878). The accused, however, were acquitted, the evidence proving to be a flimsy web of inventions. On this occasion the Jewish side was sustained by the learned Daniel Chwolson (1819–1911), a convert to Christianity, who remained in literary contact with the Jewish scholars of his time and made a name for himself among the foremost students of Oriental literature.

Chwolson was all too readily led astray by the Karaite scholar Abraham Firkovich (1786–1874), who collected in the Crimea and in the Orient a number of Karaite, Samaritan, and Rabbanite manuscripts and old inscriptions. In his zeal for the cause of his own sect, Firkovich did not scruple to forge dates and inscriptions so as to give his own people the appearance of greater antiquity. The grammarian Simhah Pinsker (1801–1864) likewise put far too implicit faith in the finds of his Karaite friend. It remained for a younger scholar, Albert (Abraham) Harkavy (1839–1919), librarian at St. Petersburg, to discriminate between truth and fiction in the finds of Firkovich, and he made notable contributions in the fields of Jewish history and literature. All these scholars enjoyed the esteem of the exponents of Jewish learning in the West. So did also the bibliographer Isaac Benjacob (1801–1863) at Vilna. Eliezer Lipmann Silbermann (1819–1882), though born in Königsberg and settled in Lyck, Prussia, was of Russian descent; he founded in 1856 the first Hebrew weekly (Ha-Maggid, 'The Intelligencer') and was instrumental in organizing a society for the publication of old Hebrew works (Mekize Nirdamim, 'The Awakeners of the Sleeping').

The interest in Jewish learning differentiated all these men from the group of Jewish Russian intellectuals, who took the leap from the old into the new without any transition. The trend was towards Hebrew letters as a fine art and the break with rabbinism. In Russia the transformation did not express itself in the making of new prayer-books and in ritual reforms. No half-way stations pleased these stormers; the modern life beckoned from without, Israel must step into it, preferably in a Hebrew form, but if necessary in Russian. At best, the Jew was to be a Jew at home and a 'man' abroad. So sang in purest Hebrew verse Judah Loeb Gordon (1831–1892), who from 1872 on acted as secretary of the Society for the Spreading of Enlightenment among the Jews of Russia. The society was founded in 1863 by Baron Joseph Günzburg (1812–1878) and his son Horace (1833–1909), who succeeded his father in the presidency. The seat of the society was at St. Petersburg; but there was a branch at Odessa, which went still further in the direction of Russianizing Jewish education in the interest of obtaining for the Jews in Russia full emancipation.

The novel was introduced into Hebrew literature by Abraham Mapu (1808–1867), and he injected into it a purely secular tone. The younger Solomon Abramovich (1836–1917), or, as he was known by his pseudonym, 'Mendele the

Bookseller,' created the novel and short story in the popular dialect of the Jewish Russian Pale.

To Moses Loeb Lilienblum (1843–1910) the 'ways of the Talmud' were nothing but superstition and his early Jewish education 'a sin against youth'; Perez Smolenskin (1842–1885) pictured himself as 'one astray in the ways of life' and from the pages of the literary periodical 'The Dawn' (Ha-Shahar) he battled against 'dark' orthodoxy. Both came back—not to orthodoxy, but to Jewish nationalism, and Smolenskin sooner than Lilienblum; in Vienna, whither he transplanted himself in 1868, he gained the perspective which taught him the folly of 'the wisdom of Berlin.' Over against the western movement of reform he scorned the casting aside of the Messianic hope, which to him was expressive of Israel's character as an 'everlasting people.' With the same force he insisted on the cultivation of the Hebrew language without which Judaism cannot exist, and against the ruthless destroyers he maintained that it was 'time to plant,' to build up.

Nor was orthodoxy quite dead to new stirrings. Israel Lipkin (died 1883) organized in 1842 at Vilna and in 1848 at Kovno societies for the study of religious morals ('Musar'). The influence of this movement for a deeper religious feeling among young students for the rabbinate impressed itself with specific force upon the talmudic school (yeshibah) at Slobodka (in 1925, the institution was in part transferred to Hebron, Palestine).

About 1860, two hundred thousand Jews or more were to be found in Rumania, the Danubian state immediately bordering upon Russia. It was in 1859 that Rumania really became a state through the union of the two principalities, Moldavia and Wallachia, which elected Alexander Cuza as their common prince under Turkish suzerainty. Jews had dwelt in these parts from remotest times; but by far the greatest part of Rumanian Jewry descended from immigrants from Poland, who commenced to arrive at the earliest in the first half of the seventeenth century. The stream continued uninterruptedly, especially after the partitions of Poland; Galicia contributed its quota; then Russia during the harsh rule of Nicholas I. The opening up of the ports of the Black Sea and of the lower Danube for international commerce, in 1829, brought into the country richer Jews from abroad, Sephardim from the south and German-speaking Jews from the north. The great mass lived in the cities and villages under the same conditions as obtained among the Jews of Poland and the southwestern provinces of Russia, either as artisans and middlemen or as unskilled laborers and petty traders.

In the Convention of Paris of 1858 there had been embodied a pledge, carelessly worded, that legislative steps would be taken by the principalities towards the political enfranchisement of the non-Christian population. Whatever designs prince Cuza entertained for a gradual emancipation of the Jews in Rumania, they were frustrated by his enforced abdication in 1866. Charles of Hohenzollern-Sigmaringen was elected prince, and the National Assembly met to frame a new constitution. Crémieux, then on a tour to Turkey, stopped at Bucharest, where he conferred with the ministers of state and a number of the deputies, and seemed to have carried the majority in favor of Jewish political rights. But the enemies of the Jews organized a street demonstration, during which a new synagogue, in course of construction, was demolished and an old synagogue invaded and desecrated. Crémieux reported to Paris that in Rumania the liberal party, while loudly professing sympathies with the revolution of 1848, was, on religious and social questions, still committed to the ideas of the fifteenth or sixteenth century.

The chief of the 'liberal' cabinet, John Bratianu, in his fight with the conservative aristocracy, leaned for support mainly on the commercial and industrial middle classes, and these, constituting the majority in the chambers, were determined to keep down Jewish competition. Old laws were resuscitated, and large numbers of Jews were expelled from rural places in the districts of Jassy, Bacau, and other parts of Moldavia; those that fled to the cities were sent across the border as 'vagabonds.' It happened that a group of Jews of Galatz, who proved to be foreigners, were convoyed across the Danube. As the Turkish frontier guards refused to receive them, the Rumanian police cast them into the river (July, 1867). Great indignation was aroused abroad, especially in France and Great Britain, and Bratianu resigned office (1868). The expulsions nevertheless continued under the conservative régime of his successors. In the years 1871–1872, during the Catargiu ministry, there was a sequence of mob attacks on the Jews in a number of cities. The government was rather lukewarm in punishing the culprits, while it redoubled its persecution of the Jews by enacting fresh restrictive legislation.

The prince was powerless to intervene, despite the assurances of sympathy he had given the American consul, Benjamin F. Peixotto (1834–1890), grand master of the order B'nai B'rith, whom President Grant had appointed for the express purpose of protecting the Jews of Rumania. The Alliance Israélite Universelle summoned a gathering of representative Jews from Europe and America to Brussels (1872). As a consequence of their efforts the Powers instructed their consuls to make representations to the Rumanian government. But with Russia as an open abetter and Austria, not wishing to be outdone by her rival Russia, friendly, Rumania stood committed to her policy of denying civil and political rights to her Jews. It insisted upon considering them as 'aliens,' though they were subjects of no other country and though they were held amenable to all the duties within the state, including service in the army.

In the Russo-Turkish War of 1877–1878 Rumania sided with Russia and achieved independence. The Treaty of San Stefano, forced upon Turkey by Russia, was viewed unfavorably by the other great Powers, and the Congress of Berlin was summoned to settle the Eastern Question. The 'Alliance' sent its delegates to confer with the plenipotentiaries of the Powers with a view to righting the condition of their Rumanian coreligionists. France moved that the independence of Rumania should be made conditional upon

the granting of equality of rights to all her subjects irrespective of religious differences. England (through Disraeli),
Germany (through Bismarck), Austria and Italy, all seconded
the motion; at last even Gorchakov, the Russian representative, joined in, although unwillingly. Thus the principle that
differences of religious beliefs cannot serve as a hindrance to
the enjoyment of political rights was embodied in the Treaty
of Berlin for all the Balkan principalities. Unfortunately, the
phrasing of the article left a technical loophole for the
Rumanian government to hark back to the Rumanian law
that the Jews were aliens and that their admissibility to
citizenship rested with the legislature. Some eight hundred
Jews, who had served in the late war, were naturalized in
1879; in the sequel, individual Jews were naturalized by
special acts of parliament. Yet, despite reminders from England and France, the bulk of the Jews of Rumania were
denied citizenship under the legal fiction that they were
'aliens.'

The internal conditions were not calculated to improve
under this constant stress of governmental hostility. Barring
individual cases, the general cultural tone was not a high
one. When Meir Loeb Malbim (1809–1879) accepted the post
of chief rabbi at Bucharest in 1860, he found much simple
piety, but also a tendency on the part of some to be derelict
in religious observance. The intrigues of the laxer element
brought about his imprisonment by the authorities, and he
was released only on condition that he would leave the country. It is true, Malbim did not remain long in his subsequent
charges; he was far too exacting in his dealings with the lay
heads. It was at Bucharest that he began his commentary
on the Scriptures, characterized by a fine perception of the
niceties of the Hebrew language and marking Malbim as
second to Luzzatto among Jewish Bible students of the
nineteenth century.

CHAPTER XCIII

GERMAN ANTI-SEMITISM AND RUSSIAN POGROMS

(1878-1894)

I<small>N</small> the very year in which Bismarck championed the cause of the Jews in the Balkans, a turn was effected by the powerful chancellor in the home politics of the empire which, with full intent, unleashed the furies of an organized movement against the Jews. Bismarck was first and foremost a Prussian; in his own way he brought about the unification of Germany by the exclusion of Austria, and William I. (1861–1888), king of Prussia, was crowned at Versailles German emperor. With the aid of the National Liberals he led for seven years the onslaught on the Catholic Party (the 'Kulturkampf'). He was no Liberal, however, and when Liberalism, having done its work, showed itself unyielding on questions of military expenditure and imperial taxation, he quickly made peace with Rome. The 'journey to Canossa' had been taken; the Liberal era was at an end.

For fifteen years there had been in existence a Social-Democratic party. It consisted of the Marxists, the followers of Karl Marx (1818–1883), who was a Jew by birth only, and the Working Men's Association, founded by Ferdinand Lassalle (1825–1864), a nominal Jew. In 1878 the emperor was twice shot at by men remotely connected with the socialist-republican agitation. The crime served Bismarck, who was determined to crush the resurgent forces of democracy, as a pretext for inaugurating a change of policy, and the greater part of the National Liberal Party went over to the Opposition. None attacked the Chancellor more fiercely than the Jew Eduard Lasker (1820–1884), a skilled parliamentarian who had helped to form the liberal party. The Jews were indebted to the Liberals for their emancipation, and were bound to liberal doctrine by their economic interests. Bismarck dropped the hint, which subservient creatures took up, to bring the Liberals to heel by striking at the Jews.

The court-preacher Stöcker at once formed a Christian Socialist Workingmen's Union, in order to invest the Chancellor's proposed social legislation with a Christian and monarchist character and thus take the wind out of democracy's sails. Those that actually joined the new party were not the workingmen, but the middle class people, who responded to the pastor's agitation against Jewish 'domination' in business, the press, and politics. Thus was born the modern 'Anti-Semitic' movement, which aimed at the revocation of the political rights held by the Jews. The thing was old, but the name was new, and it was brought into vogue by an obscure publicist (1879–1880). Back of it was the assumption that 'Semitic' and 'Aryan' were racial terms and that of the two races the Semitic was the inferior—a conception most sharply advanced by the French scholar Ernest Renan in 1855, though subsequently (1883) he denied that the modern Jews were Semites or at all a distinct race. But the Anti-Semites proceeded along the lines of the theory that the Jews were an alien race of which the European nations must rid themselves and which at all events they must subdue. 'The Jews,' wrote the historian Treitschke, 'are our misfortune.'

In 1881, a petition, signed by a large number of persons, was submitted to the Chancellor, recommending a number of discriminations against the Jews, which as a matter of fact the government had been quietly carrying out for some time. While the petition was still circulating in the country, seventy-six men, belonging to the highest scholarly, legislative, administrative, and mercantile circles, issued a counter-declaration in which the agitation against the Jews was described as a national disgrace. But the passions had been aroused; Jews were attacked in the streets of Berlin; at Neustettin a new synagogue was burned down. However, the elections of 1881 brought into the Imperial Diet eight Jewish deputies, while of the Anti-Semites only Stöcker obtained a seat. The movement had meanwhile spread into

Austria, where it was led by von Schönerer; in Hungary Istóczi fanned the flames of hatred, with the result that upon the disappearance of a Christian girl in Tisza-Eszlar, fifteen Jews were arrested on the charge of ritual murder (1882). In the same year a Congress of German and Austro-Hungarian Anti-Semites met at Dresden and passed resolutions urging the sovereigns of the principal states of Europe to take rigorous joint measures against the growing preponderance of the Jews, in particular to exclude them from the army and to forbid Jewish immigration from the east.

On March 13, 1881, the emperor Alexander II. died as the victim of revolutionary bomb throwers on the very eve of granting a semblance of constitutional government. The new czar, Alexander III. (1881–1894), was completely swayed by his former tutor, Pobiedonostzev, whom he appointed presiding officer of the Holy Synod—a man who believed that autocracy was superior to western parliamentarism and that religious unity through the Greek Orthodox Church must be imposed on all Russia. For the Jews this cynical doctrinaire developed a definite enough programme: a third might be converted, a third emigrate, and a third perish.

The Anti-Semitic agitation of Germany communicated itself to Russia, and here it led, beginning with Easter and continuing into the summer of 1881, to excesses, 'pogroms' (as the Russians call these riots), against the Jews throughout the southern provinces. There is no question but that the pogroms were centrally organized, although it is not known just how and by whom. It is equally certain that the government had no direct hand in them and that the guiding spirits had not as yet acquired that skill of which they later gave evidence. The riots occurred altogether too simultaneously to have been spontaneous; they had generally the same type. First, there were forebodings, veiled threats; then an altercation with one or the other of the Jewish inhabitants, which served as a signal. Suddenly, there appeared a mob of petty artisans and laborers, supported by peasants from the outlying districts. The Jewish quarter was invaded, dwellings were demolished, looted, and burned down, furniture was destroyed. The fleeing Jews were beaten, neither age nor sex being spared; many were wounded and killed. The police was either unwilling or powerless to interfere; the troops, called out too late, were passive. These scenes were repeated in a hundred localities during the year 1881; among the larger centers it suffices to mention Elisavetgrad (April 27–28), Kiev (May 8–9), Odessa (May 15–17).

The victims of the pogroms were for the most part people in modest circumstances. There was an immediate need to find for these unfortunates shelter and food, before there could be any thought of rehabilitation; relief committees at Kiev and other centers addressed themselves nobly to their huge task. A veritable panic seized the Jews of southern Russia; by the end of the summer ten thousand fugitives reached the Galician town Brody. Spain, repentant of the act of 1492, generously offered to receive them; but, however kindly the government was, it was questionable how the Spanish populace would take to the strangers.

Since 1869 there had been in progress a slow but steady emigration of Russian Jews, regulated by the Paris 'Alliance' with the aid of a Königsberg committee. A small number were placed in Germany, the majority—four thousand annually—found their way to America. This was the beginning of the third wave of Jewish immigration into America, coming on the top of the early Portuguese and the more recent German. Stray wanderers from the East of Europe had made a home for themselves in the New World before 1869—the Beth Hamidrash Hagadol, a congregation of Russian Jews in the city of New York, was formed in 1852. These waves of immigration, however, were insignificant as compared with the stream that from now on, year in and year out for two decades, poured through the open gates of the American continent.

The 'Alliance' took care of the fleeing humanity as soon as it crossed the frontier, and especially at the ports of embarkation. Organizations in America were active in receiving and distributing the arrivals, and in finding employment for them. Michael Heilprin (1823–1888), born in Russian Poland

and since 1856 in America, threw himself heart and soul into the work of relief. Emma Lazarus (1849–1887), an American Jewess of Sephardic descent and a gifted poet, was moved by contact with the new immigrants to a warm interest in Jewish history and literature, to which she had previously been a stranger. She looked for salvation in a complete regeneration of her people: 'Let but an Ezra rise anew, to lift the banner of the Jew!'

The Russian government made it appear as if the excesses were uncontrollable outbursts of popular indignation against the Jewish exploiters. The cause lay in the Jews, and the new minister of the interior, Ignatiev, ordered the provincial governors to submit reports as to the necessary measures. Drenteln, the governor-general of Kiev, as if to right himself for culpably permitting the excesses in his own residence, held that the Christian population was no match for the mentally superior Jewish trader and that therefore everything should be done to induce the Jews to leave Russia. The milder Totleben, in Vilna, merely advised that the Jews should be restrained from settling in rural localities. The machinery for preparing new repressions was being set in motion, when a pogrom burst upon the Polish capital (December 25–27, 1881), in which fifteen hundred Jewish dwellings were destroyed and twenty-four Jews wounded. The only protest possible for Russian Jewry was to assemble in the synagogues, on a given day, January 20, 1882, to abstain from food and drink, and to intone the old medieval penitential prayers (selihoth).

Abroad, public opinion was outspoken in condemnation of the brutal persecutors and in sympathy with the persecuted. Meetings were held, at the Mansion House in London under the chairmanship of the Lord Mayor (February 1, 1882) and at Paris under the presidency of the poet Victor Hugo (May 31), which were attended by representatives of the Protestant and Catholic clergy, men of letters and science, eminent politicians. Resolutions were passed which denounced Jewish rightlessness in Russia as the cause of all the evil, and committees were formed to solicit funds in aid of the sufferers. In the House of Commons, Gladstone, while personally sympathizing with the unfortunate Jews of Russia, nevertheless declared that the British government could not interfere in the internal affairs of a friendly power and that any intervention would only serve to aggravate the evil. The government of the United States of America instructed its representative in St. Petersburg to make known its hope that the Imperial Government would find means to cause the persecution of 'these unfortunate fellow-beings' to cease.

Jewish opinion in Russia was divided. To large circles the task of the moment seemed to be to systematize the emigration which was going on in a hurried fashion. Yet, the leaders were fearful that to encourage emigration might be construed as disloyalty or lack of patriotism, and still others thought that it would be a concession to the policy of Ignatiev who had announced that the western frontier was open to the Jews.

While a meeting of Jewish notables was being held in St. Petersburg, a most cruel pogrom broke out on Easter Monday (April 10, 1882) at Balta, an important commercial center in Podolia. Twelve hundred and fifty dwellings and shops were demolished, there was much destruction and looting of property and wares; fifteen thousand Jews were beggared, forty killed or maimed, about one hundred and seventy wounded, more than twenty women violated, while many lost their minds from fright. The depression which settled upon Russian Jewry was augmented by the promulgation in the month of May, 1882, of the 'Temporary Rules' (the 'May Laws'), which confined the Jews to the towns and townships of the Pale and forbade their settling in the villages. Ignatiev, the author of these laws, was relieved of his office; but his successor, the no less reactionary Dmitri Tolstoi, was relentless in carrying them out.

Sporadic pogroms still continued, but on the whole they were quickly suppressed by the authorities; so much had the protests from the West accomplished. Still the government was bent upon creating fresh disabilities; the number of Jewish surgeons serving in the army was greatly reduced

(1882); the Jewish Technical School at Zhitomir was closed (1884); only a small percentage of Jews (ten per cent. of all the scholars) were admitted to the secondary schools and universities situated in the Pale, and still less outside the Pale and in the two capitals (1887); Jewish graduates of the law schools were not admitted to the bar as public or private attorneys (1889). All the while Jews were being expelled from villages in the Pale—even when they had been settled there before 1882—from the interior, and from the capitals. A commission, headed by Pahlen, labored for five years to study the conditions of the Jews in Russia and to propose new measures. Though a majority was in favor of cautious and gradual reforms, it was overborne by the reactionary powers in the government.

Under the shock of the first pogroms, in the autumn of 1881, Lilienblum sounded the call for a return to the ancient land of the fathers, should it take a whole century to carry it through. In 1882, Leo Pinsker (1821–1891), son of Simhah Pinsker (p. 685), published a brochure, in which he admonished his fellow-Jews to look for salvation in 'self-emancipation,' in the creation of a national retreat somewhere on the earth, preferably on the banks of the Jordan, but if necessary on those of the Mississippi. While the brochure was still under the press, a group of young Jews, specifically university students, formed themselves at Kharkov as the circle of the BILU (abbreviation for: Beth Iaakob Leku Unelkah, 'O house of Jacob, come ye, and let us go'). Their plan was to establish an agricultural colony in Palestine. A few hundred adherents were won in Russia, but only forty arrived in Jaffa. Half were given employment in the 'Alliance' colony Mikveh Israel, and half were settled in the recently founded colony Rishon le-Zion ('A Harbinger unto Zion').

The young pioneers could not accustom themselves to the climate and the hardships of tilling the long-neglected soil; the majority departed, making room for less educated but more hardy colonists. The Palestinian movement made strides in Russia from year to year. The 'Lovers of Zion'

(Hobebe Zion), with centers in Odessa and Warsaw, were numerous enough in 1884 to send delegates to a meeting at Kattowitz in Prussian Silesia; a memorial fund in honor of the one hundredth anniversary of the birth of Moses Montefiore was created for the support of the Palestinian colonies. The movement, though started by the intellectuals, enjoyed the warm-hearted support of so orthodox a rabbi as Samuel Mohilever (1824–1898) of Bielostok, who was instrumental in the founding of a number of colonies, among them Rehoboth.

Vastly larger were the numbers of those who singly or in groups, but nevertheless by the thousands, crossed the Atlantic. Wherever they settled, they found their countrymen who had preceded them. In every port of debarkation the refugees were aided by committees from among the older Jewish residents, and frequently enough high-minded Christians expressed their sympathy by proffers of help. In these years of stress the religious strife in Europe had abated; the reformers and the orthodox, while pursuing their parallel paths, unitedly responded to the call of the hour.

In America, the religious division was still crystallizing. For a time it was thought that an organic union of all American Israel might be effected. Maimonides College (p. 681) had been intended to serve a general need; in the same manner had been conceived the Hebrew Union College as well as the Union of American Hebrew Congregations, founded in 1873. In 1885, the coming to America of Alexander Kohut (1842–1894) and his criticism of American Reform served as an impetus for the eastern and western reformers to come together. The meeting took place in Pittsburgh and a platform was adopted in which the tenets of Reform were formulated. The chief moving spirit at this conference was Kaufmann Kohler (1843–1926), who had come to America in 1869 and, after ministering to congregations in Detroit and Chicago, succeeded his father-in-law Einhorn as rabbi of Temple Beth-El in New York City in 1879. The radical tone of the Pittsburgh platform shocked the conservatives and convinced them that the idea of one institution serving

both camps must be given up. Accordingly, in 1886, Sabato
Morais of Philadelphia opened the Jewish Theological
Seminary in the city of New York. Morais held office as
non-resident head of the faculty; the chair of Talmud was
occupied by Kohut. In 1889 Kohut completed his Talmudic
Dictionary in eight volumes, a labor of sixteen years.

In Germany Frederick III., who succeeded his father, the
aged emperor William I., in 1888, was stricken with a mortal
disease, and after a reign of three months was followed by
William II. The young monarch early gave assurance that
all religious confessions stood with him on an equal footing,
which meant, so far as the Jews were concerned, that there
would be no attempt to take away from them their rights as
citizens. Of course, the reactionary elements in the government exercised their discretion in keeping the Jews from
certain appointments. The Anti-Semitic propaganda was little checked. In Hesse Böckel agitated, at Berlin Ahlwardt;
pamphlets were written attacking talmudic morality or
trumping up charges against supposed dishonest transactions of Jewish industrialists. There were a number of Anti-
Semitic factions, now at cross-purposes, now united; another
Congress was held at Bochum (1889).

At Xanten, the scene of Jewish suffering during the First
Crusade (p. 363), the blood accusation was revived (1891).
The Conservative Party made common cause with the Anti-
Semites, and a number of them were seated in the Reichstag
(1892). The Anti-Semites published a 'Catechism,' a compilation of all sorts of charges against the Jews, which was
widely disseminated. In the schools, teachers digressed to
harangue their pupils, among whom there were naturally
Jews, against the 'enemies' of the German people—liberals,
democrats, Catholics, and Jews. There were, of course, large
circles ashamed of the disreputable tactics of the Anti-
Semites. At the end of 1890, the jurist Gneist and the leader
of the Opposition in the Reichstag, Heinrich Rickert, together with a number of men eminent in politics and scholarship, founded a defensive society against Anti-Semitism.
During the Xanten trial this society published a book by the

Berlin theologian Hermann L. Strack on the origin and history of the 'blood superstition' among all peoples. In 1893, the German Jews created an organization of their own, the Central Society of German Citizens of the Jewish Faith, to institute court proceedings against libelers of the Jewish religion and to oppose vigorously curtailment of Jewish political rights.

In 1890, the Russian Home Office, now administered by Durnovo with Plehve as assistant, was preparing, in strict secrecy, new repressive measures against the Jews. However, the secret leaked out. A resolution of inquiry was passed in the House of Representatives at Washington in August; in December, a meeting of protest was held in the Guildhall in London and a petition sent on to St. Petersburg. Russian Jews were leaving their homes in ever larger numbers; they were landing in American ports by the hundreds weekly. President Harrison took the ground, and made it known in diplomatic correspondence, that, apart from humanitarian considerations, the evil treatment of the Jews of Russia gave concern to other governments because of the problems created by mass immigration. Notwithstanding, the Russian government carried out its project and expelled thousands of Jews from Moscow, Kiev, and other cities of the interior (1891).

Whatever thoughts there had been in the minds of western Jews that the Russian government might be prevailed upon to relent, it was now realized that nothing remained but to get the Jews out of Russia, So reasoned Baron Maurice de Hirsch (1831–1896). Accordingly, he caused to be incorporated in London the Jewish Colonization Association (ICA), which he endowed with a capital of two million pounds; at his death it received a further legacy of six million pounds. At the same time he established, under the laws of the state of New York, the Baron de Hirsch Fund, with an initial capital of two and a half million dollars, for the aid of Jewish immigrants from Russia and Rumania, and another fund of twelve million francs in Galicia for the relief of the Jews there.

Baron de Hirsch thought that, within twenty-five years›
some three million Jews could be transplanted from Russia.
The Russian government desired greater speed making for
expatriation of the bulk of Russian Jewry in half the time.
What was really accomplished, was, that up to 1894, six
thousand Jews were settled in the Argentine republic, half
in the capital Buenos Aires and half in colonies (Moise-
ville, Mauricio, Clara). Subsequently the settlement increased considerably. The Baron realized that the task was
far more stupendous than he had imagined. He urged his
Russian coreligionists to be patient, but the wave kept on
rolling. Before the end of the century close upon a million
Jews had left eastern Europe (Russia, Galicia, Rumania).
The largest number by far came to the United States of
America; the remainder to Great Britain and her colonies,
and a small body to Palestine. It was an unparalleled exodus, incomparably greater than the Spanish, and the end
was not yet when Alexander III. died in 1894.

CHAPTER XCIV

ZIONISM

(1894-1904)

ON October 15, 1894, Captain Alfred Dreyfus (born 1859), an Alsatian Jew attached to the French general staff, was arrested on the charge of having furnished staff secrets to the German government. He was condemned by a court martial for high treason and sentenced to life imprisonment in a fortress. On January 5, 1895, he was publicly degraded on the Champ de Mars in Paris; he protested his innocence, crying out: 'Long live France! Long live the army!' The mob shouted madly: 'Death to the traitor!'

It was a cabal deftly contrived by the clerical-royalist enemies of the Third Republic, in league with the generals of the army. Drumont had in 1886 made himself the spokesman of the Jesuits by inveighing in his brochure, 'La France Juive,' against the republic as being under Jewish domination. From 1892 on he published a sheet, 'La Libre Parole,' in which it was insinuated that Jewish army officers were guilty of treasonous acts. The charge against Dreyfus was based on a copy of a certain secret document ('bordereau') alleged to be in his handwriting. Thanks to the investigations of Scheurer-Kestner and colonel Picquart, it was brought to light in 1897 that the document was in reality the work of Esterhazy, a dissipated major in the French army and a spy in the pay of Germany. Dreyfus had meanwhile been conveyed to Devil's Island near the Guiana coast; there he was kept under close surveillance and under horrible conditions intended to break down his spirit.

The number of those at home convinced of his innocence grew daily; the novelist Zola arraigned the enemies of justice in an open letter addressed to the president of the republic (which became famous through the phrase constantly repeated,'J'accuse'). France was divided into two camps, Dreyfusard and anti-Dreyfusard. Colonel Henry, of the general staff, committed fresh forgeries to fasten the guilt upon the hated Jewish captain; when brought to bay, he took his own life (1898). All sorts of obstacles were placed in the way of reopening the case, the government fearing to break with the nationalists. After the death of President Faure (1899), Waldeck-Rousseau formed a ministry with the aid of the socialists, and Dreyfus was brought back and retried. He was once more condemned by the Council of War at Rennes; President Loubet granted a pardon. A year later the Court of Cassation quashed the verdict and pronounced Dreyfus innocent.

The Damascus libel of 1840 and the Mortara outrage of 1858 had suggested to the Jews of Paris to form the Alliance Israélite Universelle; the Dreyfus case at the end of the century was in its very initial stages the birth-hour of Zionism. Theodore (Benjamin Zeeb) Herzl (1860–1904) was then residing in Paris as permanent correspondent of a Vienna daily, the 'Neue Freie Presse.' He had been but little concerned with Jewish matters; his knowledge of Judaism was meager. He attended the sessions of the court when Dreyfus was first tried and witnessed the degradation of the Jewish captain. It seemed to him that France had revoked the principles of her Great Revolution. He felt keenly the blow struck at the whole Jewish people in the person of one Jew. Suddenly, as if by inspiration, he was an altered man; the Jewish question preoccupied his thoughts, and it presented itself to him neither as an economic nor as a religious, but as a political and national one. The Jews, he reasoned, were a nation and one united nation. From this premise he drew the conclusion that the Jews must concentrate and form a state of their own—in the Argentine or in Palestine. Feverishly, as if in a trance, he wrote in Paris his 'Jews' State,' at a time when he knew neither of Hess nor of Pinsker (1895).

The whole scheme, he thought, was quite simple. Let the Jews be granted sovereignty over a section of the earth sufficient for their just national needs, and they will take care of everything else. Negotiations for chartered territorial concession were to be carried on by an organization called 'The Society of Jews,' which would also work out the constitution—a democratic monarchy or an aristocratic republic—for the future state. Another organization, 'The Jewish Company,' with its seat in London and under the protection of the British Government, at the moment still free from the taint of Anti-Semitism, was to regulate the migration, liquidate Jewish holdings in the lands of the dispersion, and build up the new community. The capital necessary for the transaction he estimated at fifty million pounds to be raised by popular subscription.

Before making public his project, Herzl obtained an interview with Baron de Hirsch; but neither by word of mouth nor by correspondence was he able to make an impression upon the Jewish magnate. Herzl's closest friends feared for his sanity; they mocked him by pointing to the example of Sabbatai Zevi. 'What was not possible then, can be done now with our technical progress,' was the rejoinder. Once more, during the coming Passover at Vienna, the parallel with the seventeenth century visionary was brought home to him; but this time encouragingly, the resemblance being in the magnetic personal charm which both possessed. The man who recalled it was the eminent talmudist Meir Friedmann (1831–1908), the colleague of the historian of talmudic literature, Isaac Hirsch Weiss (1815–1905), in the Vienna Beth ha-Midrash.

There was one man in Paris who understood Herzl and before long was completely won over, the compatriot exile Max Nordau (1849–1923), a physician by profession, but then already a European celebrity as a critical writer. Herzl also corresponded with the chief rabbi of Vienna, Moritz Güdemann (1835–1918), a graduate of the Breslau seminary and a scholar of solid reputation, who had made noteworthy contributions in the field of Jewish cultural history. Güdemann and Herzl met by appointment in Munich (August, 1895). The rabbi listened and was apparently convinced: 'It may be that you are the one called by God.'

The Anti-Semitic movement in Austria was then on the ascendant; in September, on the eve of the Jewish New Year, Herzl witnessed the carrying of the municipal elections in Vienna by the union of Anti-Semites and Clericals. The council chose Lueger, a vehement Anti-Semite, for burgomaster; the emperor declined to sanction the election, but Lueger was repeatedly reëlected, and two years later the government accepted him. The Anti-Semites administered the city to their own satisfaction and to the hurt of the Jewish inhabitants in every way they could.

Herzl did not share the views or the tactics of the Viennese Jews, who regarded Anti-Semitism as an evil that would pass away and were organizing an opposition liberal party. Still he lent his aid to the unsuccessful efforts of Joseph Bloch (1850–1925) to rewin his seat in parliament. Despite profound differences, Herzl honored in Bloch the champion of the Jewish cause, who had refuted the attacks on the Talmud by the Anti-Semitic Catholic professor Rohling, and had confounded other agitators spreading the notion that the Jews were given to the practice of killing Christian children for ritual purposes. Güdemann was showing signs of lukewarmness towards Herzl's scheme; nevertheless, thanks to an introduction by the rabbi, Herzl met Narcisse Leven (1833–1915), then vice-president of the Paris Alliance. Leven was not to be moved; he sent Herzl on to the chief rabbi of France, Zadoc Kahn (1839-1905). At the rabbi's house Herzl again met Leven, who accentuated his French patriotism; so did also Hartwig Derenbourg (1844–1908), like his father Joseph Derenbourg (1811–1895) a noted Oriental scholar. The rabbi himself seemed willing enough to follow Herzl, but he knew that the leading French Jews would remain hostile.

Nordau counseled Herzl to go to London. There Israel Zangwill (1864–1926), who had attracted attention by his ghetto stories, introduced him to the Maccabaeans, an association of Jewish intellectuals founded in 1892. Herzl spoke; but English patriotism was put forward as an objection by his audience. Herzl came in contact with a number of representative Jews. Colonel Albert Goldsmid (1846–1904), chief of the English branch of the 'Lovers of Zion,' had been born the son of baptized Jewish parents and then returned to Judaism; he was naturally sympathetic to Herzl's scheme, but was prevented by his official position from lending a hand. Sir Samuel Montagu, subsequently Lord Swaythling (1832–1911), kept an open ear. The chief rabbi, Hermann Adler, thought the project should be laid first before the Russo-Jewish Committee of London.

In the spring of 1896 the 'Jews' State' was issued from the press. In Jewish circles of Vienna the feeling was that the whole thing might be but a jest. On the other hand, the appeal struck home in student associations and among the Jews of the East. People announced that they were ready to emigrate; in Bulgaria Herzl was acclaimed as the Messiah. A leader of Galician Hasidim offered to turn into the movement millions of his followers through Poland. It was taken for granted that the call was for Zion and for no other territory; the more Herzl came into contact with those who stood closest to the masses, the more he grew himself to be a Zionist. He regretted that he was unable to count upon the support of those in commanding positions, and so go straightway to the sultan of Turkey and offer a sum to help the Ottoman government over its financial difficulties in return for concessions in Palestine. As it was, all he could do in the summer of 1896 was to present himself in Constantinople to several high officials.

To meet the attacks of the Anti-Zionists—Güdemann had come out with a pamphlet against National Judaism in the name of the Jewish religion—Herzl started in June, 1897, largely with his own funds, the Zionist weekly, 'Die Welt.' Already he was making preparations for a Zionist Congress to meet in Munich. However, in consequence of a declaration of protest, signed by the rabbi of Munich and four other colleagues on behalf of the Association of German Rabbis (July, 1897), the Congress met in Basel in the last three days of August.

It was by no means an all-Jewish Congress summoned to debate the very existence of Jewish nationality or the need for a Jewish state. These two things were taken for granted by the two hundred delegates who were all Zionists. It remained to define Zionism and to create the organization for bringing it into effect. A platform was adopted—the 'Basel Programme'—the first paragraph of which read: 'Zionism aims at establishing for the Jewish people a publicly and legally assured home in Palestine.' Thus Zionism stepped out into the open, announcing itself as a political movement with a definite object to be achieved only through political negotiations. Two financial institutions were at once contemplated and before long created: the Jewish Colonial Trust (1899) and the Jewish National Fund (1901). To be a member of the Zionist organization one subscribed to the Basel Programme and paid a 'shekel' (twenty-five cents) as an annual contribution. An active propaganda was developed to augment the number of shekel payers and to win adherents among the masses.

At the Second Congress (1898) the slogan went forth for the conquest of the communities, so that the management of the congregations, which in Europe formed a unit in every city, should pass out of the hands of those hostile to the movement. But this Congress already showed that among the Zionists themselves there were differences. The delegates from the East, chiefly recruited from the old Lovers of Zion, demanded that until the Charter had been obtained colonization in Palestine should be continued; the strict 'politicals' were opposed to what they called 'infiltration.' Then a rift was preparing between socialist and bourgeois Zionists. The question of Jewish education along national lines created further division; the orthodox feared a jeopardizing of the religious interests. However, Moses Gaster (born 1856), the learned London haham, made solemn declaration that the cultural labor would in no wise trench upon the sphere of religion.

Herzl had been introduced by Hechler, chaplain to the British embassy at Vienna, to grand duke Frederick of

Baden. From the beginning this universally esteemed prince evinced a deep interest in Zionism; thanks to his good offices, Herzl was admitted to an audience at Constantinople (October 18) with the German emperor then on his way to Palestine, and once more in the imperial camp before Jerusalem (November 2). Though William II. said neither Yes nor No to the Zionist project, it meant something that a monarch interested in near-Eastern developments gave it a hearing. Zionism was now a question with which European politics must reckon.

Nor were Herzl's audiences with the sultan Abd-ul-Hamid II. (1876–1909) in May, 1901, and with the grand vizir in July, 1902, fruitful of results. All that Turkey was willing to grant was that individual Jews might settle in various parts of the Ottoman empire, but by no means as compact bodies. When therefore the English government began to take notice of the Zionist movement and made an offer of the district of El-Arish in the Sinaitic peninsula, Herzl's imagination was stirred by the project. He was warned, however, not to consider the colony as a 'jumping-off-station' or attempt a raid into the sultan's territory after the manner of Jameson in the Transvaal. Lord Cromer, the British agent in Cairo, was favorable; an expedition was dispatched to look over the tract. In the end the Egyptian government realized that too much Nile water would have to be drawn off for purposes of irrigation, and the project fell through.

The Zionist leader had staked his private fortune, his time, his energy, every ounce of his bodily strength on the movement of his creation; then already the cardiac affection had developed which was to cut off his career prematurely. The number of societies had grown and spread over all the continents of the world; the enthusiasm manifested itself in a revival of literature and art and in the upbuilding of a manly spirit through the cultivation of physical exercise in gymnastic societies. At the fifth Congress a radical socialistic faction was formed; but it was offset by the constitution cf the orthodox party, the Mizrahi, under the leadership of Isaac Jacob Reines (1839–1915), head of a talmudical school

at Lida. Still they all worked together, under the spell of
Herzl's magnetic personality and the sustaining zeal of his
indefatigable co-workers.

At every Congress, Nordau challenged attention by his
eloquence and grim humor, his biting scorn for the opponents
of Zionism, his scathing denunciation of rampant Anti-
Semitism. To the record of ritual murder trials two had been
added but recently, at Polna in Bohemia (1899) and at
Konitz in Prussia (1900). In Galicia, thanks to Polish economic oppression, half a million Jews were kept in a state of
pauperism. In Rumania, an Anti-Semitic League, organized
in 1895 and using any means to attain its end, strove to
render the situation of the Jews unbearable and thus to force
them out of the country. In Russia, Plehve became minister
of the interior in 1902 and made it known that he would
drown the socialist revolution, which had raised its head, in
Jewish blood. In the spring of 1903, the whole civilized world
was shocked by the bloody pogrom of Kishinev, in the province of Bessarabia.

This massacre, which cast into the shade all previous anti-
Jewish excesses in Russia, was thoroughly organized. A
Russianized Moldavian, Krushevan, had since 1897 been
conducting an anti-Jewish campaign in a newspaper edited
by him and subsidized by the government. The agitation
grew more virulent upon the discovery of the dead body of
a Christian boy, early in the year 1903, in a townlet of the
neighboring Kherson province. It was later proved that the
murderers were the boy's own relatives. Without awaiting
an investigation, Krushevan fastened the crime upon the
Jews. The plot to let loose a pogrom was hatched in secret,
with Krushevan, the vice-governor Ustrugov, and an officer
from the St. Petersburg Department of Police as leading
spirits. Printed broadsides were distributed which spoke of
an imperial ukase sanctioning a bloody judgment on the
Jews during the three days of Easter; in public inns and tea-
rooms men conversed openly on the preparing pogrom.

On Easter Sunday, which was the last day of Passover,
at noon, amid the tolling of church bells, numerous bands

throughout the city commenced to demolish Jewish dwellings and shops. Street gamins preceded and broke the windows; then the adults entered and cast wares and furniture into the street for the mob to destroy on the spot or to plunder. In the evening the murderous work began; bestialities were committed the like of which had been unknown in the earlier pogroms. From their hiding-places in cellars and garrets the Jews were dragged forth and tortured to death. Many mortally wounded were denied the finishing stroke and left to perish in their agony; in not a few cases nails were driven into the skull or eyes gouged out. Babes were thrown from the higher stories to the street pavement; the bodies of women were mutilated; young maidens and older matrons were dishonored. The drunken mob invaded the synagogues; the sacred scrolls were torn into shreds, trampled under foot and defiled. In one sanctuary, the aged beadle, wrapped in his prayer shawl, defended with his body the holy Ark until he was struck down. Jews who attempted to beat off the attackers with clubs were quickly disarmed by the police; but the mob was unmolested.

The slaughter continued on Monday; on the third day at last word was received from St. Petersburg to order the troops out, and the pogrom ceased. The Jewish victims counted forty-five dead, eighty-six with heavy and five hundred with light wounds; fifteen hundred houses and shops were destroyed or looted. All over Europe and America the world stood aghast. The Christian conscience was aroused, and platforms and pulpits rang with denunciation of the horror. In Russia, the novelist Leo Tolstoi arraigned the government as the chief culprit, and named the crime of Kishinev a direct outcome of its propaganda of falsehood and violence. The Jews of Russia had a mingled feeling of wrath and shame—wrath against the tormentors and shame for the victims who sold their lives cheaply without resistance. This feeling was voiced in matchless Hebrew diction by the poet Hayim Nahman Bialik (born 1873). In his 'Tale of the Slaughter' he portrayed his people's agony,

scourging the craven, dumb submission of the victims and
calling forth the very indignation of Heaven.

Herzl took it upon himself to beard the lion in his den. In
the beginning of August he arrived in St. Petersburg and had
an interview with Plehve, ostensibly to ask for a withdrawal
of the contemplated suppression of the Zionist societies in
Russia, in reality to induce the Russian government to use
its influence at Constantinople in favor of Zionism. Plehve
temporized on the score of diplomatic engagements. He was
willing to tolerate Zionist activity so long as it had to do
with the creation of a Jewish center in Palestine and mass
emigration from Russia; but if the movement undertook to
make nationalist Jewish propaganda within Russia, it would
be strictly checked as subversive of Russian national interests.

At the Sixth Zionist Congress, which was held in Basel at
the end of August, 1903, Herzl had a surprise in store: the
offer by the British colonial secretary of a stretch of land in
Uganda in British East Africa for purposes of Jewish colonization under a charter of complete internal autonomy.
After stormy debates the project was put to a vote; of the
five hundred delegates, one hundred and eighty-five voted
No and demonstrated their opposition to the majority by
withdrawing from the hall. Upon their return home, the
Russian delegates who made up the opposition met in Kharkov and sent an ultimatum to the leader to drop the Uganda
plan in advance of the next Congress. Herzl was grieved by
this infringement on the authority of the Congress. To prove
his sincere devotion to Zion as the ultimate goal—Uganda
was only to serve as a temporary shelter in the face of the
pressing need of the hour—he renewed negotiations with the
Turkish government. In the spring of 1904 he had an audience with Pope Pius X. (1903–1914). Here he struck a blank
wall of uncompromising Catholic opposition to Jewish possession of Palestine. Peace was patched up between the
leader and the opposition at a meeting in the month of April;
but Herzl's system was undermined. The malady from which
he suffered grew worse daily; on July 3 (Tammuz 20), 1904,
the creator of political Zionism was no more.

CHAPTER XCV

THE 'BLACK HUNDREDS' AND THE RUSSIAN
REVOLUTION

(1905-1912)

THE death of the Zionist leader did not halt the progress of the movement. David Wolffsohn (1856–1914), originally from Russia but long resident in Germany where he engaged in mercantile pursuits, succeeded as president. He managed well enough the administrative machinery and was not without skill in holding together the warring factions. It was beyond his power to prevent the secession of the Territorialists, who abandoned all hope of obtaining Palestine. In all it was a minority that followed Zangwill when he started in 1905 the Jewish Territorial Organization, though adherents were won outside of the Zionist ranks. This organization, called ITO by abbreviation, dispatched commissions to spy out a land suitable for colonization, now to Cyrenaica in Northwest Africa (1908), now to Mesopotamia (1909); but the project did not prove feasible. Then, abandoning the charter idea and the scheme of an autonomous colony altogether, the ITO interested itself in the plan of Jacob H. Schiff (p. 720) to divert American immigration from the Atlantic seaboard to the interior with Galveston, Texas, as port of entry.

Wolffsohn, seconded by Nordau and other early associates of the deceased leader, was a believer in political action as a prerequisite for Palestinian colonization. Yet, before long, in consequence of the Turkish revolution in 1908 and the nationalist Young Turk régime, the prospects of coming to terms in that quarter became almost hopeless. Wolffsohn then receded from Herzl's position and spoke of the future Palestinian settlement as a national home rather than a state. The Russian and German Zionists at last forced the issue in 1911, when Otto Warburg (born 1859), a botanist of distinction. was made chairman of the executive committee, and colonization on a small scale became the programme for Palestinian Zionist activity. Thus, in addition to the colonies previously founded and maintained by the generosity of Baron Edmond de Rothschild (born 1845), twenty-nine new settlements were opened up between 1902 and 1914 with the funds of the Zionist Organization. In 1906, a Hebrew high school was started at Jaffa and a school for the arts and crafts (Bezalel) at Jerusalem. In 1909, a beginning was made with the wholly Jewish town Tel Aviv, close by Jaffa.

From the outset, political Zionism found a most censorious critic in Asher Ginzberg (born 1856), better known by his pen-name Ahad Haam ('One of the People'). Trenchantly he pointed out the weakness of the western formulation of Zionism, which meant but a craving for the full measure of social and political activity denied to the Jews through Anti-Semitism, and which was therefore negative. Nor was he entirely satisfied with the eastern kind of Zionism which primarily was concerned with remedying the economic evil. To Ahad Haam Zionism must be positive and spiritual; a Jews' State would be of small moment unless it were a Jewish State; material comfort was a secondary consideration. The Palestinian settlement should be grounded in a gathering not so much of the dispersed people as of the scattered energies of the Jewish people. It was to serve as a place of refuge for the Jewish culture, a center from which the influence would radiate to the Dispersion. In Palestine Judaism would be regenerated, not by means of revolutionary reforms, but by steady evolution, in adjustment to the very exigencies of the new life.

A part of this spiritual renascence was realized in the system of Palestinian education established by Zionist agencies and in the living Hebrew speech developed in the homes and schools. None labored more valiantly and stubbornly for the revival of spoken Hebrew than Eliezer Ben-Jehuda (1858–1922). From the time he settled in Palestine (1882) he insisted by example and propaganda that Hebrew should be the language of conversation for old and young. He steadily occupied himself with the coinage of new words in order to enlarge the Hebrew vocabulary in accordance with modern needs. More important was his publication, begun in 1910, of a Hebrew Thesaurus, through which he effected a veritable gathering of the dispersed wealth of the Hebrew language from all corners of the vast literature throughout the ages.

Ahad Haam was a pure Zionist in that he denied the feasibility of the Jews constituting themselves as national groups in the lands of the Dispersion. The theory of national autonomy, characterizing Jewish communal life before the era of emancipation and now to be restored, found a sponsor in the publicist and historian, Simon Dubnow (born 1860). An attempt to translate the theory into practice was made in Russia in the year 1905, when in consequence of the Russian débacle in the war with Japan revolution broke out. The czar announced his intention to summon persons elected by the population to share in the drafting and discussing of legislation, at the same time commanding the ministers to invite suggestions from public bodies or private persons. In April, Jewish communal leaders of all parties met in Vilna and formed a Union for the attainment of full rights for the Jewish people in Russia. The programme included not only civil and political, but also national rights, the latter meaning freedom of national and cultural self-government in all its manifestations, with wide communal autonomy and the right for the Jews to use their own language and to organize their own schools. An executive committee, with its seat in St. Petersburg, was made up of twenty-two members elected by the Union.

The reactionary forces in Russia determined to defend their vested interests by perfecting an organization, that of the 'Genuine Russians,' with provincial branches named 'Black Hundreds.' They met the cry, 'Down with Absolutism' with the counter-cry, 'Down with the Constitution and with the Jews.' In the Jews they saw the abetters of constitutional reforms. In the Easter season of 1905, bloody pogroms were instituted in Bielostok and Zhitomir. This time the Jews resisted the attackers manfully, having organized themselves for self-defense. After the Russian defeat in the battle of Tsushima (May 27–28), the more the Jews were active in the parties of the Constitutional Democrats (Cadets), the Socialist Democrats, and the Socialist Revolutionaries, the greater were the excesses engineered by the Black Hundreds. In the summer and autumn, there was a veritable orgy of pogroms in more than fifty localities. Thus did the reactionaries hope to intimidate the radical elements.

Nevertheless the majority of seats in the first Russian parliament, the Imperial Duma, was held by liberals and radicals. Twelve Jewish deputies were returned, of whom eight associated themselves with the Cadets. While the Duma was sitting, one of the bloodiest pogroms, with a repetition of the Kishinev bestialities, was enacted in Bielostok (June 14–15, 1906). Following an interpellation, the minister of the interior Stolypin feebly defended the government. He was answered by the liberal deputy Prince Urusov, formerly governor of Kishinev and assistant minister of the interior, who revealed the secret that the appeals to riot had been printed at government expense in the central Police Department at St. Petersburg.

The Jews had been given the franchise; beyond that their disabilities remained in force. The Jewish deputies demanded that an end should be made to the legal enslavement of the Jews. But the Duma was far too occupied with its unsuccessful struggle to enlarge its own powers at the expense of the throne; before long it was dissolved (July 21). Stolypin, now master of the situation, advised the emperor to pacify the non-revolutionary elements of Jewry by making concessions; but Nicholas preferred to leave Jewish disabilities as they stood. By deft manipulation of the electoral law and by intimidation at the polls from the quarters of the Black Hundreds, Stolypin succeeded in modifying the membership of the second Duma and still more so of the third (1907). The number of Jewish deputies dwindled down to three and at last to two.

For the next seven years black reaction was supreme in the highest governing circles; the throne was in perfect solidarity with the Union of Genuine Russians which constituted a 'second government.' The Jewish deputies in the Duma rightly protested that their people were experiencing greater harshness than even under the cruel régime of Plehve. The freedom of movement, guaranteed by the constitution, was declared inapplicable to the Jews who must remain penned up in the Pale. In the spring of 1910, twelve hundred Jewish families were expelled from Kiev. The 'numerus clausus' for Jewish students in the higher schools was reintroduced. In 1911, this ruling was extended to apply also to pupils presenting themselves for final examinations after private preparation outside school (externs).

The height of persecution was reached in the Beilis trial (1911–1913). The body of a murdered Christian boy in Kiev was found in the vicinity of a brick-kiln owned by a Jew. The Black Hundred immediately raised the cry of ritual murder; Mendel Beilis, a laborer employed in the kiln, was arrested. While the government had not yet made up its mind about the character of the murder, Stolypin, who accompanied the czar to Kiev, was assassinated. The assassin was a young revolutionary whose grandfather, a Jewish writer, had joined the Greek Orthodox Church. Then the minister of justice ordered the prosecution of Beilis, though the preliminary investigation failed to produce any evidence against him or any other Jew. As a matter of fact, it was known that the actual murderer belonged to a criminal gang of thieves. For two years a wild anti-Jewish campaign was carried on, in society, on the streets, in the press, and in the Imperial Duma.

Protests by Christian theologians in Europe and America, and even by sober-minded and honest Russians, failed of their effect on a government bent upon convicting, in the person of Beilis, the entire Jewish people. Nevertheless, Beilis was acquitted, though the judges had been carefully selected from among the Genuine Russians and the jury consisted of ignorant persons who believed in the ritual murder legend. The government vented its spleen on the liberal-minded public men who had joined in protesting against the hideous libel. Twenty-two lawyers of the St. Petersburg Bar Association were convicted on the charge of agitating against the government, one month before the outbreak of the World War.

The Russian revolution of 1905 had its repercussions in Austria. The franchise was reformed so as to protect racial minorities; the members of each race were to vote in separate 'compartments' for their own national representatives in parliament. Altogether eight nationalities were recognized according to language: Germans, Czechs, Poles, Ruthenians, and so forth. For the Jews to accept membership in one or the other of these nationalities it meant, in Vienna for example, to vote for the Christian Socialist, hence Anti-Semitic, candidates, if they would not support the Socialists. In Bohemia, the Jews found themselves between the Czechs and Germans, and in Galicia between the Poles and Ruthenians, so that whichever of the two races they chose to go with, the other was certain to resent it. In Galicia and Bukowina, moreover, where the mass of the Jews spoke their own dialect, they should have really formed their own group. However, there was no unanimity among the Jews themselves; only four Jewish deputies from Galicia and Bukowina constituted themselves as the 'Jewish Club,' while ten others adhered to the German and Polish parties.

In the elections to the local Galician Diet, the Poles, whether of the conservative and nationalist or the socialist party, categorically refused to recognize a 'third nation.' In 1910, almost half of the Jewish voters in Galicia and Bukowina named in the registers their own dialect as their national language. During the parliamentary election of 1911 it came to a clash between the assimilationists and the Jewish nationalists. In the Galician town Drohobicz Jewish Laborers attacked the office of the successful candidate, Löwenstein, who had been elected on the Polish ticket. The Jewish Club ceased to exist, only one of its members having been reëlected. The Polish deputies, both in parliament and in the local Diet, were careful not to go too far in their animosity against the Jews in order not to alienate their Jewish supporters. Nothing, however, prevented the Poles from crowding out the Jewish petty traders by the establishment of rural coöperative stores and by withholding the lease of salt-mines and breweries from Jews. The economic condition of Galician Jewry grew worse daily.

The same situation developed in Russian Poland from the time of the organization of the National Democratic party and its entry into the Duma under the leadership of Dmowski. Besides the small body of 'Poles of the Mosaic Faith,' there were the mass of the politically undeveloped Hasidim, and the Zionists and nationalists who clamored for recognition of Jewish national rights. These the Poles to a man refused to countenance, maintaining that there could not be two nations on the Vistula. Under the cloak of Polish nationalism, an economic boycott was instituted in 1909–1910 against the Jews; the slogan went forth, 'Do not buy from Jews!' The antagonism became acute during the elections of 1912 to the fourth Duma. Although the Jews of Warsaw numbered two hundred thousand souls, they were ready, in order not to provoke the Poles, to support any Polish candidate who was not an Anti-Semite. Instead, the Polish electoral committee named as its candidate an out-and-out Anti-Semite, the National Democrat Kucharzewski. The Jews, still bent upon respecting Polish susceptibilities, refrained from putting forward a candidate of their own and voted for the socialist Jagello, who was elected. The result was that the bitterness of the Poles was increased and that the economic boycott was carried out with the utmost severity.

CHAPTER XCVI

THE EXODUS TO AMERICA

(1905-1914)

THE untoward turn which events took in Russia, beginning with 1905, had precipitated another exodus. Between that year and 1914, America alone received about three-quarters of a million Jewish immigrants from Russia. The effect of this mass immigration, whether in England and its dependencies or in the United States of America, was twofold, as one looked at it from without or from within. On the external side, the congestion of the new-comers at one particular spot, whether the East End in London or the East Side in New York, and their predominance in particular trades brought about legislative counter-measures. In England, the agitation began as early as 1902 and took the form of anti-alien legislation; in 1905 a law was passed in restraint of the immigration of alien paupers.

In America, the movement to restrict immigration likewise gained momentum. The head-tax was raised from fifty cents for every immigrant (1882) to two (1903) and then to four dollars (1906). In 1906, President Roosevelt appointed to membership in his Cabinet Oscar S. Straus (1850–1926) as secretary of commerce and labor. Straus had served previously as minister and ambassador to Turkey; the new office carried with it the supervision of immigration. From 1906 to 1913 bills were brought in, both in the Senate and in the House of Representatives, embodying a literacy test for immigrants and the requirement of certificates of character issued in the home country. The latter provision would have militated against the admission of Jews from Russia and Rumania, since in those countries it was exceedingly difficult, if not altogether impossible, for the Jews to procure such certificates. The bill, as finally passed by the two Houses of the Congress, dropped the certificate of character clause; but the literacy test remained. President Taft vetoed the bill

(February 14, 1913); when reintroduced in the new Congress, it was similarly vetoed by President Wilson (July 28, 1914).

The fight for liberal immigration laws was carried on, in conjunction with other Jewish organizations, chiefly by the American Jewish Committee, called into existence in 1906. The first chairman of this representative body was Mayer Sulzberger (1843–1923) of Philadelphia, distinguished as a jurist, erudite man of letters, a lover of Jewish literature, author of papers and learned monographs on the ancient polity of the Hebrews, easily the foremost Jewish layman in America. Among his principal associates were Louis Marshall (born 1856) of New York City, who succeeded to the chairmanship in 1912, and Cyrus Adler (born 1863), then of the Smithsonian Institution in Washington. Prominent in the formation of the Committee was Jacob H. Schiff (1847–1920), chief of the banking firm of Kuhn, Loeb & Co., acknowledged head of American Jewry, universally beloved for his varied and vast philanthropic gifts, far-sighted in counsel, warmly attached to the cause of his people at home and abroad. Of this princely Jew it may be truly said that nothing Jewish was alien to him; he stood above the parties and worked for peace within the household of Israel and for just treatment of his people wheresoever their rights were denied or infringed upon. Oscar S. Straus and the versatile Joseph Jacobs (1854–1916), previously secretary of the Russo-Jewish Committee in England, lent valuable aid in the formation of the American Jewish Committee.

This Committee brought to a head the question of the admission of Jewish citizens from America to Russia in accordance with the terms of the treaty of 1832. The subject had occupied the attention of the Department of State for forty years, during which time every diplomatic expedient was tried to counter the evasive answers of the czar's government. President Taft was reluctant to go to extremes; at a luncheon tendered at the White House on February 15, 1911, to representatives of the American Jewish Committee, the Union of American Hebrew Congregations, and the Independent Order B'nai B'rith, the president announced that the government could do nothing. The Jewish delegation left depressed in spirit. 'We are still in exile (galuth),' said one of the company. Schiff answered: 'This means a fight.' Congress, however, was impressed by the arguments showing Russia's deliberate discrimination against a class of American citizens. A resolution was passed in the House of Representatives calling for an abrogation of the treaty, and before the Senate had taken action, President Taft gave notice to Russia of the proposed termination of the treaty. On January 1, 1913, the abrogation went into effect.

The translation of so many hundreds of thousands of East-European Jews to England and America was necessarily productive of an internal transformation of Jewish life, both among immigrants and old-time residents. The new-comers adjusted themselves to the strange language and customs— the children quite rapidly, the elders more slowly. But even where, as in congested districts and among the older generation, the imported speech was kept up, it received an admixture from the English vocabulary, while Slavic elements went into disuse. In every large city newspapers in the spoken dialect were published, with an enormous circulation; the immigrants created their own theaters and places of amusement. The native Jews strove to speed the process of 'Anglicizing' or 'Americanizing' the foreigner, while the latter brought into the community at large an intenser Jewish atmosphere. The religious education of the children of foreign-born parents was conducted according to the traditional manner, in private (heders) or public schools (Talmud Torahs), with stress on mastering the Hebrew tongue. The religious needs of the foreign population were served by imported rabbis, who, of course, remained strangers to the English speech. It was a question of time when these ministers would prove unequal to the task of guiding the second generation, which was English-speaking.

In England, orthodoxy appeared to be in the saddle. Both the Portuguese (Gaster) and the Ashkenazic (Hermann Adler, 1839–1911) chief rabbis led their communities along traditional lines. Of the two, Gaster, being a Rumanian by birth, stood nearer to the foreign Jew in sentiment. Adler, while helpful in every way, was looked upon by the immigrants as the representative of officialdom with its 'Anglican' cast. Aside from the reform congregations of moderate scope from the middle of the nineteenth century, there was developed a radical movement under the leadership of Claude G. Montefiore (born 1858), the exponent of a Judaism stripped of all its national implications, who in 1901 founded the Jewish Religious Union. This organization established in 1910 the Liberal Jewish Synagogue, which remained outside the jurisdiction of the 'United Synagogue.' The headship of the chief rabbi was equally repudiated in the East End by the organization of the 'Upholders of the Law' (Mahazike ha-Dath); in 1898 they opened a large synagogue in Spitalfields. Jews' College, opened in 1856, graduated in the course of its existence many an able minister. It had a notable scholar as principal in the person of Michael Friedländer (1833–1910), whose place was worthily filled by his successor Adolf Büchler (born 1867). But the influence of the College was slow to reach the foreign population. Outside Jews' College, Jewish scholarship was brilliantly cultivated by the 'readers' in Rabbinic Hebrew at the two universities: at Oxford by Adolf Neubauer (1831–1907), from 1868 on sublibrarian in the Bodleian Library; at Cambridge, successively, by Solomon Schiller-Szinessy (1820–1890), Solomon Schechter (1850–1915), and Israel Abrahams (1858–1925).

Schechter was born in Rumania. After pursuing studies in Vienna, under the guidance of Friedmann (p. 704), and in Berlin under Israel Lewy (p. 682) and other scholars, he was invited to London in 1882 by Claude G. Montefiore; in 1890 he received his Cambridge appointment. Before he departed from England, he had established for himself an international reputation through the identification of a leaf of the Hebrew Ben Sira which reached Cambridge (1896), and subsequently through the find of the hoard of ancient manuscript fragments in the store-room of a Cairo synagogue (Genizah; 1897). Schechter was singularly prepared to take the lead in sifting and editing the numerous treatises and documents, through which a flood of light was shed upon obscure chapters of Jewish history.

Painstaking and accurate a scholar as Schechter was, he was far too human to withdraw himself cloistrally into the domain of pure knowledge. Out of the prodigious store of his information and reading he had something to tell to English-speaking Jewry, and he told it in a style all his own, scintillating with wit, brilliantly delightful. He was an eastern Hasid transplanted to the West; he abhorred middle-class religious smugness no less than official formalism. The show of religion was for him no substitute for genuine piety, nor the subversive estimates of Judaism by modern Christian scholars a measure of the true worth of the Torah. He pleaded for a liberalism which was Jewish, not borrowed, for a ministry well-prepared, for an orientation consummately thought out, for the historical continuity of Jewish life, for fealty to the whole of Israel—'catholic' Israel—rather than to provincial Judaism, for the revival of Jewish nationalism in complete attachment to the inherited religious values.

This programme Schechter unfolded forcefully in popular essays and addresses, in learned theological publications, in his academic teaching, and in his converse with laymen. He found a much wider field for his activity in the United States, where, in 1902, he took over the direction of the New York training school for rabbis founded by Morais and now reorganized as the Jewish Theological Seminary of America. The school was placed on a sounder financial basis through an endowment fund contributed by Schiff and other far-sighted men who realized that, as the immigrants became 'Americanized,' they must be supplied with English-speaking rabbis, trained in a spirit of respect for the orthodox traditions of the new-comers. The older orthodox or con-servative congregations, likewise, availed themselves of the services of the graduates of the New York seminary, while the reform synagogues, or Temples, took their ministers from the Cincinnati school. Kohler was elected to the presidency of the Hebrew Union College in 1903 and served actively until 1921. Freed from ministerial duties, he had the leisure to prepare a text-book of systematic Jewish Theology, which appeared both in German and in English.

The two wings of American Jewry were represented in the preparation of the Jewish Encyclopaedia, which was completed in 1905. Another literary achievement, under the joint auspices of the Jewish Publication Society of America (organized in 1888) and the Central Conference of American Rabbis (instituted in 1889), was the new English version of the Scriptures, projected in 1892 and completed in 1917, the publication being made possible chiefly through the generosity of Jacob H. Schiff. A third institution of Jewish learning, the Dropsie College for Hebrew and Cognate Learning, was opened at Philadelphia in 1908, with Cyrus Adler as president. This institution was unique in that it was a strictly graduate school leading to the degree of Doctor of Philosophy and open to students without distinction as to creed, color, or sex. The college was founded in accordance with the provisions of the last will and testament of Moses Aaron Dropsie (1821–1905) of Philadelphia.

Jewish literary efforts were furthered in Germany through the establishment of a Society for the Promotion of Jewish Learning ('Gesellschaft zur Förderung der Wissenschaft des Judentums') in 1902. This organization took in hand the preparation of a series of works, learned in substance but popular in form, comprising the whole range of Jewish knowledge. The Union of German Jews, effected in 1904, was to serve defensive purposes against the infringement of Jewish rights, though organized Anti-Semitism seemed to be losing ground in German politics. The Relief Society of German Jews ('Hilfsverein der deutschen Juden'), called into being in 1901, developed a useful activity in helping Eastern Jews. In common with the Jewish National Fund and public-spirited Jews of Russia and America, the German society interested itself in the creation of a technical school at Haifa. But when the building was approaching completion, a difference of opinion developed as to the language of instruction—German or Hebrew. The institution was finally opened in 1924 under entirely different conditions.